A Guide to

European Union Law

AUSTRALIA
LBC Information Services—Sydney

CANADA and USA
Carswell—Toronto

SINGAPORE and MALAYSIA
Sweet & Maxwell Asia
Singapore and Kuala Lumpur

A Guide to

European Union Law

by

P. S. R. F. Mathijsen

Advocaat
Professor of Law, University of Brussels.
Former Director-General with the Commission
of the European Communities

Seventh Edition

LONDON • SWEET & MAXWELL • 1999

First edition 1972
Second edition 1975
Third edition 1980
Fourth edition 1985
Fifth edition 1990
Sixth edition 1995

Published by Sweet & Maxwell Limited of
100 Avenue Road, London NW3 3PF

Typeset by Mendip Communications Ltd, Frome, Somerset
Printed in England by Clays Ltd, St. Ives plc

A CIP catalogue record
for this book is available
from the British Library

ISBN 0 421 63500 2

No natural forests were destroyed to make this product:
only farmed timber was used and re-planted

to Beverly

Acknowledgments

It was, as always, very exciting and demanding to try to get everything right and to have the manuscript and the corrected proofs delivered in time; without help this would have been quite impossible. In other words, this book could not have been published without the faithful backing of several persons whose names I would like to mention here.

I am grateful to Sweet & Maxwell for having once again considered it worthwhile to publish a new edition of the "Guide" which first appeared in 1972, and to the editorial staff for its much needed help.

I am very much indebted to my secretary Nicole Thielen for researching, reading, correcting, typing and helping in many ways.

Then there are those who gave me a hand with a couple of chapters. Although I am, of course, responsible for the final text, I wish to express my sincere thanks to Herr Marcus Pohlman who revised the material for the environment and Mr Sam Pieters who provided most of the data concerning telecommunications. I also wish to thank Professor Tony Joris who, once again, was most helpful with advice on the Institutions.

The Office for Offical Publications of the European Communities in Luxembourg and its Director General M. Lucien Emringer, were most generous in supplying the documents I needed. There are also the many officials from the European Institutions who did provide me with up-to-date information on the latest developments of Community and Union law. I am glad to report that all these anonymous contributors were always ready to answer my queries, thereby showing that the Community and its servants are, indeed, "at the disposal" of the citizens.

The victim of the writing was, as always, my dear wife—to whom this edition is dedicated—who withstood, during all those months, the infernal pressures and demands which come with writing under time and occupational constraints. Her strength and daily care prevented many things from collapsing. She also took it upon herself to read and help correct the proofs and gave me, at the same time, the satisfaction of knowing that at least one person in my large family, read the entire book!

P. S. R. F. Mathijsen

Foreword

It gives me great pleasure to write a Preface to the Seventh Edition of Professor Mathijsen's magisterial *Guide to European Union Law*. This is partly because of the quality and relevance (the latter indeed increasing in Britain) of the work itself. Had it not possessed such attributes it would hardly have achieved nearly thirty years—the First Edition was in 1972—of respect and updating.

It is also because Pierre Mathijsen was during my years as President of the European Commission one of the most able of a group of distinguished Directors-General with which the Commission was then blessed. Most of them had been "present at the creation" of the European institutions. I came to Brussels at the beginning of 1977, having had considerable experience, both as Home Secretary and as Chancellor of the Exchequer, of working with the higher ranks of the British Civil Service, which then perhaps had a higher morale than it does today, and of which I was a great admirer. I thought however that the administrative qualities and professional advice of this group was well up to what I had experienced in London. Professor Mathijsen was a little younger than some of the founding Directors-General although he had joined the service of Europe back in 1952. But he was ready by my day to assume the new post in the important Directorate-General dealing with the fairly newly-established Regional Fund.

Throughout his administrative years he retained his deep jurisprudential knowledge and interest, as exemplified in this series of volumes. He is thus eminently qualified by both academic knowledge and practical experience to provide a guide to the law of the European Union. It is essential that such a coming together of fifteen states (soon to be more), doing some things in common but also retaining strong individual identity, should operate within a firm rule of law, impartially applied between nations, companies and individuals. The European Court, essential to the process, has in my experience earned the respect of the most jurisprudentially distinguished of British judges. Professor Mathijsen's successive editions, always kept up to date, are an invaluable guide for those who, either as lawyers or businessmen, function within the jurisdiction of that Court.

Roy Jenkins
June 10, 1999

Preface

Contrary to some other publication-dates of the "Guide", the present one bears good omens for the development of the European Union, and if it were not for the very high level of unemployment, the scene in front of our European eyes would be rather encouraging, even satisfying. The single Union currency, the euro, is a reality; most Member States were able to accept the disciplines imposed by the Economic and Monetary Union and to weather (thanks partly to that) the Asian financial crisis. The Amsterdam Treaty was ratified by all fifteen Members States and, last but not least, accession negotiations were launched with six of the 11 applicants from Central and Eastern Europe. This clearly shows that the implicit dynamism of the Communities has not lost anything of its impetus, that the responsibilities of the Union continue to grow and that its geographic expansion is still under way. Those are, without doubt, promising signs.

This seventh edition tries, like the preceding ones, to capture for the reader, in simple and concentrated form, a picture of the present stage of development of Union law and the so-called *acquis communautaire*. This book endeavours to cover all the main areas of Community legislation, both institutional and material; the set-up has remained mainly unchanged. Most parts were entirely rewritten, while the others were updated and completed. Also, as in the other editions, all legal technicalities were put in the footnotes in order to make the main text as readable as possible.

Once again I ask for comments from readers about the usefulness (or lack of it) of this book for their work. Readers' suggestions are indispensable for improving the quality of the "Guide".

P. Mathijsen
Brussels, May 5, 1999

Table of Contents

Table of Cases

Court of Justice of the European Communities

Chronological List of Cases

Court of First Instance of the European Communities

Alphabetical List of Cases

Commission Decisions

National Courts

Belgium

France

Table of Treaties and Conventions

1957 Treaty establishing the European Community (E.C. Treaty) (formerly European Economic Community; modified as European Community (E.C.) by the Treaty on European Union (Maastricht) and as modified by the Treaty of Amsterdam (October 2, 1997)) (March 25, 1957, Rome) TS I (1973) Cmnd 5179—*cont.*

Table of Secondary Legislation of the European Communities

Directives

Decisions

Commission Notices

Table of National Legislation

BASIC STATISTICS

COUNTRY	AREA Km^2	POP. (1996) MILLION	GPD (1996) BIL. ECU
Austria	83,900	8.055	173.7
Belgium	30,500	10.143	208.4
Denmark	43,100	5.251	137.7
Finland	337,100	5.117	97.7
France	544,000	58.256	1,217.5
Germany	356,900	81.818	1,854
Greece	132,000	10.465	96.8
Ireland	70,300	3.616	55.3
Italy	301,300	57.333	956.5
Luxembourg	2,600	413	13.8
Netherlands	41,200	15.494	309.2
Portugal	92,400	9.921	81.9
Spain	504,800	39.242	462.7
Sweden	450,000	8.838	197.1
United Kingdom	244,100	58.694	902.5
Europe 15	**3,234,200**	**372.654**	**6,764.0**
CANDIDATE COUNTRIES			
Bulgaria	110,912	8.340	9.9
Czech Republic	79,283	10.321	36.1
Estonia	45,100	1.476	2.8
Hungary	93,000	10.212	33.42
Latvia	63,700	2.479	3.4
Lithuania	65,200	3.707	3.5
Poland	312,677	38.609	- 90.2
Romania	237,500	22.608	27.3
Slovakia	48,593	5.368	13.3
Slovenia	20,215	1.990	14.2
USA	9,372,600	227.431.350	5,961.0
Canada	9,976,100	22.000	457.4
Japan	377,800	110.000	3,628.9

Abbreviations

ACP	African, Caribbean, and Pacific countries party to the Lomé Convention.
Bull.	Bulletin of the European Communities edited by the Secretariat of the Commission; there are 11 issues per year (July–August are published together).
Bull. Suppl.	Supplement to the Bulletin.
CAP	Common agricultural policy.
Cedefon	European Centre for the Development of Vocational Training.
CEN	European Committee for Standardization.
CFSP	Common foreign and security policy.
C.M.L.R.	Common Market Law Reports.
C.M.L.Rev.	Common Market Law Review.
Competition Report	Report on Competition Policy.
Dec.	Decision.
Dir.	Directive.
EAGGF	European Agricultural Guidance and Guarantee Fund.
EBRD	European Bank for Reconstruction and Development.
E.C.R.	Official reports in English of cases decided by the Community Courts (Court of Justice: numbered I–... and Court of First Instance: II–...). A further distinction was established in 1994: Community personnel cases are published in a separate volume "Reports of European Community Staff Cases" E.C.R.–S.C. Those volumes are divided into three sections: I/A: Abstracts of decisions in staff cases;

	I/B: Summary of decisions given on appeal in staff cases; II: Judgments and Orders in staff cases (full text in the language of the case). In other words, judgments in staff cases are no longer translated in other official languages.
ECSC	European Coal and Steel Community.
EC	European Community.
EDF	European Development Fund.
EEA	European Economic Area.
EEIG	European Economic Interest Grouping.
EFTA	European Free Trade Association.
EIB	European Investment Bank.
E.L.Rev.	European Law Review.
EMI	European Monetary Institute.
EMS	European Monetary System.
EMU	Economic and Monetary union.
ERDF	European Regional Development Fund.
ESF	European Social Fund.
Euratom	European Community of Atomic Energy.
FIFG	Financial instrument for fisheries guidance.
GATT	General Agreement on Tariffs and Trade (UN).
Gen.Rep.	General Report on the activities of the Communities, published yearly by the Commission. The year mentioned after the word Report refers to the period covered by the Report.
GSP	Generalized system of preferences.
IBRD	International Bank for Reconstruction and Development (World Bank) (UN).
J.O.	*Journal Officiel*: French edition of the *Official Journal of the European Communities.* *Remarks* 1. This Journal was published under the name *Journal Officiel de la Communauté Européenne*

du Charbon et de l'Acier from 1952 to April 19, 1958; on April 20, 1958, the first issue of the *Journal Officiel des Communautés Européennes* appeared, without modifying the structure of the Journal itself; this lasted until December 31, 1967.

References to publications in the *Journal Officiel* for the period 1952 to July 1, 1967, are made by mentioning the page and the year or vice versa such as J.O. 849/65. Between July 1 and December 31, 1967, each issue is paged separately.

2. After January 1, 1968 (see O.J. 1968, L.30), the Journal was divided into two separate editions designated by the letters "L." (legislation) and "C." (communications).

Legislative texts are published in the edition marked "L." and are again subdivided in two categories:

I. Acts for which publication is a condition for their application (see EEC, Art. 191);

II. Acts for which publication is not required.

All other texts appear in the edition marked "C" except "Notices and public contracts" which are published in O.J. Supplement.

References to publications in the *Journal Officiel* after January 1, 1968, are made by mentioning the letter "L." or "C.", the year, the No. of the issue and the page, *e.g.* J.O. 1970, 31/1.

3. Starting on January 1, 1973, the Journal is also published in the Danish and English languages.

4. In accordance with Article 155 of the Act of Accession, provision was made in Council Regulation 857/72 of April 24, 1972, for Special Editions of the *Official Journal* for the publication *inter alia* of the English text of acts of the institutions of the Communities adopted and published before accession. Consequently an authentic English translation now exists of the most important Community acts.

This special edition was published in November and December 1972 and a subsequent

	edition was published in 1974 (see O.J. 1972, L.101/1). All references to an O.J. publication prior to January 1, 1973 are necessarily in the Special Edition. 5. The numbering of pages is the same in the nine languages of the Community and probably 12 after enlargement to Finland, Norway and Sweden (for Austria the language is German).
Merger Treaty	Treaty of April 8, 1965, establishing a Single Council and a Single Commission of the European Communities.
O.J.	*Official Journal of the European Communities*; see J.O. above.
OECD	Organization for Economic Cooperation and Development.
Reg.	Regulation.
R&TD	Research and technological development.
Rules	Rules of Procedure of the Court of Justice (O.J. 1975, L.102/1).
Stabex	System for the stabilization of ACP and OCT export earnings.
Sysmin	System for the stabilization of export earnings from mining products.
TAC	Total allowable catch.
TACIS	Programme for technical assistance to the Commonwealth of Independent States.
TENs	Trans-European networks.
UN	United Nations.
WEU	Western European Union.

PART ONE: THE UNION, THE COMMUNITIES, THE ACTS AND THE LAW

Chapter One
The European Union and the European Communities

INTRODUCTION

The reader who approaches the "European" subject for the first time will be easily forgiven if she or he feels confused about the terminology. The more so, since the names "European Union", "European Community(ies)", "Common market" and "Internal market" are often used indiscriminately to designate the same concept. As this book hopes to make clear, they do not cover the same "thing"; but some clarification is certainly called for at the outset, the more so since reference is also made, in this context, to the Treaty on European Union or Maastricht Treaty, the Amsterdam Treaty, the Economic and Monetary Union and the euro.

The "European Union", originally established among 12 Member States by the Maastricht Treaty,[1] constitutes a "new stage in the process of creating an ever closer union among the peoples of Europe".[2] It adds new dimensions, new fields of activity, to the ones provided for by the Treaties establishing the three European Communities, *i.e.* the Coal and Steel Community, Euratom and the European Economic Community. Consequently, the Maastricht Treaty modifies those Treaties, it does not replace them. But it also has specific features of its own and it has its own objectives concerning the European Union, which will be examined later. In addition to those features, it encompasses or, as the Maastricht Treaty says, it is "founded on", three elements: the European Communities, a Common Foreign and Security Policy, and Co-

[1] It was signed at Maastricht, The Netherlands, on February 7, 1992 and entered into force on November 1, 1993, ([1993] O.J. L293/61) after having been ratified by the parliaments of the then 12 Member States, in certain cases after it was approved by referendum. It was modified by the Amsterdam Treaty. Consolidated version: [1997] O.J. C340/145.

[2] Art. 1 (ex A.2) TEU.

operation in the fields of Justice and Home Affairs.[3] These elements constitute the so-called three pillars of the European construction. The second pillar contains what has been called the "declaration of independence" of the Union: "to safeguard the common values, fundamental interests, independence and integrity of the Union".[4]

The expression "European Communities" refers to the European Coal and Steel Community (ECSC) in existence since 1952 and the European Atomic Energy Community (Euratom) set up in 1958, at the same time as the European Economic Community (EEC) also referred to as the Treaty of Rome; it was in that city that the latter two treaties were signed in March 1957. When reference is made to the "*Community*", it is the EEC which is generally meant; the other two Communities no longer play an independent role; for all practical purposes they have been absorbed into the EEC, which explains why the name "Community" is mostly used in the singular.[5] To complicate matters, the Maastricht Treaty has changed the name "European Economic Community" into "European Community" (E.C.).

The "Common Market", often confused with the Community itself, of which it is the main feature, means the so-called "basic freedoms" (free movement of goods, workers, establishment, services, capital and payments) together with the various policies implemented by the Community itself or together with the Member States (commercial, agricultural, competition, environmental, etc.). The Common Market does not include, for instance, external relations, except for the common commercial policy.

The "Internal Market" is part of the Common Market and is defined in the Treaty as "an area without frontiers in which the free movement of goods, persons, services and capital is ensured".[6] The completion of the internal market at the end of 1992 was the object of the Single European Act[7] (SEA) signed in February 1986.

This book is mainly about the European Community (E.C.) whose nature will be discussed in this chapter. The Common Market and

---

[3] This third element was amended by the Amsterdam Treaty and renamed: "Police and Judicial Cooperation in criminal matters".

[4] Art. 11(1) (ex J.1) TEU.

[5] The Court of Justice, however, still refers to itself as the "Court of Justice of the European Communities".

[6] Art. 14(2) (ex 7a(2)), E.C.

[7] This Act is called "single" because it is the combination of two different instruments, which were, for practical purposes, put together into a single one. The first instrument contains modifications to the three European Treaties, while the second constitutes, in fact, an Agreement among the Member States concerning co-operation in the field of external relations.

the Internal Market will be examined in detail further on. But, it seems necessary to start with a brief overview of the European Union itself.

1. THE EUROPEAN UNION

The Union has political rather than legal significance; indeed, it is the ultimate objective of the European integration, the precise scope of which is, as yet, not determined in detail. However, since all the nationals of the Member States are now "citizens" of that Union, which grants them certain rights, it certainly is not meaningless from the legal point of view.[8] As was just mentioned, the Union could be compared to a structure comprising specific features and based on three pilars: the European Communities and, next to it, the Common Foreign and Security policy, and the Police and Judicial Co-operation in criminal matters. Since the Member States were not ready to include these last two elements within the "European Community", with its institutions endowed with sovereign powers, other ways had to be found. Thus a special status was agreed upon for those two elements, outside the E.C. Treaty, but still inside the European integration process. The result was the above described construction.

This structure is held together by

> "a single institutional framework which shall ensure the consistency and the continuity of the activities carried out in order to attain the objectives while respecting and building upon the *acquis*

[8] Contrary to the European Communities, the Union has no legal personality. For the rights granted to the citizens, see "Part Two—Citizenship of the Union" in Title II of the E.C. Treaty, Arts 17 to 22 (ex 8 to 8e) E.C. It provides, *inter alia*, for the right to move and reside in the territory of all the Member States (Art. 18(1) (ex 8a(1))), the right to vote and to stand for municipal elections in the Member State in which she or he resides (Dir. 94/80, laying down detailed arrangements for the exercise of the right to vote and to stand as a candidate in municipal elections by citizens of the Union residing in an Member State of which they are not nationals: [1994] O.J. L368/38, see Case C–323/97, *Commission v. Belgium* [1998] E.C.R. I–4291 (Art. 19(1) (ex 8b(1)) E.C.) and also for election to the European Parliament (Art. 19(2) (ex 8b(2)) E.C.). In third countries where their own State is not represented, citizens are entitled to diplomatic and consular protection from any Member State (Decision regarding protection for the citizens of the E.U. by diplomatic and consular representatives [1995] O.J. L314/73) (Art. 20 (ex 8c) E.C.), the citizen also has the right to petition the European Parliament and to apply to the Ombudsman (Art. 21 (ex 8d) E.C.). It should be noted that the Council may propose to the Member States to extend those rights (Art. 22 (ex 8e) E.C.).

communautaire.[9] The Union shall, in particular, ensure the consistency of its external activities as a whole in the context of its external relations, security, economic and development policies."[10]

The main objectives of the Union can be summarised as follows:[11]

(a) to promote economic and social progress, which is balanced and sustainable; the means to achieve this objective are: economic and social cohesion, and economic and monetary union;
(b) to assert its identity on the international scene, through the implementation of a common foreign and security policy which might lead to a common defence (policy).

This last objective is of particular interest since it provides for joint action towards third countries, when until now the Member States had a strong tendency to act individually in that area. The necessity for an external identity follows from the role the Community plays in the international commercial and economic fields, where it acts as an equal to the United States and Japan. This international economic role is not matched, unfortunately, by a comparable international political presence. This is *inter alia* what the Union will try to remedy.

Besides to two above mentioned objectives, the Treaty provides for the introduction of the "citizenship of the Union" to strengthen the protection of the rights and interests of the nationals of the Member States, to maintain an area of freedom, security an justice and to maintain in full the *acquis communautaire*.

Other "novelties" introduced by the Maastricht Treaty are, besides the Union citizenship, more extensive social policies, a reinforcement of the principle of subsidiarity,[12] a wider role for the European Parliament and the upgrading of the Court of Auditors.

The E.U. Treaty also makes it clear that, in order to be or become a member of the Union, a State must have a government "founded on the principles of democracy".[13] On the basis of this provision it

---

[9] "Acquis Communautaire" means everything that was decided and agreed upon since the establishment of the Communities, whatever the form in which this was done, whether legally binding or not. It refers to the body of rules which govern the Communities in whatever field of activity.

[10] Art. 3 (ex C) TEU.

[11] Art. 2 (ex B) TEU.

[12] See Protocol on the application of the principles of subsidiarity and proportionality, annexed to the E.C. Treaty: [1997] O.J. C340/105.

[13] Arts 49 and 6(1) (ex O and F.1) TEU.

should be possible to eject a member from the Union if it no longer fulfills that condition.

Of particular interest is the recognition of what the Court has stated for years, namely that the fundamental rights, as guaranteed by the European Convention for the Protection of Human Rights and Fundamental Freedoms and as they result from the constitutional traditions common to the Member States constitute "general principles of Community law".[14]

See in this context the new competence for the European Council introduced by the Treaty of Amsterdam. It allows the latter to determine the existence of a serious and persistent breach by a Member State of the principles of liberty, democracy, respect for human rights and fundamental freedoms, and the rule of law; principles which are common to all Member States.[15]

2. The European Communities

In 1951 the drafters of the Treaty establishing the European Coal and Steel Community coined the word "supranational" to describe the particular character of the functions fulfilled by the members of the High Authority.[16] The term was from the start also used to designate the specific nature of the Community itself and of the law it embodied. It was understood to mean that the Community was more than a grouping of member nations and that its law was more than their national laws. And, although the Community was set up by an international treaty concluded among sovereign States, the signatories were conscious of having created something very different indeed from other entities set up by the Law of Nations. The contracting States were not merely accepting mutual obligations,[17] they were limiting their own sovereign rights, transferring some of them to institutions over which they had no direct control and

---

[14] Art. 6(2) (ex Art. F.2) TEU. Requested by the Council to deliver an opinion pursuant to Art. 300.6 (ex Art. 228.6) on whether accession of the E.C. to the Human Rights Convention is compatible with the Treaty, the Court decided that "as Community law now stands, the Community has no competence to accede to that Convention": [1996] E.C.R. I–1763, because the Convention attributes jurisdiction to the Court of Human Rights.

[15] Art. 6(1), TEU, see also in Part Two under Council.

[16] Arts 9(5 and 6) ECSC "They shall abstain from any act incompatible with the supranational character of their function" and "Each Member State undertakes to respect this supranational character." The concept did not refer to the Community itself.

[17] Case 26/62, *Van Gend en Loos v. Nederlandse Administratie der Belastingen* [1963] E.C.R. 1 at 12; [1963] C.M.L.R. 105.

endowing the Community with powers they did not always possess themselves. Furthermore, the Treaty did not only create new rights and obligations for the Member States, it also directly included their citizens, who thereby became subjects of the Community.[18]

By contrast with ordinary international treaties, the European Treaties thus created their own legal system to which the term "international" does not apply; the term "supranational" did therefore indicate the difference, and, indeed, Community law is not international law.

Furthermore, it follows from the terms and the spirit of the European Treaties that the Member States, as a corollary, may not give precedence to their national law over a legal system accepted by all of them on the basis of reciprocity. Indeed, the executive force of Community law cannot vary from one State to another in deference to domestic law without jeopardising the attainment of the objectives of the Treaties.[19] The law of the European Communities cannot, therefore, be regarded as national law either. It is different, independent, it is separate, it is not national law; since it is common to 15 nations, it is truely "supranational." The term has now fallen into disrepute and was even eliminated from the ECSC Treaty.[20] This, however, does not change the specific nature of the Communities and the law they created. More importantly, the concept is now universally accepted and expressed by the words "Community Law".

Community law is to be found mainly in the European Treaties (also referred to as "primary" Community law) and in the implementing legislation or the "secondary" Community law, not to be confused with the "*acquis communautaire*".[21]

Primary Community law consists of the Treaties establishing the European Coal and Steel Community (ECSC), the European Atomic Energy Community (Euratom) and the European Community (E.C.), as they were amended over the years.[22] The first two can be

---

[18] Forty years later, the Maastricht Treaty formally confirmed this by providing for a "citizenship" of the European Union. See now: Arts 17 to 22 (ex TEU, Art. 8) E.C.

[19] Case 6/64 *Costa v. ENEL* [1964] E.C.R. 585 at 594.

[20] The Merger Treaty repealed Art. 9 of the ECSC Treaty and replaced it by a text which is identical in the three European Treaties. And since the term "supranational" did not appear in the two Treaties of Rome, it was entirely left out.

[21] See n.9, above.

[22] Chronologically, amendments were introduced by: the Convention on certain institutions common to the three Communities (March 25, 1957), the Treaty establishing a Single Council and a Single Commission of the European Communities (April 8, 1965), the Decision creating the Communities' own resources (April 21, 1970), the Treaty amending certain budgetary provisions (April 22, 1970), the Treaty on the accession of Denmark, Ireland and the United Kingdom (January 22,

considered as sectoral treaties, while the third one, the E.C. Treaty, covers the economic and social fields in general. (Hereinafter "Treaty" refers to the E.C. Treaty only.)

By "secondary legislation" is meant the subsequent texts, which implemented, and in certain cases, complemented the original Treaties. Community law has gradually evolved over the past half century, from the 100 Articles of the ECSC Treaty, into an impressive body of law comprising thousands of regulations, directives, decisions, agreements and other measures, and above all the case law of the Court of Justice and the Court of First Instance.

It is impressive, not only because of its sheer volume, but because of its specific character and its growth potential. It is worthwhile considering this particular aspect of Community law: except for the original three Treaties just mentioned, none of the Community acts finds its origin with the traditional institutions, bodies and organs with which lawyers and citizens were familiar and over which they exercise, through democratic elections, some sort of control. Community regulations, directives, decisions, etc., are issued outside most citizens' own countries, according to complex and remote procedures they cannot grasp and over which they have no say.[23] They are nevertheless directly involved. On the other hand, if those measures may impose upon them obligations, they also grant them rights which they can ask the national courts to uphold against fellow-citizens, undertakings and even their own government. And indeed, those rights arise not only where they are expressly granted by Community law, but also as a consequence of the obligations which this law, in a clearly defined way, imposes upon the Member States and the institutions of the Community.[24] Those citizens can also challenge the legality of Community measures in the Community courts, when they are directly and individually concerned: they are definitely part of the system!

1972), the Treaty amending certain financial provisions (July 22, 1975), the Act concerning the direct election of the European Parliament (September 20, 1976), the Treaty on the secession of Greenland (September 20, 1976), the Treaty on the accession of Greece (May 28, 1979), the Treaty concerning the accession of Portugal and Spain (March 9/30, 1985), the Single European Act (February 17/28, 1986), the Maastricht Treaty or Treaty on European Union (February 7, 1992), the Treaty concerning the accession of Austria, Finland, (Norway) and Sweden (June 24, 1994), and, finally, the Treaty of Amsterdam (October 2, 1997).

[23] In order to remedy this situation, Art. 1 (ex A) of the E.U. Treaty provides that that Treaty marks a new stage in the process of creating an ever closer union among the peoples of Europe, "in which decisions are taken as openly as possible and as closely as possible to the citizens". It should be noted, however, that this situation also prevails within most Member States!

[24] See n.17 above.

The apparent aloofness of the European authorities combined with this direct involvement might be bewildering. However, the direct election of the members of the European Parliament and the increasing number of cases involving Community law introduced by private parties, both in the European and in the national courts, seems to indicate a familiarity with at least some aspects of this new system of law. But, if democratic control by the citizens of the Union is to become a reality, some knowledge of the basic rules and procedures is required. And, this applies not only to the law student, but also to the practitioner, the politician and the general public. Unless one realises what the objectives are and what means and procedures have been provided for attaining them, no participation is possible, no criticism is justified, no suggestion can be pertinent.

The objectives are clearly set out in the Treaty:

> "The Community shall have as its task, by establishing a common market and an economic and monetary union and by implementing common policies or activities referred to in Articles 3 and 4, to promote throughout the Community a harmonious, balanced and sustainable development of economic activities, a high level of employment and of social protection, equality between men and women, sustainable and non-inflationary growth, a high degree of competitiveness and convergence of economic performance, a high level of protection and improvement of the quality of the environment, the raising of the standard of living and quality of life, and economic and social cohesion and solidarity among Member States."[25]

The means to implement these far-reaching objectives are, first, the establishment, functioning and development of a common market and of an economic and monetary union, and, secondly, the implementation of common policies and activities referred to in the Treaty.[26]

The Treaty provides precise rules and timetables for the common market and the economic and monetary union, but the policies, as shall be seen, are described in rather general terms. However, notwithstanding this vagueness, Community activities have penetrated more and more social, economic and related fields, some of which were not, until recently,[27] explicitly provided for in the Treaty.

---

[25] Art. 2 (ex 2) E.C.

[26] Arts 2 and 3 (ex 2 and 3) E.C.

[27] Education, culture, public health and industry, which were added by the Maastricht Treaty are examples of fields wherein the Community was active, although they were not mentioned as such. The same applies to Regional Policy, the European

Community law, it seems, is in the process of integrating the entire economies of the Member States.

The dynamic development of the Communities are not the only proof of their vitality; notwithstanding economic recession and political turmoil, they not only held together, but they expanded their field of activity and are in the process of developing geographically and politically. This seems to indicate that they fulfill a basic need and respond to a profound aspiration.

Further Reading

Alan Dashwood, "The Limits of European Community Powers" (1996) 21 E.L.Rev. 113.

Stephen Hall, "Loss of Union Citizenship in Breach of Fundamental Rights" (1996) 21 E.L.Rev. 129.

Erica Szyszczak, "Making Europe More Relevant to its Citizens" (1996) 21 E.L.Rev. 349.

J. H. H. Weiler, "The European Union Belongs to its Citizens: Three Immodest Proposals" (1997) 22 E.L.Rev. 150.

O. Shaw, "The Many Pasts and Futures of Citizenship in the European Union" (1997) 22 E.L.Rev. 554.

Alan Dashwood, "States in the European Union" (1998) 23 E.L.Rev. 201.

Monetary System, Economic and Monetary Union and Political Co-operation which were introduced into the Treaty by the SEA. Activities in those fields were made possible, in the meantime, through unanimous ad hoc decisions of the Council based on Art. 308 (ex 235) E.C.

Chapter Two
History

Every institution is the product of a series of historical events, and at the same time reflects the convictions, hopes and concerns of those who were instrumental in establishing it. The European Communities are no exception to this rule. For a full understanding and a correct interpretation of the European Treaties some knowledge of the historical background seems therefore necessary.

Although the expression "United States of Europe" was already used by Victor Hugo in 1849,[1] there seems to be no need to go that far back. The end of the Second World War provides a fair starting point. Some, more recent events, such as the Maastricht Treaty on European Union and the Agreement on the establishment of the European Economic Area are covered in more detail, because although they are indeed "history", they are much more recent and therefore less well known; furthermore they will play an increasing role in the development of the European Community.

1. Churchill's Speech

The agreement made at Yalta in 1945 by the United Kingdom, the United States and the U.S.S.R. left Europe more divided than ever and the growing antagonism among the victorious "Allies" spelt only more tensions and catastrophies. It was on September 19, 1946, in a speech at Zurich University, that Winston Churchill proposed a "sovereign remedy", *i.e.* to "recreate the European family, or as much of it as we can, and provide it with a structure under which it can dwell in peace, in safety and in freedom. We must build a kind of United States of Europe". And he went on to "say something that will astonish you. The first step in the recreation of the European family must be a partnership between France and Germany"; at that time it needed a lot of courage and foresight to make such a suggestion. As will be seen, it was this (British) idea which also

[1] See Henri Brugmans, *L'Idée Européenne*, 1920–1970 (Bruges, 1970).

inspired the French Government in 1950 to propose the establishment of the European Coal and Steel Community. Towards the end of his Zurich speech, Churchill also proposed to start by setting up a regional structure and to form a Council of Europe.[2]

2. Marshall Plan—OEEC

If Churchill's words were well received, the European states in those days lacked the necessary stamina to proceed with such far-reaching plans, since they were preoccupied with their daily fight for economic survival. Once again the United States came to the rescue. In another famous university speech, at Harvard this time, George Marshall, United States Secretary of State, announced on June 5, 1947, that the United States would do "whatever it is able to do to assist in the return of normal economic health in the world". This offer was accepted by 16 European countries on July 15, 1947, and so the Marshall Plan was born; but more important for the future of European integration was the setting up of the Organisation of European Economic Co-operation (OEEC)[3] in 1948; this was in response to the American request for an agreement among Europeans.

3. Robert Schuman: May 9, 1950

In the meantime, Churchill's words about a partnership between France and Germany had not been forgotten and on May 9, 1950, Robert Schuman, French Foreign Minister, declared that a united Europe was essential for world peace and that a gathering of the European nations required the elimination of the century-old opposition between France and Germany. As a first practical step towards this end he proposed "to place the whole Franco-German coal and steel production under one joint High Authority, in an organization open to the participation of the other countries of Europe". He described this pooling of production as the "first stage of the European Federation". Germany, the Netherlands, Belgium, Luxemburg and Italy accepted in principle and negotiations started at once.

---

[2] The Treaty establishing the Council of Europe was signed in London on May 5, 1949.

[3] In 1961, it became the Organisation for Economic Co-operation and Development (OECD), with the participation of the USA and Canada.

4. European Coal and Steel Community

The negotiations progressed rapidly and were simplified by the fact that all the future partners had accepted the proposed principles; the work consisted mainly in giving them legal form. A sense of urgency was probably added to the existing goodwill by the communist invasion in South Korea. The Treaty establishing the European Coal and Steel Community (ECSC) was signed in Paris, on April 18, 1951. Ratification by the national parliaments met with little opposition and on July 25, 1952, the Treaty entered into force.

5. European Defence Community

The following two years were difficult. It has been said that the easing of the international political situation—Stalin died on March 5, 1953, and July 27, 1953 marked the end of the Korean war—diminished the necessity for "closing the ranks". In any case, two additional proposals for close co-operation among the "Six"—in the form of the European Defence Community and a European Political Community—failed miserably.

6. EEC and Euratom

Undaunted by those setbacks, the Benelux countries proposed in 1955, to their partners in the Coal and Steel Community, to take another step towards economic integration by setting up a common market and jointly developing transportation, classical and atomic energy. This led to the conference of Messina in the same year, at which Mr Spaak, Belgian Foreign Minister, was asked to report on the feasibility of those plans. At that time an invitation was issued also to the British Government to join the negotiations of the Six; alas, to no avail.[4]

The "Spaak Report" was ready in 1956, and was discussed in Venice, where the decision was taken to start negotiations for drafting treaties that would establish a "common market" and an

---

[4] See Hans Joachim Heiser, *British Policy with regard to the unification efforts on the European Continent* (Leyden, 1959), p. 96.

Atomic Energy Community. With incredible speed (June 1956–February 1957) these two complex treaties were prepared for signature in Rome on March 25, 1957, and on January 1, 1958, the European Economic Community (EEC) and the European Atomic Energy Community (Euratom) became a reality. In 1961, the British Government decided to apply for negotiations to determine whether satisfactory arrangements could be made to meet the needs of the United Kingdom, of the Commonwealth and of EFTA. The Government were "baulked in their objective, so that it was not possible to determine whether satisfactory conditions of entry could be obtained".[5]

7. Treaty Establishing a Single Council and a Single Commission

On April 8, 1965, the institutional set-up of the Communities was simplified by the so-called "Merger Treaty", the Treaty establishing a Single Council and a Single Commission of the European Communities. It entered into force on July 1, 1967. Until that date, there were three Councils and three Commissions (one for each Community), while the Convention on certain institutions common to the European Communities, adopted together with the EEC and Euratom Treaties, provided for a single Court of Justice and a single Assembly. The Convention and the Merger Treaty were repealed by the Amsterdam Treaty, which, however, retained the essential elements of its provisions.[6]

8. The Customs Union

The Customs Union became fully operative in the EEC on July 1, 1968. It meant that tariff and quota restrictions between Member States had by then been completely abolished and that the replacement of the national external tariff by the common external tariff had been completed. The Community was 18 months ahead of the schedule laid down in the Treaty.[7] This left differences in taxation and measures with equivalent effect to tariffs and quotas as obstacles to free trade.

---

[5] *The United Kingdom and the European Communities*, 1971 (Cmnd. 4715), para. 6.
[6] Amsterdam Treaty, Art. 9(1).
[7] Twelve years, see EEC, Art. 8 and Acceleration Decisions ([1960] J.O. 1217 and [1962] J.O. 1284).

9. Community's Own Resources

The replacement of Financial Contributions from Member States by the Community's Own Resources[8] inaugurated a new era in the history of the Community. It became, in a certain way, financially independent and the Treaty amending Certain Budgetary Provisions of the ECSC, EEC and Euratom Treaties and of the Merger Treaty, conferred specific budgetary powers upon Parliament. The Community's own resources are provided by the agricultural levies, the customs duties, a percentage of the VAT collected by the Member States and, since February 1988,[9] a rate applied to an additional base, representing the sum of the GNP at market prices.

10. British, Danish and Irish Membership

After a debate in both Houses of Parliament, at the end of which the Government's decision was approved in the Commons by a majority of 426, the British Government applied to the Council for membership of the Communities on May 10, 1967. By December of the same year it was clear, however, that the "Six" could not reach the unanimity necessary under the Community Treaties to return a reply to Britain's application. Thus ended the second endeavour of the United Kingdom to enter "Europe". The British Government, however, decided to maintain its application for membership and it was discussed at many meetings of the Council of the Communities in the following two years.

At the meeting of Heads of State or Government, on December 1 and 2, 1969, at The Hague, it was finally agreed to open negotiations between the Communities and the States which had applied for membership. Other important decisions taken at this "Summit" concerned the economic and monetary union and the Community's own resources, *i.e.* Community's direct income system.

The Treaty of Brussels relating to the accession of the United Kingdom, Ireland, Norway and Denmark was signed on January 22, 1972; this Treaty entered into force on January 1, 1973, except for Norway which, as a result of a referendum on the subject, did not

---

8 Decision 70/243 of April 21, 1970 ([1970] J.O. L94/19; [1970(I)] O.J. 224). It became effective on January 1, 1971, after ratification by the six national Parliaments.

9 [1988] E.C. Bull. 2–13.

ratify the Treaty. Consequently, several provisions of this Treaty and of the "Act concerning the conditions of accession and the adjustments to the Treaties" attached thereto were modified by the Council Decision of January 1, 1973, adjusting the documents concerning accession of the new Member States to the European Communities (hereinafter referred to as the "Adaptation Decision").

11. Further Enlargement

On June 12, 1975, Greece applied for membership of the Communities and the Treaty of Accession, together with an Act concerning the conditions of accession and the adjustments to the Treaties were signed at Athens on May 28, 1979[10]; it was ratified by the Greek Parliament on June 28, 1979. Greece became a member on January 1, 1981. On March 28, 1977, Portugal[11] and on July 28, 1977, Spain[12] applied for membership. Formal negotiations with Portugal started on October 16, 1978, and with Spain on February 5, 1979. They were successfully concluded at the European Council of March 29 and 30, 1985 and the third enlargement became effective on January 1, 1986, bringing the total of Member States to 12.

12. Direct Election of Parliament, Declaration on Democracy and Fundamental Rights

On September 20, 1976, the representatives of the Member States in Council agreed on the conditions for direct election and signed an Act concerning the Election of the Representatives of the Assembly by Direct Universal Suffrage[13] which was subsequently ratified by the then nine national parliaments. The first elections were held in June 1979,[14] giving the European Communities their democratic legitimacy.

On April 5, 1977 the European Parliament, the Council and the Commission issued a Joint Declaration on Fundamental Rights[15] with which the Heads of State and of Government associated themselves in their Declaration on Democracy in which they confirmed their will to ensure that the values of their legal, political

---

[10] [1979] O.J. L291/1.
[11] [1977] E.C. Bull. 3–8 and Suppl. 5/78.
[12] [1977] E.C. Bull. 7/8–6 and Suppl. 9/78.
[13] [1976] O.J. L278/1.
[14] See below, European Parliament.
[15] [1977] O.J. C103/1.

and moral order are respected and to safeguard the principles of representative democracy, of the rule of law, of social justice and of respect for human rights. They stated that the application of these principles implies a political system of pluralist democracy.[16]

On June 19, 1983, the ten Heads of State and Government signed the Solemn Declaration on European Union expressing, *inter alia*, their determination "to achieve a comprehensive and coherent common political approach" and their will to transform the whole complex of relations between their States into a European Union.[17]

13. Secession of Greenland

On February 1, 1985, Greenland ceased to be part of the European Communities to which it had belonged since January 1, 1973, as part of the Kingdom of Denmark. Greenland has enjoyed a special status within the Kingdom since the Home Rule Act of 1979 and the Greenland Government has exclusive competence, *inter alia*, for fishing, agriculture and stock farming.

Greenland's special features, *i.e.* remoteness, climatic conditions and the cultural particulars of its non-European population pleaded in favour of new arrangements after the people of the island had decided in 1982, by referendum, to withdraw from the Community and to seek a new type of relationship. The Treaty provisions applicable to overseas countries and territories provided an appropriate framework for these relations, although additional specific provisions were needed.[18]

14. The Completion of the Internal Market by 1992

In June 1985, the Commission sent a White Paper to the European Council entitled "Completing the Internal Market".[19] This was the beginning of Operation 1992. It lays down a comprehensive programme and timetable for the abolition of barriers of all kinds in inter-state trade, the harmonisation of rules, the approximation of

---

[16] [1978] E.C. Bull. 3–5; in other words a State without pluralistic democracy cannot be a member of the European Communities.

[17] [1983] E.C. Bull. 6–24. See also Draft Treaty establishing the European Union, [1984] E.C. Bull. 2–7.

[18] See Commission opinion on the status of Greenland ([1983] E.C. Bull. 1–13) and text of amending treaty with various Council regulations ([1985] O.J. L29/1).

[19] White Paper from the Commission to the European Council (Milan, June 28–29, 1985), COM(85) 310 final.

legislation and tax structures and the strengthening of monetary co-operation. To complete the internal market, the White Paper provides for removal of physical, technical and fiscal barriers. It was, *inter alia*, to make the implementation of this comprehensive programme possible that the Member States decided to amend the existing Treaties through the Single European Act.

15. The Single European Act (SEA)[20]

It was signed at Luxemburg on February 17, and at The Hague on February 28, 1986; it entered into force on July 1, 1987. The SEA's objective is the completion of the so-called "internal market" defined as "an area without internal frontiers in which the free movement of goods, persons, services and capital is ensured".[21] It provides, *inter alia*, for the strengthening of the decision-making process of the Community by extending qualified majority voting, the inclusion in the Treaty of chapters on Economic and Social Cohesion (Regional Development), Research and Technological Development and Environment. It also provides for closer involvement of the European Parliament in the legislative procedures. The SEA makes reference to a treaty on Economic and Monetary Union and to co-operation in the sphere of Foreign Policy.

16. The Treaty of European Union (Maastricht Treaty)

The Treaty was signed in Maastricht on February 7, 1992 and came into force on November 1, 1993. It contains seven parts. Title I provides for a European Union, sets out its objectives, *inter alia*, the establishment of an economic and monetary union ultimately including a single currency, a common foreign and security policy including the eventual framing of a common defence policy, the introduction of a citizenship of the Union, co-operation on justice and home affairs, the maintenance of the *acquis communautaire* and the respect of the principle of subsidiarity.

It also "institutionalizes" the European Council, which shall

[20] The act was designated as "single" because it combines two different instruments: the first one provides for modifications to the three European Treaties and the second constitutes an agreement between the Member States to jointly formulate and implement a European foreign policy.

[21] Art. 14(2) (ex 7a) E.C.

provide the necessary impetus and define the general political guidelines, and it indicates that to be a member of the Community a State's government must be founded on the principles of democracy, while the fundamental rights are considered to be general principles of Community law. Titles II, III and IV contain amendments to the three European Treaties. The main novelties are the following.

Economic policy. The European Council defines broad guidelines and the Council monitors and assesses the economic development in the Member States (= multilateral surveillance procedure), possible financial assistance, excessive public budgetary deficits must be avoided and the Council may make recommendations and impose fines in case those recommendations are not put into practice. The economic policy is examined in detail in Chapter Twenty-four under Economic and Monetary Union.

Monetary policy. The primary objective is to maintain price stability; this shall be the main task of the European System of Central Banks (ESCB) and the European Central Bank (ECB). The objectives must be attained in three stages.

The first stage started on July 1, 1990, and ended on December 31, 1993. It provides for convergence and co-ordination of the economic policies of the Member States.

The second stage, which started on January 1, 1994, saw the setting up of the European Monetary Institute (EMI) whose task it is to strengthen the co-operation between central banks and the monetary policies of the Member States, monitor the functioning of the European Monetary System (EMS), facilitate the use of the ECU, etc.

The third stage which started on January 1, 1999 saw the establishment of the euro, which replaced the ECU, first as a currency in its own right, and later as the single currency of the Member States. The monetary policy is examined in more detail in Chapter Twenty-four under Economic and Monetary Union.

New Community fields of action are: education, culture, public health, consumer protection and Trans-European networks. See Part V.

The *co-decision procedure* for the European Parliament and an increase of cases where decisions are taken by the Council with qualified majority. See Part II.

Finally, the Maastricht Treaty contains provisions on *a common foreign and security policy* and on co-operation in the field of *justice and home affairs*. These two new fields of action were not incorporated in the European Community Treaty, but are part of the European Union.

17. The European Economic Area (EEA)

The Agreement for establishing the EEA was signed in Oporto on May 2, 1992 between the seven[22] European Free Trade Area (EFTA) countries and the European Community and its Member States. Following a referendum in Switzerland, this country dropped out. The signature was held up by an Opinion delivered by the Court on the conformity of the draft agreement with the Treaty.[23] Following that Opinion the Agreement, instead of setting up an EEA Court, now provides for an EEA Joint Committee to settle disputes between the two sides and to ensure the uniform interpretation of the Agreement by keeping under permanent review the decisions of the Court of Justice and of the newly created EFTA Court. The first case was introduced before that Court on April 27, 1994. The latter's jurisdiction is confined to the EFTA countries. Decisions of the Committee will have no impact on the case law of the Court of Justice. The autonomy of the Community legal system is thus preserved. In case parties cannot agree on a uniform interpretation, they may agree to apply to the Court of Justice for an interpretation of the rules at issue.[24]

The Agreement, which entered into force on January 1, 1994, establishes an integrated structure based on common rules and equal conditions of competition together with the necessary means to implement it. The free movement of goods, persons, establishment, services, capital and payments is achieved on the basis of existing Community legislation as it has evolved over the years (*acquis communautaire*). Subject to a limited number of exceptions and transitional provisions, it is now applicable in the EFTA countries. In addition to the basic freedoms, the Agreement provides for co-operation in areas, which are directly relevant to the economic activity, such as research and development, social policy, social security, consumer protection, the environment, statistics, and company law. It also provides for a permanent information and

[22] Austria, Finland, Iceland, Lichtenstein, Norway, Sweden and Switzerland. See [1994] O.J. L1/1.
[23] Opinion 1/91 of December 14 [1991] E.C.R. I–6079 and Opinion 1/92 of April 10 [1992] E.C.R. I–2825.
[24] Twenty-Sixth General Report (1992), p. 421.

consultation process covering all stages of the preparation of Community instruments. It includes surveillance and enforcement rules.[25]

The Agreement provides for an EEA Council, comparable to the European Council, an EFTA Surveillance Authority, comparable to the European Commission,[26] and an EEA Joint Parliamentary Committee. The EEA has its own decision-making procedure.[27]

18. Accession of Austria, Finland and Sweden

At the December 1992 Edinburgh European Council meeting it was agreed that negotiations with Austria, Finland and Sweden could start in early 1993, to be followed by similar talks with Norway once the Commission had delivered its opinion on that country's application. It will be remembered that the Treaty provides that "any European State may apply to become a member of the Community. It shall address its application to the Council, which shall act unanimously after consulting the Commission and after receiving the assent of the European Parliament, which shall act by an absolute majority of its component members."[28] The Maastricht European Council of December 1991 added a proviso to that by noting "that any European State whose system of government was founded on the principle of democracy could apply to become a member of the Union".[29] After all, they had just agreed on the contents of the Union Treaty which does provide that "the Union shall respect the national identities of its Member States, whose systems of government are founded on the principles of democracy".[30] Never mind if that Treaty would only enter into force nearly two years later; it probably was already clear at that time that, as the Commission states in its report "Europe and the challenge of enlargement",[31] that accession would take place on the basis of the Treaty on European Union.[32]

It is very interesting to note that the Commission drew up a set of

[25] [1992] Bull. 5, 77; for a more detailed summary see the press release which was issued after the signature, *ibid.* 130.
[26] See Rules of Procedure of the EFTA Surveillance Authority [1994] O.J. L113/19.
[27] See, *e.g.* Decisions of the EEC–EFTA Joint Committee [1994] O.J. L12/32 and of the EFTA Surveillance Authority [1994] O.J. C158/5 and [1994] O.J. L138/39.
[28] Art. 49 (ex 0) TEU.
[29] Twenty-Third General Report (1992), p. 249.
[30] Art. 61 (ex F.1) TEU.
[31] [1992] Bull. 12, 8.
[32] Twenty-Third General Report (1992), p. 249.

criteria with which applicant States should comply. First they must fulfil the three basic conditions of European identity, democratic status and respect for human rights.

Secondly, they must accept the *acquis communautaire* in its entirety, but must also, subject to transitional and temporary arrangements, be able to implement it. This presupposes that the country in question possess a functioning and competitive market economy and an adequate legal and administrative framework. On the basis of the Commission's report, the Lisbon European Council of June 1992 invited the institutions to speed up preparatory work on negotiations with EFTA countries stating that official negotiations could begin as soon as the Maastricht Treaty had been ratified[33] and the second package of financial[34] and structural[35] measures had been agreed upon. Consequently, the Commission adopted opinions on Sweden's application in July 1992,[36] and on Finland's in November.[37] Norway formally applied in November 1992 but withdrew following a negative referendum. The Commission's opinion on Austria's accession was delivered in July 1991.[38] The three countries became Member States of the European Union on January 1, 1995. They thereby accepted all the provisions of the Treaty on European Union and the *acquis communautaire* in its entirety. This enlargement, which marks a significant step forward in the history of European integration, brings the number of Member States to 15 and the number of European citizens to 368 million.

19. The Treaty of Amsterdam

The inter-governmental conference (IGC) which was provided for in the Treaty on European Union, opened in Turin on March 29, 1996, after the agenda was adopted by the European Council. The main titles were: (1) a Union closer to its citizens, (2) the institutions in a more democratic and efficient Union and, (3) a strengthened capacity for external action by the Union. On all three accounts the conference failed miserably. The Treaty was supposed to prepare the Community for further expansion by the inclusion of the countries from Central and Eastern Europe. This does require, in the first place, a profound reform, as suggested in the "Agenda 2000", of the

---

[33] November 1, 1993.
[34] See "Financing Community activities", Chapter Twelve.
[35] See "Economic and Social Cohesion", Chapter Twenty-Eight.
[36] [1992] E.C. Bull. 7/8, 74.
[37] [1992] E.C. Bull. 11, 76.
[38] [1991] E.C. Bull. 7/8, 80.

Common Agricultural Policy and of the structural funds, besides the long overdue reform of the institutions. Where the latter is concerned, the only progress that was achieved, concerns the European Parliament, which saw its direct participation in the legislative field enlarged.[39] None of the other subjects was even touched upon at Amsterdam, as if the lack of reforms were to be kept as an excuse for postponing enlargement! The difficulties encountered with the ratification of the Treaty on European Union had clearly shown that the citizens had to be associated with the activities of the Community institutions. One of the ways to achieve this is by more openness. And although the E.U. Treaty now provides that decisions must be taken "as openly as possible and as closely as possible to the citizen", nothing much has changed. As will be seen, it is still difficult to accede to the archives of the institutions, but impossible to get hold of preparatory documents for Community legislation. By refusing to communicate drafts, under the pretext that they might be amended or have not yet been approved by the hierarchy, the institutions ignore the obligations the Treaties impose upon them. What has become of the much heralded transparency, democracy and openness?

It also provides that one year before the E.U. membership exceeds twenty a conference of representatives of the governments of the Member States shall carry out a comprehensive review of the composition and functioning of the institutions.

The Amsterdam Treaty entered into force on May 1, 1999.

Further Reading

O'Keeffe, Twomey, *Legal Issues of the Maastricht Treaty* (Chancery, London, 1994).

Sally Langrish, "The Treaty of Amsterdam: Selected Highlights" (1998) 23 E.L.Rev. 3.

Amaryllis Verhoeven, "How Democratic need European Union Members Be? Some Thoughts After Amsterdam" (1998) 23 E.L.Rev. 217.

[39] See, however, Protocol on institutions with the prospect of enlargement of the European Union, annexed to the four Treaties which provides that on accession, the Commission shall comprise one national of each of the Member States, and that Member States which have two nationals will give up one, on the condition that the weighting of the votes in the Council has been modified in a manner acceptable to all Member States.

Chapter Three
Community Acts

The main lines of the decision-making process within the Community will be outlined in respect of the role played therein by Parliament, the Council and the Commission. With regard to the various forms which the Community acts can take, it should be pointed out that the actual practice does differ from what the Treaty provides. The tendency is to multiply the forms of the decisions, the procedures leading up to them and the bodies issuing them. Besides the "Communiqués", "Declarations" and "Conclusions" of the European Council, there are, for instance "Programmes"[1] and "Resolutions". These are issued not only by the Council, but also by the Representatives of the Governments of the Member States in Council or by the Council and the Representatives of the Governments. To this the Maastricht Treaty has added the "Council meeting in the composition of the Heads of State or of Government". Since, generally speaking, these acts do not directly create rights and obligations for those who are subject to community law, not all of the above-mentioned measures constitutes acts whose legality the Court can review. Neither are they always issued on the basis of a Commission proposal, although often there will be one. Nor is Parliament or the Social and Economic Committee or the Committee of the Regions necessarily consulted. Nonetheless those acts shape essential Community policies and consequently, the development of the Community itself. It sometimes appears that the more important the decision, politically speaking, the less formal the procedures and the forms.

Nevertheless, the acts expressly provided for by the Treaty still play an essential role and the conditions laid down for the decision-making process and for the contents of those acts must be seen as so many guarantees for lawfulness and judicial control and protection.

The above-mentioned developments seem to run counter to the Treaty provisions which invest the Council—since "Maastricht"

[1] Some programmes, however, are provided for in the Treaty, see, *e.g.* Art. 54 EEC.

and "Amsterdam", more often together with Parliament—and the Commission with the responsibility for implementing the objectives of the Community. To carry out this task they were empowered to make regulations, issue directives, take decisions, conclude international agreements, make recommendations and deliver opinions. It may only be done, however, "in accordance with the provisions of the Treaty".[2] Furthermore, each one of those acts fulfils a specific function in the development of Community law and the Treaty therefore explicitly provides in several cases which kind of act must be adopted. Different procedural rules apply to various categories and, more important, the extent of the legal protection afforded legal and natural persons varies widely from one category to another.[3]

1. Acts Provided for in Article 249 (ex 189) E.C.

A *regulation* has general application, it is binding in its entirety and is directly applicable in all the Member States. Regulations are adopted by the Council or by the Council together with Parliament under the "co-decision" procedure, by the Commission and by the European Central Bank.[4] The criterion for the distinction between a regulation and other acts, especially decisions, must be sought in the "general application". Being essentially of a "legislative nature, a regulation is applicable not to a limited number of persons, defined or identifiable,[5] but to categories of persons viewed abstractly and in their entirety".[6]

Secondly, a regulation is, as was mentioned, "binding in its entirety." This distinguishes it from a directive which only imposes on the Member States to which it is addressed the obligation to achieve specific results. The Court has considered that, since the regulation is binding in its entirety, it cannot be accepted that a Member State should apply in an incomplete and selective manner

---

[2] Art. 249 (ex 189) E.C.

[3] It should be noted that it is not the name given to an act which classifies it in one of the above-mentioned categories, but rather the contents and objectives of its provisions. See Case 15/70 *Chevalley v. Commission* [1970] E.C.R. 975 at 980(10). The Court has also admitted that the same act can contain provisions pertaining to different categories. See Joined Cases 16–17/62 *Producteurs de fruits v. Council* [1962] E.C.R. 471 at 479, [1963] C.M.L.R. 160.

[4] Protocol on the statute of the ESCB and of the ECB, Art. 34(1).

[5] Joined Cases 789–790/79 *Calpak v. Commission* [1980] E.C.R. 1949 at 1961(9); [1981] 1 C.M.L.R. 146.

[6] Joined Cases 16–17/62 *Producteurs de fruits* (n.3 above).

provisions of a Community regulation so as to "render abortive certain aspects of Community legislation".[7]

Finally, a regulation is "directly applicable" in all the Member States. This means that it does not require a national measure to become binding upon institutions, States, undertakings and natural persons. There are, however, cases where regulations provide for national administrative implementation measures.[8] It also means that the national authorities and national legal or administrative measures, even those posterior to the Community act, cannot prevent its application.[9] By this is meant the precedence of Community law over national law.[10]

Direct applicability must not be confused with "direct effect". Community measures have direct effect when they create rights for those who are subject to Community law. This is the case every time Community rules impose an obligation upon a Member State, an Institution or a natural or legal person.[11] The beneficiaries of those obligations can invoke them in the national courts and tribunals and the latter are under Treaty obligation to uphold them. This applies even when these obligations conflict with national measures, whether anterior or posterior.

Not all Community provisions have direct effect, but the Court considers that a regulation, by reason of its very nature and its function in the system of sources of Community law, has direct

---

[7] Case 128/78 *Commission v. U.K.* [1979] E.C.R. 419 at 428(9); [1979] 2 C.M.L.R. 45.

[8] See also Joined Cases C–143/88 and C–92/89, *Zuckerfabrik Süderdithmarschen and Zuckerfabrik Soest* [1991] E.C.R. I–415 at 540(16); [1993] 3 C.M.L.R. 1 "In cases where national authorities are responsible for the administrative implementation of Community regulations, the legal protection guaranteed by Community law includes the right of individuals to challenge, as a preliminary issue, the legality of such regulation before national courts and to induce those courts to refer questions to the Court of Justice for a preliminary ruling."

[9] See Case 230/78 *Eridania v. Ministry of Agriculture* [1979] E.C.R. 2749 at 2772(35). Certain provisions contained in a regulation might need national implementing measures to become applicable, but the regulation itself does not have to be transformed into national law by a national measure.

[10] The French Conseil d'Etat only recognised this basic principle in 1989, 37 years after the first Community was established!

[11] For a more extended analysis of direct effect, see Chapter Four, "Community Law, 2. Direct effect."

effect, *i.e.* it is capable of creating individual rights which national courts must protect.[12]

Directives can be issued by the Council or by the Council together with Parliament ("co-decision") and by the Commission. They constitute the appropriate measure when existing national legislation must be modified or national provisions must be enacted, in most cases for the sake of harmonisation. Directives are binding upon the Member States to which they are addressed, as to the results to be achieved. Although this means that Member States are obliged to take the national measures necessary to achieve the results set out in the directive, they are free to decide how they transpose this piece of Community legislation into national law. It is for instance indifferent whether the national measures are administrative in nature as long as they are binding and as long as they fully meet the requirements of legal certainty.[13]

Although directives are not directly applicable, since they normally require implementing measures, their provisions can nevertheless have direct effect. This must be ascertained on a case by case basis, taking into account their nature, background and wording. According to the Court those provisions are capable of producing direct effect in the legal relationship between the addressee of the act, *i.e.* the Member State and third parties.[14] In the absence of full transposition, a public authority may not rely on that directive against an individual; this has been established in order to prevent a Member State from taking advantage of its own failure to comply with Community law.[15] Neither can a national judge eliminate a national provision contrary to a non-transposed directive.[16] However, an individual, on the other hand, can invoke the

---

[12] It is for the national legal system to determine which court or tribunal has jurisdiction to give this protection and, for this purpose, to decide how the individual position thus protected is to be classified. Case 43/71 *Politi v. Italy* [1971] E.C.R. 1039 at 1048(9); [1973] C.M.L.R. 60. See also Case 93/71 *Leonesio v. Italian Ministry of Agriculture and Forestry* [1972] E.C.R. 287 at 295 (22–23); [1973] C.M.L.R. 343.

[13] Case 239/85 *Commission v. Belgium* [1986] E.C.R. 364; [1988] 1 C.M.L.R. 248.

[14] Case 9/70 *Grad v. Finanzamt Traunstein* [1970] E.C.R. 825 at 839(5); [1971] C.M.L.R. 1. The Court used as an argument the fact that Art. 234 (ex 177) empowers the national courts to refer to the Court of Justice all questions regarding the validity and interpretation of all acts of the institutions without distinction, which implies that individuals may invoke such acts before the national courts. See also Case 111/75 *Mazzalai v. Ferron del Renon* [1976] E.C.R. 657 at 666; [1977] 1 C.M.L.R. 105 and Case 51/76 *Nederlandse Ondernemingen v. Inspecteur der Invoerrechten en Accijnzen* [1977] E.C.R. 113 at 127(23). This last decision is referred to in many subsequent judgments.

[15] Case C–91/92 *Facini-Dori v. Recreb* [1994] E.C.R. I–3325; [1994] 1 C.M.L.R. 665.

[16] *ibid.*

non-transposed or partly transposed directive against the Member State to which it is addressed. Indeed, a directive imposes obligations upon a Member State, but cannot and does not impose obligations upon private parties.[17] However, once the directive has been properly transposed into national law, Member States are entitled to impose criminal penalties for breach of national legislation implementing a directive, even if the directive makes no such provision.[18] This is what is referred to as "vertical direct effect of a directive" as opposed to "horizontal direct effect". The latter would occur if parties could claim rights, under a directive, in their bilateral relationship. Since a directive may not of itself impose obligations on an individual, it may not be relied upon as against such a person.[19]

In other instances, however, where a question concerning the interpretation of a directive was raised in a case involving two persons, the Court did not hesitate to give an answer to the preliminary question. By doing so, the Court seems to be admitting that the directive can be relied upon in the relationship between two "third parties".[20]

The obligation imposed upon Member States to transpose directives into national legislation[21] makes these Member States responsible for the consequences of failure to do so.[22] This follows from the principle, inherent in the system of the Treaty, of State liability for loss and damage caused to individuals as a result of a breach of Community law for which the State can be held responsible.[23] Indeed, Community law requires the Member States to make good damage caused to individuals through failure to transpose a directive, provided that three conditions are fulfilled. First, the

---

[17] Case C–168/95 *Arcaro* [1996] E.C.R. I–4705; [1997] 1 C.M.L.R. 179.

[18] Joined Cases C–58, etc. 95, *Gallotti* [1996] E.C.R. I–4345; [1997] 1 C.M.L.R. 32.

[19] Case 152/84 *Marshall* [1986] E.C.R. 723 (15,16); [1986] 1 C.M.L.R. 688.

[20] Case 262/84 *Beets-Proper v. Van Lanschot Bankiers* [1986] E.C.R. 773; [1987] 2 C.M.L.R. 616.

[21] This obligation follows from Art. 10 (ex 5) E.C. and Art. 249(3) (ex 189.3) E.C. This obligation also imposes upon the Member States, according to the Court, not to take any measure liable seriously to compromise the result prescribed in the directive, during the period after the adoption of the directive, but preceding the expiration of the time limit provided for the transposition: Case 129/96, *Wallonia* [1997] E.C.R. I–7411.

[22] Joined Cases C–6/90 and C–9/90 *Francovich and Others* [1991] E.C.R. I–5357; [1993] 2 C.M.L.R. 66.

[23] See Joined Cases C–6/90 and C–9/90, *Francovich and Others* [1991] E.C.R. I–5357(35); [1993] 2 C.M.L.R. 66 and Joined Cases C–46/93 and C–48/93, *Brasserie du Pêcheur and Factortame* [1996] E.C.R. I–1019(31); [1996] 1 C.M.L.R. 889.

purpose of the directive must be to grant rights to individuals.[24] Second, it must be possible to identify the content of those rights on the basis of the provisions of the directive. Finally, there must be a causal link between the breach of the State's obligation and the damage suffered.[25]

As for a *decision*, it is binding in its entirety upon those to whom it is addressed. The addressee can be a Member State or a legal or natural person. A decision can be taken by the Council or the Council together with Parliament under the so-called "co-decision" procedure, by the Commission and by the ECB. Decisions are normally of an administrative nature, implementing other Community rules, *e.g.* granting of an exception or authorisation or imposing fines.[26]

There are no requirements as to the form of a decision, so that it may be doubtful whether a given act constitutes a binding decision or not. Obviously, the institutions must ensure that a decision is recognisable as a binding act by its very form.[27] Being binding in its entirety, a decision can have direct effect.[28]

Finally the Treaty provides for *recommendations and opinions* which have no binding force. However, according to recent case law, recommendations should not be dismissed as having no legal effect whatsoever. They do not, it is true, create rights which can be invoked in the courts, but the national judges must take recommendations into consideration when solving cases submitted to them. This is especially so if the recommendations can help with the interpretation of other national or Community legal measures.[29]

There are cases where the Court annulled a recommendation, pointing out that an action for annulment is available in the cases of

---

[24] This is another expression of the so-called *Schutznorm* theory which one also finds in the Court's case law concerning reparation of damage cause by the Community's non-contractual liability. The Court explains its restrictive approach to State liability for breach of Community law, by referring to the reasons already given by the Court to justify the strict approach to non-contractual liability of Community institutions: see Joined Cases 83/76, etc., *HNL and Others* [1978] E.C.R. 1209; [1978] 3 C.M.L.R. 566.

[25] Case C–192/94, *El Corte Ingles v. Blazquez Rivero* [1996] E.C.R. I–1283; [1996] 2 C.M.L.R. 507.

[26] See Case 226/87 *Commission v. Greece* [1989] 3 C.M.L.R. 569, where the Court rejected the Greek Government's contention that the Commission decision adopted pursuant to Art. 90(3) (now 86(3)) should merely be considered a non-binding opinion.

[27] Case 28/63 *Hoogovens v. High Authority* [1963] E.C.R. 231 at 235; [1964] C.M.L.R. 125.

[28] Case 9/70 *Grad* (n.14 above) at 837(5); [1971] C.M.L.R. 1.

[29] Case 322/88 *Grimaldi v. Fonds des maladies professionnelles* [1989] E.C.R. 4407; [1991] 2 C.M.L.R. 265.

all measures adopted by the institutions, whatever their nature or form, which are intended to have legal effects. This applies to a Commission *Communication* which sets out to specify the manner of application of a provision of a directive.[30]

Generally speaking, recommendations aim at obtaining a given action or behaviour from the addressee. An opinion, on the other hand, expresses a point of view, often at the request of a third party. Having no binding effect, the legality of recommendations and opinions cannot be reviewed by the Court. Neither can they be submitted to the Court for a preliminary ruling concerning their validity or interpretation. The Court has nevertheless agreed to examine whether recommendations had legal effects when a Member State failed to take the recommended action.[31]

The sequence in which the acts are mentioned in the Treaty does not indicate a hierarchy, it was therefore decided at Maastricht that the intergovernmental conference to be convened in 1996 would examine to what extent it might be possible to review the classification of Community acts with a view to establishing an appropriate hierarchy between the different categories of acts.[32]

A major problem exists as a result of the profusion of regulations, directives and decisions, often amending existing ones. Without even mentioning the quality and transparency of Community legislation, the citizen is confronted by an ever increasing array of measures it becomes impossible to understand in the absence of systematic codification. The Community institutions are aware of this and have concluded an Interinstitutional Agreement on the accelerated working method for official codification of legislative texts.[33] Unfortunately not much has been achieved so far and it seems that the method that was chosen creates, in fact, more confusion.[34] The same problem exists with the Treaties themselves: too many of them and

---

[30] Case C–325/91 *France v. Commission* [1993] E.C.R. I–3283.

[31] *ibid.*

[32] Declaration 16 annexed to the Maastricht Treaty. However, nothing was done.

[33] [1996] O.J. C102/2.

[34] For instance, when an act was modified several times, the simple solution would have been to include all the amendments in the text and re-issue it without further ado; unfortunately, the Council has decided that the act including all the amendments (it had previously agreed upon) has to be re-submitted and needs a new decision on the part of the institutions, at which occasion more often than not, new amendments are proposed, discussed and introduced! It so becomes a never ending process. See, however, the Declaration on the quality of the drafting of Community legislation adopted by the Amsterdam Intergovernmental Conference, which provides for guidelines for improving the quality of the drafting of Community legislation and for the institutions to make best efforts to accelerate the codification of legislative texts ([1997] O.J. C340/139).

too many amendments; the Amsterdam Intergovernmental Conference, therefore, adopted a Declaration in the consolidation of the Treaties, according to which the aim is to draft a consolidation of all the relevant Treaties, including the treaty on European Union. However, this will be done for "illustrative purposes" only and "shall have no legal value"![35]

2. Regulations, Directives and Decisions must be Reasoned

Regulations, directives and decisions must state the reasons on which they are based and must refer to the proposals and opinions which were required to be obtained pursuant to the Treaty.[36]

"Reasons" should be understood as referring both to the legal provision which entitles the institution to take the measure and the reasons which motivated the institution to act. The mention of the provision is particularly important since, as was mentioned, the Community institutions may only exercise those powers which are explicitly provided for by the Treaty. Problems do arise when the act can be based on several Treaty provisions, and a choice must be made by the legislator. According to the Court, it may not depend simply on a institution's conviction as to the objective pursued, but must be based on objective factors which are amenable to judicial review. Those factors include in particular the aim and content of the measure.[37]

As for the motives which prompted the institution to act, they must be mentioned in order to make it possible for the interested parties and for the Court to reconstruct the essential elements of the institution's reasoning,[38] thereby permitting the parties to defend their rights, the Court to exercise its control, and the Member States,

[35] [1997] O.J. C340/140.

[36] Art. 253 (ex 190) E.C.

[37] Case C–300/89, *Commission v. Council* [1991] E.C.R. I–2867; [1993] 3 C.M.L.R. 359; in that case the Council could base the act on two different Treaty provisions; one of them involved the co-operation procedure with the Parliament; the use of both provisions jointly would have excluded this procedure and therefore the involvement of the Parliament. In those cases recourse to a dual legal basis is excluded. The Court decided that the act must be based on Art. 95 (ex 100a) E.C. rather than on Art. 175 (ex 130s).

[38] Case 14/61 *Hoogovens v. High Authority* [1962] E.C.R. 253 at 275; [1963] C.M.L.R. 73. Case C–331/88, *Fedesa and others* [1990] E.C.R. I–4023 at 4066 (30); [1991] 1 C.M.L.R. 507: an effect of Council legislation must be mentioned in the latter's reasoning as one of its objectives only if it was the genuine or main ground for the act. If it is merely a side effect it does not have to be mentioned.

and in the same way all the interested citizens, to know the conditions under which the institution has applied the Treaty.[39]

To attain those objectives, it is sufficient for the act to set out, in a concise but clear and relevant manner, the principal issues of law and fact upon which it is based and which are necessary in order that the reasoning which has led the institution to its decision may be understood.[40] The extent of this requirement depends on the nature of the measure in question. The condition can also be considered as fulfilled when reference[41] is made to the reasons developed in an earlier act.[42]

If an act is not sufficiently "reasoned", this constitutes a ground for annulment: infringement of an essential procedural requirement which can be invoked in an action for review of the legality of the act concerned by the Court of Justice. The Court can and must of its own motion take exception to any deficiencies in the reasons which would make such review more difficult.[43]

As for the reference to the required proposals and opinions, a simple mention is considered sufficient; the institutions are not required to indicate whether or not the opinion was favourable[44] still less to refute dissenting opinions expressed by the consultative bodies.[45]

3. Publication and Entry into Force[46]

Since regulations are of a legislative nature and therefore concern an unidentifiable group to whom they apply, they must be published in the *Official Journal* which appears in the eleven official languages[47]

---

[39] Case 24/62 *Germany v. Commission* [1963] E.C.R. 63 at 69; [1963] C.M.L.R. 347.

[40] *ibid.* See also Joined Cases 36, 37, 38 and 40/59 *Geitling v. High Authority* [1960] E.C.R. 423 at 439.

[41] Case 75/77 *Mollet v. Commission* [1978] E.C.R. 897 at 906(12).

[42] Case 1/69 *Italy v. Commission* [1969] E.C.R. 277 at 285(9); [1970] C.M.L.R. 17. See, however, Case 73/74 *Papiers peints v. Commission* [1975] E.C.R. 1491 at 1514 (31); [1976] 1 C.M.L.R. 589.

[43] Art. 230 (ex 173) E.C., Case 18/57 *Nold v. High Authority* [1959] E.C.R. 41 at 52 and Case 158/80 *Rewe v. Hauptzollamt Kiel* [1981] E.C.R. 1805 at 1834 (27); [1982] 1 C.M.L.R. 449 where Regulation 3023/77 was declared void for not containing a statement of the reasons on which it is based.

[44] This, however, is no secret since both the Commission's proposals and the Parliament's opinions are published in the *Official Journal*.

[45] Case 4/54 *I.S.A. v. High Authority* [1954–56] E.C.R. 91 at 100 (6).

[46] Art. 254 (ex 191) E.C.

[47] The official languages of the institutions of the Community are Danish, Finnish, German, English, French, Greek, Italian, Dutch, Spanish, Swedish and Portuguese. In the case of discrepancies among the languages, the requirement of a uniform

of the Community. They enter into force on the day specified in the act or, in the absence thereof, on the twentieth day following their publication.[48] This rule raises the question of possible retroactive effect. In this regard, the Court ruled that:

> "Although in general the principle of legal certainty precludes a Community measure from taking effect from a point in time before its publication, it may exceptionally be otherwise where the purpose to be achieved so demands and the legitimate expectations of those concerned are duly respected."[49]

Directives and decisions on the other hand concern only a limited number of persons—Member States or natural or legal persons—and must therefore be notified directly to those to whom they are addressed. However, since the Court may review the legality of decisions at the request of parties which are not addressees of such acts, when the latter are of direct and individual concern"[50] to them, it is important that they be informed of the contents of all such decisions. The same applies to directives; as was seen, citizens may invoke them in the national courts and request the latter to ask the Court of Justice for a preliminary ruling on their validity or interpretation. Consequently directives are always published in the *Official Journal* as are decisions which may affect the rights of third parties.[51]

---

interpretation across the Community, excludes the consideration of one such text in isolation, obliging it to be interpreted in the light of the other versions in the other official languages: Case 9/79 *Koschnisket* [1979] E.C.R. 2717(16); [1989] 1 C.M.L.R. 87.

48 A typical example is Regulation 17 giving effect to the principles of competition: the regulation was adopted by the Council on February 6, 1962, published in the *Official Journal* on February 21, 1962 and, since it did not mention the date of entry into force, it became effective on March 13, 1962. See also Case 98/78, *Racke v. Hauptzollamt Mainz* [1979] E.C.R. 69 at 84 (15) and Case 99/78, *Decker v. Hauptzollamt Landau* [1979] E.C.R. 101 at 109 (3).

49 Case 337/88, *SAFA* [1990] E.C.R. I–1 at 18(12); [1991] 1 C.M.L.R. 507. See also Case 331/88, *Fedesa and others* [1990] E.C.R. I–4023 at 4069(45), [1991] 1 C.M.L.R. 872 and Joined Cases C–260 and 261/91, *Diversinte* [1993] E.C.R. I–188.

50 Art. 230 (ex 173(2)) E.C.

51 See in this respect Joined Cases 73–74/63 *Handelsvereniging Rotterdam v. Minister van Landbouw* [1964] E.C.R. 1 at 14; [1964] C.M.L.R. 198 and Case 130/78 *Salumificio v. Amministrazione delle Finanze* [1979] E.C.R. 867; [1979] 3 C.M.L.R. 561.

4. Enforcement[52]

Decisions of the Council and the Commission which impose a pecuniary obligation[53] on persons other than Member States and judgments of the Court of Justice[54] are enforceable.

Enforcement of Community acts is governed by the rules of civil procedure in force within the Member State where it is carried out. The following steps must be taken. The institution which wants to enforce a decision presents it for verification of authenticity to the national authority which the Government of each Member State has designated for this purpose[55] and made known to the Commission and the Court of Justice. The authority then appends to the decision an order for its enforcement.[56] This institution can then proceed to enforcement in accordance with national law, by bringing the matter directly before the competent national authorities. From that

---

[52] Art. 256 (ex 192) E.C.

[53] For instance decisions of the Commission imposing fines pursuant to Art. 15 of Regulation 17, for violation of the competition rules ([1959–1962] O.J. 87).

[54] Art. 244 (ex 187) E.C.

[55] *Austria*: Bundesministerium für Auswertige Angelegenheiten, Abteilung IV/3 "Legalisierungsbüro". *The Netherlands*: Law of February 24, 1955, Stb 73, modified by Law of January 13, 1960, Stb 15: Minister of Justice is addressee of request; Griffier of Hoge Raad implements. *Belgium*: Law of August 6, 1967: Greffier en Chef of the Court of Appeal at Brussels. *Finland*: Ministry of Justice, 1994 Act No. 1554/94 concerning the European Union. *France*: Décret No. 57/321 of March 13, 1957, *Journal Officiel*, March 19, 1957, 2885, designates (1) persons who have received delegation from the Prime Minister and (2) Secrétariat Général du Comité Interministériel. *Germany*: Bundesgesetzblatt, February 3, 1961, II, 50: Minister of Justice. *Italy*: Decree of December 2, 1960, *Gazzetta Officiale*, February 21, 1961, No. 46, 738: Minister of Foreign Affairs. *Luxembourg*: Reg. of October 17, 1962, Memorial of October 31, 1962, No. 58, 1028: verification by Minister of Foreign Affairs, and order for enforcement appended by Minister of Justice. *United Kingdom*: European Communities (Enforcement of Community Judgments) Order 1972, S.I. 1972 No. 1590, which provides for the registration in the High Court of England and Northern Ireland and the Court of Session in Scotland of Community judgments and orders to which the Secretary of State has duly appended an order for enforcement. *Ireland*: S.I. 1972 No. 331; enforcement order appended by the Master of High Court. *Denmark*: by the Minister of Justice; *Greece*: the head of the tribunal of first instance at Athens. *Spain*: B.O.E. No. 160, July 5, 1986, 17843 Minister of Justice. *Portugal*: Diano da Republica, Law No. 104/88 of August 31, 1988 verification of authenticity: Minister of Foreign Affairs; apposition of formula: through Minister of Justice, competent tribunal. *Sweden*: Domstolverket (National Courts Administration), Ordonance SFS 1995:105.

[56] In the United Kingdom "order for enforcement" means an order by or under the authority of the Secretary of State that the Community judgment to which it is appended is to be registered for enforcement in the United Kingdom (S.I. 1972 No. 1590).

moment on, the national rules of civil procedure apply with the exception that suspension of the enforcement may only be decided by the Court.

An action brought before the Court against the decision which is being enforced has no suspensory effect.[57]

As for infringement of Community law by national and legal persons when the Community legislation does not specifically provide any penalty, the Treaty requires the Member States to take all measures necessary to guarantee the application and effectiveness of Community law. While the choice of penalties remains within their discretion, they must ensure that the infringements are penalised under conditions, both procedural and substantive, which are analogous to those applicable to infringements of national law of a similar nature and importance, and which in any event, make the penalty effective, proportionate and dissuasive.[58]

5. Binding Acts not Provided for Under Article 249 (ex 189) E.C.

Community acts are not limited to regulations, directives and decisions. As was pointed out, judgments of the Court are also binding upon the parties and can be enforced. The same principle now also applies to Member States. If the Commission considers that a Member State has not taken the measures required to comply with a judgment of the Court, it shall, after having given that State the opportunity to submit its observations, issue a reasoned opinion specifying the points on which that State has not complied with the judgment. If the Member State concerned still fails to comply with the judgment, the Commission may bring the case before the Court while specifying the amount of the lump sum to be paid by the Member State. The Court may then impose such penalty.[59] As for agreements concluded by the Community with third countries or international organisations, they are binding upon the institutions of the Community and on the Member States.[60]

---

[57] When the Commission takes a decision imposing fines on a person, it usually does not seek enforcement in case an appeal has been lodged against the decision. The Court has approved this practice but only on condition that interest is paid in respect of the period of suspension and that a bank guarantee is lodged covering the amount of the fine; see Case 86/82R *Hasselblad v. Commission* [1982] E.C.R. 1555; [1984] 1 C.M.L.R. 559.

[58] Case 326/88, *Hansen*: [1990] E.C.R. I–2911.

[59] Art. 228(2) (ex 171(2)) E.C.

[60] Art. 300(7) (ex 228(7)) E.C.

The same applies to agreements concluded by the Member States among themselves regarding matters connected with the Treaty.[61] Somewhat different is the position of international agreements concluded by the Member States with third countries: in so far as, under the Treaty, the Community has assumed the powers previously exercised by Member States in the area governed by such international agreement, the provisions of that agreement have the effect of binding the Community.[62] These agreements can be submitted to the control of legality exercised by the Court when the Community is a party[63] to them and they constitute rules of law relating to the application of the Treaty[64]; the result being that regulations, directives and decisions can be annulled in case of infringement of these rules.

Finally, there are the decisions of the Representatives of the Governments of the Member States in Council; these cannot be submitted to the Court, since they do not emanate from the Council or the Commission, but they can be binding within the whole Community.[65] However it will have to be established on a case by case basis whether those decisions are binding only for the Member States or also for the institutions of the Community and even for natural or legal persons. Although those "decisions", not provided for under the Treaty, constitute a flexible instrument to solve a number of questions within the scope of the Treaties, they are not without danger for the institutional equilibrium. Besides immunity from the Court's control, these acts do not require a Commission proposal or an opinion of Parliament. Of course, nothing can prevent the latter from trying to exercise its political control over these acts anyway.

Binding acts not provided for under Article 249 (ex 189) can have

---

[61] See, *e.g.* Art. 293 (ex 220) E.C.

[62] Joined Cases 21 to 24/72 *International Fruit Company v. Produktschap voor Groenten en Fruit* [1972] E.C.R. 1219 at 1227 (18); [1975] 2 C.M.L.R. 1.

[63] See, *e.g.* Case 22/70 *Commission v. Council* [1971] E.C.R. 263; [1971] C.M.L.R. 335.

[64] Art. 230 (ex 173) E.C.

[65] See, *e.g.* the "acceleration" decisions by which the Member States agreed to establish the customs union within a shorter time limit than provided for under the Treaty ([1960] J.O. 1217 and [1962] J.O. 1284). These decisions are not to be confused with decisions of the Member States such as the appointment of the Members of the Commission (Art. 11, Merger Treaty) or of the Judges of the Court of Justice (Art. 167 EEC).

"direct effect"; this applies in the first place to international agreements.[66]

Finally, there are the *joint actions* and *common positions* provided for by the Treaty on European Union under the "Provisions on a Common Foreign and Security Policy". Joint actions address specific situations where operational action by the Community is deemed to be required.[67] Common positions define the approach of the Union to a particular matter of geographical or thematic nature.[68] Both acts are binding upon the Member States. Indeed, joint actions commit the Member States in the position they adopt and in the conduct of their activity, while Member States must ensure that their national policies conform to the common positions.

6. Other Forms of Community "Acts"

A form often used is the *resolution*, either of the Council,[69] or of the Council and of the Representatives of the Governments of the Member States.[70] These resolutions are not to be confused with the decision of the Representatives of the Governments of the Member States in Council or of Ministers in Council.[71] In the first place the decisions of the Representatives of the Member States are legally binding upon the latter, while resolutions sometimes only constitute a political commitment; secondly, the fact that the Member States act within the institutional framework is intended to indicate that the matter directly concerns the implementation of the Treaty. Resolutions, generally speaking, concern matters directly connected with the Community, but not explicitly provided for under Community law.

[66] See Joined Cases 21–24/72 *International Fruit Company v. Produktschap voor Groenten en Fruit* [1972] E.C.R. 1219; [1975] 1 C.M.L.R. 1 and Joined Cases 190 and 291/81 *Singer and Geigy v. Amministrazione delle Finanze* [1983] E.C.R. 847 concerning direct effect of GATT rules.

[67] Art 14(1) (ex J.4) TEU.

[68] Art. 15 (ex J.5) TEU.

[69] See, *e.g.* Council Resolution of February 6, 1979 concerning the guidelines for Community Regional Policy ([1979] O.J. C36/10) and the conclusions of the Council of December 4, 1984, concerning measures necessary to guarantee the implementation of the conclusions of the European Council concerning budgetary discipline. [1984] E.C. Bull. 12–24. In one case, the Court was asked to interpret a Council resolution in a request for a preliminary ruling: Case 9/73 *Schlüter v. Hauptzollamt Lörrach* [1973] E.C.R. 1135 at 1162.

[70] See, *e.g.* [1991] O.J. C178/1. Another form used is the "Conclusions", [1991] O.J. C188/4.

[71] See, *e.g.* [1991] O.J. 188/2.

There is also the *programme* or programmes of action, which intend to lay down general principles for future action both by the Member States and by the institutions of the Community. Such programmes are generally adopted by the Council and by the Representatives of the Governments of the Member States meeting in Council, either by a decision,[72] a *declaration*[73] or a resolution.[74]

Other matters are decided upon by decisions which are not formal binding acts[75] in the sense of Article 249 (ex 189) E.C., since they are not provided for under the Treaty; they are used to settle questions related to Community affairs but do not impose rights or obligations upon the institutions of the Community nor on natural or legal persons.[76] Once again, these "decisions" are not to be confused with the decisions taken by the Governments of the Member States in pursuance of the Treaty provisions such as the appointment of the Judges and Advocates-General of the Court of Justice and the members of the Commission.

Further Reading

Rosa Greaves, "The Nature and Binding Effects of Decisions under Article 189 E.C.", (1996) 21 E.L.Rev. 3.

Paul Craig, "Directives, Direct Effect, Indirect Effect and the Construction of National Legislation", (1997) 22 E.L.Rev. 159.

Klaus Lackhoff and Harold Nyssens, "Direct Effect of Directives in Triangular Situations", (1998) 23 E.L.Rev. 397.

Roger Van den Bergh and Hans-Bernd Chafer, "State Liability for Infringement of the E.C. Treaty: Economic Arguments in Support of a Rule of 'Obvious Negligence', (1998) 23 E.L.Rev. 552.

---

[72] See, *e.g.* [1982] O.J. L236/10.
[73] See, *e.g.* [1973] O.J. C112/1.
[74] See, *e.g.* [1977] O.J. C139/1.
[75] Other languages such as Dutch and German use a word ("Besluit; Beschluß") which clearly distinguishes this act from an Art. 249 (ex 189) E.C. decision ("Beschikking; Entscheidung").
[76] See, *e.g.* [1973] O.J. L207/46.

Chapter Four
Community Law

As was pointed out at the beginning of this book, the Treaties establishing the European Communities are more than classical international agreements creating mutual obligations between the High Contracting Parties. Indeed, by ratifying those Treaties the Member States intended to do more than that, although they most probably did not, at that time, foresee all the conclusions which the Court has, over the years, drawn from the specific nature of those Treaties. Hence the question: what is it that distinguishes them from other international agreements?

In the first place, they have created quasi-governmental bodies (the institutions) independent from the national public authorities and endowed with legislative, administrative and judicial sovereign rights which were transferred to them by the Member States. Furthermore, the Treaties lay down basic principles which are either worked out in the Treaties themselves or implemented by the acts of the institutions. Treaties and acts constitute a set of rules which directly, *i.e.* without interference or intervention, impose obligations upon, and consequently create rights for, the Member States and the natural and legal persons within the Community. The Treaties therefore present many analogies with national constitutions. It can therefore be said that, although they started out as international treaties, these texts have become the "Constitution" of the European Union.[1]

As was shown, the rules embodied in the Treaties (the latter being referred to as "primary" Community law) are constantly being expanded and implemented by new treaties, made more specific, implemented, interpreted and applied by the various acts and measures of the institutions (known as "secondary" Community law). The European Treaties have therefore, as was ascertained by the Court, established a specific legal order. Indeed,

[1] The word "Union" is used here in a global sense, encompassing also the three Communities established by the three European Treaties.

"by creating a Community of unlimited duration, having its own institutions, its own personality, its own legal capacity and capacity of representation on the international plane and, more particularly, real powers stemming from a limitation of sovereignty or a transfer of powers from the States to the Community, the Member States have limited their sovereign rights, albeit within limited fields, and have created a body of law which binds both their nationals and themselves".[2]

It took years before all national courts and tribunals came to share the view that the European Treaties create a separate legal order. But at the time several of them were quick to agree, as was the German Supreme Administrative Court. It stated that Community law constitutes "a separate legal order, whose provisions belong neither to international law nor to the municipal law of the Member States".[3]

1. Direct Applicability

Community law, being distinct from national law, is also independent from it. This means that rights can be conferred and obligations imposed directly by Community provisions, *i.e.* without interference or intervention from national authorities. There is indeed no necessity for Member States to intervene in order to ensure that decisions, regulations and, in certain cases, directives have binding effect throughout the Community.[4] Referring to regulations, the Treaty uses the words "shall be . . . directly applicable in all Member States".[5] The latter should not be taken too literally. The territory of

[2] Case 6/64 *Costa v. Enel* [1964] E.C.R. 585 at 593; [1964] C.M.L.R. 425. It should be pointed out that the unlimited duration only applies to the EC and Euratom Treaties; the ECSC Treaty has a duration of 50 years (Art. 97).

[3] C.M.L. Rev. 1967, 483.

[4] This is what is meant by s.2(1) of the European Communities Act of 1972: these provisions "are without further enactment to be given legal effect or use in the United Kingdom." In other words "reception" of Community law into the sphere of national law is not and cannot be required. Anyway reception is only required by those who adhere to the dualist theory, and furthermore "if one accepts, as is logical and in one view inevitable, that Community law is *sui generis* then, in strictness the monist/dualist argument is excluded, since it is an argument properly limited to international law strictly so called", which is not the case with Community law. John Mitchell, "British law and British membership", *Europarecht*, April-June 1971, 109.

[5] Art. 249(2) (ex 189(2)) E.C.

the Community is defined in the Treaty and thereby the geographical application of Community law. However, as the Court has indicated, this does not preclude Community rules from applying outside the territory of the Community, when the activity in question retains sufficient links with the Community.[6]

In addition, Member States are committed not to interfere with the application of Community law. This also follows from the Treaty which provides *inter alia* that Member States "shall abstain from any measure which could jeopardise the attainment of the objectives of this Treaty".[7]

More important than the acceptance of the "legal autonomy" of the Community legal order in regard to national law, is the understanding of its *raison d'être*. The European Treaties, it will be remembered, aim at establishing within the territories of the Member States a single market characterised *inter alia* by the basic freedoms and constituting a geographical area wherein Community rules apply with the same force and with exactly the same meaning and effect for all who operate therein.[8] Therefore, the very nature of the law created by the European Treaties implies uniform interpretation and application. Without those characteristics there can be no Community. Community law is either uniform in all the Member States or it is not. This does not mean that Community rules should not take into account the specificities of the various Member States or of their regions; as long as the fundamental principles are safeguarded, the way of implementing them must be adapted to local circumstances. Indeed, applying the same rule to different situations constitutes a discrimination just as much as applying different rules to comparable situations.[9]

2. Direct Effect

If the consequence of direct applicability for the Member States is non-interference, for the citizens it means, in most cases, the

---

[6] See Case C–214/94 *Boukhalfa v. Germany* [1996] E.C.R. I–2253; [1996] 3 C.M.L.R. 22: it concerned a Belgian citizen, a local resident employed in the German embassy in Algiers, who claimed the same employment conditions as the German employees.

[7] Art. 10(1) (ex 5(1)) E.C.

[8] Case 6–64 *Costa* (n.2 above) at 594, and Case 166/73 *Rheinmühlen v. Einfuhr- und Vorratstelle Getreide* [1974] E.C.R. 33 at 38(2); [1974] 1 C.M.L.R. 523.

[9] Case 52/79 *Procureur du Roi v. Debauve* [1980] E.C.R. 833 at 858(21); [1981] 2 C.M.L.R. 362 and Case 279/80 *Webb* [1981] E.C.R. 3305 at 3324(16); [1982] 1 C.M.L.R. 719.

possibility of invoking those Community rules in their national courts and tribunals, *i.e.* direct effect. This allows them to protect the rights which those Community rules confer upon them.[10] Applicability of Community law must indeed be understood in two ways: on the one hand, the obligations and prohibitions (*i.e.* obligations to abstain) imposed upon national authorities, institutions and persons, and, on the other hand, the rights of those in favour of whom those obligations have been provided. Indeed, in law, every obligation has a right as its corollary, although this right is not always clearly specified. It is, of course, the same in Community law. Obligations imposed upon Member States, generally speaking, have as their corollary rights for the citizens of the Community. For instance by prohibiting the Member States from hindering the free movement of goods, the Treaty grants the persons within the Community the right to move goods unhindered from one Member State to another.

It is this kind of right that the national courts and tribunals must, by virtue of the direct effect of most Community provisions, uphold in pursuance of the Treaty.[11] The question has been raised whether the national judge must, of his own volition, apply Community rules with direct effect. The Court accepted the domestic law principle of judicial passivity in civil cases and the concomitant rule that in civil suits it is for the parties to take the initiative.[12] On the other hand, a Member State may not prevent a national judge from raising the question of the compatibility of national law with Community rules.[13] It is thus not only regulations, which, because they are "directly applicable"[14] are, as such, suited to "grant to the citizens rights which the national tribunals are under obligation to protect",[15] but all binding Community acts whatever their nature or

[10] This was clearly stated by the Court in Case 43/75 *Defrenne v. Sabena* [1976] E.C.R 455 at 474(24); [1976] 2 C.M.L.R. 98; the same was already apparent in Case 2/74 *Reyners v. Belgium* [1974] E.C.R. 631 at 651(25); [1974] 2 C.M.L.R. 305, although less clearly stated.

[11] Art. 10 (ex 5) E.C. This provision refers to "Member States", but this expression covers all the national authorities whether legislative, administrative or judicial. See Case 33/76 *Rewe v. Landwirtschaftskammer Saarland* [1976] E.C.R. 1989 at 1997(5); [1977] 1 C.M.L.R. 533.

[12] Joined Cases C–430 and 431/93 *van Schijndel* [1995] E.C.R. I–4705.

[13] Case C–319/93 *Peterbroeck* [1995] E.C.R. I–4599.

[14] Art. 249 (ex 189) E.C. See above Chapter Three "Community Acts".

[15] Case 93/71 *Leonesio v. Italian Ministry for Agriculture and Forestry* [1972] E.C.R. 287 at 293(5); [1973] C.M.L.R. 343.

form.[16] Consequently, the question which provisions of Community law have direct effect should be put this way: "Which Community provisions which impose a clear and unconditional obligation upon a Member State, an institution or a person do not have direct effect?"[17] The answer is: only those which leave to the addressee of the obligation a discretionary latitude. For instance, with regard to Article 90(2), the Court stated that:

> "Its application involves an appraisal of the requirements, on the one hand, of the particular task entrusted to the undertaking concerned and, on the other hand, the protection of the interests of the Community. This appraisal depends on the objectives of general economic policy pursued by the States under the supervision of the Commission. Consequently . . . Article 90(2) cannot at the present stage create individual rights which the national courts must protect."[18]

In other words, the obligation is subject to a Commission appreciation and cannot therefore have direct effect.

However, the Court made it clear that in cases where the latitude is limited in time, the expiration of the time-limit suffices to give direct effect to Community rules. This applies notwithstanding the absence of implementing regulations which were to be adopted by the institutions or by the national authorities. The Court found also that, even in the areas in which they have no direct effect, the Community provisions cannot be interpreted as reserving to the national legislature exclusive powers to implement those rules. Indeed, such implementation may be relieved by a combination of Community and national measures.[19]

The fact that the European Treaties have created a new legal order, directly applicable and conferring upon the citizens of the Community rights which the national courts must uphold, was not only

---

[16] *e.g.* provisions of dirs., decs. or agreements; for directives, see Case 21/78 *Delkvist v. Anklagemyndigheden* [1978] E.C.R. 2327 at 2340(21); [1979] 1 C.M.L.R. 372; for decisions see Case 33/76 *Rewe* (note 11 above) and for agreements see Joined Cases 21–24/72, *International Fruit Company v. Produktschap voor Groenten en Fruit* [1972] E.C.R. 1219 at 1227; [1975] 2 C.M.L.R. 1. More recently Case 18/91 *Kziber* [1991] E.C.R. I–221.

[17] Originally, the question was put the other way round: see Case 28/67, *Molkerei Zentrale Westfalen v. Hauptzollamt Paderborn* [1968] E.C.R. 143 at 153; [1968] C.M.L.R. 187. See however Case 43/75 *Defrenne* (n.10 above) at 471. If the acts were not clear and unconditional, nobody could establish what the exact obligation is and ask for it to be upheld; that goes without saying.

[18] Case 10/71 *Ministère Public Luxembourgeois v. Müller* [1971] E.C.R. 723 at 730 (14–16).

[19] Case 43/75 *Defrenne* (n.10 above) at 480(68).

ascertained by the Court, but also recognised from the beginning by most national jurisdictions. Indeed, in the first place, the judiciaries of all the Member States have implicitly recognised this fact for many years, by making extensive use of the possibility offered them by the Treaty to ask the Court for a preliminary ruling on questions concerning Community law raised before them.[20]

By referring those questions to the Court, they accepted that Community rules do apply within the territory of their jurisdiction and may confer rights which they must uphold.

In the second place, the fact that Community law constitutes a new legal order was recognised explicitly, years ago, by the highest national courts and tribunals. This was the case *inter alia* for the Italian Corte Costituzionale, the German Bundesverfassungsgericht and the Belgian Cour de Cassation. Although of historical value only at this stage of the development of Community law, these decisions were extremely important at the time when the novelty of those issues often resulted in provoking adverse reactions from national judges. All the implications of the autonomy of the Community legal order did not always become immediately clear either. In many cases it was a lengthy process of adaptation and learning in which the Court played an important role.[21]

3. Precedence

In retrospect it might seem evident that the autonomy of the Community legal order, the necessity for its uniform interpretation and application in all the Member States automatically implies that Community provisions have precedence over national legislation in case of conflict. Since national courts and tribunals are under obligation, as was just seen, to apply Community rules alongside the provisions of national law, it is not unlikely that conflicts will result from this simultaneous application. The European Treaties contain no explicit provisions regarding the solution to be applied in such cases.[22] Attempts were therefore made to solve such conflicts in accordance with provisions of national law. However, few national legal systems provide for conflict rules of this nature.

In the United Kingdom, for instance, the European Communities Act 1972 provides for the necessary precedence by accepting the

[20] Art. 234 (ex 177) E.C.
[21] First General Report (1967), p. 563.
[22] One could, however, argue that Art. 10 (ex 5) E.C. constitutes a legal ground on which to base this precedence.

"legal effect" of Community provisions in the United Kingdom.[23] The same applies to the decisions of the Court regarding the meaning or effect of any of the Treaties, or the validity, meaning or effect of any Community instrument.[24] In relation to statute law, this means that the directly applicable Community provisions shall prevail even over future Acts of Parliament, if the latter are inconsistent with those instruments. It also means that by ratifying the European Treaties, the United Kingdom, like any other Member State, must refrain from enacting legislation inconsistent with Community law.[25]

In the Netherlands, the Basic Law (Constitution) not only provides that the provisions of international treaties have precedence over existing national laws and regulations; it also specifies that the same applies to measures enacted by the institutions set up under those treaties and adds that this precedence applies in case of conflict between an existing Community rule and subsequent national law.[26]

The French Constitution provides, in general terms, that treaties or agreements, duly ratified or approved, shall, upon their publication, have authority superior to that of laws, subject, however, for each agreement or treaty, to its application by the other party.[27]

The German Constitution provides that the Federal Republic may,

---

[23] European Communities Act 1972, s.2(1). See Case C–213/89 *Factortame and Others* [1990] E.C.R. I–2433; [1990] 3 C.M.L.R. 1, where the Court held that "a court [in a dispute governed by community law] which would grant interim relief, if it were not for a rule of national law, is obliged to set aside that rule", at E.C.R. I–1274(21).

[24] *ibid.*, s.3(1).

[25] *ibid.*, s.2(4) provides therefore that present and future enactments shall be construed and have effect subject to s.2. See *Hansard*, February 15, 1972, Vol. 831. This basic principle derives not only from the obligations explicitly accepted by the Member States when they became members of the Community, but, as was explained, from the very nature of the Community and Community law. Indeed, the existence of the Community depends upon the simultaneous and uniform application throughout the Community of all the provisions of the Treaties and the acts of the institutions. This was clearly stated over and over again by the Court. See, *e.g.* Case 83/78 *Pigs Marketing Board v. Redmond* [1978] E.C.R. 2347 at 2371(56); [1979] 1 C.M.L.R. 177 and Case 128/78 *Commission v. U.K.* [1979] E.C.R. 419 at 428(9); [1979] 2 C.M.L.R. 45.

[26] Arts 66 and 67 Dutch Constitution; these provisions were incorporated in the Constitution in 1953.

[27] Art. 55 French Constitution of 1958. In a judgment of 1962, the French Cour de Cassation held that a contested action had been carried out under an EEC decision and regulation which are "acts regularly published and having acquired force of international treaties" (*Gazette du Palais*, December 9 to 11, 1970, 6–7). See also *Administration des Douanes v. Jacques Vabre* [1975] C.M.L.R. 336, where the French Supreme Court clearly stated that the Treaty has an authority greater than that of national acts and is binding on the national courts. See, however, the

by legislation, transfer sovereign powers to inter-governmental institutions[28] and refers to the precedence of the general rules of international law.[29] It is only with difficulty that one can equate Community measures with the latter.

The Italian Constitution is even less precise. It only provides that "Italy's legal system conforms with the general principles recognised by international law."[30]

These German and Italian texts and even the French Constitution form a rather meagre legal basis for the obligation that national courts should give precedence to Community law over national law in case of conflict between the two. And what about those Member States whose Constitution contains no provisions in this respect? Furthermore, in certain cases the above mentioned constitutional provisions were not considered by national judges as obliging them to accept the precedence of Community provisions over national rules.[31]

However, even in the case of the Dutch Constitution, which is so explicit about precedence, doubts might subsist as to the precise consequences. Furthermore, if the sole legal basis for supremacy of Community law over national law were national law itself, this supremacy would be at the mercy of the next constitutional amendment.

Other grounds had therefore to be found which would be accepted by all national jurisdictions without reference to their particular

---

decision of the Conseil d'Etat *Syndicat Général des Fabricants de Semoules v. Direction des Industries Agricoles* [1970] C.M.L.R. 395. It was only in October 1989 (31 years after the EEC Treaty came into force) that this French highest administrative jurisdiction finally recognised the precedence of Community law over national law!

[28] Art. 24(1) German Constitution. See, however, German Constitutional Court on the Treaty of Maastricht, October 12, 1993, 89 BverfGE 155, at 185. As a former German Judge of the Court of Justice wrote: "[i]n the past, after some hesitations, the German Constitutional court assented to the developing supranational power of the European Community, though with provisions for extreme situations. The judgment on the Treaty of Maastricht reversed this situation fundamentally. The [German] Court returned to a nationalistic view of democracy and opened up ways of leaving the European Union regardless of juridical bonds and declared German authorities competent to ignore Community law. It is uncertain whether this tendency to re-nationalisation will continue or whether it will be overcome by another change in the case law of the Constitutional Court." Manfred Zuleeg, "European Constitution under Constitutional Constraints: The German Scenario", (1997) 22 E.L.Rev. Feb.

[29] *ibid.*, Art. 25.

[30] Art. 10(1) Italian Constitution.

[31] By a ruling of March 1, 1968 (*Recueil Dalloz-Sirey*, 1968, *Jurisprudence*, 286) the French Conseil d'Etat ruled that a French Court is bound to ensure that application of the national *lex posterior* to an existing Community rule, whatever the meaning

national legal orders. This ground was obviously the Community legal order itself. It was indeed accepted by all the Member States which "have adhered to the Treaty on the same conditions, definitively and without any reservations other than those set out in the supplementary protocols".[32] The Court has always considered that the wording and the spirit of the Treaty make it impossible for the Member States to accord precedence to a unilateral and subsequent measure over a legal system accepted by them on the basis of reciprocity. The Court also added that "the executive force of Community law cannot vary from one State to another in deference to subsequent domestic laws, without jeopardising the attainment of the objectives of the Treaty set out in Article 5, 2 [now 10.2] and giving rise to the discrimination provided by Article 7 [repealed by the Treaty of Amsterdam]".[33]

Therefore, "the law stemming from the Treaty, an independent source of law, could not, because of its special and original nature, be overridden by domestic legal provisions, however framed, without being deprived of its character as Community law and without the legal basis of the Community itself being called into question".[34] This also applies, of course, with regard to national constitutional provisions. The Court states that the effect of a Community measure cannot be affected by allegations that it runs counter to fundamental rights as formulated by the Constitution of a State.[35]

To put it simply: either Community law stands by itself, is uniformly applied and has precedence over domestic law, or it does not subsist. This view is now generally accepted in all the Member States.[36]

The general principle of Community law's precedence over national law having been established, it is necessary to examine some of its more concrete consequences. As far as any national court or

---

and scope of Community law (Second General Report (1968), 453). The Commission considered this ruling incompatible with the legal obligations deriving from the Treaty (1968, J.O. C71). See also Cour de Cassation, October 22, 1970, *Contributions Indirectes v. Ramel* [1971] C.M.L.R. 315.

[32] Joined Cases 9 and 58/65 *San Michele v. High Authority* [1967] E.C.R. 1 at 30.

[33] Case 6/64, *Costa v. ENEL* [1964] E.C.R. 585 at 594; [1964] C.M.L.R. 425. This was once again emphasised by the Court in Case 128/78, *Commission v. U.K.* ("Tachographs"): [1979] E.C.R. 419 at 429; [1979] 2 C.M.L.R. 45.

[34] *ibid.* See also Case 11/70, *Internationale Handelsgesellschaft v. Einfuhr- und Vorratsstelle für Getreide* [1970] E.C.R. 1125 at 1134(3); [1972] C.M.L.R. 255.

[35] *ibid.* and Case 4/73, *Nold v. Commission* [1974] E.C.R. 491; [1974] 2 C.M.L.R. 338.

[36] It might be of interest to mention some of the earliest and most important rulings of national courts since they constitute essential steps towards recognition of the Community legal order and its implications. In Belgium reference must be made to a

tribunal is concerned, the Court has described its obligations as follows. Directly applicable rules of Community law are a direct source of rights and duties for all those affected thereby. The latter include any national court whose task it is, as an organ of a Member State, to protect, in cases within its jurisdiction, the rights conferred upon individuals by Community law. In accordance with the principle of precedence, Treaty provisions and directly applicable Community measures, by their coming into force, automatically render any conflicting provisions of current national law inapplicable.

It follows that every national court, in cases within its jurisdiction, must apply Community law in its entirety and protect the rights which the latter confers upon natural or legal persons. In other words, it must set aside any conflicting provision of national law, whether prior or subsequent to the Community provision. It is not necessary for the national court to request or await the prior setting aside of such national provisions by legislative or other means.[37]

As far as legislative bodies are concerned, the Court indicated that the principle of precedence precludes the valid adoption of new national legislative measures to the extent that they would be incompatible with Community provisions.[38]

As far as other national authorities are concerned, it is clear that respect for the precedence of Community law and the obligations resulting for Member States from the Treaty[39] not only prevent them from enacting measures which are incompatible with Community provisions, but also impose upon them the obligation to abolish all existing contrary measures, whatever their nature. Although these measures are inapplicable their maintenance gives rise to an ambiguous situation: "by maintaining, as regards those subject to the law who are concerned, a state of uncertainty as to the possibilities which are available to them of relying on Community law".[40]

---

decision of 1971 of the Cour de Cassation in the case *Belgian State v. Fromagerie Franco-Suisse* [1972] C.M.L.R. 373: the primacy of the Treaty results from the very nature of international treaty law. In France, Cour de Cassation, 1975, *Administration des Douanes v. Jacques Vabre et al.* (*ibid.*, 336) and finally also the French Conseil d'Etat: *Maurice Boisdet* September 24, 1990: [1991] 1 C.M.L.R. 3.

37 Case 106/77 *Amministrazione delle Finanze dello Stato v. Simmenthal* [1978] E.C.R. 629 at 643–644 (14–18 and 21, 22, 24); [1978] 3 C.M.L.R. 263.

38 *ibid.*, at 17. See also Case 230/78 *Eridania v. Minister of Agriculture and Forestry* [1979] E.C.R. 2749.

39 Art. 10 (ex 5) E.C.

40 Case 167/73 *Commission v. France* [1974] E.C.R. 359 at 372(41); [1974] 2 C.M.L.R. 216. See also Case 159/78 *Commission v. Italy* [1979] E.C.R. 3247; [1980] 3 C.M.L.R. 446 and Case 61/77 *Commission v. Ireland* [1978] E.C.R. 417 at 442; [1978] 2 C.M.L.R. 466.

It follows from the preceding remarks that autonomy of the Community legal order, direct effect and precedence of Community rules over national measures all result from the particular nature of Community law.

A final aspect which needs to be mentioned in this respect is the reference by the Court to the usefulness[41] or effectiveness[42] of Community acts to justify the right of individuals to rely on obligations imposed by directives. Those acts are not directly applicable, since the choice is left to the national authorities as to the form and method of implementing the obligations imposed upon them. In other words, the implementation is left, within limits, to their discretion. Consequently, directives have no direct effect and persons cannot invoke them in national courts. However, the Court admits, as was seen before,[43] that provisions of directives can have direct effect, especially after the time limit set for their implementation has elapsed. Similarly, interested parties have the right to ask national courts to determine whether the competent national authorities, in exercising the choice which is left to them, have kept within the limits of their discretionary powers.[44] However, whether national authorities have or have not exercised their discretionary power, *e.g.* to make a derogation, is a matter for the discretion of the legislative or administrative authorities of the Member State; it cannot, therefore, be subject to legal review on the basis of the provisions of the directive. "It is the duty of the national court before which the directive is invoked to determine whether the disputed national measure falls outside the margin of the discretion of the Member State."[45]

And, as was discussed above in the chapter on Community Acts, under "directives", Member States, which breach Community law, are, under given conditions, liable for the harm caused to individuals by this breach. Those legal and natural persons can ask the national judge to order the State to compensate them for any damage caused by the infringement of Community law on the part of the State.

---

[41] Case 51/76 *Nederlandse Ondernemingen v. Inspecteur der Invoerrechten en Accijnzen* [1977] E.C.R. 113 at 127(29); [1977] 1 C.M.L.R. 413.

[42] Case 38/77 *ENKA v. Inspecteur der Invoerrechten en Accijnzen* [1977] E.C.R. 2203 at 2211(9); [1978] 2 C.M.L.R. 212.

[43] See Chap. Three "Community Acts".

[44] Case 38/77 *ENKA* (n.42 above) at 2212(10).

[45] Case 51/76 *Nederlandse Ondernemingen* (n.41 above) at 127(29).

4. Sources of Community Law

As was previously indicated, the Community legal order has its own sources, which consist not only of the European Treaties and the acts of the institutions issued in pursuance of the powers conferred upon them (regulations, directives, decisions and agreements),[46] but also of the rules relating to the application of this primary and secondary Community law. These rules comprise international law, in so far as applicable,[47] and the general principles of law,[48] including the fundamental rights. The latter play an important role, as the Court pointed out: "respect for fundamental rights forms an integral part of the general principles of law protected by the Court of Justice", and added that "the protection of such rights, whilst inspired by the constitutional traditions common to Member States, must be ensured within the framework . . . and objectives of the Community".[49] A reference to those fundamental rights is to be found in

---

[46] See above, Chapter Three "Community Acts".

[47] Agreements concluded by the Community with third States or international organisations Art. 300 (ex 228) E.C., are, of course, governed by the rules of international law. But according, to the Court (see, *e.g.* Case 30/88 *Greece v. Commission* [1989] E.C.R. 3711; [1991] 2 C.M.L.R. 169) "the provisions of an agreement concluded by the Council under Articles 228 [now 300] and 238 [now 310] of the Treaty, form, as from the entry into force of the agreement an integral part of the Community legal system". On the other hand, as the Court pointed out, when exercising their rights to lay down Community rules, the institutions are not bound by provisions of international law, unless the Community itself has assumed the rights and obligations resulting for the Member States from international agreements to which they are parties, and unless the provisions of those agreements have direct effect within the Community: Joined Cases 21–24/72 *International Fruit Company v. Productschap voor Groenten en Fruit* [1972] E.C.R. 1219 at 1226(8); [1975] 2 C.M.L.R. 1. See also *ibid.*, at 1227(18), and Joined Cases 89, etc./85 *Woodpulp Products v. Commission* [1988] E.C.R. 5233; [1988] 4 C.M.L.R. 901, "the conduct of the Commission is covered by the territoriality principle as universally recognised by public international law". As for Treaty precedence over agreements concluded between Member States before its entrance into force, see Case 10/61 *Commission v. Italy* [1962] E.C.R. 1 at 10; [1962] C.M.L.R. 187.

The precedence of Community law over all other applicable provisions, including international law, is recognised by the European Communities Act 1972, ss.2(1) and (4).

[48] See Case 159/82 *Verli-Wallace v. Commission* [1983] E.C.R. 2711 at 2718(8) and below, Chapter Eight, "The Courts", Court of Justice, Grounds for annulment.

[49] Case 11/70 *Internationale Handelsgesellschaft v. Einfuhr- und Vorratstelle Getreide* [1970] E.C.R. 1125 at 1134(4); [1972] C.M.L.R. 255. See also Case 25/70 *Einfuhr- und Vorratstelle v. Köster* [1970] E.C.R. 1161 at 1176(36); [1972] C.M.L.R. 255, where the Court found that a system of licences for import and export, involving a deposit, did not violate any right of a fundamental nature and Case 44/79 *Hauer v. Land Rheinland-Pfalz* [1979] E.C.R. 3727; [1980] 3 C.M.L.R.

the Treaty on European Union, which provides that the Union is founded on the principles of liberty, democracy, respect for human rights and fundamental freedoms, and the rule of law, principles which are common to the Member States. The same Treaty adds that "the Union shall respect fundamental rights, as guaranteed by the European Convention for the Protection of Human Rights and Fundamental Freedoms signed in Rome on November 4, 1950 and as they result from the constitutional traditions common to the Member States, as general principles of Community law".[50]

Forty-two years ago, I drafted an article to be inserted in the Treaty Chapter on the Court of Justice, which would indicate the sources of law to be applied. Although different words would be used today, its basic indications still seem to be applicable:

> "1. The Court whose function it is to ensure the rule of law in the execution of this Treaty, shall apply:
> (a) the provisions of this Treaty and of the judicial acts issued by the institutions;
> (b) the conventions to which the Community is a party or which are undertaken on its behalf;
> (c) the customary law of the Community;
> (d) the general principles of the law of the Community;
> (e) the municipal law of the Member States in case of explicit or tacit reference.
> 2. In case of reference to international law, the Court shall apply Article 38, paragraph 1, of the Statute of the International Court of Justice.
> 3. As auxiliary means for the determination of the applicable law, the Court shall apply the decisions of international tribunals, those of the Community and the doctrine."[51]

5. Application of National and International Law by the European Courts

The question of the applicability of national law by the Community institutions was raised on several occasions before the Court. The

42, where the Court examined whether a Community regulation violates the right of property and the free exercise of professional activity. Also the inviolability of the domicile in Case 46/87R *Hoechst v. Commission* [1987] E.C.R. 1549; [1991] 4 C.M.L.R. 410.

[50] Art. 6(2) (ex F.2) TEU.

[51] P. S. R. F. Mathijsen, "*Le droit de la Communauté Européenne du Charbon et de l'Acier; une étude des sources*", Martinus Nijhoff, 's-Gravenhage, 1957, 193.

latter, however, decided that it lacked the competence to apply the internal law of the Member States.[52] Consequently, the Court cannot accept a claim that by taking a decision an institution has violated national law. Neither can the Court decide on the interpretation of a national provision.[53] Application of national law by the Court, however, takes place where the Treaty refers explicitly to national concepts.[54] This is the case, for instance, where the Treaty refers to companies and firms formed in accordance with the law of a Member State.[55] Also when the Treaty provides that, in the case of non-contractual liability, the Community shall make good any damage caused by its institutions or servants "in accordance with the general principles common to the laws of the Member States".[56] Similarly, when the Court is called upon to solve a question for which there are no Treaty provisions, it must solve the problem "by reference to the rules acknowledged by the legislation, the learned writings and the case law of the member countries".[57]

In numerous cases the Court was called upon to apply International law.

6. Application of Community Law by the National Courts

As was pointed out above, Community law does not require national courts to raise of their own motion an issue concerning the breach of provisions of Community law, where examination of that issue would oblige them to abandon the passive role assigned to them by going beyond the ambit of the dispute defined by the parties.

---

[52] See, *e.g.* Case 1/58 *Stork v. High Authority* [1959] E.C.R. 17; Joined Cases 36–40/59 *Geitling v. High Authority* [1960] E.C.R. 423. See, however, Joined Cases 17 and 20/61 *Klöckner v. High Authority* [1962] E.C.R. 325 and Case 159/78 *Commission v. Italy* [1979] E.C.R. 3247.

[53] Case 78/70, *Deutsche Grammophon v. Metro* [1971] E.C.R. 487 at 498(3); [1971] C.M.L.R. 631.

[54] See Case 50/71 *Wünsche v. Einfuhr- und Vorratstelle Getreide* [1972] E.C.R. 53 at 64(6); [1973] C.M.L.R. 35.

[55] Art. 48 (ex 58) E.C. See, *e.g.* Case 18/57 *Nold v. High Authority* [1959] E.C.R. 41 at 48.

[56] Art. 288 (ex 215) E.C.

[57] Joined Cases 7/56 and 3–7/57 *Algera et al. v. Common Assembly* [1957–1958] E.C.R. 39 at 55. Another example is the definition of "misuse of power" (Art. 230 (ex 173) E.C.) based on a comparative study by the Advocate General of this concept in the municipal law of the Member States: Case 3–54 *ASSIDER v. High Authority* [1954–1955] E.C.R. 63 at 74.

However, where by virtue of domestic law, courts must raise of their own motion points of law based on binding domestic rules, which have not been raised by the parties, such an obligation also exists where binding Community rules are concerned.[58] The situation is the same, if domestic law confers on courts a discretion to apply of their own motion binding rules of law. Indeed pursuant to the principle of cooperation laid down in Article 10 (ex 5) of the Treaty, it is for the national courts to ensure the legal protection which persons derive from the direct effect of provisions of Community law.[59]

The basic rule remains, however, that it is the national judge who is, in the first place, responsible for the implementation, application, and interpretation of Community law when the parties refer to it in disputes brought before him.

In 1993, the Commission published a Notice on the co-operation between the Commission and the national judges according to which the national judge can, *inter alia*, call upon the Commission for any help he might need in cases before him involving Community law.[60]

7. Conclusions

As shown by the foregoing considerations, the Community legal order grew and developed mainly at the hands of the Community judges.[61] Over the years, the Court has played an essential role in consolidating its autonomy *vis-à-vis* municipal and international law, by emphasising its orginality and by imposing its precedence. It goes without saying that this task would have been impossible without the co-operation, understanding and adaptability of the national judges; for example by asking for preliminary rulings they gave the Court the opportunity to fulfil its task. But the Community Court was and still is the driving force.

It should be clear also that the task of the Court is not limited to applying, developing and interpreting Community law *stricto sensu*. According to the Treaty,[62] the Court shall ensure that "the law" is observed. The term "law" in this provision and as it is understood by the Court refers to the concept of what is right, much more so than to

[58] Case 33/76 *Rewe* [1976] E.C.R. 1989; [1997] 2 C.M.L.R. 1.

[59] Case C–213/89 *Factortame* [1990] E.C.R. I–243; [1990] 3 C.M.L.R. 375.

[60] [1993] O.J. C39/6. See also Case C–91/95P *Tremblay* [1996] E.C.R. I–5547; [1997] 4 C.M.L.R. 211.

[61] Of course, the Member States did also contribute to the consolidation and development of Community law; see, *e.g.* the Convention on the Law applicable to Contractual Obligations ([1980] O.J. L266/1).

[62] Art. 220 (ex 164) E.C.

anything that is described and analysed in this book. Seen in this light, the European Communities appear, beyond all the limitations, ambiguities, hesitations and conflicts, as a legal, political, social and economic system which, thanks to its balanced institutional structure and inherent potential, constitutes the only possible solution for Europe's problems and the only hope for its development.

Further Reading

D. Wyatt and A. Dashwood, *European Community Law*, (3rd ed., Sweet & Maxwell, London, 1993).

Pavlos Eleftheriadis, "Aspects of European Constitutionalism", (1996) 21 E.L.Rev. 32.

Mark Hoskins, "Tilting the Balance: Supremacy and National procedural Rules", (1996) 21 E.L.Rev. 365.

Brend Meyring, "Intergovernmentalism and Supranationality: Two Stereotypes for a Complete Reality", (1997) 22 E.L.Rev. 221.

John Temple Lang, "The Duties of National Courts under Community Law", (1997) 22 E.L.Rev. 3.

Manfred Zuleeg, "The European Constitution under Constitutional Constraints: The German Scenario", (1997) 22 E.L.Rev. 19.

John Temple Lang, "The Duties of National Authorities Under Community Constitutional Law", (1998) 23 E.L.Rev. 109.

P. Craig and G. de Burca, "*E.U. law; text, cases and materials*", second edition, Oxford University Press, 1998.

P. J. G. Kapteyn and P. Verloren van Themaat, *Introduction to the Law of the European Communities*, (3rd ed., by Laurence W. Gormley, Kluwer Law International, 1998).

Antonio Goucha Soares, "Pre-emption, Conflicts of Powers and Susidiarity", (1998) 23 E.L.Rev. 132.

PART TWO: THE INSTITUTIONS AND BODIES AND THE FINANCING OF ACTIVITIES

Introduction

Among the various bodies established by, or in pursuance of, the Treaties,[1] five are referred to as "institutions": the European Parliament, the Council, the Commission, the Court of Justice and the Court of Auditors.[2] What distinguishes an institution from other Community bodies is the fact that the former, generally speaking, can "act", *i.e.* take generally binding decisions[3] and that their Members are either elected nationally (Council and Parliament) or appointed by the governments of the Member States or by the Council. The other organs, on the other hand, operate in specific fields and either have a purely advisory task or take decisions which are not generally binding.

Only the Community itself, the EIB, the Supply Agency, the ECB and a few other organs have legal personality and capacity.[4] When the Community acquires or disposes of property or is party to legal proceedings (outside the Court of Justice) it is represented by the Commission. On the other hand, agreements with one or more States or international organisations, are negotiated by the Commission and concluded by the Council for the Community.[5]

The first European institutions, *i.e.* the High Authority, the Common Assembly, the Special Council of Ministers and the Court

---

[1] Bodies set up by the Treaty are, for instance, the Economic and Social Committee (Art. 7 (ex 4) E.C.), the Committee of the Regions (*ibid.*), a European System of Central Banks and a European Central Bank (Art. 8 (ex 4a) E.C.), the European Investment Bank (Art. 9 (ex 4b) E.C.), the Monetary Committee (Art. 114 (ex 109c) E.C.) and the Committee of Permanent Representatives (Art. 207(1) (ex 151(1) E.C.). For bodies set up by the institutions in pursuance of powers conferred upon them by the Treaty see, for instance, the European Environmental Agency (Reg. 1210/90: [1990] O.J. L120/1).

[2] The Court of Auditors was upgraded to institution by the Maastricht Treaty.

[3] This follows from the wording of Art. 7 (ex 4(1)) E.C.: "each institution shall act within the powers conferred upon it by this Treaty".

[4] Art. 281 (ex 210) and 282 (ex 211) E.C.; see Joined Cases 43/59, etc. *Lachmüller v. Commission* [1960] E.C.R. 463 at 472: "that personality is one of public law"; See also Case 22/70 *Commission v. Council* [1971] E.C.R. 263 at 274(4); C.M.L.R. 335, where the Court decided that having this legal personality "means that in its external relations the Community enjoys the capacity to establish contractual links with third countries over the whole field of objectives defined in Part I of the Treaty." For the EIB, see Art. 107 (ex 106) E.C., and for the Supply Agency, Euratom, Art. 54; see also Court Ruling 1/78 [1978] E.C.R. 2151. Other organs with legal personality are the European Centre for the Development of Vocational Training, the European Foundation for the Improvement of Living and Working Conditions and the European Environment Agency.

[5] Art. 228 300(1) and (2) (ex (1) and (2)) E.C.

of Justice were set up by the Treaty of Paris of 1951 establishing the European Coal and Steel Community.[6] Similar institutions: an Assembly, a Council, a Commission and a Court of Justice, were set up by the Treaties of Rome establishing the European Economic Community and the European Community for Atomic Energy (Euratom). This meant 12 institutions: three of each kind. However, the Convention on certain institutions common to the European Communities[7] provided for a single Assembly and a single Court of Justice for the three Communities.

Nonetheless this left three Councils and the High Authority plus two Commissions, beside the one Assembly and the one Court; a total of eight institutions. A further rationalisation was introduced by the so-called "Merger Treaty"[8] which established the "Council of the European Communities" to replace the three Councils and the "Commission of the European Communities" to replace the High Authority and the EEC and Euratom Commissions. The remaining four institutions exercised from then on, the powers and jurisdiction conferred by the Treaties on the various institutions they replaced, in accordance with the provisions of the relevant Treaties.[9] A fifth institution was added by the E.U. Treaty by "upgrading" the Court of Auditors. It might be interesting to note that, according to the Preamble of the Merger Treaty, the merger of the institutions is seen as a step in the direction of the "unification of the three Communities".

---

[6] Art. 7 ECSC.

[7] This Convention was annexed to the EEC and Euratom Treaties and signed, together with them, at Rome on April 25, 1957. It was repealed by Art. 9(1) of the Amsterdam Treaty which, however, retained its essential elements.

[8] Treaty establishing a single Council and a single Commission of the European Communities, signed at Brussels on April 8, 1965. This Treaty was also repealed by the Amsterdam Treaty, Art. 9(1). Its essential provisions were, however, retained, and according to Art. 11(2) there will be no change in the legal effects of the Acts in force adopted on the basis of the treaties.

[9] Convention, Arts 1 and 3; Merger Treaty, Arts 1 and 9.

Chapter Five
The European Parliament

As indicated above, the European Treaties originally referred to this institution as the "Assembly" and for a long time there was strong opposition from the Council and several Member States to the use of the term "Parliament".

In 1962 the Assembly decided to call itself the "European Parliament"[1] and since then the other institutions, including the Court of Justice, except for a while the Council,[2] adopted that denomination. As for the Community acts which require consultation of the Assembly, they have, except for the first few years, always referred to the "European Parliament".[3]

Finally, the name was formally changed in the Treaty, albeit in a indirect way, by the SEA, which refers to the institutions "designated as referred to hereafter" and the reference is always to the "European Parliament"![4]

Whether the Assembly was well advised in modifying its name, and having it formally changed to "Parliament", can be questioned. Not so much because the institution does not, indeed, have the powers which are characteristic of democratic parliaments, *i.e.* the power to legislate and to raise taxes, but, because the name "Parliament" has created the illusion that democratic control, as understood nationally, already exists within the Community. And although the SEA and even more the Treaty of Maastricht and the Treaty of Amsterdam have extended, as shall be seen hereafter, the powers of Parliament in the legislative field, the European Parliament is not yet a parliament in the generally accepted sense of the word.

[1] Resolution of March 30, 1962 (J.O. 1962, 1045). On March 20, 1958 the Assembly had decided to call itself the "European Parliamentary Assembly".

[2] See, *e.g.* the answer to the parliamentary question No. 398/77 in which the Council stated that the denomination of any one of the institutions could only be amended by a treaty amending the existing Treaties ([1977] O.J. C270/18).

[3] See, *e.g.* Reg. 214/79 concerning the European Regional Development Fund ([1979] O.J. L35/1).

[4] Art. 3(1) SEA.

1. The Members of Parliament

Parliament consists presently[5] of 626 "representatives of the peoples of the States brought together in the Community".[6]

(1) Election of the Members

Until the first direct elections in 1979, the members of Parliament were designated by the respective national Parliaments from among their members.[7] And although the ECSC Treaty[8] already provided for election by direct universal suffrage, it was not until September 20, 1976, that the Act concerning direct election[9] was finally adopted by the representatives of the Member States in Council.[10] Elections by direct universal suffrage should be held "in accordance with a uniform procedure in all Member States".[11] Parliament is to draw up proposals and the Council, after obtaining the assent of Parliament, shall lay down the appropriate provisions, which it shall recommend to Member States for adoption in accordance with their respective constitutional requirements. For the Member States, nothing binding, in other words. Since it was not possible until now to agree on such procedures, the 1979, 1984, 1989, 1994 and 1999 elections were held in accordance with the method of voting decided nationally.[12]

The Maastricht Treaty has introduced the right for citizens of the Union residing in a Member State of which they are not a national to

---

[5] *i.e.* 1994: at the Edinburgh European Council it was agreed to increase the number of members to reflect German unification to 567.

[6] Art. 189 (ex 137) E.C., which provides that the number shall not exceed seven hundred.

[7] This was done according to a procedure laid down by each Member State. See former Art. 138 EEC which lapsed on July 17, 1978 in accordance with Art. 14 of the Act concerning direct election. MEPs receive a uniform salary of euro 5,677 (Council Dec. of April 27, 1999).

[8] Art. 21(3) ECSC.

[9] Act concerning direct election of representatives of the European Parliament by direct universal suffrage annexed to the Council Decision of September 20, 1976 ([1976] O.J. L278/1).

[10] For this form of decision-making see under Council.

[11] Art. 190(4) (ex 138(3)) E.C. and Act concerning direct election, Art. 7(1) and (2).

[12] Act concerning direct election, Art. 7(2): "pending the entry into force of the uniform electoral procedure and subject to other provisions of the Act [Art. 9] the electoral procedure shall be governed in each Member State by its national provisions".

All the Member States apply, with some variations, a proportional representation system via party lists.

vote and to stand in elections for Parliament. A Council directive lays down detailed arrangements.[13]

In the 1999 Parliament, the 626 seats were distributed nationally as follows: 99 for Germany, 87 for each of the other larger States (France, Italy and the United Kingdom), 64 for Spain, 31 for the Netherlands, 25 for Belgium, Greece and Portugal, 22 for Sweden, 21 for Austria, 16 for Denmark and Finland, 15 for Ireland and six for Luxemburg. The main criteria for the allocation of seats is the population of the States concerned.

(2) The Member's Mandate

Members of the European Parliament (MEPs) are elected for a term of five years. Anyone can stand for Parliament,[14] it being understood that, upon election, the rules concerning incompatibility[15] apply.

Before 1979 MEPs had to be members of a national Parliament; presently, the Act concerning direct election simply states that there is no incompatibility between the two offices.[16] However, Belgium and Greece have created an incompatibility at national level and many political parties have done the same in their internal rules. Although it must be admitted that fulfilling two mandates is an extremely demanding task, it seems that the disjunction between the two (only very few MEPs have a double mandate) has somehow estranged the European Parliament from the national ones, thereby not only eliminating a chance for political integration, but also decreasing the political clout of the MEPs. The necessity of closer links between the MEPs and the national MPs is now generally recognised. To that effect a Protocol on the role of national parliaments in the European Union was annexed to the Treaties.

During the sessions of Parliament, the MEPs enjoy the privileges and immunities accorded to members of national parliaments when in their own countries, and immunity from detention and legal proceedings when on the territory of another Member State.[17]

---

[13] See Council Directive laying down detailed arrangements: [1993] O.J. L329/34.

[14] Including, *e.g.* in the U.K., peers and ministers of religion who are excluded from election to Westminster.

[15] Act concerning direct election, Art. 6(1) and (2).

[16] *ibid.*, Art. 5.

[17] Protocol on the Privileges and Immunities of the European Communities attached to the Merger Treaty, Art. 10. See, *e.g.* Case 149/85, *Wybot v. Faure* [1986] E.C.R. 2403; [1987] 1 C.M.L.R. 819 from which it follows that Parliament is always "in session".

2. Tasks and Powers

As all the other institutions, the European Parliament "shall exercise the powers conferred upon it by this Treaty". Previously, Parliament only had "advisory and supervisory" powers, but this changed with the SEA and even more with the Maastricht and Amsterdam Treaties. The former introduced the "co-operation" procedure, while the latter, as shall be seen, provided for the so-called "co-decision" power. It should be noted, however, that since 1970, Parliament has enjoyed certain deciding powers in the budgetary field.[18] Nonetheless, as was just mentioned, Parliament does not fully exercise the attributes of an elected representative body, *i.e.* legislation and the raising of taxes.

The tasks and powers of Parliament, in the order in which they appear in the Treaty, are the following:

(a) to participate in the legislative process;
(b) to set up a temporary Committee of Inquiry;
(c) to receive petitions and designate an Ombudsman;
(d) to put questions to the Council, to the Commission and to the Presidency of the Common Foreign and Security policy;
(e) to adopt its rules of procedure;
(f) to discuss the annual General Report submitted by the Commission;
(g) to vote a motion of censure when it disapproves of the activities of the Commission;
(h) to approve the nomination of the President and the members of the Commission;
(i) to participate in the budgetary procedure;
(j) to initiate procedures in the Court of Justice against the Council or the Commission, in case the latter fail to act, or to protect its own rights, and to intervene in other cases;
(k) to participate in other activities of the Community.

(1) Participation in the legislative process

It is in this area that the SEA, and more so the Maastricht Treaty, introduced the most far-reaching changes. The SEA increased the cases wherein Parliament must be consulted by the Council before the latter adopts an act, and introduced the "co-operation procedure". The Maastricht Treaty, on the other hand, provided for the

---

[18] Art. 272 (ex 203) E.C.

so-called "co-decision procedure". Presently there are four different procedures[19]: consultation, co-operation, assent and co-decision.

(a) Consultation

Until recently, this was the general rule and practically all Treaty provisions dealing with acts of the Council would read: "the Council shall, on a proposal from the Commission and after consulting the European Parliament, . . ."[20]

Presently there are 11 such instances[21] in the Treaty. Generally speaking the Treaty previously provided for consultation on all important matters such as Community policies (*e.g.* agriculture, transport, competition) and association agreements.[22] However, the Council has, for many years, agreed to consult Parliament also in cases where it is not specifically provided for in the Treaty.

When the Council enacts regulations, directives or decisions, the consultation of Parliament is initiated by the Council on the basis of a proposal submitted to it by the Commission. As long as the Council has not acted, the Commission may alter its proposal at any time during the procedure leading to the adoption of the Act.[23] This, for example, allows the Commission when Parliament has expressed an opinion on the proposal, to take it into account by submitting a modified proposal. In February 1990 the Commission proposed a "Code of conduct" that would ensure more effective co-operation in the decision-making process, with a bigger role for Parliament in the field of external relations.[24]

---

[19] Besides the budgetary powers, see n.18 above.

[20] See, *e.g.* Art. 37(2) (ex 43(2)) E.C.

[21] Art. 8 (ex G) TEU: third pillar; Art. 39 (ex K11) TEU: police and judicial co-operation in criminal matters; Art. 42 (ex K14) TEU: Council may refer action under police and judicial co-operation to E.C., Title IV, the so-called "passerelle clause"; Art. 11 (ex 5a) E.C.: close co-operation under the first pillar; Art 13 (ex 6a) E.C.: combat discrimination; Art. 18 (ex 8a) E.C.: additional rights for citizens; Art. 19 (ex 8b) E.C.: citizenship; Art. 22 (ex 8e) E.C.: citizenship; Art. 128 (ex 109q) E.C.: guidelines on employment; Art. 130 (ex 109s) E.C.: establishment of the new employment Committee; Art. 133(5) (ex 115(5)) E.C.: extension of the Article to international negotiations and agreements.

[22] Art. 310 (ex 238) E.C.

[23] Art. 250(2) (ex 189a(2)) E.C.

[24] [1990] E.C. Bull. 4–81: the Code stipulates that the Commission will take care to remind the Council not to come to a "political agreement" before Parliament has given its opinion, keep the House informed of the guidelines set out in the Council and ensure that, in accordance with the principles laid down by the Court, Parliament is reconsulted should the Council substantially amend a Commission proposal. The Commission also undertakes to set up its contact with Parliament and the Council concerning the choice of the legal base to be adopted for its

Parliament's opinions have no binding force. However, mention must be made, in the acts, of the fact that Parliament was consulted.[25] But, the Treaty does not require the Council to mention whether the opinion was favourable or not, nor to refute, in the latter case, the arguments brought forward by Parliament against the proposal.[26]

It should also be noted that where the Council acts on a proposal from the Commission, unanimity is required for an act constituting an amendment to that proposal.[27] This seems to indicate that the power of the Council to adopt an act which differs from the Commission's proposal is limited to amending the latter, while respecting the essential content of the proposal. In the case where the Council introduces a modification, the question arises whether Parliament must be consulted again, this time on the amended text. According to the Court, this is only necessary when the amended text is substantially different from the one on which Parliament gave its opinion.[28]

It should be pointed out that Parliament, acting by a majority of its Members, may "request the Commission to submit any appropriate proposal on matters on which it considers that a Community act is required for the purpose of implementing the Treaty".[29] The question has been raised as to whether this right to request proposals infringes upon the "exclusive" right of initiative of the Commission. This seems unlikely since it is only a "request", and on the other hand, the Council has had the same right from the beginning[30] and this was never considered as limiting the Commission's freedom to decide on the opportunity of making proposals.

---

proposals and to take individual decisions on any amendment adopted at second reading by Parliament, which the Commission does not wish to incorporate in its proposal. Parliament, for its part, undertakes to adopt any appropriate operational and statutory measures to make the inter-institutional process more effective, and ensure in particular that opinions on the proposals linked with the creation of a frontier-free area before the end of 1992 are adopted swiftly. (Report of proceedings: [1990] O.J. Annex 3–389.)

25 Art. 253 (ex 190) E.C.

26 See Case 6/54 *Government of the Kingdom of the Netherlands v. High Authority* [1954–56] E.C.R. 103 at 111. The Commission, on the other hand, undertook, starting with the July 1973 session of Parliament, to inform it systematically of actions taken on the opinions.

27 Art. 250(1) (ex 189a(1)) E.C.; however, this rule does not apply during the so-called co-decision procedure Art. 251(4) and (5) (ex 189b(4) and (5) E.C.).

28 See Case 41/69 *ACF Chemiefarma v. Commission* [1970] E.C.R. 661 at 689(69), Case 817/79 *Buyl v. Commission* [1982] E.C.R. 245 and Case 65/90 *Parliament v. Council* [1992] E.C.R. I–4593. Text not considered different in Case C–65/93 *Parliament v. Council* [1995] E.C.R. I–643; [1996] 1 C.M.L.R. 4.

29 Art. 192(2) (ex 138b(2)) E.C.

30 Art. 208 (ex 152) E.C.

It is clear, however, that Parliament has a different view on the matter, and considers this right to request proposals as a sharing of the Commission's right of initiative.[31] The Commission itself has pointed out that it is the Treaty which confers on it the power to initiate legislation in the areas covered by the Treaty and that it is, therefore, legally and politically responsible for its proposals, regardless of the fact that they are drawn up at the request of another institution or economic operators.[32]

Finally, mention must be made of the fact that, when provided for in the Treaty, consultation of Parliament constitutes an "essential procedural requirement", and failure of the Council to comply with it constitutes a ground for annulment of the act by the Court of Justice.[33]

(b) "Procedure referred to in Article 252" (ex 189c) E.C.[34]

The term "co-operation procedure" was introduced into the Treaty by the SEA, but eliminated again by the Maastricht Treaty, which uses the expression: "acting in accordance with the procedure referred to in Article 189c [now 252]". This procedure is, in fact, just a more elaborate consultation procedure.

Roughly speaking, the co-operation procedure means that, after having consulted Parliament on a Commission's proposal, the Council adopts a "common position" (instead of a decision, which would otherwise be the case). This common position is then communicated to Parliament, and the latter can either:

(a) approve it, or take no decision, after which the Council adopts the act in accordance with the common position; or
(b) propose amendments by an absolute majority, and the Commission then re-examines its original proposal in the light of those amendments; the Commission re-transmits its

---

[31] Rules of Procedure, Rule 36B, entitled "Legislative initiative".

[32] See answer to written question No. 3471/92: [1993] O.J. C292/22.

[33] See Cases 138/79 *Roquette Frères v. Council* and 139/79 *Maizena v. Council* [1980] E.C.R. 3333 and 3393, where the Court annulled a regulation because the Council, although it had transmitted the Commission's proposal to Parliament for its opinion, adopted the regulation without having received it. However, see also Case C–65/93, *Parliament v. Council* [1995] E.C.R. I–643: Parliament was duly consulted, but, according to the Court, failed to meet the obligation of genuine cooperation by adjourning the last plenary session during which the draft could have been adopted. No reproach to the Council which adopted the measure without having received the Opinion of Parliament, because of urgency.

[34] Art. 252 (ex 189c) E.C. After the modifications introduced by the Amsterdam Treaty, the co-operation procedure only applies in the following four areas of EMU: Art. 99(5) (ex 103(5) E.C.): detailed rules for the multilateral surveillance

proposal to the Council, together with the amendments of Parliament it has not accepted and its opinion on them; the Council then takes its final decision; or Parliament can:

(c) reject the common position, but the Council then may, nonetheless, adopt its common position unanimously.

The Treaty also provides for time-limits within which the various institutions must make their decision.

(c) Assent Procedure

The assent procedure was introduced by the SEA[35] and extended by the Maastricht Treaty.[36] It constitutes, in fact, a veto right,[37] rather than a right of co-decision, where Council and Parliament decide "together", as under the conciliation procedure.[38] When assent is required, the Council may only act after it has obtained the agreement of Parliament.

(d) "Procedure referred to in Article 251" (ex 189b) E.C.

The introduction of this co-decision procedure by the Maastricht Treaty on the E.U. and the extension of its scope[39] and of the role of

---

procedure; Art. 102(2) (ex 104a(2)) E.C.: definition for the prohibition of privileged access; Art. 103(2) (ex 104b(2)) E.C.: definitions for the prohibitions of overdraft and assuming commitments of regional or local authorities; Art. 106(2) (ex 105a(2)) E.C.: harmonisation of denominations of all coins.

[35] Arts 8 and 9 SEA: respectively action on application for membership of the Community, and international agreements; these are the only two cases introduced by the SEA.

[36] It was reduced by the Amsterdam Treaty and now only applies in the four following cases: Art. 7(1) (ex F.1(1)) TEU: serious and persistent breach by a Member State; Art. 49 (ex O) TEU: accession of new members; Art. 190(4) (ex 138(3)) E.C.: procedure for election of MEPs; Art. 300(3) (ex 228(3)) E.C.: certain international agreements.

[37] Indeed Parliament can only refuse its assent and cannot discuss the case with the Council.

[38] See hereunder: co-decision procedure.

[39] It now applies in 22 cases: Art. 12 (ex 6) E.C.: rules to prohibit discrimination on grounds of nationality; Art. 18 (ex 8a) E.C. provisions to facilitate the exercise of the right to move and reside; Art. 40 (ex 49) E.C.: measures for free movement of workers; Art. 44(1) (ex 54(2)) E.C.: directive to attain freedom of establishment; Art. 46(2) (ex 56(2)) E.C.: co-ordination directive in the field of freedom of establishment; Art. 47(1) (ex 57(1)) E.C.: directive on mutual recognition of diplomas; Art. 47(2) (ex 57(2)) E.C.: harmonisation concerning self-employed; Art. 71(1) (ex 75(1)) E.C.: transport rules; Art. 80 (ex 84) E.C. sea and air transport; Art. 95(1) (ex 100a(1)) E.C.: harmonisation in view of internal market; Art. 137 (ex 118) E.C.: minimum requirements for Member States to fulfil objectives of social policy; Art. 141 (ex 119) E.C.: measures to ensure equal opportunity and equal

the Parliament in it, by the Treaty of Amsterdam, represents a real break-through for the European Parliament. Where, before those Treaties, its function was purely consultative, the Parliament now shares with the Council real legislative power. Indeed, although the expression "co-decision" does not appear in the Treaty, the procedure provides, in certain cases, for joint decisions. The consequence is that many acts are no longer designated as "Council" regulations, directives or decision, but as regulations, directives or decisions of the "European Parliament and the Council". The procedure creates a kind of interplay between the Parliament and the Council reminiscent of that which exists between the two chambers of many national parliaments.

The rather lengthy and complex procedure can best be described on the more familiar basis of the three classical phases in Community legislation: the Commission proposal, the role of the Parliament and the Council decision.

Phase One

(a) The Commission submits a proposal to the Parliament and the Council[40];
(b) The Parliament gives its opinion to the Council;
(c) The Council adopts, by a qualified majority, a "common position", which is communicated to the Parliament (unless the Parliament has not proposed any amendments,[41] or all the amendments have been accepted by the Council, in which case it adopts the proposed act and this ends the procedure).[42]

---

treatment; Art. 148 (ex 125) E.C.: implementation Social Fund; Art. 149 (ex 126) E.C.: education, vocational training, youth; Art. 150 (ex 127) E.C.: measures to achieve *id.*; Art. 151(5) (ex 128(5)) E.C.: incentives concerning Culture; Art. 152(4) (ex 129(4)) E.C.: incentives concerning Public Health; Art. 153(4) (ex 129a(2)) E.C.: support of Member States' policies in the field of Consumer Protection; Art. 156 (ex 129d) E.C.: TENs; Art. 162 (ex 130e(2)) E.C.: ERDF; Art. 166(1) (ex 130i(1)) E.C.; Art. 172 (ex 130o) E.C.: R&D; Art. 175(1) (ex 130s(3)) E.C.: action in the fields of Environment; Art. 255 (ex 191a) E.C.: general principles for transparency; Art. 280(4) (ex 209a) E.C.: countering fraud; Art. 285 (ex 213a) E.C.: statistics; Art. 286(2) (ex 213b) E.C.: supervisory body on data processing.

[40] In the other procedures, the proposal is sent to the Council, which then consults the Parliament on it.

[41] This right of Parliament to propose amendments, which in turn determines what steps the Council may take, is one of the novelties introduced by the Amsterdam Treaty: before that, the opinion could be ignored by the Council as purely consultative.

[42] This constitutes an important simplification of the procedure enhancing Parliament's powers.

Phase Two

The Parliament can:

(a) approve the common position or abstain from taking a decision, in which case the act is deemed approved in accordance with that common position, and this ends the procedure[43];
(b) reject, by an absolute majority of its component members, the common position, in which case the act is deemed not to have been adopted, this also ends the procedure[44];
(c) propose amendments by an absolute majority of its component members; the amended text is then forwarded to the Council and the Commission, which delivers an opinion on those amendments.

Phase Three

(a) the Council can, within three months, approve all the amendments, by qualified majority,[45] in that case the act is deemed adopted (however, unanimity is required for the amendments on which the Commission has delivered a negative opinion)[46]; if the Council does not adopt all the amendments, the "Conciliation Committee" is convened;
(b) the Conciliation Committee[47] will try to reach agreement,

---

[43] Previously, the common position then had to be adopted formally by the Council. This constitutes another simplification enhancing Parliament's power.

[44] Previously, the Parliament would inform the Council of this rejection, the Council could then convene the Conciliation Committee to explain further its position, after which the Parliament could confirm its rejections, with the consequence that the act would be deemed not to have been adopted. This also constitutes a simplification enhancing Parliament's power.

[45] As will be seen, there are a number of cases wherein the Council must decide unanimously throughout the whole co-decision procedure: for instance, Art. 18(2) (ex 8a(2)) E.C.: provisions to facilitate the exercise by the citizens of the Community of the right to move and reside freely within the territory of the Community; Art. 42 (ex 51) E.C.: measures in the field of social security needed to provide freedom of movement of workers; Art. 47(2) (ex 57(2)) E.C.: harmonisation directives concerning free movement of the self-employed; Art. 151 (ex 128) E.C.: measures in the field of culture.

[46] This is logical, because, where the Council acts on a proposal from the Commission—and this negative opinion is equivalent to a proposal—it may only amend it unanimously: Art. 250(1) (ex 189a(1)) E.C.

[47] The Conciliation Committee is composed of the members of the Council, or their representatives, and an equal number of MEPs. The Conciliation Committee is given six weeks, extendible with another two, to reach agreement.

supported in that task by the Commission, on a joint text[48] by qualified majority of the Council members and majority of the Parliament members; if agreement cannot be reached on a joint text, the proposed act is deemed not to have been approved;

(c) if a joint text is agreed upon, the Council and the Parliament can, each according to its own procedure, adopt it, thereby terminating the procedure; if either of the two institutions fails to approve the proposed act, it shall be deemed not to have been approved. This also ends the procedure.[49]

It follows from this procedure that the Parliament now is in a position to put an early end to the procedure with either a positive[50] or a negative[51] outcome.

Some acts adopted under the co-decision procedure need implementing measures, which are normally adopted by the Commission; no special procedure is provided for the adoption of such measures, as far as a possible involvement of the Parliament is concerned. It is clear, however, that such implementing measures can be extremely important, since they often determine the actual content of the adopted act. A *modus vivendi*[52] was adopted by the three institutions in 1995 containing guidelines to overcome difficulties which had arisen for reasons connected with the question of committee procedure (comitology). It provides that drafts submitted by the Commission to the committee provided for in the basic act, shall be sent, at the same time and under the same conditions, to the appropriate committee of the Parliament, which then delivers an opinion. Parliament shall be informed by the Commission when the implementing measure is not in accordance with that opinion or when the Commission must submit a proposal to the Council. The latter informs Parliament and will take due account of any unfavourable opinion. The same applies to the Commission.

Besides the opinions given following consultation, Parliament has

---

[48] The Committee will address the common position on the basis of the proposed amendments.

[49] Under the Maastricht Treaty, the Council could, at that point, still adopt the common position, unless the Parliament again rejected it by an absolute majority of its component members. This last "shuttle" was abolished at Amsterdam.

[50] By not proposing amendments in phase one, and by approving the common position or abstaining in phase two.

[51] By rejecting the common position in phase two and by refusing to agree within the conciliation committee, or failing to approve the proposed act at the end of the procedure.

[52] [1996] O.J. C102/1.

always formulated resolutions whenever it considered it necessary.[53] According to the Rules of Procedure, such resolutions must, however, concern matters falling within the activities of the Community.

With a view to furthering the inclusion of Parliament in the decision-making process, a Code of Conduct has laid down, since 1990, a number of reciprocal commitments of Parliament and Commission.[54]

Which one of the four above-mentioned procedures is to be applied is, of course, indicated in the Treaty provision on which the institution bases the act. A problem might arise when the institution's power is based on two different Treaty provisions. The Court held that in such cases the act must be adopted on the basis of the two relevant provisions.[55] However, in case this would result in divesting the procedure of its essential element, *i.e.* Parliament's intervention in the legislative process, that rule is not applicable. For instance, if one of the provisions requires the co-operation procedure, and the other requires the Council to act unanimously, after merely consulting Parliament, the essential element of the co-operation procedure would be undermined. Consequently, the dual legal basis is excluded. Which one should be used depends, of course, on the content of the act to be adopted.[56]

(2) Setting up of a Temporary Committee of Inquiry

Parliament may, at the request of a quarter of its members, set up a temporary Committee of Inquiry to investigate alleged contraventions or maladministration in the implementation of Community law.[57]

---

[53] Rules of Procedure, Art. 47 ([1981] O.J. C90/49, 65). In 1998, the Parliament was consulted 215 times, participated in 38 co-operation procedures and in 41 co-decisions procedures, it gave 21 assents, issued 135 opinions and, adopted 213 own-initiative reports and resolutions.

[54] The Code provides, *e.g.* for individual Commission decisions on any amendment adopted at second reading. See [1990] E.C. Bull. 5–80.

[55] Case 165/87 *Commission v. Council* [1988] E.C.R. 5545; [1990] 1 C.M.L.R. 457.

[56] Case 300/89 *Commission v. Council* [1991] E.C.R. I–2867 at 2897, [1991] 1 C.M.L.R. 2867.

[57] Art. 193 (ex 138c) E.C. See, for example, Decision of Parliament of July 17, 1996 setting up a temporary committee of inquiry to investigate alleged contraventions or maladministration in the implementation of Community law in relation to BSE: [1996] O.J. C239/1.

There are, however, a certain number of limitations. In the first place, as the name indicates, such a Committee is only temporary, which means that it shall cease to exist on the submission of its report. Secondly, the investigation does not supersede actions undertaken by other institutions or bodies on the basis of the powers conferred on them by the Treaty. When for example the Court of Auditors submits a special report,[58] the latter cannot be contradicted by the Report of the Committee of Inquiry, and to avoid this, Parliament must consult this institution before setting up the Committee.

The same applies, and this is the third limitation, where facts are being examined before a court and while the case is still subject to legal proceedings. Anyway, detailed provisions governing the right of inquiry must be determined by common agreement of Parliament, Commission and Council.[59]

(3) Right of Petition and Appointment of an Ombudsman

The right of petition[60] is granted not only to citizens of the Union, but also to "any natural or legal person residing or having its registered office in a Member State". Petitions may be sent concerning a matter which comes within the Community's field of activity by persons directly affected by them. A right of petition has been in existence for quite some time[61] and is widely used.

An Ombudsman must be appointed by Parliament[62] empowered to receive, from the same category of persons, complaints concerning instances of maladministration in the activities of the institutions. If the Ombudsman finds such a case, he shall refer the matter to the institution concerned which shall inform him of its views within three months. He then sends a report to Parliament and to the institution with, if needed, suggestions for remedies.

---

[58] Art. 248(4) (ex 188c(4)) E.C.

[59] Decision of the Parliament, the Council and the Commission on the detailed provisions governing the exercise of the Parliament's power of inquiry: [1995] O.J. L78/1.

[60] Art. 194 (ex 138d) E.C.

[61] See Rules of Procedure, Rule 128.

[62] Art. 195 (ex 138e) E.C. See Regulation and General Conditions established by Parliament [1994] O.J. L113/15. Council Decision approving those acts [1994] O.J. L54/25 and Parliament's Resolution on the role of the Ombudsman [1995] O.J. C249/226. See also Parliament's Decision appointing the first Ombudsman [1995] O.J. L225/17.

(4) Oral or Written Questions

The Treaty provides that the Commission shall reply orally or in writing to questions put to it by Parliament or by its members.[63]

Parliament's right to obtain answers to its questions constitutes an important aspect of its supervisory powers. It has been widely used.[64] This right, and the use of it, were considerably extended over the years, both as to form and addressees. The most important extension was probably the right to obtain answers from the Council,[65] especially when one takes into account that it was introduced in 1958 unilaterally by Parliament and accepted by the Council. It was again extended by the Maastricht Treaty to include the Council of the Common Foreign and Security Policy.[66]

To the written and oral questions/answers provided for in the Treaty, Parliament added, in 1962, the oral questions followed by a debate.[67] This was accepted by the Commission and the Council with the proviso that, where the latter is concerned, the debate may not be concluded by a vote on a resolution concerning the debate in question. Finally, in 1973, Parliament introduced the Question Time, in which the Council and the Commission agreed to participate. In this case, only the answers from the Commission can give rise to a debate.

It is clear from the foregoing that Parliament succeeded in including the Council in its work, far beyond what is provided for in the Treaty. Indeed, not only the Council as such accepted to participate, but also the Presidency of the Common Foreign and Security Policy.[68]

As indicated, there are differences in the ways the above mentioned procedures are applied to the Council and to the Commission. This distinction reflects the particular character of the relationships existing between Parliament, on the one hand, and the other two institutions, on the other. Indeed, as far as the Commission is concerned, the relationship is one of political supervision and co-operation. The latter sometimes becomes a conspiracy against the

---

[63] Art. 197 (ex 140) E.C.

[64] During 1997 a total of 5,440 questions were put: 4,231 written questions were tabled (3,838 to the Commission and 393 to the Council); 1,024 oral questions were put during question time (689 to the Commission and 335 to the Council); Oral questions within debate numbered 185 (140 to the Commission and 45 to the Council).

[65] Rules of Procedure, Rules 44, 45 and 46. See Art. 197(4) (ex 140(4)) E.C.

[66] For the Common Foreign and Security Policy see Part VI.

[67] Rules of Procedure, Rule 47. See n.64 above.

[68] Art. 21(1) (ex J7(1)) TEU.

Council which after all often wields the ultimate legislative power within the Community. Where the Council is concerned, the relationship should rather be seen as political co-operation and partnership, especially after the modifications introduced by the Maastricht Treaty.[69] This relationship tends to find expression in a dialogue between the two institutions. Besides the ones already mentioned, each incoming President of the Council presents at the beginning of his mandate a "Programme of the Presidency", and a survey of significant developments at the end of his six-months term. Similarly, a representative of the Council presents an oral report to Parliament twice a year, on the activities of the Council.

(5) The General Report

According to the Treaty, Parliament must "discuss in open session the General Report" on the activities of the Community,[70] which the Commission publishes annually.[71] It is submitted to Parliament before the opening of its session, *i.e.* the second Tuesday in March.[72] In the old days, the discussion of the General Report gave rise to a general debate on all the facets of Community life, since the Report covers the activities of all the institutions and bodies of the Community. It should be noted that the work of the other institutions and of the EIB is described in detail in their own reports.

The General Report is supplemented by an annual Report on the Agricultural Situation of the Community,[73] a Report on the Development of the Social Situation in the Community,[74] and a Report on Competition Policy.[75] The Commission also presents an Annual Report on the Regional Fund.

All those reports constitute an invaluable source of information on the activities of the Community, the problems encountered and the solutions adopted or proposed. They are less important, however,

---

[69] The author is convinced that the co-decision procedure and this co-operation shall ultimately lead to the establishment of a kind of bicameral structure in the legislative field, the Council acting as a Senate.

[70] Art. 200 (ex 143) E.C.

[71] Art. 18 Merger Treaty.

[72] Art. 196 (ex 139) E.C. The Commission has always scrupulously respected this obligation.

[73] This practice was started in 1975 at the request of Parliament.

[74] Art. 145 (ex 122) E.C.

[75] Undertaking given by the Commission to Parliament on June 7, 1971; see Resolution concerning the competition rules [1971] O.J. C66/11.

for the supervisory task of Parliament, since the latter is kept well informed through the permanent contacts it maintains, mainly with the Commission through the work of the Parliamentary Committees in which the Commission always participates.

However, the discussion of the General Report no longer takes place[76]; it was replaced by the discussion on the annual legislative programme of the Commission presented to Parliament at the beginning of each year by the President of the Commission. On the basis of this programme Parliament would like the Commission to agree with it on an annual Legislative Programme.[77]

(6) The Adoption of the Rules of Procedure

The Rules of Procedure have played an important part in the development of Parliament's position within the Community. Parliament used the Rules of Procedure as an instrument to increase its powers, often with success.[78] The latest modifications were introduced in view of the entering into force of the Maastricht Treaty.[79]

However, as shall be seen in respect of the approval of the designated members of the Commission, it seems that Parliament has attributed to itself many more powers than provided for under the Treaty. And since those Rules do not, of course, bind the other institutions, it remains to be seen whether they will comply with what are, after all, only Parliament's wishes.

(7) The Motion of Censure

Parliament has the power to "dismiss" the members of the Commission, as a body, by adopting a motion of censure in case it disagrees with activities of the Commission.[80] This is by far the most impressive power of control vested in Parliament; but, although

---

[76] Rules of Procedure, Rule 29B simply states that the Report shall be submitted to the Committees, which may submit specific and fundamental questions to the plenary.

[77] Rules of Procedure, Rule 36A. For the 1994 legislative programme see Joint Declaration, Council Declaration and Parliament's Resolution [1994] O.J. C60/1.

[78] A good example is the right to put questions to (and obtain answers from) the Council. It is still not provided for by the Treaty (see Art. 140) but the Council does answer the questions put to it by Parliament.

[79] See minutes of the sitting of Wednesday, September 14, 1993, P.E. 174.510. See consolidated version, including interpretation of the rules [1997] O.J. L49/1. See also Decision on public access to Parliament's documents [1997] O.J. L263/27.

[80] Art. 201 (ex 144) E.C. Rules of Procedure, Art. 34 E.C. [1995] O.J. L293/1.

motions have been tabled in the past, never yet has one been carried.[81] The procedural requirements are cumbersome indeed. First, the Treaty prescribes a "reflexion time": Parliament shall not vote on the motion until at least three days after the motion was tabled and shall decide by open vote. Secondly, the Treaty requires that a majority of the representatives cast their vote and that two-thirds of them vote for the motion. Finally, the motion must be moved by one-tenth of the members of Parliament.

It must be underlined, however, that the censure only affects the Commission. The Council, which is the legislator within the Community remains outside Parliament's reach. Furthermore one may wonder whether such a motion can have practical effect. It shall depend, partially at least, on the reaction of the dismissed Commissioners. Indeed, they shall remain in office until they are replaced[82] and continue to exercise their functions normally.[83] Since their replacement depends on a decision of the governments of the Member States, further developments can no longer be controlled by Parliament. The governments could not, however, renominate the same persons, since the President and the members of the Commission, after having been nominated by the governments, must be approved as a body by Parliament before they can be appointed.

(8) Approval of the President and Members of the Commission

The person the Member States intend to appoint as President of the Commission is nominated by their governments by common accord; the nomination must be approved by Parliament, in practice, after this person has made a statement to Parliament, followed by a debate.[84] The other members of the Commission are nominated by the governments without prior consultation of Parliament, but by common accord with the nominee for President. The President and the members thus nominated are subject, as a body, to a vote of approval of the Parliament.[85] In conformity with Parliament's wish,

[81] The first motion was tabled in November 1972; it was later withdrawn. In order to avoid the motion of censure, the Commission can resign, as it did on March 16, 1999.

[82] Art. 215 (ex 159) E.C.

[83] This follows from the fact that the Maastricht Treaty eliminated a provision in pursuance of which the dismissed Commissioners could only "deal with current business until they are replaced" (see Art. 201(2) (ex 144(2)) E.C.).

[84] Rules of Procedure, Rule 29A(3).

[85] Art. 214(2) (ex 158(2)) E.C.

those members appear "before the appropriate committee according to their prospective field of responsibility".[86] The problem is not only that this is not provided for by the Treaty, but that, as shall be seen, portfolios are only officially attributed by the Commission itself, after it takes office. If this were to be decided beforehand, this would mean that the Member States decide in fact on this attribution. This would violate the principle of the independence of the Commission and its members so clearly provided for in the Treaty.[87]

(9) Participation in the Budgetary Procedure

The budgetary procedure and the role of Parliament in it can best be described as follows.[88]

(a) The Commission consolidates in a "preliminary draft budget" the estimates of expenditure drawn up by the various institutions; the draft also contains an estimate of the revenues. The Commission places it before the Council not later than the first of September preceding the budget year.

(b) After having consulted the Commission, the Council, by a qualified majority, establishes the draft budget and forwards it to Parliament, not later than October 5.

(c) Parliament can take one of several actions:

  (i) approve the draft budget within 45 days: the budget then stands as finally approved;

  (ii) within 45 days refrain from amending the draft nor propose modification: the budget is deemed to be finally approved.

  (iii) amend and/or propose modifications:

  - with regard to expenditure necessarily resulting from the Treaty or from acts adopted in accordance with it ("obligatory expenditure"), Parliament, by an absolute majority of the votes cast, may only propose modifications;
  - with regard to other expenditure, Parliament may, by a majority of its members, adopt amendments, but within

---

[86] Rules of Procedure, Rule 29A(1).

[87] Art. 213(2) (ex 157(2)) E.C.

[88] Arts 272–280 (ex 203–209a) E.C. These provisions were modified a first time by the Treaty of 1970 amending Certain Budgetary Provisions.

a maximum rate of increase which shall be communicated by the Commission.[89]

The draft budget together with the amendments and the proposed modifications is then returned to the Council.

(d) The Council then, in turn, has various options:
  (i) with regard to the proposed modifications, it may reject them by a qualified majority;
  (ii) with regard to the amendments, it may modify them within 15 days by a qualified majority; in the absence of such majority, the amendments stand.

If the Council accepts the proposed modifications and does not modify the amendments, the budget is deemed to be finally adopted and Parliament is informed accordingly. If, on the other hand, one or more proposed modifications are rejected or modified, or amendments modified, the modified draft budget is returned to Parliament.

(e) At this stage the powers of Parliament are limited to the expenditures other than those resulting from the Treaty or from acts adopted by the institutions ("non-compulsory" expenditure). Parliament may, within 15 days, amend or reject the modifications made by the Council to Parliament's amendments, acting by a majority of its members and three-fifths of the votes cast. Parliament then adopts the budget and the President of Parliament declares that the budget has been finally adopted.[90]

Parliament may, on the other hand, if there are important reasons, reject the draft budget acting by a majority of its members and two-thirds of the votes cast[91] and ask for a new draft to be submitted to it.

---

[89] Art. 272(9) (ex 203(9)) E.C. This maximum rate is a result from the trend of the GNP within the Community, the average variation in the budgets of the Member States, and the trend of the cost of living. With regard to Parliament's power to increase non-compulsory expenditures, see Case 34/86, *Council v. Parliament* [1986] E.C.R. 2188 at 2210; [1986] 3 C.M.L.R. 94.

[90] See Case 34/86, *Council v. Parliament*, n.81 above. See also Case C–41/95 *Council v. Parliament* [1995] E.C.R. I–4411, where the Court annulled the act of the President of the Parliament of December 15, 1994, declaring the final adoption of the budget for 1995; for the new adoption see [1996] O.J. L67/1.

[91] Art. 272(8) (ex 203(8)) E.C. This happened in 1979, see Bull. 12–1979, 93 and 120, and in 1984, see Bull. 12–1984, 28.

It follows from this lengthy procedure, that Parliament has the last word with regard to the non-compulsory expenditures[92] and does actually adopt the budget of the Community.[93]

In order to avoid the repetition of the numerous conflicts which arose between the Council and Parliament regarding the adoption of the Community budget, an Interinstitutional Agreement[94] came into force in July 1988; it covers budgetary discipline and improvements in the budgetary procedure. Its main feature is a medium-term (five years) Financial Perspective.[95] Consequently the powers of Parliament in this field were somewhat restricted.

Parliament's role in the budgetary field does not end with the adoption of the budget: it also exercises control over its implementation. In this task Parliament (and the Council) are assisted by the Court of Auditors.[96]

As shall be seen when discussing the financing of the Community's activities, the Commission is entrusted with the implementation of the budget, on its own responsibility and in accordance with the so-called financial regulations.[97]

The Commission submits annually the accounts of the preceding year together with a financial statement of the assets and liabilities of the Community to the Council and to Parliament.[98] The latter receive from the Court of Auditors a statement of assurance as to the reliability of the accounts and an annual report.[99] It is Parliament, which, on a recommendation from the Council, gives a discharge to the Commission in respect of the implementation of the budget.[1]

---

[92] Those non-compulsory expenditures have increased tremendously over the years: in 1997, they represented 55 per cent of total expenditures.

[93] It could happen, of course, that the budget is not voted in time for the beginning of the financial year; in that case a sum equivalent to no more than one-twelfth of the budget appropriations for the preceding year may be spent each month: Art. 273 (ex 204) E.C.

[94] See [1988] O.J. L185 and [1998] E.C. Bull. 6, 112–114 and 121. The Agreement was approved by Parliament in June 1988.

[95] [1988] O.J. L185 and C187. For the 1995–99 financial perspective see [1994] O.J. C395/1 Proposals for 2000–2006, see COM(1998)164 final.

[96] See below for an analysis of this institution.

[97] Art. 274 (ex 205) E.C. which refers to Art. 279 (ex 209) E.C.

[98] Art. 275 (ex 205a) E.C.

[99] Art. 248 (ex 188c(1)) E.C.

[1] Art. 276 (ex 206(1) E.C. In 1984, Parliament refused to give a discharge to the Commission with regard to the implementation of the 1982 budget; see Bull. 11–1984, 67.

(10) Procedures in the Court of Justice

Until recently, Parliament could only play a rather secondary role in the proceedings before the Community Courts. It could intervene in cases before the Courts,[2] institute third party proceeding to contest a judgment and bring an action against the Council and/or the Commission for failure of the latter to act and thereby infringing the Treaty.[3] However, its locus standi has been considerably enhanced by the case law of the Court. Although the right to request the Court to review the legality of Community acts has been granted by the Treaty only to the Council and the Commission,[4] the Court accepted the admissibility of an action brought by Parliament against an act of the Council when that action aims at upholding Parliament's prerogatives.[5] It did so on the ground that the Court must be able to maintain the Community's institutional balance and, consequently, review the observance of the Parliament's prerogatives when called upon to do so by Parliament.

(11) Participation in other Community Activities

Several agreements of association between the Community and third States provide for a joint Parliamentary Committee. This is the case with the EEC–Turkey Association,[6] the EEA, and also with the so-called European Agreements with the candidate countries from Central and Eastern Europe.[7] These parliamentary Committees are composed of members of Parliament and members of the national parliaments of the associated States. These Committees constitute discussion forums rather than decision-making bodies. Similarly, the ACP–EEC Convention provides for a Joint Assembly.[8]

---

[2] See, *e.g.* Resolution of December 14, 1979 ([1980] O.J. C4/52) to intervene in Cases 138/79, *Roquette Frères v. Council* [1980] E.C.R. 3333 and 139/79 *Maizena v. Council* [1980] E.C.R. 3393.

[3] Art. 232 (ex 175) E.C. See, *e.g.* Case 13/83 *Parliament v. Council* [1985] E.C.R. 1556; [1986] 1 C.M.L.R. 138.

[4] Art. 230 (ex 173) E.C. See Case 302/87 *Parliament v. Council* [1988] E.C.R. 5637.

[5] Case C–70/88 *Parliament v. Council* [1990] E.C.R. I–2067, [1992] 1 C.M.L.R. 91. See also Case C–65/90 *Parliament v. Council* [1992] E.C.R. I–4616.

[6] See Art. 27 of the Agreement ([1964] O.J. 3687).

[7] The first agreements were signed on December 16, 1991.

[8] The fourth Lomé Convention was signed on December 15, 1989; for meetings of the Joint Assembly, see General Report (1998).

3. Internal Organisation

The internal organisation of Parliament is comparable to that of any national parliament. It is based on a double structure: the political parties (called "Groups") and the parliamentary committees.

(1) The Political Groups

Representatives sit in multinational political groups.[9] However, the Act concerning direct election provides that representatives shall vote on an individual basis and that they shall not be bound by any instruction nor receive a binding mandate.[10]

The Rules of Procedure require for the formation of a political group 21 representatives when they belong to one single Member State, 15 when they come from two Member States and 10 when the number of Member States of origin is three or more.[11] Clearly the rule was made to encourage the formation of transnational groups which is one of the characteristics of the European Parliament.

(2) Parliamentary Committees

The Rules of Procedure provide that Parliament can set up standing or temporary committees, which in turn, may appoint one or more subcommittees.[12] The chairmen of all the Committees form the Conference of Committee Chairmen which makes recommendations to the Committee of Chairmen about the work of the Committees. The Conference of Committee Chairmen can be

---

[9] The situation at the end of 1998 was the following:

Party of the European Socialists	215
European People's Party	181
Union for Europe	55
European Liberal Democrat and Reform Party	41
Confederal Group of the European United Left/Nordic Green Left	33
Green Group in the European Parliament	28
European Radical Alliance	19
Group of Independents for a Europe of Nations	18
Non-affiliated	36

[10] Act concerning direct elections, Art. 4(1); ([1976] O.J. L278/1).

[11] Rules of Procedure, Rule 36.

[12] Rules of Procedure, Rules 109 and 114. In 1999 the Parliament decided to set up 17 Committees: Foreign Affairs, Human Rights, Security and Defence; Agriculture and Rural Development; Budget; Economic and Monetary Affairs; Industry, External

instructed to carry out specific tasks.[13] Their members are elected by Parliament after nominations have been submitted by the political groups. Generally speaking, the Committees prepare the Resolutions to be adopted by Parliament in plenary session. It is within the Committees that the real parliamentary work is carried out. When Parliament is consulted by the Council on a Commission proposal, the latter is examined by the relevant Committee(s), which include(s) its findings and recommendations in a Report. The role of the drafter of this Report, *i.e.* the Rapporteur is, consequently, very important. Parliament expresses its Opinions in the form of "Resolutions".[14]

(3) The Bureau

Parliament elects its President[15] and 14 Vice-Presidents, which together form the "Bureau", *i.e.* the executive body. The Bureau drafts the agenda of the sessions, decides on matters of competence and makes the preliminary draft of Parliament's budget.[16]

The Rules of Procedure also provide for a "Conference of Chairmen"[17] consisting of the Bureau and the Presidents of the political groups. This enlarged Bureau constitutes the ultimate centre of decision-making for all internal matters of Parliament.

Parliament has its own staff of 3.491 permanent and 602 temporary posts, grouped in a Secretariat headed by a Secretary General.

Trade, Research and Energy; Legal Affairs and Internal Market (including verification of credentials and immunities); Employment and Social Affairs; Regional Policy, Transport and Tourism; Environment, Public Health and Consumer Protection; Youth, Culture, Education, Sports and the Media; Development and Co-operation; Civil Liberties and Home Affairs; Budgetary Control; Constitutional Affairs; Fisheries; Women's Rights and Equality of Opportunities; Petitions. A temporary committee on Employment was established by the Parliament on July 21, 1994.

[13] Rules of Procedure, Rule 24B.

[14] *ibid.* Arts 37–44.

[15] Art. 197(1) E.C.

[16] Rules of Procedure, Rules 5–7, 12 and 50.

[17] *ibid.* Rule 23.

(4) Sessions and Meeting Place(s)

Parliament holds annual sessions, *i.e.* lasting 12 months, but actually sits only during 12 part-time sessions, which last five days.[18] Parliament meets, without requiring to be convened, on the second Tuesday in March. Parliament may also meet in extraordinary[19] session and has instituted so-called "additional" sessions.

At the Edinburgh European Council in December 1992, it was decided that the

> "European Parliament shall have its seat in Strasburg, where 12 periods of monthly plenary sessions, including the budget session shall be held. The periods of additional plenary sessions shall be held in Brussels. The Committees of the European Parliament shall meet in Brussels. The Secretariat of the European Parliament and its departments shall remain in Luxemburg."[20]

This most unfortunate decision from the point of view of efficiency and costs, can only be explained by petty nationalistic and political motives. It is shocking that those considerations prevailed over common sense, which would have required Parliament to work in one single place, instead of being dispersed over three locations. This decision puts an end to the long struggle of Parliament to streamline its activities.[21]

Members of the Commission may (and do) attend all meetings and the Council is represented at all the plenary sessions. The minutes of the meetings are published in the *Official Journal of the European Communities* and the full debates in an annex thereto.

Except for the adoption of a motion of censure and certain

---

[18] Parliament is understood to be "in session" even when not actually sitting, and this until the session is declared closed; see Case 101/85, *Wagner v. Fohrman and Krier* [1964] E.C.R. 195 and Case 149/85, *Wybot v. Faure* [1986] E.C.R. 2391.

[19] Art. 196 (ex 139) E.C.

[20] Conclusions of the Presidency: Decision taken by common agreement between the Representatives of the Governments of the Member States on the location of the seats of the institutions and of certain bodies and departments of the European Communities, Art. 1(a): [1992] E.C. Bull. 12–24. This Decision was incorporated in the Protocol on the location of the institutions and of certain bodies and departments of the E.C. and of Europol: [1997] O.J. C340/112.

[21] Parliament's decisions to hold its sessions wherever it decides was successfully attacked by Luxembourg: Case 230/81 *Luxembourg v. Parliament* [1983] E.C.R. 255; [1983] 2 C.M.L.R. 726, Case 108/83 *Luxembourg v. Parliament* [1984] E.C.R. 1945; [1986] 2 C.M.L.R. 507: Parliament has no right to decide on the location of its departments, and Case 358/85 *France v. European Parliament* [1986] E.C.R. 2149; [1988] 3 C.M.L.R. 786 and Case C–345/95, *France v. European Parliament* [1997] E.C.R. I–5215.

decisions within the co-operation, co-decision and budgetary procedures, Parliament acts by a majority of the votes cast.[22] There is a quorum when the majority of the representatives are present; however, as long as there is no request to do so, the number of members present is not ascertained.[23]

4. Conclusion

Although not fully equipped yet with all the attributes of a parliament, the European Parliament has, over the years, thanks to its determination and strongly supported by the popular claim for more democracy within the Community, succeeded in increasing its powers. It is rapidly becoming an institution with a status equal to that of the Council and the Commission. In fact, Parliament wields more power than would appear from the Treaty provisions.

Further Reading

Francis Jacobs and Richard Corbet, *The European Parliament*, Longman Group U.K. Ltd, 1991.

Epaminondes Marias, "The Right of Petition to the European Parliament after Maastricht", 169 (1994) E.L.Rev.

---

[22] Art. 198 (ex 141) E.C.
[23] Act concerning direct election, Art. 6(1) and (2); see n.10 above.

Chapter Six
The Council

To attain the objectives assigned to the Community, the Treaty provides for several means. First, there is the establishment of a common market and an economic and monetary union, together with the implementation of various common policies and activities.[1] This is a task of the Community as such. Secondly, the Treaty provides for the adoption of an economic policy based on the close co-ordination of the Member States' economic policies, on the internal market and on common objectives. They constitute activities of the Member States and the Community acting together, and shall also include the irrevocable fixing of exchange rates leading to the introduction of a single currency (ECU), and the definition and conduct of a single monetary policy and exchange rate policy.[2]

Quite a programme! It shall be examined in detail in Parts Three, Four and Five of this book, but it is important at this juncture to notice the distinction the Treaty makes between the "tasks of the Community" and the "activities of the Member States and the Community", both being destined to implement the Treaty objectives.[3]

This distinction was introduced by the Maastricht Treaty and indicates that certain tasks can only be accomplished by the Community institutions and the Member States acting together, but each one in its own sphere. It calls for closer integration of the policies of the Member States with those of the Community proper.

[1] Arts 2 and 3 (ex 2 and 3) E.C.
[2] Arts 4(1) and (2) (ex 3a(1) and (2)) E.C.
[3] The objectives of the European Community are set out in Art. 2 (ex 2) E.C.
- a harmonious, balanced and sustainable development of economic activities,
- a high level of employment and of social protection,
- equality between men and woman,
- a high degree of competitiveness and convergence of economic performance,
- a high level of protection and improvement of the quality of the environment,
- the raising of the standard of living and quality of life,
- economic and social cohesion and solidarity among Member States.

This is particularly relevant for the Council. Indeed, it is within this institution that the two spheres come together: the Council is an institution of the Community, but it is composed of the representatives of the Member States. In other words, it is at the same time inter-governmental and supranational. This dichotomy does often create frictions between the general interest of the Community and the interests of the individual Member States, which can only be resolved by what the Treaty refers to as "solidarity among the Member States".[4]

As indicated at the beginning of this section, the Treaty provides *grosso modo* for two means in order to fulfil the objectives of the Community: one is the establishment of the common market[5] and of an economic and monetary union, the other the implementation of common policies and activities, mainly the adoption of an economic policy.[6]

If the activities provided for in the Treaty for the establishment of the common market typically come within the ambit of the Community institutions, the situation is different with regard to the activities in the economic policy field. Those must necessarily be based "on the close co-ordination of Member States' economic policies"[7] and, as was pointed out above, this co-ordination necessarily takes place within the Council. And indeed, according to the Treaty, the Council is to: "ensure co-ordination of the general economic policies of the Member States".[8] On the other hand, the Council is also the Community's lawmaker, which is expressed in the Treaty by the words: it shall "have power to take decisions".

1. Organisational Aspects

(1) Members of the Council

The Council consists of representatives of each Member State at ministerial level, authorised to commit the government of that Member State.[9] These last words were added by the Maastricht

---

[4] Art. 2 (ex 2) E.C.

[5] Art. 3 (ex 3) E.C. summarises the activities of the Community connected with the establishment of the common market.

[6] See Art. 4(1) and (2) (ex 3a(1) and (2)) E.C.

[7] Art. 4(1) (ex 3a(1)) E.C.

[8] Art. 202 (ex 145) E.C. first indent.

[9] Art. 203 (ex 146) E.C.

Treaty to allow members of State governments in federal States to represent their central government, but ensures that whoever represents a government within the Council, for example a regional minister, she or he can indeed commit the said central government.

Being representatives of the Member States, the members of the Council act on instruction from their government. They do not, however, constitute an intergovernmental conference of ministers, nor are they in a position similar to that of their colleagues within international organisations, where decisions are necessarily taken unanimously and only bind those States which afterwards ratify them. The Council can somehow be compared to the Senate in a federal State, but without the House of Representatives! The members of the Council do indeed represent the interests of their respective States, but at the same time, they must, as an institution of the Community, act in the interest of the latter. It is not evident that this is always clearly perceived by all participants.

It is left to each government to decide which one of their members shall represent it at the Council meetings, and although the Treaty refers to "a" representative, it sometimes happens that two or more ministers are present at the same meeting. Besides the so-called "General Affairs" Councils—usually composed of the ministers of Foreign Affairs[10]—numerous specialised Council meetings take place to deal with specific subjects such as agriculture, economy and finance (the so-called "Ecofin"), the environment, etc. Normally those meetings are attended by the ministers nationally responsible for those matters. Consequently, it is not unusual to have various Council meetings in session at the same time.

The office of President of the Council is held, for periods of six months, in turn by each Member State.[11] This applies also, of course, to the presidency of the Council acting within the Common Foreign and Security Policy.[12] The same rotation applies to all the subordinate bodies of the Council, such as the Committee of Permanent

---

[10] This is a left-over of the now outdated (it is to be hoped) concept according to which Community affairs are "foreign" affairs when, in law and in fact, they are internal affairs of all the Member States.

[11] Art. 203 (ex 146) E.C. provides that the order in which the presidency is to be assumed by the various Member States is decided by the Council acting unanimously. See Decision of January 1, 1995 [1995] O.J. L1/220. The order is the following, starting on January 1, 1996: Italy, Ireland, The Netherlands, Luxembourg, United Kingdom, Austria, Germany, Finland, Portugal, France, Sweden, Belgium, Spain, Denmark, Greece. The Council may decide, at the request of the Member States, that a Member State assumes the presidency during a period different from the one resulting from the order established above.

[12] See Part VI.

Representatives,[13] the working groups and other meetings of the ministers.

The meetings of the Council are always attended by the Commission represented by its President and/or the Commission member who is more particularly responsible for the subject under discussion. Commission officials also attend the meetings and participate in the work of Coreper and other Council bodies.

(2) Voting Procedure

The voting procedure provided for under the Treaty is one of the more interesting aspects of the European Communities, since it provides for the possibility of taking, by a majority vote, decisions which are binding on all the Member States. Under the majority voting system no single Member State has a veto right. This system has allowed the Community to move steadily towards the implementation of its objectives. This system is unique, and it differentiates the Community from other bodies established under international law, since the latter only operate on the basis of unanimous decisions.

The basic rule with regard to voting in the Council is that the latter acts "by a majority of its members",[14] save as otherwise provided in the Treaty.[15] Since most Treaty provisions do provide otherwise, the general rule is in fact the exception.

The other voting procedures are:

(a) Qualified Majority when the Council is acting on a Proposal from the Commission

This is usually the case, and for this purpose the votes of the members of the Council are weighted.[16] Out of a total of 87, at least

---

[13] See below.

[14] Art. 205(1) (ex 148(1)) E.C. There being 15 members, the majority or simple majority is eight. This figure determines the quorum.

[15] Art. 205(1) (ex 148(1)) E.C.

[16] Art. 205(2) (ex 148(2)) E.C.:

Belgium	5	Luxembourg	2
Denmark	3	Netherlands	2
Germany	10	Austria	4
Greece	5	Portugal	5
Spain	8	Finland	3
France	10	Sweden	4
Ireland	3	United Kingdom	10
Italy	10		

62 votes in favour are required for the adoption of the act.[17] Since the five largest countries (population wise), *i.e.* Germany, Spain, France, Italy and the United Kingdom only have 48 votes among them, they cannot, together, impose their will on the rest,[18] neither, for that matter, can the others. To get a qualified majority, a combination of large and small or medium-sized countries is needed, which preserves some balance among the Member States. Several attempts have been made to modify this situation, especially by larger Member States, which are of the opinion that they are under-represented vote-wise. Concretely speaking, they are of the opinion that the blocking minority is too high. When there were twelve Member States this minority was 23—which means two large and one small or medium-sized member—and some Member States wanted to keep it at that after the enlargement with Austria, Finland and Sweden. At that point the total amount of votes became 87 and the required amount for a majority vote 62, so that the blocking minority is now equal to 26. This figure leaves the four larger Member States even farther behind a controlling majority/blocking minority.

An important element is also that, according to the Rules of Procedure of the Council,[19] a vote is taken at the initiative of the President or at the request of one of the Members of the Commission, if the Council so decides by simple majority.

A compromise, similar to the infamous Luxembourg compromise, was reached at Ioannina (Greece) on March 29, 1994, which, in a nutshell, provides that majority decisions should try to muster 65 votes (instead of the legal 62!) when Members representing 23 to 25 votes indicate that they oppose the measure. It is then up to the President to find a solution, with the help of the Commission! This "decision" was published in the *Official Journal of the European Communities*, but in the "C" series, and not in the "L" (= Legislation) one, which seems to indicate that the Council itself knew that it could not modify the Treaty with a simple decision.[20] Notwithstanding that, a Declaration was adopted by the Amsterdam

[17] There are a few cases where different majorities are provided for; see, *e.g.* Arts. 104(13) (ex 104c(13)) and 122(5) (ex 109k(5)) E.C.

[18] There have, however, been several attempts by some of the "big four" to strengthen their position by introducing new rules for majority voting. This, in the view of the smaller countries, would upset the delicate political balance set up in 1958, which made it a Community of equals. It might, indeed, seem strange that a country like Luxembourg with 350,000 inhabitants would have two votes, while Germany with 88 million has 10.

[19] Rules, Art. 7.1.

[20] [1994] O.J. C105/1.

Intergovernmental Conference "relating to the Protocol on the institutions with the prospect of enlargement of the European Union"[21] according to which the Ioannina compromise is extended until the entry into force of the first enlargement. It also provides that a solution must be found for the special (?) case of Spain.

As for the above mentioned Protocol, it concerns in the first place the composition of the Commission. It is generally agreed that, after a new enlargement, the larger Member States no longer can claim two members on the Commission. However, those States will only give up this privilege if "the weighting of the votes in the Council has been modified, whether by re-weighting of the votes or by dual majority, in a manner acceptable to all Member States, taking into account all relevant elements, notably compensating those Member States which give up the possibility of nominating a second member of the Commission".[22] This constitutes one of the most scandalous "horse-trading deals" ever encountered in the Communities' history: it shows publicly how certain Member States view the complete "independence" of the members of the Commission, which those Member States have undertaken "to respect".[23] Exchanging a member of the Commission for an extra vote in the Council is a cynical confusion of roles: a vote may be used to defend the national interest, a member of the Commission may never be "used" for that. Have the Member States already forgotten that over and over again they have committed themselves to respect the independence of the members of the Commission and "not to seek to influence the Members of the Commission in the performance of their task"?

The number of cases in which majority voting is provided was increased, first by the SEA, especially for decisions on harmonisation of national legislations in view of the completion of the internal market[24] and later by the Maastricht Treaty and by the Amsterdam Treaty. More important, the practice within the Council has changed: more and more decisions are taken by majority vote when the Treaty so provides. A few years ago, unanimity was the rule in practically all cases, even when not required by the Treaty, except in budget and staff matters.

---

21 [1997] O.J. C340/142.
22 [1997] O.J. C340/111.
23 Art. 213(2) (ex 157(2)) E.C.
24 Art. 95(1) (ex 100a) E.C.

(b) Qualified Majority when the Council acts without a Proposal from the Commission

In that case there is the additional requirement that at least ten Member States vote in favour of the measure; in other words, a two-thirds majority of the Members is required.

(c) Unanimity

In many cases the Treaty provided for unanimity until the end of the transitional period[25] and majority thereafter. Unanimity is also required when the Council, acting on a proposal from the Commission, wants to adopt an act which constitutes an amendment to that proposal.[26]

As indicated, unanimity had become the common practice,[27] although it is only required in a limited number of cases.[28] Fortunately, this is no longer the case. Abstentions by members

---

[25] The transitional period ended on December 31, 1965.

[26] Art. 250(1) (ex 189a(1)) E.C.; this rule does not apply in the case of Art. 251(4) and (5) (ex 189b) E.C. but applies in the case of Art. 215(3) (ex 189b) E.C.

[27] This practice finds its origin in the Arrangement regarding majority voting adopted by the Council at its meeting of January 28 and 29, 1966, at Luxembourg. This arrangement is sometimes improperly referred to as "Luxembourg Agreement" or "Luxembourg Accord": it is no such thing, it is only an internal arrangement of the Council which ended the most serious crisis the Community has known and which was started by the over-nationalist government of Général De Gaulle. The arrangement provided, *inter alia*:

> "1. Where, in the case of decisions which may be taken by majority vote on a Commission proposal and *very important interests of one or more partners are at stake* (emphasis supplied), the members of the Council will endeavour, within a reasonable time, to reach solutions which can be adopted by all the members of the Council while respecting their mutual interests and those of the Community, in accordance with Article 2 of the EEC Treaty."

For the French, the discussion must be continued until unanimous agreement is reached; this was not accepted by the other five and the question always remained: what happens in the event of failure to reach complete agreement? This is the reason why the Luxembourg arrangement was, in fact, an agreement to disagree. Anyway, after the SEA and the Maastricht and Amsterdam Treaties, one should be able to assume that the Luxembourg arrangement is dead. It should be remembered, however, that the arrangement only concerned cases where majority voting is provided for. This means that where unanimity is required, each Member State has indeed a veto right.

[28] Art. 72 (ex 76) E.C.: transport; Art. 88(2) (ex 93(2)) E.C.: aids to be considered compatible; Art. 187 (ex 136) E.C.: association with ACP countries; Art. 245 (ex 188) E.C.: approval of Court's rules of procedure and, Art. 296(2) (ex 223) E.C.: protection of security interests.

present in person or represented do not prevent the adoption by the Council of acts which require unanimity.[29]

A final observation concerning the voting procedure of the Council is that, in case of urgency, acts may be adopted by "written procedure".[30]

(3) Committee of Permanent Representatives—COREPER[31]

The creation of this Committee stems from the fact that the Council meets no more than a few days a month and that, with the increase of Community business, a more permanent presence was required. The permanent representatives—high level civil servants with the rank of Ambassador—closely follow the various Community activities on a day-to-day basis. They are not deputies of the Council members, they have no decision-making power, although they may now adopt procedural decisions in cases provided for in the Council's Rules of Procedure; they constitute an organ within the Council structure. Their task is to prepare the work of the Council and to carry out the tasks assigned to Coreper by the Council.[32] They meet several days each week. And, although they have, as was said, no decision-making power, once Coreper has reached agreement, for instance, on a proposal from the Commission, it can safely be assumed that the Council will decide accordingly. This is expressed by the fact that in such cases the matter is put on the agenda of the Council as an "A" point.[33] The practice is that the Council accepts all those A points at the beginning of its meeting, thereby transforming them into legal binding acts. It must, however, be emphasised that the Council is in no way bound to accept those A points and any Council member is free to ask for a discussion on the subject, in which case it is placed on the agenda of the next Council meeting, but this time as a "B" point. It may also happen that a member maintains a "reserve", due, for example to the need of a national parliamentary scrutiny. This reserve can, however, be lifted in time for the next council meeting allowing the latter to adopt it as an "A" point.

---

[29] Art. 205(3) (ex 148(3)) E.C.; this means that when a member of the Council is absent and not represented by another member, there can be no unanimity vote.

[30] Rules of Procedure, Art. 6.

[31] COmité des REprésentants PERmanents. It is subdivided into Coreper I, composed of the deputy permanent representatives, which handle, *inter alia* the agricultural policy, and Coreper II, formed by the Ambassadors.

[32] Art. 207(1) (ex 151(1)) E.C.

[33] Rules of Procedure, Art. 2(6).

When no agreement can be reached at Coreper level, but it is thought that a solution can be found at the ministers level, the matter is placed on the Council's agenda as a "B" point, *i.e.* a subject on which discussion is needed.

Coreper is assisted in its work by a whole series of working groups, some permanent, some temporary, which, in turn, prepare the work of Coreper. These working groups are composed of civil servants from the Member States and convene whenever necessary. When a Commission proposal is sent to the Council, it first comes before Coreper, which can examine it and agree on it directly, but normally sends it to one of the working groups. The latter examines it and reports to Coreper.

All the meetings of Coreper and of the working groups are attended by the Commission; it would be more correct to say that the Commission participates in their work. Indeed, real negotiations often take place inside those working groups (and at Coreper level) in order to arrive at a text which is acceptable to all Member States, or at least to enough of them to reach a qualified majority. This might result in the Commission modifying its proposal.[34] Those meetings are presided over by a national from the country which holds the office of President at the Council.

One great advantage of these working groups composed of national civil servants, is that the national view is clearly expressed in Brussels, while the national administrations are directly confronted with the views of the Commission and of the other Member States.

In the same way, it can be said that the Permanent Representatives fulfil a double function: they defend the national interests within the Community and at the same time represent the Community's point of view at home. They thus constitute an indispensable link between the national administrations and the European institutions.

(4) Secretariat and Rules of Procedure

According to the Treaty, the Council is assisted by a General Secretariat, under the responsibility of a Secretary General.[35] The latter is also the "High Representative for the common foreign and security policy.[36] He is assisted by a Deputy Secretary General responsible for the running of the General Secretariat. Both are

---

[34] Art. 250(2) (ex 189a(2)) E.C.

[35] Art. 207(2) (ex 151(2)) E.C.

[36] Art. 18.3 (ex J.8) TEU (which did not provide for same).

appointed by the Council. The latter also decides on the organisation of the Secretariat. It is, like the Commission's departments divided in Directorates General whose competences correspond to the main activities of the Community.

The Rules of Procedure were adopted in December 1993.[37]

At the beginning of 1999, the Council's establishment plan comprised 2,417 permanent posts and 18 temporary ones.

Mention should be made here of public access to Council documents.[38]

2. Tasks and Powers of the Council

(1) Decision-making

(a) Principles

The Council is, by definition, the institution endowed with decision-making powers,[39] although it now shares this competence, in many cases, with the European Parliament. Those powers, however, have to be exercised "in accordance with the provisions of [the] Treaty". And, the most important provision concerning the exercise of power by the institutions of the Community is to be found at the very beginning of the Treaty: "each institution shall act within the limits of the powers conferred upon it by this Treaty".[40] This means, as was pointed out earlier on, that the institutions only have "attributed" powers. Consequently, the Council is not endowed with a general regulatory competence; it can only act when this is specifically provided for in a Treaty provision, reason why the latter must always be mentioned in the Community acts.[41] There are, however, cases where action by the Council appears necessary to attain one of the objectives of the Community, while the Treaty has

---

[37] [1993] O.J. L304/1, amended [1995] O.J. L31/4, [1997] O.J. L341/67 and [1998] O.J. L337/40.

[38] Decision 93/731 on public access to Council documents [1993] O.J. L340/43, Rules of Procedure, Art. 22 amended [1993] O.J. L304/1 and Code of Conduct concerning public access to Council and Commission documents [1993] O.J. L340/41; see also Cases T–194/94, *The Guardian* [1995] E.C.R. II–2765; [1995] 3 C.M.L.R. 359; C–58/94 *Netherlands v. Council* [1994] E.C.R. I–2169; [1996] 2 C.M.L.R. 996 and T–179/95 *Svenska Journalist Forderbundet* [1998] E.C.R. II–2289.

[39] Art. 202, second indent (ex 145) E.C.

[40] Art. 7 (ex 4) E.C.

[41] Art. 253 (ex 190) E.C. See under: "Community Acts".

not provided the corresponding powers. In such a case, the Council may, acting unanimously on a proposal from the Commission and after consulting Parliament, take the appropriate measures.[42] Several stringent conditions have to be fulfilled, and this possibility may not, therefore, be considered as an unlimited opportunity for the institutions to increase their powers of decision. Indeed, the appropriate measures may only be taken when action is necessary "to attain the objectives of the Treaty", which indicates that the powers granted in such case are purely complementary. Also, the required unanimity within the Council should provide the necessary guarantees; indeed, the extension of the Community's powers will, almost inevitably, reduce the powers of the Member States in the same proportion. This necessarily constitutes a break on the extension of the powers of the Community. Furthermore, the Commission's proposal and the opinion of Parliament should ensure that the Community's interests are sufficiently taken into consideration. And, finally, there is always the judicial control of the Court.[43] It does, however, constitute a way of supplementing the Treaty provisions without going through the cumbersome procedure of amending it.

Beside the fact that the Council may only act when this is expressly provided for in the Treaty, there is another limitation which results from the balance of powers among the Community institutions. Indeed, in most cases, the Council can only use its decision-making power on the basis of a proposal from the Commission. And although there are many cases where the Commission must, in pursuance of the Treaty,[44] make a proposal to the Council,[45] and although the Council (and the Parliament) may "request the Commission . . . to submit to it any appropriate proposal",[46] it is not only the impossibility to act without a proposal that constitutes a limitation of the Council's decision-making power, but also, and

[42] Art. 308 (ex 235) E.C. (See Cmn. 5109, para. 15); at the 1972 Paris Summit it was agreed that for the purpose of carrying out the tasks laid down in the different programmes of action, "it was desirable to make the widest possible use of all the dispositions of the Treaty, including Art. 235".

[43] See Case 8/73 *Hauptzollamt Bremerhaven v. Massey-Fergusson* [1973] E.C.R. 897, where the Court accepted the use of Art. 235, and Case 242/87 *Commission v. Council* [1989] E.C.R. 1449, *id.*; [1991] 1 C.M.L.R. 478.

[44] In case the Commission were to fail to make a proposal when this is required for by the Treaty, the Court could be called upon to establish that this failure constitutes an infringement under Art. 232 (ex. 175) E.C.

[45] This is the case each time the Treaty provides that the Council, acting on a proposal from the Commission, "shall . . .," *e.g.* Art. 26 (ex 22) E.C. as opposed to: the Council "may", on a proposal from the Commission, *e.g.* Art. 12 (ex 6) E.C.

[46] Art. 208 (ex 152) E.C. and 192 (ex 138b) E.C.

probably more so, the content of the proposal. And indeed, although the Council is empowered, acting unanimously, to adopt an act which constitutes an amendment to the Commission's proposal, the Council is still bound by its general content.[47]

It could only depart from it if the Commission accepts to modify its original proposal.[48]

Particularly important therefore, is the Commission's exclusive right of legislative initiative: when the Council meets to "make regulations, issue directives, take decisions",[49] it practically always does so on the basis of a proposal put before it by the Commission and which is, one might presume, formulated in such a way as to further the Community's interest.

Related to the principle of "conferred powers" is the question of "implied powers". In several cases the Court has admitted that "rules established by international agreements or by law are considered to imply those rules without which the first either would have no sense or could not be reasonably or successfully applied".[50] This prudent approach to a very delicate question—especially in the context of the transfer of powers from the Member States to the Community—can certainly not be considered as opening the door to extensive Treaty interpretation in regard to the powers of the institutions. The principle of "conferred powers" therefore stands.

Altogether, it appears that, as far as the decision-making powers of the Council are concerned, the built-in system of limitations, safeguards and controls is indeed impressive. First, there are the limitations resulting from the system of conferred powers.

Secondly, there is the fact that the Council cannot legislate without a proposal from the Commission.

Thirdly, there is the obligation to involve Parliament and this can take, as was seen in the chapter on the European Parliament, various forms: simple consultation, co-operation, assent, agreement (in budgetary matters) and, more and more, co-decision. Finally, there is the judicial control of the Court.[51]

---

[47] Art. 250(1) (ex 189a(1)) E.C. If the Council were to modify the proposal substantially, it would no longer be an amendment. One must apply here, by analogy, the Court's view on the requirement of renewed consultation of Parliament in case the Council modifies the proposal on which Parliament was consulted, in such a way as to affect its substance. Case 41/69 *ACF Chemiefarma v. Commission* [1970] E.C.R. 661 at 662(3).

[48] Art. 250(2) (ex 189a(2)) E.C.

[49] Art. 249 (ex 189) E.C.

[50] Case 8/55 *Fédération Charbonnière de Belgique v. High Authority* [1954–1956] E.C.R. 245 at 299 and Case 22/70 *Commission v. Council* [1971] E.C.R. 263 at 280(72); C.M.L.R. 335.

[51] Art. 230 (ex 173) E.C.

(b) Scope

Being the Community law-maker, the Council's decision-making power covers the whole spectrum of the Community's activities. The Council may share these powers with the Commission, on which it can bestow, in the acts which it adopts, powers for adoption of the necessary acts for the implementation of the rules it lays down.[52] On the other hand, many of the Council's powers must be shared with Parliament. This has always been the case with the budgetary powers[53] and with all the matters which are now decided upon in pursuance of the so-called "co-decision" procedure, which is becoming more and more the rule.[54] Both were examined in some detail in the previous chapter concerning the European Parliament.[55]

The exact scope of the Council's decisions-making power in the other fields of activity shall be examined in the various sections in Parts Three, Four, Five and Six dealing with those activities.

(2) Co-ordination of Economic Policies

Beside having the power to take decisions in all the cases provided for by the Treaty, the Council has, as was seen, the task to "ensure co-ordination of the general economic policies of the Member States".[56]

As was pointed out at the beginning of this section, beside establishing a Common Market, the Community's task is to establish an economic and monetary union (EMU) and implement the common policies and activities referred to in the Treaty.[57]

The economic and monetary policy is probably the most important addition introduced by the Maastricht Treaty; it shall be examined in some detail in Part Four, but mention should be made here of the fact that the "co-ordination of the economic policies of the Member States" constitutes a necessary complement to the establishment of the common market. As will be seen, the latter consists of the basic freedoms[58] and a number of common policies.

---

[52] Art. 202, third indent (ex 145) E.C.
[53] Art. 272 (ex 203) E.C.
[54] Art. 251 (ex 189b) E.C.
[55] See above.
[56] Art. 202, first indent (ex 145) E.C.
[57] Arts 3 and 4 (ex 3 and 3a) E.C.
[58] Freedom to move goods, to accept work, to provide services, to establish oneself, to transfer capital and payments in any of the Member States.

The list of the latter has grown with the SEA and the Maastricht Treaty. It now encompasses: Transport, Competition, Fiscal matters, Harmonisation, Economic and Monetary Policy, Employment, Commercial Policy, Social Policy, Education, Vocational Training, Youth, Culture, Public Health, Consumer Protection, Trans-European Networks, Industry, Economic and Social Cohesion, Research and Technological Development, Environment and Development Co-operation. Although it is not listed in the E.C. Treaty, external relations have always played an extremely important role.

It is clear from this long list that those are policies which, with the exception maybe of competition and commercial policy, cannot be implemented by the Community alone. In other words they "do not fall within the [Community's] exclusive competence". Consequently, in those areas "the Community shall take action, in accordance with the principle of subsidiarity, only if and in so far as, the objectives of the proposed action cannot be sufficiently achieved by the Member States and can therefore, by reason of the scale or effects of the proposed action, be better achieved by the Community".[59]

It is important to note that the principle of subsidiarity does apply in all cases except those where the Community has "exclusive" competence, such as commercial policy, agricultural market organisations, protection of fishing resources, competition and, in the future, monetary policy. The principle is understandable, *i.e.* the Community only acts when it can do so better than the Member States acting individually. However, the implementation of this principle is far from clear, only experience will show how to apply it.[60]

As was pointed out, most of the above-mentioned activities of the Community require the active co-operation of the Member States, and, it follows that it is the task of the Council to co-ordinate this co-operation. But, it is extremely difficult to describe with great precision how this task is to be carried out. Indeed, while the activities of the Community with regard to the establishment of the common market are described in the Treaty with some precision (the Treaty indicates whether the Council must act through regulations, directives, decisions or agreements) and contains an indication as to the time-table for their implementation (such as the EMU phases),[61]

[59] Art. 5(2) (ex 3b(2)) E.C. The principle of subsidiarity must also be seen in connection with Art. 1 TEU, which provides that "decisions are taken as closely as possible to the citizen".

[60] See the Protocol on the application of the principles of subsidiarity and proportionality: [1997] O.J. C340/105.

[61] Art. 116 (ex 109e) E.C.

the situation is rather different when it comes to the co-ordination of the economic activities of the Member States.

Although regulations, directives and decisions are by no means excluded, the Treaty refers, as far as the Council is concerned, to "broad guidelines",[62] "multilateral surveillance",[63] "recommendations",[64] "general orientations",[65] "adoption of measures to contribute to the objectives referred to",[66] besides the "resolutions", "declarations", "work programmes", "multiannual framework programmes"[67] and "general action programmes"[68] provided for in various Treaty provisions.

Clearly, the Council's task with regard to co-ordination of economic policies is ill-defined as regards its means. And although most of these "measures" can only be taken on the basis of a proposal from the Commission and after consultation of Parliament, it is not easy to determine whether or not they constitute binding acts submitted to the judicial control of the Courts. Nevertheless, this loose system has, so far, worked in a rather satisfactorily way: to be effective, co-ordination needs to be flexible. However, one does get the impression that the more important the decisions, the more informal they sometimes are. A typical example is the setting up of the European Monetary System (EMS) which was not even provided for in the Treaty.

As for the obligations imposed upon the Member States in those fields, they are often just as vague. The Treaty mentions, for example that they "shall regard their economic policies as a matter of common concern".[69]

The question can therefore be asked whether the procedures provided in the Treaty for implementing the co-ordination of the economic policies by the Council correspond to the requirements of a democratic exercise of powers.

---

[62] Art. 99 (ex 103(2)) E.C. See Council Recommendation of July 6, 1998 on the broad guidelines of the economic policies of the Member States and of the Community [1998] O.J. L200/34.
[63] Art. 99 (ex 103(2)) E.C.
[64] Art. 97 (ex 102) E.C.
[65] Art. 111(2) (ex 109) E.C.
[66] Art. 150(4) (ex 127(4)) E.C.
[67] Art. 166 (ex 130i) E.C.
[68] Art. 175(3) (ex 130s(3)) E.C.
[69] Art. 99(1) (ex 103(1)) E.C.

3. The European Council

As pointed out above, there came a time when Council decisions were no longer taken by majority voting although this was provided for in the Treaty. Furthermore, the subjects to be decided upon became more and more political because, with the evolution towards economic co-operation, they were of vital importance for the general economic development of the Member States themselves. Consequently, the decision-making process within the Community came virtually to a halt. It became obvious that new impulses had to be given and new methods of decision-making had to be found. Since the Council is already a gathering of high-level politicians, the solution was sought more and more in the so-called Conferences of Heads of State or of Government.[70] At the 1974 "Summit", as those Conferences were also called, the participants "recognised the need for an overall approach to the internal problems involved in achieving European unity and the external problems facing Europe—consider it essential to ensure progress and overall consistency in the activities of the Communities and the work on political co-operation—and [have] therefore decided to meet, accompanied by the Ministers of Foreign Affairs, three times a year and, whenever necessary, in the Council of the Communities and in the context of Political Co-operation".[71]

Consequently, since 1975, the Heads of State or of Government meet, at first three times, but since a few years twice a year, as the "European Council". It is composed of the Heads of State or of Government of the Member States and the President of the Commission and is assisted by the Ministers of Foreign Affairs and a member of the Commission. It is presided over by the Member State which holds the presidency of the Council. The secretariat is provided by the Secretaries-General of the Council and of the Commission.

The existence of the European Council was formally recognised for the first time by the SEA[72] and its task was defined in the

[70] The original idea was to organise gatherings of heads of government and the denomination "heads of State or government" was made necessary by the fact that in France the function of head of government is assumed by the Head of State. The first such conference was held at Paris on February 10/11, 1961; see Communiqué in [1961] E.C. Bull. 3–13, and the second in Bonn on July 19, 1961, where it was decided to hold such meetings at regular intervals; see Communiqué in [1961] E.C. Bull. 7–40.

[71] Eighth General Report (1974), 297.

[72] Art. 2 SEA and Art. 4 (ex D) Maastricht Treaty: "The European Council shall bring together the Heads of State or of Government of the Member States and the President of the Commission. They shall be assisted by the Ministers for Foreign

Maastricht Treaty: "provide the Union with the necessary impetus for its development and . . . define the general political guidelines thereof". It also provided that the European Council shall submit to the European Parliament a report after each of its meetings and a yearly written report on the progress achieved by the Union.[73]

The European Council has so far limited itself to issuing general guidelines which have been acted upon by the Council and the Commission. Since the Council can also meet in the composition of Heads of State or of Government, it becomes in fact the European Council, capable of taking binding decisions, on the condition that all the rules of the Treaty applying in such a case are observed, *i.e.* proposal from the Commission, consultation of Parliament and voting procedure. The Maastricht Treaty did indeed provide for such a case where the conditions necessary for the adoption of a single currency have to be assessed.[74]

At the European Council meeting of June 1977 in London, agreement was reached on a framework for the organisation of its meetings.[75] It was also agreed that for "discussions aimed at reaching decisions or issuing statements there should be a record of conclusions, which should be issued on the authority of the Presidency".[76] At the beginning of each meeting the European Council hears a statement by the President of Parliament, which is often followed by a debate. After each meeting, the President of the European Council makes an oral report to Parliament, sometimes followed also by a debate.

One of the tasks attributed to the European Council is to define the principles of, and general guidelines for, the "*Common Foreign and Security Policy*" which was provided for by the E.U. Treaty and modified by the Amsterdam Treaty.[77] The European Council decides on common strategies to be implemented by the Union—not by the Member States—in areas where the Member States have important interests in common. The reference to "the" Member States seems to indicate that the matter must concern all of them. The common strategies are recommended to the European Council by the Council.

Affairs of the Member States and by a Member of the Commission. The European Council shall meet at least twice a year, under the chairmanship of the Head of State or of Government which holds the Presidency of the Council." (The last half of the last sentence does not appear in the SEA.) Now Art. 4 TEU.

[73] Art. 4 (ex D) TEU.

[74] Art. 121(2) and (3)) (ex 109j) E.C.

[75] [1977] E.C. Bull. 6–83.

[76] Those "conclusions" are published in the Bulletin of the European Communities issue by the Commission's Secretariat General.

[77] Art. 13(1) (ex J.3(1)) TEU.

When deciding on a common strategy, the European Council must set out their "objectives, duration and the means to be made available by the Union and the Member States". The implementation of the common strategies is the task of the Council, which acts by way of "joint actions" and "common positions". Joint actions[78] address specific situations where operational action by the Union is deemed to be required, while common positions[79] define the approach of the Union to a particular matter of a geographical or thematic nature. Since they concern mainly foreign policy, they will be examined in Part Six: the Union in the World.

The European Council may also decide on the progressive framing of a common defence policy,[80] which might lead to a common defence. The Western European Union (WEU) is now considered "an integral part of the development of the Union, providing the Union with access to an operational capability" in the context of humanitarian and rescue tasks, peacekeeping tasks and tasks of combat forces in crises management, including peacemaking. The competence of the European Council to establish guidelines also obtains in respect of the WEU for those matters for which the Union avails itself of the WEU.

The Treaty of Amsterdam introduced a new competence for the European Council allowing it to determine the existence of a *serious and persistent breach by a Member State* of the principles of liberty, democracy, respect for human rights and fundamental freedoms, and the rule of law; principles which are common to all the Member States.[81] Where such a determination is made, the European Council, acting by a qualified majority, may decide to suspend certain rights deriving from the application of the Treaty. Before imposing such sanctions, the European Council must obtain the assent of the Parliament. The latter shall decide by a two-third majority of the votes cast, representing a majority of its members.

It appears that the European Council, or, as the Treaty puts it, the Council meeting in the composition of Heads of State or Government, is acting more and more like an operational and law-making body of the Union.

---

78 Art. 14 (ex J.4) TEU.
79 Art. 15 (ex J.5) TEU.
80 Art. 17 (ex J.7) TEU.
81 Art. 6(1) (ex F) and 49 (ex O) TEU.

4. Representatives of the Governments of the Member States meeting in Council

Decisions taken by the Representatives of the Member States meeting in Council are not "decisions" in the sense of binding acts provided for in the Treaty. They are often taken in the form of a "Resolution" and concern acts which are not explicitly provided for under the Treaty but are directly connected with the Community activities. They form part of the so-called *acquis communautaire*[82] and all new Member States are required to accept them.[83]

Those acts are not to be confused with certain decisions which must be taken, in accordance with the Treaty, by "common accord of the Governments of the Member States"[84]; in certain cases after consulting Parliament.[85] The latter are binding and therefore submitted to the judicial control of the Court.

Further Reading

Inger Osterdahl, "Openness v. Secrecy: Public Access to Documents in Sweden and the European Union", (1998) 23 E.L.Rev. 336.

---

82 See Maastricht Treaty, Art. 2 (ex B) fifth indent.

83 See, *e.g.* U.K Act of Accession, Art. 3(1): "The new Member States accede by this Act to the decisions and agreements adopted by the Representatives of the Governments of the Member States meeting in Council. They undertake to accede from the date of accession to all other agreements concluded by the original Member States relating to the functioning of the Communities or connected with their activities."

84 Art. 223 (ex 167) E.C.: the Judges and the Advocates General's appointment. *Id.* Art. 214(2) (ex 158) for the Commissioners.

85 See, *e.g.* Art. 214(2) (ex 158(2)) E.C.

Chapter Seven
The Commission

The Commission's main function is to "ensure the proper functioning and development of the common market"[1] and all the other tasks provided for under the Treaty result from that. The Commission, for example is the "guardian of the Treaty", *i.e.* it makes sure that all those who are subject to Community law act in accordance with it. The Commission also administers the Community's finances, negotiates its international agreements, represents the Community both inside and outside its borders and exercises the power of decision which the Treaty or the Council have conferred upon it.

It constitutes the moving power of the Community's activities, and its uninterrupted presence at Brussels, the main seat of the Community institutions,[2] its competent staff and its world-wide relations create the necessary conditions for it to play a major role within the institutional system of the Community.

More important, however, is the fact that it embodies and represents the common or Community interest and is responsible for ensuring that this interest prevails when decisions are taken by Member States, the Council or natural and legal persons alike. Those various tasks will be examined in more detail after a short analysis of some organisational aspects.

[1] Art. 211 (ex 155) E.C.

[2] Brussels was only the temporary seat of the Commission until the Edinburgh European Council decided at its meeting of December 1992, that "The Commission shall have its seat in Brussels". Conclusions of the Presidency, Annex 6 to Part A, Art. 1(c), [1992] E.C. Bull. 12–24.

1. The Members of the European Commission

The Treaty provides that the Commission consists of 20 members,[3] but adds that that number may be altered by the Council.[4] The members are appointed for a period of five years,[5] renewable, in accordance with a procedure which, under the Maastricht Treaty, involves both the governments of the Member States and Parliament.[6]

The governments first nominate by common accord the person they intend to appoint as President of the Commission. This nomination must be approved by the Parliament.[7]

Secondly, they nominate, in consultation with the nominee for President, the other persons whom they intend to appoint as members of the Commission.

Thirdly, all those persons are subject, as a body, to a vote of approval of Parliament.[8]

Finally, after approval by Parliament, they shall be appointed by the governments of the Member States.

The requirements for designation as member of the Commission

---

[3] Since there are 15 Member States, the countries with the largest population, *i.e.* Germany, Spain, France, Italy and the U.K., each have two Commissioners. In fact the Treaty only provides that only nationals of the Member States may be members of the Commission, that the Commission must include at least one national of each of the Member States and not more than two having the same nationality. Everyone agrees that 20 members is too many. See, however, Protocol on institutions with the prospect of enlargement of the European Union, annexed to the four Treaties which provides that on accession, the Commission shall comprise one national of each of the Member States, that Member States which have two nationals will give up one, on the condition that the weighting of the votes in the Council has been modified in a manner acceptable to all Member States.

It also provides that one year before the E.U. membership exceeds twenty, a conference of representatives of the governments of the Member States shall carry out a comprehensive review of the composition and functioning of the institutions.

[4] Art. 213(1) (ex 157(1)) E.C.

[5] Art. 214(1) (ex 158(1)) E.C.

[6] Art. 214(2) (ex 158(2)) E.C.

[7] Under the old Art. 158(2) the Parliament was only consulted.

[8] In 1994, the proposed candidates appeared before the appropriate committees according to their respective fields of responsibility (Rule 29A(1)). This might seem difficult since the portfolios, in theory at least, are attributed by the Commission after the members have taken up their duties. However, many a government lets it be known in advance that the member of its nationality should have such or such a portfolio. In such a case, there is not much left of the so-called independence of the members, neither of the obligation imposed upon the Member States to refrain from

are very broadly defined: nationality, competence and independence,[9] the latter being, by far, the most important. And, indeed it is this independence that characterises the Commission in comparison with the Council and Parliament: the Commission represents the general, *i.e.* the Community interest and its main task is to ensure that this interest prevails under all circumstances.

It will be remembered that it was in connection with this independence that the ECSC Treaty introduced the term "supranational".[10] Although the word did not reappear in the subsequent Treaties, the substance of the concept, of course, remains. The required independence applies not only to the qualities of the candidate-Commissioner, but the Treaty also specifies that the members of the Commission shall, in the general interest of the Community, be completely independent "in the performance of their duties".[11] And, since the most obvious problem with regard to this independence is the relationship between the Commissioner and his own Government which nominated him,[12] the Treaty explicitly imposes upon the Member State the obligation "to respect this principle and not to seek to influence the members of the Commission in the performance of their duties".[13]

As for the members of the Commission, they are bound by certain obligations both during and after their term of office.[14] And in order to underline the importance of the independence and the other

---

trying to influence them. Maybe that is the reason why the Intergovernmental Conference in Amsterdam felt it necessary to declare that "it considers that the President of the Commission must enjoy broad discretion in the allocation of tasks within the college, as well as in any reshuffling of those tasks during a Commission's term of office". [1997] O.J. C340/137.

Parliament also expects the President-designate to present the programme of the Commission, which shall be followed by a debate (Rules of Procedure, Rule 29A(3)). In July 1994 the President-designate, Jaques Santer, Prime Minister of Luxembourg, won endorsement by 260 votes to 238 and 23 abstentions! This vote expressed the frustration of the EMPs at only being "consulted" after the Governments had made the decision.

[9] Art. 213(1) (ex 157(1)) E.C.

[10] Art. 9 ECSC: "The members of the High Authority will refrain from any action incompatible with the supranational character of their duties. Each Member State undertakes to respect this supranational character."

[11] Art. 213(2) (ex 157(2)) E.C. See [1995] O.J. L19/5.

[12] Art. 214(2) (ex 158) E.C.

[13] Art. 213(2) (ex 157(2)) E.C.

[14] *ibid.* They shall neither seek nor take instructions from any government or any other body, they may not engage in any other occupation, and they must behave with integrity and discretion as regards the acceptance, after they have ceased to hold office, of certain appointments or benefits.

obligations, the Treaty provides that the members of the Commission shall, when entering upon their duties, give a solemn undertaking to respect the obligations arising from their office.[15]

Once the members have been nominated, they form a college: the Commission, and they do not fulfil an individual role under the Treaty. They are jointly responsible for everything the Commission does.

A last remark concerning this all-important aspect of the duties of the members of the Commission: in the event of any breach of the above-mentioned obligations, the Court of Justice may, on application by the Council or the Commission, rule that the member concerned be, according to the circumstances, either compulsorily retired or deprived of his rights to a pension or other benefits in its stead.[16]

2. The Commission's Tasks and Powers

The Commission's tasks and powers, as provided for in various Treaty provisions, derive from its main responsibility, which is "to ensure the proper functioning and development of the common market".[17]

These tasks and powers shall be examined in detail hereunder in the order in which they are provided for in the Treaty. They can be summarised as follows:

(a) ensure that the provisions of the law of the Community are applied;
(b) formulate recommendations and deliver opinions;
(c) exercise its own power of decision;
(d) participate in the Community's legislative process;
(e) exercise the powers conferred upon it by the Council;
(f) negotiate international agreements and represent the Community;

---

[15] Art. 213(2) (ex 157(2)) E.C. the solemn undertaking is given before the Court of Justice during a special session. Each member undertakes to perform his duties as specified in the Treaty: complete independence in the general interest of the Community, no instructions, no action incompatible with the office, integrity and discretion; they also formally take note of the fact that the governments of the Member States have undertaken to respect their independence. One can only hope that the Commissioners strictly adhere to those obligations.

[16] Art. 213(2) (ex 157(2)) E.C.

[17] Art. 211 (ex 155) E.C.

(g) implement the budget, and
(h) publish an annual report on the activities of the Community.

(1) Enforcement of Community Law

It is the Commission's responsibility to "ensure that the provisions of this Treaty and the measures taken by the institutions pursuant thereto are applied".[18] The measures taken by the institutions are referred to as "secondary legislation", the Treaties being the primary legislation. Both impose obligations upon the Member States, the institutions and the natural and legal persons operating within the Community. It is the Commission's task to ensure that they all abide by the law. For this purpose the Commission is endowed with certain powers consisting mainly in the right to obtain information and to institute proceedings against trespassers.

The right to obtain information is provided for, in a general way,[19] and by various Treaty provisions and Community acts.[20] Furthermore, the general obligation imposed upon the Member States to "facilitate the achievement of the Community's tasks"[21] should provide the necessary legal ground for the Commission to obtain all the required data.

Based upon the information obtained,[22] the Commission can then, if necessary, start the following actions.

---

[18] Art. 211 (ex 155) E.C., first indent.

[19] See Reg. 2186/93 obliging Member States to draw up harmonised business registers and Case C–426/93 *Germany v. Council* [1995] E.C.R. I–3723: is a measure necessary to allow the Commission to carry out its task: no infringement.

[20] See, *e.g.* Art. 88(3) (ex 93(3)) E.C. (plans to grant or alter aids). As for acts see, *e.g.* Reg. 17, Arts 4 and 5 (first Reg. implementing Arts 85 and 86 (now 81 and 82), [1959–62] O.J. Spec. Ed. 87).

[21] Art. 10 (ex 5) E.C. See Case C–5/94 *R. v. Ministry of Agriculture* [1996] E.C.R. I–2553; [1996] 2 C.M.L.R. 391: Member States are obliged, in accordance with the first para. of Art. 5 to take all measures necessary to guarantee the application and effectiveness of Community law.

[22] The Commission can also obtain information through complaints from Member States or from natural or legal persons; see, *e.g.* Reg. 17, Art. 3 ([1959–1962] O.J. 87.) See Case T–182/87 *Smanor* [1998] E.C.R. II–271, Order of the CFI: refusal of the Commission to start proceedings against Member States for failure to fulfil an obligation; natural or legal persons are not admissible when challenging a refusal of the Commission to start a 226 (ex 169) procedure and Case T–83/97 *Sateba* [1997] E.C.R. II–1523; [1998] 4 C.M.L.R. 528: the procedural position of a party complaining to the Commission on the basis of Reg. 17 for violation of Reg. 99/63: [1963] O.J. 127, 2269, is fundamentally different from the one of a complainant for failure by a Member State: Art. 226 (ex 169) E.C.

(a) With regard to Member States[23]

When the Commission considers that a Member State has not fulfilled an obligation under Community law:

(a) it shall[24] remind the government in question of its obligations and invite it to take the necessary measures or submit its observations, all within a time-limit set by the Commission, usually two months;
(b) if no action is taken by the Member State and no observations are received, or if those that were submitted do not convince the Commission, it shall deliver a "reasoned opinion" on the matter, and lay down a time-limit within which the Member State must comply;
(c) if the Member State does not comply, the Commission may[25] bring the matter before the Court;
(d) if the Court finds that the Member State has indeed failed to fulfil its obligation, "the State shall be required to take the necessary steps to comply with the judgment".[26]

The main question is, of course, what happens after that, namely when the Member State fails to implement the Court's judgment. Until the entering into force of the Maastricht Treaty, there was nothing the Community institutions could do, except start the procedure all over in order to have the Court ascertain that the Member State did not comply with the judgment.[27]

The Treaty now provides that in case the Commission considers that the Member State has not taken the necessary measures to comply with the judgment, it shall, after having given the Member

---

[23] Art. 226 (ex 169) E.C.

[24] The terms used here indicate that, once the Commission has determined that a Member State has indeed failed to fulfil an obligation under the Treaty (and in this determination the Commission enjoys discretionary power: it must, among other things, weigh the political implications) there is an obligation for the Commission to act. The existence of this obligation is essential within a system where the plea of *non adimpletus contractus* is inadmissible; see Joined Cases 90 and 91/63 *Commission v. Luxembourg and Belgium* [1964] E.C.R. 625 at 631; [1965] C.M.L.R. 58.

[25] At this point the Commission's powers are entirely discretionary.

[26] It is interesting to note that Art. 226 (ex 169) E.C. refers to the judgment of the Court rather than to the Treaty obligation which was the point of departure of the whole proceedings. The Court cannot impose upon the Member States obligations which differ from what the Treaty prescribes; anyway, in its judgments based upon Art. 226 (ex 169), the Court only ascertains that the Member State "has failed to fulfil its obligation under the Treaty"; see, *e.g.* Joined Cases 227 to 230/85, *Commission v. Belgium* [1988] E.C.R. 12; [1989] 2 C.M.L.R. 797.

[27] See, *e.g.* Joined Cases 227 and 230/85, n.26 above, at 11.

State the opportunity to submit its observations, issue a reasoned opinion specifying the points on which the Member State has not complied and fixing a time-limit to do so. In case of non-compliance, the Commission may bring the matter before the Court and "specify the amount of the lump sum or penalty payment to be paid", which it considers appropriate in the circumstances.[28]

If the Court finds that the Member State has, indeed, not complied with its judgment, it may impose a lump sum or payment.

So now,[29] finally, there exists a coercive measure against Member States which flout Community law.[30] So much for the responsibility of the Member State towards the Community, but there is also the responsibility for the damages caused by the infringement to natural or legal persons. The Court decided that where a breach of Community law by a Member State is attributable to the national legislature acting in a field in which it has a wide discretion to make legislative choices, individuals suffering loss or injury thereby, are entitled to reparation, where the rule of Community law breached is intended to confer rights upon them, the breach is sufficiently serious and there is a direct causal link between the breach and the damage sustained by the individual.[31] As was pointed out above, the Commission enjoys a large discretionary power when deciding whether or not to pursue a Member State before the Court. It should also be noted that, in most cases, problems with the implementation of Community law by the Member States are settled out of court.

(b) With regard to the Institutions

The institutions concerned here are the Council and the Parliament and also, although not an institution, the ECB. The Commission can initiate a court action against those bodies when it is of the opinion that their acts infringe a Community provision[32] or when a failure of those bodies to act is considered by the Commission to be

---

[28] Art. 228(2) (ex 171(2)) E.C.

[29] The ECSC Treaty also provided for some kind of coercive measures (See Art. 88 ECSC), but they were never applied.

[30] No figures are published concerning Art. 224 (ex 169) E.C. cases brought because of non-implementation of Court judgments, but the total amount of actions brought by the Commission against a Member State was 121 in 1997, of which 37 did not result in a judgment. See General Report (1997), p. 418.

[31] Joined Cases C–46 and 48/93 *Brasserie du Pêcheur and Factortame* [1996] E.C.R. I–1029; [1996] 1 C.M.L.R. 889. *Id.* in Case C–5/94 *Heddley Lomas* [1996] E.C.R. I–2553 and C–66/95 *Sutton* [1997] E.C.R. I–2163; [1997] 2 C.M.L.R. 382.

[32] Art. 230 (ex 173) E.C. Those cases are brought either by governments (25), Community institutions (6), or by individuals (4); total: 35.

an infringement of the Treaty.[33] These actions will be examined in more detail in the Chapter on the Court of Justice.

(c) With regard to Legal or Natural Persons

The Commission has been endowed with important powers as regards undertakings both public[34] and private, legal and natural persons. Those powers apply mainly in the competition and transport fields, where the Commission may impose fines and penalties[35] in case of violation, or order enterprises to disinvest themselves when investigating mergers and acquisitions.[36]

(2) Formulating Recommendations and delivering Opinions

The Treaty provides[37] that the Commission shall formulate recommendations or deliver opinions on matters, dealt with in the Treaty, if it expressly so provides[38] or if the Commission considers it necessary. The so-called "Notices" and "Communications" of the Commission[39] fall under this category. It should be remembered that recommendations and opinions have no binding force,[40] so that in fulfilling this task the Commission acts in a purely informative or advisory capacity. The most that can be said is that the Commission binds itself politically. The Treaty provides for several cases where an opinion of the Commission is required[41] and others where it is referred to as a possibility.[42]

---

[33] Art. 232 (ex 175) E.C. Same comment as for Art. 230 (ex 175) E.C.: none in 1997.
[34] Art. 86 (ex 90) E.C.
[35] See Reg. 17 (implementing Arts 81 and 82 (ex 85 and 86) E.C.; Art. 15 E.C. ([1959–62] O.J. 87); Reg. 11 (implementing Art. 75(3) (ex 79(3) E.C.); Reg. 1017 (applying the rules of competition to transport by rail, road and inland waterways), Art. 22 E.C. and Reg. 4064/89 (the Merger Reg: [1989] O.J. L395/1); see, *e.g.* the *Nestlé/Perrier* case [1992] O.J. L356/1.
[36] Reg. 4064/89, Art. 8(4) E.C., see preceding note.
[37] Art. 211 (ex 155) E.C., second indent.
[38] Art. 209 (ex 153) E.C. (on rules governing the committees), Art. 49 TEU, opinion on applications for accession.
[39] See, *e.g.* Communication of the Commission following the famous *Cassis de Dijon* judgment [1980] O.J. C256/2.
[40] Art. 249 (ex 189) E.C.
[41] See, *e.g.* Art. 134 (ex 115) E.C. (recommending methods for co-operation), Art. 140 (ex 118) E.C. (opinion on problems arising at national level in the social field).
[42] Art. 77 (ex 81) E.C. reduction of charges and dues in respect of crossing of frontiers.

The Commission's recommendations and opinions must concern matters dealt with in the Treaty.

(3) Exercise of Power of Decision

The Treaty refers to the Commission's "own power of decision".[43] This is not without importance since, as pointed out, the decision-making institutions within the Community are in principle the Parliament and the Council acting jointly and the Council. The fact that the Commission also exercise a decision-making power might create the impression that the legislative power is shared by more than two institutions. Although those institutions may issue acts which are binding for the subjects of Community law, a distinction must be made between "legislative" power, which is the prerogative of Parliament and Council acting jointly, or the Council, and "executive" and/or "implementing" power, which befalls the Commission. Both the Legislator and the Executive may make regulations, issue directives and take decisions.[44] It should be remembered that in both cases the powers are, of course, "conferred" powers, *i.e.* the institutions were not endowed with a "general" decision-making power. They only enjoy those powers which have explicitly been conferred upon them by the Treaty.[45] The Parliament, the Council and the Commission do not operate on quite the same level, although it must be recognised that no clear cut distinction exists between the two.[46]

The power of decision directly entrusted by the Treaty to the Commission concerns the "functioning and development of the common market",[47] *inter alia*, the administration of the customs union,[48] the application of safeguard clauses and of the various common policies such as competition[49] and agriculture,[50] the

---

[43] Art. 211 (ex 155) E.C., third indent.
[44] Art. 249 (ex 189) E.C., which makes no distinction between the institutions.
[45] See above the Chapter Six "The Council": "decision-making".
[46] See, *e.g.* Directive 80/723 on the transparency of financial relations between Member States and public enterprises, [1980] O.J. L195/35 and Joined Cases 188 to 190/80, *France, Italy and United Kingdom v. Commission* [1982] E.C.R. 2545; [1982] 3 C.M.L.R. 144, where the Court ruled that the Directive in question was in conformity with the Treaty.
[47] Art. 211 (ex 155) E.C.
[48] Art. 134(1) (ex 115(1)) E.C.
[49] Arts 81(3) (ex 85(3)), 85(2) (ex 89(2)), 86(3) (ex 90(3)) and 88(2) (ex 93(2)) E.C.
[50] Art. 37 (ex 43) E.C.

execution of the Community budget[51] and, to some extent, the external relations.[52]

When exercising its right to act, the Commission has, in certain cases, a choice as to the form of the measure,[53] in other instances no form is prescribed[54] and sometimes a given act is required.[55]

Decisions of the Commission are taken by a majority of its members[56] and when at least eleven members are present.[57] The Commission may not delegate its power of decision either to one of its members or to its civil servants[58]; nor may the Commission delegate its powers to autonomous bodies.[59] The Rules of Procedure of the Commission are published in the Official Journal.[60]

(4) Exercise of Powers conferred by the Council

Most Commission decisions are based upon powers provided for by acts of the Council. Indeed, in accordance with the Treaty,[61] the Council may confer upon the Commission the powers necessary for the implementation of the rules it lays down. This delegation of powers must necessarily be limited. As the Court indicated, the "basic elements to be dealt with" must be adopted by the Council in accordance with the procedures laid down by the Treaty. The provisions implementing the basic regulations may be adopted by the Commission (or the Council) according to a different procedure.[62] In fact and in law, it is not a "delegation" of legislative power, since it only concerns "implementation" and, furthermore,

---

[51] The Commission is responsible for implementing the budget and administering the various Community funds: social fund, regional fund, cohesion fund, etc.

[52] See Part Six: "The Union in the World".

[53] See, *e.g.* Art. 86(3) (ex 90(3)) E.C.: the Commission shall address "appropriate directives or decisions"; of course, the form depends on the content of the act.

[54] See, *e.g.* Art. 38 (ex 46) E.C.: the Commission shall fix the amount of the charges.

[55] See, *e.g.* former Art. 45(2) E.C.: "Directives issued by the Commission".

[56] See, *e.g.* Art. 219 (ex 163) E.C.

[57] Rules of Procedure, Art. 6 [1993] O.J. L230/15.

[58] See however Decision 68/183 authorising certain management measures to be taken within the framework of the common organisation of the agricultural markets, [1968] O.J. L89/13. This Decision is based on Art. 27 of the Rules of Procedure of the Commission. See Case 8/72, *Cementhandelaren v. Commission* [1972] E.C.R. 977; [1973] C.M.L.R. 7, concerning the legality of a document signed by a Director-General rather than by a Commissioner.

[59] See Case 9/56, *Meroni v. High Authority* [1957 and 1958] E.C.R. 133.

[60] [1993] O.J. L230/15, amended by [1995] O.J. L97/82.

[61] Art. 211 (ex 155) E.C., first indent.

[62] Case 25/70 *Koster* [1970] E.C.R. 1161 (6).

the Member States, via the committees, which are part of the Commission's procedure, play an important, sometimes even a decisive, role. It is most interesting to note that in 1996, for instance, "the Commission adopted—in addition to numerous decisions—2,341 regulations and 2,806 directives, being legal acts with general application, whereas the Council adopted 484 acts in total".[63] In 1997, the Council adopted a decision laying down the procedures for the exercise of implementing powers conferred on the Commission.[64] As was explained above, the Council only meets a few days a month and has neither the opportunity nor the means to work out the detailed rules for implementing the Community legislation it enacts. This is therefore, normally, entrusted to the Commission. However, the Council may also impose conditions and procedural requirements for the exercise by the Commission of this delegated power. Generally, the main requirement imposed by the Council is an obligation for the Commission to consult a Committee composed of representatives of the Member States, before deciding. The principles and rules concerning this consultation are laid down in the so-called "Commitology" decision of the Council.[65] There are three kinds of committees which the Commission might have to consult before taking an implementing decision.

(a) the *Consultative Committee* which formulates a non-binding opinion, although the Commission is supposed to take it into account and mention it in the minutes;
(b) the *Management Committee* which is widely used in the implementation of the common agricultural policy. When this Committee, by a majority vote (the same as for the Council), emits a negative opinion, the Commission takes a decision which becomes applicable. It is, however, referred to the Council. What happens after that, is decided beforehand in the Council's decision which the Commission must implement:
  (i) either the Commission may postpone the application of the measure for one month, during which time the Council may, by a majority vote, modify or annul it; or
  (ii) the Commission must postpone the application for a maximum of three months during which time the Council may modify or annul the measure. If no decision is taken by

[63] Georg Haibach *Comitology after Amsterdam, a comparative analyses of the delegation of legislative power* Eipascope, European Institute of Public Administration, No. 1997/3, p. 2.
[64] [1997] O.J. L197/33.
[65] Decision 87/373 [1987] O.J. L197/33.

the Council within the given time-limit, the Commission's measure becomes definitive.

(c) the *Regulatory Committee* which must concur with the proposed measure before it can be taken. In case the Committee expresses a negative opinion or no opinion, the Commission must make a proposal to the Council, which can take a decision by a majority vote, unless the Council wants to modify the proposal, in which case unanimity is required. If no decision is taken by the Council within a maximum of three months, there are two possibilities, one of which must be provided for in the Council's decision which the Commission must implement:

(i) either the Commission may take the proposed decision; this is known as "net" (*filet*) procedure;

(ii) or, although the Council could not muster the required qualified majority, a simple majority voted against it, in which case the Commission may not take its proposed decision. This constitutes the so-called "counter-net" (*contre filet*), which in fact annuls the power conferred by the Council and imposes immobility on the Community.

As for the choice of the Council between the two procedures (one of which must be provided for in the decision which confers the power of implementation), there are no indications in the Commitology decision.

The procedures described above are quite complex and lengthy so much so that they seem ridiculous. This is the more surprising since the Council had received quite clear instructions from the governments for a speedy and efficient procedure. Those instructions were given at the time of the signature of the SEA. In the "Declaration on the powers of implementation of the Commission" attached to the SEA,[66] the Representatives of the governments of the Member States request the Council to "give the Advisory Commitee procedure in particular a predominant place in the interest of speed and efficiency in the decision-making process, for the exercise of the powers of implementation conferred on the Commission". The question is, of course, what is to be understood by "advisory committee"? Were the Member States referring to the Consultative Committee mentioned above or to the committees in general? Whatever the answer, it can certainly not be said that the present Commitology is speedy and efficient.

---

[66] First declaration adopted by the Conference at the time of signing the Act and annexed thereto: 1986.

(5) Participation in the Legislative Process

As was pointed out in the Chapters on the Parliament and on the Council, the latter can, in most cases, only legislate on the basis of a proposal submitted by the Commission. By submitting drafts for regulations, directives and decisions, the Commission participates, as the Treaty calls it, "in the shaping of measures taken by the Council and by the European Parliament".[67]

Whenever the Commission makes such a proposal in pursuance of the Treaty, it exercises its exclusive right of initiative in the law-making process of the Community. There are cases, however, where the Commission is required to make a proposal within a given time-limit,[68] but in most cases the Commission must use its own judgment as to the suitability of making a proposal.[69]

Although the Commission enjoys the exclusive right of initiative, the Treaty provides that both the Council[70] and Parliament[71] may "request" the Commission to submit to it any appropriate proposals. Of course, it is only a request, but it will be difficult, in many cases, for the Commission to ignore it; nonetheless, neither Council nor Parliament[72] can take legislative initiatives. When the Commission makes a proposal at the request of another institution, it remains nevertheless politically responsible for the proposal. The submission by the Commission of a proposal for legislation constitutes the start of the decision-making process in which the three institutions, Commission, Parliament and Council, each play an essential role. The roles of Parliament and the Council have been described in the Chapters concerning those institutions, and it is therefore necessary to briefly describe the role of the Commission. This role doesn't start with the submission of the proposal, nor does it end with it.

Before drafting its proposal, the Commission must, in certain

[67] Art. 211 (ex 155) E.C., third indent.
[68] See, *e.g.* Art. 37(1) (ex 43(1)) E.C. "immediately this Treaty enters into force".
[69] See, *e.g.* Art. 89 (ex 94) E.C.
[70] Art. 208 (ex 152) E.C.
[71] Art. 192 (ex 138b) E.C.: the Treaty requires that such request be voted by a majority of the members of Parliament, and when it considers that a Community act is required for the purpose of implementing the Treaty. Although one could argue that the latter goes without saying, Parliament shall have to show, in each case, that an act is indeed required; such an obligation is not imposed on the Council.
[72] In the Parliament's Rules of Procedure reference is made to "legislative initiative" (Rule 36B), but it is clear from the content that it remains, even for Parliament, a request addressed to the Commission to take the initiative. The only case of a parlimentarian initiative under the Treaty concerns proposals for election by universal suffrage: Art. 190(3) (ex 138(3)) E.C.

cases, consult the Economic and Social Committee,[73] but, probably of more importance are the informal consultations of national experts undertaken by the Commission. This allows the Commission to judge the possible reactions of each of the Member States, which is essential, especially in cases of majority voting in the Council.

In most cases the Commission will issue preparatory documents, such as Green Papers which contain a description of a given problem and the possible legislative solutions envisaged by the Commission. Those papers are widely distributed or sent to selected groups in order to obtain reactions and proposals.[74] The Green Paper is usually followed by a White Paper which contains the broad lines of the legislation the Commission is planning to propose. Here again, the Commission is looking for reactions from interested parties. The purpose of those consultations is, in general, to fulfil an obligation provided for in the E.U. Treaty, namely that decision should be "taken as closely as possible to the citizen",[75] but also, and for practical purpose, to allow the Commission's staff to gather the necessary information they need to draft their proposals.

Once a draft proposal has been approved by the Commission, it is, generally speaking, published in the *Official Journal*,[76] in order to allow all interested parties to comment on it. In certain cases the Commission will organise consultations of certain groups[77] and/or organise hearings. Although those consultations are quite time-consuming, they constitute for the Commission an invaluable source of information in view of the drafting of the definitive proposal or its modification in case it was already submitted. All this to indicate that there is much more to the drafting of a proposal for Community legislation than the terms of the Treaty suggest: "the Council shall, on a proposal from the Commission, . . ."

The Commission's proposal constitutes the basis for the consultation of Parliament by the Council, and the Commission will closely follow the work of Parliament and more particularly that of the parliamentary Committees which examine the draft. Representatives of the Commission are always present when those Committees meet. This allows the Commission both to explain its position in drafting the proposal and to better understand Parliament's reactions to it. The Commission is therefore fully prepared to eventually

---

[73] Art. 37 (ex 43) E.C. For the Committee see below.
[74] They are available under the reference COM, followed by the year in brackets and a number. They are always available on Internet for a limited time.
[75] Art. 1 (ex A) TEU.
[76] Proposals are published in the "C" series of the O.J., or available from the Commission and known as "COM" documents.
[77] See, *e.g.* [1994] O.J. C199/10.

modify its proposal, which it may do as long as the Council has not acted, at any time during the procedures leading up to the adoption of a Community act.[78] Parallel to the discussions within Parliament, the Commission is present when the proposal is discussed within the Council, either by Coreper or by the working groups set up by the latter. In many cases those groups are composed of the same national civil servants which were consulted informally by the Commission before the proposal was drafted; undoubtedly this allows for a smoother discussion within the Council.

The proposal of the Commission also constitutes the basis for the final decision of the Council. If the latter wishes to adopt an act constituting an amendment to the proposal, unanimity is required.[79] As pointed out before, the right of the Council to modify the proposal is certainly not unlimited: the modification may not, as the Court indicated, alter the substance of the proposal,[80] unless, of course, the Commission accepts the modification. This would be the case when, during the discussion in the Council on the proposal, the Presidency makes a compromise proposal to break a dead-lock; it is not unusual for the Commission itself to suggest such a compromise to the Presidency. As was pointed out in the Chapter on the Parliament, such modifications, even when they are accepted by the Commission, might still have to be re-submitted to Parliament for another opinion on the modified proposal.[81]

Finally, it must be noted that the Commission might be called upon to justify its proposal not only before Parliament,[82] but also before the Court, since the latter has recognised the right of applicants, in an action concerning the legality of an act, to bring proceedings not only against the Council for having adopted the act, but also against the Commission for having proposed it.[83]

---

[78] Art. 250(2) (ex 189a(2)) E.C. See, for instance, the amended proposal for a Council Directive amending Dir. 91/440 on the development of the Community railways [1998] O.J. C321/6.

[79] Art. 250(1) (ex 189a(1)) E.C.

[80] See, *e.g.* Case C–65/90 *Parliament v. Council* [1992] E.C.R. I–4593.

[81] *ibid.*

[82] During the discussions in Parliament about the proposal or through parliamentary questions.

[83] Joined Cases 63–69/72 *Werhahn v. Council* [1973] E.C.R. 1229 at 1247(8).

(6) External Relations

The external relations of the Community will be analysed in detail in Part Six of this book, it may therefore suffice here to point out two aspects which concern the Commission in particular.

Where the Treaty provides for the conclusion of international agreements, mainly within the framework of the Community's commercial policy, the Commission makes recommendations to the Council. The latter may then authorise the Commission to open the necessary negotiations and formulate directives for such negotiations. The Commission negotiates the international agreements in consultation with special committees appointed by the Council to assist it in this task.[84]

The Council, the Commission or a Member State may obtain the opinion of the Court as to whether an agreement is compatible with the provisions of the Treaties. Where the opinion is adverse, the agreement may only enter into force after the Treaty has been amended.[85] As to the word "agreement", the Court held that it covers "any undertaking entered into by a subject of international law, which has binding force".[86]

Besides negotiating international agreements, the Commission is entrusted with maintaining all appropriate relations with all international organisations,[87] and more particularly with the United Nations, and its specialised agencies.[88]

It is also the specific task of the Commission to establish close co-operation with the Council of Europe[89] and the Organisation for Economic Co-operation and Development (OECD).[90]

---

[84] Art. 300(1) (ex 228(1)) E.C.

[85] Art. 300(6) (ex 228(6)) E.C. which refers to Art. 48 E.U. See, *e.g.* Court Opinion 1/91 on the compatibility of the Treaty establishing a European Economic Area, [1991] E.C.R. I–6079.

[86] Opinion 2/92 concerning the competence to participate in the Third Revised Decision of the OECD on National Treatment [1995] E.C.R. I–521. The Court also decided that the fact that certain questions could be dealt with by means of other remedies, for instance Art. 173 E.C. does not preclude the Court from being asked an opinion under Art. 300(6) (ex 228(6)) E.C.

[87] Art. 302 (ex 229) E.C.

[88] *ibid.*

[89] Art. 303 (ex 230) E.C.

[90] Art. 304 (ex 231) E.C.

(7) Implementation of the Community Budget

The budgetary procedure and the role of the Commission in it were examined in the Chapter on the European Parliament.[91] The role of the Commission is formally limited to drafting its own budget and consolidating the estimates of the other institutions in a "preliminary draft budget" to be submitted to the Council.[92] The Commission must also determine, after consultation of the Economic Policy Committee, the maximum rate of increase for the "non-compulsory" expenditures.[93] Once the budget is adopted, it falls to the Commission to implement it in accordance with the regulations laid down by the Council.[94] Detailed rules are laid down in these regulations for each institution concerning its part in effecting its own expenditure.[95]

Afterwards, the Commission must seek discharge in respect of the implementation of its part of the budget. To this end, it must submit annually to the Council and to Parliament the accounts for the preceding financial year relating to the implementation of the budget, together with a financial statement of the assets and liabilities of the Community.[96] In exercising their powers of control over the Commission's implementation of the budget, the Council and Parliament are assisted by the Court of Auditors, which forwards to them an annual report after the close of each financial year.[97] The Council and Parliament examine the accounts, the financial statement and the report. Discharge is given to the Commission by Parliament on a recommendation from the Council, acting by a qualified majority.[98]

As part of the implementation of the budget, the Commission administers the European Agricultural Guidance and Guarantee Fund, the European Social Fund, the European Regional Development Fund and the Cohesion Fund. The Commission is also responsible for administering the European Development Fund for

---

[91] See above under European Parliament 2(9).
[92] Art. 272(2) and (3) (ex 203(2) and (3)) E.C.
[93] *ibid.* at 9.
[94] Art. 279 (ex 209) E.C. Financial Regulation of December 21, 1977 applicable to the general budget of the E.C.: [1977] O.J. L356/1, last amended by Reg. 97/2444 [1997] O.J. L340/1.
[95] Art. 274 (ex 205) E.C.
[96] Art. 275 (ex 205a) E.C.
[97] Art. 248 (ex 188c) E.C. See also below the Court of Auditors.
[98] Art. 276 (ex 206) E.C. In 1984, Parliament refused to give discharge for the 1983 budget implementation; [1994] E.C. Bull. 12–67. In 1987 it deferred the discharge in respect of the implementation of the 1985 budget; Twenty-Second General Report (1988), 75.

the African, Caribbean and Pacific States financed by direct contributions from the Member States and for the "banking activities" of the ECSC.[99]

The Commission is also empowered to borrow on the world financial markets and loan money for the financing of atomic energy projects[1] and to finance infrastructure and industrial projects.[2] The borrowing is done by the Commission, but the administration of the resources is delegated to the European Investment Bank.

(8) Publication of the Annual General Report

Each year, one month before the opening of the session of Parliament, the Commission must publish a General Report on the activities of the Community.[3] This report covers the activities of all the institutions and organs of the Community, and as such is an invaluable source of information. Several areas, however, are covered very summarily because they are the object of separate reports either from the Commission or from other institutions or bodies.[4]

3. The Commission's Staff

The Commission must adopt its rules of procedure so as to ensure that both it and its departments operate in accordance with the provisions of the Treaty.[5]

The departments consist of Directorates-General and Services whose responsibilities correspond more or less to the various tasks assigned to the Community.[6]

With regard to the Community staff, two texts should be

[99] Arts 54 and 56 ECSC.
[1] Art. 172(4) Euratom and [1977] O.J. L88/9.
[2] See [1978] O.J. L298/9.
[3] Art. 212 (ex 156) E.C.
[4] For those reports see above Chapter Five, "The European Parliament", Task and Powers, (5) The General Report.
[5] Art. 218(2) (ex 162(2)) E.C. For the Rules of Procedure see above, n.60.
[6] Arts 3 and 4 E.C. See also Declaration (32) adopted by the Conference of the Representatives of the Governments of the Member States convened in Turin on March 29, 1996 to adopt the amendments to be made to the Treaties concerning the organisation and functioning of the Commission; the Conference noted the intention to undertake, in parallel with the reorganisation of the tasks within the college, a corresponding reorganisation of its departments: [1997] O.J. C340/137. Presently there are twenty four Directorates General.

mentioned; the Protocol on the Privileges and Immunities of the European Communities[7] and the Staff Regulations of Officials and the Conditions of Employment of other Servants of the European Community.[8] It might be worth mentioning at this point that the Community civil servants don't pay taxes to the Member State whose citizens they are, on their Community salaries, but that they pay income tax to the Community itself.[9]

Officials are recruited directly by the various institutions; in other words, they are not seconded by the national administrations[10]; this should guarantee their independence and objectivity.

Access to documents: the access of the public to Commission documents is, as for the other institutions, provided for and a refusal to grant access must, according to the Court of First Instance, state reasons for refusal.[11]

Further Reading

Maselis Ignace, and Hans M. Gilliams, "Rights of Complainants in Community Law", (1997) 22 E.L.Rev. 103.

Bonnie Anne, "Commission Discretion under Article 171(2) E.C.", (1998) 23 E.L.Rev. 537.

Buitendijk, G.J. and M.P.C.M. van Schendelen, "Brussels Advisory Committees: A Channel for Influence", (1995) 20 E.L.Rev. 37.

White, Simone, "Proposed Measures Against Corruption of Officials of the European Union", (1996) 21 E.L.Rev. 465.

---

[7] Protocol (No. 34) on the privileges and immunities of the E.C. (1965).

[8] Reg. 259/68 [1968] L56/1, amended several times.

[9] Although the income tax rate might be lower than the national ones, Community officials cannot deduce anything from their Community income: the whole income is taxed, contrary to what happens in the Member States.

[10] It goes without saying that when recruiting officials, the Community institutions must take the nationality of the candidates into account, and although "no post may be reserved for a given nationality" (Staff Reg. Art. 27), a "geographical distribution" must exist, based upon the size of the population of the respective Member States. At the beginning of 1998, there were 18,441 permanent and 965 temporary posts at the Commission and altogether 22,000 officials in the various institutions and other bodies of the Community.

[11] [1994] O.J. L46/58 and Case T–124/96, *Interporc* [1998] E.C.R. II–231. See also Notice on the internal rules of procedure for processing requests for access to files: [1997] O.J. C23/3.

Chapter Eight

The Courts

The tasks of the Community Courts[1] is to ensure that in the interpretation and the application of the Treaty "the law is observed".[2] As the Court of Justice (hereafter referred to as the "Court") pointed out,[3] the Community is "based on the rule of law, inasmuch as neither its Member States nor its institutions can avoid a review of whether measures adopted by them are in conformity with the basic constitutional charter, the Treaty. The Treaty established the Court as the judicial body responsible for ensuring that both the Member States and the Community institutions comply with the law". The same applies, of course, *mutatis mutandis*, to the natural and legal persons who are subjects of the law of the Community.

The above quote from one of the Court's judgments contains several essential elements. In the first place, there is the statement that the Community is "based on the rule of law", in other words, the law prevails over all other considerations. This basic rule is not always well perceived by the Member States and there lies, therefore, a particular task for the Courts in ensuring the application of the law. From there the need for the judges to be totally independent,[4] the more so since, as was explained above, the Council tends to act as an inter-governmental conference where every member fights for his country's interests, Parliament does not have all the required powers to exercise an effective democratic control and the Commission, which besides its overwhelming administrative task must also fulfil a

---

[1] See Decision establishing a Court of First Instance [1988] O.J. L319/1, and Art. 225 (ex 168a) E.C.

[2] Art. 220 (ex 164) E.C.

[3] Case 294/83 *Les Verts v. Parliament* [1986] E.C.R. 1357 at 1365; [1987] 2 C.M.L.R. 343. See also Art. 6(1) E.U.: "The Union is founded on . . . the rule of law"; this provision was inserted by the Amsterdam Treaty.

[4] See Art. 223 (ex 167) E.C.: "the Judges and the Advocates-General shall be chosen from persons whose independence is beyond doubt." Before taking up his duties "each judge shall, in open court, take an oath to perform his duties impartially and conscientiously and to preserve the secrecy of the deliberations of the Court". (Protocol on the Statute of the Court, Art. 2.)

political function, is bound to accept compromises in the implementation of Community legislation by the Member States.

The second important element in the Court's statement is the reference to the Treaty as the "basic constitutional charter". The Treaty must indeed be viewed as the constitution of the Community, *i.e.* the basic legal text from which all other rules derive. This is expressed, *inter alia*, by the fundamental principle that "each institution shall act within the limits of the powers conferred upon it by this Treaty".[5] In other words the Treaty is the only source of Community legislation and activities.

And, finally, there is the reminder that the last word with regard to the legality of all Community acts lies with the courts. In other words, whatever the institutions decide, whatever the natural and legal persons do, they are all, in the last resort, subject to the control of the courts.

The task of the courts is complicated by the fact that Community law is basically social and economic law, which is essentially evolutive and in constant need of adaptation. This fact is best rendered probably by the formula the Court has often used: "at the present stage in the development of Community law."[6] The necessary adaptations, however, must be carried out in conformity with the general principles laid down by the Treaty. And, indeed, very few of the 250 articles of the Treaty are drafted with detailed precision, most of them lay down general rules and procedures for their implementation. Consequently, when called upon to state what the Community law is in a given field, it is in the first place by reference to the objectives of the Community that the courts will decide. It can therefore be said that existing rules are defined and new ones are formulated via teleological interpretation. Indeed, the task of the courts is not only to interpret, but also to formulate the law in the absence of explicit provisions. This, of course, is not particular to the Community courts, since "wherever there are courts, the law grows at the hand of the judges".[7] This is especially true for the Community.

Although the courts can only express themselves when called upon to do so, they have, over the years built an impressive set of rules and principles which are of prime importance for the shaping of Community law. This was done mainly through judgments interpreting the Treaty or the Community acts at the request of national judges when confronted with questions concerning Community

---

[5] Art. 7(1) (ex 4(1)) E.C.

[6] See, *e.g.* Case 27/80 *Fietje* [1980] E.C.R. 3839 at 3853(8); [1981] 3 C.M.L.R. 722.

[7] Schwarzenberger, *International Law*, p. 24.

rules applicable in cases pending before them. Which shows how important a role the national judge plays in the implementation and interpretation of Community law.

A. The Court of Justice

1. The Judges and Advocates-General

The Court consists of 15 Judges[8] and is assisted by eight Advocates-General,[9] the latter are not "members" of the Court.

The Judges and the Advocates-General shall be chosen from persons "whose independence is beyond doubt and who possess the qualifications required for appointment to the highest judicial offices in their respective countries[10] or who are jurisconsults of recognised competence".

The Judges and the Advocates-General are appointed for a term of six years by common accord of the Governments of the Member States.[11]

The President of the Court is elected by the Judges from among their number, for a term of three years; he may be re-elected.[12]

The 15 Judges are grouped in six chambers of three, five or seven Judges each.[13] Most cases brought before the Court are heard by a chamber. However, when a Member State or an institution that is a

---

[8] Each of the 15 Member States designates one judge. Every three years there is a partial replacement of the Judges and of the Advocates-General; eight and seven Judges are replaced alternatively and four Advocates-General shall be replaced on each occasion. Art. 223 (ex 167) E.C. Retiring Judges and Advocates-General are eligible for reappointment (Art. 223 (ex 167) E.C. The number of Judges may be increased by the Council at the request of the Court Art. 221 (ex 165) E.C.

[9] Presently, there are nine Advocates-General: until the enlargement with Austria, Finland and Sweden, there were 12 Member States and 13 Judges (two Italians). After enlargement there would have been 16 Judges, which is not possible: the second Italian Judge was therefore appointed Advocate-General until the end of his mandate on October 5, 2000; after that there will be, as the Treaty provides, eight Advocates-General. Five of the latter are nominated by the five largest Member States, while the other three are nominated, in turn, by the other ten. See Art. 223 (ex 167) E.C.

[10] Those qualifications are thus determined by reference to national law.

[11] Art. 223 (ex 167) E.C. Several other provisions regarding the Judges and Advocates-General are to be found in the Statute of the Court, which is attached as a Protocol to the Treaty.

[12] Art. 223 (ex 167) E.C.

[13] Art. 221 (ex 165) E.C.

party to a proceeding so requests, the Court must sit in plenary session.[14]

2. The Task of the Advocates-General

The position of the Advocate-General is a particularly interesting one: he is not a member of the Court, he is independent and he does not participate in the deliberations of the Court. This allows him to carry out his own examination of the case and express a personal opinion, something a Judge cannot do. He can also examine any related question, even not brought forward by the parties. Consequently the submissions presented by the Advocate-General during the oral proceedings does not reflect the Court's views, but when the Court follows the proposal of the Advocate-General they sometimes constitute a precious source of information concerning the reasoning which led to the Court's decision. The submissions of the Advocates-General are published, together with the judgment, in the Court's Reports.

3. The Court's Jurisdiction

Although the task of the Court is defined in a short and sibylline text: ensure that, in the interpretation and application of the Treaty, "the law is observed", its jurisdiction is multiple. In order of appearance in the Treaty, this jurisdiction consists mainly of the following:

- (a) to "find" whether or not a Member State has failed to fulfil an obligation under the Treaty[15];
- (b) to "exercise unlimited jurisdiction" with regard to penalties provided for in regulations[16];
- (c) to "review the legality" of binding Community acts or failure of the institutions to act[17];
- (d) to "give preliminary rulings"[18];
- (e) to grant compensation for damage caused by the institutions or their servants[19];

---

[14] *ibid.* at 3.
[15] Art. 228 (ex 171) E.C.
[16] Art. 229 (ex 172) E.C.
[17] Arts 230 (ex 173) and 232 (ex 175) E.C.
[18] Art. 234 (ex 177) E.C.
[19] Arts 235 (ex 178) and 258 (ex 215) E.C.

(f) to decide in disputes between the Community and its servants[20];

(g) to decide in disputes concerning obligations of Member States under the Statute of the EIB or measures adopted by the organs of the EIB and obligations of the national central banks[21];

(h) to "give judgment" pursuant to an arbitration clause in a contract concluded by or on behalf of the Community[22];

(i) to decide in disputes submitted under a special agreement between the parties[23];

(j) to decide on the inapplicability of a regulation when the latter is at issue in a proceeding before the Court[24];

(k) to "prescribe" any necessary interim measure,[25] and

(l) to decide on appeal against judgments of the Court of First Instance.[26]

The most important aspects of this multiple jurisdiction shall be examined in some detail hereunder.

(1) Finding that a Member State has failed to fulfil an obligation under the Treaty

Both the Commission and a Member State[27] may bring such a matter before the Court. For the Commission, the possibility to initiate an action of this kind[28] constitutes its main instrument for fulfilling the task of "guardian of the Treaty". Before going to court, the Commission must formally request the Member State to fulfil its obligations and give it the opportunity to submit observations.

In the absence of a positive reaction, the Commission must deliver a reasoned opinion and only if the State does not comply with that opinion, may the Commission refer the matter to the Court.

Similarly, a Member State which considers that another Member

---

20 Art. 236 (ex 179) E.C.

21 Art. 237 (ex 180) E.C.

22 Art. 238 (ex 181) E.C.

23 Art. 240 (ex 182) E.C.

24 Art. 241 (ex 184) E.C.

25 Art. 242 (ex 186) E.C.

26 Art. 225(1) (ex 168a(1)) E.C.

27 Such actions are rare: one or two a year; the first such action was brought in 1977, Case 58/77 *Ireland v. France* [1977] O.J. C142/8.

28 In 1997, *e.g.* 121 such actions were brought before the Court by the Commission; during the same year 46 judgments were delivered, of which 41 were in favour of the Commission. See General Report (1997), 418.

State has failed to fulfil an obligation under the Treaty, must first bring the matter before the Commission. The Commission then gives each State the opportunity to submit its own case and its observations on the other party's case both orally and in writing. The Commission must, after that, deliver a reasoned opinion within three months after the date the matter was brought before it. The absence of such an opinion cannot prevent the matter from being brought before the Court.

In cases against a Member State, the Court can only "find" that the State has failed to fulfil an obligation. However, if the State does not take the necessary measures to comply with the judgment of the Court, the Commission can again issue a reasoned opinion[29] after having given the State the opportunity to submit its observations. If the Member State fails to take the necessary measures within the time-limit set by the Commission, the latter may bring the case before the Court and "specify the amount of the lump sum or penalty payment to be paid by the Member State which it considers appropriate in the circumstances".[30] This possibility was introduced by the Maastricht Treaty and puts an end to an embarrassing situation in which Member States simply ignored the Court's finding.

With regard to cases brought by a Member State against another Member State, attention must be drawn to the obligation undertaken by the Member States "not to submit a dispute concerning the interpretation or application of the Treaty to any method of settlement other than those provided for therein".[31] The principal method provided for in the Treaty being the recourse to the Court, this obligation guarantees, together with the preliminary ruling, uniformity in the interpretation and application of Community law. It should be noted that the Court also has jurisdiction in disputes between Member States which relate to the subject matter of the Treaty, when such a dispute is submitted to it under a special agreement.[32]

---

[29] This reasoned opinion must specify the points on which the Member State concerned has not complied with the judgment of the Court. Art. 228(2) (ex 171(2)) E.C.

[30] *ibid.*

[31] Art. 292 (ex 219) E.C.

[32] Art. 239 (ex 182) E.C.

(2) Unlimited Jurisdiction with regard to Penalties provided for in Regulations

In order to ensure compliance with the obligations laid down in the regulations it issues, Parliament and the Council acting together, or the Council, may make provisions for penalties to be imposed on natural and legal persons in case of infringement.[33] Those persons have, of course, the right to ask the Court to review the legality of the imposed penalties[34] or to reduce them, but, much more important, they can also, in those proceedings, contest the validity of the regulation itself on which the penalties are based.[35]

The unlimited jurisdiction of the Court must be explicitly provided for in the regulation[36]; it allows the Court not only to annul the penalty, but also to increase or decrease it.[37]

The Treaty also attributes unlimited jurisdiction to the Court in two other cases: claims for damages resulting from the non-contractual liability of the Community[38] and disputes between the institutions and their servants.[39] The latter, however, have been transferred to the Court of First Instance[40] with, of course, a possibility of appeal to the Court.

---

[33] Art. 229 (ex 172) E.C. See, *e.g.* Arts 75(3) (ex 79(3) and 83(2)(a) (ex 87(2). It has been argued that Art. 229 also attributes to the Council and the Parliament acting jointly, or to the Council, a general competence to provide for penalties in the regulations they issue. This would, in my view, be contrary to the principle of the specifically conferred powers.

[34] Art. 230 (ex 173) E.C.

[35] Art. 241 (ex 184) E.C.

[36] See, *e.g.* Regulation 11, Art. 18 ([1959–1962] O.J. 60) and Reg. 17, Art. 17 ([1959–1962] O.J. 87).

[37] See, *e.g.* Case 27/76 *United Brands v. Commission* [1978] E.C.R. 207; [1978] 1 C.M.L.R. 429, where the fine was reduced from one million units of account to 850,000, because part of the decision was annulled. There are no examples of the Court increasing a fine; undertakings upon which a fine has been imposed automatically go to court and ask for a reduction, which they obtain most of the time; consequently, the Commission probably takes that into account when deciding on the importance of the fine. See, however, Guidelines on the method of setting fines [1998] O.J. C9/3.

[38] Arts 235 and 288 (ex 178 and 215) E.C.

[39] Art. 236 (ex 179) E.C.

[40] Council Decision of October 24, 1988 [1988] O.J. L319/1.

(3) Review of the Legality of an Act or Failure to act

(a) Appeal for Annulment[41]

In reviewing the legality of Community acts, the Court[42] gives judicial protection to all those who are subject to Community law, against arbitrary action by the institutions. It also insures that the activities of the Community remain within the boundaries laid down by the Treaty and that institutions respect the balance of powers within the Community.

Proceedings for annulment must be instituted within two months[43] of the publication of the measure in the *Official Journal of the European Communities*,[44] or of its notification[45] to the plaintiff, or, in the absence thereof, of the day on which it came to the knowledge of the latter, as the case may be.[46]

(b) Acts Submitted to the Control of Legality

The "acts" referred to are, on the one hand, acts other than recommendations and opinions, adopted by the European Parliament and the Council acting jointly, by the Council, by the Commission and by the ECB[47] and, on the other hand, acts of the European Parliament "intended to produce legal effects". From this one can deduce that the latter, normally have no legal effect, while the first category, generally speaking, do have legal effects.[48] They are regulations, directives and decisions.

---

[41] Art. 230 (ex 173) E.C.

[42] The following remarks apply also to the Court of First Instance.

[43] As was seen in the chapter on Community Acts, to those two months must first be added automatically 15 days (to allow the interested parties to receive the O.J.) and secondly the time-limit for distance; for the UK, for instance, this means an extra month altogether.

[44] Art. 254(1) (ex 191(1)) E.C.

[45] Notification necessarily involves the communication of a detailed account of the contents of the measure notified and of the reasons on which it is based: Case C–143/95 P, *Socurte* [1997] E.C.R. I–1.

[46] Art. 230 (ex 173) E.C.

[47] The ECB (European Central Bank) was added by the Maastricht Treaty in Art. 230 (ex 173) E.C. and also in Arts 232 (ex 175), 233 (ex 176), 234 (ex 177), 237 (ex 180), 241 (ex 184) and 288 (ex 215) E.C.

[48] Art. 173(1) refers to acts "other than recommendations and opinions"; those acts are: regulations, directives and decisions, see Art. 249 (ex 189). Since, according to that provision the recommendations and the opinions "have no binding force", one must accept that the other acts do have such force. The question is whether there are other binding acts. No doubt there are, international agreements being one example. See Case C–39/93/P *SFPI* [1994] E.C.R. I–2681(27), where the Court stated that an institution empowered to find that there has been an infringement and

It is clear from the case law of the courts that the form in which such acts are cast is, in principle, immaterial as regards the question whether they are open to challenge or not.[49]

Who may Lodge an Appeal for Annulment?

With regard to the admissibility of court actions, all the Member States apply a principle well coined in French as "*pas d'intéret pas d'action*". As the Court of First Instance decided, "a claim for annulment is inadmissible unless that applicant has an interest in seeing the contested measure annulled" and "such an interest can be present only if the annulment of the measure is of itself capable of having legal consequences".[50] The same principle applies within the Community. However, Member States, designate the governmental authorities of the States which are members of the Communities, and

---

to inflict a sanction in respect of it, and to which private persons may make complaints, necessarily adopts a measure producing legal effects when it terminates an investigation initiated upon a complaint by such person, and Case T-154/94, *Comité des Salines* [1996] E.C.R. I–1377(32); [1997] 1 C.M.L.R. 943.

[49] In Case 22/70 *Commission v. Council* [1971] E.C.R. 263 at 277(42); [1971] C.M.L.R. 335, the Court ruled that: "an action for annulment must therefore be available in the case of all measures adopted by the institutions, whatever their nature or form, which are intended to have legal effect". Again, in Case 60/81 *IBM v. Commission* [1981] E.C.R. 2639 at 2651(9); [1981] 3 C.M.L.R. 635, the Court ruled that "any measure the legal effects of which are binding on, and capable of affecting the interests of, the applicant by bringing about a distinctive change in his legal position is an act . . . under Article 173". See also Case 108/83 *Luxembourg v. Parliament* [1984] E.C.R. 1945; [1986] 2 C.M.L.R. 507, where the Court annulled a Resolution of the latter and Case C–325/91 *France v. Commission* [1993] E.C.R. I–3283, where the Court annulled a Commission Notice. On the other hand, in Cases C–66/91 and C–66/91 R *Emerald Meats v. Commission* [1991] E.C.R. I–1143 at I–1151(28), the Court held that a "communication (in this case a telex) which is from a department of the Commission and merely indicates procedures to ensure the proper administration of the system and, for the rest, announces the Commission's intention to adopt certain measures, cannot be considered to be a decision capable of having legal effects with regard to the applicant". See also Case C–303/90 *France v. Commission* [1991] E.C.R. I–5340, where the Court annulled a "Code of conduct"; Case C–192/89, *Sevince* [1990] E.C.R. I–3461; [1992] 2 C.M.L.R. 57, a decision of an Association (E.C.–Turkey) Council forms an integral part of the Community law system; Case C–366/88 *France v. Commission* [1990] E.C.R. I–3595; [1992] 1 C.M.L.R. 205, where the Court annulled Commission's Internal instructions. As for the Court of First Instance, it declared inadmissible an action for annulment against a letter, stating that it had no influence on the applicant's legal position; Case T–113/89 *Nefarma v. Commission* [1990] E.C.R. II–797; [1991] 2 C.M.L.R. 818; *id.* in Case T–2/92; *Rendo v. Commission* [1993] E.C.R. (March 29, 1993); [1992] 2 C.M.L.R. 217.

[50] Joined Cases T–480 and 483/93, *Antilian Rice Mills* [1995] E.C.R. II–2310(59).

not authorities of regions and autonomous communities[51]; the Council, the Commission, and, under certain conditions, Parliament, the Court of Auditors[52] and the ECB[53] for the purpose of protecting their prerogatives, are considered to have an overall interest in the correct implementation of Community law. They therefore have, subject to a two month time limit, an unlimited right to ask the Court to review the legality of any Community act.[54]

Natural and legal persons, on the other hand, must prove their interest in obtaining such review.[55] Obviously, they have this interest when it concerns "a decision addressed to that person".[56] But when an act having a general application (regulation, directive, agreement) is at stake, it is assumed that those acts concern everybody and therefore nobody in particular. Consequently, they cannot, normally, be challenged directly in Court by individuals or undertakings, unless they can show that these acts contain provisions which in reality have an "individual" rather than a "general" application. Or, as the Treaty puts it: that it is in fact a "decision, which, although in

[51] Case C–95/97, *Wallonia* [1997] E.C.R. I–1787 and Case C–180/97, *Regione Toscana* [1997] E.C.R. I–5247.

[52] Art. 230(3) (ex 173 E.C. which did not provide for it).

[53] Art 230(3) (ex 173(3)) E.C.

[54] All Member States have at one time or another appealed for annulment of an act of the Commission; appeals by Member States against Council acts are rare: Case 151/73 *Ireland v. Council* [1974] E.C.R. 285; [1974] 1 C.M.L.R. 429. Appeals of the Commission against the Council are not uncommon: Case 242/87 *Commission v. Council* [1989] E.C.R. 1449; [1991] 1 C.M.L.R. 478. The Court has also accepted appeals by a Member State against an act of Parliament, although this is not explicitly provided for under the Treaty: Case 230/81 *Luxembourg v. Parliament* [1983] E.C.R. 255 at 281; [1983] 2 C.M.L.R. 726, where the Court concluded that such an appeal is provided for under the ECSC Treaty, and Case 108/83 *Luxembourg v. Parliament* [1984] E.C.R. 1945; [1986] 2 C.M.L.R. 507. See also Case 34/86 *Council v. Parliament* [1986] E.C.R. 2155; [1986] 3 C.M.L.R. 94 and Joined Cases 358/85 and 51/86 *France v. Parliament* [1988] E.C.R. 4846; [1990] 2 C.M.L.R. 406. The Court has also admitted appeals by Parliament against acts of the Council when that action aims at upholding Parliament's prerogatives: Case C–70/88 *Parliament v. Council* [1990] E.C.R. I–2067; [1992] 1 C.M.L.R. 91.

[55] Case 77/77 *BP v. Commission* [1978] E.C.R. 1513 at 1525(13); [1978] 1 C.M.L.R. 265.

[56] Art. 230(4) (ex 173(4)) E.C.

the form of a regulation[57] or a decision addressed to another person, is of direct and individual concern to the former".[58]

The interpretation of the Treaty provisions concerning the locus standi of persons is, of course, essential in determining the extent of the legal protection enjoyed by individuals and undertakings within the Community. Hence the importance of the case law of the Court in this field.[59] It can be said that without resorting to extensive interpretation, the Court has given those Treaty provisions a meaning which allowed a wide access to the Court.[60]

Nonetheless, the opportunities for natural and legal persons to appeal directly for annulment of a Community act are much more

---

[57] See, *e.g.* Joined Cases 41–44/70 *International Fruit Company v. Commission* [1971] E.C.R. 411 at 422(21); [1975] 2 C.M.L.R. 515, where the Court held that Art. 1 of Reg. 983/70 "is not a provision with a general application, but must be analysed as a bundle of individual decisions". See also Case 138/79 *Roquette Frères v. Council* [1980] E.C.R. 3333.

[58] An act is of "direct" concern when it affects somebody's legal position, when there is a causal relationship between the act and the modified legal position of the individual. On the other hand those persons are, according to the Court, individually concerned only "if that decision affects them by reason of certain attributes which are peculiar to them or by reason of circumstances in which they are differentiated from all other persons and by virtue of these factors distinguishes them individually just as in the case of the person addressed". Case 25/62 *Plaumann v. Commission* [1963] E.C.R. 95 at 107; [1964] C.M.L.R. 29. This is not the case when plaintiff is affected by the act because he belongs to a category designated abstractly and as a whole: Case 42/71 *Nordgetreide v. Commission* [1972] E.C.R. 105 at 110(5); [1973] C.M.L.R. 177. See also Case 72/74, *Union Syndicale v. Council* [1975] E.C.R. 401 at 410(17); [1975] 2 C.M.L.R. 181. Or, as the Court put it in Case C–321/95 *Greenpeace* [1998] E.C.R. I–1651: "where the specific situation of the appellant was not taken into consideration in the adoption of the act". See Case C–386/96 *Dreyfus v. Commission* [1998] E.C.R. I–2309, where the applicant was recognised as being "individually", but not "directly" concerned. On the other hand, a region, for instance, cannot be "individually" concerned: Case T–609/97 *Regione Puglia*, not yet published.

[59] For an overview of the case law on this point see the opinion of the Advocate-General in Case 358/89 *Extramet Industries v. Council* [1991] E.C.R. I–2501 at 2515; [1990] 2 C.M.L.R. 406 and more recently Case C–321/95 P *Greenpeace*: see n.58 above, at para 7.

[60] For instance, the words "another person" in Art. 230 was interpreted by the Court as including also Member States since no limitation as to the meaning of those words is to be found in the Treaty. Natural and legal persons can therefore appeal against an act of an institution addressed to a Member State, when they are directly and individually concerned: Case 730/79 *Phillip Morris v. Commission* [1980] E.C.R. 2671 at 2687; [1981] 2 C.M.L.R. 321. The Court also accepted that a measure entitled by its authors a Regulation can contain provisions which are capable of being not only of direct but also of individual concern to certain natural or legal persons: Joined Cases 16 and 17/62 *Producteurs de fruits v. Council* [1962] E.C.R. 471 at 479. See also Cases 101/76 *Koninklijke Scholten Honig v. Council and Commission* [1977] E.C.R. 797; [1980] 2 C.M.L.R. 669, and 169/84 *Cofaz v. Commission* [1986] E.C.R. 408.

limited than for the Member States and the institutions.[61] However, other means exist whereby persons and enterprises can obtain a Court ruling, if not on the legality, at least on the applicability of a Community act. For the plaintiff the results will be identical if the Court finds with him.[62]

Grounds for annulment

There are four grounds for annulment which may be invoked by the plaintiff.[63]

(i) **Lack of competence.** This ground embodies the basic principle, several times referred to above, according to which the institutions of the Community may only exercise those powers which have been explicitly granted to them by the Treaty. They enjoy "conferred powers", not general powers. In case an institution were to legislate without the necessary conferred powers, the Court can annul the decision for lack of competence. For the Court this requirement is so important that it has accepted to review it, even after the time-limit for instituting the proceedings had lapsed.[64]

It follows that every Community act must clearly indicate on which Community provision it is based[65]; it follows also that the choice of this provision is of essential importance.[66]

(ii) **Infringement of an essential procedural requirement.** If the Council were to take a decision without a proposal from the Commission or without consulting Parliament,[67] when this is required by the Treaty, the Council would have infringed an essential procedural requirement. The Court would have jurisdiction on that ground to annul the Act. The same would apply if the Commission, for instance, were to make a proposal without asking for the opinion of the Economic and Social Committee, when this is required by the Treaty.

---

[61] Joined Cases 16 and 17/62, *Producteurs de fruits*, see n.60 above at 478.

[62] See below "Preliminary Ruling", "Compensation for Damages" and "Exception of Illegality".

[63] Those grounds find their origin in French administrative law.

[64] Joined Cases 6 and 11/69 *Commission v. France* [1969] E.C.R. 523 (11–13); [1970] C.M.L.R. 43.

[65] See below: infringement of an essential procedural requirement.

[66] See, *e.g.* Case C–131/87 *Commission v. Council* [1989] E.C.R. 3764; [1991] 1 C.M.L.R. 780.

[67] See, *e.g.* Case 139/79 *Maizena v. Council* [1980] E.C.R. 3393 (36).

Also, failure to mention sufficient reasons in a Community act constitutes a ground for annulment.[68]

(iii) Infringement of the Treaty or of any rule of law pertaining to its application. It could, of course, be argued that the two grounds examined above also constitute infringements of the Treaty, since they are violations of obligations provided therein and that this ground, in fact, covers all possible illegalities. However, the Treaty mentions four grounds and those must therefore be examined separately.

In the expression "infringement of the Treaty", the word "Treaty" must be understood to cover not only the Treaties themselves, but also the "secondary legislation", *i.e.* the acts of the institutions, whatever their form, as long as they are binding. When examining the meaning of "acts" submitted to the control of legality, it was pointed out that acts are binding when they bring about a distinctive change in the legal position of a party subject to Community law.[69] The word Treaty can, therefore, also cover parts of the "*acquis communautaire*".

As for the expression "any rules relating to its application", it refers to the general principles of law and to international law.[70] The general principles include those which are particular to the Member States, based on comparative studies of the 15 legal systems,[71] and those principles which the Court formulates on the basis of the wording, the contents and the systems of the Treaty. They comprise also the "fundamental rights"[72]; this is now explicitly mentioned in the Maastricht Treaty: "The Union shall respect fundamental rights, as guaranteed by the European Convention for the Protection of Human Rights and Fundamental Freedoms signed in Rome on

---

68 See Chapter Three under "Community acts": acts must be reasoned.

69 See Case 60/81 *IBM v. Commission* see n.49 above.

70 See, *e.g.* Case 8/55 *Fédération Charbonnière de Belgique v. High Authority* [1954–1956] E.C.R. 245 at 299. See also Joined Cases 21 to 24/72 *International Fruit Company v. Produktschap voor Groenten en Fruit* [1972] E.C.R. 1219 at 1226(6); [1975] 2 C.M.L.R. 1, and Case 41/74, *Van Duyn v. Home Office* [1974] E.C.R. 1337 at 1351(22); [1975] 1 C.M.L.R. 1 and more recently, Case C–162/96 *Racke* [1998] E.C.R. I–16 06 (25–27): "The Court is obliged to examine whether the validity might be affected by reason of the fact that it is contrary to rules of international law." However, in other cases the Court did not accept arguments based on international law; see, *e.g.* Joined Cases 90 and 91/63, *Commission v. Luxembourg and Belgium* [1964] E.C.R. 625 at 631; [1965] C.M.L.R. 58.

71 Case 4/73 *Nold v. Commission* [1974] E.C.R. 491 at 507(13); [1974] 2 C.M.L.R. 338: "In safeguarding those rights, the Court must draw inspiration from the constitutional traditions of the Member States."

72 *id.* "fundamental rights form an integral part of the general principles of law".

November 4, 1950 and as they result from the constitutional traditions common to the Member States, as general principles of Community law."[73] They often constitute an important part of the legal considerations which lead to the Court's rulings.

The following general principles have been referred to several times by the courts: the protection of legitimate expectation,[74] the right to be heard,[75] freedom of trade union activity,[76] legal certainty,[77] equal treatment,[78] proportionality,[79] non-discrimination[80] and good administration.[81]

(iv) **Misuse of power.**[82] There is misuse of power when a public

---

[73] Art. 6(1) and (2) (ex F.1 and F.2) TEU.

[74] See, *e.g.* Case 112/77 *Töpfer v. Commission* [1978] E.C.R. 1019 at 1033(19) and Case T–336/94 *Efisol* [1996] E.C.R. II–1343: the company was issued an import quota, but subsequently refused an import licence; according to the Court, those are two independent stages, and the company was not justified in assuming that because it had obtained a quota, it would also obtain a licence. See, however, Case T–115/94 *Opel Austria* [1997] E.C.R. II–39, where the Court found an infringement of applicant's legal expectation.

[75] See, for instance, Case C–32/95 P *Lisrestal* [1996] E.C.R. I–5373: the right to be heard "in all proceedings initiated against a person and which are liable to culminate in a measure adversely affecting that person" constitutes a fundamental principle of Community law.

[76] See, *e.g.* Case 175/73 *Union Syndicale, Massa et Kortner v. Council* [1974] E.C.R. 917 at 925(9 and 14); [1975] 1 C.M.L.R. 131.

[77] See, *e.g.* Case 21/81, *Openbaar Ministerie v. Bout* [1982] E.C.R. 381 at 390(13); [1982] 2 C.M.L.R. 371.

[78] See, *e.g.* Case 148/73 *R. Louwage v. Commission* [1974] E.C.R. 81 at 89(12).

[79] See, *e.g.* Case 122/78 *Buitoni v. FORMA* [1979] E.C.R. 677 at 684(16); [1979] 2 C.M.L.R. 665. In Case C–131/93 *Commission v. Germany* [1994] E.C.R. I–3303, the Court developed three tests to determine whether or not a measure was "proportional": it must be an appropriate and effective way to achieve the legitimate aim; it must be necessary, *i.e.* there is no less restrictive alternative and the adverse effect is not excessive when weighed against the aim of the measure. However, a looser test was applied in Case 34/79 *Henn and Darby* [1997] E.C.R. 3795: "not manifestly inappropriate" and a more rigorous test was applied in Case C–178/84 *Commission v. Germany* [1987] E.C.R. 1227: "no less-restrictive alternative available".

[80] Case 27/95 *Woodspring* [1997] E.C.R. I–1847: "the principles of proportionality and non-discrimination have been recognised by the Court as forming part of the general principles of Community law".

[81] See, *e.g.* Joined Cases 33 and 75/79 *Kuhner v. Commission* [1980] E.C.R. 1677 at 1698(25).

[82] Maybe better known by its French equivalent: "détournement de pouvoir". For more details concerning the meaning of this ground, see the comparative study of the law of the original 6 Member States made by the Advocate General in his Opinion in Case 3/54 *ASSIDER v. High Authority* [1954–1956] E.C.R. 63 at 75.

authority uses its lawful powers to attain an objective for which the powers were not intended. Although this ground has been invoked many times, the Court seldom accepts this as a ground for the annulment of an act.[83]

Consequences of the annulment of an act by the Court

Unless the Court also enjoys unlimited jurisdiction, for example in the case of penalties, it may only, when the action is well founded, declare the act void.[84] And, the institution whose act has been declared void is then "required to take the necessary measures to comply with the judgment of the Court".[85]

Since, theoretically, annulment means that the act is to be considered as never having existed—the Court's declaration has effect *ex tunc* and *erga onmes*—the institution must endeavour to recreate the situation which would have existed had the act not been issued.[86] This might be impossible, especially when the nullity affects an act of general application such as a regulation. For this reason the Treaty provides that in the case of a regulation, the Court may, if it considers this necessary, "state which of the effects of the regulation which it has declared void shall be considered as definitive"[87] or that the act or the implementing measures remains valid until replaced.[88]

In certain cases where an annulment *ex tunc* would have unacceptable financial consequences for Member States, the Court

[83] One rare example is Case 92/78 *Simmenthal v. Commission* [1979] E.C.R. 777 at 811(106); [1980] 1 C.M.L.R. 25.

[84] Art. 231 (ex 174) E.C.

[85] Art. 233 (ex 176) E.C. These measures involve "the removal of the effects of the illegalities found in the judgment annulling the act" and "the institution may thus be required to take adequate steps to restore the applicant to its original situation or to avoid the adoption of an identical measure": Joined Cases T–480 and 483/93 *Antillian Rice Mills* [1995] E.C.R. II–2310 (60).

[86] If this is not possible, compensation might have to be paid; if it concerns the annulment of an imposed penalty, interests might have to be paid; if an official was wrongly refused a promotion, he should be paid the difference in salary he would have received had he been properly promoted, etc.

[87] Art. 231 (ex 174) E.C.

[88] See, *e.g.* Case 275/87, *Commission v. Council* [1988] E.C.R. 259 where the act was annulled only because the legal basis chosen by the Council was not considered by the Court to be the right one. In Case C–22/96 *Parliament v. Council* [1998] E.C.R. I–3231, the Court annulled Dec. 95/468 since it could not be adopted on the basis of Art. 308 (ex 235), but the judgment "maintains the effects of the implementing measures already adopted by the Commission on the basis of that decision".

has decided that the annulment would have no retroactive effect.[89] This is referred to as the *temporal effect of judgments*.

In other cases, the institution might have to compensate for the irreparable damage caused by the annulled act.[90]

It should also be noted that annulment does not necessarily affect the act as a whole. If the nullity concerns only one or certain provisions and the others can remain operative, the rest of the act will stand.[91]

(c) Appeal against Failure of an Institution to act[92]

In the case of an appeal for failure to act,[93] the Court is called upon to establish that by failing to act the European Parliament,[94] the Council, the Commission or the ECB have infringed the Treaty. The latter covers also the Community's secondary legislation; whether it also covers "any rule of law relating to its application"[95] has not been tested in Court. It seems, however, that if acting in violation of such rules can be challenged in Court, failure to act in violation of such rules should also be open to challenge.[96] The more so, since, although there is a difference between the outcome of an action for annulment

[89] See 43/75 *Defrenne v. SABENA* [1976] E.C.R. 455: the direct effect of Art. 119 cannot be relied on in order to "support pay periods prior to the date of this judgment" and more recently C–308/93 *Sociale Verzekeringsdienst* [1996] E.C.R. I–2097.

[90] Art. 233 (ex 176) E.C.; see below compensation for damage caused by an institution, Art. 288 (ex 215) E.C.

[91] See, *e.g.* Case 319/82 *Société de Vente de Ciments et Bétons v. Kerpen & Kerpen* [1983] E.C.R. 4173 at 4184(12); [1985] 1 C.M.L.R. 511.

[92] Art. 232 (ex 175) E.C.

[93] Such an appeal is admissible only if the Plaintiff has first called upon the institution to act, and the latter has not defined its position within two months; the Plaintiff then has another two months to bring his action. In case the institution, within those two months, defines its position by refusing to act, this position does not become an act which can only be challenged under Art. 230 (ex 173) E.C., since the failure has not ceased. See Case 302/87 *Parliament v. Council* [1988] E.C.R. 5615; this constitutes a reversal from previous case law: Case 8/71 *Komponistenverband v. Commission* [1971] E.C.R. 705 at 710(2).

[94] One might wonder why the Treaty does not provide for a failure by Parliament and the Council acting jointly, as is provided for under Art. 230 (ex 173) E.C.

[95] Art. 230 (ex 173) E.C.

[96] If the Community is bound by an international agreement to take some action and fails to do so, there is no reason why this failure should not be open to challenge in Court.

and the one for failure to act,[97] the Court considers that "both provisions merely prescribe one and the same method of recourse".[98]

Actions for failure may be brought by the Member States and the institutions not only when an institution fails to take a binding measure, but, in general, when an institution doesn't fulfil an obligation under the Treaty. For instance if the Commission were to fail to submit a proposal to the Council when this is required by the Treaty.

On the other hand, natural and legal persons may only challenge a failure to act when it concerns a binding act of which they would have been the addressee.[99] This is not the case when the Commission is asked to refer a matter to the Court.[1]

(4) Preliminary Ruling

The preliminary ruling,[2] presupposes direct effect, *i.e.* the possibility for an interested party to invoke Community rules in national courts and the obligation for the national judge to uphold any rights resulting from the rule. The purpose of this procedure is to guarantee uniformity in the interpretation and application of Community law.[3] Indeed, the responsibility for applying Community law rests, in the first place, with the national judge. For instance, when applying Community competition rules, the national courts are acting as Community courts of general jurisdiction.[4] In order to avoid that different judges give different interpretations, the Court has been endowed with the exclusive competence to interpret,[5] as last resort, the law of the Community. As pointed out before, in a common market the economic operators, wherever they are, must be assured

---

[97] Under Art. 231 (ex 174) E.C., the Court annuls the act; under Art. 233 (ex 176) E.C., the institution must take the necessary measures to implement the judgment.

[98] Case 15/70 *Chevalley v. Commission* [1970] E.C.R. 975 at 979(6).

[99] Case 15/71 *Mackprang v. Commission* [1971] E.C.R. 797 at 804(4); [1972] C.M.L.R. 52.

[1] Case T–277/94 *AITEC* [1996] E.C.R. II–351.

[2] Art. 234 (ex 177) E.C.

[3] 2 See Case 6/64 *Costa v. ENEL* [1964] E.C.R. 585 at 594; [1964] C.M.L.R. 425, and Case 28/67 *Molkerei-Zentrale Westfalen v. Hauptzollamt Paderborn* [1968] E.C.R. 143 at 153; [1968] C.M.L.R. 187.

[4] Case T–51/89 *Tetra Pak* [1990] E.C.R. II–309; see also Case C–2/88 *Zwartfeld* [1990] E.C.R. I–3365: the judicial authorities of the Member States are responsible for ensuring that Community law is applied and respected in the national legal system.

[5] As for methods of interpretation, see, *e.g.* Case 75/63 *Hoekstra v. Bedrijfsvereniging Detailhandel* [1964] E.C.R. 177 at 184, [1964] C.M.L.R. 319, and Case 53/81 *Levin v. Staatssecretaris van Justitie* [1982] E.C.R. 1035 at 1048(9).

of being able to compete under similar conditions. This can only be ensured if they are all submitted to the same rules interpreted in the same way everywhere. The same applies to the validity of the Community's secondary legislation and therefore only the Court can decide on its validity.[6]

But, the preliminary ruling also constitutes, in the hands of the Court, the ideal instrument to define and develop the law of the Community. Indeed, when the Court interprets a provision of Community law, this interpretation must be accepted and applied by national courts.[7] Furthermore, it can be assumed that parties in

---

[6] Art. 234(b) (ex 177(b)) E.C.

[7] See 1972 European Communities Act, s.3(1) and Case 33/76 *Rewe v. Landwirtschaftskammer Saarland* [1976] E.C.R. 1989 at 1997(5); [1977] 1 C.M.L.R. 533, where the Court based this obligation on Art. 5 (now Art. 10) of the Treaty. According to the Court, Art. 234 (ex 177) E.C. calls for "judicial co-operation" between the Court and the national courts: Joined Cases 110 and 111/78 *Ministère Public and A.S.B.L. v. Van Wesemael* [1979] E.C.R. 35 at 51(25); [1979] 3 C.M.L.R. 87, and Case 811/79 *Amministrazione delle Finanze v. Ariete* [1980] E.C.R. 2545 at 2553(6); [1981] 1 C.M.L.R. 316: the preliminary ruling of the Court is binding on the national court as to the interpretation of the Community provision.

The respective tasks of the Court and the national courts have been clarified over the years:

(a) the Court has no jurisdiction under Art. 234 (ex 177) E.C. to apply the Treaty to a specific national case: Case 6/64 *Costa v. ENEL* [1964] E.C.R. 585 at 592; [1964] C.M.L.R. 425; similarly, the Court is not competent to decide on the compatibility of a national provision with Community law: Case 10/71 *Ministère Public Luxembourgeois v. Muller* [1971] E.C.R. 723 at 729(7). It may nonetheless furnish the national court with the interpretative criteria necessary to enable it to dispose of the dispute: Case 106/79 *Vereniging Boekhandels v. Eldi Records* [1980] E.C.R. 1137 at 1147(7); [1980] 3 C.M.L.R. 719, or to determine whether the national rules are compatible with Community law: Joined Cases 95 and 96/79 *Kefer and Delmelle* [1980] E.C.R. 103 at 112(5); [1982] 2 C.M.L.R. 77;

(b) the considerations which may have led a national court to its choice of questions, as well as the relevance which it attributes to such questions in the context of a case before it, are excluded from the review by the Court: Case 53/79 *ONPTS v. Damiani* [1980] E.C.R. 273 at 281(5); [1981] 2 C.M.L.R. 548;

(c) the Treaty does not prescribe a particular form in which a national court must present its request for a ruling; the Court must derive from the wording of the request, the questions which relate exclusively to the interpretation of the Community provisions: Case 5/69 *Volk v. Vervaecke* [1969] E.C.R. 295 at 301(2/4); [1969] C.M.L.R. 273; however, the reference by the national court must contain enough legal and factual information for the Court to be able to base its answer on the facts and circumstances of the case: Case C–157/92 *Pretore di Genoa v. Banchero* [1993] E.C.R. I–1085.

(d) it is not for the Court to appropriate for itself an assessment of the jurisdiction of the national court to refer the question or of the presence of a legal interest requiring protection on the part of the applicant in the main action: Case 65/81 *Reina v. Landeskreditbank Baden-Württemberg* [1982]

subsequent cases involving provisions which have been interpreted by the Court will not lightly contest that interpretation, although they remain free to do so. In other words, even if the Court's interpretation is *de jure* limited to the case under review, it has *de facto* effect *erga omnes*.[8]

Besides ensuring uniform interpretation, the preliminary ruling does also provide private parties with access to the Court, when they have no locus standi to directly ask the Court to control the validity of Community acts.[9]

Requests for a preliminary ruling must emanate from a national court or tribunal.[10] The national court *may*, or when there is no

---

E.C.R. 33; [1982] 1 C.M.L.R. 744; and it is for the national court to decide at what stage in the proceedings it is appropriate to refer a question to the Court: Case 72/83 *Campus Oil Limited v. Minister for Industry and Energy* [1984] E.C.R. 2727 at 2745(10); [1984] 3 C.M.L.R. 544.

(e) the Court has jurisdiction to give a ruling only when there is a genuine dispute before the national court: Case 104/79 *Foglia v. Novello* [1980] E.C.R. 745 at 760(11); [1981] 1 C.M.L.R. 45.

[8] See Case 66/80 *International Chemical Corporation v. Amministrazione delle Finanze dello Stato* [1981] E.C.R. 1191 at 1215(13); [1983] 2 C.M.L.R. 593; see, however, Case 61/79 *Amministrazione delle Finanze dello Stato v. Denkavit Italiana* [1980] E.C.R. 1205 at 1223(17); [1981] 3 C.M.L.R. 694 where the Court states that its interpretation applies even to relationships arising before the judgment.

[9] See Joined Cases 21–24/72 *International Fruit Company*, n.70 above at 1226(6): the jurisdiction of the Court to give rulings on the validity of measures adopted by the institutions extends to all the grounds capable of invalidating those measures, including the fact that they are contrary to a rule of international law and see Case 145/79 *Roquette Frères v. French Customs Administration* [1980] E.C.R. 2917 at 2946(52) where the Court ruled that when it declares a regulation void under an Art. 234 (ex 177) E.C. procedure, it may, by analogy with Art. 231 (ex 174), state which of the effects of the regulation shall be considered as definitive. In Case 162/96 *Racke* [1998] E.C.R. I–3655, the Court stated that Art. 234 (ex 177) E.C. does not contain any limitation of the grounds on which the validity may be contested.

[10] Whether a national organ which transmits a request for a preliminary ruling is a court of law must be determined on the basis of national law: see, *e.g.* Case 61/65 *Vaasen v. Beambtenfonds Mijnbedrijf* [1966] E.C.R. 261 at 273; [1966] C.M.L.R. 508. The Court has, however, laid down criteria to help in this determination: Case 138/80 *Borker* [1980] E.C.R. 1975 at 1977(4); [1980] 3 C.M.L.R. 638: the Court can only be requested to give a ruling by a court which is called upon to give judgment in proceedings intended to lead to a decision of a judicial nature. Arbitrators in disputes between parties to a contract under a clause inserted in that contract cannot be considered as a "court or tribunal": Case 102/81 *Nordsee v. Reederei Mond* [1982] E.C.R. 1095 at 1110(13); but in Case 109/88 *Handels- og Kontorfunktionaerernes Forbund i Danmark v. Dansk Arbejdsgiverforening acting on behalf of Danfoss* [1989] E.C.R. 3220; [1991] 1 C.M.L.R. 8, the Court ruled that an industrial arbitration board which (1) hears disputes on the application of one party without the need for the other party's agreement, (2) whose composition

judicial remedy against its decision *must*,[11] request such a ruling. This is the first distinction to be applied: there is no obligation for the national judge to refer a question to the Court when there exists a possibility of appeal against his decision. In that case he "may" decide to refer the question, or give himself the necessary interpretation of the Community rule. After all, it is the national judge who is, in the first place, responsible for applying and therefore also interpreting that rule. As for the *validity* of Community law, the national judge may decide that it is valid and apply it; he may not, however, decide that it is invalid and consequently refuse to apply it. Only the Court may declare a Community act invalid.[12]

As for the question "when" do the Treaty provisions concerning the preliminary ruling apply, the answer is: each time the national judge considers that, in order to give judgment in a case pending before him, he needs a decision on a "question". And, there is a question, when, having to apply a Treaty provision, the national judge finds himself confronted with a problem concerning its interpretation. The same can happen when he has to apply secondary

procedure is laid down by statute, and (3) which applies objective rules, is a "court or tribunal". Similarly, an appeals committee set up by a professional body and which may affect the exercise of rights granted by Community law is considered a "court": Case 246/80 *Broekmeulen v. Huisarts Registratie Commissie* [1981] E.C.R. 2311 at 2328(17); [1991] 3 C.M.L.R. 706. In Joint Cases C–69 to 79/96 *Garofalo* [1997] E.C.R. I–5603, the Court specified a number of factors to be taken into account in order to determine whether a body is a "court or tribunal": it depends on whether the body is established by law, is permanent, its jurisdiction is compulsory, the procedure before it is *inter partes*, it applies rules of law and finally, whether it is independent; in the case in question, the Court found that when it issues an opinion in the context of an extraordinary petition, the Consiglio di Stato is a court or tribunal.

[11] Art. 234 (ex 177) E.C. The particular purpose of the third paragraph of Art. 234 (ex 177) is to prevent a body of national case law that is not in accord with the rules of Community law from coming into existence in any Member State; Joined Cases 35 and 36/82 *Morson and Jhanjan v. State of the Netherlands* [1982] E.C.R. 3723 at 3734(8); [1983] 2 C.M.L.R. 221. The obligation to refer a question to the Court does not exist however, when it is raised in interlocutory proceedings and the decision to be taken is not binding on the court or tribunal which later has to deal with the substance of the case; Joined Cases 35 and 36/82 *Morson*, see *ibid.* at 3734(10). There are situations where the obligation to refer does not apply: (1) the question raised is not relevant, (2) the Community measure has already been interpreted or (3) the correct application of Community law is so clear (*acte clair*) that there is no room for any reasonable doubt; Case 283/81 *CILFIT v. Ministry of Health* [1982] E.C.R. 3415 at 3428(8–16); [1983] 1 C.M.L.R. 472.

[12] Case 314/85 *Foto-Frost v. Hauptzollamt Lübeck-Ost* [1987] E.C.R. 4199. However, a national judge may, under certain circumstances, grant interim measures concerning national measures based on a Community regulation which is the object of an Art. 234 (ex 177) E.C. procedure concerning the validity of said act: Case C–465/93 *Atlanta* [1995] E.C.R. I–3781.

Community law and a question is raised concerning the validity or the interpretation of that rule. A second distinction must indeed be made here between the Treaty on the one hand and the acts of the institutions and of the ECB on the other. A question concerning validity may only be referred to the Court when it concerns secondary Community law; indeed, the Court cannot rule on the validity of the Treaty, the constitution of the Community.

As to the precise meaning of the words "where such a question is raised", this condition is fulfilled as soon as a difference of opinion arises concerning the interpretation (and the validity) of a provision of Community law which is invoked by one of the parties. According to the Court, questions can be raised by one of the parties to the dispute, but also by the national court or tribunal itself.[13]

However, the possibility or obligation to refer a question only exists when the national judge considers that a decision on the question is necessary to enable him to give judgment. In other words, it is his decision. Neither the Court,[14] nor national law,[15] nor a Community rule[16] can deprive him of this right. It is also within his discretionary power to decide whether the question has been raised in good faith, or whether it is a purely procedural move initiated by one of the parties, for instance to delay judgment.[17] There is therefore nothing automatic in the procedure of the preliminary ruling.

Once the national judge has decided to refer a question to the Court, he suspends the proceedings in the national court, and awaits the answer from the Court before resuming them.

In his reference the national judge formulates a question or questions to be answered by the Court. And it is then for the latter to decide whether or not this question is to be answered. Indeed, the Court does not feel under obligation to answer any question put to it. In the first place, the question must be formulated in such a way that

---

[13] Case 126/80 *Salonia v. Poidomani and Giglio* [1981] E.C.R. 1563 at 1577(7); [1982] 1 C.M.L.R. 64.

[14] Case 5/77 *Tedeschi v. Denkavit* [1977] E.C.R. 1555 at 1574(17); [1978] 1 C.M.L.R. 1.

[15] Case 166/73 *Rheinmühle v. Einfuhr-und Vorratstelle Getreide* [1974] E.C.R. 33 at 38(4); [1974] 1 C.M.L.R. 523.

[16] Case 127/73 *BRT v. Sabam* [1974] E.C.R. 51 at 63(23); [1974] 2 C.M.L.R. 238.

[17] See opinion of the Advocate-General in Case 6/64 *Costa v. ENEL* [1964] E.C.R. 585 at 607; [1964] C.M.L.R. 425, where mention is made of a "preliminary inquiry of legality" by the national judge concerning the relevance of the question to the solution of the dispute.

the Court can understand the circumstances and facts of the case wherein the problem arises, if not it will refuse to consider it.[18]

It should be noted also that the "summary and urgent character of a procedure in the national court does not prevent the Court from regarding itself as validly seized" to give a preliminary ruling.[19] However, a national court is not required to refer to the Court (even when no judicial review is available against its decision) a question raised in interlocutory proceedings for an interim order. But, this only applies if each party is entitled to institute proceedings or require proceedings to be instituted on the substance of the case. Furthermore, it should be possible during those proceedings to re-examine the question provisionally decided in the summary proceedings and to refer the question to the Court.[20]

It is clear from the abundance of requests for preliminary rulings[21] that here lies an essential function of the Court, not only in regard to the development of Community law, but also as an instrument at the disposal of natural and legal persons confronted with Community measures whose legality they cannot directly challenge in the Court. Indeed, when in a preliminary ruling an act of the institutions or of the ECB is declared to be invalid, it becomes inapplicable. This has for the plaintiff practically the same consequences as an annulment.

Recently the Court indicated that the Preliminary ruling procedure could not be used to have the Court examine the validity of a

---

[18] Joined Cases C–320, 321 and 322/90 *Telemarsicabruzzo v. Circostel* [1993], C–321/90 *Telaltitalia v. Circostel* [1993] and C–322/90 *Telelazio v. Circostel* [1993] all of January 26, 1993; where the Court rejected the questions as inadmissible since they did not contain sufficient information for the Court to interpret the competition rules in relation to a dispute which was not explained. See also Case C–157/92 *Pretore di Genova v. Banchero* [1993] E.C.R. I–1086, where the Court found the questions inadmissible for the same reasons.

[19] Case 107/76 *Hoffman-La Roche v. Centrafarm* [1977] E.C.R. 957 at 973(4); 2 C.M.L.R. 334.

[20] *ibid.* at 973(5). See Case 36/74 *Walrave v. Union Cycliste Internationale* [1974] E.C.R. 1405; [1975] 1 C.M.L.R. 320: in a decision in summary proceedings, the President of the Arrondissementsrechtbank at Utrecht gave an interim order which was subject to the proviso that the plaintiff initiate proceedings in the same court within a period of six weeks so as to be able to request the Court to make a preliminary ruling, which was done.

[21] In 1998, *e.g.* 264 preliminary questions were filed in the Court as against 147 appeals for annulment; Court Report (1998), 199.

Community act when the interested party could have "without any doubt[22] challenged it by virtue of Article 173 of the Treaty".[23]

The following should also be noted with regard to the preliminary ruling.

First, the competence of the Court does not apply to purely internal situations; however, if the Member State has applied the Community rules (provided for in a directive) also to purely internal situations, then the Court is competent to interpret the Community rules in an internal case.[24] Secondly, intervention by a private party in a preliminary ruling procedure is not admissible since those proceedings are not contentious in nature.[25] And, thirdly, an application for revision of a preliminary ruling cannot be made. Only the national judge could submit to the Court new elements susceptible to lead to a different answer.[26]

(5) Compensation for Damages caused by Institutions

The Court has jurisdiction in disputes relating to compensation for damages resulting from the non-contractual liability of the Community.[27] Indeed, the Treaty provides that "in the case of non-contractual liability, the Community shall, in accordance with the general principles common to the laws of the Member States, make good any damage caused by its institutions or by its servants in the performance of their duties".[28] In one of its first judgments concerning claims for redress, the Court held that an administrative measure which had not been annulled could not constitute on the part of the administration a wrongful act inflicting damage upon those whom it affects.[29] In later judgments, however, the Court modified its position, indicating that actions for annulment and claims for damages were different proceedings. In providing for an appeal for damages the Treaty introduced an autonomous form of

---

[22] See Case C–241/92 *Accrington* [1996] E.C.R. I–6699, where a preliminary question was admitted because there were doubts as to the standing of the plaintiff to challenge the regulation. *Id.* Case C–408/95 *Eurotunnel v. SeaFrance* [1997] E.C.R. I–6315.

[23] Case C–188/92 *TWD Textilwerke Deggendorf* [1994] E.C.R. I–846 at 855 (24/25) and Case C–178/95 *Wiljo* [1997] E.C.R. I–585.

[24] Case C–28/95 *Leur-Bloem* [1997] E.C.R. I–4161.

[25] Case C–181/95, *Biogen v. Smithkline* [1996] E.C.R. I–717.

[26] Case C–116/96 Rev: *Reisebüro Binder* [1998] E.C.R. I–1891.

[27] Art. 235 (ex 178) E.C.

[28] Art. 283 (ex 215) E.C. For a rare successful action see Joined Cases C–104/89 and C–37/90 *Mulder v. Council and Commission* [1992] E.C.R. 3131.

[29] Case 25/62 *Plauman v. Commission* [1963] E.C.R. 95 at 108; [1964] C.M.L.R. 29.

action subject to conditions on its use dictated by its specific nature. Indeed, its end is not the abolition of a particular measure, but the compensation for damages inflicted by the measure or action of the administration.[30] Undoubtedly, this is true, but this action is, nevertheless, often used to obtain just that, albeit under the motto of the non-applicability of a measure considered to be illegal and giving rise to compensation of damages, since the latter implies the illegality of said measure.

Indeed, the Court indicated that the non-contractual liability of the Community presupposes the unlawful nature of the act, besides actual damage and a causal relationship between the act and the damage.[31] On the other hand, the unlawful nature of an act does not automatically make the Community responsible for compensation in case of damage. The cases in which compensation is granted are rather rare.[32]

In the case of legislation involving measures of economic policy, the Community does not incur non-contractual liability unless a sufficiently flagrant violation of a superior rule of law for the protection of the damaged party can be shown.[33] Furthermore, in many cases the Court has considered that the institution enjoyed wide discretionary powers (*e.g.* in the field of agricultural policy) in which case it must be shown that the institution has gone beyond the limits assigned to the exercise of its powers.[34] As for the damage for which compensation is sought, it must be certain and have been assessed or, at least, be assessable. The Court has, however, accepted the admissibility of an action in which it is asked to declare the Community liable for imminent damage foreseeable with sufficient certainty, even if the damage cannot yet be precisely assessed. The Court also admits that the damage be fixed by agreement between

---

[30] Case 5/71 *Zuckerfabrik Schöppenstedt v. Council* [1971] E.C.R. 975 at 983(3).

[31] Case 51/81 *De Franceschi v. Council and Commission* [1982] E.C.R. 117 at 134(9).

[32] Joined Cases 83 and 94/76 *HNL v. Council and Commission* [1978] E.C.R. 1209 at 1224(4); [1978] 3 C.M.L.R. 566. A rare case where compensation was granted is T–20/94, *Hartmann* [1997] E.C.R. II–595.

[33] Joined Cases 197, etc. 80 *Ludwigshafener Walzmühle v. Council and Commission* [1981] E.C.R. 3211 at 3246(19).

[34] See Joined Cases 83 and 94/76, 4,15 and 40/77 *HNL v. Council and Commission* [1978] E.C.R. 1209; [1978] 3 C.M.L.R. 566: in case of wide discretionary powers, the Community does not incur liability unless the institution concerned has manifestly and gravely disregarded the limits on the exercise of its power.

the parties.[35] The Community courts have exclusive jurisdiction to hear cases concerning compensation based on the non-contractual liability of the Community.[36] This would also include compensation for moral prejudice.[37]

A problem might arise with measures taken by the Member States on the basis of a Community act. The Court has indicated that it has no jurisdiction when the application for compensation is, in fact, based on such national measures. The Member States could, of course, be sued in the national courts for faulty application of Community law if this were the case.[38] On the other hand, when the damage caused by the national implementing measure finds its origin in the underlying Community act, the liability of the Community can be established by the Court on the basis of Community law.[39]

It should be noted that actions for compensation for damage are subject to a five year period of limitation.[40] Of great importance for the natural and legal persons is the fact that when the Court allocates damages caused by an act of the institutions considered by the Court to be illegal, the latter becomes virtually inapplicable. The action for compensation of damages constitutes, therefore, next to the preliminary ruling, an instrument for challenging the legality of Community acts for those who have no locus standi under the direct appeal procedure.

---

[35] Case 256/81 *Pauls Agriculture v. Council and Commission* [1983] E.C.R. 1707 at 1721(15) and Case 59/83 *Biovilac v. EEC* [1984] E.C.R. 4057 at 4075(9). Case 145/83 *Adams v. Commission* [1985] E.C.R. I–3539. The President of the Court referred to "serious and irreparable loss": Case C–110/97 *Netherlands v. Commission* [1997] E.C.R. I–1795.

[36] Joined Cases 106 to 120/87 *Asteris v. Hellenic Republic and Commission* [1988] E.C.R. 5531; [1990] 1 C.M.L.R. 575. The Court ruled that a question relating to the application of Art. 215(2) (now 288(2)) cannot be determined in proceedings for a preliminary ruling: Case 101/78 *Granaria v. Hoofdproduktschap voor Akkerbouwprodukten* [1979] E.C.R. 623 at 638(10); [1979] 3 C.M.L.R. 124.

[37] Case T–485/93, *Dreyfus* [1996] E.C.R. II–1101 (74).

[38] See Joined Cases 106 to 120/87, n.36 above.

[39] Case 126/76 *Dietz v. Commission* [1977] E.C.R. 2431; [1978] 2 C.M.L.R. 608. See also Case 101/78 *Granaria*, n.36 above at 640(3) and Case 310/81, *EISS v. Commission* [1984] E.C.R. 1341.

[40] Protocol on the Statute of the Court, Art. 43. See Joined Cases 256, etc. 80 and 5/81 *Birra Wührer v. Council and Commission* [1982] E.C.R. 85.

(6) Other Cases within the Court's Jurisdiction

The objection of illegality[41] gives, according to the Court,

> "expression to a general principle conferring upon any party to proceedings the right to challenge, for the purpose of obtaining the annulment of a decision of direct and individual concern to that party, the validity of previous acts of the institutions which form the legal basis of the decision which is being attacked, if that party was not entitled under Article 173 [now 230] of the Treaty to bring a direct action challenging those acts by which it was thus affected without having been in a position to ask that they be declared void."[42]

Although the Treaty refers to a "regulation", the Court mentions "acts" in general.[43]

For the Court it is clear from the wording and the general scheme of the Treaty that, although this is not specified, a declaration of inapplicability is only possible in proceedings brought before the Court itself under some other provision of the Treaty and that the plea may only be used against a measure which is the basis for the act in dispute. In other words, the objection of illegality does not constitute an independent action and may only be sought incidentally.[44]

The objection of illegality constitutes, with the request for a preliminary ruling and the claim for compensation for damage, the third way for natural and legal persons to challenge a measure whose legality they cannot directly ask the Court to review.[45]

JURISDICTION OUTSIDE THE ECSC, EURATOM AND E.C. TREATIES

Basically, the jurisdiction of the Court of Justice is limited to the above mentioned three Treaties as successively amended by other Treaties and acts, including the Amsterdam Treaty. The Treaty on

---

[41] Art. 184 E.C. See, *e.g.* Case 258/80 *Rumi v. Commission* [1982] E.C.R. 487.

[42] Case 15/57 *Hauts Fournaux de Chasse v. High Authority* [1957–1958] E.C.R. 211 and Case 9/56 *Meroni v. High Authority* [1957–1958] E.C.R. 133. As was seen above, the important words are: "if that party was not entitled . . . to bring a direct action challenging those acts"; the same rule applies here as in the case of the preliminary ruling. Those "indirect" ways may only be used if the "direct" way should be closed.

[43] Case 92/78 *Simmenthal v. Commission* [1979] E.C.R. 777 at 800(39); [1980] 1 C.M.L.R. 162.

[44] See Case T–154/94 *Comité des Salines* [1996] E.C.R. II–1377.

[45] Art. 220 (ex 173) E.C.

European Union now provides[46] for jurisdiction of the Court with regard to the *Provisions on Police and Judicial Co-operation in Criminal Matters*.[47] The Court may be asked to give preliminary rulings on the validity and interpretation of framework decisions and decisions, on the interpretation of conventions established under the said *Provisions* and on the validity and interpretation of the measures implementing them.[48] The Court also has jurisdiction with regard to the *Provisions on Closer Cooperation*,[49] under the conditions laid down by the E.C. Treaty.[50] The latter provides that Member States which wish to establish closer co-operation among themselves, may be authorised "to make use of the institutions, procedures and mechanisms laid down by that Treaty". There are, however, certain conditions which must be fulfilled. Among other things, such co-operation may not affect Community policies, actions or programmes and may not constitute a discrimination or a restriction of trade, etc.[51]

The Court's jurisdiction also applies with regard to amendments to the E.U. Treaty[52] and admission of new members and consequent adjustments to the Treaty.[53]

EUROPEAN INVESTMENT BANK AND THE EUROPEAN CENTRAL BANK[54]

It is interesting to note that the Board of Directors of the ECB may enjoy the powers conferred upon the Commission with regard to the fulfilment by the Member States of their obligations under the Treaty. Also that decisions of the Board of Governors of the EIB may be challenged in the Court by the Member States, the Commission or the Board of Directors. As for decisions of the Board of Directors they may, in certain cases be challenged by the Member States and the Commission.[55] New since the entering into force of the Maastricht Treaty, is the Court's jurisdiction in disputes concerning the fulfilment by national central banks of their obligations under the Treaty and the Statute of the European Systems of Central Banks

---

[46] Art. 46 (ex L) TEU.
[47] Arts 29 to 42 TEU.
[48] Art. 35 TEU.
[49] Arts 43 to 45 TEU.
[50] Art. 11 (ex 5a) E.C.
[51] Similar provisions are to be found in Art. 40 TEU.
[52] Art. 48 (ex N) TEU.
[53] Art. 49 (ex O) TEU.
[54] Art. 237 (ex 180) E.C.
[55] See Case 85/86 *Commission v. EIB* [1987] E.C.R. 1313; [1989] C.M.L.R. 103.

(ESCB).[56] The Council of the ECB enjoys the same powers *vis-à-vis* the national central banks as the Commission may exercise in case of failure by a Member State to fulfil a Treaty obligation.[57] Similarly, if the Court finds that certain obligations have not been fulfilled, the central bank must take the necessary measures to comply with the judgment. There is, however, an important difference: the Council of the ECB does not have the possibility to ask the Court to impose a lump sum or penalty payment in case the national central bank fails to implement the Court's judgment.[58]

ATTRIBUTION OF COMPETENCE

Competence may be attributed to the Court either pursuant to an arbitration clause contained in a contract concluded by or on behalf of the Community[59] or in any dispute between Member States which relates to the subject-matter of the Treaty, if the dispute is submitted under a special agreement.[60] In the case of a contract, the arbitration clause is necessary since the Treaty provides that disputes to which the Community is a party shall not, on that ground, be excluded from the jurisdiction of the courts of the Member States.[61]

In this context mention must be made of the attribution of jurisdiction to the Court by the Protocol on the Interpretation of the Convention on Jurisdiction and the Enforcement of Judgments in Civil and Commercial Matters[62] concluded between the Member States.[63]

---

[56] Art. 237 (ex 180) E.C.

[57] See above, Commission 3(1).

[58] Art. 228(2) (ex 171(2)) E.C.

[59] Art. 238 (ex 181) E.C. See Case C–114/94 *IDE* [1997] E.C.R. I–803.

[60] Art. 239 (ex 182) E.C.

[61] Art. 240 (ex 183) E.C.

[62] See Art. 3 of the Protocol of June 3, 1971 annexed to the Convention of Brussels of September 27, 1968 ([1978] O.J. L304). See, *e.g.* Joined Cases 9 and 10/77 *Bavaria Fluggesellschaft and Germanair v. Eurocontrol* [1977] E.C.R. 1517; [1980] 1 C.M.L.R. 566. See also Protocol of the Convention of February 29, 1968 on the Mutual Recognition of Companies and Bodies Corporate: [1968] O.J. L204/28; Convention of December 18, 1975 concerning the European Patent for the Common Market. Art. 46 TEU. (ex Art. L): powers of the Court regarding the E.U. Treaty; Protocol integrating the Schengen *acquis*, Art. 2(1) 3 [1997] O.J. C340/94.

[63] This Protocol does not constitute a "special agreement" in the sense of Art. 239 (ex 182) E.C., since it does not concern a "subject matter of the Treaty".

INTERIM RELIEF AND MEASURES

Actions brought before the Court have no suspensory effect.[64] However, the Court may, if it considers that circumstances so require, order the suspension of the contested act.[65]

A decision ordering a suspension or other interim measures is conditional on the existence of circumstances giving rise to urgency and of factual and legal grounds establishing a prima facie case for the interim measure.[66] According to the Court, this urgency must be assessed in relation to the need to prevent serious and irreparable damage to the applicant.[67] Since interim measures may only be granted in respect of a case pending before the Court,[68] the plaintiff must also show the grounds, on which the substantive application is made, "not to be manifestly without foundation".[69]

Owing to the urgency pleaded in requests for interim measures, the President of the Court was given powers to decide on them himself,[70] although, where the case is important or complex he may refer the request to the full Court.

Interim measures can be prescribed against persons, institutions and Member States.[71] Generally speaking, the Presidents have been rather reluctant to grant interim measures and the Court considers that they should only be ordered in exceptional circumstances.[72]

The interim measures prescribed by the Court have been extremely varied, and indeed, the Treaty only refers to any "necessary" interim measure.[73] The Court has, for instance, ordered the parties to start negotiations to agree upon an alternative solution,[74]

---

[64] Art. 242 (ex 185) E.C.

[65] *ibid.*

[66] Rules of Procedure, Art. 83(2). For suspension of an act, see Case T–41/96R *Bayer AG* [1996] E.C.R.

[67] See, *e.g.* Cases 113/77R and 113/77 R–/Int *NTN TOYO v. Council* [1977] E.C.R. 1721 at 1725(6); [1979] 2 C.M.L.R. 257 and Case 32/89 R *Greece v. Commission* [1989] E.C.R. 985 at 989(13); [1991] 1 C.M.L.R. 377. See, however, Case C–149/95P(R), *Atlantic Container Line* [1995] E.C.R. I–2169, where the appeal of the Commission against the suspension was dismissed.

[68] Art. 243 (ex 186) E.C.

[69] Case 3/75R, *Johnson & Firth Brown v. Commission* [1975] E.C.R. 1 at 6(1); [1975] 1 C.M.L.R. 638.

[70] Rules of Procedure, Art. 85.

[71] For persons see, *e.g.* Case 3/75R, note 69 above; for institutions, see, *e.g.* Case 113/77R, note 67 above and for Member States, see, *e.g.* Joined Cases 31/77 R and 53/77R *Commission v. U.K.* [1977] E.C.R. 921 at 925; [1977] 2 C.M.L.R. 359.

[72] Case 113/77R n.71 above.

[73] Art. 243 (ex 186) E.C.

[74] Case 61/77R *Commission v. Ireland* [1977] E.C.R. 937 at 943(34); [1978] 2 C.M.L.R. 466.

authorised a Member State to take temporary measures but with the consent of the Commission,[75] and suspended the application of a measure on condition that a party continues to provide security.[76]

(7) Appelate Jurisdiction

Since 1989, the Court also functions as court of appeal from decisions of the Court of First Instance.[77] An appeal may be brought before the Court within two months of the notification of the contested decision. This decision may concern a final decision, a decision disposing of the substantial part of the substantive issues only, or a decision disposing of procedural issues concerning a plea of lack of competence or inadmissibility.[78]

The appeal may be brought by the unsuccessful party, the interveners when the decision directly affects them, the Member States and the Community institutions.[79]

An appeal to the Court shall be limited to points of law. It "shall lie on the grounds of lack of competence of the Court of First Instance, a breach of procedure before it which affects the interests of the appellant as well as the infringment of Community law by the Court of First Instance".[80] If the appeal is well-founded, the Court shall quash the decision. It may then either give final judgment itself, or refer the case back to the Court of First Instance,[81] which is then bound by the decision of the Court of Justice on matters of law.

---

[75] *ibid.*

[76] Case 113/77R, n.71 above. See also Case C–149/95P(R) *Atlantic Container Line* [1995] E.C.R. I–2169, where the appeal of the Commission against the suspension was dismissed.

[77] Council Decision of October 24, 1988 establishing a Court of First Instance of the European Communities [1988] O.J. L319/1. Art. 225 (ex 68a) E.C.

[78] Protocol on the Statute of the Court of Justice as modified by the above-mentioned Council Decision: Art. 49(1).

[79] *ibid.* Arts 49(2) and (3).

[80] *ibid.* Art. 51. Limitation to points of law, see Case C–53/92P *Hilti* [1994] E.C.R. I–667 and Case 91/95P, *Tremblay* [1996] E.C.R. I–5547.

[81] *ibid.* Art. 54. However, it is not for the Court of Justice, when ruling on questions of law in the context of an appeal, to substitute, on grounds of fairness, its own assessment for that of the Court of First Instance exercising its unlimited jurisdiction to rule on the amount of fines.

4. The Procedure

The rules concerning the procedure before the Court are laid down in the Protocol on the Statute of the Court annexed to the Treaty and in the Rules of Procedure which the Court adopts after having received the unanimous approval of the Council.[82] The Rules contain, apart from the rules "contemplated" by the Statute, "any other provision necessary for applying and, when necessary, for supplementing it".[83] The procedure before the Court, for which no fees are charged, consists of two parts: a written and an oral one. The language of the proceedings must be one of the twelve official languages of the Community and is determined by the applicant.[84]

(1) The Written Procedure[85]

The procedure starts with the submission to the Court of a written *application* addressed to the Registrar.[86] The Statute and the Rules contain various requirements as to form, content and accompanying documents of the application.[87] The Member States and the institutions are represented by an agent appointed for each case; other parties must be represented by a lawyer entitled to practice before a court of a Member State.[88] It is important to note that the application must state all the grounds on which it is based, since parties may not, in the course of the proceedings, raise fresh issues, unless these are based on matters of law or of fact which come to light in the course of the written procedure.[89] The time limit within which the application

[82] Art. 245 (ex 188) E.C.; the present Rules of Procedure of the Court of Justice were adopted on June 19, 1991: [1991] O.J. L176/1 and Corrigendum [1992] O.J. L383/117, and have been modified several times, lastly in [1995] O.J. L44/61. See also Annex II to the Rules: Extension of time limits on account of distance [1991] O.J. L176/22 and the Supplementary Rules, *ibid.* at 4.

[83] Art. 44 Protocol.

[84] Art. 29(2) Rules; the languages are: Danish, Dutch, German, English, Finnish, French, Greek, Irish, Italian, Portuguese, Spanish and Swedish. This is one more than the "official" languages of the Community.

[85] Arts 18 *et seq*. Statute, and Rules, Title II, Chap. I.

[86] See Instructions to the Registrar [1982] O.J. C39/35.

[87] Art. 19 Statute and Rules, Arts. 18 *et seq*.

[88] Art. 17 Statute. The application must also state an address for service at the place where the Court has its seat. It shall also give the name of a person who is authorised and has expressed willingness to accept service; Rules, Art. 38(2). Proceedings brought by a litigant in person are inadmissible: Case C–174/96P *Lores* [1996] E.C.R. I–6401.

[89] Rules, Art. 42(2); see Case 139/79 *Maizena v. Council* [1980] E.C.R. 3393 at 3424(32).

must be filed is also essential; appeals for annulment must be instituted within two months of the publication of the measures or of its notification to the plaintiff.[90] This time limit was extended by Annex II to the Rules of Procedure for parties living outside Luxembourg.

The fact that an application is lodged with the Court is published in the *Official Journal*; besides the names of the parties, the subject-matter of the dispute and the claims of the applicant, "a summary of the contentions and of the main arguments" are also published.[91]

The application is notified to the defendant who then has one month to file a *defence*.[92] The plaintiff's application and the defence may (but need not) be supplemented by a *reply* from the applicant and a *rejoinder* from the defendant. The time limit within which those pleadings have to be lodged is fixed by the President of the Court.

Before formally closing the written part of the procedure, the Court, at the suggestion of the Judge Rapporteur[93] or the Advocate-

---

[90] Art. 230(3) (ex 173(3)) EEC. If publication in the *Official Journal* allows the date to be determined with some precision (*i.e.* the moment it becomes available), the matter is more delicate with letters, especially when they are not registered, see Case 108/79 *Belfiore v. Commission* [1980] E.C.R. 1769 at 1781(7). Since the arrival of the O.J. varies with circumstances and from country to country, 14 days are automatically added to the two months: Rules of Procedure, Art. 8(1): "The period of time allowed for commencing proceedings against a measure adopted by an institution shall run . . . where the measure is published, from the 15th day after publication thereof in the *Official Journal*"; this provision was complemented (clarified ?) by an amendment to the Rules: [1977] O.J. L103/1: ". . . that period shall be calculated, for the purposes of Article 81(1)(a), from the end of the 14th day after publication thereof . . .". This, however, doesn't specify when the 14 days start running: it probably does not include the date mentioned on the *Official Journal*.
The additional days are the following:
Belgium: 2,
Germany, France (Europe) and The Netherlands (Europe): 6,
Denmark (Europe), Spain, Ireland, Italy, Austria, Portugal (except Azores and Madeira), Finland, Sweden and the U.K.: 10,
Other countries and territories outside Europe: 2 weeks,
Azores and Madeira 3 weeks,
Other countries, Departments and territories: 1 month.
In Case 107/83 *Klopp* [1984] E.C.R. 2971, the Court pointed out that "the modern methods of transport and telecommunications facilitate proper contact with the . . . judicial authorities" so that distance "does not prevent the application of the rules of ethics in the host Member State". Is it not time that the Court, on the basis of those facts and taking into account the Fax and E-mail, puts an end to this difference in treatment, which, in fact, amounts to discrimination?

[91] Rules, Art. 16(6).

[92] Rules, Art. 40(1).

[93] Rules, Art. 9(2).

General, may decide to prescribe measures of inquiry,[94] *i.e.* interrogation of the parties, request for information, hearing of witnesses,[95] etc.

In a procedure for a preliminary ruling, the parties, the Member States, the Commission and, where appropriate, the Council, are entitled to submit statements of case or written observations to the Court.[96]

Finally, it should be noted that the Member States and the institutions may always *intervene* in cases before the Court; legal and natural persons have the same right when they establish an interest in the result of a case. It should be noted that the submissions made in an application to intervene must be limited to "supporting the submissions of one of the parties"; in other words, the intervening party is bound by the submissions already made by the parties to the dispute: he is either for or against, there is no other alternative.[97]

(2) The Oral Procedure

The oral procedure[98] starts with the reading of the report of the Judge-Rapporteur (although in practice this is no longer strictly the case), the hearing by the Court of agents, legal advisers or council and of the Opinion of the Advocate-General, as well as the hearing of witnesses and experts, if any. The reading of the Opinion of the Advocate-General indicates the end of the oral part of the procedure.[99] The judgment[1] is, in turn, read in open Court, at a later date. It is published in the European Court Reports (E.C.R.). Court Judgments are now designated with the letter "C", before the number of the case and published in part "I" of the E.C.R. The

[94] For details, see Rules, Arts 45–54.

[95] The rules contain several provisions concerning witnesses: the Court may impose penalties in case of default (Art. 24 Statute); the Court may have a witness heard by the judicial authorities of the place of his permanent residence (Art. 26 Statute); Member States must treat any violation of an oath by a witness in the same manner as if the offence had been committed before one of their courts with jurisdiction in civil procedure and prosecute the offender before their competent court at the instance of the Court (Art. 27 Statute).

[96] Art. 20 Statute.

[97] Art. 37 Statute.

[98] See Art. 18(4) Statute and Rules, Art. 55–62.

[99] Rules, Art. 59. In fact only the operative part of the conclusions is read in court.

[1] For the prescribed content of the judgment, see Rules, Art. 63. The judgment always contains a decision on the costs which are normally born by the losing party; Rules, Arts 69 *et seq*. Here also only the operative part is read.

judgments of the Court of First Instance (CFI) are preceded by the letter "T" (for Tribunal) and published in part "II" of the E.C.R. In case of appeal, the number is followed by the letter "P" (*Pourvoi*) and summary procedures are indicated by the letter "R" (*Référé*).

(3) Costs

There are, generally speaking, no court costs in respect of proceedings before the European courts.[2] On the other hand, the Treaty provides that "the Court shall adjudicate upon costs".[3] Normally, the unsuccessful party shall be ordered to pay the costs, if they have been applied for in the successful party's pleadings.[4] Recoverable costs include, *inter alia* "expenses necessarily incurred by the parties for the purpose of the proceedings, in particular the travel and subsistence expenses and the remuneration of agents, advisors and lawyers".[5] Member States and institutions which intervene bear their own costs. The Courts may order other interveners to bear their own costs.[6]

There is no taxation of the lawyers costs in the judgment. In case of dispute, the courts decide by order.[7]

(4) Special Forms of Procedure

The Statutes and the Rules contain provisions for several special forms of procedure[8] such as a summary procedure (examined above under "other cases within the Court's jurisdiction"), intervention,

[2] See however, Rules, Art. 72.

[3] Statute, Art. 35.

[4] Art. 62(2) Rules. See Case T–174/95 *Svenska Journalistförbundet v. Council* [1998] E.C.R. II–2293, where the Court ordered the successful party to bear part of its own costs in view of the abuse of procedure committed by the applicant who had published an edited version of the defence on the Internet with an invitation to the public to send their comments to the Agents of the Council.

[5] Rules, Art. 73(b).

[6] Rules, Art. 69(4).

[7] See, for instance, Order of the CFI of September 17, 1998, in Case T–271/944 *Branco* [1998] E.C.R. II–742: of the 2,633,319 ESC asked for, the CFI granted 1,170,000.

[8] See Arts 36 *et seq.* Statute and Rules, Arts 83 *et seq.*

judgment by default, rectification, third party proceedings,[9] interpretation and revision.[10]

B. The Court of First Instance (CFI)

As provided for in the SEA,[11] the Council attached to the Court of Justice[12] "a court with jurisdiction to hear and determine at first instance, subject to a right of appeal to the Court of Justice on points of law only and in accordance with the conditions laid down by the Statute, certain classes of action or proceedings brought by natural or legal persons".[13] This Court of First Instance started functioning in November 1989.

(1) Members of the Court of First Instance

There are 15 members chosen from persons whose independence is beyond doubt and who possess the ability required for appointment to judicial office. They are appointed by common accord of the Governments of the Member States for a term of six years. The membership is partially renewed every three years, and retiring members are eligible for re-appointment.[14] They elect their President for three years. There are no appointed Advocates-General, but the members of the Court of First Instance may be called upon to perform the task of Advocate-General; their task is identical to that of the Advocates-General of the Court of Justice[15] and they may make their submission in writing.[16]

The CFI normally sits in (extended) chambers of three or five judges or a single judge.[17] It sits in plenary session "whenever the legal difficulty or the importance of the case or special circumstances

---

[9] See Case 292/84 T.P. *Bolognese v. Scharf and Commission* [1987] E.C.R. 3563; for a rectification see Order of June 25, 1996 in Case C–441/93 *Panagis Pafitis* [1996] E.C.R. I–3083; [1996] 2 C.M.L.R. 551, and for a judgment by default: Case T–85/95 *Branco* [1995] E.C.R. II–47: failure to file a defence.

[10] See, *e.g.* Case C–185/90 P-Rev. *Walter Gill v. Commission* [1992] E.C.R. I–993.

[11] Art. 11 SEA.

[12] Council Decision of October 24 [1988] O.J. L319/1 modified in 1989 [1989] O.J. L241/1; consolidated [1989] O.J. C215/1; modified [1993] O.J. L144/21.

[13] Art. 225(1) (ex 168a(1)) E.C.

[14] Art. 225(3) (ex 168a(3)) E.C.

[15] Decision of October 24, Art. 2(3); see n. 12 above.

[16] *ibid.*, Art. 9(46(3)).

[17] *ibid.*, Art. 2(4). Council Decision 99/291/E.C.

so justify". It establishes its Rules of Procedure in agreement with the Court of Justice; those rules require unanimous approval of the Council.[18]

(2) Jurisdiction

The Court of First Instance exercises at first instance the jurisdiction conferred by the Treaty on the Court in[19]:

(a) disputes between the institutions and their servants[20];
(b) actions brought against the Commission by undertakings concerning ECSC levies, production, prices and agreements and concentrations[21];
(c) actions brought by natural or legal persons for the review of legality of acts of the institutions, for failure to act, for compensation of damages or following an arbitration clause[22];
(d) actions brought pursuant to the Euratom Treaty.[23]

(3) Procedure before the Court of First Instance

The procedure before the CFI is governed by Title III of the Statute of the Court of Justice, with the exception of the provisions concerning the preliminary ruling.[24] Further and more detailed provisions are laid down in the Rules of procedure established by the CFI.[25]

---

[18] Art. 225(1) (ex 168a(4)) E.C.

[19] Some elements of this jurisdiction only entered into force on March 7, 1994 [1994] O.J. L69/29.

[20] See above under "Court of Justice, (6) other cases within the Court's jurisdiction" and Art. 236 (ex 179) E.C. The first case is T–159/89, *Vitranyani v. Commission* [1993] 1 C.M.L.R. 41. Another 153 cases were transferred from the Court of Justice; Decision of October 24, 1988, Art. 14.

[21] Decision, Art. 3(1)(b) and Arts 33, 35, 40, 42 ECSC.

[22] *ibid.*, at (c) and Arts 230(2) (ex 173(2)), 232(3) (ex 175(3)), 235 (ex 178) and 238 (ex 181a) E.C.

[23] *ibid.*, at (d) and Arts 146, 148, 151 and 153 Euratom.

[24] Statute of the Court of Justice, Art. 46(1)

[25] Art. 225(4) (ex 168a(4)) E.C. See [1991] O.J. L.136/1. On the basis, for instance, of Art. 102(2) of those Rules, the extension of the time limit above the two months for initiating proceedings, allotted on account of the distance which (in theory) separates the plaintiff from the Court in Luxembourg, are the same as for the Court of Justice: see Annex II to the Rules of Procedure of that court [1991] O.J. L176/1 and Corrigendum [1992] O.J. L383/117.

Interestingly, the Court of First Instance may dispense with the written procedure.[26]

Where a case is referred back by the Court of Justice, the Court of First Instance shall be bound by the decision of the Court of Justice on points of law.[27]

Further Reading

Brown and Jacobs, *The Court of Justice of the European Communities* (Sweet & Maxwell, London, 1994).

David W. K. Anderson, *References to the European Court* (Sweet & Maxwell, London, 1995).

David Edward, "How the Court of Justice Works", (1995) 20 E.L.Rev. 539.

David W. D. Scorey, "A New Model for the Communities' Judicial Architecture in the New Union", (1996) 21 E.L.Rev. 224.

Lord Howe of Aberavon, "Euro-Justice, Yes or No?", (1996), 21 E.L.Rev. 187.

Takis Trimidas, "The Court of Justice and Judical Activism", (1996) 21 E.L.Rev. 199.

Walter van Gerven, "The Role and Structure of the European Judiciary Now and in the Future", (1996) 21 E.L.Rev. 211.

Editorial, "Single Judges in the Court of First Instance?", (1998) 23 E.L.Rev. 107.

Editorial, "The Select Committee on single judges in the Court of First Instance", (1998) 23 E.L.Rev. 303.

David O'Keeffe, "Is the Spirit of Article 177 under Attack? Preliminary References and Admissibility", (1998) 23 E.L.Rev. 509.

---

[26] *ibid.*, Art. 9 (46 *et seq.*).

[27] Decision Art. 9(52). The first judgment was given on January 30, 1990, only two weeks after the formal hearing; *York von Wartenburg v. Parliament* [1990] E.C.R. II–31.

Chapter Nine
The Court of Auditors

The Court of Auditors[1] was set up by the Treaty amending Certain Financial Provisions of the European Treaties and the Merger Treaty.[2] Previously a simple organ of the Community, it was "upgraded" to "institution" by the Maastricht Treaty.[3] Its task is to "carry out the audit". Since it is an institution, albeit without the power to issue binding acts, which could be challenged in the courts, it has nonetheless the power to go to court, like the Parliament and the ECB, for the purpose of protecting its prerogatives.[4]

1. Members of the Court of Auditors

The Court of Auditors consists of 15 members appointed for a term of six years by the Council, after consultation of Parliament. They are chosen from among persons who belong or have belonged, in their respective countries, to external audit bodies or who are especially qualified for this office.

Their independence, like that of the members of the Commission and the Judges, must be beyond doubt. Similarly, they must be completely independent in the performance of their duties, not take any instructions, engage in no other occupation, give a solemn undertaking on entering upon their duties and behave with integrity and discretion during and also after their term of office.[5]

---

[1] Art. 246 (ex 118a) E.C.

[2] This Treaty was signed at Brussels on July 22, 1975, but entered into force only on June 1, 1977 ([1977] O.J. L359/20), see Art. 15.

[3] Art. 7(1) (ex 4(1)) E.C.

[4] Art. 230(3) (ex 173) E.C., which did not provide for it.

[5] Art. 247(2) to (5) (ex 188b(2) to (5)) E.C. The only difference between their nomination and that of the members of the Commission, is that the latter are appointed by the Member States, and not, as here, by the Council.

2. Tasks of the Court of Auditors[6]

The Court of Auditors examines the accounts of all revenue and expenditure of the Community and of all bodies[7] set up by the Community, unless this is explicitly excluded.

It must present Parliament and the Council with a "statement of assurance as to the reliability of the accounts and the legality and regularity of the underlying transactions".

It shall examine the legality and regularity of all income and expenditure and whether the financial management was sound. The auditors have the right to examine all records and visit all the premises of the Community; with regard to the Member States, the audit must be carried out in liaison with the national audit bodies. The institutions and the Member States must forward to the Court of Auditors any document and information necessary to carry out its task.

The Court of Auditors draws up an annual report which is published, with the observations of the various institutions, in the *Official Journal*. Although this is not provided for in the Treaty, the Court of Auditors also publishes its own replies to those observations, which leaves the institutions at a disadvantage, since they have no possibility of making their views on those answers known. It may also submit special reports on specific questions and deliver opinions at the request of another institution.

Its role can best be summarised, in the words of the Treaty, as "assisting the European Parliament and the Council in exercising their powers of control over the implementation of the budget".[8]

The Court of Auditors is situated in Luxembourg.

---

[6] Art. 248 (ex 188c) E.C.

[7] See Reports on the financial statements and management of 10 bodies set up by the Community [1998] O.J. C406/1 to 55.

[8] Art. 248(4) (ex 188c) E.C. For the Special Reports see, *e.g.* [1994] O.J. C13/1 concerning business and innovation centres.

Chapter Ten
Other Bodies of the Community

1. The Economic and Social Committee (ESC)

The Economic and Social Committee[1] plays a consultative role mainly within the decision-making process of the Community: it must be consulted by the Council or by the Commission where the Treaty so provides. It may be consulted by the Parliament. If the Council fails to consult it when it is provided for by the Treaty, the final act can be annulled by the Court for infringement of an essential procedural requirement[2]; the required consultation must also be referred to in the relevant Community act.[3]

The Committee may also be consulted, either by the Council or the Commission, in all cases in which they consider it appropriate. At the 1972 Paris Summit meeting, the Heads of State or Government decide to invite "the Community institutions to recognise the right of the Economic and Social Committee in future to advise on its own initiative on all questions affecting the Community".[4]

The Committee is composed of 222 members appointed for four years by the Council in their personal capacity[5]; they may not be bound by mandatory instructions. The members are representatives of various categories of economic and social activities, in particular: producers, farmers, carriers, workers, tradesmen, craftsmen, members of the professions and the general public.[6]

---

[1] Art. 257 (ex 193) E.C.

[2] See Chapter Eight "Court of Justice, Grounds for annulment".

[3] Chapter Three "Community Acts: Regulations, etc., must be reasoned".

[4] See the own-initiative opinions in [1988] O.J. C95, C134 and C318.

[5] The large countries each nominate 24 members, Spain 21, Belgium, Greece, The Netherlands, Austria, Portugal and Sweden 12, Denmark, Ireland and Finland nine and Luxembourg six. See Case 297/86 *CIDA v. Council* [1988] E.C.R. 3549; [1989] 3 C.M.L.R. 851, asking for annulment of the Council's decision nominating the members. Case T–382/94 *Confindustria* [1996] E.C.R. II–519, Art. 258 (ex 194) E.C.

[6] For further information on the Committee's composition and activities, see its annual report and the accounts published in the Bulletin of the European Communities.

The Economic and Social Committee has its seat in Brussels.

For public access to ESC documents, see Decision of March 27, 1997.[7]

2. The Committee of the Regions

This Committee was established by the Maastricht Treaty and is composed of representatives of regional and local bodies; it has an advisory status.[8]

Like the Economic and Social Committee, it has 222 members,[9] but also an equal number of alternate members, appointed for four years by the Council on proposal from the respective Member States. The members may not be bound by any mandatory instructions; they must be completely independent in the performance of their duties, in the general interest of the Community.

There are several cases where consultation of the Committee of the regions is provided for by the Treaty.[10]

See decision of September 17, 1997 concerning public access to documents of the Committee of the regions.[11]

3. The Consultative Committee of the ECSC

The ECSC Treaty[12] provides for the creation of a Consultative Committee attached to the High Authority, now the Commission. It consists of between 72 and 96 members made up of an equal number of producers, workers, consumers and dealers. They are appointed for two years in their personal capacity by the Council from a list drawn up by representative organisations also designated by the

---

[7] [1997] O.J. L339/18.

[8] Art. 263 (ex 198a) E.C.

[9] For the numbers of seats attributed to each Member State; see Art. 263(2) (ex 198a(2)) E.C., they are the same as for the ESC.

[10] Implementation of the transport policy: Art 71(1) (ex 75) E.C.; the social provisions: Art. 137(3) (ex 118) E.C.; education, vocational training and youth: Art. 150(4) (ex 127) E.C.; public health: Art. 152(4) (ex 129) E.C.; Trans-European Networks: Art.156 (ex 129d) E.C.; economic and social cohesion: Art.158 (ex 130a) E.C.; actions outside the structural funds: Art 159(3) (ex 130b) E.C.; definition of tasks, priority objectives and organisation of the structural funds: Art. 161(1) (ex 130d) E.C.; implementing decisions concerning the ERDF: Art. 162(1) (ex 130e) E.C. and the environment: Art. 175(1) (ex 130s) E.C.

[11] [1997] O.J. L351/70.

[12] Arts 18 and 19 ECSC.

Council. The functions of the Consultative Committee are comparable in every respect to those of the Economic and Social Committee.[13]

4. The Scientific and Technical Committee of Euratom

This Committee, set up by the Euratom Treaty,[14] is attached to the Commission; it consists of 33 members appointed for five years in their personal capacity by the Council after consultation with the Commission. It has an advisory status. The Commission must consult it *inter alia* before setting up the Joint Nuclear Research Centre and before working out the basic standards for the protection of the health of workers and the general public against dangers arising from ionising radiations.[15]

5. The European System of Central Banks and the European Central Bank (as its forerunner the European Monetary Institute)

The European Monetary Institute (EMI), the European System of Central Banks (ESCB) and the European Central Bank (ECB) were established by the Maastricht Treaty.[16] They exercise their powers and carry out their tasks to implement the Economic and Monetary Policy of the Community which will be examined hereafter within that framework. The institutional aspects shall be briefly described here.

Institutional Provisions concerning the EMI, ESCB and the ECB

The EMI[17] took up its duties at the start of the second stage of the EMU. It had legal personality and was directed and managed by a

---

[13] See, *e.g.* opinion on the market of solid fuels in the Community ([1992] E.C. Bull. 3–49) and Resolution on coal policy in the internal market ([1992] O.J. C94).

[14] Art. 134 Euratom.

[15] See, *e.g.* Directive 84/467/Euratom [1984] O.J. L265.

[16] Art. 8 (ex 4a) E.C. and Statute of the ESCB and of the ECB annexed to the Treaty.

[17] Art. 117 (ex 109f) E.C. See Decision 9/97 concerning public access to administrative documents of the EMI [1998] O.J. L90/43.

Council consisting of a President and the Governors of the national central banks, one of whom was Vice-President appointed by the Council.

The President was appointed by the European Council on the recommendation of the *Committee of Governors* (which was dissolved at the start of the second stage), after consulting Parliament and the Council. The President was chosen from among persons of recognised standing and professional experience in monetary and banking matters. Its Statute is laid down in a Protocol annexed to the Treaty.

At the start of the third stage it was replaced by the ECB[18]; as was decided by the European Council on October 29, 1993, the seat of the EMI, and consequently of the ECB is in Frankfurt.

The ESCB,[19] which began operation at the start of the third stage, is composed of the ECB and the national central banks; it has legal personality.

The ECB, which replaced the EMI at the start of the third stage, is headed by a *Governing Council* and an *Executive Board*.[20]

The Governing Council consists of the members of the Executive Board and the Governors of the national central banks. The Executive Board comprises the President, the Vice-President and four other members of the Governing Council. They are appointed for eight years from among "persons of recognised standings and professional experience in monetary and banking matters", by common accord of the governments of the Member States. The appointments are decided by the latter at the level of the European Council, on a recommendation of the Council. The latter must first consult Parliament and the Governing Council.

The meetings of the Governing Council may be attended, without voting right, by the President of the Council and a member of the Commission.[21] The President of the ECB shall be invited to attend meetings of the Council when the latter discusses matters relating to the objectives and tasks of the ESCB.

Clearly everything has been provided to establish close links both with the highest national monetary institutions and the highest political decision-making authorities within the Community.

The ECB addresses an annual report to Parliament, the European Council, the Council and the Commission. This report is presented

---

[18] Art. 123(2) (ex 1091(2)) E.C.

[19] Art. 107 (ex 106) E.C.

[20] Art. 112(1) (ex 109a(1)) E.C. Rules of Procedure [1998] O.J. L338/28.

[21] Art. 113(1) (ex 109b(1)) E.C.

by the President to the Council and to Parliament, which may hold a general debate on that basis.

A *Monetary Committee* with advisory status was set up to promote co-ordination of the policies of Member States to the full extent needed for the functioning of the internal market.[22] Its tasks are to keep under review the monetary and financial situation of the Member States and the Community and the general payments system of the Member States and to report thereon to the Council and the Commission, deliver opinions, contribute to the work of the Council regarding movement of capital, the guidelines for the economic policies of the Member States, access to financial institutions, commitments of public authorities, government deficits and the transitional provisions of the Economic and Monetary Union (EMU). At the start of the third stage the monetary Committee was replaced by an *Economic and Financial Committee*, with similar tasks.[23]

The composition of the Committee is decided by the Council on a proposal from the Commission and after Consulting the ECB and the Monetary Committee.

6. The European Investment Bank

(1) Task

The task of the European Investment Bank (EIB)[24] is to contribute to the balanced and steady development of the common market in the interest of the Community. It does so by having recourse to the capital market and utilising its own resources on a non-profit-making basis. Notwithstanding this obligation, it follows from the decision of the Board of Governors that there was, for 1996 alone for instance, a so-called operating surplus of one billion ECUs.[25]

The capital of the Bank is subscribed by the Member States, which are liable only up to the amount of their share of the capital subscribed and not paid up.[26] The subscribed capital is paid up by the Member States to the extent of slightly more than 9 per cent.[27]

---

[22] Art. 114(1) (ex 109c(1)) E.C.

[23] Art. 114(2) (ex 109c(2)) E.C.

[24] Art. 226 (ex 198d) E.C. and Protocol annexed to the Treaty. Those provisions were not modified by the Amsterdam Treaty.

[25] [1997] O.J. C211/6.

[26] Art. 4, Statute.

[27] Art. 5(1), Statute.

However, instead of "paying up", the Board of Governors decided in June 1997 that the remaining contributions would be financed using part of the proceeds of the operating surplus for 1996. The legality of this measure can be questioned.[28]

At the occasion of the last increase in the capital of the EIB, the Board of Governors took a number of related decisions laying down a "Strategic Framework for the Bank".[29] This follows the invitation of the Amsterdam European Council to the Bank to step up its activities, with special reference to a number of sectors, in order to promote the creation of employment. Accordingly, the Bank introduced its Amsterdam Special Action Programme (ASAP), involving the creation of a special SME window, the development and reinforcement of EIB activities in the sectors of education, health, urban environment and environmental protection and, a new impetus to the financing of trans-European networks and other large infrastructure networks. It is against this background that the Board of Directors has discussed the strategic framework, the main pillars of which are the following:

- concentration on 'peripheral economic areas';
- continuing support to key E.U. policy areas such as development of TENs, international competitiveness, SMEs, energy and the environment.

This must be viewed in the light of recent developments, *i.e.* recognition that the disciplines of EMU must be accompanied by a concerted policy to reduce unemployment and the Council's decision on enlargement.[30]

The EIB shall grant loans and give guarantees which facilitate the financing of:

(a) projects for developing less-developed regions[31];
(b) projects for modernising and converting undertakings, under certain conditions; and
(c) projects of common interest to several Member States which cannot be financed by individual States.

---

[28] [1997] O.J. C211/16.
[29] [1998] O.J. C269/9.
[30] For further details on this important document, see [1998] O.J. C269/89.
[31] The Commission finances similar projects with the European Regional Development Fund (ERDF), hence the need for close co-operation between the Commission and the EIB.

In carrying out its task the Bank must facilitate the financing of investment programmes in conjunction with assistance from the structural funds[32] and other Community financial instruments.[33]

The EIB grants loans to its members (the Member States), and private and public undertakings for investment projects to be carried out, unless authorised by the Board of Governors, in the European territories of the Member States.[34] As far as possible, loans are granted only on condition that other sources of finance are also used.[35] When granting a loan to a body other than a Member State, it is conditional on an adequate guarantee, for example, from the Member State where the project is to be carried out.[36] The necessary funds are borrowed on the international capital markets or those of the Member States.[37]

(2) Procedure for Granting Loans

Requests for loans are sent either directly or through the Commission or the Member State concerned. Decisions regarding applications for loans or guarantees[38] are taken by the Board of Directors on a proposal from the Management Committee. Before deciding on the financing of a project the Bank must secure the opinion of the interested Member State and the Commission. If the latter delivers an unfavourable opinion, the Board of Directors may not grant the loan (or guarantee) unless its decision is unanimous, the director nominated by the Commission abstaining.

Originally the bank was mainly intended to provide financial resources for the economic development of Southern Italy, the Mezzogiorno. This is still the case today, but other regions have been added, first by the successive enlargements of the Community and secondly by the economic crisis of the 1970s. About three-quarters

[32] The ERDF, the Social Fund and the Guidance Section of the European Agricultural Guarantee and Guidance Fund (EAGGF).

[33] *e.g.* the Cohesion Fund.

[34] Art. 18(1), Statute.

[35] *ibid.* at (2).

[36] *ibid.* at (3). See Council Decision of April 14, 1997 granting a Community guarantee to the EIB against losses under loans for projects outside the Community: Central and Eastern European countries, Mediterranean countries, Latin American and Asian countries and South Africa [1997] O.J. L102/33.

[37] In 1997, the EIB granted loans totalling 26.2 billion ECUs and it borrowed a total of 23 billion ECUs.

[38] The Bank may also guarantee loans contracted by public or private undertakings or other bodies; Art. 18(4), Statute.

of the Bank's loans go to the development regions of the Community[39] as a means of increasing economic and social cohesion. From there the necessity to co-ordinate those activities vary closely with those of the other structural funds.

(3) Internal Structure of the EIB

The Bank is directed and managed by a Board of Governors, a Board of Directors and a Management Committee. The Board of Governors consists of the Ministers of Finance of the Member States. It lays down general directives for the credit policy of the Bank; it also decides on possible increases in the subscribed capital,[40] on grants of special interest-bearing loans to the Bank to finance specific projects by Member States and on the granting of loans for investment projects to be carried out entirely or partially outside the European territory of the Member States.

The Board of Directors consists of 25 directors and 13 alternates nominated by each Member State and the Commission and appointed by the Board of Governors for five years. The Management Committee consists of a President and seven Vice-Presidents appointed for six years by the Board of Governors. The Management Committee is responsible for the current business of the Bank under the authority of the President and the supervision of the Board of Directors. The officials and other employees of the Bank are not servants of the Community, but under contract to the Bank.

A Committee of three members verifies annually that the operations of the Bank have been conducted and its books kept in a proper manner.

The Bank has legal personality and its members are the Member States. Its Statute is laid down in a Protocol annexed to the Treaty.

The EIB is submitted to the jurisdiction of the Court.[41]

In 1997, the Management Committee adopted Rules on public access to documents.[42]

---

[39] In 1998, out of 17 billion euros lent in the Community, 72 per cent went in loans for regional development.

[40] 98 billion euros.

[41] See, *e.g.* Case C–370/89 *SGEEM v. EIB* [1992] I E.C.R. 6211.

[42] [1997] O.J. C243/13.

7. The European Bank for Reconstruction and Development (EBRD)

The Agreement establishing the EBRD entered into force on March 28, 1991.[43] The EBRD was set up to finance economic development projects in Central and Eastern Europe. With a capital of euro 10 billion it promotes the development of the private sector, to which at least 60 per cent of its committed funds must go; however, it presently accounts for less than half that figure, due in particular to the slow development of the private sector in the countries in which the Bank is active, to the difficulties which privatisation programmes are encountering and to the limited scale of private-sector projects compared with those in the public sector. The capital was contributed initially by 41 shareholders, *i.e.* 39 countries, the E.C. in its own right and the EIB. The bulk (over 75 per cent) comes from Europe (51 per cent from the Community and its Member States; the balance is contributed by the non-European countries, in particular America and Japan). The Bank has the right to grant loans to acquire holdings using funds raised on capital markets. The Community maintains its support to the Bank, particularly by providing almost euro 40 million from the Phare and Tacis budgets for financing its technical assistance operations.

[43] [1991] O.J. L107/52. See General Reports: Twenty-fourth, 51; Twenty-fifth, 22 and Twenty-seventh, 28.

Chapter Eleven
Decentralised Community Agencies

1. Europol

It was established in 1995 by a Council act consisting in a convention concluded by the Member States and based on the E.U. Treaty, the "Europol Convention".[1] It became operational on October 10, 1998, after ratification by the 15 Member States. Some of its tasks are now provided for in the E.U. Treaty, such as the collection, storage, processing, analysis and exchange of relevant information including information held by law enforcement services.[2]

The Council, on the other hand, must promote cooperation through Europol, and was given five years to:

- enable Europol to facilitate, support and encourage the coordination and carrying out of specific investigative actions, including operational actions of joint teams comprising representatives of Europol in a support capacity;
- allow Europol to ask the competent authorities of the Member States to conduct and co-ordinate their investigations in specific cases and develop specific expertise which may be put at the disposal of said authorities to assist them in investigating cases of organised crime;
- promote liaison arrangements between prosecuting/investigating officials specialising in the fight against organised crime in close co-operation with Europol.

A protocol on the interpretation, by way of preliminary ruling[3] by the Court of Justice of the Europol Convention was accepted by all the Member States, except the U.K.

[1] [1995] O.J. C 316/2.
[2] Art. 30 (ex K.2) TEU.
[3] See under "Court of Justice".

2. The European Agency for Safety and Health at Work

The Agency[4] started work in 1996 and is based in Bilbao, Spain.

The object of the Agency is to encourage improvements in the working environment. It shall provide the Community bodies, the Member States and those involved in health and safety at work with the technical, scientific and economic information of use in the field of safety and health at work.

The Agency is managed by a Director and has a Board, which is made up of representatives of the governments, employers and workers from the Member States and representatives of the Commission.

3. The Office for Harmonisation in the Internal Market (Trade Marks, Designs and Models)

The Office for the Harmonisation in the Internal Market (OHIM) was established on December 22, 1993.[5] The Office shall grant a uniform Community-wide protection which shall allow its owner to prohibit the use of the mark, design or model for similar goods and services.

Before granting the protection, the Office shall examine whether any absolute motive prevents the grant from being made; the latter can also be withdrawn, for instance, if the owner does not make use of it for five years, or if someone else proves prior claim. The protection is granted for a renewable period of 10 years, to anyone having his domicile in one of the Member States, or in one of the countries party to the Paris Convention on the protection of industrial property rights. There is a right to appeal at every stage of the procedure, before the appeal chamber.[6] It is possible to appeal the decisions of the appeal chamber in the Community courts. In some cases, national courts are competent to hear the appeals.

The Community protection does not replace the existing national

---

[4] Reg. 2062/94 [1994] O.J. L216/1.

[5] Reg. 40/94 on the Community Trade Mark [1994] O.J. L11/1.

[6] See Order of the President of the CFI of June 19, 1997, Case T–159/97 R *Chaves Fonsica Ferrao v. OHIM* [1997] E.C.R. II-1049, concerning the independence of the members of the appeal chamber. See also Rules of Procedure of the Board of Appeal: Reg. 216/96, [1996] O.J. L28/11.

protections, and the economic operators have the choice between the two. They shall be able to present their request in one of the eleven languages of the Community, but the working languages shall be limited to German, English, French, Spanish or Italian.

The Office is situated in Alicante (Spain), and started operating on April 1, 1996.

4. THE EUROPEAN AGENCY FOR THE EVALUATION OF MEDICINAL PRODUCTS

The Council laid down Community procedures for the authorisation and supervision of medicinal products for human and veterinary use and for establishing a European Agency for the Evaluation of Medicinal Products.[7]

Since 1995, the Community has had a twin-track approach to drug licensing. Companies will be able to submit a conventional medicine either to the EMEA (the "centralised" route) or to one of the 15 national regulatory agencies (the "decentralised" route).

In 1993 the existing Community pharmaceutical legislation was amended to create a new "mutual recognition" procedure for the authorisation of human and veterinary medicinal products, based on the principle of mutual recognition of national authorisations with binding Community arbitration in the event of disagreement between Member States.[8] At the end of the mutual recognition procedure, there will be only one brand name approved per market and authorisation granted (national marketing authorisation), which is consistent with the current provisions of Community law. A supplementary protection certificate for medicinal products was created in 1992[9]; the Court decided that it could only be granted if a market authorisation had been given by the Member State in which the application is made.[10]

A fee, the amount of which was laid down by the Council,[11] has to be paid to the Agency for each request of authorisation.

The Agency is situated in London.

---

[7] Reg. 2309/93 [1993] O.J. L214/1. See, for instance, Summary of Community decisions on marketing authorisations in respect of medicinal products, taken pursuant to Art. 12 or 34 of Reg. 2309/93.

[8] Dirs 93/39, 93/40 and 93/41, O.J. L214/22, 31 and 40.

[9] Reg. 1768/92, [1992] O.J. L182/1.

[10] Case C–110/95 *Yamanouchi* [1997] E.C.R. I–3251; [1997] 3 C.M.L.R. 749.

[11] Reg. 297/95, [1995] O.J. L35/1; amended by Reg. 2743/98, [1998] O.J. L345/3.

5. The Office for Veterinary and Plant-Health Inspection and Control

In 1991 the Commission approved the establishment of the Office for Veterinary and Plant-Health Inspection and Control.[12] This Office is not an independent body, but part of the Commission services: Directorate General XXIV: Consumer Policy and Consumer Health Protection. It is indeed "decentralised" in so far as the Office is situated in Dublin. As its title indicates, it carries out inspections within the Union and outside to ensure that in the food chain the rules on hygiene and food safety are respected.

6. The European Monitoring Centre for Drugs and Drug Addiction (EDMC)[13]

The Centre's objective is to provide the Community and its Member States with objective, reliable and comparable information at European level concerning drugs and drug addiction and their consequences. Its tasks are:

(a) collection and analysis of existing data;
(b) improvement of data-comparison methods;
(c) dissemination of data; and
(d) co-operation with European and international bodies and organisations and with non-Community countries.

It has legal personality, has a Management Board, a Director and a Scientific Committee and is submitted to the jurisdiction of the Court. It became operational in December 1993, *i.e.* after the Member States agreed on its location: Lisbon.

7. The European Training Foundation

The purpose of this foundation[14] is to help the countries of central and eastern Europe with professional training. It must therefore

---

[12] Com. Dec. of December 18, 1991.
[13] Reg. 302/93, [1993] O.J. L36/1, modified by Reg. 22/94, [1994] O.J. L341/7.
[14] Reg. 1360/90: [1990] O.J. L131/1.

define the requirements, serve as a clearing house for information in this field, examine the possibility of creating joint enterprises, finance projects, fix the conditions for such financing, control the expenditure, disseminate information and exchanges and fulfil any other task assigned to it by the Commission.

It is managed by a Management Council, a Consultative Committee and a Director. With regard to non-contractual liability it is submitted to the jurisdiction of the Court. See the Decision of the Governing Board on public access to EFT documents.[14a]

Its seat is in Turin.

8. European Centre for the Development of Vocational Training

The Centre was set up in 1975.[15] It is a scientific and technical body entrusted with promoting, at Community level, the exchange of information and experience, the distribution of documentation and the launching of research and experimental projects to facilitate the attainment of vocational training objectives set by the Treaty.

The Centre is endowed with legal personality to ensure its independence.

The Management Board consists of representatives of the Member States, worker's organisations, employer's organisations and the Commission.

The Centre has its own budget.[16] Its seat was recently transferred from Berlin to Thessaloniki.

9. Translation Centre for Bodies of the Union

A Translation Centre will be set up within the Commission's Translation Departments located in Luxembourg and will provide the necessary translation services for the operation of the bodies and departments whose seats have been determined by the Decision of October 29, 1993, with the exception of the translators of the European Monetary Institute.[17]

[14a] [1997] O.J. C369/10.

[15] Reg. 337/75, [1975] O.J. L39/1; last modified, [1995] O.J. L41/1.

[16] See statement of revenue and expenditure for 1994 ([1994] O.J. L35/1), which constitutes an annex to the Community budget.

[17] Declaration of the Member States, [1993] O.J. C323/5. Reg. 2965/94; [1994] O.J. L314/1 amended by Reg. 2610/95, [1995] O.J. L268/1.

The seat of the Centre is in Luxembourg.

10. The European Environment Agency and the European Environment Information and Observation Network

The objective of the Agency[18] is to provide the Community and the Member States with objective and reliable information at the European level in order to allow them to take the necessary measures to protect the environment, to evaluate their implementation and to ensure that correct information reaches the public on the state of the environment. Its main tasks are:

(a) establish an Information and Observation Network;
(b) provide the information necessary to formulate and implement efficient environmental policies;
(c) register, check and evaluate environmental data;
(d) ensure the comparability of the data at European level;
(e) integrate the European information into international programmes;
(f) disseminate the information;
(g) precipitate the development of methods for calculating the damage caused to the environment; etc.

The agency is situated in Copenhagen.

11. Community Plant Variety Office

This Office was set up by the Regulation on Plant Variety Rights[19] and the rules for the proceedings before the Office were published in 1995.[20]

The Parliament and the Council created a supplementary protection certificate for plant protection products,[21] indicating that the

[18] Reg. 1210/90, [1990] O.J. L120/1.
[19] Art. 30 of Reg. 2100/94 on Community Plant Variety Rights, [1994] O.J. L227/1, amended by Reg. 2506/95, [1995] O.J. L258/37.
[20] Reg. 1239/95, [1995] O.J. L121/37, amended by Reg. 448/96, [1996] O.J. L62/3. See also Dir. 91/414 concerning the placing of plant protection products on the market, [1991] O.J. L230/1 and Dir. 97/57 establishing Annex IV, [1997] O.J. L265/87.
[21] Reg. 1610/96, [1996] O.J. L198/30.

competitiveness of the plant protection sector, by the very nature of the industry, requires a level of protection for innovation, which is equivalent to that granted by the Council when creating a supplementary protection certificate for medicinal products.[22]

The Office is situated at Angers (France).

12. The European Foundation for the Improvement of Living and Working Conditions

It was set up in 1975 with seat in Ireland.[23] The Foundation deals specifically with the following issues: men at work; organisation at work and particularly job design; problems peculiar to certain categories of workers; long-term aspects of the improvement of the environment; and spacial distribution of human activities and their distribution in time.

The structure is similar to that of the CEDEFOP.[24]

13. Euratom's Agency

Established in the Euratom Treaty, the Agency has a right of option on ores, source materials and special fissile materials produced in the territories of the Member States and an exclusive right to conclude contracts relating to the supply of those materials coming from inside or outside the Community.[25] However, the Agency is entitled to refuse to purchase on grounds of origin of fuel[26] and is not obliged to guarantee disposal of uranium output accumulated by Community producers.[27]

The Agency has legal personality and is situated in Brussels.

---

22 See above under European Agency for the Evaluation of Medicinal Products.

23 Reg. 1365/75, [1975] O.J. L139/1, amended [1993] O.J. L181/3.

24 See Statement of revenue and expenditure, n.16, *id.* See also Case T–589/93 *Ryan-Sheridan*, Staff Cases [1996] E.C.R. II–77.

25 Article 52(2)(b), Euratom. See also Arts 53–56 *ibid.*

26 Joined Cases T–149 and T–181/94, *Lippe-EMS* [1997] E.C.R. II–161; [1997] 3 C.M.L.R. 136.

27 Case C–357/95P, *ENU* [1997] E.C.R. I–1329; [1997] 3 C.M.L.R. 95.

14. The European Monitoring Centre on Racism and Xenophobia

The Centre was set up in 1997[28] and its task is to provide the Community and the Member States with objective, reliable and comparable data at European level on the phenomena of racism, xenophobia and anti-Semitism. It must study the extent, development, causes and effect of the said phenomena in the following fields:

- free movement of persons,
- information, TV and the media,
- education, vocational training and youth,
- social policy, including employment,
- free movement of goods, and
- culture.

Further Reading

Jackie Jones, "The Committee of the Regions, Subsidiarity and a Warning" [1997] 22 E.L.Rev. 312.

[28] Reg. 1035/97, [1997] O.J. L151/1.

Chapter Twelve
Financing Community Activities

1. Financial Contributions of the Member States and the Community's own Resources

The Decision on the Replacement of Financial Contributions from Member States, which was the original way of financing Community activities, by the Community's own Resources[1] inaugurated a new era in the history of the Communities. On the one hand, it made them, in a certain way, financially independent, with all the economic and political consequences this entails. On the other hand, the Treaty of April 22, 1970 amending Certain Budgetary Provisions of the ECSC, EEC and Euratom Treaties and of the Merger Treaty, conferred at the same time certain budgetary powers upon Parliament, as a necessary complement to the transfer of resources to the Community.[2]

In 1975 the budgetary provisions were again modified and complemented by the creation of the Court of Auditors.[3]

The Decision of April 21, 1970

The main features of this decision can be summarised as follows:

(a) Both the agricultural levies and the Common Customs Tariff duties constitute own resources to be entered in the budget of the Community;

(b) The transfer of revenue from customs duties takes place progressively over a period of four years. From then on the

[1] Dec. 70/243 of April 21, 1970, [1970] J.O. L94/19; [1970] (1) O.J. 224; it became effective on January 1, 1971 after ratification by the six national Parliaments.

[2] This Treaty became effective on January 1, 1971. The budgetary powers of Parliament are analysed above under "The European Parliament, (9) Participation in the budgetary procedure".

[3] Treaty amending Certain Financial Provisions of the Treaties establishing the European Communities and the Merger Treaty of July 22, 1975 [1977] O.J. L359/1.

budget of the Community is, save other revenue,[4] entirely financed from own resources.

(c) Since revenue accruing from the duties and levies does not suffice to cover the expenditures of the Community, revenue from the Value Added Tax is also allocated.[5]

As from January 1, 1980, the Community's expenditures were entirely financed by the revenue accruing from the agricultural levies, the customs duties and a percentage of the VAT collected in the Member States.

A decision on the system of the Community's own resources, adopted in June 1988,[6] introduced the changes adopted by the European Council at Brussels, in February 1988:

(a) the overall ceiling on own resources is set at 1.20 per cent of total Community GNP for payments (1.30 per cent for commitments), it will be 1.27 per cent in 1999;
(b) customs duties on ECSC products are to be paid to the Community;
(c) the costs of collecting traditional own resources will be deduced from the Member States' payments;
(d) the third source (VAT) will be collected at a rate of 1.4 per cent applied to a VAT base limited to 55 per cent of GNP to take account of the situation of Member States where consumption accounts for a high proportion of GNP; this is to be reduced from 1995 to 50 per cent;
(e) a fourth resource, based on a GNP scale, is introduced.[7]

The Brussels European Council resolved a long standing feud about the Community's own resources which had become insufficient to cover the expenditures. This "liberated" the Community and

---

[4] Other revenues are, *e.g.* the fines imposed upon enterprises for violation of the competition rules and the income-tax levied on the salaries of the officials.

[5] Dir. 77/388 ([1977] O.J. L145/1). The revenue results from the application of a rate not exceeding 1.4 per cent of the basis used for assessing VAT, determined in a uniform manner for the Member States. The decision to increase the rate from 1 per cent to 1.4 per cent from January 1, 1986 and to 1.6 per cent on January 1, 1988 was taken by the European Council at Fontainebleu in June 1984; see [1984] E.C. Bull. 6–11. The Decision of April 21, 1970 was implemented by Reg. 2892/77 ([1977] O.J. L336), see the Commission's report on the implementation of this Regulation: COM(88) 99 final.

[6] Dec. 88/376, [1988] O.J. L185 and [1988] E.C. Bull. 3–105. See Reg. 3464/93 implementing Dec. 88/376, [1993] O.J. L317, and Commission proposal for replacing Dec. 88/376: General Report (1993) 377.

[7] For details see, *e.g.* [1988] E.C. Bull. 2, 13 *et seq*. This resource will become the most important Community resource.

allowed it to go ahead with the completion of the internal market by the end of 1992.

It should also be noted that the "budget correcting mechanism" introduced in 1976 to enable payments to be made to Member States which, due to special economic conditions, are considered to bear a disproportionate burden in financing the budget,[8] will remain applicable. Furthermore, an adjustment was made to offset the effect of the introduction of the fourth resource. Compensation to the United Kingdom[9] is financed on the basis of a GNP scale, Germany's contribution is reduced by a third, and for Spain and Portugal abatement arrangements are applied in accordance with their Act of Accession.[10]

2. The Community Budget, Revenue and Expenditure

As the Commission remarked about the budgetary procedure of 1988: "Thanks to the new instruments governing Community finances the problems which have beset the budgetary procedure in the past were very largely avoided."[11] The Commission was referring to the Interinstitutional Agreement on budgetary discipline and improvement of the budgetary procedure[12] and the Regulation amending the implementing regulation of the Decision of April 21, 1970 creating the Community's own resources.

All items of revenue and expenditure of the three Communities must be included in estimates to be drawn up for each financial year

---

[8] *i.e.* the U.K. General Report (1980), 59; [1980] E.C. Bull. 5–7 and Reg. 2744/80, [1980] O.J. L284/4.

[9] In 1980 agreement was reached on the United Kingdom's contribution to the budget: the financial correcting mechanism was modified to allow a reduction for the U.K. and supplementary Community expenditures were provided for to help reduce certain regional disparities in the U.K. This compensated 66 per cent of the difference between the U.K. VAT transfers and its receipts from the Community. The correction for 1990 was 2,430 million ECUs.

[10] Act of Accession, Arts 187 and 374.

[11] General Report (1988), p. 66.

[12] This agreement came into force on July 1, 1988; [1988] O.J. C142. A novelty is the Financial Perspective 1988–92; another important aspect of the agreement is the mutual obligation to comply with the financing objectives set by the European Council for certain priority policy areas (structural funds, integrated Mediterranean programmes, framework research programme). See [1988] E.C. Bull. 6–112. A new Agreement was signed on October 29, 1993 [1993] O.J. C331 and a new financial framework laid down for 1993–1999 at the Edinburgh European Council; see General Report, 1993, 375.

and be shown in the budget.[13] The revenue and expenditure shown in the budget must be in balance.[14] The financial year runs from January 1 to December 31.[15] The structure of the general budget and the form in which it is to be presented are determined by Financial Regulations.[16] The budget consists of separate sections dealing with the revenue and expenditure of each institution. The section dealing with the Commission provides for expenditure in the following fields: 1. Common agricultural policy (markets, set-aside, income aids, fishery fund), 2. Structural operations (structural funds, support frameworks, fishery guidance, cohesion fund, etc.), 3. Internal policies (all the Community policies described in Part Three of this book), 4. External action (EDF, food aid, co-operation with third countries, common foreign and security policy, etc.), 5. Administrative expenditure of the institutions (salaries, pensions, etc.), 6. Reserves and 7 Compensation. The total budget for 1999 stands at euro 96.928 million in commitment appropriations, and euro 85.557 million in payment appropriations. The latter represents 1.09 per cent of GNP, compared with the own resources ceiling of 1.27 per cent of GPD.

(1) Commitment and Payment Appropriations

The Community budget contains "non-differentiated" and "differentiated" appropriations. Under the former, commitments can be made during the financial year and the corresponding payments can be made practically at the same time, *i.e.* during that financial year and the next. The differentiated appropriations consist of both commitments, *i.e.* the maximum that may be committed during that financial year, and the corresponding payments which may be disbursed either during that same year or at any time thereafter. This system is particularly suited for medium and long term operations such as research projects and infrastructure investments. The advantage of this method is that the total amount of the Community's financial participation can be committed at the start of the

[13] One important item not covered by the Community budget is the European Development Fund (resources destined to finance aid to developing countries); the activities of the European Investment Bank do not appear on the budget either.
[14] Art. 268 (ex 199) E.C. and Art. 20 Merger Treaty.
[15] Art. 272 (ex 203) E.C.
[16] See [1977] O.J. L356/1, Arts 15 and 16. This Regulation was amended in June 1988; see [1988] O.J. L185/3. An up-to-date version was published in [1991] O.J. C80/1.

project but the payments only have to be made as the work progresses over the years.[17]

(2) Compulsory and Non-compulsory Expenditure

The Treaty of July 22, 1975 amending certain financial provisions of the existing Treaties introduced the concept of "expenditure necessarily resulting from this Treaty or from acts adopted in accordance therewith",[18] otherwise referred to as "compulsory" expenditures. A budgetary item is considered compulsory when the principle and the amount of the expenditure (either a figure or a precise mechanism for arriving at it) are statutorily prescribed in the Treaties, secondary legislation, international conventions or private contracts.[19]

A typical example of compulsory expenditures are those of the agricultural fund. Non-compulsory expenditures are practically speaking all the others: regional, social, research and staff appropriations. In practice however, the expenditures are classified in one or the other category in a rather pragmatic way, by agreement between the Council and Parliament. One now even finds "non-privileged" non-compulsory expenditure.[20]

As was pointed out before, the distinction is important with regard to the budgetary powers of Parliament. The final decision concerning non-compulsory expenditure belongs to Parliament, although the possible increase is limited by the maximum annual rate which is established by the Commission on the basis of objective criteria,[21] while the recent Interinstitutional Agreement has imposed a discipline on all the institutions.

---

[17] The commitment and payment appropriations are now used for all expenditures.
[18] Art. 272(4) (ex 203) E.C.
[19] D. Strasser, *The Finances of Europe* (New York, 1977), p. 33. Another definition given by the Council reads: "expenditure in respect of which, by virtue of existing enactments, no budgetary authority, be it the Council or the European Parliament, has the right freely to determine the appropriations". See also the Joint Declaration of Parliament, Council and Commission of June 1982 [1982] E.C. Bull. 6–7.
[20] General Report (1988), 69.
[21] Art. 272(9) (ex 203(9)) E.C.

3. Financial Framework and Inter-institutional Agreement

The Edinburgh European Council of December 1992 agreed on the resources for the financing of the Community in the period 1993–99. This will allow the Community to finance its internal and external policies.

On October 29, 1993, the European Commission, the Council and the European Parliament concluded an Interinstitutional Agreement on budgetary discipline and improvement of the budgetary procedure. This Agreement renews, in accordance with the conclusions of the Edinburgh European Council, the previous Agreement concluded on June 29, 1988. It is intended to ensure, besides what is indicated in the title itself, that, in the medium term, Community expenditure develops within the limits of the own resources. It covers all expenditure.

The Agreement does not, of course, alter the respective budgetary powers of the various institutions as laid down in the Treaty and as described above, in the Chapter on the European Parliament.

The Agreement provides, in the first place, the 1993 to 1999 *Financial Perspective*, which constitutes the reference framework for the interinstitutional budgetary discipline. For each of the years and for each heading and subheading it establishes amounts of expenditure in terms of appropriation commitments, while overall annual totals of expenditure are shown for both commitments and payments appropriations. Each of the absolute amounts represents an annual ceiling on Community expenditure. Yearly adjustments and revisions are provided for.

The Agreement also creates three "reserves". The first is to cover the impact on agricultural expenditures of unforeseen movements in the dollar/ECU parity; the second serves to guarantee loans to non-member countries and the third is destined for emergency aid to non-member countries and foremost for humanitarian operations.

The second main subject of the Agreement is the *improvement of the budgetary procedure*. The institutions, for instance, agree that all expenditure under headings 2 and 3, is "non-compulsory" expenditure: the agricultural guarantee and structural operations. Parliament and Council accept the maximum rate of increase for those expenditures deriving from the budgets established within the ceilings set by the financial perspective. This puts an end to the recurring conflicts between the two budgetary authorities. They also undertake to respect the allocations of commitment appropriations provided in the financial perspective for the Structural Funds and the Cohesion Fund.[22]

Annex two to the Agreement provides for Interinstitutional Collaboration in the budgetary sector. An ad hoc conciliation procedure is set up for compulsory expenditure. The conciliation includes the so-called "trialogue" between the three institutions to seek agreement. The Commission is asked, for instance, to identify appropriations connected with new or planned legislation and will make careful estimates of the financial implications of the Community obligations based on legislation.

The last Annex to the Agreement concerns rules for the treatment of food aid expenditure.

The enormous advantage of the multi-annual planning of expenditure is obvious: it gives the Community a solid base for its future planning and it eliminates the inter-institutional haggling from which the Community suffered for many years.

At the Berlin European Council of March 24–25, 1999[23] it was decided that the new financial perspective should be established for a duration of seven years covering the period 2000–2006. It should be drawn up on the basis of the working assumption of the accession of new Member States starting from 2002. The European Council also hopes that a new Interinstitutional Agreement can be established between the European Parliament, the Council and the Commission on terms ensuring strict budgetary discipline, while preserving the overall balance of powers between the institutions and clearly ring-fencing pre-accession and accession-related expenditure for the entire duration of the financial perspective.

The financial perspective agreed upon in Berlin provides the following amounts for commitments; only the total amount and those for agriculture and the structural funds are given below.

Year	2000	2001	2002	2003	2004	2005	2006
Total	91995	93385	93805	93005	91465	90795	90260
Agriculture	40920	42800	43900	43770	42760	41930	41660
Structural	32045	31455	30865	30285	29595	29595	29170

[22] The Cohesion Fund was established in 1994, Reg. 1164/94; [1994] O.J. L130/1. While awaiting the formal adoption of that Reg., the Council adopted Reg. 792/93 establishing a cohesion financial instrument which enabled projects to be financed from April 1, 1993 [1993] O.J. L79.

[23] See Presidency conclusions: DN: DOC/99/1, March 26, 1999.

Upon enlargement this financial perspective should be adjusted, taking account of the actual number of acceding countries and the maximum amounts set out in the Berlin conclusions.

Further Reading

European Commission, "*European Union Public Finance*", Brussels, Luxembourg, 1995.

PART THREE: THE INTERNAL MARKET

Introduction

Over the past ten to twelve years, the scope of the E.C. Treaty has been continuously extended, first by the Single European Act (SEA) of 1987, then by the Treaty on European Union (TEU or the so-called Maastricht Treaty) of 1992, and finally by the Treaty of Amsterdam (in force since May 1, 1999). Indeed, each time new responsibilities were added to the list of activities of the Communities.[1]

This extension results from the built-in dynamism of the Treaties establishing the European Communities and the political will of the signatories. According to the Preamble of the Amsterdam Treaty the latter were "determined to lay the foundation of an ever closer union among the peoples of Europe".[2] However, the same parties deleted another recital: "[i]n view of further steps to be taken in order to advance European integration", which had become politically unacceptable to certain Member States. Was this then the end of European integration, as was advocated by the so-called Eurosceptics? A few months later, even before the Amsterdam Treaty had been ratified, the greatest step towards this integration was taken when most Member States transferred their monetary sovereignty to the newly set-up European Central Bank! This only shows that the trend is irreversible, even if the ultimate goal is not definitively fixed.

The objectives of the European Community, as set out in the latest Treaty, are to promote throughout the Community:

- a harmonious, balanced and sustainable development of economic activities,
- a high level of employment and of social protection,
- equality between men and women,
- sustainable and non-inflationary growth,
- a high degree of competitiveness and convergence of economic performance,
- a high level of protection and improvement of the quality of the environment,
- the raising of the standard of living and quality of life, and
- economic and social cohesion and solidarity among Member States.

---

[1] Art. 3 (ex 3) E.C. The EEC Treaty provided for 11 activities, the Treaty on European Union increased this to 20 and the Treaty of Amsterdam added a recital on employment.

[2] E.C., Preamble, first recital.

To achieve those objectives, the Community institutions must:

- establish a common market and an economic and monetary union, and
- implement common policies and activities.

Those two means are of a rather different nature, but essentially complementary. The Internal Market which will be examined in this Part Three is included in the common market, which constitutes one of the two elements of the first means.

Chapter Thirteen
The Free Movement of Goods

In the introduction it was pointed out that the Treaty provides for two means to implement the far-reaching objectives of the Community: the common market together with the economic and monetary union, on the one hand, and the common policies and activities, on the other.

The "common market" is nowhere described as such in the Treaty, but it encompasses the "internal market" and the various common policies such as agriculture, competition, regional development, environment and various others.

The "internal market" is defined in the Treaty as "an area without internal borders in which the free movement of goods, persons,[1] services and capital is ensured in accordance with the provisions of this Treaty".[2]

The first of those freedoms: the free movement of goods, means that goods can be shipped unimpeded across the whole Community.[3] This freedom constitutes the point of departure of all the other freedoms and of most, if not all, of the common policies and activities. It is important to see this, since it allows one to understand the logical link, which exists between the many subjects which shall be discussed hereafter. The central idea is that the whole Community constitutes one single economic area similar to a national market,[4]

---

[1] The free movement of "persons" as such, does not exist; it consists of the free movement of "workers" (Arts 39 (ex 48) to 42 (ex 51)) E.C., and the free movement of "self-employed persons". The latter is expressed by the freedom of "establishment" (Arts 43, (ex 52) to 48 (ex 58)) and the freedom to "provide services" (Arts 49 (ex 59) to 55 (ex 66)) E.C. If furthermore, one distinguishes between the free movement of capital and the free movement of payments (Arts 56 (ex 73b) to 60 (ex 73g)) E.C., one comes to a total of six basic freedoms, which constitute the internal market and the nucleus of the common market and the Community itself.

[2] Art. 14(2) (ex 7a(2)) E.C.

[3] For a geographical description of the Community see Art. 299 (ex 227) E.C.

[4] Similar words were used by the Court with regard to the common agricultural policy: Joined Cases 80 and 81/77 *Commissionnaires Réunis v. Receveur des Douanes* [1978] E.C.R. at 946(29).

wherein trade can develop without obstacles. These therefore had to be eliminated.

It is generally admitted that free trade contributes to the creation of wealth, *i.e.* employment and rising standards if living, which are objectives of the Community. Any producer within the Community now has a potential market of around 380 million customers, which should allow him, *inter alia*, to fully use the advantages of the economies of scale, and every consumer is free to "shop" wherever he can obtain the best conditions.

The establishment of this single market required not only the elimination of all existing obstacles to free trade, *i.e.* tariff, as well as non-tariff barriers and indirect obstacles such as state monopolies, agreements between undertakings, abuses of dominant position, mergers and acquisitions, state aids and fiscal discriminations. It also, of course, called for the adoption of measures to prevent the creation of new barriers.

Under the heading "free movement of goods" the Treaty provides in Title I of Part Three, that the "Community shall be based upon a customs union which shall cover all trade in goods and which shall involve the prohibition between Member States of customs duties on imports and exports and of all charges having equivalent effect, and the adoption of a common customs tariff in their relations with third countries".[5] The same Title also provides that "quantitative restrictions on imports and all measures having equivalent effect shall be prohibited between the Member States".[6]

The elimination of the tariff barriers will be very briefly examined in the next section on the Customs Union, and the non-tariff barriers will be analysed in the section on the elimination of quantitative restrictions and measures having equivalent effect. On the other hand, the competition rules, the tax provisions and the approximation of laws, which also guarantee equal market access for all, will be examined in Part Four "Other Community policies".

1. The Customs Union

The free movement of goods thus requires in the first place the creation of a customs union involving;

- the prohibition of customs duties and of all charges having equivalent effect, and

[5] Art. 23 (ex 9) E.C.
[6] Art. 28 (ex 30) E.C.

– the adoption of a common customs tariff in the relations with third countries.[7]

By "goods" must be understood "products which can be valued in money and which are capable, as such, of forming the subject of commercial transactions".[8] They are both industrial and agricultural[9] goods, whether originating in the Member States or imported from third countries.[10] Where imported goods are concerned, as soon as the import formalities have been complied with and all customs duties and charges have been paid—and not reimbursed—those imports are "in free circulation" just like Community goods. There is one exception: it concerns protective measures which the Commission might authorise a Member State to take to ensure that goods imported from third countries into another Member State do not obstruct its own commercial policy measures taken in accordance with the Treaty.[11]

(1) Prohibition of Customs Duties and Charges Having Equivalent Effect

Customs duties on imports and exports and charges having equivalent effect are prohibited between Member States.[12] The Amsterdam version of the relevant Treaty provisions is quite different from the preceding ones. The latter set out in detail how those duties and charges were to be abolished progressively; nothing of the sort in the actual Treaty text, although those rules will necessarily apply to any new Member State. The Customs Union among the original six

[7] Without this CCT products from third countries would all enter the Community through the country with the lowest tariffs, since, once inside, those products can circulate freely throughout the whole Community. This would deflect trade from the other Member States. See also Art. 134 (ex 115) E.C.: measures of commercial policy and deflexion of trade.

[8] Case 7/68 *Commission v. Italy* [1968] E.C.R. 423 at 428. See also the definition in case C–2/90 *Commission v. Belgium* [1992] E.C.R. I–4466(26): "all objects, which are being shipped across a frontier for the purpose of commercial transactions, are subject to Article 30 [now 28] E.C. whatever the nature of those transactions" (here negative value of the product).

[9] See "Agriculture" below; the inclusion of agricultural products was not evident at the onset.

[10] The inclusion of imported products into the Customs Union is what distinguishes the latter from a "free trade area" where only products originating within the Member States are included; this is because there is no CCT; see EFTA Treaty, Article 4.

[11] Art. 134 (ex 115) E.C.

[12] Art. 25 (ex 12 and 13) E.C.

Member States was established over a period of ten-and-a-half years, shorter than the twelve years provided for in the original Treaty.

The ban applies also, as indicated, to "charges having equivalent effect". The latter have been defined by the Court as any levy imposed by a Member State on a product at the occasion of it crossing a border, and which, although not formally designated as a customs duty (*i.e.* appearing on a tariff list), alters its cost price, and thus produces the same restrictive effect on the free movement of goods as a customs duty.[13]

Unless the charge is a consideration for a benefit provided for the importer or exporter,[14] it is prohibited.[15] The concept "charge having an equivalent effect" gave rise to an abundant case law and in one of its first judgments, the Court stated that the Treaty provisions on this point create, for the citizens of the Community, individual rights which the national courts must uphold.[16] In other words, those provisions have "direct effect".[17]

(2) The Common Customs Tariff (CCT)

The CCT constitutes, in the first place, a measure of commercial policy towards the third countries. As was pointed out, the setting up of the CCT had to coincide with the elimination of customs duties and charges among the Member States. This was necessary in order to avoid deflexion of trade. Consequently, it also constitutes an integral part of the Customs Union, which could not have been established without it.

The CCT was adopted by a Council regulation[18] and gradually introduced in parallel with the elimination of the customs duties. Since that time, Member States no longer have jurisdiction over the duties they levy on the goods entering their territory from third countries. They may not modify them, neither interpret[19] them, nor

[13] Case 29/72 *Marimex v. Amministrazione Finanziaria Italiana* [1972] E.C.R. 1309 at 1318(6); [1973] C.M.L.R. 486.

[14] This is not the case, for instance, when the service is rendered in the general interest such as health inspections or charges covering the costs of customs activities: Case C–16/94 *Dubois* [1995] E.C.R. I–2421; [1995] 2 C.M.L.R. 771.

[15] Case 89/76 *Commission v. Netherlands* [1977] E.C.R. 1355.

[16] Case 26/62 *Van Gend & Loos v. Dutch Fiscal Administration* [1963] E.C.R. 1 at 12; [1978] 3 C.M.L.R. 630.

[17] See the Chapter on "Community Law" above.

[18] Reg. 950/68 O.J. L172/1; it was replaced by Reg. 2658/87 [1987] O.J. L256/1 and is regularly updated. See [1997] O.J. L321/1.

[19] Case 38/75 *Nederlandse Spoorwegen v. Inspecteur der Invoerrechten en Accijnzen* [1975] E.C.R. 1439 at 1449(4); [1976] 1 C.M.L.R. 167.

may they keep the proceeds[20] which now belong to the Community as "own resources". Modification or suspension of CCT duties is an exclusive Community matter[21] and is decided by the Council.[22]

Important reductions were introduced following multilateral trade negotiations pursuant to the General Agreement on Tariffs and Trade (GATT, now WTO) such as the Kennedy Round (1964–67), the Tokyo Round (1973–79) and the Uruguay Round (1988–93).

Mention should also be made of the possible exception to the CCT where tariff quotas at reduced rate or zero-rate are provided for.

It should be noted however that, from a commercial point of view, a reduction of customs tariffs is less important than the elimination of non-tariff trade barriers, which are much more difficult to detect. This applies also to trade within the Community itself.

In terms of trade, the creation of the Customs Union has resulted in shifts in the trade patterns, since, generally speaking, industrial goods are less expensive for Community users and consumers when imported from other Member States than from third countries. Also trade among the Member States has grown much faster than trade between the Community and third countries. In relation to the latter, the Community uses the CCT as an instrument to guarantee the effectiveness of its commercial and external policy.

One should also remember that setting identical levels for each external tariff is only a first step towards establishing the CCT. Indeed, the latter also calls for uniform interpretation, continuing administration, harmonisation of customs rules, simplification of checks and formalities and, generally speaking, the reinforcement of the structure of the Customs Union.[23] The Council is to take measures in order to strengthen customs co-operation between Member States and between the latter and the Commission.[24]

---

[20] Except for 10 per cent, which they may keep to cover administrative costs: Council Decision 88/376 [1988] O.J. L185/24.

[21] Case C–126/94 *Cadi Surgelés* [1996] E.C.R. I–5647; [1997] 1 C.M.L.R. 795.

[22] Art. 26 (ex 28) E.C.

[23] See the Convention on the use of information technology for customs purposes and Agreement on provisional application between certain Member States [1995] O.J. C316/33 and 58.

[24] Art. 135 (ex 116) E.C. See Decision of the Parliament and the Council adopting an action programme for customs in the Community (Customs 2000) [1997] O.J. L33/24.

2. Prohibition of Quantitative Restrictions[25]

As was mentioned, the elimination of customs duties and charges having equivalent effect is not sufficient to guarantee the free circulation of goods within the Community. There are indeed many other ways of hindering imports and exports; quotas are one such way, but they have since long been abolished between the Member States. The worst offenders are the so-called "measures having equivalent effect". These are all the measures, which have an effect equivalent to quantitative restrictions on imports and exports, and are not covered by other provisions adopted in pursuance of the E.C. Treaty.[26] They are often referred to as "invisible" trade barriers, since they are, generally speaking, difficult to detect and only discovered by their effects on trade. The latter is disrupted to the prejudice of traders and consumers alike and they must therefore be hunted down by all parties concerned.

The Court[27] has defined those measures as "all trading rules[28] enacted by Member States,[29] which are capable of hindering, directly or indirectly, actually or potentially, intra-Community trade". This means that the prohibition applies not only when this trade is prevented, but already when it is simply made unnecessarily difficult.[30] Secondly, it means that the hindrance does not have to be actual. It suffices that it can be shown that the possibility exists that interstate trade may be hampered. In other words, one does not have to wait till the measure has produced its effects. And it is not necessary that those trading rules should have an appreciable effect on intra-Community trade.[31] Thirdly, the word "indirect" means that there is an infringement of the principle of the free movement of goods even when the hindrance is only indirectly attributable to the measure.

It is interesting to ascertain that the above mentioned Court formula has also been used in various judgements applying the

---

[25] Art. 28 (ex 30) E.C.

[26] See Dir. 70/50 [1970] O.J. L13/29.

[27] Case 8/74 *Procureur du Roi v. Dassonville* [1974] E.C.R. 837 at 852(5).

[28] This includes rules of a temporary nature: Case 82/77 *Openbaar Ministerie v. Van Tiggele* [1978] E.C.R. 25 at 40(20).

[29] The prohibition also applies to measures adopted by the Community institutions: Case 114/96 *Kieffer and Thill* [1997] E.C.R. I–3629.

[30] This means that there are cases where it may or should be made difficult: Case 6/81 *Industrie Diensten Groep v. Beele* [1982] E.C.R. 707. See also below "Exception to the free movement of goods".

[31] Case 16/83 *Prantl* [1984] E.C.R. 1299.

Community competition rules.[32] This similarity should not surprise, since the competition rules and the provisions concerning the Customs Union have an identical objective: the free movement of goods.

The question must be asked, however, to which goods does the principle of free movement apply? According to the Court, it concerns goods, which have been "lawfully produced and marketed in one of the Member States".[33] Those goods must "be admitted in all the other Member States". This is, because of its far-reaching implications, the most important rule concerning the free movement of goods. It means that Member States must recognise as equivalent to their own legislation concerning the production and marketing of goods, that of all the other Member States. This is referred to as the principle of "mutual recognition". Without it, free circulation of goods could only be achieved through harmonisation of all the national regulations and standards. Obviously this is impossible.[34] The Community therefore chose to combine mutual recognition with a more efficient mechanism for harmonisation; and the latter only where absolutely necessary. The procedure for the approximation of the national laws and regulations was also simplified by the SEA.[35] This allowed the internal market to be completed by December 31, 1992.[36]

However, in the absence of harmonisation, even mutual recognition does not always provide the solution. Indeed, according to the Court, the basic principle of the free movement cannot yet fully be applied under all circumstances. Therefore, "in the absence of common rules relating to the production and marketing of [a given product], it is for the Member States to regulate all matters relating to the production and the marketing of [said product] on their own territory".[37]

Consequently, "obstacles to movement [of goods] within the

---

[32] Joined Cases 56 and 58/64 *Consten and Grundig v. Commisssion* [1966] E.C.R. 299 at 341.

[33] Case 120/78 *Rewe v. Bundesmonopolverwaltung für Branntwein*; the so-called "*Cassis de Dijon*" case [1979] E.C.R. 649 at 664(14); [1979] 3 C.M.L.R. 494. Of course, this rule does not apply to goods imported from third countries once they have been put into "free circulation": Art. 24 (ex 10) E.C. In *Dassonville*, the Court referred to "an authentic product which has been put into free circulation 'in a regular manner' in another Member State". See n.27 above.

[34] See Commission White Paper on the Completion of the Internal Market (COM(85) 510 final).

[35] The SEA introduced Art. 95 (ex 100a) E.C., which provided that such measures could be adopted by a majority vote, rather than unanimity, as was the case before.

[36] Art. 14 (ex 7a) E.C.

[37] *Cassis de Dijon* at 662(8); see n.33 above.

Community resulting from disparities between the national laws relating to marketing of the products in question, must be accepted in so far as those provisions may be recognised as being necessary in order to satisfy mandatory requirements"[38] of the public interest.

Those *mandatory requirements* are for instance, the "effectiveness of fiscal supervision", the "protection of public health", the "fairness of commercial transactions", and the "defence of the consumer".[39] Others are, according to the case law: "legitimate elements of economic and social policy",[40] the "fight against inflation",[41] the "protection of the environment",[42] the "promotion of culture"[43] and the "safeguard of press diversity".[44]

The mandatory requirements are to be distinguished from the *exceptions* to the free movement of goods provided for in the Treaty.[45] The latter render the principle of the free movement inapplicable as soon as the necessary conditions are fulfilled. Those exceptions will always exist since they are provided for in the Treaty itself. The mandatory requirements are a creation of the courts and they may only be relied upon "in the absence of common rules". Since more and more common rules are being adopted, they will cease to be applicable over time. They do not constitute exceptions to the basic principle of the free movement of goods, they only justify a temporary suspension of the total and strict applicability of a basic rule.

What is the rationale behind those "mandatory requirements"? The principle of the free movement of goods is embodied in the Treaty in the form of obligations imposed upon the Member States. Since every obligation implies a corresponding right for the beneficiaries of those obligations—in this case the natural and legal persons within the Community, the latter simultaneously acquired a corresponding right: the right to free trade. On the other hand, no right is unlimited and the limitations result from the necessity to protect the public interest. The Member States as the guardians of this public interest, are entitled to impose the measures necessary to it. Those measures can, in the absence of common rules, constitute obstacles to the free movement of goods, and must be temporarily accepted.

Those measures, however, "must only be accepted in so far as

---

[38] *ibid.*
[39] *ibid.*
[40] Case 155/80 *Oebel* [1981] E.C.R. 1983 at 2008(12).
[41] Case 181/82 *Roussel Laboratoria v. Netherlands* [1983] E.C.R. 3849 at 3870(24).
[42] Case 302/86 *Commission v. Denmark* [1988] E.C.R. 4627.
[43] Joint Cases 60, 61/84 *Cinéthèque* [1985] E.C.R. 2605.
[44] Case C–368/95 *Familiapress v. Bauer Verlag* [1097] E.C.R. I–3689.
[45] Art. 30 (ex 36) E.C.

[they] may be recognised as being necessary".[46] The Member State imposing them must prove that they serve a purpose which is in the general interest, and such as to take precedence over the requirements of the free movement of goods, which constitutes one of the fundamental rules of the Community. They must demonstrate the need for their measures, based for instance, on international scientific research.[47] This means, according to the Court, that those measures must be "reasonable".[48] This is where the expression the "rule of reason" finds its origin. The latter is sometimes identified with the *Cassis de Dijon* judgment, but wrongly so. The basic rule of that judgment is, as was mentioned, that all goods legally produced and marketed in one Member State must be admitted in all the others. Furthermore, if Member States may, under strictly limited circumstances, prohibit the marketing of such products, this prohibition must be open to appeal under a procedure, which is readily accessible and can be completed within a reasonable period.

Except in the case of mandatory requirements, all restrictions on inter-State trade resulting from national measures having equivalent effect to quantitative restrictions are and remain prohibited.[49] It should be noted that a measure "does not escape this prohibition simply because the competent authority is empowered to grant exemptions, even if the power is freely applied to imported products". This is particularly the case with measures, which discriminate between national and non-national products. In such a case even mandatory requirements cannot justify such measures. On the other hand, even measures which apply indistinctly the domestic

---

[46] Case 58/80 *Dansk Supermarked v. Imerco* [1981] E.C.R. 181.

[47] Case C–42/86, *Ministère Public v. Bellon* [1990] E.C.R. I–4878.

[48] Case 8/74 *Dassonville*, n.27 above.

[49] Case 27/80 *Fietje* [1980] E.C.R. 3839 at 3854(14). In numerous cases the court was called upon to rule on the compatibility of national measures. For instance are prohibited: fees charged for veterinary inspection: Case 46/76 *Bauhuis v. Netherlands* [1977] E.C.R. 20(51); freezing of all prices at a level so low that imports can only be done at a loss: Joined Cases 16 to 20/79 *Joseph Danis* [1979] E.C.R. 3327; systematic veterinary and public health inspection: Case 251/78 *Denkavit* [1979] E.C.R. 3369; mandatory description on product making it necessary to modify the label: *Fietje* same n.; fixing of minimum and maximum limits for dry matter contained in a product; Case 130/80 *Kelderman* [1981] E.C.R. 527; requirement as to indication of origin: Case 207/83 *Commission v. U.K.* [1985] E.C.R. 1207; allowing only certain national producers to use a specific shape of wine bottle: Case 16/83 *Prantl* [1984] E.C.R. 1299; health checks on animal feeding-stuffs: Case 73/84 *Denkavit* [1985] E.C.R. 1013. On the other hand the detailed declaration of imports and exports required by a directive is not prohibited: Case C–114/96 *Kieffer and Thill* [1997] E.C.R. I–3629.

and imported products can have restrictive effects on the latter,[50] if in practice they produce protective effects by favouring typical national products and, by the same token, operating to the detriment of certain types of products from other Member States.[51] In such a case the potential effect on inter-State trade is indirect.

It might appear that the Court modified its position in the now famous *Keck and Mithouard* case,[52] especially since it used the words "contrary to what has been ruled until now". It concerned a French law, which prohibits the resale of goods at a loss. The Court stated that this law did not constitute a "trading rule"—this expression was used to define measures having equivalent effect in the *Dassonville* case. And although it was recognised that the law could limit the sale of imported products, the Court concluded that it constituted a measure, which applies without distinction to operators and all products within the national territory. It was not a measure intended to regulate "trade" but rather selling arrangements[53]; it did not therefore constitute a measure having equivalent effect to quantitative restrictions.[54]

The judgment met violent criticism as being a reversal of the standing case law and accepting hindrances to intra-Community trade, rather than liberating it. On close examination this criticism seems unfounded. Indeed, the Court, when asked to interpret the expression "measures having equivalent effect to quantitative restrictions", always referred to State rules regulating intra-Community trade. The word "trade" cannot be applied to the "marketing" of products and, the object of the measures in question is to regulate the way products, whatever their origin, are marketed, *i.e.* sold, within a given Member State. Such measures have nothing to do with the prohibition of measures having equivalent effect. Such measures are justified under Community law and they reflect certain choices relating to particular national or regional socio-cultural characteristics. It is for the Member States to make those choices in compliance with the requirements of Community law.[55] The latter

---

[50] Case 53/80 *Officier van Justitie v. Kaasfabriek Eyssen* [1981] E.C.R. 409, where the national measures applied only to products destined for the domestic market.

[51] Case 16/83 *Prantl* [1984] E.C.R. 1299; [1985] 2 C.M.L.R. 238.

[52] Joined Cases C–267 and 268/91 [1993] E.C.R. I–6097; [1995] 1 C.M.L.R. 101.

[53] This expression was used in the Joined Cases C–418/93, etc. *Semeraro* [1996] E.C.R. I–2975; [1996] 3 C.M.L.R. 648.

[54] The Court's position was clearly restated in the judgment in the case mentioned in the preceding note, at I–3004(11–13) and also in Joined Cases C–69 and 258/93 *Punto Casa and PPV* [1994] E.C.R. I–2355.

[55] Case 418/93 *Semerano*, n.53 above.

may not be used by market operators to oppose any State measure which regulates (limits) their commercial freedom.[56]

3. Prohibition of Discriminating or Protective Internal Taxation

No Member State may impose, directly or indirectly, on the products of other Member States any internal taxation of any kind in excess of that imposed directly or indirectly on similar domestic products nor any internal taxation of such a nature as to afford indirect protection to other products.[57]

The above mentioned prohibition supplements, within the system of the Treaty, the provisions on the abolition of customs duties and charges having equivalent effect. Their aim is to ensure free movement of goods between the Member States in normal conditions of competition by the elimination of all forms of protection which results from the application of internal taxation which discriminates against products from other Member States.[58]

What distinguishes a (protective) internal taxation from a charge having an effect equivalent to a customs duty is that the first is imposed on both imported and domestic products, whilst the second is imposed exclusively on the imported product.

The Court has defined as "similar" products those which "have similar characteristics and meet the same needs from the point of view of the consumer".[59] Similarity is not a question of strictly identical nature, but of similarity and comparability in the use of the products. For instance, spirits obtained by the distillation of cereals and sugar-cane are similar to spirits obtained from wine and marc.[60] In such a case the taxes imposed in the imported products may not be higher than the one imposed on the domestic ones.

As for protective taxation, it affects products which, without being similar, are nevertheless in competition, even partial, indirect or potential with national products. According to the Court the prohibition applies to a national system of taxation affecting differently imported whisky and domestic production of spirits obtained from wine. Such differences affect the market in the

---

[56] *Keck* Case, n.52.
[57] Art. 90 (ex 95) E.C.
[58] Case 169/78 *Commission v. Italy* [1980] E.C.R. at 399(3); [1981] 2 C.M.L.R. 673.
[59] Case 45/75 *REWE* [1976] E.C.R. 181; [1976] 2 C.M.L.R. 1.
[60] Case 169/78 *Commission v. Italy* [1980] E.C.R. at 409; [1981] 2 C.M.L.R. 673.

products in question by reducing the potential consumption of imported products.[61]

Although the Treaty refers explicitly only to imports, the prohibition extends, according to the Court, also to exports.[62]

4. Exceptions to the Free Movement of Goods

Every rule has its exceptions. They can be found either in the legal provisions laying down the rule, or in the interpretation of the rule by the courts. The same applies, of course, to the basic rule concerning the free movement of goods. The E.C. Treaty provides for several exceptions.

The most important one concerns the prohibition of quantitative restrictions and measures having equivalent effects.[63] Restrictions on imports, exports and transit of goods may be justified on grounds of public morality,[64] public policy or public security,[65] the protection of health and life of humans, animals and plants,[66] the protection of national treasures possessing artistic, historic or archeological value,[67] or the protection of industrial and commercial property.[68]

---

[61] Case 216/81 *Cogis* [1982] E.C.R. at 3713(11); [1983] 1 C.M.L.R. 685.

[62] Case 142/77 *Larsen* [1978] E.C.R. at 1557(21); [1979] 2 C.M.L.R. 680.

[63] Art. 30 (ex 36) E.C.

[64] See Case 34/79 *R. v. Henn and Darby* [1979] E.C.R. 3795; [1980] 1 C.M.L.R. 246; prohibition of imports of pornographic articles.

[65] See Case 7/78 *R. v. Thompson* [1978] E.C.R. 2247; [1979] 1 C.M.L.R. 47: export ban on silver alloy coins.

[66] The Court considers that "health and the life of humans ranks first among the interests protected by Article 30 (ex 36) E.C.": Case 104/75 *De Peijper* [1975] E.C.R. 613 at 635(15); [1976] 2 C.M.L.R. 271. This ground for exception has given rise to numerous Court rulings: see Case C–293/94 *Brandsma* [1996] E.C.R. I–3159: prohibition of import of biocidal products containing dangerous substances which have not yet been the subject of Community legislation, is justified even if they have already been authorised in another Member State. In Case C–42/90 *Bellon* [1990] E.C.R. I–4863, the Court added that a Member State may prohibit the marketing of a foodstuff containing certain preservatives, provided that the principle of proportionality underlying the last sentence of Art. 36 is observed and authorisation can be obtained under a procedure which is readily accessible and which can be completed within a reasonable period, where the additive meets a genuine need and represents no danger to public health.

[67] See Case 7/68 *Commission v. Italy* [1968] E.C.R. 423. See also Directive 93/7 on the return of cultural objects unlawfully removed from the territory of a Member State [1993] O.J. L74/14 and Reg. 3911/92 on the harmonisation of controls on the export of cultural goods [1993] O.J. L395/1.

[68] See Case 144/81 *Keurkoop v. Nancy Keen Gifts* [1982] E.C.R. 2853; [1983] 2 C.M.L.R. 47 and Joined Cases C–427, 429 and 436/93 *Bristol-Myers* [1996] E.C.R. I–3457; [1997] 1 C.M.L.R. 1151: the exhaustion principle does not apply in the cases provided for in Dir. 89/104 Art. 7(2).

It should be noted that, according to the relevant Treaty provision, the prohibition or restriction "may not constitute a means of arbitrary discrimination or disguised restriction on trade between Member States".[69] The Court also considered that those exceptions are not designed to reserve certain matters to the exclusive jurisdiction of the Member States. They permit national laws to derogate from the principle of the free movement of goods to the extent to which such derogation is and continues to be justified for the attainment of the objectives referred to.[70] And where Community directives[71] provide for the harmonisation of the national measures necessary to safeguard those objectives, recourse to the exceptions will automatically cease.

The Treaty provides that in case difficulties arise in a Member State, the Council may decide upon "measures appropriate to the economic situation",[72] in particular if they arise in the supply of certain products. Such measures could have effects equivalent to quantitative restrictions. Although this text was introduced by the Amsterdam Treaty and has consequently not been tested yet in court, there is no doubt that it would apply in situations similar to those created by the oil crises of the 1980s.[73]

Another exception was already pointed out in relation to goods imported from third countries and which are in free circulation; the Commission may authorise Member States to take protective measures to avoid deflection of trade or economic difficulties.[74] Such measures would normally consist in import restrictions limiting intra-Community trade.

Finally, mention must be made in this context of the possibility for Member States to take such measures as they consider necessary for the protection of the essential interests of their security which are connected with the production or trade in arms, munitions and war material. A list of the products benefiting from these exceptions was drawn up by the Commission on April 15, 1958 and has never been published.[75] Similarly, Member States may be called upon to take certain measures[76] in the event of serious internal disturbances

---

69 Art. 28 (ex 36) E.C. See Case 40/80 *Commission v. U.K.* [1982] E.C.R. 2793.

70 Case 5/77 *Tedeschi v. Denkavit* [1977] E.C.R. 1555.

71 See, *e.g.* Dir. 70/54 [1970] O.J. 840 and Dir. 74/63 [1974] O.J. L38/31.

72 Art. 100(1) (ex 103) E.C.

73 See for instance Case 72/83 *Campus Oil* [1984] E.C.R. 2727; [1984] 3 C.M.L.R. 544.

74 Art. 134 (ex 115) E.C.

75 Art. 296 (ex 223) E.C.

76 Art. 297 (ex 224) E.C.

affecting the maintenance of law and order,[77] in the event of war, serious international tension constituting a threat of war, or in order to carry out obligations they have accepted for the purpose of maintaining peace and international security.[78]

In both those cases, the measures taken by the Member States may limit the free movement of goods.

In the latter case the Treaty simply provides that the Member States shall consult each other with a view to taking steps together to prevent the functioning of the common market being affected. If, in both cases, the measures affect competition in the common market, the Commission shall, together with the Member State concerned, examine how those measures can be adjusted. In case the Commission or a Member State considers that another Member State is making improper use of the powers provided in the above mentioned circumstances, they may bring the matter directly before the Court, which shall give its rule in camera.[79]

5. Theory and Reality of the Free Movement of Goods

What explains that seven years after the completion of the internal market on December 31, 1992, people still experience difficulties when moving goods within the Community? The answer, of course, is not a simple one. In the first place there are the legal exceptions just examined. Secondly there are the many remaining measures having equivalent effect. Obviously, there is a task here for all the interested parties: users, consumers and traders. They are in the front line, they are the ones who experience the negative effects of those measures; it is up to them to make the necessary representations to the national authorities and to the Commission.

It is, of course, up to the latter to make sure that the Member States "recognise the technical specifications, standards and rules applicable in other Member States and the validity of tests carried out by approved laboratories in other Member States offering adequate guarantees of reliability and efficacity".[80] So the Commission continues to monitor the compliance by Member States with the

[77] One may think of the situation prevailing in Northern Ireland.
[78] Think about the intervention in former Yugoslavia.
[79] Art. 298 (ex 225) E.C.
[80] General Report (1992) 48.

principle of free movement of goods, mainly through the procedure[81] under which the Member States have to inform the Commission of *technical standards and regulations* which they intend to introduce. The other institutions[82] are, of course, also involved in the fight against old and new[83] obstacles to intra-Community trade.

When the Commission is of the opinion that proposed standards or regulations will infringe the principle of free trade, it issues a "detailed opinion", which is binding upon the Member States concerned.

From the above it follows that standards and technical regulations play a very important role in the functioning of the internal market. Consequently, the Council laid down provisions on the introduction and implementation of technical regulations and standards[84] and adopted Resolutions on a new approach to technical harmonisation and standards[85] and on the role of European standardisation in the European economy.[86] The Commission, on the other hand, co-operates extensively with the European standardisation bodies. The Community only lays down the essential safety requirements[87] to which products placed on the market must conform in order to enjoy freedom of movement. It is for the standardisation bodies to establish the necessary technical specifications. National administrations are obliged to assume that products manufactured in conformity with harmonised standards are in conformity with the essential requirements laid down by the directives.

There are other areas where the principle of "mutual recognition" cannot work, mainly on account of the complexity of the required regulations. In such cases, the Commission continues to make the

---

[81] Dir. 83/189 [1983] O.J. L109/8, incorporated. [1994] O.J. L1/572, last modified by Dec. 96/139 [1996] O.J. 132/31. See Case C–194/94 *CIA* [1996] E.C.R. I–2201: definition of "technical regulations" under Dir. 83/189.

[82] See Dec. 3052/95 of the European Parliament and the Council establishing a procedure for the exchange of information on national measures derogating from the principle of the free movement of goods within the Community [1995] O.J. L321/1. This Dec. applies as from January 1, 1997.

[83] See Thirteenth Annual Report Monitoring the Application of Community Law 1995 (COM(96) 600 final, 26) where the Commission points out that with regard to the notification procedure under Dir. 83/189, as amended by Dir. 88/182 "the Commission received 382 drafts of technical regulations . . . This figure compares with 385 in 1993 and 389 in 1994—clear evidence that, despite the completion of the internal market at the end of 1992, Member States are still adopting large numbers of technical regulations which could undermine the single market and the integrity of the benefits it has brought to all sectors of the economy".

[84] Decision 80/45 [1980] O.J. L14/36.

[85] Resolution of May 7, 1985 [1985] O.J. C136/1.

[86] Resolution of June 18, 1992 [1992] O.J. C173/1.

[87] See, *e.g.* Dir. on General Product Safety—Product safety Dir. [1992] O.J. L228/24.

necessary proposals for harmonising national laws. Examples are foodstuffs, motor vehicles and the chemical sector.

Further Reading

Wouter P. J. Wils, "The Search for the Rule in Article 30 EEC: much ado about nothing?", (1993) 18 E.L.Rev. 475.

Thomas von Plehwe, "European Union and the Free movement of Cultural Goods", (1995) 20 E.L.Rev. 431.

Rosa Greaves, "Advertising Restrictions and the Free Movement of Goods and Services", (1998) 23 E.L.Rev. 305.

Chapter Fourteen
The Free Movement of Workers

Introduction: The Free Movement of Persons

The free movement of persons constitutes one of the fundamental freedoms guaranteed by the Treaty and the relevant provisions may not, according to the Court, be interpreted restrictively[1]; furthermore, they have direct effect.[2] Although Title III of the Treaty mentions the free movement of "persons", this term is not to be found again in this part of the Treaty, except in the new Title IV added by the Treaty of Amsterdam. This freedom must be understood as referring to both "workers"[3] (anyone who pursues an activity as an employed person) and "self employed persons" (professionals, trades people, etc.). The latter expression covers both natural and legal persons and their "free movement" consists in "freedom of establishment" and "freedom to provide services".

Those three freedoms (workers, establishment and services) do not confer unlimited rights (no right is unlimited). Workers' rights and the right to establish and to provide services in other Member States consist solely in the right to be treated in the same way as the nationals of that State. Without going into details, each one of those three freedoms confers directly on the persons concerned the right to enter the territory of another Member State, to reside there with their families, and to exercise their activities under the same conditions as the nationals of the host Member State.[4]

The basic principle underlying the three freedoms is non-discrimination: workers from other Member States have the same rights as national workers and professionals can exercise their profession, but under the same conditions as the nationals. However, it must be clear

[1] Case 53/81 *Levin v. Staatssecretaris van Justitie* [1982] E.C.R. 1035 at 1049(3) [1982] 2 C.M.L.R. 454.

[2] Case 48/75 *Royer* [1976] E.C.R. 497 at 51231; [1976] 2 C.M.L.R. 619.

[3] Arts. 39 to 42 (ex 48 to 51) E.C.

[4] This follows from the rule prohibiting discrimination between nationals and non-nationals, also called "equal treatment".

that for a worker, a tradesman or a professional to move from one place to another within his own country, is not quite the same thing as moving to another country. She or he is bound to face new administrative requirements resulting from the simple fact that each Member State has its own legal system, language and habits. Since there are differences, the implementation of the principle of non-discrimination would not suffice; the Treaty therefore provides for a number of specific rights, which will be examined in the corresponding sections.

Now, discrimination occurs when two parties in exactly the same position are treated differently, but also when the same treatment is applied to parties in different positions. Can one say that a worker, tradesman or professional from another Member State is in exactly the same position as the nationals? Doesn't the fact of being "foreign" constitute necessarily, a certain difference, which justifies a slightly different treatment? This is the case, for instance, with national rules concerning the control of foreigners. The Court found that "the application of such legislation, where it is based upon objective factors, cannot constitute 'discrimination on ground of nationality' " prohibited under the Treaty.[5]

It should be remembered that Community law only applies when trans-frontier activities are concerned. In other words, those provisions cannot be invoked in purely national situations.[6] Consequently the provisions regarding free movement of persons only apply to individuals and firms from other Member States.

Part Two of the E.C. Treaty, which establishes the citizenship of the Union, provides that every citizen of the Union "shall have the right to move and reside freely within the territory of the Member States".[7] How does this "freedom" correspond with the one just described but which is limited to workers and self employed persons? As long as the Council has not "adopted provisions with a view to facilitating the exercise of the rights referred to" above, this general right to move and reside remains "subject to the limitations and conditions laid down in [the] Treaty and by the measures adopted to give it effect".[8] Those limitations and conditions are the ones which

---

[5] Former Art. 7 E.C.

[6] See Case 175/78 *R. v. Sanders* [1979] E.C.R. 1129 at 1135(10); [1979] 2 C.M.L.R. 216, where the Court held that Art. 39 (ex 48) E.C. does not prevent a Member State from limiting the free movement of persons within their own territory. See also Case 180/83 *Moser v. Land Baden-Württemberg* [1984] E.C.R. 2539; [1984] 3 C.M.L.R. 720, where it concerned a national who had never resided or worked in another Member State.

[7] Art. 18(1) (ex 8a)) E.C.

[8] *ibid.* at 2.

apply to the above mentioned two categories and which will be examined in the following sections.

The only measures "adopted to give effect" are those, which grant the right of residence to nationals of the Member States who do not enjoy this right under other provisions of Community law and to members of their families,[9] and to students and members of their families.[10]

Free movement of persons was also facilitated by the issue of a "European Passport"[11] *i.e.* a passport of uniform pattern (format and colour) and by the implementation of the "Schengen" Agreement of 1985[12] on the gradual abolition of controls at the common frontiers and the Convention of 1990 applying the Schengen Agreement.[13]

The Treaty of Amsterdam integrated the Schengen *acquis* into the framework of the European Union.[14] This in itself is an interesting legislative exercise worth looking at. The Treaty of Amsterdam provides that the *acquis*, which literally means everything that was acquired in the way of applicable provisions by the law of the signatories to the Schengen agreements, shall immediately apply from the date of entry into force of the Treaty as Community law in those same States. However, since those provisions were not adopted in conformity with the provisions of the E.C. Treaty, the Council, acting unanimously, shall determine, in conformity with the relevant provisions of the Treaties "the legal basis for each of the provisions

---

[9] Dir. 90/364 on the right of residence [1990] O.J. L180/26; the right is granted provided that the beneficiaries are covered by sickness insurance in respect of all risks in the host Member State and have sufficient resources to avoid becoming a burden on the social assistance system of the host Member State.

[10] Dir. 93/96 [1993] O.J. L317/59, on the right of residence for students enrolled in a recognised educational establishment for the principal purpose of following a vocational training course, and provided the student has sufficient resources and is covered by sickness insurance.

[11] Several Resolutions were adopted by the Representatives of the Governments of the Member States, meeting within the Council; [1981] O.J. C241/1, amended by [1995] O.J. C200/1; [1982] O.J. C179/1; [1986] O.J. C185/1.

[12] Agreement of June 14, 1985; originally it fell outside the Community framework and was signed by the Benelux countries, Germany and France which published the agreement, see *e.g. Moniteur Belge* of April 29, 1986 (the text can also be obtained from the Benelux Secretariat in Brussels, fax 02/513.42.06), and Convention of June19, 1990 applying the Schengen Agreement on the gradual abolition of checks at their common borders and the movement of persons.

[13] The authentic French, German and Dutch texts are published, *inter alia* in the Dutch *Tractatenblad* [1990] at 145.

[14] Consolidated version of the Treaty establishing the European Community, Protocol (No. 2) integrating the Schengen *acquis* into the framework of the European Union [1997] O.J. C340/93.

or decisions which constitute the Schengen *acquis*".[15] In the meantime the *acquis* shall be regarded as acts based on Title VI of the Treaty on European Union: "Provisions on Cooperation in the Field of Justice and Home Affairs." This so-called third pillar of the European Union was replaced by the "Provisions on Police and Judicial Cooperation in Criminal Matters", which is much narrower.[16] Some of the provisions of the third pillar are now to be found in the new Title IV of the E.C. Treaty: "Visas, Asylum, Immigration and other Policies related to the Free Movement of Persons".

This new Title provides for an "area of freedom, security and justice"[17] to be established progressively with the aim of ensuring the free movement of persons as provided for by the establishment of the internal market.[18] This free movement entails, *inter alia*, the absence of any control on persons, citizens of the Union and nationals of third countries, when crossing internal borders. It might be of interest to note the new expression "flanking measures" used in the Treaty, with respect to external border controls,[19] asylum,[20] refugees and displaced persons,[21] immigration[22] and measures to prevent and combat crime. For the latter, a reference is made to the E.U. Treaty, which provides for the progressive adoption of measures establishing minimum rules relating to the constituent elements of criminal acts and to penalties in the fields of organised crime, terrorism and illicit drug trafficking.[23]

In this area also exceptions are, of course, provided for; they

---

[15] *ibid.* Art. 2(1).

[16] Arts 29 to 42 TEU. According to the consolidated text published in the *Official Journal of the European Communities* [1997] O.J. C340/162, those Articles replace Arts K.1 to K.14; however the contents of the new Articles do not correspond at all to the old ones. Worse are the references in the new Title IV of the E.C. Treaty, to the old Title IIIa and Arts 73i to 73q, which are nowhere to be found in the official Treaty texts published by the Office for *Official Publications of the European Communities* in 1993. The answer is that those provisions were first introduced in the E.C. Treaty by the Amsterdam Treaty and afterwards renumbered. But the reference "ex Article 73j" for instance, is misleading and will therefore not be used in this book: "ex" means: "before Amsterdam".

[17] Art. 61 E.C.

[18] Art.14(2) (ex 7a(2)) E.C.

[19] Art. 62(1) E.C. which provides for standards and procedures for carrying out checks at those borders, and rules on visas.

[20] Art. 63(1) E.C. measures on asylum in accordance with the Geneva Convention of July 28, 1951 and the Protocol of January 31, 1967 relating to the status of refugees.

[21] Art. 63(1) E.C. promoting, *inter alia* a balance of effort between the Member States in receiving and bearing the consequences of receiving refugees and displaced persons.

[22] Art. 63(1) E.C. long term visas and residence permits and repatriation of illegal residents.

[23] Art. 31(e) (ex K.3, which has a different content!) E.C.

concern the responsibility incumbent upon Member States with regard to maintenance of law and order and the safeguarding of internal security.[24] One might wonder why the Treaty does not refer here to the classical "public policy and public security", which constitute exceptions to the basic freedoms and have acquired a specific meaning on the basis of the case law of the courts. Another exception to the rules of this new Title IV, is the case of a Member State being confronted with an emergency situation characterised by a sudden inflow of nationals of third countries. In such a case the Council may adopt provisional measures for no longer than six months.[25]

The Treaty now also provides for judicial co-operation in civil matters having cross-border implications. They include systems for cross-border service of judicial and extrajudicial documents, co-operation in taking evidence and the recognition and enforcement of decisions in civil and commercial cases. Also is provided, the promotion of compatibility of the rules applicable in the Member states concerning the conflict of laws and of jurisdiction and of the rules on civil procedure. This, of course, constitutes a very important step forward in European integration since, until now, national civil and commercial matters fell outside Community law, except for the competence attributed to the Court of Justice.[26]

The Treaty also provides for co-operation between the administrations of the Member States in the areas covered by this new Title IV, as well as between those departments and those of the Commission.[27]

Much more important, and probably worrisome if it were not limited to a transitional period of five years, is the first breach in the exclusive right of proposal of the Commission. Indeed, where measures are to be taken by the Council in the areas covered by the Title, it shall act unanimously "on a proposal from the Commission or on the initiative of a Member State". After the five year period, one reverts to the exclusive right of initiative of the Commission, the latter having to "examine any request made by a Member State that it submit a proposal to the Council".[28] The explanation of this oddity is, of course, that the subject matter covered here, was always purely national or at the most, intergovernmental. Bringing it into the

---

[24] Art. 64(1) E.C.

[25] Art. 44(2) (ex 54(2)) E.C.

[26] See, for instance, Art. 3 of the Protocol of June 3, 1971 annexed to the Convention of Brussels of September 25, 1968 [1978] O.J. L304.

[27] Art. 66 E.C.

[28] Art. 67 E.C.

Community orbit necessitates progressivity. Nevertheless, it is to be considered a *faux pas*, which could have far reaching consequences.

On the other hand, the Treaty of Amsterdam enlarges the jurisdiction of the Court of Justice in that it introduces the preliminary question into this area, from which it was excluded until now. And, although certain acts such as measures taken by Member States to maintain law and order are excluded from the Court's jurisdiction, this "communitarisation" of a sector closely related to one of the basic freedoms, reinforces the uniform application of the law.

The Free Movement of Workers

The principle of freedom of movement of workers forms, according to the Court, one of the foundations of the Community and, consequently, has to be given a broad interpretation.[29] Access to employment in another Member State is a fundamental aspect of the free movement of persons within the European Union. A wide area of labour mobility represents a large number of opportunities for workers to find work and for the employer to find people with adequate skills, thereby enhancing employment and economic growth. The purpose is to open European labour markets to all E.U. workers, which is one of the tangible aspects of European integration. As shall be seen, the right of access to national labour markets includes a right to equal treatment with respect to working conditions, as well as the right to social, economic and cultural integration of the migrant worker and her or his family in the host State.[30]

Before going any further, it is of course necessary to define the term "worker". The more so, since as already mentioned, Title III of the E.C. Treaty is called "Free movement of persons, services and capital", but in the context of the internal market, it must be accepted that "persons" has no legal meaning. Anyway the term only appears in a title and, as is well known, *titulus non lex*. What should be remembered is that the Treaty, with regard to free movement, only knows "workers" and "self-employed" natural and legal persons. The free movement of the latter finds its expression in the freedom of establishment and in the freedom to provide services. However, those three freedoms must be considered, according to the

---

[29] Case C–344/95 *Commission v. Belgium* [1997] E.C.R I–1035.
[30] Internet: http.//europa.eu.mt/comm

Court, as based on the same principles, where entry, residence and treatment are concerned.[31]

As for "workers" their definition could simply be stated as "employed persons". This means that the Treaty does not know the category "employees"; consequently, a bank teller and a university professor, for instance, are both workers, and so are football players,[32] as far as the E.C. Treaty is concerned. There is, however, a basic condition in order to be recognised as "worker": the person in question must be covered by social security. There is a definite link between "worker" and social security and, a definition of worker is to be found in the Regulation on the application of social security schemes to employed persons and their families moving within the Community.[33]

The definition of worker gave rise to an abundant case law of the Court, which has always maintained that the term "has a Community meaning and, inasmuch as it defines the scope of one of the fundamental freedoms of the Community, must be interpreted broadly".[34] The Court further indicates that the concept must be defined in accordance with objective criteria which distinguish the employment relationship by reference to the rights and duties of the persons concerned and, that "the essential feature of an employment relationship is that for a certain period of time a person performs services for and under the direction of another person in return for which he receives remuneration".[35]

However, the Court added that freedom of movement is guaranteed only for persons pursuing or wishing to pursue an economic[36] activity and that, consequently, it only covers the pursuit of an effective and genuine activity.[37] The latter is defined by the Court as excluding "activities on such a small scale as to be regarded as purely marginal and ancillary". Clearly, it is up to the national authorities to decide whether or not an activity fulfils those criteria.

The Court also added that neither productivity nor the origin of the funds used for the remuneration can have any consequence with

---

[31] Case 48/75 *Royer* see n.2.

[32] Case C–415/93 *Bosman* [1995] E.C.R. I–4921; [1996] 1 C.M.L.R. 645.

[33] Reg. 1408/71 [1971] O.J. L149/2. See Art. 1(a)(i). This Regulation was modified dozens of times lastly by Reg. 123/98 [1998] O.J. L168/1.

[34] Case 344/87 *Bettray v. Staatssecretaris van Justitie* [1989] E.C.R. 1621 at 1644(11); [1991] 1 C.M.L.R. 459.

[35] *ibid.* at 1645(12).

[36] See Case 36/74 *Walrave v. Union Cycliste* Internationale [1974] E.C.R. at 1417(5); [1975] 1 C.M.L.R. 320, concerning the nationality of the motorcycle pacemakers and cyclists. A minister of the Church is a typical example of a person pursuing a non-economic activity.

[37] Case 53/81 *Levin* n.1 above, at 1050(17).

regard to the question whether or not the person is to be regarded as a worker. The same applies to the nature of the legal relationship between the employee and the employer.[38] Furthermore, the employment must not be necessarily full-employment: free movement also applies to persons who pursue an activity on a part-time basis and, who by virtue of that fact, obtain a remuneration lower than the minimum guaranteed wage in a given sector.[39] The Court also determined that the motives which may have prompted a worker to seek employment are of no account and must not be taken into consideration.[40]

Barriers to the Free Movement of Workers and their Remedies

"Barriers" is maybe not the right word, since it conveys the idea that movement is prevented. However, in the case of persons, the same principle prevails as was applied by the Court in the case of the free movement of goods, *i.e.* that the prohibition of the Treaty also covers actions which make the movement between Member States more difficult than movement within a given State. One should probably refer to "hindrance" or "restriction" of the free movement.

It is interesting to read what the Commission publishes on the Internet concerning free movement of workers. "Historically, cross border mobility in the E.U. has been low. But even today[41] free movement is not yet a daily reality for Europe's citizens. Presently around five million European citizens [out of a total of nearly 350 million] reside in another Member State. Less than two per cent of the working population in the E.U. consists of people from one Member State working in another, although there are considerable variations between the Member States. While much has been achieved in this field, there is still much to be done in order to guarantee the effectiveness of the right to practice a profession in another Member State under the same conditions as nationals of that State. The way in which rules and regulations are applied raises a number of difficulties. Moreover, there is a lack of administrative flexibility towards the special situation of migrants and the level of co-operation between Member States is sometimes insufficient. There is a lack of knowledge and information about the rights and opportunities for workers moving from one Member State to another".

---

[38] Case 152/73 *Sotgiu v. Deutsche Bundespost* [1974] E.C.R. 153.
[39] See also Case 96/80 *Jenkins v. Kingsgate* [1981] E.C.R. at 925(11); [1981] 2 C.M.L.R. 24.
[40] Case 53/81 *Levin* n. 1 above, at 1052(22).
[41] This text was published in September 1998.

This sobering assessment will hopefully underline the importance of understanding the Community provisions applicable in this field.

The main barriers to the free movement of workers within the Community are: (i) discriminatory conditions of work and employment for non-nationals, (ii) law, regulations and administrative action, which impose on workers from other Member States obligations which are different from those governing nationals, and (iii) lack of co-ordination among the social security systems with harmful consequences for the migrant worker. As shall be seen hereunder, the Treaty provides for remedies for each one of those obstacles; those remedies have been expressed in the form of rights granted to any person who desires to exercise an economic activity as an employed person and, is a national of one of the Member States.[42] Those rights have been implemented by directives and regulations issued by the Council and, since the Maastricht Treaty, by the European Parliament acting jointly with the Council.[43]

With regard to the free movement of workers, the Treaty starts[44] by providing in a general way that it "shall entail[45] the abolition of any discrimination based on nationality between workers of the Member States as regards employment, remuneration and other conditions of work and employment". This statement is followed by a list of rights, which shall be briefly examined hereafter. Before doing so it should be noticed that the rights enumerated in that list are not simply examples of what is meant by non-discrimination. Indeed, equality of treatment is one thing, freedom of movement is another,[46] although it is obvious that the latter would have practically no meaning without the former. The Treaty provides that the worker enjoys the following rights.

The right "*to accept offers of employment actually made*". This, however, does not mean that the worker, in order to benefit from the freedom to move, must have in his possession a duly executed employment contract. Freedom of movement also extends to persons who "seriously wish to pursue activities as an employed person".[47]

The right "*to move freely within the territory of Member States*".

[42] Reg. 1612/68 on freedom of movement of workers within the Community [1968] J.O. L175/1; [1968] O.J. Spec. Ed. 475, as amended by Reg. 312/76 [1976] O.J. L39/2. See Case C–85/96 *Martinez Salo* [1998] E.C.R. 12.05.

[43] See Art. 40 (ex 49) E.C. which refers to the "procedure referred to in Article 251"; the latter constitutes the so-called "codecision" procedure.

[44] Art. 39(2) (ex 48(2)) E.C.

[45] The use of this term indicates that the list that follows is not exhaustive.

[46] See Case 36/75 *Rutili v. Minister for the Interior* [1975] E.C.R. at 1231(27).

[47] Case 53/81 *Levin* n.1 above, at 1052(21).

This means, in the first place the right to enter and, in the second place, the right to remain in, any Member State[48] for the purpose of employment. Taking into account the fact that the right to enter and to move can also be claimed by a person "looking" for a job, the question was raised how long this person could go on "looking". The answer given by the Court is six months, subject to appeal, unless the person in question provides evidence that she or he is continuing to seek employment and that there is a genuine chance of being engaged.[49] Workers must be admitted on the basis of an official identification,[50] *i.e.* an identity card or passport, showing in particular their nationality[51]; no visas may be required.

The right "*to stay in the Member State for the purpose of employment*". This requires the national authorities of the host State to deliver to the worker a "residence permit" in the form prescribed.[52] This permit constitutes proof of the worker's right to reside in the Member State in question; this right is not conferred by the issue of the permit; the right stems from Community law.[53] The worker must, however, report his presence to the national authorities in conformity with national law, the Court having determined that a Member State has the right to be informed about the presence of foreigners on its territory,[54] but added that the time limit for reporting and the penalties for failing to do so, had to be reasonable.

The right "*to employment in accordance with the provisions governing employment of nationals*". This is, by far the most important right of the migrant worker; it is the embodiment of the principle of non-discrimination on the basis of nationality, which according to the Treaty applies to "employment, remuneration and other conditions of work and employment". It means *inter alia* that she or he must have access to all economic activities, including professional football,[55] within the territory of the host State under the same conditions as the nationals. Save exceptions, no such

---

[48] Dir. 68/360 on the abolition of restrictions on movement and residence within the Community of workers of Member States and their families: [1968] J.O. L257/13, [1968] O.J. Spec. Ed. 485. The provisions of that Directive are directly applicable.

[49] Case C–292/89 *Queen v. Immigration Appeal Tribunal* [1991] E.C.R. 1773 at 1780(18); [1991] 2 C.M.L.R. 373 where the Court found that an obligation to automatically leave after three months, infringes Community law.

[50] Case C–376/89 *Giagounidis* [1991] E.C.R. I–1069; [1993] 1 C.M.L.R. 537.

[51] Dir. 68/360 Art. 2(2) see n.48 above.

[52] *ibid.*, Annex.

[53] Case 48/75 *Royer* [1976] E.C.R. 497; [1976] 2 C.M.L.R. 619. For the meaning of "residence", see Case C–216/89 *Reibold v. Bundesanstalt für Arbeit* [1990] E.C.R. I–4163.

[54] Case 118/75 *Watson and Belmann* [1976] E.C.R. 1185; [1976] 2 C.M.L.R. 552.

[55] Case 13/76 *Dona v. Mantero* [1976] E.C.R. 1333; [1976] 2 C.M.L.R. 578.

activity may be reserved for nationals. Not only access, but also the conditions of employment must be the same as those which apply to nationals. This applies particularly to remuneration and other conditions of work and employment.[56] This also means that no overt or covert discriminatory criteria may be applied to workers from other Member States. This applies also to individual and collective employment agreements.[57]

Important are the words "and other conditions of work and employment"; they fulfill a role comparable to the terms "and charges having an equivalent effect" prohibited with regard to customs duties and quantitative restrictions. It allowed the Council in its implementing legislation and the Court in its answers to preliminary questions, to give a broad interpretation of the rights covered by the free movement of workers. They include conditions as regards dismissal, reinstatement or re-employment, social and tax advantages, access to training in vocational schools and retraining centers, membership of trade unions and the exercise of the rights attached thereto, including the right to vote, eligibility for workers' representative bodies in the undertaking. The migrant worker shall also enjoy all the rights and benefits accorded to national workers in matters of housing, including ownership.

Furthermore, the spouse and the children under the age of 21 years or dependent on him shall have the right to take up any activity as an employed person throughout the territory of the same State, even if they are not nationals of any Member State. The worker's children shall be admitted to the host State's general educational,[58] apprenticeship and vocational training[59] courses under the same conditions as the nationals of that State, if such children are residing in its territory.[60] They must also have access to special employment

[56] Art. 39(2) (ex 48(2)) E.C.; this provision is similar to para. 3(c).

[57] Reg. 1612/68 [1968] O.J. L257/2; [1968] O.J. Spec. Ed. 68 475, on freedom of movement of workers within the Community; incorporated [1994] O.J. L1/325.

[58] Dir. 77/486 on the education of the children of migrant workers: [1977] O.J. L199/32 and Council conclusions concerning the implementation of Dir. 77/486 [1985] O.J. C165/1.

[59] Vocational training: "Any form of education which prepares for a qualification for a particular profession, trade or employment or which provides the necessary training and skills for such a profession, trade or employment": Case 293/83 *Gravier v. City of Liége* [1985] E.C.R. 593; [1985] 3 C.M.L.R. 1. See also Art. 150 (ex 127) E.C.

[60] Reg. 1612/68, Art. 12 see n. 131. Concerning education and training facilities and the rights of children of a deceased worker: Case 131/85 *Gül v. Regierungspräsident* [1986] E.C.R. 1573 at 1590(20); [1974] 2 C.M.L.R. 423, and Case 152/82 *Forcheri v. Belgium* [1993] E.C.R. 2323 at 2336(18); [1984] 1 C.M.L.R. 334; the right only applies to vocational training not of university level; children of migrant workers

programmes.[61] Generally speaking, the rights constituting the free movement of workers, especially the right of entry, movement and residence also apply to the worker's family, even if the latter are not nationals of a Member State.[62]

The right "*to remain in the territory of a Member State after having been employed in that State*" subject to the conditions embodied in the implementing regulation of the Commission.[63] Those conditions are the following: the worker, at the time of termination of his activity as an employed person must have reached the age laid down by law of the host Member State for entitlement to an old-age pension; the worker must also have been employed in that State for at least the last twelve months and has resided there continuously for more than three years. The latter does not apply in case of incapacity resulting from an accident at work or an occupational disease. No formalities may be required for the exercise of this right and the worker is entitled to a residence permit which shall be issued and renewed free of charge or on payment of a sum not exceeding the dues and taxes payable by nationals.

If the worker has acquired the right to remain in the territory of a Member State, the members of his family shall be entitled to remain there permanently even after his death.

Social security

The rights just mentioned would, however, be useless if the migrant worker, when moving from one Member State to another would lose, even partially, the benefits acquired under social security regulations of the first Member State .The Treaty therefore provides that all the rights acquired or periods acquired under the laws of the several countries where the worker exercised his activity shall be

---

should be eligible for finance by the state on the same conditions as nationals, Case 42/87 *Commission v. Belgium* [1988] E.C.R. 5453 [1989] 1 C.M.L.R. 457. On the other hand the obligation to pay tuition for ordinary schools is acceptable, even if it is not required from nationals, since those schools do not provide vocational training: Case 263/86 *Belgium v. Humbel* [1989] E.C.R. 5383; [1989] 1 C.M.L.R. 393, but scholarships may not be refused: Case 235/87 *Mattencci v. Communaute Francaise of Belgium* [1988] E.C.R. 5606; [1989] 1 C.M.L.R. 357.

[61] Case C–278/94 *Commission v. Belgium* [1996] E.C.R. I–4307; [1997] 1 C.M.L.R. 1040: tide-over allowances to young people seeking their first employment may not be subject to them having completed their secondary education in an establishment subsidised or approved by that Member State.

[62] Case 32/75 *Cristin v. SNCF* [1965] E.C.R. at 1095(19).

[63] Reg. 1251/70 on the right of workers to remain in the territory of a Member State after having been employed in the State [1970] O.J. L142/24; [1970] O.J. Spec. Ed. 402.

aggregated for the purpose of acquiring and retaining the right to benefit and of calculating the amount of benefit.[64] Those benefits will be paid to the worker by the Member State of residence.

The purpose of the Treaty therefore is not to harmonise the existing social security systems of the different Member States into a single Community social security system, but to co-ordinate them. As the Court pointed out, the Treaty allows for separate systems to exist "creating separate claims against separate institutions against which the beneficiary has direct rights" either under national law alone or under national law supplemented by the Treaty. The Council must take such measures as are necessary to provide freedom of movement to workers and it "shall make arrangements to secure for the migrant workers and their dependents" the aggregation and payments just mentioned.[65] Those measures gave rise to an abundance of case law, which is not surprising considering the complexity and the scope of the matter. The following branches of social security are covered by the Council's regulations: sickness[66] and maternity,[67] invalidity,[68] old age,[69] survivors' family benefits,[70] unemployment,[71] family allowances,[72] accidents at work and occupational diseases[73] and death grants.[74] However, social "assistance" is not included, which, of course, does not simplify matters, since it is difficult to distinguish "assistance" from "security".[75]

---

[64] Art. 42 (ex 51) E.C.

[65] Reg.1408/71 on the application of social security schemes to employed persons and their families moving within the Community: [1971] O.J. L149/71; [1971] O.J. Spec. Ed. 71415, last amended by Reg. 1290/97 [1997] O.J. L176/1 and Reg. 574/72 fixing the procedure for implementing Reg. 1408/71. The Commission issued about two dozen Decisions on the interpretation of the various provisions of those Regulations; see directory of community legislation in force issued by the European Communities.

[66] Case 41/77 *R. v. Warry* [1977] E.C.R. 2085; [1977] 2 C.M.L.R. 783.

[67] Case 69/79 *Jordens-Voster v. Bedrijfsvereniging* [1980] E.C.R. 75; [1980] 3 C.M.L.R. 412.

[68] Case 2/72 *Murru v. Caisse Regionale d'Assurance Maladies de Paris* [1972] E.C.R. 333; [1972] C.M.L.R. 888.

[69] Case 1/72 *Frilli v. Belgium* [1972] E.C.R. 457; [1973] C.M.L.R. 386.

[70] Case 65/81 *R. v. Landeskreditbank Baden-Württemberg* [1982] E.C.R. 33; [1982] 1 C.M.L.R. 744.

[71] Case 76/76 *Di Paolo v. Office National de l'Emploi* [1977] E.C.R. 315; [1977] 2 C.M.L.R. 59.

[72] Case C–114/88 *Delbar v. Caisse d'Allocations Familiales* [1989] E.C.R. 4067.

[73] Case 268/78 *Pennartz v. Caisse Primaire d'Assurance Maladies des Alpes-Maritimes* [1979] E.C.R. 2411; [1980] 1 C.M.L.R. 682.

[74] Case 22/81 *R. v. Social Security Commissioner* [1981] E.C.R. 3357; [1982] 1 C.M.L.R. 427.

[75] See however Case 35/77 *Beerens v. Rijksdienst voor Arbeidsvoorziening* [1977] E.C.R. 2249; [1978] 2 C.M.L.R. 320.

Nearly thirty years after the adoption of the first implementing measures, the Court is still called upon to interpret them, which shows how complicated the matter indeed is. To give an example, in a 1998 judgment the Court decided that the rules concerning the free movement of goods preclude national rules under which social security institutions in a Member State refuse to reimburse to an insured person on a flat-rate basis the cost of a pair of spectacles purchased in another Member State, on the ground that prior authorisation is required for the purchase of medical products in other Member States, while it is not required for products purchased within that State.[76]

An Administrative Commission and an Advisory Committee on Social Security for Migrant Workers[77] were set up to help the Member states and the Commission with the implementation of the measures adopted in favour of migrant workers. Many more measures were adopted by the Community in the social field, but since they do not pertain in particular to migrant workers, they are analysed in the Chapter on Social Policy.

Exceptions to the Free Movement of Workers

There are two exceptions to the free movement of workers: one concerns limitations to the specific rights just examined, justified on grounds of public policy, public security or public health,[78] the other excludes the "employment in the public service" from the application of the Treaty rules.[79]

The meaning of the concepts "public policy", "public security" and "public health" which limit free movement[80] was defined by a Council directive[81] and the extensive case law on the Court on those subjects.[82]

With regard to "public policy"—but this also applies to the other two exceptions—the Court stated that this concept must, in the

[76] Case C–120/95 *Decker v. Caisse de Maladie des Employés Privés* [1998] E.C.R. I–1831.

[77] Reg. 1408/71 Arts 80 to 83, n.65 above. Internal Rules in [1995] O.J. C163/3.

[78] Art. 39(3) (ex 48(3)) E.C.

[79] Art. 39(4) (ex 48(4)) E.C.

[80] Reg. 1612/68, n.60 above and Dir. 68/360, n.48 above.

[81] Dir. 64/221 on the co-ordination of special measures concerning the movement and residence of foreign nationals which are justified on the grounds of public policy, public security or public health: [1964] O.J. 850 (63–64) [1964] O.J. Spec. Ed.117; incorporated [1994] O.J. l1/325.

[82] See for instance Case 36/75 *Rutili v. Minister for the Interior* [1975] E.C.R. 1219; [1976] 1 C.M.L.R. 140.

Community context and where, in particular, it is used as a justification for derogating from the fundamental principles of equality of treatment and freedom of movement for workers, be interpreted strictly, so that its scope cannot be determined by each Member State without being subject to control by the institutions of the Community. Restrictions can only be imposed on a migrant worker if his presence or conduct constitutes a genuine and sufficiently serious threat to public policy. A Member State's decision, whether it concerns refusal of entry[83] or expulsion,[84] must be based on the individual circumstances of any person under the protection of Community law and not on general considerations.

Furthermore, and this is essential, in each Member State, nationals of other Member States should have adequate legal remedies available to them in respect of the decisions of the administration based on the protection of public policy.[85] Those remedies should be the same as are available to nationals of the State concerned in respect of acts of the administration. The remedies can have suspensive effects. In order to be able to exercise his right of appeal, the worker in question must, of course, be given a precise and comprehensive statement of the grounds for the decision.

Concerning the non-applicability of the free movement of workers to *employment in the public service*, the exception does indeed allow the Member States to refuse access of non-nationals to certain activities in the public service; however, once they have been admitted, the exception cannot be invoked to justify discrimination on the ground of nationality.[86]

In one of its recent judgments,[87] the Court mentions that the Commission having found that, in certain Member States, a large number of posts regarded as belonging to the public service had no connection with the exercise of power conferred by public law or with the safeguarding of the general interests of the State, decided to implement a strategy. The latter was based upon a communication on the "Freedom of movement of workers and access to employment

---

[83] Case 41/74 *Van Duyn v. Home Office* [1974] E.C.R. 1337; [1975] 1 C.M.L.R. 1.

[84] Case 98/79 *Pecastaiug v. Belgian State* [1980] E.C.R. 691; [1980] 3 C.M.L.R. 685, a person against whom an expulsion order has been issued may exercise all the remedies available to nationals in respect of acts of the administration.

[85] See Joined Cases C–65 and C–11/95, *R. v. Secretary of State for the Home Department, ex p. Singhgara and Radiom* [1997] E.C.R. I–3343; [1997] 3 C.M.L.R. 703.

[86] Case 152/73 *Sotgiu v. Deutsche Bundespost* [1974] E.C.R. 153; [1975] 1 C.M.L.R. 91.

[87] Case C–290/96 *Commission v. Greece* [1996] E.C.R. I–3285.

in the public service—Commission action in respect of the application of Article 39(4) (ex 48.4)".[88]

In that communication, the Commission gave a list of commercial services carried out by entities, access in which should be open to nationals of other Member States. They concern; public transport, supply of water, electricity and gas, railways, airlines and shipping lines, posts and telecommunications, radio and television, public health care services, State education and research for non-military purposes conducted in public establishments. Having been informed recently of an Opera's refusal to engage a musician on the ground of his nationality, the Commission, in letters to certain Member States, added national, municipal and local musical orchestras to the list.

The Court stated that the fact that some posts in those areas may, in certain circumstances, be covered by the exception of the Treaty, cannot justify a general prohibition of access to non-nationals in those areas.[89]

Further Reading

Mel Cousins, "Equal Treatment and Social Security", (1994) 19 E.L.Rev. 123.

David O'Keefe, "The Free Movement of Persons and the Single Market", (1992) 3 E.L.Rev. 17

A. Mattera, "La libre circulation de travailleurs à l'intérieur de la Communauté Européenne", 47 (4–1993) Revue du Marché Unique Européen.

A Lyon-Caen et S. Simitis, "L'Europe sociale à la recherche de ses références", 109 (4–1993) Revue du Marché Unique Européen.

Luigi Daniele, "Non-Discriminatory Restrictions to the Free Movement of Persons", (1997) 22 E.L.Rev. 191.

Jorg Monar, "Justice and Home Affairs in the Treaty of Amsterdam: Reform at the Price of Fragmentation", 23 (1998) E.L.Rev. 320.

---

[88] [1988] O.J. C72/2.

[89] Practically identical judgments were delivered in Cases C–473/93 *Commission v. Luxembourg* [1996] E.C.R. I–3207; [1996] 3 C.M.L.R. 981 and C–173/94 *Commission v. Belgium* [1996] E.C.R. I–3265.

Chapter Fifteen
Freedom of Establishment

Introduction: Free Movement of Self-Employed Persons

If the free movement of workers finds its expression in the principle of non-discrimination and the right to enter, move, reside and remain, with their family, in another Member State, the free movement of self-employed people and legal persons, finds its implementation in the right of establishment and the right to provide services. The expression "free movement of self-employed persons" is not to be found in the Treaty. The right of the self-employed to move within the Community is provided for under "establishment" and "services".

The three freedoms mentioned above: free movement of workers, right of establishment and the right to provide services, show great similarities in so far as they consist mainly, where the Member States are concerned, in the prohibition of discrimination with their own nationals, and the obligation to admit and let the beneficiaries of those freedoms circulate, reside and remain in their territory. See, for instance, a directive on the abolition of restriction on the movement and residence within the Community of nationals of Member States with regard to establishment and the provision of services.[1] As shall be pointed out many implementing directives and regulations, including those concerning social security, apply without distinction to all the beneficiaries of the three freedoms. Even the exceptions provided for in the Treaty are practically the same for all three categories. The main differences are that free movement of workers does only concern individuals, while establishment and services also apply to undertakings, and, secondly, that establishment and services require professional qualifications, both for legal and natural persons, in order to accede to the "regulated" professions.

As for the self-employed, they can be defined, according to the

[1] Dir. 73/148 [1973] O.J. L172/14.

Court, as "any person who is insured against sickness or old age under one of the social security schemes organized for the benefit of self-employed".[2] It will be noted that the Treaty refers to "nationals of Member States" when defining the beneficiaries of the two freedoms, establishment and services.[3] The Court determined that this cannot be interpreted as excluding from the benefit of Community law own nationals who want to establish themselves in their own country after having resided in another Member State.

Self-employed persons are not only those exercising what is called the "professions" such as doctors, nurses, dentists, vets, midwives, architects and lawyers, but also tradespeople, *i.e.* those engaged in personal service sectors such as hotels, restaurants and taverns,[4] transport and travel agencies,[5] commercial agents,[6] retail trade,[7] and many others.[8]

For both freedoms, *i.e.* establishment and the provision of services, the Treaty did provide for the Council to draw up "general programmes"[9] for the abolition of existing restrictions. Those programmes were indeed adopted and constituted the basis for the many directives facilitating the exercise of those freedoms. They concern in the first place the harmonisation of the qualifications required from self-employed persons so that they may perform so-called "regulated" activities, *i.e.* activities subject to certain conditions.

As the Court pointed out, "when the taking up or pursuit of a specific activity is subject to certain conditions in the host Member State, a national of another Member State intending to pursue that activity, must in principle comply with them. However, national measures liable to hinder or make less attractive the exercise of fundamental freedoms guaranteed by the Treaty, must fulfil four conditions: they must be applied in a non-discriminatory manner, they must be justified by imperative requirements in the general interest, they must be suitable for securing the attainment of the

---

[2] Joined Cases C–4 and 5/95 *Stöber and Piosa Pareira v. Bundesanstalt für Arbeit* [1997] E.C.R. I–511 at 543(28); [1997] 2 C.M.L.R. 213.

[3] See Art. 43 (ex 52) and 49 (ex 59) E.C.

[4] Dir. 68/368 [1968] O.J. L260/19.

[5] Dir. 82/470 [1982] O.J. L213/1.

[6] Dir. 86/653 [1986] O.J. L382/17; concerning the right to a commission, see Case C–104/95 *Kontogeorgas* [1996] E.C.R. I–6643; [1997] 1 C.M.L.R. 1093.

[7] Dir. 68/363 [1868] O.J. L260/496.

[8] References can be found in the directory of Community legislation in force and other acts of the Community institutions, published by the Office for Official Publications of the European Communities.

[9] Ex Arts 54(1) and 63(1) E.C. Those programmes were indeed adopted and implemented by numerous directives.

objective which they pursue, and they must not go beyond what is necessary in order to attain it".[10] The fact that one Member State imposes less strict conditions than another Member State does not mean that the rules of the latter are disproportionate and hence incompatible with Community law.[11]

The directives facilitating the exercise of the freedom of establishment of self-employed people concern, in the second place, the mutual recognition of diplomas, certificates and other evidence of formal qualification.

Freedom of Establishment

In accordance with Chapter Two of Title III of the Treaty, restrictions to the freedom of establishment of nationals of a Member State in the territory of another Member State are prohibited; the prohibition also applies to the setting-up of agencies, branches and subsidiaries by nationals of any Member State established in the territory of any Member State.[12] The last words "established in the territory of any Member State" also apply, of course, to undertakings; they refer to the Treaty requirement that in order to "be treated in the same way as natural persons who are nationals of Member States", a company or firm must fulfil two conditions. In the first place, it must have been formed in accordance with the law of a Member State, and, in the second place, it must have its registered office, central administration or principal place of business within the Community, *i.e.* established in the territory of any Member State.[13]

It will be noted that the Treaty only requires "establishment" in one of the Member States, but not that a company or firm has the "nationality" of one of the Member States, in order to enjoy the freedom of establishment. This would have been extremely difficult, if not impossible, to establish anyway; it therefore suffices that the company or firm fulfils the above mentioned two conditions.

The Treaty defines the freedom of establishment as including the right to take up and pursue activities as a self-employed person and to set up and manage undertakings, in particular companies and firms in another Member State, under the conditions laid down for

---

[10] Case C–55/94 *Gebhard* [1995] E.C.R. I–4165; [1996] 1 C.M.L.R. 603.

[11] Case C–3/95 *Reisebüro Broede v. Sandker* [1996] E.C.R. I–6529(42); [1997] 1 C.M.L.R. 224.

[12] Art. 43 (ex 52) E.C.

[13] Art. 48(1) (ex 58(1)) E.C.

the nationals. The latter are defined as entities "constituted under civil or commercial law, including co-operative societies, and other legal persons governed by public or private law, save for those which are non-profit-making".[14]

As mentioned before, the freedoms provided for in the Treaty do not confer absolute rights, (no rights are absolute) but rights which are limited or "regulated" in the same way as the rights applying to the nationals. Or, as the Treaty states it in this case, "under the conditions laid down for its own nationals by the law of the country where such establishment is effected".[15]

In fact, establishment in another country, can mean that the person in question keeps his main interests[16] in one Member State and opens an agency, branch or subsidiary in another. The Court expressed it as follows: "the right of establishment includes freedom to set up and maintain, subject to observance of the professional rules of conduct, more than one place of work within the Community."[17] It can also mean, and probably in the first place, that the legal or natural person in question moves its entire business to another Member State.[18] In the latter case, the distinction with the right to provide services is rather clear-cut; in the former case the separation line is rather blurred.

As is the case with the free movement of workers, the Treaty explicitly provides that, besides the right to be treated without discrimination in the Member State of establishment, the beneficiary of the freedom enjoys certain specific rights, such as that to remain[19] in the territory of the host State, also after having pursued its activities,[20] and to acquire and use land and buildings situated in the

---

14 *ibid.*, para.2

15 *ibid.*

16 For taxation purposes it is sometimes important to be able to establish in which country the main interests are situated; see the rather amusing Case C–297/89 *Ryborg* [1991] E.C.R. I–1966; [1993] 1 C.M.L.R. 218, where the Court had to decide whether a person "resides" in the country where he works, or the one where his girl-friend lives and where he spends all his nights.

17 Case 107/83 *Ordre des Avocats du Barreau de Paris v. Klopp* [1984] E.C.R. 2971 at 2987(10); [1985] 1 C.M.L.R. 99.

18 Case 81/87, *R. v. Treasury and Commissioners of Inland Revenue, ex parte Daily Mail and General Trust PLC* [1988] E.C.R. 5483 at 5510(16).

19 Dir. 73/148 on the abolition of restrictions on movement and residence within the Community for nationals of Member States with regard to establishment and the provision of services.

20 Dir. 75/34 concerning the right of nationals of Member States to remain in the territory of another Member State after having pursued an activity in a self-employed capacity: [1975] O.J. L14/10. See also Dir. 90/365 on the right of residence for employees and self-employed persons who have ceased their occupational activity [1990] O.J. L180/28.

territory of another Member State (with some possible reservations for agricultural land[21]). There is, therefore, an evident link with the free movement of capital needed to acquire that real estate.

In order to attain freedom of establishment, the Treaty imposes various obligations on the Council and Commission and on the Member States. The former is to act by means of directives; as was indicated above, two legislative programmes were adopted by the Council. One concerns the mutual recognition of diplomas and the coordination of the conditions of access to certain professions, and the other one established harmonised rules for firms and companies. As for the Member States, their main obligation concerns the abolition of those administrative procedures and practices the maintenance of which would form an obstacle to freedom of establishment. Reference is made both to the conditions for setting up agencies, branches and subsidiaries and the conditions governing the entry of personnel belonging to the main establishment, into managerial and supervisory posts in such agencies, branches and subsidiaries. Interesting is that this entry of personnel is not limited to nationals of the Member States; this is particularly important for undertakings from third countries.

The directives referred to were, over the years, adopted in implementation of the General Programme previously provided for in the Treaty[22]—these programmes disappeared from the Treaty with the Treaty of Amsterdam, for the simple reason that they have been mostly implemented.

One directive which might interest many readers concerns the right of residence for students.[23] This Directive confers upon students from other Member States the right of residence under a few general conditions. They have to assure the authorities of the host State that they have sufficient resources for him- or herself and the family, if any, so as to avoid becoming a burden for that State; they must be enrolled in a recognised vocational training course or university and must be covered by sickness insurance.

---

[21] Art. 44(e) (ex 54(e)) E.C., which refers to Art. 33(2).

[22] Ex Art. 54(1): [1962] O.J. 2/36: General Programme for the abolition of restrictions on freedom of establishment; the programme, among others, defined the persons to whom the right of establishment applies, refers to the right of entry and residence in the host Member State, and details which restrictions have to be removed (they include rules which are applicable without discrimination to nationals and others but hinder the latter more).

[23] Dir. 93/96 [1996] O.J. L317/59.

Required Qualifications for Natural Persons

Where the taking-up of a specific activity is not subject to any rules in the host State, a national of any other Member State will be entitled to establish himself and pursue that activity there without further ado. On the other hand, freedom of establishment and the right to provide services require that the natural or legal person claiming those rights has the necessary qualifications, if those are required in the host Member State. This is the case for the performance of professional activities. The latter are indeed "regulated" in all the Member States. The diversity of the national requirements concerning those qualifications constituted the main obstacle to the freedom of establishment and of services. And, although the fact of requiring certain qualifications for the performance of professional activities is not only legitimate but constitutes a vital condition for the protection of the general interest, free movement of persons could not become effective without a minimum of harmonisation. Consequently, the Treaty provides that Council and Parliament acting jointly,[24] issue the necessary directives. Firstly, for the "mutual recognition of diplomas, certificates and other evidence of formal qualification".[25] Secondly, for the "coordination of the provisions laid down by law, regulation and administrative action in Member States concerning the taking up and pursuit of activities as self-employed persons". The latter implies, in most cases, "amendment of the existing principles laid down by law governing the professions with respect to training and conditions of access for natural persons".[26]

Those directives concern the following professions:

Doctors: provisions concerning both training and recognition of diplomas are now to be found in the same directive.[27] The Court was called upon to interpret the applicable provisions, and decided, for instance, that the rights also apply to own nationals who have acquired the necessary qualifications in another Member State in accordance with Community law, and who want to establish themselves as general practitioner in their own country, even if that

---

[24] Most existing directives and regulations were issued by the Council, since the co-decision procedure was only introduced by the Maastricht Treaty, which entered into force on November 1, 1993.

[25] Art. 47(1) (ex 57(1)) E.C.

[26] Art. 47(2) (ex 57(2)) E.C.

[27] Dir. 93/16 to facilitate the free movement of doctors and the mutual recognition of diplomas: [1993] O.J. L165/1, last modified [1998] O.J. L119/15.

practice there is subject to additional training requirements.[28] The most important aspect of this judgment is the recognition by the Court that the right to practice flows directly from the directive.

Nurses responsible for general care.[29] It might be interesting to very briefly mention here the sort of training details contained in this kind of directives. To become a nurse one must first have a general school education of at least ten years and secondly, have followed a full-time training programme set out in the Annex to the directive and comprising a three year course or 4.600 hours of theoretical and practical instruction. The directive goes on to define where and under which supervision the instruction must have been received. In fact, this is the only way of guaranteeing that the nurse from another Member State is at least as good as the national ones.

Dental practitioner.[30] The same kind of detailed training programme applies, of course, for this profession also.

Veterinary surgeons.[31] It was mentioned above that the freedom of establishment derives directly from the directives. However, the Court decided that a person could not rely on the provisions of an implementing directive prior to the date on which the Member States are required to have taken the measures necessary to comply with said directive.[32] The Court also decided, and this is important because it applies to all the directives on the mutual recognition of diplomas, that they can be invoked if they impose clear, complete, precise and unconditional duties on each Member State, which leave it no discretion. Consequently, an individual may, in proceedings before the national court, rely upon those provisions where they have not been implemented by the Member State concerned or have been implemented incompletely.[33]

With regard to doctors, nurses, dentists and vets, the mutual

---

28 Case 246/80 *Broekmeulen v. Huisarts Registratie Commissie* [1981] E.C.R. 2311; [1982] 1 C.M.L.R. 91. See also Joined Cases C–69 to 79/96 *Garofalo and Others v. Ministero della Sanita* [1997] E.C.R. I–5603; [1998] 1 C.M.L.R. 1087 concerning specific training in general medicine and the right to engage in general practice. See also Council Resolution on migrant doctors within the Community: [1997] O.J. C241/1.

29 Dir. 77/452 recognition of diplomas and Dir. 77/453 co-ordination of provisions concerning training: [1977] O.J. L56/1 and [1977] O.J. L56/8, both incorporated [1994] O.J. L1/572.

30 Dir. 78/686 recognition of diplomas and Dir. 78/687, co-ordination of provisions, both incorporated [1994] O.J. L1/572.

31 Dir. 78/1026 diplomas and Dir. 78/1027 co-ordination: [1978] O.J. L233/1 and 10, incorporated [1994] O.J. L1/371 and 572; see also Statements on diplomas [1978] O.J. C308/1.

32 See Case 271/82 *Auer v. Ministère Public* [1983] E.C.R. 2727; [1985] 1 C.M.L.R. 123.

33 Case 5/83 *Rienks* [1983] E.C.R. 4233; [1985] 1 C.M.L.R. 144.

recognition also applies to diplomas which are evidence of training which does not meet the minimum requirements and which was completed after the implementation of the relevant directives, but has commenced before the said implementation.[34]

Midwives.[35] Here also, training details are to be found in the directives in question.

The directives concerning the above mentioned professions were amended to take account of the changes in the titles of diplomas or in the designation of certain medical specialisations which had taken place in some Member States and to protect the holders of former qualifications.[36] They were again modified following the unification of Germany[37] and the enlargement to Austria, Finland and Sweden.

Pharmacists.[38] With regard to the directives concerning pharmacists, the Court stated that mere administrative practices which lack appropriate publicity cannot be regarded as the valid fulfilment of the obligations imposed by the Treaty on the Member States.[39]

Architects.[40] A directive concerns the mutual recognition of diplomas including measures to facilitate the effective exercise of the right of establishment and freedom to provide services, while a Council recommendation—and this is something that is not provided for the other professions—concerns holders of a diploma in architecture awarded in a third country.[41]

Lawyers: currently they are required, in order to practise in another Member State the law of that State, to either sit an aptitude test or complete an adaptation period before they can establish themselves in another Member State on the basis of recognition of their diploma.[42] In the absence of specific Community rules in the matter, each Member is free to regulate the exercise of the legal profession in its territory. There exists, however, a number of

---

[34] Dir. 81/1057 [1981] O.J. L385/25 supplementing Dirs 75/362, 77/452, 78/686 and 78/1026 concerning mutual recognition of diplomas of doctors, nurses, dentists and vets, respectively, with regard to acquired rights.

[35] Dir. 80/154 diplomas, and 80/155 co-ordination [1980] O.J. L33/1 and 8; incorporated [1994] O.J. L1/572.

[36] Dir. 89/594 [1989] O.J. L341/19; see also [1993] O.J. L165/1.

[37] Dir. 90/658 [1990] O.J. L353/73.

[38] Dir. 85/432 co-ordination and Dir. 85/433 diplomas [1985] O.J. L254/34 and 37.

[39] Case C–167/90 *Commission v. Belgium* [1991] E.C.R. I–2535.

[40] Dir. 85/384 diplomas and measures to facilitate establishment and services.

[41] [1985] O.J. L223/28. It should be noticed that a Council "Recommendation", which, by definition, is not binding, is nonetheless published in the "L" series of the O.J., this is awkward, since "L" stands for legislation.

[42] Dir. 89/48 on a general system for the recognition of higher-education diplomas.

directives destined to facilitate the effective exercise by lawyers of freedom to provide services.[43]

The so-called lawyers directive[44] was adopted in February 1998 and will become effective on December 15, 1999. It will allow a lawyer to become established in a Member State and to practise the host's country law immediately after simply proving that she or he is already registered as a lawyer in another Member State, without the need for either a test or an adaptation period. Moreover, after effectively and regularly pursuing for a period of three years an activity involving the law of the Member State in question, including Community law, a lawyer will be entitled to gain admission to the profession in the host Member State and so acquire the professional title of that Member State. For example, under the directive, a Danish "advokat" could become established in Germany, practise immediately German law as an "advokat" and, after three years, obtain the German title of "Rechtsanwalt".

This profession by profession approach took years. The main difficulty was, as already pointed out, the education and training needed to qualify for a "regulated" profession. It would have been totally impossible to achieve the required harmonisation for all the sectors in which self-employed persons are active. As was pointed out in the chapter on free movement of goods, the same problem was encountered with products from other Member States. The harmonisation approach was partially abandoned and complemented by the principle of "mutual recognition". Something similar happened with the free movement of the self-employed persons: the Council adopted "a general system for the recognition of higher education diplomas awarded on completion of professional education and training of at least three years duration", followed by adaptation periods or an aptitude test in the Member State of establishment. A second directive extended the system of mutual recognition to professional education and training of less than three years duration

[43] Dir. 77/249 [1977] O.J. L78/17, see Case C–294/89 *Commission v. France* [1991] E.C.R. I–3591; [1993] 3 C.M.L.R. 569 and Dir. 98/5 to facilitate practice of the profession of lawyer on a personal basis in a Member State other than that in which the qualification was obtained [1998] O.J. L177/36. See Case 2/74 *Reyners v. Belgian State* [1974] E.C.R. 631; [1974] 2 C.M.L.R. 305; Case 71/76 *Thieffry v. Conseil de l'Ordre des Avocats de Paris* [1977] E.C.R. 765; [1977] 2 C.M.L.R. 373 and Case 107/83 *Ordre des Avocats du Barreau de Paris v. Klopp* [1984] E.C.R. 2971; [1985] 1 C.M.L.R. 99.

[44] Dir. 98/5 to facilitate practice of the profession of lawyer on a permanent basis in a Member State other than that in which the qualification was obtained [1998] O.J. L77/36.

acquired at an establishment of higher education or at similar establishments.[45]

See, for instance, a directive on the abolition of restrictions on movement and residence within the Community for nationals of Member States with regard to establishment and the provision of services.[46] Other directives were adopted for the production and processing activities. They concern among others: agriculture,[47] activities in the wholesale trade and intermediaries in commerce, industry and small craft industries,[48] manufacturing and processing industries falling within Industries and Small Craft Industries (ISIC) Major groups 23–40,[49] mining and quarrying,[50] food manufacturing and beverage industries,[51] exploration prospecting and drilling for petroleum and natural gas.[52]

Required Qualifications for Legal Persons

As for "legal persons", the right of establishment is, according to the Court, "generally exercised by the setting up of agencies, branches and subsidiaries", as is expressly provided by the Treaty.[53] This free movement of companies and firms obviously requires that the safeguards for the protection of the interests of the members and the public, which are required by Member States, be equivalent throughout the Community. The Treaty therefore entrusts the Council and the Commission to take the necessary action, while it provides that the Council must act by means of directives.[54] Those provisions were given a wide interpretation by the institutions and the result was an ambitious legislative programme aiming at harmonising the national laws applying to undertakings, the so-called "company law directives".

---

[45] Dir. 89/48 [1989] O.J. L19/16; Dir. 92/51 on a second general system for the recognition of professional education and training to supplement Dir. 89/48 [1992] O.J. L209/25 last amended [1997] O.J. L184/31.

[46] Dir. 73/148 [1973] O.J. L172/14.

[47] See for instance Dir. 71/19 laying down detailed provisions for the attainment of freedom of establishment in respect of self-employed persons providing agricultural and horticultural services.

[48] Dir. 64/222 [1964] O.J. 56 857 and Dir. 64/224 [1964] O.J. 869.

[49] Dir. 64/427 [1964] O.J. 117 1863, amended by Dir. 69/77 [1969] O.J. L59/8 and Dir. 64/429 [1964] O.J. 117 1880.

[50] Dir. 64/428 [1964] O.J. 117 1871.

[51] Dir. 68/365 and 68/366 [1968] O.J. L260/505 and 509.

[52] Dir. 69/82 [1969] O.J. L68/4.

[53] Case 81/87 *R. v. Inland Revenue* [1988] E.C.R. at 5511(17).

[54] Art. 44(1) and (2) (ex 54(1) and (2)) E.C.

The *first* directive concerns the co-ordination of safeguards in the case of companies with limited liability. It provides for the protection of the interests of third parties by disclosure of information concerning such companies, the particulars of persons authorised to bind the company, restriction of the grounds on which obligations are not valid and limitation of the cases in which nullity can arise.[55]

The *second* directive deals with the formation of public liability companies and the maintenance and alteration of their capital; it restricts the right of a company to acquire its own shares.[56] This restriction was extended to the acquisition of shares by companies over which the first can exercise a dominant influence.[57]

The *third* directive concerns mergers of public limited liability companies and requires publication to the shareholders of the merger plan, accounts and reports.[58]

The *fourth* directive provides for similar legal requirements concerning the financial information that must be made public, such as annual accounts.[59] Extended to banks and other financial institutions[60] and to branches in the Community of credit or financial institutions with head office in third countries.[61]

The *fifth* directive never passed the stage of the Commission proposal.[62] It concerns the structure of public limited liability companies and the powers and obligations of their organs.

The *sixth* directive is about the division operations of public liability companies either by acquisition or by the formation of new companies, or both.[63]

---

[55] Dir. 68/151 [1968] O.J. L65/8. See Case C–79/96 *Daihatsu* [1997] E.C.R. I–6843: national legislation may not restrict to certain persons the right to apply for imposition of penalties in the event of failure of a company to disclose the annual accounts.

[56] Dir. 77/91 [1977] O.J. L26/1. See Case C–44/93 *Pafitis v. TKE* [1996] E.C.R. I–1347: increase of bank capital by administrative measure not allowed; Case C–49/95 *Siemens v. Nold* [1996] E.C.R. I–6017: Art. 29 of the directive does not prohibit the grant of a preferential right to shareholders in case of capital increase, and Case C–367/96 *Kefalas* [1998] E.C.R. I–2843 the right of a shareholder to invoke Art. 25(1) is not annulled by successful violation.

[57] Dir. 92/101 [1992] O.J. L347/64.

[58] Dir. 78/885 [1978] O.J. L295/36.

[59] Dir. 78/660 [1978] O.J. L222/11.

[60] Dir. 86/635 on the annual accounts and the consolidated accounts of banks and other financial institutions [1986] O.J. L372/1.

[61] Dir. 89/117 [1989] O.J. L44/40. See also Dir. 89/299 on the own funds of credit institutions [1989] O.J. L124/16.

[62] [1983] O.J. C240/2.

[63] Dir. 82/891 [1982] O.J. L378/47.

The *seventh* directive concerns group accounts[64] and was extended to banks and other financial institutions.[65]

The *eighth* directive deals with approval of persons responsible for carrying out statutory audits of accounting documents.[66]

There is no *ninth* directive, and the *tenth* never got beyond the draft stage: it was supposed to concern cross-frontier mergers of public liability companies.[67]

The *eleventh* directive concerns disclosure requirements with respect to branches opened in a Member State by certain types of companies governed by the law of another State.[68]

The *twelfth* directive deals with single-member private limited-liability companies.[69]

Mention must also be made of three directives on the admission of shares to official stock exchange listing,[70] the requirements for the drawing up, scrutiny and distribution of particulars to be published for that admission,[71] and information to be published on a regular basis by companies whose shares were admitted.[72] Furthermore, there are directives concerning taxation in the case of mergers, divisions, transfer of assets and exchanges of shares concerning companies of different Member States,[73] and in the case of parent companies and subsidiaries of different Member States.[74]

More than twenty years ago the Commission made a proposal for a *European Company Statute*, which would allow the setting up of a company according to Community law and recognised in all the Member States. The main difficulty was the workers representation in such a company; this was still unacceptable for certain Member States. However, substantial progress was made in 1997 and it is to be expected that it will be possible to set up such a European company before long. A forerunner, although on a more modest level, is the *European Economic Interest Grouping (EEIG)*,[75] which constitutes a very simple form of association between economic entities, based on Community law. When registered in one Member State, it is recognised as a legal entity in all the others. The only

---

[64] Dir. 83/349 [1983] O.J. L193/1.
[65] Dir. 86/635 [1986] O.J. L372/1.
[66] Dir. 84/253 [1984] O.J. L126/20.
[67] [1985] O.J. C203.
[68] Dir. 89/666 [1989] O.J. L395/36.
[69] Dir. 89/667 [1989] O.J. L395/40.
[70] Dir. 79/279 [1979] O.J. L66/21.
[71] Dir. 80/390 [1980] O.J. L100/1.
[72] Dir. 82/121 [1982] O.J. L48/26.
[73] Dir. 90/434 [1990] O.J. L225/1.
[74] Dir. 90/435 [1990] O.J. L225/6.
[75] Reg. 2137/85 [1985] O.J. L199/1; incorporated [1994] O.J. L1/517.

requirement is the drafting and registration of the bylaws; it enjoys legal personality if the Member State of registration so provides. It suffers, however, from an enormous drawback constituted by the fact that all the members of an EEIG are individually responsible for its debts. A problem might arise with the denomination of an EEIG, since this is done on the basis of national law.[76]

Exceptions to the Freedom of Establishment

A first exception might, in theory, result from the restrictions on the free movement of capital. Indeed, the Treaty provides that the freedom of establishment, which includes, as already indicated, the right to take up and pursue activities as self-employed persons and to set up and manage undertakings in another Member State, is "subject to the provisions of the Chapter relating to capital".[77] In itself this reference to capital is not surprising since establishment implies that the beneficiary of the right moves all or part of his assets to another Member State. Transfer of capital from one Member State to another used to be limited: restrictions only needed to be eliminated "to the extent necessary to ensure the proper functioning of the common market".[78] This changed with the Treaty on European Union, when all restrictions on the movement of capital between Member States were prohibited.[79] Consequently, the reservation concerning capital movements, no longer has any practical significance for the freedom of establishment.

The second exception to the freedom of establishment consists in its non-applicability, so far as any given Member State is concerned, to activities which in that State are concerned, even occasionally, with the exercise of official authority.[80] (Very similar to the exception examined in the previous Chapter on the free movement of workers: that freedom does not apply to "employment in the public service".[81]) According to the Court, this second exception to the freedom of establishment cannot "be given a scope which would exceed the objective for which the exception was inserted, having regard to the fundamental character of freedom of establishment and

[76] Case C–402/96 *European Information Technology Observatory* (EITO) [1997] E.C.R. I–7515.
[77] Art. 43(2) (ex 52(2)) E.C.
[78] Ex Art. 67 E.C.
[79] Art. 56(2) (ex 73(2)) E.C.
[80] Art. 45(1) (ex 55(1)) E.C.
[81] Art. 39(4) (ex 48(4)) E.C.

the rule on equal treatment with nationals in the system of the Treaty".[82]

Finally, there is the exception resulting from the applicability of provisions laid down by law, regulation or administrative action providing for special treatment for foreign nationals on grounds of public policy, public security or public health.[83] Those concepts were clarified by implementing legislation, which applies equally, of course, to all three freedoms: workers, establishment and services.[84]

Further Reading

Eric Werlauff, "The Development of Community Company Law", (1992) 17 E.L.Rev. 207.

Julian Maitland-Walker, *Guide to European Company Laws*, Sweet & Maxwell, London (1993).

---

[82] Case 2/74 *Reyners v. Belgium* [1974] E.C.R. 631(43); [1974] 2 C.M.L.R. 305. The Belgian Government had argued that, since the profession of *avocat* is connected organically with the functioning of the administration of justice, the whole profession is excepted from the rules of the Treaty. Other governments regarded the exception limited to those activities alone, within the various professions concerned, which are actually connected with the exercise of official authority, subject to their being separable from the normal practice of the profession. The *avocat* can, for instance, be required to assume the functions of judge; it is obvious that when this becomes necessary, the foreign lawyer will not be considered.

[83] Art. 46(1) (ex 56(1)) E.C.

[84] Dir. 64/221 on the co-ordination of special measures concerning the movement and residence of foreign nationals which are justified on grounds of public policy, public security or public health [1964] O.J. 850, amended by Dir. 75/35 [1975] O.J. L14/14.

Chapter Sixteen
Freedom to Provide Services

According to the Treaty, restrictions on freedom to provide services within the Community are prohibited in respect of nationals of Member States who are established in a State of the Community other than that of the person for whom the services are intended.[1] Obviously, this does not mean that the provider of the service may not move temporarily to the State of the recipient of his services. The only requirement for being a beneficiary of the freedom to provide services, is that the provider is "established" in a Member State different from that of the recipient party. A surgeon who moves to another Member State to perform an operation, does not "establish" himself in that other State: he remains "established" in the Member State where he resides and, normally, carries out his activities. For the performance of the operation in another Member State, he therefore comes under the provisions concerning the freedom to provide services.

According to the Court, the Treaty does not only prohibit overt discrimination, but "all forms of covert discrimination which, although based on criteria which appear neutral, in practice, lead to the same result".[2]

The main difference between establishment and the provision of services, is that in the first case, a national of a Member State participates on a stable and continuous basis in the economic life of another Member State and profits therefrom, so contributing to economic and social interpenetration within the Community in the sphere of activities of self-employed persons. By contrast the provider of services pursues his activity in another State on a temporary basis. This case is also provided for by the Treaty. Indeed, according to the latter "the person providing a service may, in order to do so, temporarily pursue his activity in the State where the service is provided, under the same conditions as are imposed by that State

[1] Art. 49 (ex 59) E.C.
[2] Joined Cases 62–63/81 *Seco v. Evi* [1982] E.C.R. 223(8).

on its own nationals".[3] This means, according to the Court, that the host State should impose on the person from another Member State who provides services on its territory, the same specific requirements based on the particular nature of the service where they have as their purpose the application of professional rules dictated by the common interest. Those requirements concern the organisation of the profession, the qualifications, the rules of professional ethics, the supervision and the liability, which are binding upon any person providing that kind of service.[4]

One would have thought that it goes without saying, that requiring the person in question to be established in the country where the service is provided, would totally defeat the purpose of the freedom to provide services and, therefore, be contrary to the Treaty; however, the Court had to state this explicitly.[5]

When the provider of the services temporarily moves to another Member State, he enjoys the same rights as those, which are granted to the migrant worker and the person who establishes himself in another Member State. This means, *inter alia*, that he may be accompanied by his family. Indeed, practically all the directives, which implement the freedom of establishment, are also based on the Treaty provisions concerning the freedom to provide services.

Required Qualifications

It goes also without saying that to exercise the right to provide services, the provider must have the required qualifications to do so. The person in question is, therefore, confronted with exactly the same problem as the person wishing to establish himself in another Member State to carry out a regulated activity. This means that the provider of services must have the necessary diplomas. The directives examined in the previous chapter on the right of establishment with regard to the recognition of evidence of qualification, the harmonisation of the conditions of professional education and training and the abolition of restrictions on movement and residence, also apply to those who wish to avail themselves of the freedom to provide services.[6] The Court also admitted that a Member State may reserve

[3] Art. 50(3) (ex 60(3)) E.C.

[4] Case 33/74 *Van Binsbergen v. Bedrijfsvereniging Metaalnijverheid* [1974] E.C.R. 1299; [1975] 1 C.M.L.R. 298.

[5] Case 220/83 *Commission v. France* [1986] E.C.R. 3663.

[6] See, for instance, Dir. 73/148 on the abolition of restrictions on movement and residence within the Community for nationals of Member States with regard to establishment and the provision of services [1973] O.J. L172/14.

the exercise of a given activity to a specific profession, since this rule applies without distinction to national providers of services and to those of other Member States.[7]

Most of those directives were adopted by the Council, now by the Parliament and the Council acting jointly, in implementation of a General Programme. This programme is no longer mentioned in the Treaty, but it was adopted and implemented and was quite similar to the General Programme for the abolition of the obstacles to the freedom of establishment.

And what about the "recipient" of the services? May she or he move to another Member State to receive services? This case not being provided for in the Treaty, the question was put to the Court, which determined that the right to provide services, also means the freedom to receive services. And, in order to be able do so, the recipient is just as free to travel to any other Member State as the provider of the services.[8] There are, indeed, numerous cases where it is the receiver of the service who moves to another Member State. This is the case, for instance, for patients who go and consult a doctor, students who go to school, the business man on the so-called "business trips" and, especially, the tourists. The rights of the recipient are also recognised in the directive on the abolition of restrictions on movement and residence within the Community for nationals of Member States with regard to establishment and the provisions of services, which provides "that the freedom to provide services entails that persons providing and receiving services, should have the right of residence for the time during which the services are being provided".[9]

Definition of "Services"

The Treaty gives the following definition of services: "services shall be considered 'services' within the meaning of this Treaty where they are normally provided for remuneration".[10] The essential characteristic of remuneration lies in the fact that it constitutes consideration for the service in question and is normally agreed upon between the provider and the recipient of the service.[11] According to the Court,

[7] Case C–3/95 *Reisebüro Broede v. Sandker* [1996] E.C.R. I–6511; [1997] 1 C.M.L.R. 224.

[8] Joined Cases 286/82 and 26/83 *Luisi and Carbone v. Ministero del Tesoro* [1984] E.C.R. 377; [1985] 3 C.M.L.R. 52.

[9] Dir. 73/148 [1973] O.J. L172/14.

[10] Art. 50(1) (ex 60(1)) E.C.

[11] Case 263/86 *Belgium v. Humbel* [1988] E.C.R. 5388(17); [1989] 1 C.M.L.R. 393.

remuneration is for instance absent in the case of courses provided in an establishment of higher education which is financed out of public funds and where students pay only enrolment fees.[12]

The Treaty adds that the above definition only applies "in so far as [the services] are not governed by the provisions relating to freedom of movement for goods, capital and persons".[13] This is, at first sight a rather curious addition, since one might wonder what the free movement of goods has to do with services; indeed, the Treaty also provides that "freedom to provide services in the field of transport shall be governed by the Title relating to transport".[14] One would imagine that "services", where goods are concerned, would mainly be transport; however, one has to see that there are other ways of selling goods across a border. Those operations come, according to the Court, under the provisions concerning the free movement of goods.

The same kind of question arose with regard to television signals: are they goods or services. According to the Court, they must, in the absence of express provision to the contrary, by reason of their nature, "be regarded as provision of services".[15]

And what about the services related to movement of capital, which are also excluded from the provisions of freedom to provide services? The first service that comes to mind in this regard, is, of course, banking. Here again, the Treaty provides that "[t]he liberalisation of banking and insurance services connected with movement of capital shall be effected in step with the liberalisation of movement of capital". Since the moment the Treaty on European Union entered into force, capital movements across the Community were entirely free[16] and, consequently, so are services in those sectors, independently of the provisions on the freedom to provide services.

Finally, as regards "persons" whose free movement is excluded from the provisions concerning freedom to provide services, it concerns the freedom of establishment, since the Treaty provides that the right of a person providing services to temporarily pursue his activity in the State where the service is provided, is "without prejudice to the provisions of the Chapter relating to the right of establishment".[17] According to the Court this means that the

---

[12] *ibid.*

[13] Art. 50(1) (ex 60(1)) E.C.

[14] Art. 51(1) (ex 61(1)) E.C.

[15] Case 155/73 *Sacchi* [1974] E.C.R. 409(6); [1974] 2 C.M.L.R. 177. See also Case 52/79 *Procureur du Roi v. Debauve* [1980] E.C.R. 833; [1981] 2 C.M.L.R. 362 and Case 62/79 *Coditel v. Cine Vog Films* [1980] E.C.R. 881; [1981] 2 C.M.L.R. 362.

[16] Art. 56 (ex 73(b)) E.C.

[17] Art. 50(3) (ex 60(3)) E.C.

provisions of the Chapter on services "are subordinate to those of the chapter on the right of establishment". This means that the provisions relating to the provision of services only apply if those relating to the right of establishment do not apply. In other words, it only applies to a situation in which a person moves from one Member State to another, not for the purpose of establishment there, but in order to pursue his activity there on a temporary basis. This temporary nature has to be determined in the light of its duration, regularity, periodicity and continuity. This does not mean that the provider of services may not equip himself with some form of infrastructure in the host Member State, including an office, chambers or consulting rooms, in so far as such infrastructure is necessary for the purposes of performing the services in question.[18]

The Court gave a rather extensive interpretation of the concept "services". It determined that a national from another Member State has the same right as the nationals from the host State to obtain the financial compensation provided for by national law in case of assault.[19] It concerns here a "service" provided by the State.

The Court also stated that since the end of the transitional period, the essential requirements of the freedom to provide services are unconditionally applicable[20] and have direct effect.[21]

With regard to the kinds of services covered by the freedom, the Treaty refers to activities of an "industrial" or "commercial" character and activities of a "craftsman" and "the professions".[22]

The Exceptions, the Directives and the Companies and Firms

None of those subjects are explicitly mentioned in the chapter on the freedom to provide services, but the Treaty provides that certain provisions of the chapter on the freedom of establishment shall apply to the freedom of providing services.

Those provisions concern in the first place the *exceptions* to the freedom. The same exception apply as to the freedom of establishment.[23] Concretely speaking this means that Member States may

[18] Case C–55/94 *Gebhard v. Consiglio dell'Ordine degli Avvocati e Procuratori di Milano* [1995] E.C.R. I–4165; [1996] 1 C.M.L.R. 603.
[19] Case 186/87 *Cowan v. Trésor Public* [1989] E.C.R. 216; [1990] 2 C.M.L.R. 613.
[20] Case 33/74 *Van Binsberge* [1974] E.C.R. 1299; [1975] 1 C.M.L.R. 298.
[21] Joined Cases 110-111/78 *Ministère Public and A.S.B.L. v. Van Wesemael* [1979] E.C.R. 35; [1979] 3 C.M.L.R. 87.
[22] Art. 50(2) (ex 60(2)) E.C.
[23] Art. 55 (ex 66) E.C.

prevent nationals from other Member States from exercising activities, which, as far as any given Member State is concerned, are, in that State, connected, even occasionally, with the exercise of official authority.[24] It will be remembered that the Court decided that if the exercise is indeed only occasionally so connected, and can, furthermore be separated from the main activity, then there is no justification for excluding the whole profession.[25] Freedom to provide services may also be limited on the basis of provisions laid down by law, regulation or administrative action providing special treatment for foreign nationals on grounds of public policy, public security or public health.[26] Those exceptions must, however, be interpreted restrictively and, when applied, account must be taken of the abundant case law of the Court.

In the second place there is the obligation, already examined above, imposed upon Parliament and Council acting jointly to issue *directives* on the recognition of diplomas and the harmonisation of national provisions concerning training and conditions of access, to the regulated activities.

And finally there is the fact that *companies and firms* must be treated in the same way as natural persons which are nationals of Member States. The meaning of these terms and the legislative programme implemented by the institutions of the Community, to ensure that those legal persons possess all the required qualifications in order to protect the interests of their members and of the public, were also referred to in the previous chapter.

A final reminder: the Treaty provisions and therefore also those concerning the freedom to provide services, only apply when a transnational element is involved. In other words, the provisions examined in this chapter cannot be invoked by a person whose activities are confined within a single Member State.[27]

Financial Services

Of particular importance within a single market is the financial services sector, *i.e.* banks and the credit and financial institutions, to which should be added insurance. The free circulation of "financial

---

[24] Art. 45 (ex 55) E.C.

[25] Case 2/74 *Reyners v. Belgium* [1974] E.C.R. 631; [1974] 2 C.M.L.R. 305.

[26] Art. 46(1) (ex 56(1)) E.C.

[27] Case 52/79 *Procureur du Roi v. Debauve* [1980] E.C.R. 833(15); [1981] 2 C.M.L.R. 362.

products" is made constantly easier by the development of modern technology in the communication field. Those services were to be liberalised in step with the liberalisation of movement of capital and payments, in so far as those services are connected with such movement. Since the free movement of capital and payments is now a reality, this does no longer constitute an obstacle for the free movement of financial services. The problem lies with the rules concerning the operation of financial institutions. Free circulation of financial products needs mutual recognition by Member States of what the other States do to safeguard the interests of the public.

Consequently, some harmonisation is required of such matters as licensing, financial supervision, solvency ratio, own funds, winding up, etc. It was agreed among the Member States that any harmonisation or mutual recognition must be guided by the principle of "home country control". This means assigning the primary task of supervising the financial institutions, to the competent authorities of the Member State of origin, while the other States would communicate to the former all the necessary information; the Member State of destination of the services would play a complementary role.

The first directive adopted in this sector concerned the abolition of restrictions on freedom of establishment and freedom to provide services in respect of self-employed activities of banks and other financial institutions.[28] It was followed by a directive on the harmonisation of provisions relating to the taking up and pursuit of the business of credit institutions,[29] and the second directive on the co-ordination of laws, regulations and administrative provisions relating to the taking up and pursuit of the business of credit institutions.[30] It lays down the principle of the single banking authorisation and supervisions and control by the home Member State. It also enables banks to set up branches and other financial services freely throughout the Community.

Other directives concern: the annual accounts and consolidated accounts of banks and other financial institutions[31]; obligations regarding the publication of annual accounting documents of branches of credit institutions and financial institutions having their head offices outside the Member State where the branch is established[32]; the own funds of credit institutions[33]; the solvency ratio for

---

[28] Dir. 73/183 [1973] O.J. L194/1.
[29] Dir. 77/780 [1977] O.J. L322/30, last amended by Dir. 98/33 [1998] O.J. L204/29.
[30] Dir. 89/646 [1989] O.J. L386/1.
[31] Dir. 86/635 [1986] O.J. L372/1.
[32] Dir. 89/117 [1989] O.J. L44/40.
[33] Dir. 89/299 [1989] O.J. L124/16, last amended [1992] O.J. L110/52.

credit institutions[34]; the supervision of credit institutions on a consolidated basis[35]; the monitoring and control of large exposures of credit institutions[36]; the capital adequacy of investment firms and credit institutions[37]; the deposit guarantee schemes[38]; cross-border credit transfers.[39]

It is also interesting to note that the Court declared that the directive on consumer protection in respect of contracts negotiated away from business premises was applicable to services offered by banks.[40] The Court also stated that the harmonisation directives[41] preclude, for instance, a Member State from requiring a credit institution already authorised in another Member State to obtain again an authorisation in order to be able to grant a mortgage loan to a person residing within its territory.[42] It also follows from the directives[43] that if the banks must comply with an authorisation procedure, it may no longer be examined on the basis of economic needs of the market. Finally, it should be noted that in 1991, the Council adopted a directive on prevention of the use of the financial system for the purpose of money laundering.[44] The directive was accompanied by a statement committing the Member States to enact criminal legislation determining the penalties to be applied for infringement of those provisions.

An Advisory Committee for banking was set up in 1977[45]; it is composed of senior officials from the Member States, whose task it is to help the Commission in implementing and completing the Community banking legislation.

Insurance

Similar legislation was enacted with regard to insurance. The internal market in that sector was completed years ago with the

[34] Dir. 89/647 [1989] O.J. L386/14, last amended [1996] O.J. L85/17.
[35] Dir. 92/30 [1992] O.J. L110/52, last amended [1993] O.J. L141/1.
[36] Dir. 92/121 [1992] O.J. L29/1.
[37] Dir. 93/6 [1993] O.J. L141/1, amended [1998] O.J. L204/13.
[38] Dir. 94/19 [1994] O.J. L135/5; see Case C–233/94 *Germany v. EP and Council* [1997] E.C.R. I–2405, concerning the obligation imposed upon all credit institutions to join a deposit-guarantee scheme.
[39] Dir. 95/67 [1995] O.J. L43/25.
[40] Case C–45/96 *BHW v. Dietzinger* [1998] E.C.R. I–17.03.
[41] See, for instance, Dir. 89/646 amending Dir. 77/780 [1989] O.J. L386/1.
[42] Case C–229/95 *Parodi* [1997] E.C.R. I–3899.
[43] Dir. 89/646 [1989] O.J. L386/1, modified by Dir. 92/39 [1992] O.J. L110/52.
[44] Dir. 91/308 [1991] O.J. L166/77.
[45] Dir. 77/780 [1977] O.J. L322/30.

introduction of freedom of establishment and freedom to provide services on the basis of a single licence.[46] Laws were harmonised with regard to insurance against civil liability in respect of the use of motor vehicles,[47] direct insurance other than life insurance,[48] the activities of insurance agents and brokers,[49] co-insurance,[50] direct life insurance,[51] legal expenses insurance,[52] and on the annual accounts and consolidated accounts of insurance undertakings.[53]

Restrictions on the freedom to provide services can also result from national procedures concerning *public service contracts*. As shall be seen in the chapter on "Industry Policy", several directives were adopted to achieve the opening of all national procedures to tenders from nationals of[54] other Member States.

Further Reading

D. Wyatt and A. Dashwood, *European Community Law* (3rd ed., Sweet & Maxwell, London, 1993).

P. Annabolis, La libre circulation des services dans l'Union Europeéne, 123 (2–1994) Revue du Marché Unique Européen.

[46] Dir. 64/225 [1964] O.J. 56/868.
[47] Dir. 72/166 [1972] O.J. L103/1, several times amended.
[48] Dir. 73/239 [1973] O.J. L228/3, last amended by Dir. 95/26 [1995] O.J. L168/7 and Dir. 73/240 on the freedom of establishment in the business of direct insurance other than life insurance [1973] O.J. L87/12. See Case C–238/94, *Garcia* [1996] E.C.R. I–1673.
[49] Dir. 77/92 [1977] O.J. L26/14.
[50] Dir. 78/473 [1978] O.J. L1/403.
[51] Dir. 79/267 [1979] O.J. L63/1, last amended by Dir. 95/26 [1995] O.J. L168/7.
[52] Dir. 87/344 [1987] O.J. L185/77.
[53] Dir. 91/674 [1991] O.J. L374/7.
[54] See, for instance, Dir. 92/50 relating to the co-ordination of procedures for the award of public service contracts [1992] O.J. L209/1.

Chapter Seventeen

Free Movement of Capital and Payments

Previously the free movement of capital was only required "to the extent necessary to ensure the proper functioning of the common market".[1] This changed with the Treaty on European Union. Indeed, with regard to the free movement of capital, the Treaty provides that all restrictions shall be prohibited, not only between Member States, but also between Member States and third countries. The Treaty, however, adds that this prohibition applies "within the framework of the provisions set out in this Chapter".[2] The prohibition was reinforced by the provisions on Economic and Monetary union, which provides that before the beginning of the second stage (January 1, 1994) "each Member State shall adopt, where necessary, appropriate measures to comply with the prohibitions laid down in Article 56".[3] The other provisions of this Chapter on Capital and Payments, save one, refer exclusively to the free movement of capital with third countries,[4] from which one can deduce that the prohibition applies practically without restrictions to the free movement of capital between Member States. More modifications were introduced by the Treaty of Amsterdam which repealed ten out of the fifteen Articles of the Treaty as modified by the Treaty on European Union.[5]

The only exceptions concern the application of tax laws,[6] the prudential supervision of financial institutions, and procedures for the declaration of capital movements for purposes of administrative

[1] Art. 67 E.C., which was repealed by the Treaty of Amsterdam. However, Dir. 88/361 for the implementation of Article 67 of the Treaty is still on the books [1988] O.J. L78/5.

[2] Art. 56(1) (ex 73b(1)) E.C.

[3] Art. 116(2) (ex 109(2)) E.C.

[4] See Art. 57(1) and (2) (ex 73c(1)) E.C., and (2), Art. 59 (ex 73f) E.C., and Art. 60 (ex 73g) E.C.

[5] Arts 67 to 73a, 73e and 73h E.C. were repealed by the Treaty of Amsterdam.

[6] Art. 58(1)(a) (ex 73d(1)(a)) E.C.

or statistical information.[7] To those exceptions must be added the measures which are justified on grounds of public policy or public security. The exceptions based on those two grounds are common to all the freedoms, as was seen above.[8] In the case of freedom to move capital they refer, for instance, to national measures designed to ensure effective fiscal supervision and to prevent illegal activities such as tax evasion, money laundering,[9] drug trafficking or terrorism.[10] The Court considered that those aims could be attained by making movement of capital conditional on prior "declaration", but that prior "authorisation" would render the freedom of capital movement illusory.[11]

With regard to tax laws, for instance, Member States have the right to apply tax provisions distinguishing between taxpayers, which are not in the same situation with regard to their place of residence or with regard to the place where their capital is invested.[12] The Treaty makes no distinction between movement of capital and movement of payments, both are entirely liberated. The distinction might be difficult to make anyway when it concerns, for instance, coins, banknotes or bearer cheques. The Treaty establishes a relation between capital movement and direct investment (including real estate), establishment, the provision of financial services or the admission of securities to capital markets.[13] Without those, transfers constitute payments, and are linked mainly to goods and services.

Another distinction has to be made with regard to means of payment such as coins: could they be considered as "goods" and consequently enjoy free movement and be subject to limitations on that account? To take an example, the reader should try to decide whether gold coins such as the Krugerrands or silver alloy coins

---

7 Art. 58(1)(b) (ex 73d(1)(b)) E.C.

8 Workers: Art. 39(3) (ex 48(3)) E.C.; establishment: Art. 46(1) (56(1)) E.C., and services: Art. 55 (ex 66) E.C. which refers to Art. 46.

9 See Dir. 91/308 on prevention of the use of the financial system for the purpose of money laundering: [1991] O.J. L 44/40.

10 Joined Cases C–163, 165 and 250/94 *Sanz de Lera and Others* [1995] E.C.R. I-4821(22).

11 See also Joined Cases C-286/82 and C-26/83 *Luisi and Carbone v. Ministero del Tesoro* [1984] E.C.R. 377; [1983] 3 C.M.L.R. 52 and Joined Cases C–358 and 416/93 *Criminal proceedings against Aldo Bordessa and Others* [1995] E.C.R. I–361(25); [1996] 2 C.M.L.R. 13, where the Court already declared that the export of coins, banknotes or bearer cheques could be made conditional on prior declaration, but not on prior authorisation.

12 Art. 58(1)(a) (ex 73d(1)(a)) E.C.

13 Art. 57(2) (ex 73c(2)) E.C. See Joined Cases mentioned in n. 10, wherein the Court refers to Dir. 88/361 (see n.1) and its Annex I, which refers to physical imports or exports of financial assets.

which are legal tender in a Member State are to be regarded and to be treated as "goods".[14]

It should be clear that if the free movement of capital is closely linked with the freedom of establishment, the free movement of payments is a necessary complement to the free movement of goods, workers, services and capital. Indeed, nobody would profit from those freedoms if the financial results of the activities carried out under them could not be "brought home" to wherever in the Community the operator resides. The introduction of the euro will certainly facilitate all those transactions.

Further Reading

Derek Devgun, "Multilateral Capital Transfer Tax Treaty Relief within the European Community", (1995) 20 E.L.Rev. 451.

Jackie Jones, "The Committee of the Regions, Subsidiarity and a Warning", (1997) 22 E.L. Rev. 312.

Laurence Gormley and Jakob de Haan, "The Democratic Deficit of the European Central Bank", (1996) 21 E.L. Rev. 95.

[14] Case 7/78, *R. v. Thompson* [1978] E.C.R. 2247; [1979] 1 C.M.L.R. 47: the Court decided that silver alloy coins, which are no longer legal tender, are goods whose export may be prohibited on the grounds of public policy within the meaning of Art. 30 (ex 36) E.C.; on the other hand, silver alloy coins which are legal tender in a Member State, are by their very nature to be regarded as means of payment and the provisions concerning the free movement of goods are not applicable; the same applies to Krugerrands since certain Member States permit dealings in these coins which are therefore to be regarded as being equivalent to currency.

PART FOUR: OTHER COMMUNITY POLICIES

Chapter Eighteen
Competition Policy

Introduction

Competition policy is, according to the Commission,[1] a structural factor of great importance when it comes to helping Europe adapt to the new competitive environment brought about by globalisation. This is because:

- it seeks to make the economic structures stronger and more competitive;
- it helps, through a policy of balanced liberalisation, to safeguard equality of treatment, thereby ensuring that European businesses and consumers are provided with the best possible services at the lowest prices, and
- it plays a key role in the implementation of the single market, whose mechanisms ensure a better allocation of resources and optimum efficiency of the economy, while paying due regard to the general interest.

The campaign against restrictive practices remains at the forefront of the Commission's competition activities. The same holds true for the application of stringent rules of State aids, while its activities in the field of merger control grow by the year.

I. Competition Rules Applying to Undertakings[2]

Those rules are contained mainly in three sets of provisions: the first concern what is generally referred to as "cartels", the second; abuse

[1] Report on Competition, 1996, introduction by Mr. Karel van Miert.
[2] Art. 81 (ex 85) to 85 (ex 89) E.C. and Merger Regulation, see below.

of dominant positions and the third, concentrations. The term cartel designates all forms of co-operation among undertakings; the second expression refers to anti-competitive behaviour of (an) undertaking(s) in a dominant position, while concentrations cover the creation or strengthening of a dominant position through joint ventures, mergers or take-overs.

Whether a cartel is incompatible with the common market or whether there is abuse of a dominant position is decided by the national judge or by the Commission, but only the latter can grant an exemption from the prohibition or decide what measure must be taken to eliminate the abuse. As for concentrations, which have a Community dimension, they need to be notified only to the Commission. However, a Member State can ask for the whole or part of the case to be assigned to it when it considers that it would affect competition on a market within that State, which "presents all the characteristics of a distinct market".[3]

In other words, both the Commission and the authorities of the Member States are entrusted, in close co-operation with each other,[4] with the implementation of the Community competition rules, but only the former can impose fines for violation of those rules.

1. Cartels (Agreements, Decisions of Associations of Undertakings and Concerted Practices)—Article 81 (ex 85) E.C.

The Treaty[5] refers not only to "agreements between undertakings", but also to "decisions by associations of undertakings" and "concerted practices". They are prohibited when they affect trade between Member States and have as their object or effect the prevention, restriction or distortion of competition. And, when caught by the prohibition, they are automatically void, unless they are exempted by the Commission. Each one of these expressions needs to be clarified and interpreted.

[3] Reg. 4064/89 on the control of concentrations between undertakings [1989] O.J. L395/1, as rectified by [1990] O.J. L257/13, amended by the 1994 Act of Accession and Reg. 1310/97 [1997] O.J. L180/1.

[4] See, *e.g.* Commission Notice on co-operation between national competition authorities and the Commission in handling cases falling within the scope of Arts 85 or 86 (now 81 and 82) E.C. of the Treaty [1997] O.J. C313/3.

[5] See Art. 81 (ex 85) E.C.

(a) The Prohibition

Obviously not all agreements between undertakings are prohibited; on the contrary, the whole economy thrives on such agreements, and the Commission has done everything to encourage them, especially cross-border ones. However, such agreements are prohibited when they affect trade between the Member States and the parties to the cartel seek to restrict competition or cause it to be restricted in the common market. This basic rule seems simple enough, but what exactly is meant by "agreement", "undertaking", "decision by associations of undertakings", "concerted practices", "have as their object or effect", "may affect trade between Member States", and "distortion of competition"? Those terms will be successively examined hereafter.

(i) Agreements and Concerted Practices

An agreement is a legally binding and, therefore, enforceable commitment.[6] According to the case law of the European courts, "there is an agreement in the sense of Article 85(1) [now Article 81(1)], when the act considered by the Commission is the faithful expression of the parties' intention to conduct themselves in a certain way".[7] A concerted practice, on the other hand, is an anti-competitive parallel market behaviour of several undertakings, which is caught by the prohibition when it is the result of a "concertation" among said undertakings.[8]

The difference between an agreement and a concerted practice is important with regard to the conditions for the existence of a prohibition and the proof of an infringement. Indeed, in the case of an agreement, it is sufficient for a violation of the competition rules to occur, that the clauses of the agreement show the intention of the parties to distort competition. Whether competition was actually

---

[6] Such a commitment is not limited to certain forms; see Joined Cases 209 to 265/78 and 218/78 *Van Landewijk v. Commission* [1980] E.C.R. 3125; [1981] 3 C.M.L.R. 134. Also Case C–277/87 *Sandoz v. Commission* [1990] E.C.R. I–45: the systematic dispatching by a supplier to his customers of invoices bearing the words "exports prohibited", constitutes a prohibited agreement. *Id.* Commission Decision of January 10, 1996 *Bayer* [1996] O.J. L291/1, implicit acceptance by wholesaler through continued dealing, so agreement reached.

[7] Case T–347/94 *Mayer-Melnhof* [1998] E.C.R. II–1751(65).

[8] For an example of a concerted practice see Joined Cases 100–103/80 *Musique Diffusion Française v. Commission* [1983] E.C.R. 1825; [1983] 3 C.M.L.R. 221.

distorted is irrelevant.[9] In the case of a concerted practice, concertation is not, in itself, prohibited; it is the market behaviour, the practice, following the concertation, which is caught by the prohibition when it affects trade and distorts competition.

As for the proof of the existence of a concerted practice, the Commission must show both that the practice violates the Treaty and that there was collusion among the parties, which led to that anti-competitive behaviour. Proof that there was concertation could be, for instance, the existence of a gentlemen's agreement.[10] For example, parallel price increases by several undertakings are not in themselves prohibited; they could indeed be purely coincidental or the result of a particular market situation known as oligopoly with price leadership.[11] On the other hand, such parallel price increases are prohibited when they are the result of a concertation. Proof of such concertation will often have to be based on circumstantial evidence,[12] such as the participation in meetings with anti-competitive object.[13]

(ii) Decisions by associations of undertakings

Decisions must be understood to include the constitutive act of a trade association and its internal rules,[14] decisions made in accordance with those rules and which are binding upon the members of the association[15] and also recommendations such as the fixing of "target

---

[9] See Case 56/65 *Société Technique Minière v. Maschinenbau Ulm* [1966] E.C.R. 235 at 249; [1966] C.M.L.R. 357.

[10] Gentlemen's agreements and other arrangements, binding in honour only, are not, in this writer's view, prohibited by the Treaty whatever their content; it is only the resulting "practice" which can be prohibited. See *ACF Chemiefarma Dec.* [1969] O.J. L192/5 where the Commission considered a gentlemen's agreement to be a binding agreement in the sense of Art. 81 (ex 85) E.C. because it was concluded together with a binding agreement which referred to the former. This view was accepted by the Court: Case 41/69 *ACF Chemiefarma v. Commission* [1970] E.C.R. 661 at 693 (113,114). See also Opinion of the Advocate-General, *ibid.* at 714.

[11] In Case 85/76 *Hoffmann-La Roche v. Commission* [1979] E.C.R. 461 at 520(39); [1979] 3 C.M.L.R. 211, the Court refers to "parallel courses of conduct which are peculiar to oligopolies".

[12] See, *e.g.* Case 48/69 *ICI v. Commission* [1972] E.C.R. 619; [1972] C.M.L.R. 557 and Joint Cases 40, etc. 73 *Suiker Unie and Others v. Commission* [1975] E.C.R.1663; [1976] C.M.L.R. 295. In both cases the Court admitted the existence of a concerted practice. Not admitted in Joined Cases 29 and 30/83 *Cram and Rheinzink v. Commission* [1984] E.C.R. 1679 at 1702(19); [1985] 1 C.M.L.R. 688.

[13] Case T–327/94 *SCA Holdings v. Commission* [1998] E.C.R. II–1374.

[14] *ASPA* Dec. [1970] O.J. L148/1.

[15] *Bomee-Stichting* Dec. [1975] O.J. L329/30.

prices" by an association.[16] Whether an agreement must be regarded as one between undertakings or one between associations of undertakings is irrelevant. The same applies to the framework within which decisions of associations are taken and the classification given to that framework by the national authorities.[17]

As for the term "association",[18] it is not limited to any particular form of association. It also includes associations of associations[19] with or without legal personality and non-profit-making associations. According to the Court of First Instance, an association representing a significant number of manufacturers in a relevant sector can be directly and individually concerned by a decision addressed to another association and is therefore admissible to challenge that Commission decision in court.[20]

(iii) Undertakings

The term also covers entities without legal personality[21]; however, in the latter case they must have some kind of recognised legal status.[22] This is necessary for them to be able to carry out economic activities.[23] In other words, they must have "legal autonomy", which they can only have when they are a "legal entity". Whether or not the latter is the case, must be determined in accordance with the applicable national law.

---

[16] Case 8/72 *Cementenhandelaren v. Commission* [1972] E.C.R. 977 at 991(19); [1973] C.M.L.R. 7. See also Joined Cases 209 etc. 78 *Van Landewyck* [1980] E.C.R. 3125 at 3254(102); [1981] 3 C.M.L.R. 134.

[17] Case 123/83 *BNIC v. Clair* [1985] E.C.R. 391 at 423(17–20); [1985] 2 C.M.L.R. 430.

[18] See Joined Cases T–528/93, etc. *Metropol Television* [1996] E.C.R. II–649; [1996] 5 C.M.L.R. 386.

[19] A *de facto* association of associations was considered by the Commission to be an association of undertakings. See *Cecimo* Dec. [1969] O.J. L69/13 and Joined Cases *van Landewyck* (note 16).

[20] Case T–380/94 *AIUFASS* [1996] E.C.R. II–2169; [1997] 3 C.M.L.R. 542.

[21] Art. 43(2) (ex 52(2)) E.C. refers to "undertakings, in particular companies or firms within the meaning of the second paragraph of Article 48"; the latter (ex 58) provides that "'companies or firms' means companies or firms constituted under civil or commercial law". From this it follows that when the Treaty refers to legal persons it uses the terms "company" or "firm" and that the term "undertaking" is broader and also covers entities without legal personality. See Case T–25/96 *Arbeitsgemeinschaft Deutscher Luftfahart-Unternehmen* [1998] E.C.R. II–363.

[22] This would be the case, *e.g.* with the Dutch "vennootschap onder firma", the English "partnership" and the German "offene Gesellschaft".

[23] See, *e.g.* Case C–244/94 *Société d'Assurance* [1995] E.C.R. I–4022; [1996] 4 C.M.L.R. 536: a non-profit organisation which manages an old-age insurance scheme in keeping with the rules laid down by the authorities is an undertaking within the meaning of Art. 81 (ex 85) E.C.

The term "undertaking" also covers natural persons,[24] public enterprises and even the Member States,[25] when they carry out commercial and economic activities. Consequently, entities engaged in religious, artistic or scientific activities are not caught by the competition rules.

Besides being a "legal" entity, an "undertaking" must also be an "economic" entity, in other words have economic independence.[26] This is not the case, under certain conditions, with undertakings belonging to the same group or concern and having the status of parent company and subsidiary. When the subsidiary is not free to determine its market behaviour independently of the parent company[27] and the agreements concluded between them merely constitute an internal allocation of tasks, such undertakings form a single economic unit. Therefore, the agreement concluded between them is not an "agreement between undertakings". The same applies to agreements concluded between subsidiaries.[28]

On the other hand, when the market behaviour of the subsidiary is determined by the parent company and the subsidiary violates the competition rules, it is the parent company which is held responsible.[29] Whether the parent company in such a case is situated within the Community or not is irrelevant since the violation has its effects within the common market and is therefore caught by its rules.[30]

(iv) Which may affect trade between Member States

This criterion serves, in the first place, to determine the field of application of the Community competition rules. Indeed, it is "to the

---

[24] See *Reuter/BASF* Dec. [1976] O.J. L254/40.

[25] See Case 83/78 *Pig Marketing Board v. Redmonds* [1978] E.C.R. 2347; [1979] 1 C.M.L.R. 177.

[26] See *Christiani and Nielsen* Dec. [1969] O.J. L165/72 and more recently reaffirmed in Case T–387/94 *Asia Motor France* [1996] E.C.R. II–961; [1996] 5 C.M.L.R. 537.

[27] The question is whether or not the parent company "controls" the subsidiary; see, *e.g. Wilded Steel Mesh Cartel* Dec. [1989] O.J. L260/1: a 25% interest held by one company in a competitor does not give rise to a parent-subsidiary relationship.

[28] See *Kodak* Dec. [1970] O.J. L147/24.

[29] See Case T–309/94 *KNP* [1998] E.C.R. II–1007.

[30] See, *e.g.* Case 48/69 *ICI v. Commission* [1972] E.C.R. 619 at 662; [1972] C.M.L.R. 557; Case 6/72 *Europemballage and Continental Can v. Commission* [1973] E.C.R. 215; [1973] C.M.L.R. 199; Joined Cases 6–7/73, *Instituto Chemioterapico Italiono and Commercial Solvents v. Commission* [1974] E.C.R. 223; [1974] 1 C.M.L.R. 309; Case 27/76 *United Brands v. Commission* [1978] E.C.R. 207; [1978] 1 C.M.L.R. 429 and Case 85/76 *Hoffmann-La Roche v. Commission* [1979] E.C.R. 461; [1979] 3 C.M.L.R. 211.

extent that the agreement may affect trade between Member States, that the interference with competition caused by that agreement is caught by the prohibition in Community law found in Article 85 [now 81], while in the converse case it escapes this prohibition".[31]

In several judgments the Court held that:

> "in order that an agreement between undertakings may affect trade between Member States it must be possible to foresee with a sufficient degree of probability on the basis of a set of objective factors of law and fact that it may have an influence, direct or indirect, actual or potential, on the pattern of trade between Member States such as might prejudice the realisation of the aim of a single market in all the Member States".[32]

When an agreement, for instance, prevents undertakings from importing certain goods from another Member State or prohibits them from re-exporting those goods to other Member States, those agreements indisputably affect trade between Member States. Indeed, they limit the free movement of goods within the Community, which it is the object of the competition rules to guarantee. Another example are agreements which grant an exclusive right; the Court stated that they do not necessarily, of their very nature, contain elements incompatible with the common market. In such a case special attention must be given to the question whether or not the agreement is capable of partitioning the market in certain products between the Member States.[33]

It is also clear from the wording of the Treaty and the judgments of the Court that the effect on trade does not have to be actual; it suffices that the agreement is "capable of constituting a threat" to freedom of trade between Member States.[34]

(v) "Which have as their object or effect"

When the object of an agreement is to restrict competition, the question whether competition was indeed distorted is irrelevant.

---

[31] Case 56/65 *Société Technique Minière* (n. 9 above) at 249.

[32] Case 42/84 *Remia v. Commission* [1985] E.C.R. 2545 at 2572(22); [1987] 1 C.M.L.R. 1. See also Joined Cases 56–58/64 *Consten and Grundig v. Commission* [1966] E.C.R. 299 at 341; [1966] C.M.L.R. 418, where the Court added that the fact that an agreement encourages an increase, even a large one, in the volume of trade between States is not sufficient to exclude the possibility that an agreement "may affect" trade in the above mentioned manner. In Case 43/69 *Bilger v. Jehle* [1970] E.C.R. 127 at 135(5); [1974] 1 C.M.L.R. 382 the Court stated that trade may be affected even though the agreement does not concern imports or exports.

[33] Case 56/65 *Société Technique Minière* (n. 9 above).

[34] Joined Cases 56–58/64 *Consten and Grundig* (n. 32 above) 299 at 341.

What counts, in that case, is the intention of the parties as expressed in the wording of the agreement. The intention to distort may result from all or some of the clauses of the agreement; only those clauses which indicate that the object of the agreement is to interfere with competition will be caught by the prohibition and nullified, and not necessarily the whole agreement.[35] When the terms of the agreement do not disclose the intention of the parties to distort competition, the consequences of *implementing* the agreement must be considered. In order to be able to prove violation of the competition rules, factors must be found by the Commission, which show that competition was in fact distorted, or, at least that a danger of distortion existed.[36]

(vi) "Prevention, Restriction or Distortion of Competition"

Competition exists when the economic operators in the common market act independently from one another and have freedom of choice.[37] Operators must be understood in the broadest sense possible to include all legal and natural persons performing an economic activity. Most typical of the existence of competition is the free choice of the consumer: one can safely say that the moment this freedom is limited in one way or another, competition is distorted. As for the producers, competition exists whenever they have to take into account the market behaviour of other producers within the relevant market.[38]

The Court has further developed and specified the meaning of "distortion of competition" by indicating that in order to be prohibited, an agreement must distort competition "to an appreciable extent".[39] For instance, an "exclusive dealing agreement, even with absolute territorial protection, may, having regard to the weak position of the persons concerned in the market and the products in

[35] See Joined Cases 56–58/64 *Consten and Grundig* (n. 32 above) where the Court annulled the Commission's decision because it considered the whole agreement as void. See also Case 319/82 *Société de Vente de Ciments et Betons v. Kerpen & Kerpen* [1983] E.C.R. 4173 at 4184(12), where the Court reiterated that the consequences of the nullity of certain provisions for other parts of the agreement are not a matter for Community law, but must be determined by the national court on the basis of its own national law.

[36] See Case 56/65 *Société Technique Minière* (n. 9 above) at 251.

[37] Joined Cases 40, etc./73 *Suiker Unie and Others* (n. 12 above) at 1942(173).

[38] For the concept "relevant market" see below: "abuse of a dominant position".

[39] See Case 56/65 *Société Technique Minière* (n. 9 above). For more details as to the meaning of "appreciable" see the Commission's Notice concerning Agreements of Minor Importance [1997] O.J. C–372/13. See also Dec. *SOCEMAS* [1968] O.J. L201/4.

question, escape the prohibition" of the Treaty.[40] In other words, the *de minimis* rule also applies in Community competition law.

Another point emphasised by the Court is that the anticipated effect on competition may not be purely theoretical, but that "the competition in question must be understood within the actual context in which it would occur in the absence of the agreement in dispute. It is therefore appropriate:

> "to take into account the nature and quantity, limited or otherwise, of the products covered by the agreement, the position and importance of the [parties] on the market for the products concerned, the isolated nature of the disputed agreement or, alternatively, its position in a series of agreements, the severity of the clause intended to [limit trade] or alternatively the opportunities allowed for other commercial competitors in the same product by way of parallel re-exportation or importation."[41]

(vii) "Within the common market"

According to the Treaty the distortion of competition must take place within the common market. It follows that an agreement between undertakings situated within the Community but which limits competition in a third country is not prohibited by Community law.[42] It would be different, of course, if, as a result of this agreement, the behaviour of the parties were influenced in such a way as to cause distortion of competition and of inter-state trade within the Community.[43] Similarly, an agreement concluded between undertakings situated outside the Community, but having effect on trade between Member States and on competition within the Community, is prohibited by, and prosecutable under, Com-

---

[40] Case 5/69 *Volk v. Vervaecke* [1969] E.C.R. 295 at 303; [1969] C.M.L.R. 273 and Case 30/78 *Distillers Company v. Commission* [1980] E.C.R. 2229 at 2265(28); [1980] 3 C.M.L.R. 121.

[41] Case 56/65 *Société Technique Minière* (n. 7 above) at 250 and Case 99/79 *Lancôme v. Etos* [1980] E.C.R. 2511 at 2536(24) [1981] 2 C.M.L.R. 164.

[42] See, *e.g.* the *Rieckermann* Dec. [1968] J.O. L276/25; see, however, Joined Cases C–89 etc. /85 *Osakeyhtio and Others v. Commission* [1988] E.C.R. 5193 [1988] 4 C.M.L.R. 901, a concerted practice between undertakings situated in non-member countries affecting selling prices to purchasers established in the Community.

[43] Same idea in Joined Cases 6 and 7/73 *Commercial Solvents* (n. 29 above).

munity law.[44] The same applies, of course, when one of the parties to such an agreement is situated within the Community.[45]

Finally, it should be noted that the expression "within the Community" does not mean that agreements must concern all the Member States or even some of them. An agreement limiting competition in one of the Member States can have distorting consequences in other Member States and affect trade within the Community. This will practically always be the case when the agreement in question covers the whole territory of one Member State, since it creates what the Court calls a threshold effect with regard to imports.[46]

(b) The Nullity

Prohibited *cartels* are automatically void.[47] Consequently, no declaration to this effect is needed.[48] This statement, however, is not as absolute as it sounds: indeed, a distinction has to be made between "old" and "new" agreements.

Old agreements are those which were concluded before March 13, 1962,[49] *i.e.* the date at which Regulation 17[50] entered into force. The Court held that in those cases the general principle of contractual certainty requires, particularly when the agreement has been notified in accordance with Regulation 17, that national courts only ascertain their nullity after the Commission has taken a decision by virtue of that regulation.[51] Not all the "old" agreements had to be notified after the entry into force of the Regulation in order to be "exemptable" from the prohibition,[52] and those which had to

---

[44] This is sometimes referred to as the extra-territorial application of Community competition law. It is doubtful whether this expression is correct in the above mentioned case since it is only in "operating within the Community", territorially speaking, that the behaviour of these undertakings is caught.

[45] See, *e.g.* the *Franco-Japanese Ballbearings* Dec. [1974] O.J. L343/19.

[46] See, *e.g.* Case 8/72 *Cementhandelaren* (n. 16 above).

[47] Art. 81(2) (ex 85(2)) E.C.

[48] See Reg. 17, Art. 1 where the same is provided for the prohibition [1959–62] O.J. Spec. Ed. 13/87.

[49] Different dates apply, of course, in the new Member States: the date of accession was substituted for the original date: January 1, 1973 for Denmark, Ireland and the U.K.; January 1, 1981 for Greece, January 1, 1986 for Portugal and Spain, and January 1, 1995 for Austria, Finland and Sweden.

[50] This was the first Regulation adopted "to give effect to the principles set out in Articles 85 [now 81] and 86 [now 82]", pursuant to Art. 83 (ex 87) E.C.

[51] See Case 59/77 *De Bloos v. Bouyer* [1977] E.C.R. 2359 at 2369(8); [1978] 1 C.M.L.R. 511.

[52] See below "(c) Exemption from the Prohibition".

be notified are "provisionally valid".[53] According to a recent judgment of the Court, this provisional validity ceases when the Commission has taken a position and, when duly notified, applies only as long as the terms of the agreement remain unchanged; when amendments are introduced, these may not have the effect of reinforcing or extending the restrictive effect.[54]

As for new agreements, *i.e.* those concluded after March 13, 1962, when they are prohibited, the nullity applies without reservation, whether they were notified or not.[55] In other words, as was pointed out before, the new agreements can only be implemented at the parties' own risks. It is up to them to determine whether their agreement is prohibited and consequently void. If the agreement is implemented anyway, the possibility remains that, even years later, a national court finds that the agreement was void *ab initio*. Such a finding may also have implications for third parties. For those reasons, parties should, in case of doubt, notify their agreements to the Commission and request a negative clearance or an exemption.[56]

(c) Exemptions from the Prohibition

The Commission, and only the Commission,[57] may declare that the prohibition is inapplicable under certain limited conditions, in the case of individual cartels or categories of cartels.[58]

---

[53] Indeed they may still become void if the Commission refuses the exemption. See Case 13/61 *de Geus v. Bosch and Van Rijn* [1962] E.C.R. 45 at 52; [1962] C.M.L.R. 1. More recently Case C–39/96 *KVBBB v. Free Record Shop* [1997] E.C.R. I–2303: "provisional validity expires only when the Commission has taken a positive or negative decision on the agreement".

[54] Case C–39/96 *Boekhandels* [1997] E.C.R. I–2303; [1997] 5 C.M.L.R. 521.

[55] Some of those new agreements were exempted from notification; see Case 48/72 *Brasserie de Haecht v. Wilkin (No. 2)* [1973] E.C.R. 77 at 86(9–10); [1973] C.M.L.R. 287.

[56] See below "(c) Exemptions from the Prohibition".

[57] Before Reg. 17 came into force, only the national authorities could grant such an exemption (see Art. 84 (ex 88) E.C.). When Reg. 17 took effect, this exclusive right was transferred to the Commission: Reg. 17, Art. 9(1). See also Case 31/80 *L'Oréal v. De Nieuwe AMCK* [1980] E.C.R. 3775 at 3790(130); [1981] 2 C.M.L.R. 235.

[58] Art. 81(3) (ex 85(3)) E.C.

(i) Individual Exemptions

The Commission can only grant such an exemption when an agreement has first been notified to it[59] and the following four conditions are fulfilled:

(a) the agreement must contribute to improving the production or distribution of goods or to promoting technical or economic progress;
(b) consumers must get a fair share of the resulting benefit;
(c) the agreement may not impose on the undertakings concerned restrictions which are not indispensable to the attainment of the above objectives, and
(d) the agreement may not afford such undertakings the possibility of eliminating competition in respect of a substantial part of the products in question.

The exemption may not come into force on a date earlier than the date of notification of the cartel to the Commission[60]; it must be issued for a specific period and conditions and obligations may be attached to it. The exemption may be renewed but also revoked, even retroactively.[61]

(ii) Exemptions for Categories of Agreements; the so-called "Block Exemptions"

As indicated, the declaration of inapplicability of the prohibition can also apply to categories of agreements, of decisions by associations of undertakings and of concerted practices.[62] Those exemptions are reserved for agreements for which it can be assumed with sufficient certainty that they satisfy the conditions set by the Treaty for exemptions from the prohibition. They are granted by the Commission acting in pursuance of a Council regulation. The Council establishes the principle of the exemption and delegates to

---

[59] Reg. 17, Art. 4(1). For details concerning notifications, see Reg. 27/62, First Regulation implementing Council Regulation 17 [1962] J.O. 35/1118 and [1959–62] O.J. Spec. Ed. 132. Reg. 17 was amended by Reg. 59 [1962] J.O. 58/1655 and [1959–62] O.J. Spec. Ed. 87 by Reg. 118/63 [1963] J.O. 162/2696 and [1959–62] O.J. Spec. Ed. 249 by Reg. 2822/71 [1971] J.O. L285/49 and [1963–64] O.J. Spec. Ed. 55 and by Reg. 2526/85: [1985] O.J. L240/1. See also Notice on Procedure Concerning Notification [1983] O.J. C295/6. It is very important to note that, once notified, an agreement can no longer serve as ground for the imposition of a fine by the Commission.

[60] Reg. 17, Art. 6(1).

[61] Reg. 17, Art. 8.

[62] Art. 81(3) (ex 85(3)) E.C.

the Commission the task of working out the details.[63] This technique was used for several categories.

The first category concerns agreements to which only two undertakings are party; the so-called "exclusive dealing agreements".[64] They concern bilateral exclusive distribution and exclusive purchasing agreements and also patent licensing and know-how agreements.

The second Council Regulation concerns specialisation and, research and development agreements.[65]

The third concerns the insurance sector.[66]

The Council also adopted several regulations in the field of transport on the basis of which the Commission adopted several implementing regulations. Those are examined hereafter under "Competition Rules Applying to Various Branches of the Economy".

All the regulations granting block exemptions follow, generally speaking, the same pattern. They provide in detail which restriction may be imposed upon the parties, which other restrictions do not infringe the prohibition and which restrictions are excluded from the exemption. It should be noted that agreements which are not exempted under the block exemption may be notified to the Commission under the general procedural rules[67] in order to obtain an individual exemption.[68]

(a) **Bilateral Exclusive Distribution (Supply) Agreements.**[69] Excluded from the prohibition by this Regulation are agreements to which only two undertakings are party and whereby one party agrees to supply, only to the other party, certain goods for resale within the whole, or a defined area of, the common market within which the re-seller enjoys exclusivity. The only other obligation

[63] This delegation constitutes an example of what is provided in Art. 211 (ex 155) E.C., last indent: the Commission exercises "the powers conferred on it by the Council for the implementation of the rules laid down by the latter".

[64] Council Reg. 19/65 [1965] J.O. 36/533; [1965–66] O.J. Spec. Ed. 35. See Green Paper on Vertical Restrains, COM (96) 721 final [1997] 4 C.M.L.R., 519.

[65] Council Reg. 2821/71 [1971] J.O. L258/46; [1971-III] O.J. Spec. Ed. 1032. Modified by Reg. 2743/72 [1972] J.O. L291/144; [1972] O.J. Spec. Ed. 60.

[66] Council Reg. 1534/91 [1991] O.J. L143/1.

[67] Those procedural rules are examined under (c) "Regulation 17".

[68] See, *e.g.* the *Carlsberg* Dec. [1984] O.J. L207/26.

[69] The literature refers to those agreements as "exclusive supply agreements". See Reg. 1983/83 [1983] O.J. L173/1; corrigendum [1983] O.J. L281/24; modified by Reg. 94/103 [1994] O.J. L1/446.

which may be imposed upon the supplier is not to supply himself to users in the territory. The following restrictions may also be imposed upon the distributor:

(a) not to manufacture or distribute goods which compete with the contract goods;
(b) to obtain the contract goods only from the supplier;
(c) to refrain from seeking customers, establishing any branch or maintaining any distribution depot, outside the territory;
(d) to purchase complete ranges or minimum quantities;
(e) to sell the contract goods under trade marks, etc., presented by the supplier, and
(f) to take measures for promotion (advertise, provide guarantee, etc.).

However, the exemption does not apply:

(a) to reciprocal exclusive distribution agreements when concluded between competitors of identical goods;
(b) to non-reciprocal agreements unless one of the parties has a turnover of less than euro 100 million;
(c) when users can only obtain the contract goods from the exclusive distributor;
(d) when it is made difficult for users to obtain the goods from other dealers inside the common market.

This regulation does not apply to agreements for the resale of drinks in premises used for the resale and consumption of beer and to agreements for the resale of petroleum products.[70] The period of validity of the Regulation was extended to December 31, 1999.[71]

This regulation is accompanied by a lengthy explanatory Notice[72] from the Commission whereby the latter gives a detailed interpretation of its own legislation. This rather unusual procedure (one wonders why the regulation could not be so drafted in the first place that no further interpretation was needed) has the advantage of providing interested parties with some necessary clarification.

Mention should be made here of *Selective Distribution Agreements* whereby a producer limits the distribution of his products to a few "selected" distributors. According to the Court, "it is common ground that agreements constituting a selective system necessarily affect competition in the common market. However, it has always

[70] *ibid.* Art. 8.
[71] [1997] O.J. L214/27.
[72] [1984] O.J. C101/2.

been recognised in the case law of the Court that there are legitimate requirements, such as the maintenance of a specialist trade capable of providing specific services as regards high-quality and high-technology products, which may justify a reduction of price competition in favour of competition relating to factors other than price."[73]

On the basis of the Court and Commission Decisions[74] the prohibition of the Treaty does not apply if the following conditions are met:

(a) selection must take place on the basis of non-discriminatory qualitative criteria concerning technical ability and suitability of premises[75];
(b) those criteria must be reasonably necessary,
(c) all dealers who fulfil the conditions must be admitted, *i.e.* no quantitative criteria, and
(d) parallel imports and exports must be possible.

(b) Bilateral Exclusive Purchasing Agreements.[76] These are exempted agreements to which only two undertakings are party, and whereby one party, the reseller, agrees with the other, the supplier, to purchase certain goods specified in the agreement for resale. The reseller agrees to purchase the goods only from the supplier, or from a connected undertaking which the supplier has entrusted with the sale of his goods.

No other restrictions may be imposed upon the supplier than the obligation not to distribute the contract goods in the reseller's territory and no other restriction upon the reseller, than the obligation not to sell competing goods.

The Regulation also applies when other restrictions are imposed upon the reseller, similar to the ones provided for the exclusive supply agreements.

---

[73] See, *e.g.* Case 107/82 *AEG v. Commission* [1983] E.C.R. 3151 at 3194(33) and Case 31/80 *L'Oréal v. De Nieuwe AMCK* [1980] E.C.R. 3775.

[74] One of the first Commission decisions was *Omega* [1970] O.J. L242/22, where the admissibility of the selective system was based upon the high technical quality of the product requiring well trained staff, etc., *id.* for *BMW* [1975] O.J. L29/1. As for the case law, see Case 107/82 *AEG v. Commission* [1983] E.C.R. 3151, Case 86/82 *Hasselblad v. Commission* [1984] E.C.R. 883; [1984] 1 C.M.L.R. 559 and Case 10/86 *VAG France v. Magne* [1986] E.C.R. 4071.

[75] See, *e.g.* Case 26/76 *Metro v. Commission* [1977] E.C.R. 1875 at 1904(200); [1978] 2 C.M.L.R. 1 and Case 99/79 *Lancôme v. ETOS* [1980] E.C.R. 2511; [1981] 2 C.M.L.R. 164.

[76] [1984] O.J. L173/5; corrigendum [1983] O.J. L281/24. Amended by Reg. 94/103 [1994] O.J. L1/446.

The Regulation deals also with beer supply agreements (brewery ties) and with petroleum supply agreements (service-station agreements). It should be noted that this agreement does not provide the reseller with an exclusive area as provided for the distribution agreements. The Commission Notice mentioned under (a) above also applies to the supply Regulation, which was also extended until December 31, 1999.

(c) **Motor Vehicle Distribution and Servicing Agreements.**[77] This exemption is granted for agreements between only two undertakings, in which one agrees to supply only the other or a specified number of other undertakings within a defined territory, for resale, certain motor vehicles. Such a distribution system constitutes a so-called "selective distribution" agreement about which more hereafter.

A novelty introduced in 1995 is the "multidealership": the reseller may not be prevented from selling other marks of motor vehicles as long as he does it in separate sales premises, with separate management, within a distinct legal entity and in a way which avoids confusion between marks.[78] The regulation also protects the rights of intermediaries acting on behalf and on account of an end consumer. Such an independent reseller who undertakes to make parallel imports[79] is not caught by the Regulation, which only applies to suppliers and approved distributors.[80]

(d) **Franchising Agreements.**[81] Certain agreements are exempted, to which two undertakings are party, concerning licensing of industrial or intellectual property rights (trade marks, trade names, shop signs, utility models, designs, copyrights, know-how or patents) to be exploited for the purpose of selling special types of goods or providing services to end-users. Often the sales or the provision of services takes place in premises of uniform appearance and with the same business methods. It is interesting to note that recommended prices and a post-term non-competition obligation not exceeding one year are admitted.

---

[77] Reg. 1475/95 [1995] O.J. L145/25. See interpretation of Arts 3, 4 and 5 E.C. in Case C–230/96, *Cabour SA* [1998] E.C.R. I–2055.
[78] See Explanation Brochure IV/9509/95 EN.
[79] See Case C–41/96 *VAG* [1997] E.C.R. I–3123; [1997] 5 C.M.L.R. 537.
[80] See Case C–128/95 *Fontaine* [1997] E.C.R. I–967; [1997] 5 C.M.L.R. 39.
[81] Reg. 4087/88 [1988] O.J. L359/46.

The Regulation applies to all economic sectors including those where specific block exemptions have been adopted.

(e) **Specialisation Agreements.**[82] The Regulation exempting specialisation agreements from the prohibition is based on the second Council Regulation.[83] It concerns agreements whereby undertakings accept reciprocal obligations to leave the manufacture of certain products to other parties to the agreement or to manufacture certain products or have them manufactured jointly.

The exemption only applies if the products which are the subject of the specialisation, together with similar products of the participating undertakings, do not represent more than 20 per cent of the market. Furthermore, the aggregate annual turnover of all the participants may not exceed euro 500 million. If the latter is exceeded the agreement can be notified under the opposition procedure.

The validity of the regulation was extended to December 31, 2000.

(f) **Research and Development Agreements.**[84] This regulation is based on the second Council Regulation.[85] It exempts from the prohibition agreements entered into by undertakings for the purpose of:

(a) joint research and development of products or processes and exploitation of the results;
(b) joint exploitation of results from a prior agreement between the same undertakings, and
(c) joint research and development excluding joint exploitation.

There are, however, conditions:

(a) the joint R&D work must be carried out within the framework of a programme defining the objectives of the work and the field in which it is to be carried out;

---

[82] Reg. 417/85 [1985] O.J. L53/1; last amended by Reg. 2236/37 [1997] O.J. L306/12.
[83] See n. 65 above.
[84] Reg. 418/85 [1985] O.J. L53/5; last modified by Reg. 2236/97 [1997] O.J. L306/12.
[85] See n. 65 above.

(b) all the parties must have access to the results of the work;
(c) each party must be free to exploit the results of the joint R&D independently;
(d) joint exploitation may only relate to results which are protected by intellectual property rights or constitute know-how which contribute to technical and economic progress; furthermore, the results must be decisive for the manufacture of the product or for the application of the process, and
(e) the parties charged with the manufacturing must fulfil orders from all the parties.

The exemption is valid for a limited number of years. Where the parties to the agreement are competitors, the combined market share of the products which are the object of the research may not exceed 20 per cent of the market.

The regulation expires in December 31, 2000.

(g) Technology Transfer Agreements. The Commission Regulation[86] granting a block exemption in this field is based upon the first Council Regulation.[87] It combines the former Regulation on patent licensing agreements[88] and the Regulation on know-how licensing agreements.[89] The Commission decided that those two block exemptions ought to be combined into a single regulation covering technology transfer agreements. The object of the Regulation is to facilitate the dissemination of technology and the improvement of manufacturing processes.

The Regulation applies to the Member States' own patents, Community patents[90] and European patents[91] ("pure" patent licensing agreements). It also applies to agreements for the licensing of non-patented technical information such as descriptions of manufacturing processes, recipes, formulae, designs or drawings, commonly termed "know-how" ("pure" know-how licensing agreements) and, to combined patent and know-how licensing agreements ("mixed agreements"), which are playing an increasingly important role in the transfer of technology.

---

[86] Reg. 240/96 [1996] O.J. L31/2.
[87] Reg. 19/65 [1965] O.J. L533/65.
[88] Reg. 2349/84 [1984] O.J. L219/15.
[89] Reg. 556/89 [1989] O.J. L61/1.
[90] Convention for the European patent for the common market (Community Patent Convention) of December 15, 1975 [1975] O.J. L17/1.
[91] Convention on the grant of European patents (European Patent Convention) of October 5, 1973.

Are also covered by the exemption agreements containing ancillary provisions relating to intellectual property rights other than patents.

The exemption applies to agreements to which only two undertakings are party and which include *inter alia.* one or more of the following obligations:

(1) the licensor undertakes not to license other undertakings in the licensed territory;
(2) the licensor undertakes not to exploit himself in said territory;
(3) the licensee may not exploit in the territory of the licensor;
(4) the licensee accepts not to exploit in territories licensed to others;
(5) the licensee accepts not to pursue an active policy of putting the licensed product in territories licensed to others, particularly no advertising aimed at those territories;
(6) neither to sell the products in those territories in response to unsolicited orders[92];
(7) the licensee must use the licensor's trade mark although he may not be prevented from identifying himself as the manufacturer of the licensed product;
(8) an obligation on the licensee to limit the production to the quantities he requires in manufacturing his own products.

The Regulation exempts several other contract obligations which are generally not restrictive of competition and imposes a number of conditions for the exemption to apply. Obviously a certain number of contractual obligations are excluded from the exemption.[93] Finally, it should be noted that the so-called opposition procedure is also provided for, *i.e.* that agreements, which contain provisions not covered by the Regulation are exempted after the agreement is notified to the Commission and the latter does not oppose it within four months.

The application of Community law to patents and know-how will be further examined in the chapter on Industry Policy; however, mention must be made here of the effect the Community competition rules have on the use that can be made of "intellectual property rights". Normally such rights are used by their owner to prevent third parties from producing the products covered by such rights, and/or by reserving the use of such rights to particular (national)

---

[92] This would not prevent the licensee from selling to a third party in his own territory even if he knows the latter will sell in other territories; otherwise parallel imports might be made impossible.
[93] See Arts 3 and 5 E.C.

territories. And, although the owner acts in accordance with national law, by preventing imports and exports among the Member States, he prevents the free movement of goods within the common market. It is in connection therewith that several cases concerning the use of intellectual property rights were submitted to the appreciation of the Court,[94] which declared that such use is also contrary to the Community competition rules.[95]

The position of the Court with regard to the use of intellectual property rights can be summarised as follows: the Treaty provisions do not affect the existence of the exclusive rights attached to patents, know-how, trademarks, copyrights, registered designs, plant breeder's rights and other similar rights. They do, however, limit their use in so far as they restrict trade between Member States. On the other hand, the Court upholds the use of those rights when this is "justified by the purpose of safeguarding rights which constitute the specific subject matter of such property".[96] As will be seen in the Chapter on Industry Policy, the Court introduced another restriction in the form of the principle of the "exhaustion" of intellectual and industrial property rights, when the owner puts his product on the market in another Member State.

2. Abuse of a Dominant Position—Article 82 (ex 86) E.C.

Competition and interstate trade can, as was just seen, be adversely affected by "cartels", *i.e.* agreements between undertakings, decisions of associations of undertakings and concerted practices. However, they can also be restricted by an undertaking or undertakings in a quasi-monopoly situation called "dominant position", behaving on the market in such a way that it constitutes an "abuse". Such abuse is prohibited by the Treaty in so far as it affects trade between Member States.

Both the rules of competition concerning cartels and those applying to abuses have as their object to ensure that "competition in

---

94 See, *e.g.* Case 78/70 *Deutsche Grammophon v. Metro* [1971] E.C.R. 487; [1971] C.M.L.R. 631 and Case 262/81 *Coditel v. Cine Vog Films* [1982] E.C.R. 3381; [1983] 1 C.M.L.R. 49.

95 Joined Cases 56–58/64 *Consten and Grundig v. Commission* [1966] E.C.R. 299 at 346; [1966] C.M.L.R. 418, where the Court found that Community law does not allow improper use of rights under national trade mark law in order to frustrate the Community's laws on cartels.

96 See *Deutsche Grammophon*, n. 94.

the internal market is not distorted",[97] or, in other words, that the free movement of goods within the common market is not hindered.

The Treaty refers to "dominant position", "abuse" and "may affect trade between Member States". The latter expression was examined in relation with prohibited cartels; the other two concepts will be briefly analysed hereafter.

(i) Dominant Position

Such a position exists, according to the Court, when the economic strength of an undertaking on a given market is such that it "enables it to hinder the maintenance of effective competition on the relevant market by allowing it to behave to an appreciable extent independently of its competitors and customers and ultimately of its consumers".[98]

An undertaking is not in a dominant position merely because of the size of its market share,[99] it can also derive from a combination of several factors which, taken separately, would not necessarily be determinative. They are, for instance, the relationship between the market share of the undertaking in question and the shares of the next largest undertakings, the technological lead, the existence of a highly developed sales network and the absence of potential competition.[1] Since the Treaty refers to one or more undertakings, a dominant position can also be held by several undertakings together,

---

[97] See Art. 3(1)(g) (ex *id.*) E.C. As the Court pointed out in Case 6/72 *Europemballage and Continental Can v. Commission* [1973] E.C.R. 215 at 244(25); [1973] C.M.L.R. 199: "the restraint of competition which is prohibited if it is the result of behaviour falling under Article 85 [now 81], cannot become permissible by the fact that such behaviour succeeds under the influence of a dominant undertaking".

[98] Case 322/81 *Michelin v. Commission* [1983] E.C.R. 3461 at 3503(30); [1985] 1 C.M.L.R. 282.

[99] However, a share of 80% would normally be considered as constituting a dominant position. When the market share is not decisive other criteria must be taken into consideration. See Case 85/76 *Hoffmann-La Roche* [1979] E.C.R. 1513; [1979] 3 C.M.L.R. 211, where the Court rejected as irrelevant a number of additional criteria mentioned by the Commission, but indicated those which it considered important. See also Case 19/79 *Miller v. Commission* [1978] E.C.R. 31, where the market share of the applicant was estimated at 6% of the German market and the Court accepted that in that case, there was a danger that trade between Member States would be appreciably affected.

[1] Those criteria and others have been analysed in "Oligopolistic Dominance under the Merger Regulation" *Festschrift für Dr Jürgen Gündich*, 1999, by P. Mathijsen.

the so-called "joint" or "collective" dominance.[2] This concept was further developed by the Commission within the framework of the merger Regulation, which will be examined hereunder.

It follows from the practice of the Commission[3] and the case law of the European courts[4] that in order to determine whether an undertaking's position is dominant it must be viewed in relation to the "relevant product/service market" and to the "relevant geographic market". Indeed, logically, it is only after having defined the relevant product/service market that the Commission and the courts will be able to determine whether there does indeed exist competition, which the abuse might distort. From there the question: when does competition exist between products or services? Basically, the answer is very simple. There is competition when the end consumer has a choice between different products/services, which, because of their characteristics, their price and their intended usage are "interchangeable". The Court defined it as follows: "the concept of relevant market, in fact, implies that there can be effective competition between the products, which form part of it and this presupposes that there is a sufficient degree of interchangeability between all the products forming part of the same market in so far as the specific use of the product is concerned".[5]

Probably the best example of a non-interchangeable product is the banana. The Court of Justice was called upon to determine whether that product constitutes a relevant market on its own or whether it was part of the larger market of fresh fruits. It found that "the banana has certain characteristics, appearance, taste, softness, seedlessness, easy handling, a constant level of production, which enables it to satisfy the constant needs of an important section of the population consisting of the very young, the old and the sick".[6] And the Court concluded that "consequently, the banana market is a market which is sufficiently distinct from the other fresh fruit markets".

---

[2] See Joined Cases T–24-26/93 *Compagnie Maritime Belge* [1996] E.C.R. II–1201 (65–66); [1977] 4 C.M.L.R. 273 and Dec. of May 14, 1997, in Case IV/34.621 *Irish Sugar plc* [1997] O.J. L258/1, (11–112). See also Case T–69/89 *RTE v. Commission* [1991] E.C.R. II–485 and Joined Cases T–68/89, etc. "Flat Glass" *SIV* [1991] E.C.R. II–1403; [1992] 5 C.M.L.R. 302.

[3] See, for instance, *British Leyland* [1984] O.J. L207/11.

[4] See, for instance Case 7/82 *GVL v. Commission* [1983] E.C.R. 483; [1983] 3 C.M.L.R. 645.

[5] Case 31/80 *L'Oreal v. De Nieuwe AMCK* [1980] E.C.R. 3775; [1981] 2 C.M.L.R. 235.

[6] Case 27/72 *United Brands v. Commission* [1978] E.C.R. 207 at 273(31); [1973] C.M.L.R. 612. Another example is to be found in Case 85/76 *Hoffmann La Roche* [1979] E.C.R. 461 at 547(111).

It follows that the Commission, when examining whether or not there has been abuse, must in the first place determine the limits of the product/service market. With regard to services, an example of the difficulty this might present, is to be found, for instance, in the definition of the banking sector. The Commission ascertained, for instance, that a significant number of non-financial companies have subsidiaries involved in financial services, such as financing subsidiaries of car manufacturers, payment cards or retail banking subsidiaries of big retailers. In other words, not only "banks" offer banking services; so where are the limits?[7]

Besides defining the product/service relevant market, the Commission must also determine the geographic market. The larger this market, the more likelihood for competition; from there its importance. The limits of this market depends on the structure of the product market, especially as far as production, supply and demand are concerned.[8] The Court did underline "how necessary it is to define the market concerned in order that the relative strength for the undertakings in such a market might be considered".[9]

The limits of the geographic market do not necessarily coincide with the territories of the Member States nor of the Community, although they normally do, for the simple reason that statistics are normally available for those areas only. The Treaty refers to the "common market or a substantial[10] part of it". However, the geographic market can be very small indeed.[11]

The Commission published a "Notice on the definition of the relevant market for the purpose of the Community competition law".[12] Market definition is a tool to identify and define the boundaries of competition between firms. It serves to establish the framework within which competition policy is applied by the Commission. The main purpose of market definition is to identify in a systematic way the competitive constraints that the undertakings involved face. The objective of defining the market is to identify the actual competitors.

More difficult even is the definition of "abuse". It will be remembered that cartels are prohibited when two conditions are

---

[7] Dec. of May 20, 1998, in case No. IV/M.1016 *Price Waterhouse/Coopers & Lybrand*. See also Dec. of September 21, 1994 *Night Services* [1994] O.J. L259/20, (191.); this Dec. was annulled by the CFI.

[8] See Case 247/86 *Alsatel v. Novasam* [1988] E.C.R. 5987, where the Court did not accept the existence either of a relevant product market nor of a national geographic market, but only of a regional one.

[9] Case 85/76 *Hoffmann-La Roche* n. 99.

[10] See Case 40/73 *Suiker Unie and others v. Commission* [1975] E.C.R. 1663 at 1677.

[11] See, *e.g.* Dec. of December 13, 1995 *Eurotunnel* [1995] O.J. L354/66.

[12] [1997] O.J. C372/5.

fulfilled: trade between Member States must be affected and competition must be restricted. With regard to "abuse of a dominant position", the Treaty only refers to trade between Member States, and the term "abuse" must therefore be understood in relation to competition. According to the Court, the concept of abuse is an objective concept relating to the behaviour of an undertaking enjoying a dominant position in a given market. This behaviour constitutes an abuse when it is such as to influence the structure of the relevant market. Such behaviour must have the effect, through recourse to methods different from those which condition normal competition, of hindering the maintenance or growth of existing competition.[13]

Any behaviour of an undertaking in a dominant position, which interferes with one of the basic freedoms or with the free choice of the purchaser or consumer, or with freedom of access to the market or to an essential facility,[14] constitutes an abuse.[15] The most obvious criterion is the freedom of choice left to the other participants in the market.

It should be noted that abuse can also take place on a market different from the dominated one and without effects on the latter, but the markets must be closely linked.[16] In other words, prohibited abuses are also abuses on, and affecting, associated non-dominated markets in special circumstances.

Although the Treaty refers to abuse "of" a dominant position, this does not mean that a link of causality must exist between the dominant position and the abuse. Indeed, the strengthening of the position of an undertaking may constitute an abuse and be prohibited regardless of the means and procedures by which it is achieved.

---

[13] Case 85/76 *Hoffmann-La Roche* n. 6 above at 541(91).

[14] See, *e.g.* Dec. of January 18, 1994, Case IV/34.689 *Sea Containers v. Stena* [1994] O.J. L15/8.

[15] See, *e.g.* Dec. of June 28, 1995 *Landing fees at Zaventem* [1995] O.J. L216/8 and Case C–55/96 *Job Centre* [1998] E.C.R. I–7119: abuse of dominant position "unavoidable", caught by Art. 82 (ex 86) and Art. 86 (ex 90) E.C.

[16] Cases T–83/91 and C–333/94 *Tetra Pak* [1994] E.C.R. II–755 at 758(3) and [1996] E.C.R. I–5951.

3. Competition Rules Applying to Various Branches of the Economy

(1) Agriculture

The Treaty[17] also entrusts the Council, acting by a qualified majority on a proposal from the Commission and after consulting the European Parliament, to lay down appropriate regulations or directives to define, if need be, in the various branches of the economy, the scope of the competition provisions. One of those branches is explicitly provided for in the Treaty: the "rules on competition shall apply to production of, and trade in, agricultural products only to the extent determined by the Council".[18] In other words, the Council could, in theory, have decided that those rules do not apply to agriculture[19]; however, the Council opted for a limited application.[20]

The point of departure is that the rules of competition do apply to agriculture, but only in so far as their application does not impede the functioning of national organisations of agricultural markets—those were later replaced by the common organisations of agricultural markets—or jeopardise the attainment of the objectives of the common agricultural policy. The following cartels are exempted:

- farmers' cartels,
- farmers' associations,
- associations of such associations belonging to a single Member State, and which concern the sale of agricultural products or the use of joint facilities for the storage, treatment or processing of agricultural products

and under which there is no obligation to charge identical prices.

The Commission has sole power to determine which cartels fulfil those conditions; its decisions must be published.

---

[17] Art. 83 (ex 87) E.C.

[18] Art. 36 (ex 42) E.C.

[19] See first recital of Reg. 26/62 [1962] J.O. 30/993: "whereas one of the matters to be decided under the common agricultural policy is whether the rules on competition . . . are to apply to production of and trade in agricultural products".

[20] Reg. 26/62: see above and [1959–62] O.J. Spec. Ed. 129. See Joined Cases C–319, etc. 93 *Dijkstra* [1995] E.C.R. I–4471; [1996] 5 C.M.L.R. 178, on the interpretation of Art. 2.

(2) Transport

Although, as indicated above, the Council must, if need be, define the scope of the competition rules in the various branches of the economy, there is no obligation to do so with regard to transport. However, the Council considered that "in pursuance of the common transport policy, account being taken of the distinctive features of the transport sector, it may prove necessary to lay down rules governing competition different from those laid down or to be laid down for other sectors of the economy".[21]

The most important decision was to exclude the provision of transport services from the application of the first regulation implementing the competition rules: Regulation 17.[22] This was followed by a regulation laying down specific rules[23] of competition for transport by rail, road and inland waterway.[24] Indeed, the Council considered that "when rules of competition for those sectors are being settled, account must be taken of the distinctive features of transport" and that "the rules of competition for transport derogate from the general rules of competition".[25]

The main differences with those "general" rules of competition are the following;

- the prohibition of cartels in the transport sector is not absolute, but "subject" to different provisions of the regulation;
- there is an exception for technical agreements;
- groups of small and medium-sized undertakings are exempted;
- the Commission may declare the prohibition inapplicable to a specific series of agreements,[26] (not to cartels fulfilling certain general conditions, as is provided for by the general rules[27]);
- a complex procedure is provided for whereby cartels can be deemed exempt from the prohibition for three years from the

---

[21] Reg. 141/62 exempting transport from the application of Council Regulation No. 17 [1962] O.J. 124/2751 and [1959–62] O.J. Spec. Ed. 291, first recital.

[22] Reg. 17/62 [1962] O.J. 13/204.

[23] Indeed, they are laid down in a Council regulation "applying rules of competition to transport" and not applying "the" rules of competition to transport. See next n.

[24] Reg. 1017/68 [1968] O.J. L175/1 and [1968] O.J. Spec. Ed. 302. For the scope of this Reg. see Case C–264/95P *Union Internationale des Chemins de fer* [1997] E.C.R. I–1287; [1997] 5 C.M.L.R. 49. Art. 26 of Reg. 1017/68 on hearings was implemented by Reg. 1630/69 [1969] O.J. L209/11; this Reg. was replaced by Reg. 2842/98 [1998] O.J. L354/18.

[25] *ibid.* fourth and fifth recitals.

[26] Reg. 1017/68 Arts. 5 and 6.

[27] Art. 81(3) (ex 85(3)) E.C.

moment an application has been received and a summary thereof published in the O.J.[28]

Another regulation concerns the limitation periods in proceedings and the enforcement of sanctions under the Community rules relating to transport and competition.[29]

The other rules, particularly the procedural rules, are very similar to the general rules. Various directives and regulations were adopted by the Council and by the Commission with regard to specific transport sectors, which will be briefly mentioned hereunder.

Maritime Transport

Reference must be made here to the Council Regulation laying down detailed rules for the application of the Community competition rules to maritime transport.[30] This regulation, *inter alia* supplements and makes more precise the United Nations Code of Conduct for Liner Conference.[31] On the other hand, tramp vessel services are excluded. The regulation provides for the possibility to exempt certain technical cartels and also for block exemptions of liner conferences under well defined conditions and with specific obligations. The Regulation, however, recognises that its application to certain restrictive practices may result in conflicts with the laws and rules of third countries and prove harmful to important Community trading and shipping interests. Negotiations with those countries are therefore provided for.

The Council also adopted a regulation on the application of the competition rules to certain categories of cartels between liner shipping companies, described in shipping circles as "consortia".[32] This Regulation authorises the Commission to declare that the competition rules shall not apply to certain categories of cartels. It concerns cartels that have as object to promote or establish co-operation in the joint operation of maritime transport services between liner shipping companies, for the purpose of rationalising

---

[28] *ibid.* Art. 12.

[29] Reg. 2988/74 [1974] O.J. L319/1.

[30] Reg. 4056/86 [1986] O.J. L378/4. See Joined Cases T–24/93, etc. *Compagnie Maritime Belge Transports v. Commission* [1996] E.C.R. II–1741. Reg. 4056/86 and was amended by Reg. 3666/93 [1993] O.J. L 336/1 and was implemented by Reg. 4260/88 on the communications, complaints and applications and the hearings provided for in the Council Regulation [1988] O.J. L376/1; Section II of Reg. 4260/88 was deleted and replaced by Reg. 2842/98 [1998] O.J. L354/18.

[31] [1979] O.J. L121/1.

[32] Reg. 470/92 [1992] O.J. L55/3.

their operations by means of technical, operational and/or commercial arrangements with the exception of price fixing consortia.

Air Transport

The Treaty provides that the Title on transport shall only apply to transport by rail, road and inland waterway and that the Council may decide "whether, to what extent and by what procedure appropriate provision may be laid down for sea and air transport".[33] Having recognised that the rules on competition form part of the Treaty's general provisions which also apply to air transport,[34] the Council adopted a regulation laying down the procedure for the application of the rules on competition to undertakings in the air transport sector.[35]

In that Regulation the Council considered that air transport is characterised by features which are specific to this sector and that, furthermore, international air transport is regulated by a network of bilateral agreements between States. Those agreements define the conditions under which air carriers designated by the parties to the agreement may operate routes between their territories. On the other hand, it is clear that practices which affect competition relating to air transport between Member States may have substantial effect on trade between Member States. It was therefore necessary to authorise the Commission to take the requisite measures for the application of the competition rules to air transport.

Consequently, the Commission adopted a regulation concerning complaints, applications and hearings in the air sector.[36]

Subsequently, the Council adopted a regulation allowing the Commission to exclude from the prohibition provided by the Treaty, certain categories of cartels in the air sector.[37] Thus were excepted by the Commission several categories of cartels.

The first concerns agreements between undertakings relating to computerised reservation systems (CRS) for air transport services.[38]

---

[33] Art. 80(2) (ex 84(2)) E.C.

[34] This recognition only occurred after the Court had so decided, see Joined Cases 209 to 213/84 *Ministère Public v. Asjes* [1986] E.C.R. 1425; [1986] 3 C.M.L.R. 173.

[35] Reg. 3975/87 [1987] O.J. L374/1, amended by Reg. 1284/91 [1991] O.J. L122/2 and by Reg. 2410/92 [1992] O.J. L240/18.

[36] Reg. 4261/88 [1988] O.J. L376/10, amended by Reg. 3666/93. Section II was deleted and replaced by Reg. 2842/98 [1998] O.J. L354/18.

[37] Reg. 3976/87 [1987] O.J. L374/9 amended by Reg. 2344/90 [1990] O.J. L217/15 and by Reg. 2411/92 [1992] O.J. L240/19.

[38] Reg. 3652/93 [1993] O.J. L333/37.

The exemption applies to agreements the purpose of which is one or more of the following:

- to purchase or develop a CRS in common;
- to create a "system vendor" to market and operate the CRS; or
- to regulate the provision of distribution facilities by the system vendor or by distributors.

All kinds of conditions and obligations are attached to the exemption which applies until June 30, 1998. The validity of this Regulation was not extended.

The second category excluded from the prohibition[39] concerns:

- joint planning and co-ordination of the schedule of an air service between Community airports;
- the joint operation of a scheduled air service on a new or on a low-density route between Community airports;
- the holding of consultations on tariffs for the carriage of passengers, with their baggage, and of freight on scheduled air services between Community airports; and
- slot-allocation and airport scheduling in so far as they concern air service between airports in the Community.

The Regulation applies until June 30, 1998. The Commission has undertaken to extend the validity until June 30, 1999,[40] when it will be replaced by a new one.

A third category concerns ground handling services agreements.[42] However, this exemption was partly replaced by a directive on access to the groundhandling market at Community airports.[41]

Altogether, the main preoccupation of the Community remains the opening of the markets, *i.e.* the right of access for Community air carriers to intra-Community air routes.[43]

Rail Transport

Until very recently, the rail transport sector was characterised by the existence in all Member States of State monopolies with the effect

[39] Reg. 1617/93 [1993] O.J. L155/18 amended by Reg. 1523/96 [1996] O.J. L190/11.
[40] [1998] O.J. C369/2.
[41] Reg. 82/91 [1991] O.J. L10/7 and Reg. 3652/93 [1993] O.J. L333/37.
[42] Dir. 96/67 [1997] O.J. L272/36. See in this respect two Commission Decisions on the application of Art. 9 of the Directive to Frankfurt airport [1998] O.J. L173/32 and Düsseldorf airport, *ibid.* at 45.
[43] See Reg. 2408/92 [1992] O.J. L240/8, and Case T–260/94 *Air Inter* [1997] E.C.J. II–997. Interesting also is the Decision on the Italian traffic distribution rules for the airport system of Milan, application of Reg. 2408/92 [1998] O.J. L337/42.

that national markets were absolutely closed to operators from other Member States. The privatisations which have taken place recently have not changed this. Consequently the Community has tried to open the national market to operators from other Member States by providing for a "right of access".[44] Under the present directive this right is granted only to "international groupings" and to "railway undertakings operating international combined transport goods services".[45] Where the former are concerned they have the right of access in the Member States of establishment of their constituent railway undertakings and the right of transit in other Member States for international services between the Member States of establishment. As for the combined goods services, they have access to the infrastructure of all the Member States.

Further provisions concerning transport will be examined in the relevant chapter hereafter.

(3) Telecommunications

Telecommunications, information industries and innovation constitute one of the most important industrial sectors for the economic development of the European Union. They will be examined in the Chapter on Industry Policy.

Full competition in the telecommunications market was only introduced in 1998, after the traditional monopolies were abolished for equipment[46] and value-added services.[47] But, given the fact that the infrastructure remained governed by monopoly rights, the Council introduced the Open Network Provision Directive[48] requiring the telecommunication organisations to lease lines to new market entrants on reasonable terms and to provide open and fair access to their networks.

---

[44] Dir. 91/440 [1991] O.J. L237/25 on the development of the Community's railways, implemented by Dir. 95/19 on the allocation of railway infrastructure capacity and the charging of infrastructure fees [1995] O.J. L143/75.

[45] *ibid.*, Art. 10.

[46] Dir. 88/301 [1988] O.J. L131/73, incorporated [1994] O.J. L1/446, modified by Dir. 94/46 [1994] O.J. L268/15.

[47] Dir. 90/388 [1990] O.J. L192/10, modified by Dir. 94/46. See n. 4 above.

[48] Dir. 90/387 on the establishment of the internal market for telecommunications services through the implementation of open network provision [1990] O.J. L192/1.

From 1992 onwards, the satellite[49] and mobile[50] services and the cable television networks[51] were progressively opened up to competition.

In 1996 the Commission adopted its so-called "Full Competition Directive",[52] amending and extending its earlier Services Directive. This Directive aims at the introduction of full competition in the E.U. telecommunications market. It requires the Member States to abolish the last remaining areas of monopoly rights in that market. All exclusive/special rights for the provision of public voice telephony services and the provision of the public telecommunications network were to be abolished by January 1, 1990 (with the exception of some Member States). Similarly, all exclusive/special rights regarding the self-provision of infrastructure, the use of infrastructure run by third parties and the use of shared infrastructure for the provision of services other than public voice telephony, were to be abolished by July 1, 1996.

The Directive also introduces the basic principles for licensing new entrants to both voice telephony and telecommunications infrastructure markets. It also requires interconnection to the voice telephony service and public switched telecommunications networks to be granted on non-discriminatory, proportional and transparent terms, based on objective criteria.

Additional legislative action was taken to ensure a successful transition to full liberalisation. Among the most important are the extension of the Open Network Provision to leased lines[53] and voice telephony.[54]

The Interconnection Directive ensures to all market players the ability to obtain interconnection with the networks[55] of others where this is reasonably justifiable and in accordance with the ONP

[49] Dir. 94/46 amending Dir. 88/301 and Dir. 90/388 in particular with regard to satellite communications [1994] O.J. L268/15.

[50] Dir. 69/2 amending Dir. 90/388 with regard to mobile and personal communications [1996] O.J. L20/59.

[51] Dir. 95/51 amending Dir. 90/388 with regard to the abolition of the restrictions on the use of cable television networks for the provision of already liberalised telecommunications services [1995] O.J. L256/49.

[52] Dir. 96/19 amending Dir. 90/388 regarding the implementation of full competition in telecommunications markets [1996] O.J. L74/13.

[53] Dir. 92/44 on the application of open network provision to leased lines [1992] O.J. L165/27.

[54] Dir. 95/62 on the application of open network provisions to voice telephony [1995] O.J. L321/6.

[55] Directive on interconnection in telecommunications with regard to ensuring universal service and interoperability through application of the principles of Open Network Provision [1997] O.J. L199/32.

principles of non-discrimination, transparency, objectivity and proportionality. See also the Notice on the application of the competition rules to access agreements in the telecommunications sector.[56]

Beyond 1998, the European telecommunication policy will focus on the effective implementation of this regulatory framework and maintain it under constant review in order to take account of future changes, such as the increasing convergence between telecommunications, information technology and audio-visual sectors.

(4) Postal Services

As recognised by the Court of Justice, competition rules of the E.C. Treaty apply, of course, also to the postal sector.[57] This concerns not only cartels and abuses of dominant positions, but also State aid rules.[58] The Commission published a Notice[59] setting out the "guiding principles according to which the Commission intends to apply the competition rules to the postal sector in individual cases, while maintaining the necessary safeguards for the provision of a universal service. It also gives the enterprises and the Member States clear guidelines so as to avoid infringements of the Treaty."

The Commission also ascertains that "the traditional structures of some services of general interest, which are organised on the basis of national monopolies, constitute a challenge for European economic integration".

The Notice sets out rules concerning the duties of dominant postal operators, cross-subsidisation, public undertakings and special or exclusive rights, freedom to provide services, measures adopted by Member States, postal operators and aid, services of general economic interest and the conditions for the application of the exception provided for undertakings entrusted with the operation of such services.[60]

---

[56] [1998] O.J. C265/2.

[57] See Joined Cases C–48 and 66/90 *Nederlandse and Koninklijke PTT Nederland and PTT Post BV v. Commission* [1992] E.C.R. I–565; [1993] 5 C.M.L.R. 316 and Case C–320/91 *Procureur du Roi v. Paul Corbeau* [1993] I–2533; [1995] 4 C.M.L.R. 621.

[58] Case C–387/92 *Banco di Credito Industrial* [1994] E.C.R. I–877; [1994] 3 C.M.L.R. 473.

[59] [1998] O.J. C39/2.

[60] See Art. 86(2) (ex 90(2)) E.C.

(5) Insurance

This is another sector where special rules were established. In May 1991, the Council adopted a regulation concerning the exemption of certain categories of agreements in the field of insurance. It authorises the Commission to issue a regulation exempting this category from the prohibition.[61] On that basis the Commission issued, in December 1992, a regulation[62] exempting four types of agreements which seek co-operation with respect to:

- the establishment of common risk-premium tariffs based on collectively ascertained statistics or on the number of claims;
- the establishment of standard policy conditions;
- the common coverage of certain types of risks; and
- the establishment of common rules on the testing and acceptance of security devices.

The provisions of the Regulation also apply where the participating undertakings lay down rights and obligations for the undertakings connected with them.

The Regulation shall apply until March 31, 2003.

(6) Intellectual Property Rights

Normally, such rights are used by their owner to prevent others from producing and commercialising the product covered by the right or to limit the use of this right to particular national territories. Consequently, the owner divides the Community again into separate markets, and, although he acts in conformity with national law, he thereby prevents trade between Member States. This, of course, constitutes an infringement of the basic principle of freedom of movement of goods and it was in relation with this principle that the Court defined the implementation of the competition rules in this important sector. This subject is discussed under "Industry Policy" in Part Five, Chapter Twenty-Seven.

---

[61] Reg. 1534/91 [1991] O.J. L143/1.
[62] Reg. 3932/92 [1992] O.J. L398/7.

4. Rules Giving Effect to Articles 81 and 82 (ex 85 and 86) E.C.—Regulation 17

Regulation 17[63] is the first regulation "to give effect to the principles set out in Articles 85 and 86 [now 81 and 82]".[64] Generally speaking, it provides for procedures to be followed when the Commission takes one of the following decisions.[65]

(1) To give a "negative clearance"[66]; this is issued at the request of undertakings, which want to make certain that their cartels are not prohibited by Articles 81 (ex 85) or 82 (ex 86) E.C.
(2) To oblige undertakings to put an end to infringements either upon the application of a Member State or a natural or legal person,[67] or on its own initiative.[68] In this connection attention should be drawn to the *limitation period* of five years for enforcement procedures.[69]
(3) To issue a declaration granting an exemption from the prohibition of Article 81.1 (ex 85).[70]
(4) To undertake investigations into undertakings.[71] To this end officials authorised by the Commission are empowered to: (a) enter any premises, land or means of transport[72]; (b) to examine books and business records; (c) to take copies of or

---

[63] [1962] J.O. 13/204 and [1959–62] O.J. Spec. Ed. 87.
[64] See Art. 83 (ex 87) E.C.
[65] Lists of decisions taken by the Commission can be found in the annual Reports on Competition policy published in conjunction with the annual General Reports.
[66] Reg. 17, Art. 2; the first such decision was *Grosfillex-Fillisdorf* [1964] J.O. 915/64.
[67] *ibid.* Art. 3(2)(b). See Reg. 27, First Regulation implementing Council Regulation 17, fixing form, content and other details concerning applications [1962] J.O. 35/1118 and [1959–62] J.O. Spec. Ed. 132, last amended by Reg. 2526/85 [1985] O.J. L240/1. See Case T–575/93 *Koelman* [1996] E.C.R. II–1; [1994] 4 C.M.L.R. 636, wherein the CFI ruled that this Article does not confer upon a person who lodges an application, the right to obtain from the Commission a decision within the meaning of Art. 249 (ex 189) E.C.
[68] See Case 792/79R *Camera Care v. Commission* [1980] E.C.R. 119 at 131(18); [1980] 1 C.M.L.R. 334; the powers which the Commission holds under Art. 3 include the power to take interim measures which are indispensable for the effective exercise of its function. See also Joined Cases 228–229/82R *Ford Werke v. Commission* [1982] E.C.R. 3091, where interim measures were suspended.
[69] Reg. 2988/74 [1974] O.J. L319/1, Art. 4–6.
[70] Reg. 17, Art. 6.
[71] *ibid.*, Art. 14.
[72] *ibid.*, Art. 14(2) and (3). This right to enter premises was contested, but to no avail, by several undertakings Case 46/87R *Hoechst v. Commission* [1987] E.C.R. 1549 and Case 85/87 *Dow Chemical Nederland BV v. Commission* [1987] E.C.R. 4367. See also Explanatory Notes on authorisation to investigate: Thirteenth Report on Competition policy, 1993, 270–271.

extracts from the books and business records, and (d) to ask for oral explanations on the spot. (*Legal Privilege*. The confidentiality of written communications between lawyer and client is, however, protected when (i) such communications are made for the purpose and in the interest of the client's defence and (ii) they emanate from independent lawyers, *i.e.* lawyers who are not bound to the client by a relationship of employment.)

(5) To impose fines and penalties.[73] (The Commission published a Notice[74] on the non-imposition or reduction of fines for enterprises co-operating with the Commission during an investigation into a cartel and Guidelines on the method of setting fines.[75]).

Before deciding on a negative clearance, an obligation to put an end to an infringement or grant an exemption, the Commission must formally initiate a procedure.[76] The latter does not constitute a separate act which can be challenged in Court,[77] but once it has been opened, a national judge can no longer decide on the application of Community competition law.[78]

This opening of proceedings consists, in the first place, in informing the undertakings in question about the points to which the Commission objects. This is done by sending a "*Statement of Objections*". The Commission must also give the addressees the opportunity to express their views on them; this can be done, when requested by the parties, in the form of hearings.[79] Those hearings are

---

[73] Reg. 17 Arts. 15 and 16. The undertakings must be told, in the statement of objections, that the Commission intends to impose fines. Fines have been imposed for submitting incomplete information ([1971] E.C. Bull. 11–55) and periodic fines were imposed for each day an undertaking failed to fulfil an obligation imposed by the Commission *MA-Statuut* [1980] O.J. L318/1.

[74] [1996] O.J. C207/4. However, the conditions provided are very strict and the "co-operating" undertaking will not know before the end of the procedure whether a reduction will be granted and, if so, how much. Furthermore, the question of confidentiality does not seem to have been satisfactorily solved. See Case T–327/94 *SCA Holding v. Commission* [1998] E.C.R. II–1373 where mitigation was refused. There is one case where a fine paid was refunded. Case T–227/95 *Assidoman Kraft* [1997] E.C.R. II–1189; [1997] 5 C.M.L.R. 364.

[75] [1998] O.J. C9/3.

[76] Reg. 17, Art. 9(3).

[77] See Case 60/81 *IBM v. Commission* [1981] E.C.R. 2639 at 265; [1981] 3 C.M.L.R. 635.

[78] See Case 127/73 *BRT v. SABAM I* [1974] E.C.R. 51; [1974] 2 C.M.L.R. 251.

[79] *ibid.* Art. 19(1) and (2). See Reg. 99/63 on the Hearings provided for in Reg. 17 [1963] O.J. 127/2268 and [1963–64] O.J. Spec. Ed. 47; this Reg. was replaced by Reg. 2842/98 [1998] O.J. L354/18.

chaired by the *Hearing Officer* whose terms of reference were laid down by a Commission decision.[80]

The Commission must also invite third parties to submit their observations and therefore must publish in the *Official Journal* the essence of the decision it intends to take, and which contains a summary of the cartel or abuse, which is the object of the decision. Indeed, according to the Court, respect for the rights of the defence "requires that any person who may be adversely affected by the adoption of a decision should be placed in a position in which he may effectively make known his views on the evidence against him which the Commission has taken as the basis for the decision at issue".[81]

In the three above-mentioned cases, the Commission must also consult the *Consultative Committee on Cartels and Monopolies* composed of representatives of the Member States.

The proceedings are normally closed by a decision, but, beside settlement, this can also be done by a so-called "*Comfort Letter*" or "*Administrative Letter*".[82] There are two kinds of comfort letters: the enhanced[83] one wherein the Commission states that it sees no reason to intervene and the informal one stating that there is no reason to issue a formal decision. Before sending an enhanced comfort letter, the Commission must publish a notice in the *Official Journal* summarising the cartel and invite interested parties to comment.

Those comfort letters emanate from a top official of the Commission and therefore, do not bind the Commission. More and more undertakings ask for such letters since they involve much less delays than would be the case for a formal decision. Those comfort letters must, however, be taken into account by the national courts as important "indications".[84]

Two delicate subjects have given rise to much discussion and several judgments of the European courts, they are the business

---

[80] Dec. 94/810 on the terms of reference of hearing officers in competition procedures [1994] O.J. L330/67.

[81] Case T–450/93 *Lisrestal v. Commission* [1994] E.C.R. II–1177(42).

[82] See Case 99/79 *Lancôme v. Etos* [1980] E.C.R. 2511 at 2532, where the Court ascertained that the letter in question was dispatched without publication as laid down in Art. 19(3) of Reg. 17 and which was not published pursuant to Art. 21(1); it concluded that such a letter which is based only upon the facts in the Commission's possession and brings to an end the procedure of examination by the department of the Commission responsible for this, does not have the effect of preventing national courts before which the agreements in question are alleged to be incompatible with Art. 81 (ex 85) E.C. from reaching a different finding as regards the agreements concerned on the basis of the information available to them.

[83] Reg. 17, Art. 19(3). See "Competition Report" 1991, pt 15 and Notice on *Fluke/Philips* [1989] O.J. C188/2.

[84] See Case 37/79 *Marty v. Estée Lauder* [1980] E.C.R. 2481 at 2498; [1981] 2 C.M.L.R. 143.

secrets and the right of access to the Commission files by the undertakings involved in proceedings.

With regard to *Business Secrets*, the Court reminded the Commission of the fact that the obligation of professional secrecy is laid down in the Treaty itself. Reference can also be made to the Commission Decision on the terms of reference of hearing officers who have received delegation to decide that secret information may be communicated; such a decision may be challenged in court.[85]

As for the *Right of Access to Files*, it is generally admitted[86] and recognised by the Court[87] that due process requires that the undertakings be given access to the files held by the Commission, although this is not explicitly provided for.

As was mentioned above, the Commission can act on its own initiative or on the basis of a complaint filed by a natural or legal person. The question arose whether the Commission could reject such a complaint. The Community courts accepted that the Commission could reject a complaint where it finds that the case does not display sufficient Community interest to justify further investigation of it.[88] According to the Court, it is consistent with the Commission's obligations under Community law for it to apply different degrees of priority to the cases submitted to it. In order to do this, the Commission is entitled to refer to the Community interest, *i.e.* significance of the alleged infringement as regards the functioning of the common market, the probability of establishing the existence of the infringement and the scope of the investigation required.[89]

Finally, reference must be made to a Commission Regulation on the form, content and other details of applications and notifications under Regulation 17.[90]

The reader should be aware of the quite revolutionary White Paper of April 28, 1999 (Commission programme 99/027) in which it is proposed to amend Regulation 17 by eliminating the notification and exemption system and rendering the exemption of Article 85(3) directly applicable without prior Commission decision. Article 85, as a whole, would be applied by the Commission, national competition authorities and national courts.

---

85 [1994] O.J. L330/67. See Case 53/85 *Akzo* [1986] E.C.R. 1965; [1987] 1 C.M.L.R. 231.

86 See Competition Report 1992, at 38.

87 See Case 85/76 *Hoffmann-La Roche v. Commission* [1979] E.C.R. 461; [1979] 3 C.M.L.R. 211.

88 Case T–114/92 *Industries Musicales* [1995] E.C.R. II–147.

89 Case T–24/90 *Automec* [1992] E.C.R. II–2223. See, however, Case T–387/94 *Asia Motor* [1996] E.C.R. II–961; [1996] 4 C.M.L.R. 305, where the Court concluded that the Commission had made an error of assessment.

90 Reg. 3385/94 [1994] O.J. L377/28.

5. Control of Concentrations[91]—Merger Regulation[92] (Reg. 4064/89)

While recognising that the dismantling of the internal frontiers of the Community results in major corporate reorganisations in the form of concentrations and that this development must be welcomed as being in line with the requirements of dynamic competition, the Council indicated that they may also seriously impede competition. The Council concluded that those concentrations must therefore be controlled. This control applies to all industries, including services.

The merger Regulation covers mainly two operations: mergers and acquisitions, on the one hand, and joint ventures on the other.

Mergers are operations whereby two companies legally and economically form a single undertaking, while acquisitions are operations whereby one undertaking takes sole control of the whole or part of another. Joint ventures are transactions whereby two or more firms acquire joint control of another firm, existing or to be created. Here a distinction must be made, since the merger Regulation only applies to "concentrative" joint ventures, while "co-operative" joint ventures are subject to the control of agreements between undertakings.

What characterises a concentrative joint venture is the fact that it accomplishes "on a lasting basis all the functions of an autonomous entity [and] does not give rise to coordination of the competitive behaviour of the parties among themselves or between them and the joint venture".[93] For further details see the Commission Notice on the distinction between concentrative and co-operative joint ventures.[94]

All the operations covered by the Regulation are referred to below collectively as "mergers".

All mergers are prohibited which create or strengthen a dominant position as a result of which effective competition would be significantly impeded on the common market or in a substantial part of it.[95] Dominance therefore becomes the key word of the prohibition. The definition of "dominance" under the Merger Regulation is, of course, the same as under Article 82 (ex 86) E.C. analysed

---

[91] See Commission Notice on the notion of concentration [1994] O.J. C385/5.

[92] Reg. 4064/89 [1990] O.J. L257/14, corrected in [1990] O.J. L257/13 and amended by Reg. 1310/97 [1997] O.J. L180/1. For a consolidated text see [1997] 5 C.M.L.R. 387. This Reg. is based on Arts. 81 (ex 87) and 308 (ex 235) E.C.

[93] *ibid.*, Art. 3(2)2.

[94] [1994] O.J. C385/1.

[95] Merger Reg. Art. 2(2).

above. Summarily said, an undertaking occupies a dominant position when it can operate on the market independently of its competitors, its customers and the end consumers. There are, however, important differences; indeed, the dominant position in the case of Article 82 (ex 86) E.C. refers to an existing position, while under the merger Regulation it concerns also a future dominant position. Furthermore, as was seen, Article 82 (ex 86) prohibits a certain behaviour, while the Merger Regulation prohibits a modification of the market structure which might impede competition. The latter therefore is prospective, while the former concerns the past.

Although the Regulation refers to a dominant position held by a single undertaking, the Commission applied the prohibition of the Merger Regulation also to joint or collective dominance. This dominance includes undertakings which are not party to the merger. In other words, an undertaking operating in a given market can find itself in infringement of the Regulation because other undertakings on the same market merged. The Commission's practice was challenged in the Court, which ruled that "collective dominant positions are not excluded from the field of application of the Regulation". This put an end to a hotly disputed issue.[96]

The main features of the merger Regulation are the following:

1. Those concentrations that fall within the Regulation are concentrations with a "Community dimension", *i.e.*

(i) when only two Member States are concerned, three conditions must be fulfilled:

- the aggregate world-wide turnover of all the undertakings concerned is more than euro 5 billion;
- the aggregate Community-wide turnover of at least two of them is more than euro 250 million; and
- where each undertaking realises at least one third of its Community turnover in another Member State;

(ii) when three or more Member States are concerned, a concentration that does not meet the above mentioned thresholds has nonetheless a Community dimension when:

- the combined aggregate world-wide turnover of all undertakings concerned is more than euro 2.5 billion;

[96] Joined Cases C–68/94 *France v. Commission* and C–30/95 *SCPA and EMC v. Commission* [1998] E.C.R. I–1375.

- in each of at least three Member States the combined aggregate turnover of all undertakings concerned is more than euro 100 million;
- in each of those three Member States the aggregate turnover of at least two of the undertakings concerned is more than euro 25 million; and
- the aggregate Community-wide turnover of at least two of the undertakings concerned is more than euro 100 million;
- unless each of the undertakings concerned achieves more than two-thirds of its aggregate turnover within one and the same Member State.[97]

In other words, a concentration between two or more undertakings situated in the same Member State has no Community dimension when all of them achieve more than two thirds of their turnover in that same Member State. Indeed, in that case it is an internal affair of that Member State.

The Commission published a Notice on calculation of turnover.[98] The above mentioned thresholds will be reviewed before July 1, 2000.

Where the Commission finds that a notified concentration falls within the scope of the concentration, it must publish the fact of the notification, at the same time indicating the names of the parties, the nature of the concentration and the economic sector involved.[99]

2. A concentration is deemed to arise where two or more, previously independent, undertakings merge, or where one or more persons or undertakings, already controlling one or more undertakings, acquire direct or indirect control of the whole or parts of one or more other undertakings; the main criteria therefore is "control".[1]

3. The above mentioned concentrations must be notified[2] to the Commission not later than one week after the conclusion of the agreement or the announcement of the public bid, or the acquisition of the controlling interest; they may not be implemented until the

---

[97] Merger Reg. Art. 1.

[98] [1994] O.J. C385/21.

[99] Merger Reg. Art. 4(3).

[1] *ibid.*, Art. 3.

[2] Notification must be made by using Form CO issued by the Commission. See Annex to Reg. 3384/94 [1994] O.J. L377/1. In their notification, the parties must define the relevant product and the relevant geographic market and also the "affected market", *i.e.* a relevant market where two or more of the parties are engaged in business activities in the same product or individual group product market and would acquire a combined market share of more than 10%; this threshold applies to both horizontal and vertical relationships.

Commission has given clearance or the time-limit for Commission action has expired.[3]

4. The Commission appreciates the concentration taking into account, *inter alia*, the structure of all the markets concerned. Also, the actual and potential competition from undertakings located within or outside the Community; the market position of the undertakings concerned[4] and their economic and financial power; the opportunities available to suppliers and users, their access to supplies and markets and any legal or other barrier to entry into the relevant market. The Commission also takes into account supply and demand trends for the relevant goods and services, the interests of the intermediate and ultimate consumers and the development of technical and economic progress.[5] Finally, the Commission will take into account the restrictions ancillary to the concentration.

5. Straightforward cases will be cleared within one month from the date of notification. But, when the Commission has "serious doubts" it opens a procedure which may last no more than four months. Such a procedure is opened by a decision, after which the parties will receive a "statement of objections". The undertakings may contest the Commission's objections in writing and, if they so request, during hearings. The rights of the defence must be fully respected and the parties directly involved will have access to the file, subject to the protection of business secrets. After having consulted the Advisory Committee[6] the merger must be declared either compatible or incompatible[7] with the common market. This decision must be published in the *Official Journal*. If no decision is taken, the merger is deemed compatible. The Commission may impose conditions and/or accept modifications to the merger agreement proposed by the parties, to allow it to clear the merger.

6. The Commission may order suspension of the merger until it reaches a final decision, but within given time limits.[8]

7. The Commission has powers to investigate and to impose fines or periodic penalty payments.[9]

8. The Commission has exclusive jurisdiction over mergers with a

[3] *ibid.*, Art. 4(1). The Commission imposed a fine of 33,000 ECU on *Samsung* (South Korea) for late notification and for having put the merger into effect prematurely.

[4] See Commission Notice on the notion of undertakings concerned [1994] O.J. L385/12.

[5] Merger Reg. Art. 2(1).

[6] *ibid.*, Art. 19.

[7] In 1998, the Commission received 225 notifications; only 10 were submitted to the second stage examination.

[8] Merger Reg. Arts 7 and 10.

[9] *ibid.*, Arts 13, 14 and 15.

Community dimension; however, at a Member State's request, the Commission may and, under certain circumstances, must[10] refer the case, in whole or in part, to the competition authorities of that State. A Commission Regulation lays down rules for applications, time limits and the hearings.[11]

Another delicate problem, as with cartels, is the confidentiality of information provided to the Commission by the parties to the concentration, the so-called *Business Secrets*. It should be remembered, in the first place, that the Treaty itself requires the members of the Commission, the officials and other servants of the Community "not to disclose information of the kind covered by the obligation of professional secrecy".[12] Furthermore, the Regulation provides that information acquired shall be used only for the purpose of the relevant request, investigation or hearing. It also specifies that neither the Commission nor the competent authorities of the Member States shall disclose information they have acquired through the application of the Regulation.[13] The protection of business secrets is further guaranteed both in the merger Regulations and in the implementing Regulation. See below, "Access to File". With the adoption of the Merger Regulation, the arsenal of Community instruments at the disposal of the Community institutions and national authorities to ensure that competition is not distorted in the common market by undertakings, can now be considered complete.

6. Commission Notices of a General Nature

In order to clarify its competition policy, the Commission has issued several notices; some of them, somehow, complete the block

[10] Those conditions are that within three weeks after having received copy of the notification, the Member State communicates to the Commission who informs the parties, that a concentration affects a distinct market within its territory, which is not a substantial part of the common market and that the Commission considers that such a market is indeed affected; see Art. 9(3)(b), last indent.

[11] Reg. 447/98 on the notifications, time limits and hearings provided for in the merger Regulation [1998] O.J. L61/1.

[12] Art. 287 (ex 214) E.C., which refers "in particular [to] information about undertakings, their business relations or their cost components".

[13] Merger Reg. Art. 17. See detailed examination by the CFI in Case T–102/86 *Gencor* [1997] E.C.R. II–879, concerning requests for confidential treatment. See also Opening to the Public of Documents and Files from the Historical Archives of the Commission which are covered by the Obligation of professional or Business Secrecy [1997] O.J. C–218/3.

exemptions, although, contrary to the latter, they have no binding effect, except to a certain extent for the Commission itself. They simply provide guidance and information concerning the Commission's views on the implementation of the competition rules.

(i) Exclusive Agency Contracts made with Commercial Agents[14]

In this Notice the Commission declares that contracts concluded with commercial agents, in which those agents undertake for a specified part of the territory of the common market to negotiate transactions on behalf of an enterprise, or conclude transactions in the name or on behalf of an enterprise, are not prohibited by the Treaty.

(ii) Co-operation Agreements[15]

In this Notice the Commission first indicates that it encourages co-operation between small and medium-sized enterprises (SMEs), where such co-operation enables them to work more rationally and increases their productivity and competitiveness on a larger market.[16] The Commission then lists eight categories of agreements which have as their sole object the following co-operation and which, in its view, do not restrict competition.

1. Exchange of opinion or experience, joint market research, joint carrying-out of comparative studies of enterprises or industries, and joint preparation of statistics and calculation models.
2. Co-operation in accounting matters, joint provision of credit guarantees, joint debt-collecting associations, and business or tax consultant agencies.
3. Joint implementation of R&D projects, joint placing of R&D contracts, the sharing-out of R&D projects among participating enterprises.

---

[14] [1962] O.J. 292/1.

[15] Notice concerning agreements, decisions and concerted practices in the field of co-operation between enterprises [1968] O.J. C75/3, corrected by O.J. C84/14.

[16] See Commission Recommendation 96/280 concerning the definition of SMEs [1996] O.J. L107/4. Please note that this Recommendation was published in the "L" series of the O.J., normally reserved for legislative acts. Indeed, as will be remembered, according to Art. 249 (ex 189) E.C., recommendations "shall have no binding force".

4. Joint use of production facilities and storing and transport equipment.
5. The setting-up of consortia for the joint execution of orders, where the participating enterprises do not compete with each other as regards the work to be done or where each of them by itself is unable to execute the orders.
6. Joint selling arrangements, joint after-sales and repairs service, providing the participating enterprises are not competitors with regard to the products or services covered by the agreement.
7. Joint advertising.
8. The use of a common label to designate a certain quality, where the label is available to all competitors on the same conditions.

(iii) Import of Japanese Products[17]

The Commission reminds undertakings concluding agreements with Japanese firms and which are intended to restrict imports of Japanese products into the Community, that such agreements do not fall outside the Community competition rules because one or all of the parties are situated outside the Community. It urges the undertakings concerned to notify those agreements.

(iv) Subcontracting Agreements[18]

This form of agreement is considered by the Commission as a form of work distribution, which concerns in particular SMEs[19] and whereby technology is made available by one party to the other with restrictions as to its use. Restrictions which are not prohibited are the following.

1. Technology and equipment provided by the contractor may only be used for the purposes of the agreement, and may not be made available to third parties, and the goods and services resulting from the use of such technology may be supplied only to the contractor or used on his behalf, provided that the technology and equipment is necessary to enable the subcontractor to carry out his obligations.

---

[17] [1972] O.J. C11/13.
[18] [1979] O.J. C1/2.
[19] See Commission Recommendation concerning the definition of SMEs: n. 16 above.

2. The above proviso is satisfied where performance of the sub-contracting agreement makes necessary the use of industrial property rights of the contractor, of know-how of the contractor, of studies, plans or documents which have been prepared by the contractor or dies patterns or tools and accessory equipment which belong to the contractor and, which permit the manufacture of goods which differ in form, function or composition from other goods manufactured or supplied on the market.
3. The following restrictions are also authorised: an undertaking by either party not to reveal manufacturing processes or other know-how, an undertaking by the sub-contractor not to make use, even after expiration of the agreement, of the above, and an undertaking by the sub-contractor to pass to the contractor on a non-exclusive basis any technical improvement which he has made during the execution of the sub-contracting agreement.
4. The contractor may forbid the use by the sub-contractor of trademark, trade names and get-up in the case of goods, which are not to be supplied to the contractor.

(v) Agreements of Minor Importance[20]

There used to be two thresholds—turnover and market share—below which undertakings were considered as not in a position to distort competition. There is no longer a turnover threshold, so that large firms with small market shares can also benefit from the "exemption" provided by this Notice.

A distinction is made with regard to the market share threshold between horizontal agreements (for which a threshold of five per cent applies) and vertical agreements (10 per cent).

There is a "blacklist" of restrictions which, because of their nature, are regarded as typically incompatible with Article 81(1) (ex 85(1)). These are caught by the prohibition even when they are below the above mentioned thresholds. The restrictions in question are the following.

1. Horizontal agreements having as their object price fixing, production or sales quotas, market sharing or sharing of sources of supply, and
2. Vertical agreements fixing resale prices or containing territorial protection clauses.

[20] [1997] O.J. C372/13.

However, below the thresholds it is primarily for the national authorities and courts to intervene. The Commission will examine such agreements only if, in its opinion, this is necessary in the Community interest and, in particular, if such agreements hinder the smooth functioning of the internal market.

Where Small and Medium-sized Enterprises (SMEs)[21] are concerned, firms with an annual turnover of no more than 40 million ECUs or a balance sheet total of no more than euro 27 million and employing no more that 250 persons, agreements entered into by such SMEs need not be notified. The Commission, however, reserves the right to intervene.

(vi) Access to the Files

The right of access to the files is laid down in a Notice[22] on the internal rules of procedure for processing of requests for access to the file of cases pursuant to Articles 81 (ex 85) and 82 (ex 86) E.C., Articles 65 and 66 ECSC and Regulation 4064/89.

This Notice defines "non-communicable" and "communicable" documents.

7. Relationship between Community and National Competition Authorities and Rules

In one of its early judgments[23] the Court had to answer the question whether or not Community competition law and national competition rules could be applied simultaneously to the same cartel. The Court found that Community law and national rules consider cartels from different points of view. The former regards them in the light of the obstacles which may result for trade between Member States, while the latter proceeds on the basis of considerations which are particular to it. It follows that one and the same agreement may, in principle, be the object of two parallel proceedings.

However, if the ultimate general aim of the Treaty is to be respected, the parallel application of the national system can only be allowed in so far as it does not prejudice the uniform application throughout the common market of the Community rules on cartels, and the full effect of the measures adopted in implementation of those rules.

---

[21] See Commission Recommendation concerning the definition of SMEs, n. 16 above.
[22] [1997] O.J. C23/3.
[23] Case 14/68 *Wilhelm v. Bundeskartellamt* [1969] E.C.R. 1; [1969] C.M.L.R. 100.

The Court concluded that "consequently, conflicts between the rules of the Community and national rules in the matter of the law on cartels must be resolved by applying the principle that Community law takes precedence". As long as this rule is applied, national authorities may take action in accordance with their national law, even when an examination of the same cartel is pending before the Commission.

However, when a cartel is void under Community law, national authorities may not declare it to be valid under national law.[24] On the other hand, when applying national law, national authorities are under no obligation to take into account possible infringements of Community law, as long as the Commission has not opened proceedings. Furthermore, nothing prevents those authorities from prohibiting under national law agreements which are void under Community law. Neither are they prevented from imposing fines upon the undertakings concerned, even if fines were already imposed by the Commission. Conversely, the Commission is not prevented from imposing fines after an undertaking has been fined under national law. However, according to the Court, the Commission must take account of the penalties which have already been borne by the same undertaking for the same action, where penalties have been imposed in a Member State. The situation is different when penalties have been imposed in a third country.[25]

To take account of several judgments of the Court,[26] the Commission published a Notice on co-operation between the Commission and the national judges.[27] It should indeed be noted that it is in the first place the national judge who is responsible for applying the Community competition rules. This follows from the Treaty itself[28] and from the direct effect of those rules.[29] In such cases the national rules of procedure and admissibility apply to appeals.[30]

---

[24] This leaves open the question whether national authorities may declare void an agreement for which the Commission has granted an exemption under Art. 81(3) (ex 85(3)) E.C. If this were possible one would have the strange situation where an agreement would be void in one Member State and valid in all the others. This seems contrary to Community law in general which demands uniform application of Community decisions throughout the Community.

[25] Case 7/72 *Boehringer v. Commission* [1972] E.C.R. 1281 at 1289.

[26] See, *e.g.* Case C–234/89 *Delimitis v. Brau* [1991] E.C.R. I–991; [1992] 5 C.M.L.R. 210.

[27] [1993] O.J. C–39/6. See Case C–91/95P *Tremblay* [1996] E.C.R. I–5547; [1997] 4 C.M.L.R. 211.

[28] Art. 10 (ex 5) E.C.

[29] See Case 127/73 *BRT v. SABAM* [1972] E.C.R. 51(16); [1974] 2 C.M.L.R. 251.

[30] Case 158/80 *Rewe v. Hauptzollamt Kiel* [1981] E.C.R. 1805 at 1858; [1982] 1 C.M.L.R. 449.

The Notice on co-operation with national judges was followed a few years later by a Notice on co-operation between national competition authorities and the Commission in handling cases falling within the scope of Articles 81 (ex 85) or 82 (ex 86) of the E.C. Treaty.[31] In this Notice, the Commission expressed the opinion that national authorities should normally handle cases the effect of which are felt mainly in their territories and which appear on preliminary examination unlikely to qualify for exemption under Art. 81(3) (ex 85(3)) E.C. where the Commission retains exclusive power.

8. International Co-operation

An agreement was concluded between the Commission and the United States Government regarding the application of their competition laws. This agreement contains provisions on exchange of information, consultation, notification and other procedural aspects. It also provides for co-operation in cases where the parties to the agreement apply their competition rules to identical or related situations. They agree to take into account the important interests of the other party, referred to as "comity".

This co-operation has allowed the competition authorities of both parties to harmonise, for instance, the content and timing of their final decisions in identical cases,[32] thereby avoiding discrepancies which might create embarrassing situations when the object of the investigations concerns cases with world-wide ramifications, as is more and more the case in this period of "globalisation".

This first agreement was complemented by another agreement between the European Community and the Government of the United States of America[33] on the application of positive comity principles in the enforcement of their competition laws. On a broader front mention must be made of a Communication from the Commission to the Council "Towards an international framework of competition rules"[34] and a Recommendation of the Council concerning "co-operation between Member Countries on Anti-Competitive Practices Affecting International Trade".[35]

---

[31] [1997] O.J. C313/3.

[32] See, *e.g.* Case IV/M 877 *Boeing/McDonnell Douglas* [1997] O.J. L336/16 and *Price Waterhouse/Coopers & Lybrand* [1999] O.J. L50/27.

[33] [1998] O.J. L173/28.

[34] COM(96) 284 final, [1996] E.C. Bull. 6–125.

[35] COM(95) 130 final.

II. Competition Rules Applying to Member States

1. State Monopolies of a Commercial Character—Article 31 (ex 37) E.C.

Member States are required by the Treaty to "adjust" their monopolies of a commercial[36] character, so as to ensure that, by the end of the transitional period,[37] no discrimination regarding the conditions under which goods are procured and marketed, exists between nationals of the Member States.

However, the "article does not apply to national provisions which do not concern the exercise by a public monopoly of its exclusive right, but apply in a general manner to the production and marketing of goods, whether or not they are covered by the monopoly in question".[38] This reference to the application, in a general manner, of national legislation to the marketing of goods is particularly interesting in view of the interpretation given by the Court of the concept "measures having [an] equivalent effect [to quantitative restrictions]"[39] it is, in fact, an application of the principle developed in the famous *Keck and Mithouard* judgment.[40]

According to the Commission, "liberalisation of the traditionally monopolised sectors is a crucial step in the establishment of a real single market.[41] Nevertheless, the Commission is aware that the particular way those sectors are organised very often reflect legitimate concerns to ensure social cohesion". In its Notice on services of general interest in Europe, the Commission advocated a pragmatic and gradual approach which respects the special characteristics of

---

[36] The term "commercial" indicates that production monopolies are not affected by the Treaty. Indeed, in an internal market, production monopolies do not constitute an obstacle to free trade between Member States, this freedom being the test for the existence of competition. Neither are the common agricultural organisations affected by Art. 37, since, under Art. 38(2), the "agricultural" provisions have precedence over the rules laid down for the establishment of the common market. See Case 83/78 *Pigs Marketing Board v. Redmond* [1978] E.C.R. 2347; [1979] 2 C.M.L.R. 573. The same applies to service monopolies, see Case C–17/94 *Gervais and Others* [1995] E.C.R. I–4353.

[37] For the original six Member States this was the December 31, 1969; other dates were, of course, provided by the different accession Treaties.

[38] Case C–387/93 *Banchero* [1995] E.C.R. I–4663; [1996] 1 C.M.L.R. 829.

[39] Art. 28 (ex 30) E.C.

[40] Joined Cases C–267 and 268/91 *Keck and Mithouard* [1993] E.C.R. I–6097; [1995] 1 C.M.L.R. 101; see under "Free movement of goods".

[41] Competition Report 1996, 53.

each sector. The Commission tries to reach a consensus with other Community institutions, the Member States and the parties concerned by a parallel approach of liberalisation measures and the harmonising directives of the Council and the Parliament. One can only subscribe to this implementation of the Community competition rules in a less exclusive and strict legal way. Indeed, this means that, although the Commission intends to make use of all the legal instruments available to it, it is of the view that the objectives of liberalisation and of public service can be kept fully compatible.

At the time the E.C. Treaty came into force, about a dozen monopolies existed within the Community. The timetable provided for in the Treaty was not respected and although most monopolies were either simply abolished or adapted, it was only in 1993 that the Commission could report that the measures taken by the various governments were adequate,[42] thereby overlooking that certain sectors, like energy, were, in most Member States, in the hands of monopolies which control imports and exports.[43]

The successive accessions brought new monopolies into the Community; this was particularly the case with Greece, Portugal and Spain and lately the accession of Austria, Finland and Sweden extended the list and created problems in this field due to the extremely strict rules concerning the sales of alcohol. Interestingly enough the Swedish monopoly was not considered as being in breach of the monopoly rules, since it was not discriminatory, but rather as constituting an obstacle to trade contrary to the free movement of goods. As for the Swedish and Finish retail monopolies they were not considered contrary to Community law, taking account of the objectives pursued as long as there is no discrimination between national and imported goods.[44]

Presently, it can be said that, with certain unavoidable exceptions, the monopolies of a commercial nature existing within the Community have been "adapted" in conformity with the Treaty rules. However, the Commission considers that there still exist monopolies in the public service sector, which have not yet been adapted.[45] They concern sectors such as telecommunications, energy, postal service and transport. These were examined above under Competition Rules Applying to Various Branches of the Economy.

---

[42] Competition Report 1992, 149.

[43] See, however, Cases C–157/94, etc. *Commission v. The Netherlands, Italy, France and Spain* [1997] E.C.R. I–5699, I–5789, I–5815 and I–5851, where the Court concluded that the Commission did not prove that the existing monopolies were disproportionate or contrary to Community interest.

[44] See Case C–189/95 *Franzén* [1997] E.C.R. I–2310.

[45] Competition Report 1996, 54.

2. Public Undertakings—Article 86 (ex 90) E.C.

A public undertaking is any undertaking, whatever its public or private status, on whose economic behaviour the State can exert influence. This influence can be based, for instance, on the State's direct or indirect financial participation or on legal provisions governing the establishment of the undertaking in question. In other words, the criteria for determining whether an undertaking is a "public" one, in the sense of the Treaty, depends on whether the public authority can and, in fact, does exercise control over it.[46]

The logical consequence of the subordinate position of the public undertaking is that the public authority which controls it, is responsible for the market behaviour. Indeed, the object of the Treaty is to prevent that a Member State would exercise, through a public undertaking, an activity which it is prohibited from exercising in its capacity of public authority. This would constitute a circumvention of the Treaty rules for which the Member States remain responsible. The Treaty rules do indeed apply, in the first place, to the Member States. Very few Treaty rules apply directly to undertakings, the most important ones being the competition rules. But when a public undertaking infringes those rules it can be held directly responsible by the Commission notwithstanding the fact that it might have been induced to do so by a public authority. The same applies when national legislation imposes an anti-competitive behaviour on a public undertaking. Indeed, even such legislation does not excuse the public undertaking from implementing the competition rules.[47]

Of course, those competition rules only apply when the public undertaking is in competition with undertakings not controlled by the State.[48] Neither do they apply when the public undertaking acts for the State in the exercise of an activity which is connected by its nature, its aim and the rules to which it is subject, with the exercise of powers relating, for instance, to the protection of the environment, which are typically those of a public authority.[49]

However, in the case of infringement by a public undertaking of these competition rules, the State and its legislation can also be

46 See Dir. 80/723, Art. 2 [1980] O.J. L195/35, last amend. by Dir. 93/84 [1993] O.J. L254/16, and Case 118/85 *Commission v. Italy* [1987] E.C.R. 2599 at 2621(8).

47 See Joined Cases C–359 and 379/95P *Commission and France v. Ladbroke* [1997] E.C.R. I–6265; [1998] 4 C.M.L.R. 27. See also Commission Dec. 97/606 [1997] O.J. L244/18 breach of Arts 86 (ex 90) and 43 (ex 52) E.C.

48 Case 10/71 *Ministère Public Luxembourgeois v. Müller* [1971] E.C.R. 723.

49 Case C–343/95 *Cali & Figli v SEPG* [1997] E.C.R. I–1547.

challenged by the Commission.[50] Indeed, the Treaty[51] provides that the Member States shall neither enact, nor maintain in force any measure contrary to the rules of the Treaty, in particular to the rules on competition. This means that the State is under obligation to ensure that the undertakings it controls abide by the Treaty rules.

According to the Court of Justice, the Commission is empowered to determine that a given State measure is incompatible with the rules of the Treaty. Such powers are also essential to allow the Commission to discharge the duty imposed upon it to ensure the application of the rules on competition and to contribute to the institution of a system of undistorted competition in the common market. It would be impossible for the Commission to discharge its duty completely if it could impose penalties only in respect of anti-competitive conduct of undertakings and could not take action directly against Member States enacting or maintaining in force measures having the same anti-competitive effect.[52]

An exception is, however, provided for undertakings entrusted with the operation of "services of general economic interest". This exception only applies "in so far as the application of those rules does not obstruct the performance, in law or in fact, of the particular tasks assigned to them".[53]

The CFI reiterated that since this condition permits, in certain circumstances, derogation from the rules of the Treaty, it must be strictly interpreted. It is therefore not sufficient that the application of the Treaty provision in question simply would hinder or make the performance of the public service more difficult. Obstruction must be proved. The CFI added that the application of the exception is not left to the discretion of the Member States.[54]

In order to ensure the application of the Treaty provisions concerning public undertakings, the Commission shall, where necessary, address appropriate directives[55] and decisions[56] to Member States. This provision clearly shows that the Member State is

---

[50] *ibid*. This challenge would be based on Arts 3(g), 81 (ex 85) and 86(3) (ex 90(3)) E.C.

[51] Art. 86(1) (ex 90(1)) E.C.

[52] Joined Cases C–48/90 and C–66/90 *The Netherlands and Others v. Commission* [1992] E.C.R. I–565.

[53] *ibid*., at 2. See Communication on services of general interest: COM(96)443 final and Case C–38/97 *Autotrasporti* [1998] E.C.R. I–5955.

[54] Case T–260/94 *Air Inter* [1997] E.C.R. II–997; [1997] 5 C.M.L.R. 851.

[55] See Dir. 80/723 on the transparency of financial relations between Member States and public undertakings [1980] O.J. L195/35.

[56] See Dec. with regard to the landing fees at Zaventem [1995] O.J. L218/8.

indeed responsible for the market behaviour of the public undertaking.

Individuals may challenge decisions taken by the Commission in this context.[57] However, according to the Court, the Commission enjoys a broad discretion in the application of this Treaty provision. And since this discretion involves complex economic and social appraisals, the Court must confine itself to verifying whether the Commission complied with the rules governing procedure and the statement of reasons, whether the facts on which the contested decision was based, have been accurately stated and whether there has been any manifest error of assessment or misuse of power. But the Court cannot substitute its own economic assessment to that of the Commission.[58]

Owing to the very important role played by the public undertakings in the economy as producers of goods and services it is to be expected that the provisions of Article 86 (ex 90) will continue to be applied with increasing vigour.[59]

3. Aids Granted by States[60]—Articles 87 (ex 92) to 89 (ex 94) E.C.

(a) The Notion of Aid

Any aid granted by a Member State or through State resources in any form whatsoever which distorts competition by favouring certain undertakings or the production of certain goods is, in so far as it affects trade between Member States, incompatible with the common market.

In other words, for a measure to be regarded as aid that is subject to the principle of incompatibility with the common market, it must satisfy four conditions, which are cumulative. The measure must:

---

[57] Case C–107/95P *Bundesverband der Bilanzbuchhalter* [1997] E.C.R. I–947; [1997] 3 C.M.L.R. 1189; [1997] 5 C.M.L.R. 432. See also Joined Cases C–48 and 66/90 *The Netherlands v. Commission* [1992] E.C.R. I–565 on the rights of the defence.

[58] Joined Cases T–371 and 394/94 *British Airways and British Midlands v. Commission* [1998] E.C.R. 2405

[59] See Commission Communication to the Member States—Application of Art. 87 (ex 92) and 88 (ex 93) E.C. and of Art. 5 of Dir. 80/723 to public enterprises in the manufacturing sector [1993] O.J. C273/2. It is particularly interesting to note that this Communication, which in theory is a non-binding act, was challenged in Court by the French government; the Commission was obliged to modify it: Case C–325/91 *France v. Commission* [1993] E.C.R. I–3393.

[60] Parts of the section are based upon the Competition Report 1996, 71 *et seq*.

1. "*advantage an undertaking*". According to the Court[61] and the Commission, a measure constitutes an aid when it confers upon an undertaking an economic or financial advantage, which it would not have enjoyed in the normal course of events and which reduces the charges it would otherwise have born.[62] On the other hand, compensation for the extra costs connected with public service obligations does not constitute a state aid.[63] Similarly, the public financing of infrastructure at certain industrial sites does not involve state aid on condition that the infrastructure is open to all the firms in those areas without discrimination.[64] In this context see also the Commission Communication on State aid elements in sales of land and buildings by public authorities.[65] When the sale is the result of an open and sufficiently advertised auction, the Commission will assume that no aid was involved.

As regards *privatisations*, the Commission continues to apply the principle that there is no aid when the shares are sold to the highest bidder following an open and unconditional bidding procedure.

2. "*granted by a Member State or through State resources*". The latter must be taken in the broadest possible sense.[66] As the Commission has indicated, cross-subsidisation, for instance, between a public company operating in a non-competitive market and one of its subsidiaries operating in a market where there is free competition may constitute aid granted through state resources.[67] As for State participation in undertakings, the Commission applies the market investor principle. It allows the Commission to determine whether the transfer of public funds to public or private undertakings partially owned by the State constitutes an aid. This is the case if a private investor operating under normal market conditions would provide the funds on less favourable funds or would not provide them at all.[68]

---

[61] See, *e.g.* Case C–61/79 *Amministrazione delle Finanze dello Stato v. Denkavit Italiana* [1994] E.C.R. 709; [1981] 3 C.M.L.R. 694.

[62] See, *e.g.* Case C–387/92 *Banco Exterior de España* [1984] E.C.R. I–877 (12, 13); [1994] 3 C.M.L.R. 473.

[63] Commission Dec. *Financing of Portuguese radio and television* which is the object of an action before the CFI: T–46/97P [1997] O.J. C142/21.

[64] Report on Competition 1996, 72.

[65] [1997] O.J. C209/3.

[66] See, *e.g.* Cases 305/89 *Italy v. Commission* [1991] E.C.R. I–1603 and 234/84 *Belgium v. Commission* [1986] E.C.R. 2263; [1988] 2 C.M.L.R. 331.

[67] See Commission Decision in the *Société Française de Messageries/Chronopost and Securitpost*, I.P.(96) 126. See also Case C–39/94 *SFEI v. la Poste* [1996] E.C.R. I–3547; [1996] 3 C.M.L.R. 369.

[68] Competition report 1997, 78.

3. "*favour certain undertakings or the production of certain goods*". This is not the case with general economic, fiscal or social measures which grant an advantage to firms in the State implementing them. The distinction between those measures and State aids is difficult to establish, according to the Commission. It seems, however, that from the moment a measure only benefits certain undertakings in a given economic sector, as opposed to a measure applying indiscriminately to all undertakings, there can be little doubt about it constituting an aid.

As for distortions resulting, in the internal market, from advantages granted by general measures to the undertakings of one Member State as compared to the undertakings of other Member States, they can only be eliminated through approximation of legislation.[69]

According to the Court, for a measure to be described as "general", it is necessary, in particular, that the State should have no discretionary power enabling it to vary the application of the measure according to such considerations as the choice of recipient, the amount, or the conditions of the intervention.[70]

See also the Commission Notice on Monitoring of State Aid and Reduction of Labour Costs,[71] where the Commission clarified the distinction between general measures and aids.

4. "*distort competition and affect trade between Member States*". It seems difficult to imagine measures favouring certain undertakings of one Member State, trading across inter-State borders, which would not distort competition and trade between Member States.[72]

---

[69] See below Approximation of Laws and Arts 94 (ex 100), 95 (ex 100a) and 96 (ex 101) E.C.

[70] Case C–241/94 *France v. Commission* [1996] E.C.R. I–4551; [1997] 1 C.M.L.R. 983.

[71] [1997] O.J. C1/5. See the "Mirabel" Decision where the Commission declared incompatible the Belgian increased reduction in social security contributions in respect of manual workers granted to employers in one of the sectors most exposed to international competition [1997] O.J. L95/25.

[72] In Case 730/79 *Philip Morris v. Commission* [1980] E.C.R. 2671; [1981] 2 C.M.L.R. 321, the Court rejected the applicant's argument that in order to show that an aid falls within the terms of Art. 87(1) (ex 92(1)) E.C., the Commission must apply the tests, which determine the existence of restriction of competition under Arts 81 (ex 85) and 82 (ex 86) E.C. (relevant markets, market structure, etc.). The Court held that simpler grounds (a more favourable treatment of certain undertakings affects inter-State trade) are adequate. See, however, Case 323/82 *Intermills v. Commission* [1984] E.C.R. 3809; [1986] 1 C.M.L.R. 614: the granting of aid cannot be regarded as automatically contrary to the Treaty.

However, incompatibility of aid with the common market is "neither absolute, nor unconditional".[73]

Aids which fulfil the four above mentioned criteria are incompatible with the common market, unless they belong to the small category of compatible aids or are declared compatible by the Commission.

Mention must be made here of the *de minimis* rule for State aids, which sets a threshold figure below which the incompatibility can be said not to apply, so that a measure needs no longer to be notified in advance to the Commission.[74]

(b) Aids Compatible or Declared Compatible with the Common Market

Indeed, State aids can also constitute an instrument of structural development policy when certain legitimate objectives of economic growth cannot be attained solely by the interplay of market forces, or not within an acceptable time limit, or not without unacceptable social frictions. The Treaty, therefore, having stated the principle of their incompatibility with the common market, provides for certain categories of aid, which either are, or may be considered by the Commission[75]—or in *exceptional* cases by the Council[76]—as being compatible with the common market.

Compatible aids are those having a social character, granted to individual consumers, provided it is granted without discrimination related to the origin of the products concerned; aids to make good the damage caused by natural disasters or exceptional occurrences and aids granted to certain areas of Germany required to compensate for the economic disadvantages caused by the *previous* division of that country.

Aids which can be "declared" compatible with the common

---

[73] Case 74/76 *Iannelli v. Meroni* [1977] E.C.R. 557(11); [1977] 2 C.M.L.R. 688.

[74] [1996] O.J. C68/6; the ceiling is euro 100,000 over a three year period comprising all aid granted from whatever source, including the Community.

[75] This category of aids can be extended by the Council pursuant Art. 87(3)(e) (ex 92(3)(e)) E.C. See, *e.g.* Aid to shipbuilding: Reg. 3094 [1995] O.J. L332/1, amended by Reg. 1904/96 [1996] O.J. L251/5; pending the entry into force of the Agreement respecting normal competitive conditions in the commercial shipbuilding and repair industry, Reg. 90/684 continues to apply [1994] O.J. C375/3 amended by Reg. 2600/97 [1997] O.J. L351/18.

[76] Art. 88(2) (ex 93(2)) E.C. On application by a Member State, the Council may, acting unanimously, decide that an aid which that State is granting or intends to grant shall be considered to be compatible. This application suspends the Commission procedure.

market by the Commission pursuant to a procedure which will be examined hereafter. The Treaty provides for five categories of such aids: aids to promote the economic development of less-developed regions, aids for important projects of common European interest, aids to certain economic sectors or areas, aids to promote culture and heritage conservation and other categories of aids specified by the Council.[77] The following aids will be examined hereunder: regional, sectoral and others.

(1) Regional Development Aids

The Treaty provides for two kinds of regional development aids, which may be considered by the Commission to be compatible with the common market.[78] They are, firstly, the aids to promote the economic development of areas where the standard of living is abnormally low or where there is serious underemployment. Secondly, the aids to promote the development of certain economic areas, where such aid does not adversely affect trading conditions to an extend contrary to the common interest. The first concerns areas in general, while the second ones concern "economic" areas, which are areas economically developed, but subject to acute and temporary difficulties.

As the Commission indicates in its 1998 Guidelines,[79] regional aid is designed to develop the less-favoured regions by supporting investment and job creation in a sustainable context. It promotes the expansion, modernisation and diversification of the activities of establishments located in those regions and encourages new firms to settle there. The granting of such aid must be conditional on the maintenance of the investment and the jobs created during a minimum period. In exceptional cases those aids might have to be supplemented by operating aids.

The consequent distortions of competition must be accepted if the equilibrium between those distortions and the advantages of the aid in terms of development of the less-favoured regions can be guaranteed. Another requirement is that the aid adheres to certain principles and obeys certain rules.[80] Furthermore, it must be neutral towards the allocation of resources between the various economic

---

[77] Art. 87(3) (ex 92(3)) E.C.

[78] Art. 87(3)(a) and (c) (ex 92(3)(a) and (c)) E.C.

[79] [1998] O.J. C74/9. See also the new multisectoral framework on regional aid to large investment projects [1997] O.J. C107/7.

[80] See the Communication from the Commission to the Member States on the links between regional and competition policy [1998] O.J. C90/3.

sectors and activities. The Commission also considers that the total extent of the assisted regions must remain smaller than that of the non-assisted regions, *i.e.* less than 50 per cent of the Community population.

For the Commission, the conditions of abnormally low standard of living or serious underemployment[81] are fulfilled when a level II geographical unit[82] has a per capita GDP, measured in purchasing power standards, of less than 75 per cent of the Community average, based on the average of the last three years. As for the second exception, it allows greater latitude, and it gives the Commission power to authorise aid for the development of areas which are disadvantaged in relation to national rather than Community average.

The object of regional aid is to secure either productive investment or job creation which is linked to investment. To ensure that the investment is viable and sound, the recipient's contribution must be at least 25 per cent. The form of aid is variable: grant, low-interest loan or interest rebate, government guarantee, tax exemption, reduction of social security contributions, supply of goods and services at concessionary prices, etc. Eligible expenditure can also include transfer of technology through the acquisition of patents or know-how.

Operating aid, *i.e.* aid aimed at reducing the firm's current expenses, is normally prohibited, but there are exceptions for the outermost regions.

More details on the grant of aids will be found in the chapter on Economic and Social Cohesion.

(2) Sectoral Aids[83]

Specific rules were drawn up by the Community institutions for the following sectors.

(a) Shipbuilding

In 1998, the Council established new rules on aid to shipbuilding.[84]

---

[81] For a definition of those concepts see Case 248/84 *Germany v. Commission* [1987] E.C.R. 4013(19); [1989] 1 C.M.L.R. 591.
[82] Nomenclature of Statistical Territorial Units.
[83] Art. 87(3)(c) (ex 92(3)(c)) E.C.: "development of certain economic activities".
[84] [1998] O.J. L202/1.

(b) Steel

In 1996, the Commission adopted the sixth and last steel aid code[85] which covers the period until the ECSC Treaty expires in July 2002. It contains rules on state aids for R&D and on aid for environmental protection. The Commission also allows aids for partial closures and aligns the procedural rules of the steel aid code on new developments in the E.C.

(c) Coal

Community rules on aid to the coal industry for the period 1994 to 2002 were established by the Commission in 1993.[86] On that basis the Commission authorised various Member States: Germany, the United Kingdom, France, Spain and Portugal to grant financial assistance to cover, *inter alia* operating losses, inherited liabilities resulting from modernisation, rationalisation and restructuring, exceptional welfare aid paid to workers who lose their jobs as a result of restructuring, the technical costs of closing down mining installations, R&D projects and the protection of the environment.

From August 2002 on such aids will be examined by the Commission on the basis of the aid rules of the E.C. Treaty.

(d) Motor Vehicle Industry

In 1997, the Commission published a new "Community framework for State aid to the motor vehicle industry".[87] It contains a most interesting footnote on aids granted by Member States: in the period 1977 to 1987, State aid to the motor vehicle industry, essentially in the form of capital injections or extensive debt write-offs, is estimated at 26 billion ECUs. Between 1989, when the framework entered into force, and July 1996, the Commission approved 5.4 billion ECUs of aid. The framework is presented as an "appropriate measure" under Article 88(1) (ex 93(1)) of the Treaty and proposes to the Member States that, pursuant to Article 88(3) (ex 93(3)), they give prior notification of the most significant aid cases, *i.e.* when it concerns an aid under authorised aid schemes, that either of the following thresholds is reached: total cost of the project: euro 50

---

[85] Dec. 3855/91 ECSC establishing Community rules for aid to the steel industry [1991] O.J. L362/57.

[86] Dec. 3932/93 ECSC establishing rules for State aid to the coal industry [1993] O.J. L329/12, implemented by Dec. 94/341 [1994] L49/1.

[87] [1997] O.J. C279/1.

million, or total gross aid for the project: euro 5 million. On the other hand, any "*ad hoc*" aid must be notified. The framework also establishes guidelines for the assessment of aid, based on a cost-benefit analysis.[88]

The motor vehicle sector continues to be affected by structural over-capacity in Europe; the task of the Commission here is to prevent surplus production capacity from further distorting competition. Most aids to the motor vehicle industry are granted in the form of regional aids. In practice, a "top-up" of 3 per cent of the eligible regional investment is authorised where the recipient of the aid does not create extra capacity in a saturated market segment.[89]

(e) Synthetic fibres industry

Since 1977, the conditions under which aid may be awarded to this industry have been laid down in a Code whose terms and scope have been revised periodically. The current code came into force on January 1, 1996 and is valid until August 31, 2001.[90] It requires notification of all plans to grant aid for extrusion/texturisation, polymerisation and any linked ancillary process.

(f) Textiles and clothing

It is interesting to read what the Commission has to say about aids in this sector: "the industry was previously covered by guidelines adopted in 1971 and modified in 1977. The Commission considers, following a 1995 Court's judgment,[91] that the guidelines are no longer legally valid as the obligation of the Commission, to examine, in co-operation with Member States, existing schemes has not been complied with in the present case in textile and clothing industry."[92]

(g) Transport

The number of aid cases to transport have increased with the constant opening-up of the transport market and the resulting

---

[88] It should be noted that such a framework is addressed to the Member States and must be approved by all of them. See Case C–135/93 *Spain v. Commission* [1995] E.C.R. I–1651.

[89] In the case of *MCC–Swatch* a top-up was allowed because the special characteristics of the new Smart car will create a new production segment on the vehicle market. See Competition Report 1996.

[90] [1996] O.J. C94/7.

[91] Case C–135/93 *Spain v. Commission* [1995] E.C.R. I–1673.

[92] Competition Report 1997, 87.

increase in competition, together with the progress of the single market for transport. As the Commission points out, "under those circumstances the control of State aid is of particular importance to ensure that fair conditions of competition are maintained between public and private enterprises".[93]

Thus, the Commission published a Communication setting out guidelines for the application of State aid provisions to aid granted in the civil aviation field[94] and pays particular attention to the aids granted by the Member States to their *national airlines*. This was the case for Iberia, Olympic Airways, Air France and TAP.[95] However, the Commission decisions in this field are not always appreciated by the competitors and it was at the request of several European Airlines that the Court annulled the Decision authorising, once again, the re-capitalisation of Air France.[96]

With regard to the *maritime transport* sector, the Commission admitted in its Communication "Towards a New Maritime Strategy" that support measures may be required to maintain and to develop the Community's shipping industries. In 1997, the Commission adopted new Community guidelines for State aid in the maritime transport sector.[97]

In the *ports* sector, the Commission acts, often on the basis of complaints about public assistance, to check on the possible grant of aids.[98] The same applies to *road* transport. As for *Rail* transport the Commission is endeavouring to have the Member States implement the basic directives on the development of the Community's railways, on the licensing of railway undertakings and on the allocation of railway infrastructure capacity and the charging of infrastructure fees.[99] The aim is to arrive at a system where the only public financing of railways will be for infrastructure or compensation for public service obligations.

Finally, in the area of *inland waterways*, the Community will part finance the structural reorganisation aimed at reducing overcapacity. Measures were also provided on structural improvements

---

[93] Competition Report 1996, 80.

[94] [1997] O.J. C350/5.

[95] Competition Report. 1996, 80.

[96] Joined Cases T–371 and 394/94 *British Airways and British Midland v. Commission* [1998] E.C.R. II–2405.

[97] See also Community Guidelines on State aid to maritime transport [1997] O.J. C205/5.

[98] Competition Report 1996.

[99] Dir. 91/440 [1991] O.J. L237/25; Dir. 95/18 [1995] O.J. L143/770 and 95/19 [1995] O.J. L143/75. See also draft Directives on the so-called "Infrastructure Package".

in inland waterway transport[1] and on the systems of chartering and pricing in national and international inland waterway transport in the Community.[2]

(h) Agriculture and Fisheries

In July 1997, the Commission adopted a new version of the Community Guidelines for rescue and restructuring aid to agricultural undertakings; they involve a substantive change in policy. The former specific criteria have been replaced by criteria similar to those contained in the guidelines applicable to all sectors, *i.e.* a quid pro quo for the aid is needed in the surplus sectors in the form of an irreversible reduction or closure of capacity; derogations are provided to take into account the particular features of agriculture. The Commission also published guidelines for State aid in connection with investments in the processing and marketing of agricultural products,[3] and a communication sets out the Commission's philosophy of its policy in this field.[4]

The guidelines for the examination of State aid to fisheries and aquaculture were based to a large extend on a Council regulation laying down the criteria and arrangements regarding Community structural assistance in those sectors.

(i) Financial Sector

No specific rules govern the granting of aid in this particularly sensitive sector, but mention must be made here of the massive aids accepted by the Commission for the restructuring of the *Credit Lyonnais*.[5]

(j) Multisectoral framework on regional aid for large investment projects[6]

The aim of this framework is to limit aid for large-scale projects, of whatever sector of industry, to a level which avoids as much as

---

[1] Reg. 1101/89 [1989] O.J. L116/25, amended by Reg. 2254/96 [1996] O.J. L304/1 and implemented by Reg. 1189 [1989] OJ. L116/30.
[2] Dir. 96/75 [1996] O.J. L304/12.
[3] [1995] O.J. C29/4.
[4] [1994] O.J. C189.
[5] Competition Report 1996, 84(211). See Dec. 95/547, conditional approval on State aid granted by France to the bank Crédit Lyonnais [1995] O.J. L308/92.
[6] [1998] O.J. C107/7.

possible adverse effects on competition between regions, but which at the same time maintains the attraction of the assisted areas. The framework provides for the prior notification of all projects with a total cost of at least euro 50 million and an aid intensity of at least 50 per cent of the regional aid ceiling, or where the total aid is at least euro 50 million.

(3) Horizontal Aids

The Council adopted a regulation[7] on the application of the Community rules to certain categories of horizontal State aids; this Regulation allows the Commission to adopt regulations exempting certain categories of aid from the obligation to notify. No implementation regulations have been issued yet.

The Commission, on the other hand, published a number of "guidelines", setting out the way in which it applies the Treaty provisions on aid in various sectors.

(a) R&D

A *new* Framework for State Aid for Research and Development was published in 1996[8]; it allows the Member States to give financial support under well defined conditions.

(b) Employment and Training

In this field also the Commission published Guidelines[9] and a Framework on training aid.[10] Regarding aid to employment, the Commission makes a distinction between aid to create jobs and aid to maintain existing jobs. Clearly, the preference of the Commission goes to the former. Those aids do not have to be notified. However, the Commission let it be known that it had an *a priori* negative position with regard to employment aid targeted at certain sectors in a Notice on the monitoring of State aid and reduction of labour costs.[11]

As for aid for training, a distinction is made between specific and general training; in the Commission's opinion, the latter effectively improves the worker's employability and adaptability and thus

---

[7] Reg. 994/98 [1998] O.J. L142/1; this Regulation is based on Art. 89 (ex 94) E.C.
[8] [1996] O.J. C45/5.
[9] [1995] O.J. C334/4.
[10] [1998] O.J. C343/10.
[11] [1997] O.J. C1/10.

makes a larger contribution in the field of employment and human resource development. The framework also establishes a list of reimbursable costs and the authorised intensity of aid for training.

(c) Environment

A Community framework for State aid for environmental protection was published in 1994.[12] Aid to SMEs may be increased by as much as 10 percentage points above the rate ordinarily allowed for large enterprises.

(d) Small and Medium-Sized Enterprises

The first Guidelines were published in 1992[13] and revised in 1996.[14] The definition of an SME is interesting[15]: an enterprise with fewer than 250 employees and an annual turnover not exceeding euro 40 million or an annual balance-sheet total not exceeding euro 27 million. "Employees" means the number of actual work units (AWUs), that is to say the number of wage- and salary-earners employed full-time for a whole year, with part-time or seasonal work being counted as fractions of a unit. The turnover is *grosso modo* the amount derived from the sale of products and the provision of services, after deduction of rebates and taxes.[16]

The Commission also considers acceptable aid for the transfer of SMEs.[17]

(e) Rescue and Restructuring

Guidelines on State Aids for Rescuing and Restructuring Firms in Difficulties were published in 1997[18] with the addition of specific rules for agriculture and fisheries.[19]

---

[12] [1994] O.J. C72/3.
[13] [1992] O.J. C213/2.
[14] [1996] O.J. C213/4.
[15] When it is necessary to distinguish between small- and medium-sized undertakings, a small one is an undertaking of fewer than 50 employees, a turnover not exceeding seven million euros and conforms to the criterion of independence defined by the Commission in its guidelines.
[16] See Fourth Company Law Directive ([1978] O.J. L22/11 as amended by Dir. 94/8 ([1994] O.J. L82/33).
[17] Recommendation on the transfer of SMEs [1994] O.J. L385/14 and Commission Communication [1994] O.J. C400/1.
[18] [1997] O.J. C283/2.
[19] [1994] O.J. C368/5.

(f) Aid to Firms in Under-privileged Urban Areas

The Commission takes a favourable view of certain aid measures aimed at encouraging investment and job creation through the development of small businesses in rundown neighbourhoods.[20]

(g) General Aid Schemes

These general measures do not fall within one of the categories provided for in the Treaty as being suitable to be declared compatible with the common market. Consequently, the Commission is unable to take a definitive position on such aid schemes. It therefore requires the Member States, when implementing those schemes, to notify in advance the regional or sectoral programmes envisaged, or the significant cases of aid to be granted under those schemes. However, according to the Court, such aids constitute "existing aids", which must not be notified unless otherwise provided by the Commission Decision accepting the aid scheme. Such individual aids are covered by the Commission approved general scheme, and the Commission has no further power to adopt a decision on individual aid. But, such aids may be challenged in national courts.[21] On the other hand, when the Commission authorises a general aid scheme on condition that individual significant cases be notified with a view to an assessment of their impact on intra-Community trade and commerce, it cannot constitute blanket approval of all aid granted pursuant to that scheme, since the obligation to notify significant cases must be interpreted as a reservation on the approval contained in the decision itself.[22]

(4) Procedural Rules

In order to allow the Commission to supervise the implementation of the competition rules in the aid sector and to declare certain aids compatible with the common market, Member States must notify the Commission of any plans to grant or alter aid.[23] Until the

---

[20] SEC(96) 1706/2.

[21] Case C–278/96 *Comité des Salines* [1996] E.C.R. 2410. See also Case C–278/95P *Siemens* on the qualification of aids [1997] E.C.R. I–2507.

[22] Joined Cases T–447 etc./93, *AITEC and Others v. Commission* [1995] E.C.R. II–1971.

[23] Art. 88(3) (ex 93(3)) E.C. During the year 1997, the Commission received 714 notifications of new schemes or amendments to existing ones; it registered 135 cases of non-notified aid schemes. In 568 cases it decided not to raise objections, in 100 it

Commission has decided on the compatibility, the Member State may not put the measure into effect. However, failure to notify is not in itself enough to enable aid to be declared incompatible with the common market.[24] But, if an interested third party files a complaint with the Commission concerning a non-notified aid, the institution is obliged to examine such complaint, and even examines elements which have not been raised by the complainant.[25] Indeed, the Commission has the exclusive competence to find that an aid is illegal. The Commission is therefore obliged to take one of the following decisions[26]; either that the measure does not constitute an aid, or that it constitutes an aid, but is compatible, or, to open the procedure as provided in the Treaty.

However, Member States must notify the Commission "in sufficient time to enable it to submit its comments"[27]; the latter then has two months to take a decision.[28]

The Commission is under obligation to keep, in co-operation with Member States, under constant review all systems of aid existing in those States.[29]

(5) Recovery of Aid

When State aids have been granted illegally, the Commission can require the national authorities in question to recover the aid.[30] The same applies to Community aids. The Commission can even seek the payment of interests on the sums recovered.[31] In the event the beneficiary or the public authority which granted the aid obtains an interim order from the Court to suspend the repayment, a suspension will be conditional upon the provision of a bank guarantee; the judge

decided to initiate examination proceedings, and, as a result, it took 33 positive final decisions, 40 negative ones and 11 conditional ones: Gen. Rep. 1998, 81. See Reg. 659/99 laying down detailed rules for the application of Art. 93 (now 88) E.C.: [1999] O.J. L83/1.

[24] Case T–49/93 *SIDE* [1995] E.C.R. II–2501, where the CFI based itself on the case law of the Court of Justice; Case C–301/87 *France v. Commission* [1990] E.C.R. I–307 and Case C–354/90 *FNCE (Salmon Processor)* [1991] E.C.R. I–5505(84).

[25] Case C–367/95P *Commission v. Sytraval and Brink's France* [1998] E.C.R. I–1719.

[26] Case T–95/96 *Gestevision v. Commission*, unreported.

[27] Art. 88(3) (ex 93(3)) E.C.

[28] This time limit was set by the Court in Case 122/73 *Nordsee v. Germany* [1973] E.C.R. 1511 at 1522(4).

[29] Art. 88 (ex 93) E.C.

[30] See Commission Communication on aids granted illegally [1983] O.J. C318.

[31] Case T–459/93 *Siemens* [1995] E.C.R. II–1675.

is entitled to take into account the overall financial resources of the applicant and the Community interest in securing effectiveness of the judgment to be given.[32] The Commission may also authorise an aid which a Member State is planning to give to an undertaking, but prohibit payment thereof until the undertaking has repaid previously received aid which has been found to be unlawful by a decision of the Commission which has become final.[33]

In case of unforeseen and unforeseeable difficulties encountered by the Member State in the recuperation of the aid, the Commission and the Member State must work together in good faith with a view to overcoming the difficulties whilst fully observing the Treaty provisions and especially those on aid.[34]

However, non-recovery is acceptable in certain circumstances and under condition that the beneficiary's good faith is established and the same applies to the recovery of purely national payments.[35] In any case, there is little, it seems, the beneficiary of the illegal aid can do to prevent repayment of the aid. In the first place, the Court has decided that, under certain circumstances, a prudent operator should make sure, before accepting an aid, that it is being granted legally.[36] Therefore, "negligence" on the part of the beneficiary might be held against him. In the second place, the only possibility for the recipient who has paid back the aid, might be an action against the Member State which granted the aid, for damage caused by a breach of Community law by said Member State. Besides this problem, the beneficiary who is asked to pay back the aid, must demonstrate, as was also indicated in relation with the responsibility of Member States for breach of Community law, that three conditions are fulfilled. In the first place the Community rule breached must provide a right for the plaintiff; in the second place, the Member States must be guilty of an infringement and, finally, the damage sustained must have been caused by the said breach.

Further Reading

Marco L. Slotboom, "State Aid in Community Law: A Broad or Narrow definition?" (1995) 20 E.L.Rev. 289.

[32] Case 12/95P(R) *Transacctiones Maritimas* [1995] E.C.R. I–468; [1996] 2 C.M.L.R. 580.

[33] Joined Cases T–244 and 486/93, *TWD v. Commission* [1995] E.C.R. II–2265; [1996] 1 C.M.L.R. 332.

[34] Case C–349/93 *Commission v. Italy* [1995] E.C.R. I–343.

[35] Case C–298/96 *Ölmühle Hamburg* [1998] E.C.R. I–4767.

[36] Case C–39/94 *SFEI and Others* [1996] E.C.R. I–3549; [1996] 3 C.M.L.R. 369.

A. van Mourik, *Developments in the European competition policy* European Institute of Public Administration (Maastricht 1996).

Paul Torremans, "Extraterritorial Application of E.C. and U.S. Competition Law" (1996) 21 E.L.Rev. 280.

Robert Waltz, "Rethinking *Walt Wilhelm*, or the Supremacy of Community Competition Law over National Law" (1996) 21 E.L.Rev. 449.

Bellamy and Child, *Common Market Law of Competition*, (4th ed., 1st supp. Sweet & Maxwell, London, 1996).

C. J. Cool, C. S. Kerse, *E.C. Merger Control*, Sweet & Maxwell, London, 1996.

Valentine Korah, *Cases and Materials on E.C. Competition Law* (Sweet & Maxwell, London, 1996).

Rein Wesseling, "Subsidiarity in Community Antitrust Law: Setting the Right Agenda", (1997) 22 E.L.Rev. 35.

Wouter P. J. Wils, "The Commission Notice on the Non-Imposition or Reduction of Fines in Cartel Cases, a Legal and Economic Analysis" (1997) 22 E.L.Rev. 125.

Editorial, "Competition, the Commission and Some Constitutional Questions of More than Minor Importance" (1998) 23 E.L.Rev. 1.

James Kirkbride and Tao Xiong, "The European Control of Joint Ventures: A Historic Opportunity or a Mere Continuation of Existing Practice?" (1998) 23 E.L.Rev. 37.

Wouter P. J. Wils, "The Commission's New Method for Calculating Fines in Antitrust Cases" (1998) 23 E.L.Rev. 252.

Guisseppe B. Abbamonte, "Cross-subsidisation and Community Competition Rules: Efficient Pricing Versus Equity?" (1998) 23 E.L.Rev. 414.

Andrew Evans, "Law, Policy and Equality in the European Union: the Example of State Aid Control" (1998) 23 E.L.Rev. 434.

M. Cini and L. McGowan, *Competition Policy in the European Union*, (St Martin's Press, New York, 1998).

Lennart Ritter, W. David Braun, F. Rawlinson, *E.C. Competition Law, A Practitioner's Guide* (2nd ed., Kluwer, 1999).

Chapter Nineteen
Agriculture

The Treaty provides[1] that "common market shall extend to agriculture[2] and trade in agricultural products",[3] and that "[s]ave as otherwise provided in Articles 33 to 38, the rules laid down for the establishment of the common market shall apply to agricultural products". Nevertheless, the Treaty also provides that the "operation and development of the common market for agricultural products must be accompanied by the establishment of a common agricultural policy among the Member States".[4] In other words, an unqualified application of the rules concerning the free movement of goods to agricultural products was, from the start, deemed impossible. Special complementary rules, known as "agricultural policy", were needed. The more so, since agriculture represents, because of its particular nature,[5] difficult problems in all the Member States. Elaborate and costly national measures to aid agriculture existed practically everywhere. Consequently, the inclusion of agriculture in the common market was agreed upon, but on special terms, *i.e.* "the establishment of a common agricultural policy among the Member States"[6] and the "need to effect the appropriate adjustments by

[1] Art. 32(1) (ex 38(1)) E.C.

[2] One could, in theory, have established a common market without agricultural products, but agriculture constitutes in all the Member States a sector closely linked with the economy as a whole; see Art. 33(2)(c) (ex 39(2)(c)) E.C. The food industry, which processes more than three-quarters of the agricultural products of the Community, also constitutes its most important industrial sector.

[3] Agricultural products are defined in Art. 32(1) (ex 38(1)) E.C.: "products of the soil, of stockfarming and of fisheries and products of first-stage processing directly related to those products". They are listed in Annex II to the Treaty. In pursuance of Art. 32(3) (ex 38(3)) E.C. a number of products were added to this list in 1960. See Reg. 7a: [1961] J.O. 71/61 and [1959–62] O.J. Spec. Ed. 68.

[4] Art. 32(4) (ex 38(4)) E.C.

[5] Art. 33(2)(a) (ex 39(2)(a)) E.C. refers to the "particular nature of agricultural activity which results from the social structure of agriculture and from structural and natural disparities between the various agricultural regions".

[6] Art. 32(4) (ex 38(4)), E.C.

degree".[7] As mentioned, the common market rules shall apply to agricultural products unless otherwise provided. This means, *inter alia*, that the provisions relating to the common agricultural policy have precedence, in case of conflict, over the rules relating to the establishment of the common market, such as those on the free movement of goods.[8] On the other hand, it means that, in the absence of specific provisions, the general rules of the Treaty fully apply since the end of the transitional period.[9] As for the national measures existing at the time of the establishment of the common agricultural policy, they were replaced by a "common organisation of agricultural markets"[10] which took the form of various "European Market Organisation[s]".[11]

THE COMMON AGRICULTURAL POLICY (CAP)

It is important to mention all the objectives which the Treaty assigns to the CAP, since as the Court stated, taken separately, they appear to conflict with one another and it is up to the Community Institutions to allow, where necessary, temporary priority to one of them.[12]

"The objectives of the common agricultural policy shall be:

(a) to increase agricultural productivity by promoting technical progress and by ensuring the rational development of agricultural production and the optimum utilisation of the factors of production, in particular labour;
(b) thus to ensure a fair standard of living for the agricultural community, in particular by increasing the individual earnings of persons engaged in agriculture;
(c) to stabilise markets;
(d) to assure the availability of supplies;

---

[7] Arts 33(2)(b) (ex 39(2)(b)) E.C.
[8] Case 83/78 *Pigs Marketing Board v. Redmond* [1978] E.C.R. 2347; [1979] 1 C.M.L.R. 177.
[9] Case 48/74 *Charmasson v. Minister for Economic Affairs and Finance* [1974] E.C.R. 1383; [1975] 2 C.M.L.R. 208.
[10] Art. 34(1) (ex 40(1)), E.C.
[11] Art. 34(1)(c) (ex 40(2)(c)), E.C.
[12] Case 5/73 *Balkan-Import-Export v. Hauptzollamt Berlin-Packhof* [1973] E.C.R. 1091.

(e) to ensure that supplies reach consumers at reasonable prices."[13]

Looking back over the past 40 years it is easy to ascertain that only some of those objectives were actually attained. There is no doubt that agricultural productivity and production increased dramatically; it could be said: out of all proportion to the needs. However, one should not forget that the CAP was established by people who had lived through World War II and that the memories about the scarcity of food during that period and those who died of hunger were still very vivid. What was more natural than the strong desire "to assure the availability of supplies",[14] preferably home-grown to avoid dependency upon outside suppliers? When one adds to that the claim of the farmers organisations—which have long enjoyed and exercised an excessive influence on political decisions concerning agriculture—that the "increase of individual earnings of persons engaged in agriculture"[15] was guaranteed to them by the Treaty, one understands why it was impossible to "stabilise the markets"[16] and "to ensure that supplies reach consumers at reasonable prices".[17]

The basic principles which determined the future orientation of the CAP were adopted by the Council in 1960:

(a) free movement of agricultural products within the Community;
(b) a common price level for all agricultural products;
(c) fair earnings for those employed in agriculture, *i.e.* price support;
(d) a uniform system of levies imposed on all imported products and export restitutions;
(e) co-ordination of national measures for structural reform.

After several decades of operation, with outstanding positive results, the problems created by appalling overproduction in some sectors and the resulting unbearable costs to the Community made a revision of the CAP mandatory.[18] A first "reform" of the CAP took

---

[13] Art. 33(1) (ex 39(1)), E.C.
[14] Art. 33(1)(d) (ex 39(1)(d)), E.C.
[15] Art. 33(1)(b) (ex 39(1)(b)), E.C.
[16] Art. 33(1)(c) (ex 39(1)(c)), E.C.
[17] Art. 33(1)(e) (ex 39(1)(e)), E.C.
[18] See the Communiqué of the European Council of June 1983, [1983] E.C. Bull. 6 at 19.

place in 1984.[19] Although it was considered by the Commission as "a milestone in the development of the [agricultural] policy",[20] the Community faced a major crisis a few years later due to a combination of accumulated surplus stocks and acute budgetary difficulties. A turning point came at the meeting of the European Council in Brussels, in February 1988. The Council approved a Commission Communication entitled "The Single European Act: a new Frontier for Europe". At that meeting the Community endowed itself with the political and financial resources it needed to achieve the internal market.[21]

Notwithstanding all those efforts, the CAP continued to suffer from a fundamental deficiency: agricultural production was guided by price setting rather than by demand. Farmers continued to produce huge quantities of those products for which the Community offered the highest guaranteed prices, irrespective of the need for those products. And so, once again the Council approved, in May 1992, a number of measures "redirecting agriculture in the Community".[22]

1. The reforms of the CAP of 1992 and 1999

(1) The reform of the market organisations

It was the result of a re-examination prompted both by interior and exterior considerations. The GATT Uruguay Round[23] was definitely an incentive to try, once again, to find solutions to the

---

[19] [1983] E.C. Suppl. Bull. 4 at 19. The following adaptations were proposed: (1) co-responsibility principle, guarantee thresholds and delivery quotas for milk; (2) a prudent and, in certain cases, restrictive price policy, and for cereals a reduction of the gap between Community and World prices; (3) existing aids and premiums to be discontinued; (4) promotion of agricultural exports and (5) dismantlement of the monetary compensatory amounts. See General Report (1983), 172.

[20] General Report (1984), 164.

[21] General Report (1988), 26.

[22] General Report (1992), 169.

[23] Within those negotiations the Community was faced mainly with the American demands concerning the export supports which allowed the Community to conquer 22 per cent of the world cereal market, which the U.S. want to see reduced to 13 per cent. Then there were the so-called Cairn countries which, contrary to the U.S. do not subsidise their exports and the developing countries which claim to suffer from the Communities offensive and defensive policies. It is certain that the main reform measures: reduction of the guaranteed prices by 30 per cent, *idem* for the export restitutions and set-aside of 15 per cent of arable land, made a deal with all the interested parties possible.

above-mentioned internal problems.[24] Although not necessarily revolutionary, the 1992 reform certainly represents a re-orientation of the policy, even if it appears that the basic principles set out above were maintained, although price support was partly replaced by some sort of deficiency payments. It is interesting to note that Community expenditure trebled between 1972 and 1992 (33 billion ECUs which represents 60 per cent of the Community budget) and that 40 per cent of that goes to export restitutions, 25 per cent to stocking and 30 per cent to price and revenue support. To these Community budget expenditures have to be added the national support systems which seem to represent, according to conservative estimates, an amount at least equal to the one just mentioned. On the other hand, all this expenditure has not been able to maintain a decent income for all farmers. Faced with all these problems, the Maastricht and Amsterdam Treaties have nevertheless curiously left the Treaty provisions concerning Agriculture[25] unchanged. It was therefore up to the implementing legislation to try to remedy the shortcomings just mentioned. This was done as follows.

The basis remains the fundamental principles of the CAP (market unity which implies price unity,[26] Community preference which should not be affected by the reform, Community financial solidarity which means that the agricultural expenditure is paid by the Community budget and co-responsibility of the farmers for the management of the policy) and a guaranteed farmers support level comparable to that which had been ensured until then. The decisions that were taken in 1992 were futhermore based on the following four principles.

(a) a general reduction in guaranteed farm prices; reductions vary depending on the product, but result in improved competitiveness of Community products in relation to products sold on the world market[27];

---

[24] The main internal problems were mentioned above: surpluses, excessive costs and lower agricultural incomes; to this should be added a phenomenon which is not typical for the Community: rural exodus.

[25] Arts 39 to 47 E.C.

[26] Since the achievement of the internal market the compensatory amounts were no longer warranted and were finally abolished: Reg. 3813/92 on the unit of account and the conversion rate to be applied for the purpose on the agricultural policy: [1992] O.J. L387/1.

[27] Notwithstanding severe cuts in prices, they remain more or less uniform throughout the Community. The price system of the market organisations remains in place with its target price, which now will be more realistic when compared to the world price, the intervention price, which should be used much less extensively following their important reduction: for cereals 29 per cent in three years and thirdly, the threshold price for imports.

(b) compensation for the price reductions in the form of payments and premiums granted, not on the basis of production, but on the basis of production factors (hectare or head of livestock);

(c) measures to directly influence the quantities produced, applied in the form of quotas, set-aside of arable land or restrictions on the grant of premiums; these measures replace partly the co-responsibility measures introduced about 30 years ago;

(d) measures to encourage the restructuring of farms, *i.e.* early retirement, afforestation or reduction of yield by the use of more extensive or more environmently-friendly methods.[28]

The 1992 reform together with the reform of the Structural Funds[29] resulted in a certain shift from the previous dominance of market measures towards the provision of a greater role for rural development, the aim being to meet the challenge posed by the depopulation and abandonment of many rural areas.

On July 15, 1997, the Commission adopted a package of measures called "AGENDA 2000". This is, as was mentioned before, a key strategy document in which the Commission sets out its views on how the European Union should develop its common policies beyond the year 2000. It outlines the expected developments regarding enlargement of the E.U., amendments to the Structural and Cohesion funds, future reform of the common agricultural policy and the future of the E.U.'s finances. As far as agriculture is concerned, the Commission proposes deepening and extending the 1992 reform through further shifts from price support to direct payments, and developing a coherent rural policy to accompany this process. Once again, the Commission set out objectives for the CAP:

- increased competitiveness internally and externally in order to ensure that E.U. producers take full advantage of positive world market developments;
- food safety and food quality which are both a fundamental obligation towards consumers;
- ensuring a fair standard of living for the agricultural community and contributing to the stability of farm incomes;
- the integration of environmental goals into the CAP;
- the creation of alternative job and income opportunities for farmers and their families;
- simplification of E.U. legislation.

[28] General Report (1992), 169.
[29] See under Economic and Social Cohesion.

The document envisages new reforms for the *crop* sector: cereals, oil seeds and protein crops: (reduction of the intervention price, non crop specific area payments, set-aside, etc.), the *beef* regime (supply control measures to address the effects of the BSE crisis, decreasing the level of market support, etc.), the *dairy* regime (extension of the quota regime, gradual decrease of price support, etc.) and the so-called *Mediterranean products*: tobacco, olive oil and wine. Also proposed were differentiation and ceilings for direct payments, rural policy and integration of the environment into the Common Market Organisations. On the basis of the AGENDA 2000, the Commission made several proposals[30] in March 1998 including (1) amendments to the common market organisation in cereals and other arable crops, beef and veal, milk and olive oil, (2) a horizontal regulation laying down common rules for direct support schemes (linking support to compliance with environmental criteria, modulating aid relative to employment, and introducing a digressive formula for the highest aid payments), (3) changes in the EAGGF financing regulation, and (4) a new regulation on rural development aid.[31] The proposals provide for further reductions in market support prices and an increase in direct aid for farmers in order to make the E.U.'s agriculture more competitive in domestic and world markets, thereby reducing the risk of recurrence of expensive and unsaleable surpluses. Lower prices will benefit consumers and leave more room for price differentiation in favour of quality products, while a more market-orientated approach will prepare the way for integration of new Member States and strengthen the E.U.'s position in the coming WTO negotiating round. Most of those proposals were adopted by the Berlin European Council of March 24–25, 1999.[32]

At the time of writing, the decisions had not yet been translated into legal texts; consequently no references to Community Acts could be given. For the expenditure decided upon in Berlin see the financial perspective 2000–2006 in the Chapter on financing Community activities.

[30] General Report (1998) 1.

[31] Rural development is becoming more and more important within the agricultural policy of the Community, since the exodus from the farm takes on worrying proportions with all the consequences for the abandoned areas. The Berlin European Council of March 1999 decided to allocate an amount of euro 25 billion over the period up to 2006 for rural development as well as for veterinary and plant health measures. This aspect of the Community policy distinguishes it from policies of other countries, something the latter do not always understand and appreciate.

[32] See Presidency conclusions: DN: DOC/99/1.

(2) The Common Market Organisations

(i) Cereals. In pursuance of the Treaty, the common market organisations may include "regulation of prices", and "any price policy shall be based on common criteria and uniform methods of calculation".[33] This uniformity is guaranteed as follows: the prices are fixed for a certain standard product, for a certain product unit, for a given time period, for a well defined stage of trade, for the whole Community and is expressed in a common currency.

The market organisation for cereals was one of the first ones to be established[34]; it was modified several times and especially since the conclusion of the GATT agreements of 1994, better known as the Uruguay Round.[35] The agreement concerning agriculture was, for cereals, included in the existing regulation by an adjustment and a transitional period. Many amendments were to follow.[36]

The previous market organisation for cereals was based upon various prices: a target price, *i.e.* a price at which the Council expected that cereals can be sold within the Community, an intervention price at which the Community would buy the products that could not be sold on the open market and a threshold price for imported products. The target price and the threshold price had to be abandoned following the signature of the Uruguay Round agreement.

Imported agricultural products are henceforth submitted, like any other product, to customs duties. There are, of course, exceptions for certain products for which the import duty is based on the intervention price.[37] The introduction of other mechanisms, which do not involve the collection of customs duties, is only possible through the adoption of derogations in the basic regulations.[38]

This leaves only the *intervention price*. This is the price at which national intervention agencies shall buy the products which are offered to them. Those products must fulfil certain conditions in

---

[33] Art. 34(2) (ex 40(2)) E.C.

[34] Reg. 120/67 [1967] O.J. 2269.

[35] Reg. 1766/92 [1992] O.J. L181/22 was replaced by Reg. 3290/94 [1994] O.J. L210/1.

[36] It was destined to help farmers decide what to sow by giving them some indication as to their possible income from the product in question. This function is now taken over by the sole intervention price, which allows them to calculate what their minimum income will be from the given product if they cannot sell it on the market.

[37] Reg. 3290/94, Art. 20(2). The intervention price to be used for the calculation is that of the month in which the import duties apply: Reg. 1249/96 [1996] O.J. L161/125, Art. 2(2).

[38] Reg. 1766/92, Art. 4(1).

respect of quality and quantity, and they must have been harvested within the Community.[39] The intervention price refers to the wholesale stage for goods delivered to the warehouse before unloading. They were fixed annually by the Council for the following marketing year, around the first of July. Until 1998 they showed a slight annual increase of one ECU per ton; the price for 1999 showed no increase. At the Berlin meeting of the European Council in March 1999, it was decided to lower the intervention price by 15 per cent in two stages of 7.5 per cent in 2000 and 2001.[40]

Payment to the farmers on the basis of superfices were also agreed upon.[41] The cereal market is also characterised by the set-aside policy. In principle each farmer must set aside 10 per cent of the cultivated land during the periods 2000/2001 and 2001/2002. This set-aside is a condition for the payment of compensations.

The objectives which the Community set itself, namely to control production, is more or less achieved through a strong reduction in guaranteed prices compensated by a kind of deficiency payment, granted on condition that the required amount of land is set aside. The consequences of the lower cereal prices may be important for this sector; it might allow the producers to regain part of the market share they lost to imported substitutes because of their own high prices.

(ii) **Oil seeds and protein crops** occupy a rather special place in the agricultural market. When the common organisation was set up, the Community had to concede to the USA free entry for its products on the European market. This, of course, meant severe competition within the Community for the home-grown products. The organisation, on the other hand, is based on the same price system as for cereals, plus a production subsidy to encourage the transformation industry to use home produced rather than cheaper imported products.

Under protest from the USA against those subsidies the Community adopted a new regulation in 1991.[42] The existing system of prices and transformation subsidies was replaced by a subsidy directly paid to the producers. This resulted in huge production increases. A solution was sought in a system very similar to the one examined above for cereals: deficiency payments on condition that

---

[39] Art. 37(2) (ex 43(2)) E.C.

[40] These only constitute the main elements of the global compromise on the implementation of the Agenda 2000 reached in Berlin.

[41] Many other detailed decisions were taken concerning various Member States.

[42] Reg. 3766/91 [1991] O.J. L356/17.

15 per cent of the land would be set aside.[43] The U.S. could not accept this new arrangement and threatened again with retaliation measures. The so-called Blair House agreement was concluded in November 1992 under these conditions. It was to become the centre of a bitter controversy between France and the U.S. and its European partners. It became a major obstacle to the finalisation of the Uruguay Round, and it was only at the last minute, in the beginning of December 1993, that an agreement could be reached paving the way for a final GATT agreement which was concluded on December 15, 1993.

After this historical reminder, it is necessary to consider the legislation. The regulation setting-up the common market organisation for oils and fats was adopted in 1966.[44] It still covers *oil seeds*, although amended several times. Following a decision of a GATT panel which found against the Community, a new regulation was adopted in 1991[45] which, as mentioned, provides for payments directly to the producers and based upon the amount of cultivated land, but within certain limits. For the year 1993–94, the reform of 1992 applies.[46] The aid is now, as it is for cereals, conditioned by the set-aside of 15 per cent of the land on which the seeds were cultivated. This similarity is explained by the fact that oil seeds are cultivated on the same kind of land as cereals. But, contrary to the latter, the oil seeds have no guaranteed price nor import levies to protect them from imports. The payments provided for cereals by the Berlin Council from 2002/2003 onwards also apply to oil seeds.

(iii) Protein crops formerly regulated by a regulation of 1982[47] were, of course, also reformed in 1992,[48] in exactly the same way as is the oil seeds: reduction in prices, compensatory payments based on the number of hectares and conditioned by the set-aside of 15 per cent of the land.

A new market organisation was also introduced for *tobacco* in implementation of the reform. It is henceforth covered by a new premium scheme and production and processing quotas to restrict the grant of the premium.[49]

---

[43] Reg. 1765/92 [1992] O.J. L181/12.
[44] Reg. 136/66 [1966] O.J. L172/3025.
[45] Reg. 3766/91 [1991] O.J. L356/17.
[46] Reg. 1765/92 n. 43 above.
[47] Reg. 1431/82 [1982] O.J. L162/28.
[48] Reg. 1765/92 n. 43 above.
[49] Reg. 2075/92 [1992] O.J. L215/70.

(iv) **Beef and Veal** were the object of one of the first agricultural market organisations.[50] Closely linked with the two preceding products which constitute the basis of the animal fodder, this third category was also strongly modified by the reform. Originally it had the same price system as the above-mentioned other two organisations; it also resulted in huge surpluses. After several attempts to stem the tide,[51] the 1999 reform introduced the now classical measures: price reduction of 20 per cent in three stages and direct subsidies.[52] Similar measures apply to *sheepmeat* and *goatmeat*.[53]

(v) **Dairy products.** One very important sector within the common agricultural policy is *milk and milk products*[54] which were previously also regulated by a target and a threshold price. To dispose of overproduction, the Community tried literally everything: export restitutions, food aid, subsidies for transforming milk into fodder or industrial products, free milk distribution in schools, etc., even publicity. All to no avail; it appeared that only measures directly affecting production could help solve the surplus problem. In 1977 a co-responsibility levy[55] was introduced for the first time together with other measures such as temporary stopping of production.[56] Finally, production targets were established via a guaranteed threshold. Any production above that limit did result in a lowering of the threshold. Simultaneously the Community introduced the well-known production quotas.[57] In fact this was the real beginning of the 1992 reform! The system works as follows. A global quantity is set for the whole Community and is divided among the Member States on the basis of former production. The quantities of each Member State are then distributed among the producers in the form of "reference quantities", in fact quotas, according to two formulas from which the Member State can choose. Formula A, the individual quota is based on the quantities of milk or milk equivalents delivered by the producer to the dairy during a given year also chosen by the Member State.

---

[50] Reg. 805/68 [1968(I)] O.J. Spec. Ed. 187.
[51] See, *e.g.* Reg. 571/89 [1989] O.J. L61/43.
[52] Member States are authorised to supplement those subsidies within specific limits for each country.
[53] Reg. 2069/92 [1992] O.J. L215/59.
[54] Reg. 804/68 [1968] O.J. L148/13.
[55] Reg. 179/77 [1977] O.J. L131/6.
[56] Reg. 1078/77 [1977] O.J. L131/1.
[57] Reg. 856/84 [1984] O.J. L90/10.

Formula B is based on the quantities bought by the dairy. Overstepping the quotas means sanctions in the form of a supplementary levy.

The 1992 reform[58] extended the quota system to the year 2000 with a 2 per cent reduction in 1993–94 and 1994–95. For the rest, the market organisation continues to function around the target, intervention and threshold prices.

The co-responsibility levy was abolished in 1993[59] but the supplementary levy was maintained.[60]

The dairy reform 1999 will enter into force as from the 2005/2006 marketing year without prejudice to the decisions concerning the specific additional dairy quotas.

If one takes the two most important agricultural sectors: cereals and milk, one finds that, in the first case, the reform has appreciably reduced prices while maintaining income through deficiency payments and controlling production through set-aside of land. In the latter, the guaranteed prices are rather high, thereby maintaining the farmer's income, while the quantities are controlled through the quota system.

(3) The Structural Measures

Structural measures and assistance[61] in the agricultural field were included in the Structural Funds and their programmes with the reform of those funds examined in the chapter on Economic and Social Cohesion. They are part of objective 5: regulations concerning the improvement of agricultural structures, the improvement of processing and marketing conditions for agricultural products, and producer groups and associations thereof. The regulations concerned were reformulated in 1997.[62]

Other actions in this field concern the *protection of the environment*[63] and *forestry*.[64] The former provides for agricultural

---

[58] Reg. 3950/92 [1992] O.J. L405/1.

[59] Reg. 1029/93 [1993] O.J. 108/4.

[60] Reg. 536/93 [1993] O.J. 57/12.

[61] Total assistance from the guidance section of the Agricultural Fund for 1997 was 974,666 million ECUs.

[62] Reg. 950/97 on improving the efficiency of agricultural structures [1997] O.J. L143/9; *id.* Reg. 951/97 on improving the processing and marketing conditions for agricultural products [1997] O.J. L142/22 and Reg. 952/97 on producer groups and associations thereof [1997] O.J. L142/30.

[63] Reg. 2078/92 [1992] O.J. L215/85.

[64] Reg. 2080/92 [1992] O.J. 215/96.

production methods compatible with the requirements of the protection of the environment and the maintenance of the countryside. Its object is to reduce the harmful effects and pollution caused by agriculture, while ensuring recognition of the fundamental function performed by farmers in terms of management of the countryside and protection of natural resources. The latter introduces a Community aid scheme for forestry measures in agriculture, intended to enable farmers to adjust to the changes arising from the adjustments to the market organisations, particularly by providing economically viable alternatives to the agricultural use of land.[65] In the context of the protection of forests against atmospheric pollution and fire, the Council also adopted measures to ensure the extension, improvement and reinforcement of the mechanisms set up previously.[66]

2. Financing the Common Agricultural Policy: the EAGGF

As was mentioned at the beginning of this Chapter one of the basic principles adopted at the onset for the Community common agricultural policy was the financial responsibility of the Community for all the expenses, or financial solidarity. This includes both the expenditure for the price system and those for the socio-structural measures. The European Agricultural Guarantee and Guidance Fund (EAGGF) comprises therefore two parts: a guarantee and a guidance or structural section. The latter was included within the Structural Funds, together with the European Regional Development Fund, the Fisheries Fund and the Social Fund.

Long acclaimed as the first and only totally integrated sector of the Community, the Fund grew over the years to be not only a financial burden but a danger for the Community itself. Some Member States were no longer prepared to contribute to the open-ended system. The ever-increasing agricultural expenditures were one of the reasons, if not the main one, for the various reforms referred to above and especially the 1992 one. However, outside pressures also played a role. As mentioned, the multilateral trade negotiations within the GATT, the so-called Uruguay Round, forced the Community to strengthen its negotiation position by making some of the required adaptations to its policy with the ensuing reductions in agricultural

---

[65] See recitals to the above-mentioned regulations and General Report (1992), 171.

[66] Regs 1170/93 and 2158/92 [1993] O.J. 118/23 and [1992] O.J. 217/3.

expenditure. This however applied only to the Guarantee Section. As described above, the guaranteed price system has been severely curtailed by the latest reform and expenditures are now fixed in advance in order to avoid over-spending. The appropriations for 1998 amounted to some 40,437 billion ECUs.

A new reform became inevitable when the Community decided to enlarge to the countries of Central and Eastern Europe. The latter are still overwhelmingly agricultural and the application of the present CAP to those countries would, as the Commission expresses it mildly, "create difficulties".[67] The Commission mentions price gaps between candidate countries and higher CAP prices, the introduction of which would stimulate production, thus adding to projected surpluses. World Trade Organisation (WTO) constraints on subsidised exports would prevent the enlarged Union to sell its surpluses on third markets and the extension of the CAP would also entail an important budgetary charge, estimated at around euro 11 billion per year.

Substantial rises in agricultural prices and important direct transfers to farmers would have a negative economic and social impact on acceding countries. A reorientation of the CAP with less focus on price support and more on direct income support as well as on rural development and environment policy would help to reduce the price gap and would provide support for the structural adjustment process of acceding countries. Finally, adequate implementation and enforcement of the Community *acquis* in the candidate countries is essential for the protection of plant, animal and public health in an enlarged Union as a whole. It must be accomplished before the movement of agricultural products without border control can be established. The implementation of these measures will require substantial investment and time.

The agricultural structural measures are financed by the EAGGF Guidance Section which is examined hereafter as part of the Structural Funds under "Economic and Social Cohesion". In 1992, the commitments for the Guidance Section amounted to 2,886 billion ECUs, *i.e.* 17 per cent of the total for the Structural Funds.

It can only be hoped that the latest reform will allow an improvement of the market equilibrium and of the internal and international competitiveness of Community agriculture, as well as ensuring a greater stability in farm incomes and a more equitable distribution of the Community's resources. The reform also aimed at helping to secure quality production which is more respectful of the environment and at lower prices for the consumer.

---

[67] Agenda 2000, [1997] E.C. Suppl. Bull. 5, 98.

Further Reading

Yearly Report of the European Commission, *The Agricultural Situation in the European Union* (Office for Official Publications of the European Communities, Luxembourg).

European Commission, "The Common Agricultural Policy: promoting Europe's agriculture and rural areas: continuity and change", DG IV, Luxembourg, EUR-OP 1998.

K. A. Ingersent, A. J. Rayner, R. C. Hine, *The reform of the Common Agricultural Policy* MacMillan, Basingstoke, 1998.

Chapter Twenty
Fisheries

Community Policy

The competence of the Community in regard to fisheries is based on the same Treaty provisions as those for agriculture[1] of which they are, undoubtedly, a part. However, fisheries acquired a momentum of their own and developed into an autonomous policy. Since the Second World War, fishery products have become an important food resource, and although this sector only provides a few hundred thousand jobs, compared with millions in agriculture, the industry is also of crucial economic importance to many otherwise disadvantaged coastal areas. But, it was not until 1970 that the first decisions concerning fisheries were taken by the Community which used its powers in the following fields.

The establishment of a common market organisation,[2] based on producer organisations, a price support mechanism and protection for the Community market, a structural policy, conservation and administration of resources, and relations with third countries.

The Common Fisheries Policy is based on the principle of common access to all fishing grounds in the Community, monitoring fishing activities, the common organisation of the market, agreements with third countries and structural measures.[3]

In 1997, the Council adopted a decision on the objectives and detailed rules for restructuring the Community fisheries sector for the period 1997–2002[4] with a view to achieving a balance on a sustainable basis between resources and their exploitation. Among

[1] See Case 141/78 *France v. United Kingdom* [1979] E.C.R. 2923; [1990] 1 C.M.L.R. 6. "The powers of the Community in fishing matters are based on Article 3(d) of the Treaty in conjunction with Articles 38 *et seq.* relating to agriculture, including Annex II to the Treaty, which includes fisheries within the sphere of the common agricultural policy."

[2] Reg. 3959/92 on the common organisation of the market in fishery and aquaculture products [1992] O.J. L388/1; last modif. [1993] O.J. 76/12.

[3] This chapter is partly based upon http://europa.eu.int/pol/fish/mo_en.htm.

[4] Dec. 97/413: P [1997] O.J. L175/27.

other things, this decision sets new targets for the reduction of fishing effort in each segment of the fleet. On this basis, the Commission was able to adopt fourth-generation multiannual guidance programmes (MAGP IV).[5]

(1) Access to fishing grounds and conservation of fish stocks

Access to coastal waters, *i.e.* coastal bands six to 12 miles wide, has been reserved for fishermen from local ports to protect their fishing rights and help ensure that fishing remains an essential part of the local economy. However, the restriction is not absolute: small fishing boats from a given Member State, which have traditionally operated in the coastal waters of another continue to do so. Outside the 12-mile band, the general principle of free access to fishing grounds applies except for predetermined protected areas where the right to fish is restricted or completely withdrawn. Those decisions are based on biological advice and implemented to protect rich breeding grounds of fish for human consumption. In this domain, the Community has exclusive competence.[6]

In 1995, a new system of fishing licences—a kind of identity paper—was introduced for Community fishing boats operating in and outside E.U. waters. Moreover, a system of fishing permits provides a management mechanism to limit the fishing effort of individual vessels having access to certain fisheries.

Conservation is ensured by the fixing of Total Allowable Catches (TACs) fixed annually by the Council for all species threatened because of overfishing[7] taking into account the international agreements and arrangements made with the interested third countries. Those TACs are divided among the Member States, in the form of quotas, in pursuance of the principle of relative stability which allowed for a global equilibrium among the fishing fleets. Concretely speaking, each Member State concerned keeps a fixed percentage for each stock as originally established.[8] The accession of new Member States required of course an adaptation of the existing quotas

---

[5] [1997] E.C. Bull. 12–82.

[6] Case C–25/94 *Commission v. Council* [1996] E.C.R. I–1469: exclusive competence of the Community in matters relating to conservation of the biological resources of the sea.

[7] For the 1999 TACs see Reg. 48/99 [1999] O.J. L13 and [1993] O.J. L310/1.

[8] Reg. 894/87 relating to technical measures for the conservation of fisheries resources [1997] O.J. L132/1, modif. [1998] O.J. L171/17.

especially in so far as they concerned also non-Community waters.[9] Spain and Portugal, for instance, contested the principle of relative stability before the Court, which however, rejected most of their complaints.[10] Another problem resulted from the so-called quota hopping. This was the transfer of fishing boats from one Member State to the flag of another in order to use the quota allocated to the latter. Certain Member States therefore restricted access to their quotas. The Court has admitted that conditions be imposed in the sense that the boat in question should have some economic ties with that country; it did not admit however restrictions based on the nationality or residence of the crew, limitations to the right to land the captures in other Member States or restrict normal fishing activities.[11]

(2) Monitoring fishing activities

Since the Member States are in charge of implementing the preservation measures taken at Community level, the task of the Commission is to monitor their correct application.[12] The Commission also monitors compliance with TACs and quotas in Community and in certain international waters; the same applies to fishery agreements with third countries and international agreements. The Commission also contributes to the financing of programmes presented by Member States for the acquisition and improvement of means of monitoring and inspection.[13] Satellite technology to check vessel movements is now also being used on an experimental basis.

---

[9] Reg. 170/83 which no longer exists. See Reg. 1796/94 [1994] O.J. L187/1.

[10] Joined Cases C–63 and 67/90 *Portugal and Spain v. Council* [1992] E.C.R. I–5073.

[11] Case C–3/87 *Agegate* [1989] E.C.R. 4459; [1990] 1 C.M.L.R. 366 Case C–216/87 *Jaderow* [1989] E.C.R. 4509; [1991] 2 C.M.L.R. 556; Case C–246/89 *Commission v. United Kingdom* [1991] E.C.R. I–4607; Case C–221/89 *R. v. Secretary of State for Transport, ex p. Factortame* [1991] E.C.R. I–3956.

[12] Reg. 2241/87, establishing certain control measures for fishing activities [1987] O.J. 306/2.

[13] Council Dec. 89/631 [1989] O.J. L364/64, modif. [1992] O.J. 213/35 extending the programme to include the Mediterranean. See Council Dec. of December 20, 1993 restructuring the Community fisheries sector with a view to achieving a lasting balance between the resources and their exploitation [1994] O.J. L10/20.

(3) The common organisation of the market

In 1993, a new regulation[14] strengthened the controls and extended monitoring beyond the catching of fish, to other aspects of the CFP, such as structures, fish marketing and aquaculture. In addition all links in the fishery chain from producer to consumer, whether it be catches themselves, landings, transport or actual sales, are now monitored and documented. This provides for much more detailed checks of the data recorded in the fishermen's logbooks. Penalties are decided by national courts. They may range from, heavy fines, confiscation of fishing nets, of fish caught and even of the boat itself to temporary suspension or permanent withdrawal of fishing licences.

The common organisation of the market in fishery and aquaculture products was set up in 1970 and was, as was the rest of agriculture, reformed in 1992.[15] It comprises four elements.

(1) Common commercialisation norms for the species subject to a Community price system.
(2) Producers organisation, which, *inter alia*, constitute an exception to the competition rules.
(3) A price system based on three mechanisms:
   (i) withdrawal and selling prices for 40 species[16];
   (ii) support for private stocking of products frozen on the sea;
   (iii) compensatory payments for tuna.[17]
(4) The possibility of adopting safeguard measures in case of grave disturbances of the market.

The Community also encourages *research* with various programmes such as the Fisheries and Aquaculture Research (FAR) and AIR, an integrated programme in agriculture and agro-industry.

(4) Agreements with third countries and international conventions

Since 1976 the Community has been exclusively competent to handle international fishing negotiations. Fishing agreements were signed with a number of third countries[18] in order to safeguard

---

[14] Reg. 2847/93, establishing a control system applicable to the common fisheries policy.
[15] Reg. 3759/92 [1992] O.J. L388/1, modif. [1993] O.J. L76/12.
[16] Reg. 3595/93 [1993] O.J. L330/1.
[17] Reg. 3659/91 [1991] O.J. L348/40.
[18] See various General Reports.

traditional fishing rights of Community vessels or to seek new opportunities.

Indeed, without those agreements the general extension of fishing zones to 200 miles and the resulting substantial reduction in fishing opportunities would have had serious repercussions for Community fishermen. Furthermore, in the present circumstances of surplus capacity in Community waters, these agreements represent a means of reducing fishing efforts in those waters.

Multilateral agreements have also been concluded with a view to the Community's participation in the international agreements covering the North-West, North-East, East, Central and South East Atlantic: the North-Atlantic Salmon Conservation Organisation (NASCO), the North-East Atlantic Fisheries Commission (NEAFC), the International Commission for the South East Atlantic Fisheries (ICSEAF), the Fishery Committee for the Eastern-Central Atlantic (CECAF), the International Whaling Commission, etc.[19]

To date the Community had concluded 26 agreements, with countries from North Africa and the Indian Ocean and from the North Atlantic area. In the latter area problems have developed mainly with Canada which forced the Council to regulate access and catches for the North-West Atlantic Fisheries Organisation (NAFO) convention area.[20] Different categories of fisheries agreements exist, which are distinguished according to the type of concession offered: reciprocal arrangements, access to surplus stock, access to stocks in return for market access, access to stocks in return for financial compensation and access to stocks in return for payment and market access. For more details see the annual General Reports published by the Commission in February of each year.[21]

(5) Structural measures

The first rules laying down a common structural policy for the fishing industry were enacted in 1970.[22] Following enlargement, a

---

[19] See General Report (1989) 270.

[20] Reg. 3927/92, laying down certain conservation and management measures for fishery resources in the Regulatory Area as defined in the Convention on Future Multilateral Co-operation in the North-West Atlantic Fisheries [1992] O.J. L397/67 and Reg. 3928/92 establishing a NAFO pilot observer scheme applicable to Community fishing vessels operating on the Regulatory Area of the North-West Atlantic Fisheries Organisation (NAFO) [1992] O.J. L397/78.

[21] General Report (1993) 205.

[22] Reg. 2141/70 [1970] O.J. Spec. Ed. 703.

new regulation was adopted in 1976.[23] Those provisions enabled the Community to support financially, through the agricultural fund, fish processing and marketing development projects, building of inshore fishing vessels, refitting of vessels and extension of fish farming schemes.

In 1977 common measures were adopted to improve the conditions under which agricultural and fishery products are processed and marketed,[24] and in 1983 the Council adopted common measures for restructuring, modernising and developing the fishing industry and for developing aquaculture[25] and measures to encourage exploratory fishing.[26] Once again new structural aspects of the fisheries policy were adopted, this time in 1986,[27] to finance the construction of fishing vessels, aquaculture and structural work in coastal waters, modernisation of fishing vessels and exploratory fishing voyages, while at the same time financing programmes to reduce the capacity of the Member States' fishing fleets to bring them into line with the available fish stocks.[28]

The actions relating to the transformation and the commercialisation of products of fishery and aquaculture have as their objective the modernisation and the rationalisation of the factories, mainly sanitary conditions. Following the reform of the Structural Funds the Community established, within that framework, a Financial Instrument for Fisheries Guidance (FIFG).[29] This permitted a doubling of the available resources.

The Community fisheries suffer from overcapacity of its fleets in comparison to diminishing resources; it is essential to re-establish an equilibrium. This can only be achieved through several activities—the Community must increase the effectiveness of the TACs, reinforce the monitoring, reduce the fishing capacity, compensate the socio-economic consequence with accompanying measures and at the same time guarantee a constant supply at reasonable prices. Important changes are required while the Community, on the other hand, needs to import huge quantities to satisfy the internal demand.

Mention must also be made of the PESCA Community initiative[30]

---

[23] Reg. 101/76 [1976] O.J. L20/19.

[24] [1993] O.J. L51.

[25] Reg. 2908/83 [1983] O.J. L290 and Reg. 3166/83: L316/1.

[26] Reg. 2909/83 [1983] O.J. L290.

[27] [1986] O.J. L376.

[28] General Report (1988) 297 and Dir. 83/515 (O.J. 1983, L. 290/15).

[29] Reg. 2080/93 laying down provisions for implementing Reg. 2052/88 as regards the financial instrument of fisheries guidance: [1993] O.J. L193/1.

[30] See under Social and Economic Cohesion for the Community Initiatives.

which seeks to generate clearly focused projects to help the fishing sector to adapt and coastal areas to diversify their economic activities[31] and the Multiannual Programme to restructure the Community fishing industry for the period January 1, 1997 to December 31, 2002.[32]

Actions for the fisheries sector outside Objective 1 regions[33] will be supported, according to the decisions taken by the Berlin European Council of March 24–25, 1999, by the financial instrument for fisheries guidance (FIFG) with an amount of euro 1.1 billion over the period 2000–2006.

Further Reading

European Commission, "Improving the implementation of the common fisheries policy, an action plan", Brussels: E.C. 1998.

European Commission, "The Common Fisheries Policy", DG XIV, Luxembourg, EUR-OP 1998.

[31] In 1997, this initiative was endowed with 21,456 million ECUs. See also Dec. 97/292 on a specific measure to encourage Italian fishermen to diversify out of certain fishing activities [1997] O.J. L121/20.

[32] [1997] E.C. Bull. 4–59.

[33] See Chapter Twenty-Eight: Economic and Social Cohesion.

PART FIVE: POLICIES OF THE COMMUNITY AND THE MEMBER STATES

Chapter Twenty-one
Taxation

Title VI (ex V) of the Treaty encompasses three subjects: "common rules on competition, taxation and approximation of laws." These three spheres of activity of the Community have in common that they aim at guaranteeing the free movement of goods, which is made possible by the customs union and the prohibition of quantitative restrictions.[1] That cartels, abuses of dominant positions, mergers and acquisitions, State aids and public enterprises, can restrict the free movement of goods, seems evident. Similarly, differences in taxation according to the origin of the product, risk to prevent goods from other Member States to be commercialised in competition with national products. Finally, as shall be seen, differences between the provisions laid down by laws, regulations and administrative provisions of Member States may directly affect the establishment and functioning of the internal market, thereby rendering more difficult the free flow of goods within the Community.

In the case of distortions of competition and discriminatory taxation, the remedy is simply a prohibition with the necessary exceptions to take account of particular situations; in the case of differences between the applicable provisions of Member States, the remedy consists in approximation of laws.

Although the Treaty prohibits the direct or indirect imposition on products from other Member States,[2] of "any internal taxation of any kind", in excess of that imposed on similar domestic products,[3] the Council's power to harmonise the national laws, is limited to the legislation on turnover taxes, excise duties and other forms of indirect taxation.[4] And although the Council may only act "to the

[1] Competition policy together with Agriculture and Fisheries Policy were examined in Part Four as "Community Policies", since they fall into the exclusive competence of the Community.

[2] The expression "other Member States" includes products from third countries in free circulation; see Case 193/85 *Co-Frutta* [1987] E.C.R. 2085.

[3] Art. 90 (ex 95) E.C. Art. 90(2) has direct effect, see Case 27/67 *Finck-Frucht v. Hauptzollamt München* [1968] E.C.R. 223; [1968] C.M.L.R. 187.

[4] Art. 93 (ex 99) E.C.

extent that such harmonisation is necessary to ensure the establishment and the functioning of the internal market within the limits laid down in Article 14 (ex 7a)",[5] an impressive and exceedingly important legislative programme was implemented over the years, particularly since 1967,[6] concerning Value Added Tax (VAT). This cumulative multi-stage turnover tax system was definitively introduced in the Community in 1977.[7]

The importance of VAT for the Community derives, *inter alia*, from the fact that since 1970 a percentage of the VAT collected in the Member States belongs to the Community as "own resource".[8] With the entering into force of the internal market, which implied the elimination of the fiscal frontiers within the Community, new rules had to be adopted concerning VAT collection. Agreement was reached on transitional arrangements, which still apply. All tax checks and formalities at intra-Community frontiers would be abolished. VAT is still collected in the country of destination of the product or service in question. At the end of the transitional period, the definitive VAT system will be based on payment in the Member State in which the goods or services originated.[9]

In 1992, the Council adopted a directive on the approximation of VAT rates. The standard rate was set at not less than 15 per cent and the optional "reduced rate" at not less than five per cent. A framework for co-operation between national tax authorities in a Community without internal border controls was set up, which provides in particular for the exchange of information on intra-Community trade subject to VAT. It also provides for the introduction of a computerised network for ensuring that such exchanges are rapid and effective.[10]

Direct taxes remain within the exclusive ambit of the Member States. Nonetheless, the Council and the Representatives of the Governments of the Member States adopted a resolution on a Code

---

[5] *ibid.*

[6] First Council Directive 67/227 on the harmonisation of legislation of Member States concerning turnover tax [1967] O.J. L71/1301; [1967] O.J. Spec. Ed. 1.

[7] The Sixth Directive 77/388 on the harmonization of the laws of the Member States relating to turnover tax—Common system of value added tax: uniform basis of assessment [1977] O.J. L145/1. See Case C–155/94 *Welcome Trust v. Commissioners of Customs and Excise* [1996] E.C.R. I–3013; [1996] 2 C.M.L.R. 909.

[8] See above, Chapter Twelve: "Financing Community Activities".

[9] Dir. 91/680 supplementing the common system of value added tax and amending Directive 77/388 with a view to the abolition of the fiscal frontiers [1991] O.J. L376/1.

[10] Reg. 218/92 on administrative co-operation in the field of indirect taxation [1992] O.J. L24/1.

of Conduct for Business Taxation and Taxation of Saving.[11] The object is to reduce continuing distortions in the single market, prevent significant losses of tax revenue and help tax structure develop in a more employment-friendly way.[12] The Council also adopted a directive on the common system of taxation applicable in the case of parent companies and subsidiaries of different Member States,[13] and a directive concerning mutual assistance by the competent authorities of the Member States in the field of direct taxation.[14] Furthermore, the way in which direct taxes are applied can constitute a breach of Community law.[15] The Court pointed out that non-residents should not be taxed more heavily than residents if they derive most of their income from the State of employment.[16]

A system for the exchange of information between the competent authorities of the Member States, in the field of direct taxation, similar to the one mentioned above for indirect taxes, was set up by the so-called Mutual Assistance Directive.[17] See also the Mergers Directive on a common system of taxation applicable to mergers, divisions, transfer of assets and exchanges of shares concerning companies of different Member States.[18]

The basic Treaty provision concerning the prohibition of discriminatory taxation gave rise to an abundance of case law. There is, in the first place, the definition of the term "taxation". The fact that the Treaty refers to "any kind", indicates that it must be interpreted widely. This was confirmed by the Court.[19] Even an import surcharge, which at first sight might be viewed as a charge having an equivalent effect to a customs duty, must, according to the Court, be assessed in the light of the tax provisions, where the surcharge is added to a general duty which forms part of a general system of

---

[11] [1998] O.J. C99/1 and C2/2 for taxation of savings: *ibid.* 2/6.
[12] *ibid.*
[13] [1990] O.J. L225/6.
[14] Dir. 79/1072 [1979] O.J. L331/11.
[15] See Case C–279/93 *Schumacker* [1995] E.C.R. I–225; [1996] 2 C.M.L.R. 450.
[16] Case C–80/94 *Wielockx* [1995] E.C.R. I–2493, applying the same principle to the self-employed.
[17] Dir. 77/799 [1977] O.J. L336/15.
[18] Dir. 90/434 [1990] O.J. L225/1. See also the capital duty Dir. 69/335 [1969] O.J. L249/25 and the Parent-Subsidiary Directive [1990] O.J. L225/6.
[19] Case 20/76 *Schottle v. Finanzamt Freudenstadt* [1977] E.C.R. 247; [1977] 2 C.M.L.R. 98: taxation imposed indirectly on products must be interpreted as including a charge imposed on international transport of goods by road according to the distance covered on the national territory and the weight of the goods.

internal dues.[20] Obviously, stamp duties[21] and fees for a mark on precious metal,[22] constitute internal taxation. A distinction between the latter and customs duties and charges having equivalent effect, should be possible on the simple basis that the latter are levied, as was seen, at the occasion of a product crossing a border between Member States. Taxes, on the other hand, are levied once the products are inside the territory. The distinction, however, is not always that easy.

As for the term "indirect", the Court decided that it must also be widely interpreted.[23] For instance, although Member States are free to subject cars to a road tax which increases progressively depending on an objective criterion, the Treaty prohibits the charging on cars exceeding a given power of a special fixed tax, where the only cars subject to the special tax are imported, in particular from other Member States.[24] On the other hand, in a more recent judgment, the Court decided that a progressive tax is not prohibited solely because only imported products come within the most heavily taxed category. Such taxation only breaches the prohibition of the Treaty if it may deter consumers from purchasing the more heavily taxed imported cars, to the benefit of products of domestic manufacture.[25]

The term "similar" refers, according to the Court, to products having the same characteristics and meeting the same needs from the point of view of the consumer.[26] It is therefore necessary to determine the scope of the prohibition on the basis, not of the criterion of the strictly identical nature of the products, but on that of their similar and comparable use.

The Treaty also prohibits the imposition on the products of other Member States of any internal taxation of such a nature as to afford indirect protection to other products.[27] This provision covers all

[20] Case C–90/94 *Haahr Petroleum v. Abenra Havn and Others* [1997] E.C.R. I–4085; [1998] 1 C.M.L.R. 771.

[21] Case 77/69 *Commission v. Belgium* [1970] E.C.R. 237; [1974] 1 C.M.L.R. 203; the rate was the same, but the basis on which it was applied, resulted in heavier taxes for the imported products.

[22] Case 142/77 *Statens Kontrol v. Larsen* [1978] E.C.R. 1543; [1979] 2 C.M.L.R. 680.

[23] Case 28/67 *Molkerei-Zentrale Westfalen v. Hauptzollamt Paderborn* [1968] E.C.R. 143; [1968] C.M.L.R. 187.

[24] Case 112/84 *Humblot* [1985] E.C.R. 1367; [1986] 2 C.M.L.R. 338.

[25] Case C–113/94 *Jacquier v. Directeur Général des Impôts* [1995] E.C.R. I–4203.

[26] Case 168/78 *Commission v. France* [1981] E.C.R. 347; [1981] 2 C.M.L.R. 631 and Case 170/78 *Commission v. U.K.* [1983] E.C.R. 2265; [1980] 1 C.M.L.R. 716, where the Court considered discriminatory the imposition of higher taxes on wine than on beer.

[27] Art. 90 (ex 95) E.C.

forms of indirect taxation which protects products which, without being similar, are nevertheless in competition, even partial, indirect or potential, with certain imported products.[28]

As mentioned several times already, every rule has its exceptions, and this applies, of course, also in the case of the Treaty tax provisions. As was just mentioned in the example concerning cars, not every tax that penalises imported products more heavily than it does national products, is prohibited. The Court has developed a theory according to which discrimination can be accepted on the basis of "objective criteria", such as the nature of the products used or the production process employed, as long as it pursues "economic policy objectives", which are compatible with Community law and are not discriminatory or protective in their nature.[29] The Court considered that although the taxation resulted in restraining imports, it had an equivalent economic effect in the State itself. The reader will remember that with regard to the prohibition of measures having an effect equivalent to a quantitative restriction with regard to the free movement of goods, the Court adopted a similar position. It considered that a national measure prohibiting the sale of a product at a loss, could indeed restrict imports, but pursued an acceptable economic objective and applied without discrimination to all products.[30] The same principle applies if the object is to protect the environment.

For the sake of completeness, mention must also be made of the prohibition imposed on the Member States to repay internal taxation where products are exported to any Member State, in excess of the internal taxation effectively imposed.[31] The same prohibition applies to remissions or repayments in respect of exports to other Member States of charges other than turnover taxes, excise duties and other forms of indirect taxation, unless the measures contemplated have been previously approved for a limited period by the Council.[32]

As for *Excise Duties*, a directive was finally adopted in 1992,

[28] See the Cases mentioned in n. 26 above.

[29] Case 140/79 *Chemical Farmaceutici v. DAF* [1981] E.C.R. 1, concerned taxation which favoured the production of alcohol from agricultural products rather than from petroleum derivatives, and, although it results in restraining the importation of synthetic alcohol, it has an economic policy justification.

[30] Joint Cases C–267 and 268/91 *Keck and Mithouard* [1993] E.C.R. I–6097; [1995] 1 C.M.L.R. 101.

[31] Art. 91 (ex 96) E.C.

[32] Art. 92 (ex 98) E.C.

before the entry into force of the internal market.[33] It is based on the principle that chargeability of excise duties should be identical in all the Member States, that in the case of products subject to excise duty acquired by private individuals for their own use and transported by them, the duty must be charged in the country where they were acquired, in other cases they must be subject to excise duty in the country of destination, etc. Rates are still laid down by Member States; in other words no harmonisation has been accepted by them, except for some products,[34] with the consequence that trade is presently distorted to the advantage of States with low rates. The Directive also provides that the above mentioned mutual assistance Directive will also apply to excise duties. Notwithstanding regular attempts, it has not been possible yet to arrive at a harmonised, let alone a common, system of excise duties within the Community. It seems obvious, however, that the internal market cannot function properly if those duties and other indirect taxes are not harmonised as provided for in the Treaty.

Within the framework of the Chapter on Taxation, a word must be said about the so-called *duty free*. This system of turnover tax and excise duty exemption was set up in 1969[35] in order to allow the traveller who crosses a border between two Member States to dispense with reclaiming taxes already paid when leaving one Member State, and paying new taxes on arrival in the other Member State. The traveller was therefore allowed to purchase goods to be transported in his personal luggage at a price which does not include VAT, nor excise duty; the amounts of goods, which the traveller could thus purchase were strictly limited.

To put this system into practice, vendors at airports and on board ships and planes were allowed to purchase those goods at "duty free" prices in order to sell them at those same prices to the traveller. Unfortunately, the system was perverted and abused, since the vendors kept for themselves most of the profit which the Council had intended for the traveller. This constituted for those vendors a huge profit which distorted competition. The system, furthermore, dis-

---

[33] Dir. 92/12 on the general arrangements for products subject to excise duty and on the holding, movement and monitoring of such products [1992] O.J. L76/1, last amended by Dir. 96/99 [1996] O.J. L8/12.

[34] But see for instance, Dir. 92/84 on the approximation of the rates of excise duty on alcohol and alcoholic beverages.

[35] Dir. 69/169 on the harmonisation of provisions relating to exemption from turnover tax and excise duty on imports in international travel. See also Third Council Directive on the harmonisation of provisions relating to the rules governing turnover tax and excise duty applicable in international travel [1978] O.J. L366/28. See Case C–296/95 *EMU, The Man in Black* [1998] E.C.R. I–1605.

criminated between categories of travellers. Notwithstanding the entry into force of the internal market at the end of 1992, and the elimination of the fiscal frontiers, which were the origin of the whole system, the Council, in 1992, extended the duty free exemption to June 30, 1999. This anti-competitive and discriminatory system has now disappeared for intra-Community travellers.

A last word in this chapter on taxation ought to be said about the *prevention of tax evasion and avoidance*. On this subject the Council has, over the years, issued two Directives, one Regulation, three Resolutions and one Conclusion. The first Directive was already mentioned above: it concerns mutual assistance by the competent authorities of the Member States in the field of direct taxation.[36] The second on prevention of the use of the financial system for the purpose of money laundering was also mentioned above in the chapter on "The Freedom of Establishment" for financial institutions.[37] The Regulation concerns on-the-spot checks and inspections carried out by the Commission in order to protect the European Communities' financial interests against fraud and other irregularities.[38] It was preceded by a Resolution on the legal protection of the financial interests of the Community[39] and Conclusions concerning the fight against fraud.[40] The first Council Resolution is from 1975 and concerns the measures to be taken by the Community in order to combat international tax evasion and avoidance.[41]

And finally, there is the Resolution of the Council and of the Representatives of the Governments of the Member States, meeting within the Council, concerning the protection of the financial interests of the Communities.[42]

Further Reading

European Commission, "Tax provisions with a potential impact on environmental protection", final report of the Commission, September 1996, Luxembourg EUR-OP 1997.

Pierre Mathijsen, "Are the Present Arrangements for Duty Free Shops Legal?" (1998) 23 E.L.Rev. 452.

---

[36] Dir. 77/99 [1977] O.J. L336/15.
[37] Dir. 91/308 [1991] O.J. L166/77.
[38] Reg. 2185/96 [1996] O.J. L292/2.
[39] [1994] O.J. C355/2.
[40] [1994] O.J. C292/1.
[41] [1975] O.J. C35/1.
[42] [1991] O.J. C328/1.

Chapter Twenty-two

Approximation of Laws

"Approximation", which is the name given in the Treaty to this "activity",[1] refers to the objective to be attained. The method to be used consists in "harmonisation" measures. It is clear that the many differences existing between the laws of the Member States impede the development and functioning of the common market on which the Community is based. As indicated in the chapter on the free movement of goods, the differences between the "laws, regulations or administrative provisions of the Member States"[2] can be bridged either by mutual recognition of existing national provisions or, when this is not desirable or possible, through harmonisation. As far as mutual recognition is concerned, the chapter contained a most interesting provision which was repealed since it referred only to the year 1992. It provided that the Council, on the basis of an inventory drawn up by the Commission of national provisions which have not been harmonised, could decide that "the provisions in force in a Member State must be recognised as being equivalent to those applied by another Member State".[3] It is unfortunate that a similar, more general, provision was not kept in the Treaty. It would have greatly facilitated the indispensable approximation activity.

Harmonisation, on the other hand, consists in replacing existing national provisions by rules whose content is common to all the Member States. Those are not exactly "common rules", if by that is understood identical rules. Indeed, as was indicated, the ideal instrument to achieve the objective of approximation is the directive, and the latter, as was seen in the chapter on Community acts, is only binding as to the results to be achieved. It leaves to the national authorities the choice of form and methods.[4]

The Treaty makes a distinction between national provisions "as directly affect the establishment or functioning of the common

[1] See Art. 3(1)(h) (ex 3(h)) E.C.
[2] Art. 94 (ex 100) E.C.
[3] Former Art. 100b(1)(2) E.C.
[4] Art. 249 (ex 189) E.C.

market"[5] and rules which "have as their object the establishment and functioning of the internal market".[6] The difference between common and internal market was explained at the beginning of this book and can be summarised as follows. The common market covers most of the "activities of the Community",[7] including the "internal market", the latter consisting in the basic freedoms only.[8] And since the establishment of the internal market was bound by a time limit—the end of 1992—a method more rapid than the one applying to approximation in general, had to be devised. The Treaty on European Union—the Maastricht Treaty—introduced it.

As regards the first category, those which may directly affect the establishment or functioning of the common market, the Treaty provides for directives issued by the Council, acting unanimously on a proposal from the Commission and after consulting the European Parliament and the Economic and Social Committee. The requirement of unanimity makes the implementation of this provision extremely time-consuming, if not practically impossible. Many directives were nonetheless adopted pursuant to this method, especially in those areas of Community activity where harmonising directives were provided for by the Treaty. This was the case, for instance, for the implementation of the freedom of movement of workers and self-employed persons. It was clear, however, that another solution had to be found to expedite the establishment and functioning of the "internal" market before the end of 1992. Consequently, the Commission in its White Book on the "Completion of the Internal Market", proposed a new approach consisting both in simplifying the harmonisation procedure and replacing it, whenever possible, by "mutual recognition".

The "simplification" consisted in replacing unanimity by qualified majority. To this end the Treaty on European Union introduced a new provision providing for qualified majority and the co-operation of the European Parliament.[9] "Mutual recognition" consisted in applying to national legislation what the Court had applied to the free movement of goods. In that area the rule states that a product lawfully produced and commercialised in one Member State must be freely admitted in all the others.[10] Similarly, what is lawful in one

[5] Art. 94 (ex 100) E.C.
[6] Art. 95(1) (ex 100a(1)) E.C.
[7] Art. 3 (ex 3) E.C.
[8] Art. 14 E.C.
[9] Former Art. 100a(1) E.C. which is identical to the new Art. 95(1).
[10] See the famous cases *Dassonville* ([1974] E.C.R. 837(5)) and *Cassis de Dijon* ([1979] E.C.R. 649(14)).

Member State must be accepted as lawful in all the others: each State recognises the laws of all the others.

There are, of course, exceptions, such as health, safety, environmental protection and consumer protection where approximation still has its place. In those areas the Treaty provides that the Commission when it makes its proposals must take as a base a high level of protection "taking account in particular of any new development based on scientific facts".[11]

The Treaty also provides for exceptions in the case of protection of the environment or of the working environment".[12] The exceptions are the same as those provided for the elimination of quantitative restrictions and measures having equivalent effect where the free movement of goods is concerned.[13] These exceptions allow Member States, after the adoption of a harmonisation measure, and under the supervision of the Commission,[14] either to maintain national provisions, or to introduce national provisions based on new scientific evidence on grounds of a problem specific to a given Member State. As stated by the Court, the supervision by the Commission implies that the Member State may not apply unilateral rules derogating from the Community harmonised measures without the prior authorisation of the Commission.[15] The Treaty also provides that in case the Commission or any Member State considers that another Member State is making improper use of the exception, they can bring the matter directly before the Court, without going through the normal procedures.[16]

The chapter on approximation also contains provisions concerning a difference between the national provisions, which "is distorting the conditions of competition" and which, according to the Commission, "needs to be eliminated".[17] In that case, the Commission must first consult the Member States concerned. It is only if such consultation does not result in an agreement eliminating the distortion of competition, that the Council must act, by a qualified

---

[11] Art. 95(3) (ex 100a(3)) E.C.

[12] Art. 95(4) and (5) (ex 100a(4)) E.C.

[13] The Treaty refers to Art. 30 (ex 36) E.C.

[14] See Art. 75(5) to (10) (ex 100a(4) and (5)) E.C.

[15] Case C–41/93 *France v. Commission* [1994] E.C.R. I–1829; [1995] 3 C.M.L.R. 733.

[16] Art. 95(9) (ex 100a(9)) E.C. The normal procedures require the Commission to first give the Member State the opportunity to submit its observations and then to issue a reasoned opinion, before going to court. A Member State must first bring the matter before the Commission, which gives each of the States concerned the opportunity to submit its own case and its observations on the other party's case. The Commission can then deliver a reasoned opinion.

[17] Art. 92 (ex 98) E.C.

majority, on a proposal from the Commission. This provision seems to indicate that differences which distort competition are more urgent than differences which "directly affect the establishment or functioning of the common market", since only qualified majority is required here.

The Treaty furthermore provides that where there is fear that the adoption or amendment of existing provisions might distort the conditions of competition, the Member State wishing to proceed therewith, must first consult the Commission. The latter may make recommendations, and if the Member State does not comply therewith, other Member States are not required to amend their own provisions in order to eliminate the distortion. However, when the distortion is only detrimental to the Member State which has introduced the provision and not followed the Commission's recommendation, the Treaty does not apply.

The chapter on approximation of laws contained several articles[18] which were repealed by the Amsterdam Treaty. They concerned the issue of visas to nationals of third countries. Similar provisions are now to be found in Title IV "visas, asylum, immigration and other policies related to the free movement of persons".[19]

Since, as indicated at the beginning of this chapter, "harmonisation" is but a method to arrive at the approximation of the national provisions applicable in the various areas of activity of the Community as defined in the Treaty,[20] the many harmonisation directives are examined in the corresponding chapters of this book. For instance, the directives harmonising the conditions of access to the regulated professions are examined in the chapter on the freedom of establishment.

Finally, it should be noted that there are certain subjects which are excluded from the approximation process. One example is to be found in the field of employment. The Treaty provides that the Council may adopt "incentive measures designed to encourage co-operation between Member States and to support their action in the field of employment", but adds that those measures shall not include harmonisation of the laws and regulations of the Member States.[21] Other fields, namely those relating to fiscal provisions, the free movement of persons and the rights and interests of employed persons, are excluded from the harmonisation procedure provided

---

[18] Former Arts 100c and 100d.
[19] Art. 61 to 69 E.C.
[20] Art. 3 (ex 3) E.C.
[21] Art. 129 (ex 109r) E.C.

for the establishment and functioning of the internal market.[22] They are not, however, excluded from the normal harmonisation procedure. The vocational training policy,[23] culture,[24] public health[25] and education[26] are excluded also from the harmonisation process.

Further Reading

Piet Jan Slot, "Harmonisation", (1996) 21 E.L.Rev. 378.

Christopher M. G. Himsworth, "Things Fall Apart: The Harmonisation of Community Judicial Procedural Protection Revisited", (1997) 22 E.L.Rev. 291.

[22] Art. 95(2) (ex 100a(2)) E.C.
[23] Art. 150(4) (ex 127(4)) E.C.
[24] Art. 151(5) (ex 128(5)) E.C.
[25] Art. 152(4)(c) (ex 129(4)) E.C.
[26] Art. 149(4) (ex 126(4)) E.C.

Chapter Twenty-three

Transport

The Treaty makes it clear from the outset that the objectives set out in this Title on Transport must be pursued by the Member States. Contrary to other activities, like agriculture, the Community does not intervene directly in this field. Its role is to lay down a "common transport policy".[1] Nevertheless, the Community has an important role to play since the Treaty also provides that the objectives must be pursued "within the framework of a common transport policy", which can only be established within the Community framework. The great importance of Transport for the functioning of the common market follows, *inter alia*, from the fact that free movement of persons and of goods would have no practical effect without an integrated trans-European transport network. Such a network also responds to people's demands for cleaner environment and safer, reliable mobility.

Although this is only mentioned at the end of Title V on Transport, those provisions only apply to transport by rail, road and inland waterways. However, Parliament and Council acting jointly,[2] may decide whether, to what extent and by what procedures appropriate provisions may be laid down for sea and air transport.[3] This they have done and, as will be seen, many Community acts were adopted concerning those means of transport.

It is the task of the Parliament and the Council acting jointly[4] and,

[1] Art. 70 (ex 74) E.C.

[2] Art. 251 (ex 189b) E.C., with the exceptions mentioned in n. 4.

[3] Art. 80 (ex 84) E.C.

[4] Art. 251 (ex 189b) E.C., except where the application of provisions concerning the principles of the regulatory system for transport would be liable to have a serious effect on the standards of living and on employment in certain areas and on the operation of transport facilities; in those cases the Council shall act alone and unanimously, after consulting the Parliament and the ESC: Art. 71(2) (ex 75(3)) E.C.

taking into account the distinctive features of transport,[5] to provide for:

- common rules applicable to international transport within the Community[6];
- conditions under which non-resident carriers may operate transport services within Member States;
- measures to improve transport safety[7];
- any other appropriate provision.

Until the above mentioned provisions have been laid down, the Member States must observe a stand-still with regard to similar national provisions.

Special Features of Transport

There are several characteristics which distinguish transport from other services. One is the fact that it extends inevitably beyond the geographic borders of the Community and is subject to many international agreements and regulations: it suffices to think about sea and air transport. Furthermore, most kinds of transport require heavy investments, which, due to widely varying demand (for instance, public transportation) often remains idle and unproductive for part of the time. Then there exists an enormous discrepancy between the infrastructure needs for various means of transport. Some, like railways and inland shipping, need heavy and specially designed infrastructure, used intermittently by a limited number of carriers. The offer here largely exceeds, most of the time, the demand. Other infrastructures like roads, are used by millions of people who do not contribute directly to the costs of those infrastructures. Another characteristic is that some means of transport are (or at least were until recently) in the hands of the State, due, *inter alia*, to the fact that they are obliged to offer services which are

---

[5] It will be remembered that Reg. 141 exempting transport from the application of Reg. 17/62 [1962] J.O. 124/2751 and Reg. 1017/68 applying rules of competition to transport by rail, road and inland waterway [1968] O.J. L175/10 do also point out the "particular features" of transport.

[6] See, *inter alia*, First Council Dir. (62/2005) on the establishment of certain common rules for international transport (carrying of goods by road for hire or reward) [1962] O.J. 70/2005, incorporated [1994] O.J. L1/572.

[7] See Dir. 76/914 on the minimum level of training for some road transport drivers [1976] O.J. L357/36. The implementation of this Directive (like for the previous Dir. 74/561) by the Member States must be submitted in draft form to the Commission, which expresses an opinion or issues a recommendation.

not justified on purely economic grounds. Finally, whether nationalised or not, all forms of transport, especially public transport, are subject to severe requirements with regard to safety. Furthermore, to understand the challenges, which the Community faces in developing its Common Transport Policy, a few basic facts should be kept in mind.

The first important fact is the constant increase in demand for transport. This is due, *inter alia*, to the increase in the standards of living, which allows people to travel more and further away: for instance, the number of personal cars has doubled over the past 20 years. Secondly, there is the geographical spread of economic activities, which are no longer concentrated in the urban areas; the same applies to the population in general: "suburbia" has inevitably increased the demand for transport. Thirdly, there is the change in spread of demand across the various modes of transport. Contrary to 20 years ago, inland waterways today only carry a small percentage of the goods within the Community, railways a little over 10 per cent, while nowadays, pipelines also carry nearly 10 per cent. The contrary, as is well known, applies to road transport, which now represents nearly 80 per cent of all inland transport in the Community. It is clear that, if nothing is done (by whom?), this means of transport will continue to grow to the detriment of all the others, with all the problems this creates with regard to, for instance, the environment. The above mentioned figures are exclusive of transport by air and sea.

It might be interesting to recall that the Common Transport Policy failed to materialise for many years, so much so that Parliament had to take the Council to Court for failure to implement the Treaty provisions in this field. The Court ruled that "in breach of the Treaty, the Council had failed to ensure freedom to provide services in the sphere of international transport and to lay down the conditions under which non-resident carriers may operate transport services in a Member State".[8] The result of this Court ruling was that the Council adopted a policy approach to transport, rather than the piecemeal one used until then.

Subsequently, the Treaty on E.U. introduced new concepts with regard to transport. This is the case, for instance, with transport safety, which has become a Community responsibility. Also important was the introduction of the Trans-European Networks,[9] *inter*

---

[8] Case 13/83 *Parliament v. Council* [1983] E.C.R. 1513; [1986] 1 C.M.L.R. 138; the Court also concluded that "there is not yet a set of rules which may be regarded as a common transport policy".

[9] E.C. Treaty, Title XV, see below.

alia, in the field of transport. The Community may contribute, through the Cohesion Fund,[10] to the financing of specific projects in the area of transport.[11] Another new feature was the necessity to integrate environmental protection requirements into the definition and implementation of other Community policies, and therefore, also into the Common transport policy. The same applies to Economic and Social Cohesion, which means the Common Transport Policy must contribute to the creation of the necessary transport infrastructure in the less developed regions. If one adds to that the necessary international aspects, the conclusion can only be that there was a need for a global transport policy of the Community.

As mentioned, such a policy is based on the free movement of goods, the freedom to provide services and the right of establishment, while also taking into account other policies such as social policy.[12] The object remains to provide the carriers with the greatest possible choice while at the same time harmonising technical characteristics.[13]

Application of competition rules to transport: this subject was examined in some detail in the chapter on Competition, with special reference to maritime, air and rail transport. It was also pointed out that transport, like agriculture, is subject to specific competition rules,[14] which differ from those applying to other sectors. Mention must also be made of the application of the rules on State aid.[15] The Treaty provides that they are compatible with the Treaty if they meet the needs of co-ordination of transport or if they represent reimbursement for the discharge of certain obligations inherent in the concept of a public service.[16]

As mentioned above, the Treaty entrusts the Community institutions to lay down common rules applicable to international

---

[10] See under Economic and Social Cohesion.

[11] Art. 155(1) third indent (ex 129c(1)) E.C.

[12] See, for instance, Reg. 3820/85 on the harmonisation of certain social legislation relating to road transport [1968] J.O. L370/1 and Reg. 3821/85 on recording equipment in road transport [1985] O.J. L370/8, last amended Reg. 1056/97 [1994] O.J. L154/21.

[13] A large number of directives were adopted relating, for instance, to the type-approval of motor vehicles and their trailers [1970] O.J. L42/1.

[14] See Reg. 1017/68, above. See also Decision on the harmonisation of certain provisions affecting competition in transport by rail, road and inland waterway [1968] J.O. L175/1.

[15] Reg. 1107/70 on the granting of aids for transport by rail, road and internal waterway [1970] O.J. L130/1.

[16] Art. 73 (ex 77) E.C. See Reg. 1191/69 on action by Member States concerning the obligations inherent in the concept of a public service in transport by rail, road and inland waterway [1969] J.O. 156/1; last amended by Reg. 1893/91 [1991] O.J. L169/1.

transport, conditions for market access, measures to improve transport safety and any other appropriate provision.[17] For clarity sake the principal applicable provisions will be examined successively for the various modes of transport.

Road transport

A distinction can be made between transport of passengers and that of goods. For the former, the Community signed the Agreement on the International Carriage of Passengers by Road by means of Occasional Coach and Bus Services (ASOR).[18] The Agreement provides for harmonised liberalisation measures and simplified inspection measures by introducing a single document. Common rules were established for international transport of goods by road for hire or reward.[19] The right of non-resident carriers operating national road passenger transport services within a Member State is also provided for.[20] Where goods are concerned, market access is provided for by a basic Council regulation,[21] while various regulations concern the right of non-resident carriers with regard to road haulage services within a Member State.[22]

For both road haulage and passenger transport, the Council laid down the conditions for admission to the occupation, the mutual recognition of diplomas in order to facilitate freedom of establishment.[23] And rules regarding transport prices and terms. With regard to the latter the Treaty explicitly provides that "discrimination which takes the form of charging different rates and imposing different conditions for the carriage of the same goods over the same transport links on grounds of the country of origin or of destination

---

[17] Art. 71 (ex 75) E.C.

[18] [1982] O.J. L230/39. See also Reg. 56/83 concerning the implementation of the Agreement [1983] O.J. L10/1 and Reg. 684/92 on common rules for the international carriage of passengers by coach or bus [1992] O.J. L74/1, amended by Reg. 11/98 [1998] O.J. L4/1 and implemented as regards documents by Reg. 1839/92 [1992] O.J. L187/5.

[19] First Council Dir. 62/2005 [1962] J.O. 70/2005, last amended Reg. 881/92 [1992] O.J. L95/1. See also Dir. 76/914 on the minimum level of training for road transport drivers [1976] O.J. L357/36 and Dir. 84/647 on the use of vehicles hired without driver for the carriage of goods by road [1984] O.J. L335/72.

[20] Reg. 2454/92 [1992] O.J. L251/1 and Reg. 12/98 [1998] O.J. L4/10.

[21] Reg. 881/92 [1992] O.J. L95/1.

[22] Reg. 3118/93 laying down the conditions under which non-resident carriers may operate road haulage services within a Member State [1993] O.J. L279/1, implemented by Reg. 792/94 [1994] O.J. L92/13 and Reg. 3315/94 [1994] O.J. L350/9. See also Reg. 98/12 [1998] O.J. L4/10.

[23] Dir. 96/26 [1996] O.J. L124/1.

of the goods in question must be abolished".[24] It is up to the Council to lay down the necessary rules for implementing this principle.[25] Other subjects such as insurance against liability in respect of the use of motor vehicles,[26] the installation and use of speed limitation devices for certain categories of motor vehicles,[27] recording equipment in road transport[28] or, social harmonisation in road freight transport in the Internal Market[29] and social conditions[30] are the subject of several directives.

Special mention must be made, of course, of safety measures and technical conditions; where the latter are concerned, Community legislation is very detailed indeed. They concern, for instance, the use of safety belts,[31] safety glazing on motor vehicles and their trailers,[32] the tread depth of tyres,[33] the external projections forward of the cab's rear panel of motor vehicles of category N (!),[34] driving licences,[35] etc. The list seems unending.[36]

The Community also adhered to the European Agreement concerning the work of crews of vehicles engaged in international road transport (AETR)[37] which was the object of a famous judgment establishing the international competence of the Community in a field where no specific powers are granted by the Treaty.[38]

Competition rules applicable to transport were briefly examined in the Chapter on Competition. Let it suffice to mention that

---

[24] Art. 75(1) (ex 79(1)) E.C.

[25] Reg. No. 11 concerning the abolition of discrimination in transport rates and conditions: [1960] J.O. 52/1121 and Reg. 4058/89 on the fixing of rates for the carriage of goods by road between Member States [1989] O.J. L390/1. The Court accepted that road-haulage tariffs be approved and brought into force by the State: Case C–38/97 *Autotrasporti Librandi* [1998] E.C.R. I–5955.

[26] Dec. 93/43 [1993] O.J. L16/53.

[27] Dir. 92/6 [1992] O.J. L57/27.

[28] Reg. 3821/85 [1985] O.J. L370/8.

[29] Reg. 3820/85 [1985] O.J. L370/1.

[30] See, for instance, Dir. 96/26 on the admission to the occupation of road haulage operator; [1996] O.J. L124/1.

[31] Dir. 91/67 [1991] O.J. L373/26.

[32] Dir. 92/22 [1992] O.J. L129/11.

[33] Dir. 89/359 [1989] O.J. L226/4.

[34] Dir. 92/114 [1992] O.J. L409/17.

[35] Dir.91/439 [1991] O.J. L237/1, last amended [1997] O.J. L150/41.

[36] As mentioned already the complete list of all the Community acts in force can be found in the Directory of Community Legislation, published by the *Official Journal*, in Luxembourg.

[37] [1978] O.J. L95/1 and Reg. 2829/77 [1977] O.J. L334/11 bringing the Agreement into force.

[38] Case 22/70 *Commission v. Council* [1971] E.C.R. 263; [1971] C.M.L.R. 335.

Transport has its own competition rules[39] which apply to all forms of transport, except to maritime[40] and air transport, which have their own rules. There are no specific competition rules for road transport.

Rail transport

As is well known, rail transport requires extremely heavy expenditure on infrastructure, which, furthermore, is only used intermittently, with the consequence that all railway companies lose money[41] and, until recently, were all nationalised. While road and air transport, both for passengers and freight, increase their market share, railway transport has seen its own constantly reduced, not only in absolute, but also in relative terms. This, in turn, deprived it of the sorely needed income to modernise its infrastructure and rolling stock. Nevertheless, rail transport is needed, it is cleaner and therefore more environmental-friendly and probably safer.

How to explain this *decadence*? The railways themselves are, of course, partly to blame: inefficiency (except for a few remarkable achievements), corporatism, lack of co-operation with other railway companies[42] and conservatism. The real cause, however, is their monopoly position; in other words, there is no competition and therefore closed-off and protected markets. This can only partly be explained by the obligations of public service[43] generally imposed on the railways by the national governments. The Community is trying to put an end to this by providing, *inter alia*, for a right of access to all

---

[39] Reg. 1017/68 applying rules of competition to transport by rail, road and inland waterway [1968] J.O. 175/1. Reg. 1629/69 on the form, content and other details of complaints [1969] J.O. L209/1, Reg. 1630/69 on the hearings [1969] J.O. L209/11 and Reg. 2988/74 concerning limitation periods [1974] O.J. L319/1.

[40] Reg. 4056/86 laying down detailed rules for the application of Articles 85 (now 81) and 86 (now 82) E.C. to maritime transport [1986] O.J. L378/4.

[41] Reg. 1192 on common rules for the normalisation of the accounts of railways undertakings.

[42] Council resolution on co-operation between railway undertakings [1971] O.J. C5/1; presently there exist, save a few exceptions, no "international" trains; indeed, when crossing a border, a train acquires the nationality of the host country and is submitted to all the rules and regulations applying to "national" trains.

[43] Reg. 1191/69 on action by Member States concerning the obligations inherent in the concept of public service in the transport by rail, road and inland waterway [1969] O.J. L156/1, amended [1993] O.J. L169/1. See also Art. 73 (ex 77) E.C., which refers to the discharge of certain obligations inherent in the concept of public service.

infrastructures by third parties[44] and the creation of a high-speed rail network[45] and freight transport "freeways" across the Community.

Safety does, of course, also play an important role, for instance a general licensing system for railway undertakings was set up[46] and rules were laid down regarding the transport of dangerous goods by rail.[47] So does "combined" transport, which the Community tries to encourage and regulate.[48]

Inland waterway transport

Europe is known for its canals and natural waterways used for transport not only of goods but also of passengers. The Community legislation in this field is particularly extensive, but of interest to only a small group of people. No further mention will therefore be made here of the rules applying to this mode of transport. As already mentioned, the *Official Journal Repertory of Community Legislation in force*, contains most of the needed information.[49]

Air transport

As indicated air and maritime transport were not, at first, included under the provisions of the Treaty Chapter on Transport,[50] although the other Treaty provisions were, from the beginning applicable. However, a Court decision was needed to clarify this fact.[51] Air

---

[44] Reg. 91/440 on the development of the Community's railways [1991] O.J. L237/25; Art. 10 provides for a right of access for certain categories of users. See also Dir. 95/19 on the allocation of railway infrastructure and the charging of infrastructure fees [1995] O.J. L143/75

[45] Council resolution on the development of a European high-speed rail network [1991] O.J. C33/1.

[46] Dir. 95/18 [1995] O.J. L143/70.

[47] Dir. 96/49 on the approximation of the laws of the Member States with regard to the transport of dangerous goods by rail [1996] O.J. L235/25, amended O.J. L235/45.

[48] Dir. 92/106 on the establishment of common rules for certain types of combined transport of goods between Member States [1992] O.J. L368/38 and Council Resolution on the development of rail transport and combined transport O.J. C169/1.

[49] Office for Official Publications of the European Communities, L2985 Luxembourg.

[50] Art. 80 (ex 84) E.C.

[51] The Court based its decision on the very first words of the Title on Transport: "The objectives of this Treaty shall be pursued . . .". When a reference is made to those objectives, "it means the provisions of Articles 2 and 3" and since the fundamental provisions applicable to the whole complex of economic activities are of prime

transport, although in full expansion, suffers from the same draw-back as rail transport, namely its monopoly position, and therefore a protected national market. Indeed, some competition from foreign carriers had to be accepted on the international routes, but for a long time there were no competing national ones. This, however, has changed to a certain degree, at least in the larger Member States. The national airlines, the so-called "Flag Carriers" desperately fought to keep foreign airlines from providing air service within their territory, *i.e.* from flying passengers from one city to another within the same country. A first step was taken by opening intra-Community routes.[52]

It was only in 1987 that the Council laid down the procedure for the application of the rules on competition to undertakings in the air transport sector.[53] This was followed by various other regulations: on exemption by category for agreements and concerted practices,[54] *idem* for agreements concerning joint planning and coordination of schedules, joint operations, consultations on passenger and cargo tariffs, on scheduled air services and slot allocation,[55] agreements between undertakings relating to computerised reservation systems,[56] access to the groundhandling market at Community airports,[57] code of conduct for computerised reservation systems,[58] operation of air cargo services between Member States,[59] common rules for the allocation of slots at Community airports,[60] fares and rates for air services,[61] the limitation of noise emission[62] and, licensing of air carriers.[63]

Safety, of course, plays a very important role and several

importance for the attainment of those objectives, the object of the rules relating to the common transport policy, far from involving a departure from those fundamental rules, is to implement and complement them by means of common action: Case 167/73 *Commission v. France* [1974] E.C.R. 359, 24–25; [1974] 2 C.M.L.R. 216.

[52] Reg. 2343/90 on access for air carriers to scheduled intra-Community air service routes and on sharing of passenger capacity between air carriers on scheduled air services between Member States [1990] O.J. L217/8.

[53] Reg. 3975/87 [1987] O.J. L374/1, amended O.J. L240/18.

[54] Reg. 3976/87 [1987] O.J. L374/9, amended [1992] O.J. L240/19; Reg. 4261/88 [1988] O.J. L376/10, amended [1993] O.J. L336/1.

[55] Reg. 1617/93 [1993] O.J. L155/18, amended [1996] O.J. L190/11.

[56] Reg. 3652/93 [1993] O.J. L333/37; no longer applicable since June 30, 1998.

[57] Dir. 96/67 [1996] O.J. L272/36.

[58] Reg. 2299/89 [1989] O.J. L220/1, amended [1993] O.J. L278/1.

[59] Reg. 294/91 [1991] O.J. L36/1.

[60] Reg. 95/93 [1995] O.J. L14/1.

[61] Reg. 2409/92; [1992] O.J. L240/15.

[62] Reg. 629/89 [1989] O.J. L363/27.

[63] Reg. 2407/92 [1992] O.J. L240/1.

regulations and directives were adopted[64] including one on air carrier liability in the event of accidents. This regulation[65] goes far beyond the liability provided in the Warsaw Convention of 1929: 100,000 special drawing rights; the airline cannot excuse itself by showing there was no fault on its part (the only excuse concerns fault of the passenger); an advance payment of the euro equivalent of 15,000 special drawing rights must be paid not later than 15 days after the identity of the victim has been established.

Mention must also be made of the Agreement between the E.C. and the USA concerning the application of the "GATT Agreement on Trade in Civil Aircraft" to trade in large civil aircraft.[66] The purpose was to put an end to the financial support granted on both sides of the Atlantic to the constructors of large aircrafts (*Boeing v. Airbus*).

Maritime transport

This mode of transport has, by definition, an international aspect; there is no question, therefore, of treating this field on a purely Community basis. This applies, in the first place, to the rules of competition. Special rules had therefore to be adopted; this was done in 1986 by a Council Regulation laying down detailed rules for the application of articles 85 (now 81) and 86 (now 82) of the Treaty to maritime transport[67] and a regulation on unfair pricing practices in maritime transport.[68] The Commission adopted the usual regulation on communications, complaints, applications and hearings.[69]

Since liner shipping companies (consortia) play an important role in shipping, an exemption for certain categories of agreements was also provided for.[70] The same applies to liner Conferences: the Council adopted a regulation on the ratification by the Member States of the United Nations Convention on a Code of Conduct of Liner Conferences.[71]

---

[64] See, for instance, Dir. 93/65 on the definition and use of compatible technical specifications for the procurement of air-traffic-management equipment and systems [1993] O.J. L187/52, amended [1997] O.J. L95/16.

[65] Reg. 2027/97 [1997] O.J. L282/1.

[66] [1992] O.J. L301/32.

[67] Reg. 4056/86 [1986] O.J. L378/4.

[68] Reg. 4057/86 [1986] O.J. L378/14.

[69] Reg. 4260/88 [1988] O.J. L376/1, amended [1993] O.J. L336/1.

[70] Reg. 479/92 [1992] O.J. L55/3.

[71] Reg. 954/79 [1979] O.J. L121/1. See Commission Decision imposing fines on the Trans-Atlantic Conference Agreement for abuse of a dominant position: press release IP(98)811, of September 16, 1998.

Market access also played an important role, both within the Community: freedom to provide services to maritime transport within Member States (maritime cabotage)[72] and outside: the Council provided for co-ordinated action to safeguard free access to cargoes in ocean trades.[73]

Understandably, safety at sea was a major preoccupation. The Council recommended the ratification of several international conventions concerning safety at sea,[74] and laid down minimum requirements for vessels bound for or leaving Community ports and carrying dangerous or polluted goods.[75] Following several catastrophic accidents with ferries, rules were adopted on the safety management of roll-on/roll-off passenger ferries,[76] the setting up of a harmonised safety regime for fishing vessels of 24 meters in length or over,[77] on safety rules and standards for passenger ships,[78] on the minimum safety and health requirements for improved medical treatment on board vessels,[79] and concerning enforcement, in respect of shipping using Community ports and sailing in the waters under the jurisdiction of the Member States, of international standards for ship safety, pollution prevention and shipboard living and working conditions.[80]

Conclusion with regard to a common transport policy

As was seen, transport in the Community is the subject of an impressive array of rules and regulations. The question is, however, whether this constitutes a common policy. As was seen above, important steps were taken to liberalise transport within the

[72] Reg. 3577/92 [1992] O.J. L364/7.

[73] Reg. 4058/86 [1986] O.J. L378/21.

[74] Convention on safety in shipping [1978] O.J. L194/17; Convention on standards of training, certification and watch-keeping for sea-farers [1979] O.J. L33/31; Convention for safe containers [1979] O.J. L125/18 and the Convention for the safety of fishing vessels O.J. L259/29; Convention for the safety of life at sea and the Convention for the prevention of pollution from ships [1993] O.J. L194/5; Convention on maritime Search and Rescue (SAR) [1983] O.J. L237/34. It will be noticed that all those Council Recommendations were published in the (Legislation) series of the *Official Journal*.

[75] Dir. 93/75 [1993] O.J. L 247/19, amended [1997] O.J. L158/40.

[76] Reg. 3051/95 [1995] O.J. L320/14, amended [1998] O.J. L19/35.

[77] Dir. 97/70 [1997] O.J. L34/1.

[78] Dir. 98/18 [1998] O.J. L144/1.

[79] Dir. 92/29 [1992] O.J. L113/19.

[80] Dir. 95/21 [1995] O.J. L157/1, amended [1998] O.J. L133/19.

Community, even cabotage is now possible; another important step was the setting up by the E.U. Treaty of the Trans-European Networks, which should help to integrate the national networks into a single system. This aim has been practically achieved with regard to the road system, but is still completely lacking as far as rail transport is concerned. Nevertheless, as is shown by the Common Transport Policy Action Programme for 1995–2000,[81] there now exists a global approach to the various sectors of transport. The objective remains the establishment and functioning of an Internal Transport Market, which can only be attained through liberalisation, integration and harmonisation; it is to be seen whether, not only the Member States but also, and maybe in the first place, the undertakings presently enjoying monopoly positions are ready to accept that this is also in their own interest. Much has been achieved, much remains to be done.

Further Reading

European Commission, "The Common Transport Policy action programme 1995–2000" Communication, COM (95) 302.

European Commission, "High Level Group on Transport Infrastructure Charging" final report, 1998.

Commission Communication, "The Common Transport Policy. Sustainable mobility: perspectives for the future" COM (98) 716.

[81] COM (95) 302.

Chapter Twenty-four
Economic and Monetary Union (Policy)

The most tangible aspect of the Economic and Monetary Union (EMU) for the European citizen is, of course, the introduction of the single currency, now called the "EURO". The reader will notice that the Treaty still refers to the "ECU", notwithstanding the fact that at the meeting of the European Council in Madrid on December 15 and 16, 1995, the Governments of the 15 Member States agreed on a definitive "interpretation" of the relevant Treaty provisions and that "the name given to the European currency shall be the 'euro' ".[1] The introduction of the euro on January 1, 1999, to be substituted[2] for the national currencies of the Member States participating in this aspect of EMU,[3] constitutes a major event not only from an economic and monetary point of view, but foremost from the point of view of European integration. Indeed, a corollary of the introduction of the euro, is the setting up of the European Central Bank (ECB) to which the Member States have surrendered, as shall be seen, the definition of their monetary policies. It can be said, without exaggeration, that through this extraordinary transfer of sovereignty, the process of European integration has reached the point of no return. None of the preceding achievements, including the internal market, were secure in the absence of a single currency. Politically speaking, it was "the" decisive step on the way to European Union. At the risk of incurring the disfavour of some readers, it is submitted that this fact alone stands out as the most important decision taken by and for Europe since the end of World War II.

The introduction of the euro was the result of a rather short—10

---

[1] Reg. 1103/97 [1997] O.J. L162/1 and Case T-207/97 *Berthu v. Council* [1998] E.C.R. II-12.03. See also Council Reg. 974/98 on the introduction of the euro [1998] O.J. L139/1.

[2] National currencies will cease to exist on June 30, 2002.

[3] As of December 31, 1998, those are all the Member States except Denmark, Greece, Sweden and the U.K.

years—but complex procedure with economic, monetary and institutional aspects. Those shall be briefly described in the following sections.

Title VII of the Treaty, on "Economic and Monetary Policy" is divided into four chapters: "Economic policy", "Monetary policy", "Institutional provisions" and "Transitional provisions". It is important to note that Economic and Monetary Policy is not mentioned among the "activities of the Community",[4] but is provided for in an Article inserted into the E.C. Treaty by the Treaty on European Union and which refers to the activities "of the Member States and the Community". This clearly indicates that the policy in question is not a "Community" policy, but a "shared" one. Indeed it is based both on the close co-ordination of the Member States' economic policies and on the Community's internal market. It is also based on common objectives, which are not further defined.[5]

One thing is clear, however, namely that the economic policy envisaged, must be conducted "in accordance with the principle of an open market economy with free competition".[6] At least the basic economic philosophy is here unequivocally affirmed, and complemented in Title VII, with the "favouring of an efficient allocation of resources".

As for the monetary policy, the Treaty summarises it as including the irrevocable fixing of exchange rates[7] leading to the introduction of a single currency, and the definition and conduct of a single monetary policy and exchange rate policy. It being understood that the primary objective of both is to maintain price stability and to support the general economic policies in the Community. Here again the principle of an open market economy with free competition is asserted.[8]

And finally, the Treaty adds that this economic and monetary policy must entail compliance with the following guiding principles: stable prices, sound public finances and monetary conditions, and a

---

[4] Art. 3 (ex 3) E.C.

[5] Art. 99(2) (ex 103(2)) E.C. provides that on the basis of a conclusion of the European Council, the Council shall adopt a recommendation setting out broad guidelines of the economic policies of the Member States and of the Community.

[6] Art. 4(1) (ex 3a(1)) E.C.

[7] See Reg. 2866/98 of December 31, 1998 on the conversion rates between the euro and the currencies of the Member States adopting the euro [1998] O.J. L359/1.

[8] *ibid.* at 2.

sustainable balance of payments.[9] Those principles correspond more or less to the famous four criteria[10] which must be fulfilled by the Member States "for the adoption of a single currency".[11]

The above constitutes, in a nutshell, the economic and monetary policy of the Community; its various aspects will, as already mentioned, be examined in some more detail below.

1. Economic Policy[12]

Although no mention is made of social policy in the context of the economic and monetary policy, it is quite obvious that the social aspects cannot be dissociated from neither policies, even if this is more obvious with regard to economic policies as such.

The chapter on economic policy covers the following subjects: the conduct of economic policies by the Member States in the context of the broad guidelines set out by the Council, the monitoring of economic developments in each of the Member States by the Council, Community financial assistance to Member States in difficulties,[13] the prohibition of credit facilities[14] and of privileged access to financial institutions,[15] mutual financial guarantees for the joint execution of a specific project[16] and the avoidance of excessive government deficits. The first and the last items are, from an economic policy point of view, by far the most important.

Co-ordination of the economic policies of the Member States.[17] Member States must conduct their economic policies in the context of "broad guidelines". These shall be drafted by the Council on a recommendation from the Commission and submitted to the European Council. The latter discusses a "conclusion" on the guidelines, after which the Council shall adopt a recommendation setting them out.[18] The implementation of the guidelines forms the object of a "multilateral surveillance" by the Council.

---

[9] *ibid.* at 3.
[10] Art. 121(1) (ex 109j) E.C.
[11] *ibid.* at 4.
[12] Arts 98 (ex 102a) to 104 (ex 104c) E.C.
[13] Art. 100 (ex 103a) E.C.
[14] Art. 101 (ex 104) E.C.
[15] Art. 102 (ex 104a) E.C.
[16] Art. 103 (ex 104b) E.C.
[17] Art. 99 (ex 103) E.C.
[18] See, for instance, Council Recommendation of July 6, 1998 on the broad guidelines [1998] O.J. L200/34.

It is worthwhile noting here that none of the binding Community acts provided for in the Treaty, *i.e.* regulations, directives and decisions, are mentioned here; the terms "report" and "conclusion", in such a context, are novelties in the text of the Treaty. Furthermore, the setting out of broad guidelines for the economic policies of the Member States via a non-binding "recommendation" seems to minimise their importance. This is surprising since great importance is attached to the consistency between the economic policies of the Member States and those guidelines and since the Council may adopt detailed rules for the multilateral surveillance, in accordance with the "cooperation procedure" provided in the Treaty for binding acts.[19]

Excessive government deficits.[20] The Treaty introduces the notion of "budgetary discipline" in order to avoid excessive government deficits.[21] Two criteria are provided which allow the Commission to monitor the development of the budgetary situation and the stock of government debt. The ratio of deficit, on the one hand, and of the government debt, on the other, to gross domestic product may not exceed a reference value specified in the Protocol on the excessive deficit procedure annexed to the Treaty.[22]

In case those criteria are not observed by a Member State, the Commission prepares a report which is submitted to the Monetary Committee[23] which formulates an opinion thereon. The Commission may also address an opinion to the Council. The latter may, after having considered the observations of the Member State concerned, decide that an excessive deficit does indeed exist.[24] The Council must then make recommendations to the Member State. If the latter fails to put the recommendations into practice, the Council may decide to give notice to that Member State "to take, within a specified time limit, measures for the deficit reduction".[25] And, although failure by the Member State in question to abide by the

---

[19] Art. 252 (ex 189c) E.C.

[20] Art. 104 (ex 104c) E.C.

[21] The obligation to avoid excessive government deficits applied from the beginning of the third stage: Art. 116(3) (ex 109e(3)) E.C.

[22] The ratios are respectively three and 60 per cent. This Protocol shall be replaced by "appropriate provisions" adopted by the Council, acting unanimously on a proposal from the Commission and after consulting the Parliament and the ECB: Art. 104(14) E.C.

[23] Art 114 (ex 109c) E.C.

[24] See for instance Council Decision of June 30, 1997 abrogating the Decision on the existence of an excessive deficit in The Netherlands [1997] O.J. L177/23.

[25] Art. 104(9) (ex 104c(9)) E.C.

notice does not constitute a failure "to fulfil an obligation under this Treaty"[26] which can be brought before the Court of Justice, the Treaty provides for some measures which can be taken against the recalcitrant Member State.

These measures are the following[27]:

- require the Member State to publish additional information before issuing bonds and securities;
- invite the EIB to reconsider its lending policy towards said State;
- require a non-interest-bearing deposit with the Community, and/or
- impose fines.

All decisions are taken on a recommendation from the Commission, by a majority of two-thirds of the votes of the members, weighted as for normal Council decisions.

Prohibition of "overdraft facilities" and "privileged access to financial institutions".[28] Overdraft facilities with the Central Banks and privileged access to financial institutions for governments, regional, local or other public authorities have always been a simple means to finance deficits. They had therefore to be abolished in order to help eliminate those deficits and their recurrence.

2. Monetary Policy[29]

Expanding on the task description of the European System of Central Banks (ESCB) one can say that the primary objective of the Community monetary policies is to maintain price stability. In order to make this possible a vast programme for achieving economic and monetary union, of which a part was just described, was devised. It had to be implemented in three stages.

The *first stage* started on July 1, 1990 and ended on December 31, 1993. It consisted essentially in an attempt at greater convergence of the national economies[30] and the strengthening of the co-operation between the central banks. During that stage, all restrictions on the

[26] Art. 104(10) (ex 104c(10)) E.C.
[27] Art. 104(11) (ex 104c(11)) E.C.
[28] Arts 101 (ex 104) and 102 (ex 104a) E.C.
[29] Arts 105 to 111 (ex 106 to 109) E.C.
[30] Council Dec. 90/141 on the attainment of progressive convergence of economic policies and performance during stage one of economic and monetary union [1990] O.J. L78/23.

free movement of capital and payments between Member States and between Member States and third countries were abolished and so were the overdraft facilities and the privileged access to financial institutions, mentioned above.[31] Furthermore, the Council was to assess the progress made with regard to economic and monetary convergence, in particular with regard to price stability and sound public finances, and progress made with regard to Community law concerning the internal market.[32] Governments also had to avoid excessive deficits and start the process leading to the independence of their central bank.[33]

The *second stage* for achieving economic and monetary union started on January 1, 1994.[34] On that date the *European Monetary Institute* (EMI) was established (in Frankfurt) and took up its duties. It was replaced, five years later, by the *European Central Bank* (ECB) at the start of the third stage. Its task was to prepare the third stage; details can be found in the corresponding Treaty provisions.[35] In particular it should be noted that the EMI had to specify the regulatory, organisational and logistical framework for the European System of Central Banks (ESCB). The latter's task is to define and implement the monetary policy of the Community.[36]

The most important decision to be taken during the second stage was which Member States could participate in the single currency system. Since no other date had been set for the beginning of the third stage, the latter started on January 1, 1999, and the Council, meeting in the composition of the Heads of State or Government had to confirm, before July 1, 1998, which Member States fulfil the necessary conditions for the adoption of the single currency and whether a majority of the Member States fulfil the necessary conditions for the adoption of a single currency.[37] Although this is now history, it is of interest to note that this decision was taken on the basis of a report from the Commission and the EMI on, among other things, the achievement of a high degree of sustainable convergence. The latter was judged by reference to the fulfilment by each Member State of four criteria, *i.e.* inflation, budgetary deficit, exchange-rate fluctuations within the European Monetary System

[31] Art. 116(2) (ex 109e(2)) E.C.
[32] *ibid.*
[33] Art. 108 (ex 107) E.C.
[34] Art. 116(1) (ex 109e(1)) E.C.
[35] Mainly Arts 117 (ex 109f) and 121 (ex 109j) E.C.
[36] Art. 105(2) (ex 105(2)) E.C.
[37] Art. 121(4) (ex 109j(4)) E.C, which refers to paras 1 and 2.

and long term interest-rate levels. Those criteria were further developed in a Protocol annexed to the Treaty.[38]

The decision was taken by the Heads of State and Government on May 1, 1998,[39] and as indicated above, all the Member States, except Denmark, Greece, Sweden and the U.K., were found to fulfil the necessary conditions for the adoption of a single currency. Denmark, Greece and Sweden are "Member States with a derogation", which assume certain obligations and, will as a matter of course, integrate the single currency system, as soon as their economic policies allow.[40]

The *third stage* started on January 1, 1999. From that date on the value of the euro was irrevocably fixed, but the composition of the euro basket was not changed. On that date, the Member States participating in the single currency did no longer implement their own monetary policy. This role was transferred to the *European System of Central Banks* (ESCB). The latter is composed of the ECB[41] and of the national central banks, including those of the Member States which do not participate in the single currency. The ESCB has no legal personality (only the ECB has[42]) and its Statute is the object of a Protocol.[43] Its primary objective is to maintain price stability and to support the general economic policies in the Community. Its basic tasks are described as follows:

- to define and implement the monetary policy of the Community;
- to conduct foreign exchange operations;
- to hold and manage the official foreign reserves of the Member States[44];
- to promote the smooth operation of payments systems.

On that date also financial transactions could be carried out in euros; anyone could open a bank account in that currency. However, the euro did not become legal tender for current transactions. This will have to wait for the issuing of euro banknotes and coins.

The treaty confers upon the ECB the "exclusive right to authorise the issue of banknotes within the Community". Both the ECB and the central banks may issue such notes. Those banknotes are the "only such notes to have the status of legal tender within the Community.[45]

---

[38] Protocol No. 21 (ex No. 6) on the convergence criteria referred to in Article 121 (ex 109j) E.C.

[39] Dec. 98/317 [1998] O.J. L139/30.

[40] See Art. 122 (ex 109k) E.C.

[41] See below under Institutional provisions.

[42] Art. 107 (ex 106) E.C.

[43] Protocol No. 18, which contains also the Statute of the ECB.

[44] Art. 105(3) (ex 105(3)) E.C. allows holding and management by the Member States of foreign-exchange working balances.

[45] Art. 106 (ex 105a) E.C.

With regard to coins, the Treaty provides that they may be issued by the Member States, subject to approval by the ECB of the volume of the issue. As indicated above, measures were adopted by the Council to harmonise the denominations and technical specifications of all coins intended for circulation to the extent necessary to permit their smooth circulation within the Community.[46]

These coins and banknotes will not be issued until January 1, 2002; on that date the citizens of the participating Member States will carry two different currencies: the euro and their national currency. They will use both of them for a period of six months: until June 30, 2002 at midnight. Until then, both currencies will be legal tender at the same time but after that date only the euro will be accepted as current payment.

The Treaty also provides that the Council may conclude formal agreements on an exchange-rate system for the euro in relation with non-Community currencies.[47]

3. Institutional Provisions

Although not classified under this heading in the Treaty, the most interesting institutional provision is the one conferring upon the ECB, the power to make regulations,[48] take decisions, and make recommendations and deliver opinions. The fact that the ECB has the power to make regulations which have general application and are binding in their entirety and directly applicable in all Member States,[49] *de facto* confers upon it the status of an institution of the Community. Like all binding acts of the institutions, the regulations and decisions of the ECB must be reasoned, published in the *Official Journal of the European Communities*,[50] they must be made available to the citizens of the Union and when they impose a pecuniary obligation[51] on persons other than States, they shall be enforceable. The binding acts of the ECB are also submitted to the control of legality by the European courts.[52]

[46] Reg. 975/98 [1998] O.J. L139/6.

[47] Art 111 (ex 109) E.C.

[48] See, for instance, Reg. 2818/98 of the ECG on the application of minimum reserves and Reg. 2819/98 concerning the consolidated balance sheet of the monetary financial institutions sector [1998] O.J. L356/1 and 7.

[49] See Art. 249 (ex 189) E.C., which contains an identical definition of a regulation.

[50] This is provided in Art. 254 (ex 191) E.C. to which Art. 110 (ex108a) refers; it is therefore surprising to read that the ECB "may decide to publish its regulations and decisions".

[51] The ECB may be entitled by the Council to impose fines or periodic penalty payments on undertakings for failure to comply with obligations under its regulations and decisions: Art. 110(3) (ex 108a(3)) E.C.

[52] Art. 230 (ex 173) E.C.

The composition of the ECB was described in the chapter on Institutions and other Bodies of the Community.

An *Economic and Financial Committee* was set up, *inter alia*, to keep under review the economic and financial situation of the Member States.[53]

4. Transitional Provisions

Most of the transitional provisions provided for under this title have been incorporated in the previous sections on the three stages. They concerned, *inter alia*, the EMI which no longer exists.

5. Stability and Growth Pact[54]

This consists of a Resolution and two Council Regulations[55] concerned with safeguarding sound Government finances as a means to strengthening the price stability and for strong sustainable growth conducive to employment creation. It is also considered necessary that national budgetary policies support stability oriented monetary policies. According to the Resolution, adherence to the objective of sound budgetary positions close to balance or in surplus will allow all Member States to deal with normal cyclical fluctuations while keeping the government deficit within the reference value of three per cent of GDP.

The Resolution contains firm political guidelines issued to the Member States, the Council and the Commission, in order to implement the Growth and Stability pact.[56]

Further Reading

Lawrence Gormley and Jacob De Haan, "The Democratic Deficit of the European Central Bank": 21 (1996) E.L.Rev. 95

---

[53] Art. 114(2) (ex 109c) E.C. See Dec. 98/743 on the detailed provisions concerning the composition of the Economic and Financial Committee [1998] O.J. L358/109.

[54] Resolution of the European Council on the Stability and Growth Pact, Amsterdam June 17, 1997 [1997] O.J. C236/1.

[55] Reg. 1466/97 on the strengthening of the surveillance of budgetary positions and the surveillance and co-ordination of economic policies [1997] O.J. L209/1, and Reg. 1467/97 on speeding up and clarifying the implementation of excessive deficit procedure [1997] O.J. L209/6.

[56] See point (2) of Reg. 1466/97: n. 55 above.

M. Obstfeld "EMU: ready or not?" (University of California, Department of Economics, Berkeley, California, 1998).

O. Fanjul, "What will EMU add up to?" (Philip Morris Institute for Public Policy Research, Brussels, 1998).

D. Currie, "Will the Euro work? The ins and outs of EMU" (Economist Intelligence Unit, London, 1998).

Tim Jones, "Euro Essentials A Pocket Guide to the Single Currency" (European Voice and Citibank, The Economist Group, 1998).

Chapter Twenty-five
Social Policy

Under this heading will be examined the Social Provisions, the European Social Fund, Education, Vocational Training and Youth and also, although it is not mentioned under the same heading in the Treaty, Employment. The latter was added by the Treaty of Amsterdam.

The Community has been accused of giving absolute priority to the economic and monetary aspects of European integration, forgetting the social aspects, or even at their cost. It suffices, however, to look at the first of the European Treaties establishing the European Coal and Steel Community to realise that, from the beginning, the social preoccupations were present.[1] As for the European Economic Community, it not only contained a Title III on Social Policy with social provisions and a Social Fund, but the free movement of workers was considered as requiring such measures in the field of social security. Similarly, the Euratom Treaty contains several provisions on the health and safety of workers.[2] However, only the social provisions of the E.C. Treaty shall be examined here.

Social policy remains largely within the competence of the Member States, with the Community supporting and complementing their activities in given fields.[3] Furthermore, both are to take implementing measures which take account of the diverse forms of national practices, in particular in the field of contractual relations. The Treaty also refers to the "need to maintain the competitiveness of the Community economy"; maybe this is a hidden way of reminding the workers and their organisations of the fact that, besides all the rights mentioned in the various charters (see hereunder), workers also have "duties" with regard, for instance, to productivity and wage-restraint.

[1] ECSC, Title Three "economic and social provisions" Art. 46(5) which refers to "improving the working conditions and living standards for workers".
[2] EAEC, Title Two, Chapter Three.
[3] Art. 137(1) (ex 118) E.C.

1. Social Provisions

The social provisions[4] start with a reference to the European Social Charter of 1961 and the 1989 Community Charter of the Fundamental Social Rights of Workers (Social Charter). The former was signed at Turin in 1962 within the framework of the Council of Europe. It provides for 19 "rights" such as the right to work, to just conditions of work, to safe and healthy working conditions, to fair remuneration, to organise, to bargain collectively, to social security, to medical assistance, etc. As for the Social Charter, it was adopted at the Strasbourg European Council, on December 8 and 9, 1989. Although referred to in many Community publications, it was never published officially; only the Agreement on social policy between the Member States with the exception of the U.K. was annexed to the E.U. Treaty.[5] The purpose of that agreement is to implement the 1989 Social Charter. This led to the adoption of several directives, which were later accepted by the U.K., which also adhered to the Charter and the Agreement with the entry into force of the Amsterdam Treaty.

Most of the rights provided for in the Charter and the Agreement are now to be found in the social provisions of the Treaty. They refer to the promotion of employment, improved living and working conditions, proper social protection, dialogue between management and labour, the development of human resources with a view of lasting high employment and the combating of exclusion.

It is interesting to note that the Community and the Member States included a *credo* in the Treaty, (something that is normally done in the recitals) by affirming that they "believe" that the implementation of the objectives outlined above will ensue, *inter alia*, "from the functioning of the common market", which will favour the harmonisation of the social systems.[6] The Treaty procedures and the approximation of laws are other means to achieve the objectives set out in this chapter.

The "social provisions" refer to four different subjects: firstly, the Community is to support and complement the activities of the Member States in various fields; secondly, the Commission has the task of promoting the consultation of management and labour, thirdly, the Commission must encourage co-operation between the

---

[4] Art. 136 (ex 117) E.C.

[5] Former Protocol 14 E.C.

[6] It will be remembered that with regard to the free movement of workers and self-employed persons, a harmonisation of the social security systems was not envisaged.

Member States in given fields, and finally, Member States must ensure the principle of equal pay for male and female workers.

(1) Community Action Supporting and Complementing Member States' Activities

In the social field also, one of the first tasks of the Community is to "support and complement" the activities of the Member States by means of directives setting out minimum requirements, in the following fields:

- improvement in particular of the working environment to protect worker's health and safety; with regard to the latter, several directives on the protection of workers from certain risks at work[7] were adopted by the Council, and the Agency for Safety and Health at Work was set up[8];
- working conditions; the European Foundation for the improvement of living and working conditions[9] was created to help achieve this objective;
- the information and consultation of workers; the Council adopted a directive on the establishment of a European Works

---

[7] The basic Dir. 80/1107 concerns the protection of workers from the risks related to exposure to chemical, physical and biological agents [1980] O.J. L327/8, see [1998] O.J. L131/11. That Directive was implemented through the following "individual" directives: Dir. 82/605, exposure to metallic lead and its compounds [1982] O.J. L247/12; Dir. 83/477, exposure to asbestos [1983] O.J. L263/25, last amended [1998] O.J. L131/11; Dir. 86/188, exposure to noise [1986] O.J. L137/28, amended [1998] O.J. L131/11; Dir. 88/364, banning of certain specified agents and/or certain work activities [1988] O.J. L179/44; Dir. 89/654, concerning the minimum safety and health requirements for the workplace [1989] O.J. L393/1; Dir. 89/655, *id.* for the use of equipment [1989] O.J. L93/13, amended [1995] O.J. L355/28; *id.* for the use of protective equipment [1989] O.J. L393/18; Dir. 90/269, *id.* for the manual handling of loads where there is a risk of back injury [1990] O.J. L156/9; Dir. 90/270, *id.* for work with display screen equipment: O.J. L156/14; Dir. 92/57, *id.* at temporary or mobile construction sites [1992] O.J. L245/6; Dir. 90/394, risks related to exposure to carcinogens [1990] O.J. L196/1, amended [1997] O.J. L179/4; Dir. 90/679, *id.* biological agents [1990] O.J. L374/1, amended [1997] O.J. L335/17; Dir. 92/58, minimum requirements for the provisions of safety and/or health signs [1992] O.J. L245/23; Dir. 92/85, pregnant workers or who have recently given birth or are breastfeeding [1992] O.J. L348/1; Dir. 92/91, workers in the mineral-extracting industries through drilling [1992] O.J. L348/9; Dir. 92/104, workers in the surface and underground mineral-extracting industries [1992] O.J. L404/10; Dir. 93/103, work on board fishing vessels [1993] O.J. L307/1; Dir. 98/24, risk related to chemical agents [1998] O.J. L131/11.

[8] Established by Reg. 2062/94 [1994] O.J. L216/1.

[9] Reg. 1365/75 [1975] O.J. L139/1, last amended [1993] O.J. L181/13.

Council or a procedure for informing and consulting employees[10];

- the integration of people excluded from the labour market;
- equality between men and women with regard to the labour market opportunities and treatment at work[11]; (not to be confused with equal pay for male and female workers for equal work or work of equal value,[12] which shall be examined below).

In those areas the Council must act jointly with Parliament, according to the so-called co-decision procedure.[13] However, in some fields the Council must act alone, after consulting the Parliament, the ESC and the Committee of the Regions: on social security and social protection of workers (it will be remembered that in those fields the Member States are particularly jealous of their independence):

- protection of workers where their employment contract is terminated; several directives were adopted concerning, *inter alia*, collective redundancies,[14] safeguarding employees rights in the event of transfers of undertakings,[15] the protection of

[10] Dir. 94/45 on establishment of a European Works Council or a procedure in Community-scale undertakings and Community-scale groups of undertakings for the purpose of informing and consulting employees [1994] O.J. L254/64; extended to the U.K. by Dir. 97/74 [1997] O.J. L10/22.

[11] See, for instance, Dir. 76/207 on the implementation of the principle of equal treatment for men and women as regards access to employment, vocational training and promotion, and working conditions (the "equal treatment directive") [1976] O.J. L39/40, see Case C–180/95, *Draehmpaehl* [1997] E.C.R. I–2195; [1997] 3 C.M.L.R. 1107, and Case C–185/97, *Coote* [1998] E.C.R. I–5199. The Directive also applies after work relationship was terminated; Council Recommendation on the promotion of positive action for women [1984] O.J. L331/34; Council Dir. 86/613 on the application of the principle of equal treatment between men and women engaged in an activity, including agriculture, in a self-employed capacity, and on the protection of self-employed women during pregnancy and motherhood [1986] O.J. L359/56, Resolution on the promotion of equal opportunities for women [1986] O.J. C203/2, Council Recommendation on the balanced participation of women and men in the decision-making process, and Dir. 97/80 on the burden of proof in cases of discrimination based on sex [1998] O.J. L14/6, extended to the U.K. [1998] O.J. L205/66. This Directive applies to any kind of discrimination.

[12] Art. 141 (ex 119) E.C.

[13] Art. 249 (ex 189) E.C.

[14] Dir. 75/129 [1995] O.J. L48/29 and Dir. 98/59 [1998] O.J. L225/16. See Case C–449/93 *Rockfon* [1995] E.C.R. I–4291: definition of "establishment" company forming part of a group.

[15] Dir. 77/187 relating to the safeguarding of employee's rights in the event of transfers of undertakings, businesses or parts of businesses [1977] O.J. L61/26. See Case C–298/94 *Henke* [1996] E.C.R. I–4989; [1997] 1 C.M.L.R. 373, does not apply to

workers in the event of the insolvency of their employer,[16] and the obligation of the employer to notify an employee of the essential aspects of the contract or employment relationship by written declaration not later than two months after the commencement of employment.[17] A landmark judgment in this field is *Francovich*[18] where the Court held that a Member State is required to make good loss and damage caused to individuals by its failure to transpose a directive. Representation and collective defence of the interests of workers and employers, including co-determination; those provisions do not apply, however, to pay, the right of association, the right to strike or the right to impose lock-outs;

- conditions of employment for third-country nationals legally residing in Community territory;
- financial contribution for the promotion of employment and job creation, without prejudice to the provisions relating to the Social Fund.

(2) Consultation of Management and Labour

With regard to *Management and Labour*, the Treaty provides that a Member State may entrust them, at their joint request, with the

---

the transfer of administrative functions from a municipality to an administrative collectivity. Case C–305/94 *Rotsart de Hertaing* [1996] E.C.R. I–5927; [1997] 1 C.M.L.R. 329; the contracts of employment and the employment relationships existing on the date of the transfer of an undertaking, between the transferor and the workers employed in the undertaking transferred, are automatically transferred from the transferor to the transferee by the mere fact of the transfer of the undertaking, despite the contrary intention of the transferor or the transferee. The Directive does not apply in case of termination of a cleaning contract with an independent contractor: Case C–13/95 *Suzen* [1997] E.C.R. 1259; [1997] 1 C.M.L.R. 768; Case C–479/93, *Francovich* [1995] E.C.R. I–3843, gives a definition of insolvency under Dir. 80/987 employers who are subject to proceedings, involving their assets, to satisfy collectively the claims of creditors. Joined Cases C–171 and 172/94 *Merckx and Neuhuys* [1996] E.C.R. I–1255, concept of transfer; the criterion is whether the entity in question retains its economic identity, as indicated, *inter alia* by the fact that this operation is actually continued or resumed and Case C–319/94 *Dethier* [1998] E.C.R. I–1061, workers illegally made redundant by the transferor can turn to the transferee on the basis of Art. 4.1 of the Directive.

[16] Dir. 80/987 [1980] O.J. L283/23; Art. 4 has direct effect: Case C–235/95 *AGS Assedic* [1998] E.C.R. I–4531.

[17] Dir. 91/533 [1991] O.J. L288/32; see Joined Cases C–253 to 258/96 *Kampelmann et al.* [1997] E.C.R. I–6907: the burden of proving correctness of details notified must be determined by national law.

[18] Joined Cases C–6 and 9/90 *Francovich and Others* [1991] E.C.R. I–5357.

implementation of the above mentioned directives.[19] The Commission, on the other hand, has the task of promoting the consultation of management and labour, by doing just that, before submitting proposals in the social policy field, and following that, consulting them on the content of the envisaged proposals.[20] On that occasion management and labour may inform the Commission that they wish to initiate a dialogue at Community level, which may lead to contractual relations, including agreements. Implementation of such agreements can be done by a Council decision.[21]

It should also be noted that the above mentioned directives do not prevent any Member State from maintaining or introducing more stringent protective measures compatible with the Treaty. A similar provision exists in different other fields where the policy in question is the joint responsibility of the Member States and the Community, for instance "Environment"[22] and "Public Health"[23] protection.

(3) Encouraging co-operation between the Member States and facilitating co-ordination of their action

This is the task of the Commission and is to take place particularly in matters relating to:

- employment[24]; a Standing Committee on Employment in the European Communities was set up,[25] special measures of Community interest were introduced granting financial assistance[26];
- labour law and working conditions; various measures were taken concerning, for instance, the organisation of working

---

[19] Art. 137(4) (ex 118, which did not provide for this possibility) E.C.
[20] Art. 138 (ex 118a) E.C.
[21] Art. 139 (ex 118b, which did not provide for this possibility) E.C.
[22] Art. 156 (ex 130t) E.C.
[23] Art. 152(4)(a) (ex 129) E.C.; however, this possibility was provided for in Art. 138 (ex 118a(3)) E.C.
[24] In December 1993, the Commission forwarded to the European Council, at its request, a White Paper entitled "Growth, Competitiveness, Employment: the Challenge and Ways forward into the 21st Century".
[25] [1970] O.J. L273/25, amended [1975] O.J. L21/17.
[26] [1984] O.J. L177/1.

time,[27] safety at work,[28] wages, income and working hours,[29] industrial relations, etc.

- basic and advanced vocational training[30]; it suffices to mention here that the Commission is helped in this task by the European Centre for the Development of Vocational Training[31]; vocational training will be examined in more detail hereafter in section 3;
- social security[32]; since the task of the Community in this field is limited to encouraging co-operation between Member States, the Commission and the Council only issued "Recommendations" and "Resolutions"[33];
- prevention of occupational accidents and diseases[34];
- occupational hygiene;
- the right of association and collective bargaining between employers and workers.

As mentioned already, the role of the Community in those fields is rather limited: the Commission, acting in close contact with the

---

[27] Dir. 93/104 [1993] O.J. L307/18; Dir. 96/71 concerning the posting of workers in the framework of the provision of services [1996] O.J. L18/1; Dir. 97/81 concerning the framework agreement on part-time work concluded by UNICE, CEEP and ETUC [1997] O.J. L14/9, amended [1998] O.J. L131/10;

[28] See n. 7 above.

[29] See, for instance, Dir. 93/104 concerning certain aspects of the organisation of working time [1993] O.J. L307/18 and Reg. 2744/95 on statistics on the structure and distribution of earnings [1995] O.J. L287/3.

[30] Vocational training was, from the beginning, part of the activities of the Community.

[31] The Centre was set up in 1975, Reg. 337/75 [1975] O.J. L39/1, last amended [1995] O.J. L41/1.

[32] It will be remembered that this subject was broached under the Chapter concerning "Free Movement of Workers", for whom the Treaty secures, for the purpose of acquiring and retaining the right to benefits, aggregation of all the periods taken into account under the laws of the several Member States and the payment of those benefits in wherever Member State the beneficiary resides, while many regulations were adopted on the application of social security schemes to employed persons and their families moving within the Community, see, for instance, Reg. 1408/71 [1971] O.J. 149/2.

[33] Council Recommendations 92/441 on common criteria concerning sufficient resources and social assistance in social protection systems ([1992] O.J. L245/46 and 92/442) on the convergence of social protection objectives and policies ([1992] O.J. L245/49); it will be noticed that those non-binding acts were published in the "L" series of the O.J. normally reserved for Legislative acts; see also Council Resolution on flexible retirement arrangements (O.J. C188/1).

[34] Commission Recommendation 90/326 concerning the adoption of a European schedule of occupational diseases ([1990] O.J. L160/39). See also n. 7 above.

Member States, may act "by making studies, delivering opinions and arranging consultations"[35]; not very much indeed!

(4) The principle of equal opportunity and equal treatment of men and women[36]

The basic directive on equality of men and women[37] was annulled by the Court in so far as it grants absolute priority to women in case of equivalent qualifications. In a Communication,[38] the Commission pointed out that the Court did not condemn the implementation of positive action in general.

The principle of equal opportunity also includes the principle of equal payment for male and female workers; it only applies, of course, "for equal work or work of equal value". It concerns here an obligation imposed upon the Member States, and the Council must, acting jointly with the Parliament, adopt the necessary measures. Reference to "equal opportunity" was made above, the focus here will be on equal "pay". The latter is defined as "ordinary basic or minimum wage or salary and any consideration, whether in cash or in kind, which the worker receives directly or indirectly, in respect of his employment, from his employer".[39]

As for "equal pay", it means that "the pay for the same work at piece rates shall be calculated on the basis of the same unit of measurement" and that "pay for work at time rates shall be the same for the same job".[40] It should be noted that this Treaty provision has direct effect.

---

35 Art. 140 (ex 118c) E.C.

36 Art 141 (ex 119) E.C. See, for instance, Dir. 79/7 on the progressive implementation of the principle of equal treatment of men and women in matters of social security [1979] O.J. L6/24 and Case C–77/95 *Zuchner* [1996] E.C.R. I–5689; [1997] 3 C.M.L.R. 263: not applicable to persons not engaged in an economic activity. Also Case C–435/93 *Dietz* [1996] E.C.R. I–5223.

37 Dir. 76/207 [1976] O.J. L39/40. Case C–450/93 *Kalanke* [1995] E.C.R. I–305.

38 COM(96)88 and 93 [1996] E.C. Bull. 3–64.

39 Art. 141(2) (ex 119) E.C.

40 The second Protocol attached to the Treaty on E.U. provides that "for the purpose of Article 119 [now 141] of this Treaty, benefits under occupational schemes shall not be considered as remuneration if and in so far as they are attributable to periods of employment prior to 17 May 1990 [date of the *Barber* judgment, see below], except in the case of workers or those claiming under them who have before that date initiated legal proceedings or introduced an equivalent claim under applicable national law".

Several directives[41] were adopted by the Council to implement the above mentioned principles and many Court judgments have clarified the various concepts.[42]

2. The European Social Fund

The European Social Fund (ESF) was set up by the E.C. Treaty in 1958; its objectives were not modified neither by the Single European Act, nor by the Treaty on European Union, nor by the Amsterdam Treaty. Those objectives are to "improve employment opportunities for workers in the common market and to contribute thereby to the raising of the standards of living.[43] The E.U. Treaty did, however, modify the definition of the aim of the ESF, which now reads as follows: "to render the employment of workers easier and to increase their geographical and occupational mobility within the Community, and to facilitate their adaptation to industrial changes and to changes in production systems, in particular through vocational training and retraining". In other words, the ESF is clearly linked to employment (see hereafter), to the free movement of workers (which was examined earlier) and to the vocational training (see below).

[41] See, for instance, Dir. 75/117 on the approximation of the laws of the Member States relating to the application of the principle of equal pay for men and women [1975] O.J. L45/19; in Case 237/85 *Rummler v. Dato-Druck* [1986] E.C.R. 2101; the use of the criterion of muscular demand is not prohibited; Dir. 76/207 on the implementation of the principle of equal treatment for men and women as regards access to employment, vocational training and promotion and working conditions [1976] O.J. L39/40.

[42] Case C–262/88 *Barber* [1990] E.C.R. I–1889; [1990] 2 C.M.L.R. 513 on the notion of "remuneration"; on the fact that the benefits paid by an employer to a worker on the latter's redundancy, constitutes a form of pay; also that, unlike the benefits awarded by national statutory social security schemes, retirement pensions paid under private occupational schemes constitute consideration paid by the employer in respect of his employment and consequently fall within the scope of Art. 141 (ex 119) E.C.; also Case C–400/95 *Larsson v. Fotex Supermarked* [1997] E.C.R. I–2757; [1979] 2 C.M.L.R. 915: outside periods of maternity leave, women are not protected against dismissal of ground of absence due to illness attributable to pregnancy. The most famous cases are without doubt the *Defrenne* cases: Case 80/70 *Defrenne v. Belgium* [1971] E.C.R. 445 and Case 43/75 *Defrenne v. Sabena* [1976] E.C.R. 455. See also Case 61/88 *Commission v. U.K.* [1982] E.C.R. 2601 and Case 165/82 *Commission v. U.K.* [1988] E.C.R. 3431; [1984] 1 C.M.L.R. 44. The Court also held that when there are important differences between the pay of men and that of women, and they cannot be explained, it is up to the employer to prove that there is no discrimination: Case 109/88 *Handelsverband v. Danfoss* [1989] E.C.R. 3220.

[43] Arts 146 to 148 (ex 123 to 125) E.C.

More interesting is the addition introduced by the E.U. Treaty concerning the necessary adaptations of the working force to economic changes; from that it follows that social policy is not only about granting rights to workers and protecting them, but also about helping them to accept the consequences of a changing economic environment. It was pointed out earlier on that the Treaty enjoined the Community and the Member States to implement measures which take account of the "need to maintain competitiveness of the Community economy".[44] Although in a rather indirect way those two provisions give a clear hint as to the obligations which rest on the workers to help achieve the objectives of the Community.

As is explained in the Chapter on "Economic and Social Cohesion", since the Treaty on E.U., the ESF, together with the European Agricultural Guidance and Guarantee Fund, Guidance section, and the European Regional Development Fund, form the "Structural Funds", which with the European Investment Bank and the other existing financial instruments support the achievement of the objective of overall harmonious development.[45] The EFS will be examined in that context.

3. Education, Vocational Training and Youth

Education in this context refers to general education, *i.e.* grammar school, high school and university, while vocational training refers to the teaching of specific trades, corresponding to the distinction between workers and professionals, the latter, as was seen under the Free Movement of Persons, being only a part of the "self-employed".

Education, remains the sole responsibility of the Member States, where the content of teaching and the organisation of education systems are concerned—except for the professions.[46] The main task of the Community in this field is therefore to "contribute to the development of quality education".[47] The means at its disposal to fulfil this task are encouraging co-operation between Member States and, if necessary, supporting and supplementing their action. It is probably to be considered as normal that, even where it is their exclusive responsibility, the Member States do not hesitate to ask for

---

[44] Art. 136 (ex 117 which did not contain this provision) E.C.

[45] Arts 158 and 159 (ex 130a and 130b) E.C.

[46] See under Free Movement of the self-employed: the content of the education for the regulated professions is established by Community directives.

[47] Art. 149(1) (ex 126(1)) E.C.

the (financial) support of the Community. Where it does go very far indeed, is when the Treaty provides that the Community may "supplement" the action of the Member States. However, the Treaty adds immediately that, while doing this, the Community must not only respect the responsibility of the Member States just mentioned, but also their cultural and linguistic diversity.

Furthermore, the incentive measure to be adopted by the Parliament and the Council acting jointly, may not lead to harmonisation of the laws and regulations of the Member States.[48]

The Community action shall, according to the Treaty, be aimed at:

- developing the European dimension in education,[49] particularly through the teaching and dissemination of the languages of the Member States. The reader might wonder about this objective, with eleven official languages at the present time—with five or six more to be added in the not too far future—is this a viable proposition? Surely, everyone will want to learn or improve English, since, for all practical purposes, that is the "common" language, but such an idea is, of course, anathema in all the non-English-speaking capitals. Anyway, the Community set up the LINGUA programme[50] to promote the teaching and learning of all the languages[51];
- encouraging mobility of students and teachers; for this purpose the European Community Action Programme for the Mobility of University Students (ERASMUS)[52] and the Trans-European Mobility Scheme for University Students (TEMPUS)[53] were established; the mobility should be facilitated, *inter alia*, by encouraging the academic recognition of diplomas and periods of study[54];
- promoting co-operation between educational establishments[55];

---

[48] *ibid.* at (4).

[49] See Resolution of the Council and the Ministers of education meeting within the Council on the European dimension in education [1988] O.J. C177/5; *id.* for higher education [1992] O.J. C336/4.

[50] Council Dec. 89/489 establishing an action programme to promote foreign languages competence in the European Community [1989] O.J. L239/14.

[51] Council Resolution on the early teaching of European Union languages [1998] O.J. C1/2.

[52] Dec. 87/327 [1987] O.J. L166/20.

[53] Dec. 90/233 [1990] O.J. L131/21.

[54] See above, under "Right of Establishment" and "Freedom to provide Services". See also [1974] O.J. C98/1, Resolution on mutual recognition of diplomas, certificates and other evidence of formal qualifications.

[55] Conclusion of the Council and the Ministers of Education meeting within the Council concerning a pilot action for multilateral school partnership in the European Community [1991] O.J. C321/3.

this constitutes one of the objectives of the Community action programme SOCRATES[56];
- developing exchanges of information and experience on issues common to the education systems of the Member States; see the EURYDICE network and the ARION programme[57];
- encouraging the development of youth[58] exchanges and the exchange of socio-educational instructors;
- encouraging the development of distance education.[59]

The Treaty also provides for the Community and the Member States to foster co-operation with third countries[60] and the competent international organisations in the field of education, in particular the Council of Europe.[61]

Vocational training. The Treaty provides for the Community to implement its own vocational training policy, which, however, must "support and supplement the action of the Member States", the latter remaining responsible for the content and organisation of vocational training.[62]

Like in the field of education, measures are to be adopted jointly by the Parliament and the Council to achieve the objectives referred to in the Treaty, with the exclusion, however, of any harmonisation of the laws and regulations of the Member States. Once again, Member States accept Community support, but are not ready yet for an approximation of their national rules.

Vocational training was provided for by the Treaty from the beginning; it was referred to as one of the actions of the Member States which could be financed at 50 per cent by the ESF. It has

---

[56] Parliament and Council Dec. 819/91 establishing an action programme SOCRATES [1995] O.J. L87/10 with the objective of contributing to the development of quality education and training and the creation of an open European area for co-operation in education, including ERASMUS for higher education and COMENIUS for school education; amended by Dec. 576/98 [1998] O.J. L77/1.

[57] See EURYDICE, an education information network [1992] O.J. C336/7 and ARION programme on study visits for education specialists and administrators.

[58] See the Youth for Europe programme [1988] O.J. L158/42 and Dec. 818/95 [1995] O.J. L87/1.

[59] Conclusions *id.* on the development of open and distance learning [1992] O.J. C151/3 and on criteria for actions for open and distant learning [1992] O.J. C336/6.

[60] See Agreement between the E.U. and the U.S. establishing a co-operation programme in higher education and vocational education and training [1995] O.J. L279/13; *id.* with Canada [1995] O.J. L300/19; also Association in this field with Romania [1997] O.J. L229/5.

[61] Art. 149(3) (ex 126(3)) E.C.

[62] Art. 150 (ex 127) E.C.

become an activity on its own: see the Leonardo da Vinci action programme for the implementation of a Community vocational training policy[63] and the setting up of the *European Centre for the Development of Vocational training*.[64] The latter is a scientific and technical body entrusted with promoting, at Community level, the exchange of information and experience, the distribution of documents and the launching of research and experimental projects to facilitate the attainment of the vocational training objectives. As for the *European Training Foundation*, its purpose is to help the countries of Central and Eastern Europe with professional training.[65]

The aims of the Community action in the field of vocational training are the following:

- facilitate adaptation to industrial changes;
- improve initial and continuing vocational training;
- facilitate access to vocational training and encourage mobility of instructors and trainees;
- stimulate co-operation on training between training establishments and firms;
- develop exchanges of information and experience.

In the field of vocational training also, the Community and the Member States are to foster co-operation with third countries and international organisations.[66] No reference is made here to the Council of Europe.

4. Employment

Employment is the object of the new Title VIII, which was introduced by the Amsterdam Treaty. It is thus not part of Title XI on Social Policy, where it probably belongs; it was inserted into the E.C. Treaty immediately after the Title on Economic and Monetary Policy to function as the social "counterpart", to prevent the Treaty from looking too one-sided in favour of economic preoccupations.

The set-up of this title is similar to the various parts of Social

[63] Dec. 94/819 [1994] O.J. L340/8.

[64] Reg. 337/75 [1975] O.J. L39/1, last amended [1995] O.J. L41/1; see also Dec. 96/1025 [1996] O.J. C316/1.

[65] Reg. 90/1360 [1990] O.J. L131/1.

[66] See n. 60, above.

Policy, *i.e.* shared responsibility of the Community and the Member States for achieving the objectives; the task of the Community is limited to encouraging cooperation between the Member States through the drawing up of guidelines[67] and incentive measures decided jointly by the Parliament and the Council. Harmonisation measures are, however, excluded here also.

Furthermore, the Treaty only refers to "coordinated strategy", "promotion" of a skilled, trained and adaptable workforce, "employment policy", promoting employment as a "matter of common concern", the "objective of a high level of employment", the European Council, which must "each year consider the employment situation" and adopt "conclusions thereon", the Council and the Commission making a "joint annual report on the employment situation in the Community",[68] "exchange of information and best practice", providing "comparative analysis and advice" and promoting "innovative approaches", "evaluating experiences" and an Employment Committee. One can only hope that all this "soft" action will indeed create jobs. Clearly, it is up to the Member States to take the necessary measures and implement their own employment policy, the Community can only encourage co-operation between the Member States and support their action in the field of employment. The danger of providing for the kind of Community activity described above, is that it might create the illusion that the Community is actively engaged in combating unemployment. This is not its task; it is not equipped to do this; the principle of subsidiarity applies here to the full. The only thing the Community can do, besides trying to coordinate the actions of the Member States, is to help in training and retraining the workforce in order to make it responsive to economic change.

Unemployment is the most crucial problem facing the Community at the moment it launches the most ambitious project yet: the single currency. Not surprisingly, it is this new step on the way to economic integration that might play a decisive role in helping to create the

---

[67] The Employment Guidelines for 1998, agreed upon at the Luxembourg Job Summit of November 1997, were built on four main pillars: employability, entrepreneurship, adaptability and equal opportunity. Every year, a set of guidelines are adopted for each of the pillars, which set out a number of specific targets for Member States to achieve in their national employment policies. Those Guidelines are then transposed into concrete and administrative measures by each Member State, through their *National Action Plans for Employment* (NAPS).

[68] In fact there are two reports: the *Joint Employment Report*, the objective of which is to present the employment situation in the Member States and to assess the quality of the efforts being undertaken by them to implement their national Action Plans, and the *Employment Rates Report* on employment performance in the Member States.

necessary jobs, thanks to the greater flexibility it will generate in the trade between Member States.

Mention must also be made of the *European Employment Services* (EURES) which is a European labour market network aiming at facilitating the mobility of workers in the European Economic Area. It links more than 450 Euroadvisers—specialists in employment matters—throughout Europe.

Further Reading

European Commission, "National transposition measures at 1 January 1998. Employment and social affairs", DG V document, Luxembourg, EUR-OP 1998.

European Commission, "Social Action Programme 1998–2000", COM(98)259; Internet: europa.eu.int/comm/dg05/news/sapen. htm.

T. Hervey, *European social law and policy* (Longman European law series, London, 1998).

Laqmmy Beten, "The democratic deficit of Participatory Democracy in Community Social Law" (1998) 23 E.L.Rev. 20.

Chapter Twenty-six
Culture, Public Health, Consumer Protection

Those three subjects are treated here together because they have much in common, although they form separate titles in Part Three of the E.C. Treaty. Compared to subjects like the basic freedoms or competition, they constitute "minor" Community activities. They all tend to "complement", "supplement" or "support" the Member States' action in those fields. This means that the emphasis is on the Member States, not on the Community's activities. They, furthermore, contain very few provisions, and those are, most of the time, couched in general terms: "contribute to", "shall be ensured", "promote", etc. These activities could be called what the Amsterdam Treaty refers to as "directly related flanking measures".[1] But, are they directly related to other activities? For other areas, such as "Trans-European Networks", the Treaty itself indicates that they are to "help achieve the objectives referred to in Articles 14 (ex 7a) and 158 (ex 130a)".[2] Other subjects such as Education and Vocational Training, obviously are indispensable for the free movement of the self-employed. Nothing of the sort for the subjects examined here and, one may indeed wonder why the Treaty on European Union inserted them into the E.C. Treaty. At the next Treaty revision it will probably be the turn of Sports, Religion and Charity!

It is not because the Treaty rules, for example those on competition, apply to certain human activities, like sports, that therefore the Community must be endowed with competences in those fields. And it is not because the Community is no longer referred to as the "Economic" Community, that therefore "non-directly related" fields may be legitimately included. What about the principle of subsidiarity and the famous slogan "let's do less, but do it better"?

[1] Amsterdam Treaty, Art. 61 (ex 73Ia).
[2] Art. 154(1) (ex 129b(1)) E.C.

Anyway, the activities are in the Treaty, and they will therefore be examined.

CULTURE[3] (TITLE XII (EX IX) OF PART THREE OF THE E.C. TREATY)

Even before the insertion of the present Title into the E.C. Treaty, there were, of course, references to activities which can be classified under the heading "culture": to start with the "protection of national treasures possessing artistic, historic or archeological value", which justifies prohibitions or restrictions on imports, exports or transit.[4] Other provisions were adopted, for instance, for the return of cultural objects unlawfully removed from the territory of a Member State[5]; the harmonisation of controls on exports of cultural goods[6]; besides more mundane arrangements like the application of the Social Fund to "cultural workers",[7] special conditions of admission of young people to museums and cultural events,[8] and the protection of Europe's architectural heritage.[9]

Since the entry into force of the Treaty on E.U., the Community has a task with regard to both the cultures of the Member States, whose national and regional diversities must be respected, and the "common cultural heritage". The latter will be brought "to the fore", while the Community must "contribute to the flowering"[10] of the former. However, the Community is not to develop its own activity, but simply to encourage co-operation between the Member States and, if necessary, to support and supplement their action in the following areas. Improvement of the knowledge and dissemination of the culture and history of the European peoples; conservation and safeguarding of cultural heritage of European significance; non-commercial cultural exchanges and, artistic and literary creation, including the audio-visual sector.

The "supporting and supplementing" will be done jointly by the

---

[3] Art. 151 (ex 128) E.C.

[4] Art. 30 (ex 36) E.C.

[5] Dir. 93/7 [1993] O.J. L74/74, amended by Dir. 96/100 [1996] O.J. L60/59.

[6] Reg. 3911/92 [1992] O.J. L395/1, amended by Reg. 2469/96 [1996] O.J. L335/9; see also Reg. 752/93 laying down provisions for the implementation of Reg. 3911/92 [1993] O.J. L77/24.

[7] Resolution of the Council and of the Ministers responsible for Cultural Affairs meeting within the Council [1985] O.J. L2/2.

[8] Resolution of December 20, 1985 [1985] O.J. C348/2.

[9] Resolution of November 13, 1986 [1986] O.J. C320/1.

[10] One cannot help but think of the Chinese cultural revolution!

Parliament and the Council[11] according to the so-called co-decision procedure,[12] but with an important modification: the Council shall act unanimously throughout the procedure. Even recommendations may only be adopted unanimously. All this clearly shows that this field remains solidly in the hands of the Member States, which only consent in receiving (financial) "support" from the Community!

The Treaty also provides that the Community and the Member States (acting together), shall foster co-operation with third countries and the competent international organisations, in particular the Council of Europe.[13] Interesting is that the cultural aspects must be taken into account by the institutions in all actions under other provisions of the Treaty; whether this will have a great impact on Community legislation, remains of course to be seen.

Public Health[14] (Title XII (ex X) of Part Three of the E.C. Treaty)

Whenever it defines or implements any of its policies and activities, the Community must ensure a high level of human health protection; it shall also complement national policies. The field of action is circumscribed as follows: improving public health, preventing human illness and diseases and obviating sources of danger to human health, which shall include the fight against the "major health scourges", by promoting research into their causes, their transmission and their prevention, as well as health information and education. Reference is also made to the reduction of drug-related health damage, including information and prevention.

Although in this field also, the first task of the Community is to

---

[11] See, for instance, Decision of the Parliament and the Council establishing a programme to support artistic and cultural activities having a European dimension (kaleidoscope) [1996] O.J. L99/20; *id.* to support, including translation, in the field of books and reading (ARIANE) [1997] O.J. L 291/26; *id.* in the field of cultural heritage (RAPHAEL) [1997] O.J. L305/31; there are also at least two dozen Resolutions and Conclusions (all not binding) of the Council, or of the Council and the Ministers responsible for Cultural Affairs meeting within the Council, or of those Ministers alone, concerning electronic publishing, a European sculpture competition, the European Foundation, etc. A full list is to be found in the *Directory of Community Legislation and other Acts of the Community Institutions*, published twice a year by the *Official Journal of the European Communities*, Office for Official Publications of the European Communities, Luxembourg.

[12] Art. 251 (ex 189b) E.C.

[13] As shall be seen the Community is to establish all appropriate forms of co-operation with the Council of Europe: Art. 303 (ex 230) E.C.

[14] Art. 152 (ex 129) E.C.

"encourage co-operation between the Member States", and, if necessary lend support to their action, but it is also to develop its own activity. The latter is to be done by adopting various measures with regard to the quality and safety of organs and substances of human origin, blood and blood derivatives, the protection of human health in the veterinary and phytosanitary fields and, incentives to protect and improve human health. Each time, however, the Treaty makes sure that the Community will not tread on national toes: harmonisation is excluded and the "responsibilities of the Member States for the organisation and the delivery of health services and medical care" must be fully respected. In particular, adds the Treaty, the above measures "shall not affect national provisions on the donation or medical use of organs and blood".

Obviously, many aspects of health protection overlap with Consumer Protection which is analysed in the next section and Environment the object of which is also to protect human health. This applies, for instance, to the classification, packaging and labelling of dangerous substances,[15] restrictions on the marketing and use of certain dangerous substances and preparations,[16] pesticides,[17] asbestos,[18] biotechnology, the quality of drinking[19] and bathing[20] water. Human health is, of course, dependent also on animal health. In this field the Community has been very active, mainly within the framework of the agricultural policy.

Mention must be made of a Parliament and Council Decision setting up a Network for Epidemiological Surveillance and Control of Communicable Diseases in the Community.[21] It should also be noted that health protection projects may be co-financed in certain regions by the European Regional Development Fund (ERDF) and the European Social Fund (ESF).

Consumer Protection (Title XIV (ex XI) of Part Three of the E.C. Treaty)

The history of consumer protection starts with the Council resolution of April 14, 1975 concerning a preliminary programme for a

[15] Dir. 67/548 [1967] O.J. 196/1, last amended [1997] O.J. L343/19.
[16] Dir. 76/769 [1976] O.J. L262/201, last amended [1997] O.J. L315/13.
[17] Dir. 78/631 [1978] O.J. L206/13, last amended [1992] O.J. L154/1.
[18] Dir. 87/217 [1987] O.J. L85/40.
[19] Dir. 75/440 [1975] O.J. L194/26.
[20] Dir. 76/160 O.J. [1976] L31/1, last amended [1991] O.J. L377/48.
[21] [1998] O.J. L268/1.

protection and information policy of the consumer. It referred to a large number of areas, some of which were taken over into the E.C. Treaty by the Treaty on E.U. They are the protection of the health, safety[22] and economic interests of the consumer, and the right to information and education and to organise themselves in order to safeguard their interests.[23] Other areas not explicitly referred to in the Treaty are, under the heading protection of the economic interests: misleading advertising, unfair commercial practices[24] and furthermore, advice, help and redress.

Of great importance for both consumers and producers are the directives on general product safety[25] and liability for defective products.[26] With regard to the latter, the Court determined that, in order for a producer to incur liability for defective products, the victim does not have to prove that the producer was at fault; that, however, in accordance with the principle of fair apportionment of risk between the injured person and the producer,[27] the latter has a defence if he can prove certain facts exonerating him from liability, including that "the state of scientific and technical knowledge at the time when he put the product into circulation, was not such as to enable the existence of the defect to be discovered".[28]

The protection of the economic interests cover various areas such as the protection of the consumer in respect of contracts negotiated away from business premises,[29] consumer credit,[30] the indication of

---

[22] See, for instance, Dir. 88/378 on the safety of toys [1988] O.J. L187/1, amended [1993] O.J. L220/1.

[23] Art. 153 (ex 129a) E.C.

[24] Dir. 84/450 approximation of laws concerning misleading advertising [1984] O.J. L250/18.

[25] Dir. 92/59 [1992] O.J. L228/24.

[26] Dir. 85/374 [1985] O.J. L210/29; this Directive was consolidated by Dir. 98/37 on the approximation of the laws of the Member States relating to machinery [1998] O.J. L207/1.

[27] Preamble of Dir. 85/374.

[28] Case C–300/95 *Commission v. U.K.* [1997] E.C.R. I–2649.

[29] Dir. 85/577 [1985] O.J. L372/31 and Dir. 97/7 on the protection of consumers in respect of distance contracts [1997] O.J. L144/19. See Case C–45/96 *Ditzinger* [1998] E.C.R. I–1199.

[30] Dir. 87/102 [1987] O.J. L42/48.

the prices on non-food products,[31] unfair terms in consumer contracts,[32] package travel, package holidays and package tours.[33]

Great emphasis was put on foodstuffs following the publication by the Commission of what is sometimes referred to as the "White Paper bis" on the completion of the internal market for foodstuffs, wherein the Commission points out four areas in which it will continue to propose legislation, leaving the others to mutual recognition. It concerns mainly labelling[34] and nutritional labelling.

As with public health, consumer protection requirements must be taken into account in defining and implementing other Community policies and activities. To help therewith a Consumer Committee was set up.[35] And here also, the Community must take measures to attain the objectives stated above and to support, supplement and monitor the policy pursued by the Member States. The latter measures must be adopted jointly with the European Parliament and in accordance with the co-decision procedure.[36]

Further Reading

European Commission, "Investing in culture: an asset for all regions", Luxembourg, EUR-OP 1998.

---

[31] Dir. 88/314 O.J. L142/19 and Dir. 98/6 on consumer protection in the indication of the prices of products offered to consumers [1998] O.J. L80/27.

[32] Dir. 93/13 [1993] O.J. L95/29.

[33] Dir. 90/314 [1990] O.J. L158/59. See Case C–364/96 *Verein für Konsumenteninformation* [1998] E.C.R. I–2949. Art. 7 protects travellers who have already paid their hotel and who must pay it a second time following the bankruptcy of the travel organisation.

[34] Dir. 79/112 on the approximation of the laws of the Member States relating to the labelling, presentation and advertising of foodstuffs for the sale to the ultimate consumer [1979] O.J. L33/1, last mod. [1997] O.J. L4/21; Dir. 79/581 on consumer protection in the indication of the prices of foodstuffs [1979] O.J. L158/19; Dir. 90/496 on nutritional labelling for foodstuffs [1990] O.J. L276/40; Dir. 93/102 relating to the labelling, presentation and advertising of foodstuffs for sale to the ultimate consumer [1993] O.J. L291/14 and Reg. 54/94 [1994] O.J. L300/14; see Case C–85/94 *DIAGEME* [1995] E.C.R. I–2955, the requiring of the language of the "Taalgebiet" goes too far and Case C–385/96 *GOERRES* [1998] E.C.R. I–4431: the language must be on the label in a comprehensible language. Regulation on the protection of geographical indications and designations of origin for agricultural products and foodstuffs [1992] O.J. L208/1, amended [1997] O.J. L156/10 and Reg. 1107/96 O.J. L148/1, last amended [1998] O.J. L87/8 and Reg. 2400/96 [1996] O.J. L327/111; Dir. 76/796 approximation of laws relating to the marketing and use of certain dangerous substances and preparations [1976] O.J. L262/201, last amended [1997] O.J. L315/13.

[35] Decision of June 13, 1995 [1995] O.J. L162/37.

[36] Contrary to what is the case with culture, unanimity is not required throughout that procedure.

M. Leonard, *Making Europe popular: the search for European identity* (Demos/Interbrand Newell and Sorrell, London, 1997).

Commission Communication on "The development of public health policy in the EC", COM (98) 2305.

European Commission, "Public health in the EC: health promotion programme 1996–2000", DG V, Luxembourg EUR-OP 1997.

European Commission, "Consumer Policy Action Plan 1999–2001", COM (98) 696 final.

Chapter Twenty-seven
Industrial Policy and Trans-European Networks

In this chapter, besides the general policy, several aspects of industrial policy such as enterprise policy, intellectual and industrial property, public procurement and the Trans-European Networks will be examined.

1. General Policy

As the Commission has indicated,[1] industrial policy today is vastly different from what it was 30 years ago when some national authorities believed that barriers to shield their companies from competition from abroad was the key to prosperity. Other Member States questioned the need for an industrial policy altogether, arguing that industrial policy had no place in an open market. Now it is widely accepted that insularity can only lead to stagnation and that it is liberalisation of markets that offers the greatest benefits to both consumer and supplier, and that it will help industry to remain profitable in an increasingly global and increasingly competitive market.

Thus the key question that industrial policy now seeks to address is, what needs to be done to help business and industry to compete in the global market place. Inevitably, this is a multi-faced issue and one that cuts across many other policy areas. The response to that question will have implications for education and training, research and development, competition and environment. The Community's industrial policy is presently determined by the modifications introduced in the E.C. Treaty by the Treaty on European Union and maintained unchanged by the Amsterdam Treaty. The sole objective of the Treaty in this area is to ensure that the conditions necessary for

[1] http://europa.eu.int/comm/dg03/mission_en.htm (as of December 2, 1998); parts of this chapter are based on, or have been taken from, this publication.

the competitiveness of the industry exist.[2] This is the task of both the Community an the Member States, but the latter remain so to say "in the lead". Indeed the Treaty provides that they must "consult" each other, in liaison with the Commission, and where necessary, "coordinate" their action. Nothing very concrete. The Community may only "take any useful initiative to promote such coordination".[3]

The aim of the action of the Community and the Member States, in view of the competitiveness of the industry, and in accordance with a system of open and competitive markets, is described as follows:

- speeding up the *adjustment* of industry to structural changes (this clearly indicates that the drafters of the Treaty were aware of the new market conditions mentioned above);
- encouraging an *environment* favourable to initiative and to the development of undertakings throughout the Community, particularly small and medium-sized undertakings (a clear indication that the action is to consist in flanking measures and not in direct intervention in favour of undertakings; in this context it is noteworthy that the Treaty explicitly indicates that it does "not provide a basis for the introduction by the Community of any measure which could lead to distortion of competition"[4]; important also are the words "throughout the Community", which are also to be found in the introductory provisions of the Treaty,[5] they indicate that the less developed regions must not be forgotten, but they don't get priority; that is the task of other policies; finally, the reference to the small and medium-sized undertakings should be underlined: it is universally recognised that they are the principal creators of jobs and, as was seen in other places in this book, for instance under competition, they are the object of special measures;
- encouraging an environment favourable to co-operation between undertakings (this must be seen in relation with the competition policy of the Commission, which, as was seen, exempts from the prohibition various forms of co-operation);
- fostering better exploitation of the industrial potential of policies of innovation, research and technological development (those policies will be examined hereafter).

Although, as was indicated at the beginning of this chapter, the

---

[2] Art. 157 (ex 130) E.C.
[3] *ibid.* at 2.
[4] *ibid.* last para.
[5] Art. 2 E.C. Under the heading "economic and social cohesion", the Treaty refers to "overall" harmonious development: Art. 158 (ex 130a) E.C.

initiative in this area lies, according to the Treaty provisions, with the Member States, the Community is entrusted with the task to "contribute to the achievement of the objectives set out above through the policies and activities under other provisions of the Treaty". In other words, no specific industrial actions. However, the Treaty also provides that the Council may decide on specific measures, but then only "in support of action taken in the Member States" to achieve the objectives set out above.[6]

Following the priorities set in the White Paper on *Growth, Competitiveness and Employment*,[7] the Commission developed two kinds of actions:

- actions related to the operation of the markets, including regulations on market access and product specifications, trade policy and competition policy, and
- actions relating to factors that affect industry's capacity to adapt to change.

The main conditions necessary for the competitiveness of the Community's industry can be identified as R&D and the proper functioning of the internal market which promotes industrial co-operation and the strengthening of competition.

Promotion of intangible investment: with the growth in information-based competition, investment training and R&D has become vital. The drafters of the Single European Act were well aware of its importance when they introduced it in the E.C. Treaty. It was kept practically unchanged by the Treaty on E.U. and the Amsterdam Treaty.[8] Since it forms a separate Title in the Treaty, it will be examined hereafter.

As for the internal market, the removal of the many hidden barriers to trade continue to boost the competitiveness of E.U. companies, while the emergence of a continent-wide market enables them to reduce unit costs, forge links and partnerships across borders and innovate more rapidly and successfully. Nevertheless, as the Commission recognises,[9] the internal market remains incomplete in a number of areas, including company law, public procurement and fiscal harmonisation. One must add to that, unfortunately, the refusal of many a Member State to implement to rules governing the

[6] It seems to be the same old story: the Member States want to do it each in its own way, at the most consult each other, but gladly accept the (financial) support of the Community; see what was said about education, vocational training and youth, culture, health protection, consumer protection and trans-European networks.

[7] White Paper presented to the European Council in December 1993.

[8] It constitutes an entire Title XIX (ex XVI) of no less than ten Articles.

[9] See n.1 above.

internal market, especially with regard to the free movement of goods and services (think of transport, for instance), the right of establishment and more generally speaking the refusal of their administrations to view the territory of the fifteen Member States as one single entity where the same rules apply to all. With regard to the free movement of goods, which, after all is the corner stone, so to say, of the European construction, standards play an extreme important role. In other areas it is the telecommunication and information industries, the intellectual and industrial property rights and public procurement, which greatly influence the competitiveness of the industry. Those subjects will be briefly examined hereinafter.

Promoting open standards

The application of standards by the industry presuppose three related issues.

- regulations, *i.e.* mandatory rules adopted and enforced by governments, widely misrepresented as a weapon for imposing uniform European regulations for their own sake! They are in fact the result of the approximation of laws which aim to remove those discrepancies between existing national regulations that hinder trade. The objective is to ensure that a product accepted for sale in one Member State has free access to the whole European market, with advantages for both the consumer and the competitiveness of the industry.
- standards, *i.e.* voluntary specifications prepared by autonomous standardisation bodies made up of representatives of industry, consumer groups and administrations; equipment and appliances need to be capable of working together in the different Member States without sacrificing quality, safety or environmental principles.[10]
- certification, *i.e.* a means by which manufacturers can declare that their products conform to the appropriate quality and technical requirements. The Commission's role is to reinforce and insure the mutual equivalence and recognition of the testing, certification accreditation bodies in Europe.

---

[10] One highly successful example is the GSM standard which allows mobile telephones to work in most of the E.U.

Community Telecommunications Policy

One of the most important industrial sectors for the economic development of the European Union is comprised of *telecommunications, information industries* and *innovation*. In the field of *telecommunications*, a very intensive programme of legislation has been undertaken by the Commission, which has led to the achievement of complete liberalisation of most of the European telecommunications market,[11] since January 1, 1998, by gradually abolishing the exclusive rights traditionally held by Europe's state-owned telecommunications organisations.

European policy on the deregulation of telecommunications must be seen in the wider context of economic integration in Europe, initiated by the Treaty of Rome.

The publication by the Commission of the 1987 Green Paper on the development of the common market for telecommunications services and equipment[12] marks the actual initiation of this deregulation process. However, as early as 1984, the Commission aimed to move the sector forward by establishing common development lines, characterised by programmes on special development for the least developed regions of the E.U., shared research programmes between operators and industry and standards development programmes. The preparatory phase of the RACE programme[13] was started, which was essential for the development of communications technology.

The liberalisation of the E.U. telecommunications market proceeded in two phases. A first phase covers the period from 1987 until the publication by the Commission of its 1992 review.[14] The second phase covers the remaining period until the introduction of full competition in 1998.

Within the first five years following the 1987 Green Paper, legislation was introduced to liberalise the telecommunications

[11] Greece and Portugal have obtained transition periods for liberalising their telecommunications infrastructure.

[12] Commission Green Paper on the development of the common market for telecommunications services and equipment (COM(87) 290, June 30, 1987).

[13] Between 1987 and 1995, the main RACE programme was operational, under the second and third R&D framework programmes. The ACTS programme took over from RACE in 1994 under the fourth framework programme; see the Commission Telecom Status Report of January 1998; for the RACE programme, see [1991] O.J. C154.

[14] 1992 review of the situation in the telecommunications services sector: Communication by the Commission (SEC(92) 1048, October 21, 1992).

equipment[15] and value-added services[16] markets. Given the fact that the infrastructure remained governed by monopoly rights, the Commission introduced the Open Network Provision Directive[17] (ONP) requiring the telecommunication organisations to lease lines to new market entrants on reasonable terms and to provide open and fair access to their networks.

During the second phase, from 1992 onwards, the satellite[18] and mobile[19] services, and the cable television networks,[20] were progressively opened up to competition.

On March 13, 1996, the Commission adopted its so-called "Full Competition Directive",[21] amending and extending its earlier Services Directive.

This Directive also introduces the basic principles for licensing new entrants to both voice telephony and telecommunications infrastructure markets and requires interconnection to the voice telephony service and public switched telecommunications networks to be granted on non-discriminatory, proportional and transparent terms, based on objective criteria.

Additional legislative action has been taken to ensure a successful transition to full liberalisation. Among the most important are the extension of the open network provision (ONP) to leased lines[22] and voice telephony.[23] The Interconnection Directive[24] ensures to all market players the ability to obtain interconnection with the

---

[15] Dir. 88/301 on competition in the markets of telecommunications terminal equipment [1988] O.J. L131/73.

[16] Dir. 90/388 on competition in the markets for telecommunications services [1990] O.J. L192/10.

[17] Dir. 90/387on the establishment of the internal market for telecommunications services through the implementation of open network provision [1190] O.J. L192/1.

[18] Dir. 94/46 amending Dir. 88/301 and Dir. 90/388 in particular with regard to satellite communications O.J. [1994] L268/15.

[19] Dir. 96/2 [1996] O.J. L2059 amending Dir. 90/388 with regard to mobile and personal communications.

[20] Dir. 95/51 amending Dir. 90/388 with regard to the abolition of the restrictions on the use of cable television networks for the provision of already liberalised telecommunications services [1995] O.J. L256/49.

[21] Dir. 96/19 amending Dir. 90/388 regarding the implementation of full competition in telecommunications markets [1996] O.J. L74/13.

[22] Dir. 92/44 on the application of open network provision to leased lines [1992] O.J. L165/27.

[23] Dir. 95/62 on the application of open network provision (ONP) to voice telephony [1995] O.J. L321/6.

[24] Dir. 97/33 of the Parliament and the Council on interconnection in telecommunications with regard to ensuring universal service and interoperability through application of the principles of Open Network Provision (ONP) [1997] O.J. L199/32.

networks of others where this is reasonably justifiable and in accordance with the ONP principles of non-discrimination, transparency, objectivity and proportionality. Finally, a common framework was set up for general authorisations and individual licenses in the field of telecommunications.[25]

Beyond 1998, the European telecommunications policy will focus on the effective implementation of this regulatory framework and maintain it under constant review in order to take account of future changes, such as the increasing convergence between telecommunications, information and audio-visual sectors.

With regard to the *information industries*, the Fourth Framework Programme for research and development[26] was adopted by the Parliament and the Council in 1994 and covers the period 1995–1998. Under this framework, a very important role has been attributed to information technologies, which can be divided into three sections: the telematic applications (Telematics programme), the advanced telecommunications technologies (Acts programme), and information technologies (former Esprit programme). Actions under the Fifth Framework Programme are now under discussion.[27]

Many sectors are directly interested in the further development of information technology, *e.g.*, transport, health care, flexible and distant learning, the rural areas, linguistic research, engineering and libraries. A special aspect of this further development consists in computerised communication of data, information and documents, standardisation, dissemination and exploitation of the results of Community and national research programmes and the development of an information services market.[28]

Enterprise Policy

Activities in this area include the improvement of the business environment and administrative simplification. More specifically with regard to the supply of business services, mention must be made of the *Euro-Info-Centres*, the *Business Co-operation* Network and

---

[25] Dir. 97/13 of the Parliament and the Council on a common framework for general authorisations and individual licences in the field of telecommunications services [1997] O.J. L117/15.

[26] Dec. 94/1110 of the Parliament and of the Council concerning the fourth framework programme of the European Community activities in the field of research and technological development and demonstration (1994 to 1998) [1994] O.J. L126; amended by Dec. 96/616 [1996] O.J. L86/69 and Dec. 97/2535 [1997] O.J. L347/1.

[27] See the Commission Telecom Status Report of January 1998.

[28] See General Report, 1992, 116 *et seq.* See also General Report, 1996, 168 *et seq.*

the *Business Co-operation Centre* which aims to be a vehicle for promoting business contacts of a non-confidential nature. As for small businesses the Community set up several programmes: experimental training schemes, Euromanagement, participation in public procurement, the setting up of seed capital, etc. see, for instance, a Council decision on measures of financial assistance for innovation and job-creating small and medium-sized enterprises (SMEs)—The Growth and Employment Initiative.[29]

Obviously the qualification of "small" or "medium-sized" plays an important "access" role for all those programmes. The Commission therefore issued a recommendation concerning the definition of small and medium-sized enterprises:

- is "small", an enterprise
  - with fewer than 50 employees,
  - a turnover not exceeding euro 7 million or an annual balance sheet total of less than euro 5 million,
  - which is independent
- it is "medium-sized" when
  - it has fewer than 250 employees,
  - a turn-over of less than euro 40 million, or a balance sheet total of less than euro 27 million, and
  - it is independent.

See also the Council Resolution of April 22, 1996 on the co-ordination of Community activities in favour of small and medium-sized enterprises and the craft sector.[30]

In the chapter on freedom of establishment, mention was made of a series of directives harmonising various aspects of company law. They form the basis for equal treatment in all the Member States of companies and firms formed in accordance with the law of one of them and having their registered office, central administration or principal place of business within the Community.[31]

Intellectual and Industrial Property Rights

The first reference in the Treaty to those rights is in connection with the exceptions to the free movement of goods.[32] The expression "industrial and commercial property" can be held to cover all the

[29] [1998] O.J. L155/43.
[30] [1996] O.J. C130/1.
[31] Art. 48 (ex 58) E.C.
[32] Art. 30 (ex 36) E.C.

rights mentioned in the Paris Convention on the Protection of Industrial Property, the Munich Convention on the European Patent[33] and the Community Patent Agreement of 1989.[34] This Agreement provides that a Community patent has equal effect throughout the Community, has an autonomous character and is subject only to the provisions of the Agreement. National patents continue to exist. Community law provides for protection of data bases[35] and it was decided that the expression of computer programmes is protected by copyright.[36]

The owners of such rights enjoy a legal and absolute monopoly (but not necessarily a dominant position, this depends on the relevant market), since they can, as any property owner, claim exclusive use. But by doing so they can prevent trade between Member States since the protection is generally granted for the national territory by each Member State separately.[37] As the Court put it, in the absence of unification of national rules relating to such protection, industrial property rights and the differences between national rules are capable of creating obstacles to the free movement of products covered by such rights.[38]

The exercise of a property right granted and guaranteed by national law thus constitutes an obstacle to the full application of certain fundamental Community rules. The question therefore arose of how to reconcile the use of those individual rights with the principle of free trade. The answer given by the Court is that

---

[33] The European Patent Convention came into force in October 1977; all the Member States are party to the Convention. The European Patent Office is located in Munich. Protection can be sought in several States, with the same effect as national patents. Decisions are subject to the judicial control of the European courts [1989] O.J. L401/1. The Common Appeals Court for community patents is located in Luxembourg [1993] O.J. C325/5.

[34] Those Conventions cover: patents, utility models, industrial designs, trade marks, service marks, trade names, indication of source or applications of origin, and copyrights. There are other similar rights which protect such property, for instance know-how.

[35] Dir. 96/9 on the legal protection of data bases [1996] O.J. L77/20.

[36] Dir. 91/250 [1991] O.J. L122/42. See Reg. 40/94 [1994] O.J. L11/1.

[37] Except, of course, when a patent is issued under the Convention on the Community Patent which has the same effects, as regards the rights conferred by it, in all the Member States ([1976] O.J. L17/1).

[38] Case 24/67 *Parke, Davis v. Centrafarm* [1988] E.C.R. 55 at 71; [1968] C.M.L.R. 48. See also Case 53/87 *Cicra v. Renault* [1958] E.C.R. 6067; [1990] 4 C.M.L.R. 265. The Court accepted opposition to the import of decorative parts on the basis of national law.

See the cases reported above under Community Competition Policy, *e.g.* Case 119/75 *Terrapin v. Terranova* [1976] E.C.R. 1039; [1976] 2 C.M.L.R. 482. Also Case 40/70 *Sirena v. Eda* [1971] E.C.R. 69; [1971] C.M.L.R. 260.

the "existence" of the right is not affected by the Treaty, but that the "exercise" of such rights can, under certain conditions, be prohibited by Community law. Consequently, such exercise must be strictly limited to what is necessary to safeguard what constitutes the "specific subject-matter" of those rights.[39]

The question arose however of what is left of this specific subject-matter once the owner has used his rights in one of the Member States. The Court refers to "exhaustion of rights".[40] The proprietor of an industrial or commercial property right protected by the legislation of a Member State may not rely on that legislation in order to oppose the importation of a product which has lawfully been marketed in another Member State by or with the consent of the proprietor of the right himself or a person legally or economically dependent on him.[41] In other words, once the owner of a right has exercised it in such a way that its use by others in any one Member State is legal, he can no longer claim territorial exclusivity within the common market. The situation can, however, be different in regard to products coming from third countries.[42]

The various rules with regard to property rights and free movement of goods were restated by the Court as follows:

(1) the Treaty does not affect the existence of property rights recognised by the law of the Member States;
(2) the exercise of those rights may, nevertheless, depending on the circumstances, be restricted by the prohibitions of the Treaty;

---

[39] See Cases 15/74 *Centrafarm v. Sterling Drug* and 16/74 *Centrafarm v. Winthrop* both [1974] E.C.R. 1147 and 1183; [1974] 2 C.M.L.R. 480, where the Court defined what is the subject-matter of a patent: the guarantee that the patentee, to reward the creative effort of the inventor has the exclusive right to use an invention with a view to manufacturing industrial products and putting them into circulation for the first time, either directly or by the grant of licences to third parties as well as the right to oppose infringements (Case 15/74 at 1162) and of a trade mark (Case 16/74 at 1194); from Case 24/67 *Parke, Davis* (n. 38 above) it follows that one can legally oppose the import and distribution of an unpatented product, otherwise one's own patent becomes useless. The same applies where the holder of a specific right prevents the import of a product from another Member State where there is no longer a protection: Case 341/87 *EMI* [1989] E.C.R. 92; [1989] 2 C.M.L.R. 413. See also Case 119/75, *Terrapin v. Terranova* [1976] E.C.R. 1039; [1976] 2 C.M.L.R. 482: the protection of a trade-mark implies also the right to prevent confusion between two products bearing similar names. It is for the national courts to determine whether a risk for confusion does in fact exist.

[40] Case 15/74 *Centrafarm* (n. 30 above).

[41] Case 144/81 *Keurkoop v. Nancy Kean Gifts* [1982] E.C.R. 2853 at 2873(25); [1983] 2 C.M.L.R. 47.

[42] See EMI Cases 51/75, 86/75 and 96/75, all [1976] E.C.R. 2853 at 2873(25); [1976] 2 C.M.L.R. 235.

(3) in as much as an exception to the fundamental principles of the Treaty is provided, it applies only to the extent necessary to safeguard rights which constitute the specific subject-matter of that property;
(4) the owner of the right cannot rely on national law to prevent the importation of a product which has been marketed in another Member State by the owner or with his consent;
(5) it is the same when the right relied on is the result of a sub-division, either voluntary of publicly imposed, of a trademark which originally belonged to a single owner[43]; however, an owner can oppose the import of a product into a Member State when this product was produced in another Member State on the basis of a compulsory licence[44];
(6) even when the rights belong to different proprietors, national law may not be relied on when the exercise of those rights is the purpose, means or result of a prohibited agreement;
(7) it is compatible with the Treaty provisions concerning free trade for the owner of a trademark to prevent the importation of products from another Member State and legally bearing a name giving rise to confusion with the trademark. However, this does not apply when there is an agreement or link between the owner and the producer in the other Member State; their respective rights must also have arisen independently.[45]

---

[43] C–10/89 *SA CNL-SVCAL NV v. HAG GF AG* [1990] E.C.R. I–3711; [1990] 3 C.M.L.R. 571. Articles 30 and 36 do not prevent that a national law authorises an undertaking, owner of a trade-mark in a Member State to oppose the importation from another Member State of a similar product bearing legally in that other Member State the same or confusingly similar trade-mark even if it belonged to a subsidiary and belongs now to a 1/3 party following expropriation and C–238/89, *Pall Corporation v. Dahlhausen* [1990] E.C.R. 4827. Art. 30 must be interpreted as precluding the application of a national provision on unfair competition which enables a trader to obtain a prohibition in the territory of a Member State on the putting into circulation of goods bearing the letter R in a circle beside the trade-mark, where the trade-mark is not registered in that State but is registered in another Member State. See, however, Case 102/77 *Hoffmann-La Roche v. Centrafarm* [1978] E.C.R. 1139; [1978] 3 C.M.L.R. 217 and Case 3/78 *Centrafarm v. American Home Products* [1978] E.C.R. 1823.

[44] [1979] 1 C.M.L.R. 326. Case 19/84 *Pharmon v. Hoechst* [1985] E.C.R. 2298(25); [1985] 3 C.M.L.R. 775.

[45] Case 119/75 *Terrapin* (n. 38, above).

As was mentioned in the section on Competition Policy, the Commission issued regulations providing block exemptions for patent licensing[46] and for know-how licensing agreements.[47] Attention must also be drawn to a Directive on the legal protection of the topographies of semi-conductor products[48] and another on the legal protection of biotechnical inventions.[49]

As far as copyrights are concerned, the principle is, of course, the same: protection can only be invoked to safeguard the rights which constitute the specific subject-matter of the intellectual property.[50]

Trade marks

The matter of trade mark protection finds a legal basis in the Madrid Agreement concerning the International Registration of Marks, of June 27, 1989[51] and in several Community acts. See, for instance, the first Council Directive to approximate the laws of the Member States relating to trade marks.[52] Also the Council Regulation on the Community trade mark,[53] which provides uniform trade mark protection for the entire territory of the European Union in addition to the already existing national and international registration systems. See also the directive on the protection of Designs.[54]

The Community trade mark is obtained by filing one single application with the Community Office,[55] the Office for Harmonisation in the Internal Market (Trade Marks, Designs and Models).[56] This means that only one representative has to be appointed. Furthermore, it requires use in only one Member State of the Union. The protection lasts ten years and can be renewed. There is an implementing regulation,[57] a regulation on the fees payable to the

[46] Reg. 2349/84 ([1984] O.J. L219/15, amended by [1985] O.J. L113/34). See Case 65/86 *Bayer* [1998] E.G.R. 5249 no-challenge clause admissible under certain conditions.
[47] Reg. 556/89 [1989] O.J. L61/1.
[48] [1987] O.J. L24/36.
[49] [1989] O.J. C10.
[50] See Case 78/70 *Deutsche Gramophon v. Metro* [1971] E.C.R. 487; [1971] C.M.L.R. 631 and Joined Cases 55 and 57/80 *Musik-Vertrieb Membran v. GEMA* [1981] E.C.R. 500; [1981] 2 C.M.L.R. 44.
[51] [1996] O.J. C293/13.
[52] Dir. 89/104 [1989] O.J. L40/1.
[53] Reg. 40/94 [1994] O.J. L349/93.
[54] Dir. 98/71 [1998] O.J. L289/28.
[55] The administration fee on application is euro 975 and upon registration another euro 1,100 is due. The protection lasts 10 years; it can be renewed at the cost of euro 2,500.
[56] See under Institutions and other Organs of the Community, in Part Two.
[57] Reg. 2368/95 [1995] O.J. L303/1.

Office and a regulation laying down the rules of procedure of the Board of Appeal of the Office.[58] Interested parties should consult the *Official Journal OHIM* on evidence to be provided on claiming priority or seniority.

One of the most sensitive points is the exhaustion of trade mark rights; an exhaustive study of this question was made by the Advocate-General in one of the Court cases concerning this question.[59] In that case, the Court found that the harmonisation Directive[60] precludes, save in given circumstances, that the reliance by a trade mark owner on his rights as owner in order to prevent an importer from marketing a product which was put on the market in another Member State by the owner or with his consent, even if that importer repackaged the product and re-affixed the trade mark to it without the owner's authorisation. On the other hand, if the importer reconditions the product and puts his own name on it, the owner of the trade mark can oppose the import of a product lawfully marketed in another Member State.[61]

The basic rule, however, remains the exhaustion of rights doctrine, which provides that once an intellectual property right holder has himself placed products, or, as a result of his consent, products have been placed, on the Community market, he is deemed to have exhausted his rights. In other words, the owner cannot after that prevent another person from buying those products in one part of the single market and then selling them in another. In a recent case, the Court was asked whether the exhaustion doctrine also applied to products which had been put on the market, by the owner of the right, in a third country. In other words, whether the international exhaustion of rights doctrine applied in Community law. This question was particularly important, since certain Member States, like Austria, could have their own rules concerning international exhaustion. The Court decided[62] that, if this were recognised, then the same product would either be subject to parallel imports in one Member State and not in another, or, as a result of the Customs Union, would be put into free circulation in the whole Community. This possibility was therefor rejected by the Court.

---

[58] Reg. 216/96 [1996] O.J. L28/11.

[59] See Joined Cases 427 etc./93 *Bristol-Myers Squibb and Others v. Paranova* [1996] E.C.R. I–3457; [1997] 1 C.M.L.R. 1151.

[60] The court refers to Dir. 89/104, see n. 52 above, and particularly its Art. 7. The latter, according to the Court in another case, regulates the question of exhaustion of trade mark rights comprehensively: Case C–352/95 *Phyteron* [1997] E.C.R. I–1729; [1997] 3 C.M.L.R. 199.

[61] Case C–232/94 *MPA Pharma* [1996] E.C.R. I–3671.

[62] Case C–355/96 *Silhouette* [1998] E.C.R. I–4799.

2. Public Procurement

The purpose of the Community legislation in this field is to open the procedures for awards[63] of public contracts to competition from all undertakings situated in the Community. Discrimination in the award of supply contracts, for instance, is contrary to the free movement of goods and constitutes a measure with equivalent effect as a quantitative restriction.

A first distinction must be made between public supply, public works and public services contracts. A second distinction, historically explainable, exists between water, energy, transport and telecommunications,[64] on the one hand, and all the other fields on the other.

Public supply contracts were regulated by three directives which were consolidated and amended in a single directive which entered into force on June 14, 1994.[65] As mentioned, it concerns the award of such contracts, not the execution, which remains under national law. Furthermore it only concerns the most important contracts, *i.e.* for contracts with a value of more than euro 130,000 when the State is involved, otherwise 200,000. The directive requires publication of the intention of the public authority to award a contract via a notice in the *Official Journal* of the Community. Also is required that discrimination be avoided by references to Community norms (AFNOR, Din) rather than to national norms.

Public works contracts are covered by two directives from 1990[66] which were modified in 1993[67] and a codified version entered into force on July 1, 1993.[68]

The directive applies also to works carried out under a concession and by private persons which are, however, controlled by public authorities.

This directive also only applies to important contracts: those with a value of more than five million euros.

---

[63] For a definition of "contracting authority", see Case C–44/96 *Mannesmann* [1998] E.C.R. I–73.

[64] Dir. 90/531 on the procurement procedure of entities operating in the water, energy, transport and telecommunications sectors [1990] O.J. L297/1, replaced by Dir. 93/38 [1993] O.J. L199/89. See Case C–87/94 *Commission v. Belgium* [1996] E.C.R. I–2043; [1996] 3 C.M.L.R. 671.

[65] Dir. 93/36 [1993] O.J. L199/1, modified by Dir. 97/52 [1997] O.J. L328/1.

[66] Dir. 71/305 [1971] O.J. L185/5, modified by Dir. 89/440 [1989] O.J. L210/1 and Dir. 93/4 [1993] O.J. L38/31. See Case C–323/96 *Commission v. Belgium* [1998] E.C.R. I–5063.

[67] Dir. 93/37 [1993] O.J. L199/54, amended by Dir. 97/52 [1997] O.J. L328/1.

[68] Dir. 89/665 [1989] O.J. L395/33.

As for *public services contracts*[69] the directive entered into force on July 1, 1993. A distinction is made between priority services where all the requirements apply and non-priority services, such as cultural training services, which are only covered by a surveillance system. It applies to contracts worth at least euro 200,000.

A possibility to appeal concerning the awards made by public authorities for supplies, works and services is provided.[70]

Water, energy, transport and telecommunications have always been considered as forming a separate sector for which different rules should apply, hence their exclusion from the first series of directives. For supply and works there exists one single directive[71] which provides for different thresholds of applicability: in the telecommunication sector for supply it is euro 600,000, while for the other sectors it is euro 300,000. For works it is five million euros and for services[72] euro 400,000, except for Telecommunications where it is euro 600,000. Generally speaking in these so-called "excluded sectors", the rules are less strict: no obligation to publish each individual contract, they may be grouped and there are different possibilities: open bidding, restricted and negotiated contracts.

It will be remembered that the United States protested against the Community legislation, considering it discriminatory and contrary to the GATT rules. The dispute was settled by an Agreement in the form of a Memorandum of Understanding between the European Economic Community and the United States of America on government procurement.[73] Consequently, the Council adopted a decision concerning the extension of certain benefits in respect of the United States.[74]

At the end of 1993 all the Member States had transposed the supply and works directives into their national law; with regard to services many were lagging behind, while for the "excluded sectors" most Member States had adapted their national law.

In 1987, the Commission set up an Advisory Committee on the opening-up of public procurement.[75] The instruments are now in place and the problem is now one of implementation.

---

[69] Dir. 92/50 relating to the co-ordination of procedures for the award of public service contracts [1992] O.J. L209/1, amended [1998] O.J. L101/1.

[70] Dir. 89/665 [1989] O.J. L395/33, and for the water, energy, transport and telecommunications sectors Dir. 93/38 [1993] L199/89.

[71] Dir. 90/531 [1990] O.J. L297/1, replaced by Dir. 93/38 [1993] O.J. L199/84, amended [1998] O.J. L328/1.

[72] Dir. 92/13 [1992] O.J. L76/14.

[73] [1993] O.J. L125/1.

[74] *ibid.*, at 54.

[75] Dec. 87/305 [1987] O.J. L152/32.

3. Trans-European Networks

The concept of Trans-European Networks (TENs) was introduced by the Maastricht Treaty.

It is closely associated with Economic and Social Cohesion and with the achievement of the internal market. It expressly refers to both Community activities where the Treaty provides that the TENs are intended to help achieve the objectives of both those policies.[76] As can be seen in the section on the Economic and Social Cohesion, the Regional Development Fund may contribute to the financing of the TENs.[77]

By "networks" is meant the interconnection and inter-operability of national networks as well as access to such networks in the areas of transport, telecommunications and energy infrastructures.

Where the regional development preoccupation clearly appears, is when the Treaty provides that account shall be taken in particular of the need to link island, landlocked and peripheral regions with the central regions of the Community.

Community activity in the TENs' field shall consist of:

(a) establishing guidelines covering objectives, priorities and broad outlines of envisaged measures;
(b) implementation of measures that may prove necessary to ensure the inter-operability of the networks, in particular in the field of standardisation;
(c) support for the financial efforts made by Member States for projects of common interest; the Community may also contribute to specific projects in the area of transport infrastructure through the Cohesion Fund.[78]

As for the Member States, they must co-ordinate among themselves the policies used at national level which may have an impact on the achievement of the above-mentioned objectives.[79]

The Community may also co-operate with third countries to promote projects of mutual interest.

Wide powers have been attributed in the TENs' field to Parliament since the guidelines to be established shall be adopted by the Council together with Parliament and after consultation of the Economic and

---

[76] Art. 154(1) (ex 129b(1)) E.C.

[77] Reg. 2083/93, Art. 1(b), first indent [1993] O.J. L193/34.

[78] See Commission Decisions concerning projects to be co-financed [1993] O.J. L308/1.

[79] Art. 155(2) (ex 129c(2)) E.C.

Social Committee and the Committee of the Regions.[80] Other measures are adopted according to the co-operation procedure.

In the case of common projects which relate to the territory of a Member State, the latter's approval shall, of course, be required.

As was seen, one of the first tasks of the Community was to establish guidelines. Following the modifications introduced by the Treaty of Amsterdam, all the measures concerning the TENs are adopted according to the co-decision procedure,[81] and after consultation of the ESC and the Committee of the Regions. The first ones were adopted in 1995, according to the co-operation procedure, and concerned the telecommunications field of Euro-ISDN,[82] they were followed by guidelines for the development of energy,[83] transport[84] and telecommunications[85] networks. On the basis of those guidelines, the Commission determines which projects are of common interest,[86] after having consulted the Member State where the project is to be carried out. However, a first list of 10 priority projects in the energy field and 14 in the transport area was established by the European Council at Essen.[87] To think that it needs Heads of State or of Government to select individual projects!

During the years following the Essen European Council, steady progress was made in implementing some of the selected projects in the *transport sector*. These are of course large infrastructure projects, which take years to construct. The Commission adopted a communication seeking to clarify the application of the competition rules to new rail infrastructure projects.[88]

Where *telematics and telecommunications* are concerned, the Parliament and the Council adopted a decision on guidelines for trans-European telecommunication networks. Those guidelines cover all telecommunication networks, including satellites and mobile networks; they incorporate the guidelines adopted in 1995 for integrated services digital networks (ISDN). They also identify projects of common interest eligible for financial aid from the Community; those projects concern the basic networks, namely

---

[80] Art. 156 (ex 129d) E.C.

[81] Art. 156 (ex 129d which for measures other than guidelines provided for the co-operation procedure) E.C.

[82] Dec. 95/489 [1995] O.J. L282/16.

[83] Dec. 96/1254 [1996] O.J. L161/147, amended O.J. L152/2.

[84] Dec. 96/1692 [1996] O.J. L228/1.

[85] Dec. 97/1336 [1997] O.J. L183/12.

[86] See, for instance, for the energy sector, Dec. 96/537 [1996] O.J. L230/16 and 97/548 [1997] O.J. L225/25.

[87] See General Report 1994, 112 and 113.

[88] COM (98) 480.

ISDN and IBC (integrated broadband communications) generic services and sectoral applications.

As for *energy*, the Parliament and the Council supplemented the list of projects of common interest, in order to take account of the rapidly changing market, especially for natural gas, the acceleration towards the extension of the interconnected network across the European continent and the prospects of Union enlargement.[89]

Further Reading

Conor Quigley, *European Community Contract Law* (two vols, Kluwer Law International, 1997).

[89] Further details on the various projects can, as always, be found in the yearly General Reports of the Commission and in the Bulletin.

Chapter Twenty-eight

Economic and Social Cohesion

GENERALITIES

When Title V on Economic and Social Cohesion was added to the Treaty by the SEA, regional policy had been an important Community activity since 1975.[1] This is acknowledged by the Treaty which provides that the Community must "develop and pursue" the actions already undertaken and which should be leading to the strengthening of its economic and social cohesion.[2] It was assumed from the moment the common market was established that it could not function as an economic entity if the differences in economic development of the composing regions were excessive. That there are and will be differences is inevitable, due, *inter alia*, to geography, climate, belief and population. But, without some similarity in the levels of economic and social development the internal market simply cannot function. If the purchasing power in one part does not allow its inhabitants to acquire the goods they need, the producers in the richer parts will not be able to sell them their products. And, since economic integration of the Community is based on inter-State trade such a situation not only jeopardises the development of the common market, but makes it practically impossible to pursue the economic and monetary convergence which is a precondition for EMU.

As indicated, economic and social cohesion mainly concerns "regional policy", but other policies such as Social Policy, Agricultural Policy and Fisheries are also involved in the attainment of the objectives of this policy. Those objectives are clearly set out in the Treaty as "reducing disparities between the levels of development of

[1] The regulation setting up the European Regional Development Fund (ERDF) was adopted in March 1975: Reg. 724/75 [1975] O.J. L73/1. The Social Fund and Agricultural Fund have been in existence practically since the very beginning; they were provided for in the Treaty.

[2] Art. 158 (ex 130a) E.C.

the various regions and the backwardness of the least-favoured regions, including rural areas".[3]

The Treaty established three basic principles for the implementation of economic and social cohesion. In the first place, as with most of the Community activities, the responsibility for attaining the objectives is shared by the Community and the Member States. Indeed, the latter must conduct their economic policies and co-ordinate them (amongst themselves) "in such a way as, in addition, to attain the objectives" set out in the Treaty.[4]

Secondly, the Treaty provides that these objectives must be taken into account by the institutions when formulating and implementing other Community policies and actions, and that those policies and actions must support the achievement of the objectives. The same obligation is imposed by the Treaty with regard to other policies, such as the protection of the environment. In other words, the formulation and implementation of all Community policies must be achieved in a coherent and co-ordinated manner, with special attention given to the so-called "horizontal" policies.[5]

A third point is the indication in the Treaty that the various existing funds, *inter alia* the so-called "Structural Funds" and the European Investment Bank (EIB) must all be used to attain the objectives.

If other actions are required, they shall be decided by the Council, acting unanimously, on a proposal from the Commission and after consultation of Parliament, the Economic and Social Committee and the Committee of the Regions.[6]

Besides the provisions concerning Economic and Social cohesion, there are several other Treaty provisions which refer to underdeveloped regions,[7] which shows that from the very beginning the regional problems were taken into account.[8] Furthermore, the signatories of the Treaty were convinced that the functioning of the common market with the resulting development of economic activity throughout the Community would more or less automati-

---

[3] Art. 159 (ex 130a) E.C. The words "including rural areas" were added by the Maastricht Treaty; it establishes a clear link between regional policy and agricultural policy.

[4] Art. 159 (ex 130b) E.C.

[5] See, for instance, Communication from the Commission to the Member States on the links between regional and competition policy [1998] O.J. C90/3.

[6] *ibid.* at 3.

[7] The European Investment Bank (EIB), for instance, was set up to provide the necessary resources, *inter alia*, for "developing the less developed regions" (Art. 267(a) (ex 198e(a)) E.C.)

[8] See, *e.g.* Art. 87 (ex 92) E.C.

cally reduce regional disparities. The functioning of the common market did, indeed, achieve spectacular results in most depressed areas, as is evidenced by the doubling, even trebling of their *per capita* income. Nevertheless, this was not enough for achieving the necessary coherence among the regions in a Community where similar developments took place in the well developed areas. The result was that, although the gap between the richer and poorest regions might not have widened, it was not reduced significantly. It goes without saying that the existing discrepancies are no longer socially and politically acceptable and create a major problem for the Community as a whole. Even worse, it becomes very difficult, if not impossible to achieve the economic convergence which is required for the functioning of the EMU.[9] Indeed, as long as some of the Member States (and their number has increased with each enlargement), have to devote large proportions of their resources to the development of their less favoured regions, they will remain subject to inflation, balance of payment problems and exchange rate fluctuations.

It was at the October 1972 Paris Conference of Heads of States or of Governments that it was agreed that a high priority should be given to the aim of correcting the structural and regional imbalances which might affect the realisation of economic and monetary union.[10] The Member States undertook to co-ordinate their regional policies and invited the Community institutions to create a European Regional Development Fund (ERDF).[11] However, it was not until March 1975 that the Council adopted the regulation setting up the ERDF[12] and a Decision creating a Regional Policy Committee.[13] It is interesting to note that no reference was made to a Community regional policy. This had to wait till February 1979, when amendments to the regulation were adopted[14] together with a Resolution concerning guidelines for such a policy.[15] Finally in 1984 a Regulation was adopted concerning both a Community Regional Policy and the ERDF.[16]

---

[9] Art. 116(2) (ex 109(2)) E.C., second indent: "lasting convergence necessary for the achievement of economic and monetary union".

[10] Bull. 10 [1972] E.C., 9. This was the first "summit" in which Denmark, Ireland and the U.K. participated.

[11] See the Commission's "Report on Regional Problems in the Enlarged Community"; 1973 E.C. Bull. suppl. 8.

[12] Reg. 724/75 [1975] O.J. L73/1. It is based on Art. 235. Initially the ERDF was endowed with the equivalent of euro 375 million; in 1998 it was euro 14 billion.

[13] [1975] O.J. L73/47.

[14] [1979] O.J. L35/1.

[15] [1979] O.J. C36/10.

[16] [1984] O.J. L169/1.

Over the past years, the ERDF regulation was amended several times and one of the novelties was its inclusion into the "Structural Funds". This allowed for far-reaching co-ordination of objectives and procedures. The EIB,[17] the European Agricultural Guidance and Guarantee Fund, Guidance Section (EAGGF Guidance Section), the European Social Fund (ESF) and the Financial Instrument of Fisheries Guidance (FIFG) are also included.

The latest revision of the ERDF regulations were to be completed, together with the revision of the ESF and EAGGF, in 1999. The provisions concerning the Structural Funds are embodied in six regulations: a "framework" regulation setting out the tasks of the Structural Funds and their co-ordination among themselves and with the EIB.[18] This framework regulation is implemented by a so-called co-ordination regulation.[19] They are accompanied by four "sectoral" regulations: fisheries,[20] regional,[21] social[22] and agriculture.[23]

The Structural Funds Principles

As indicated, the Agenda 2000 concerns, besides the Community financing for the next seven years and the reform of the agricultural policy, the reform of the structural funds: the European Social Fund, the Regional Fund, the structural part of the Agricultural Fund (FEOGA), the Fisheries Fund and the Cohesion Fund. As was mentioned, all those funds constitute the so-called "Structural Funds" and the expenditure of the available amounts under those funds is closely co-ordinated.

Together with the Community financing and the reform of the CAP, the Berlin Council of March 24–25, 1999 agreed on the reform of the Structural Funds. The decisions taken in Berlin will, of course, have to be translated into amendments to the existing regulations. Obviously this will take time. It would, therefore, have been extremely difficult at this stage to give indications about the future look of those funds, were it not for the fact that the Berlin Council

[17] Art. 198d E.C.
[18] Reg. 2081/93 amending Reg. 2052/88 [1993] O.J. L193/5.
[19] Reg. 2082/93 amending Reg. 4253/88 [1993] O.J. L193/20.
[20] Reg. 2080/93 [1993] O.J. L193/1.
[21] Reg. 2083/93 [1993] O.J. L193/34.
[22] Reg. 2084/93 [1993] O.J. L193/39.
[23] Reg. 2085/93 [1993] O.J. L193/44.

adopted quite detailed arrangements.[24] Part of these are reproduced hereafter, so that the reader will have all the information presently available concerning the future operations of those funds.

(1) Structural Operations

Improving the effectiveness of the structural and cohesion funds in achieving the goal of economic and social cohesion enshrined in the Treaty is a central plank of the Agenda 2000 reforms. This goal has to be maintained in the future as priorities continue to evolve in a more diverse Union, taking account of the aim of achieving greater concentration of structural assistance, improving the financial management of the structural funds as well as simplifying their operation and administration.

Greater concentration of structural fund assistance in the areas of greatest need will be achieved by means of a substantial reduction in the number of Objectives to three. In fostering economic and social cohesion by pursuing these Objectives, the Community shall contribute to the harmonious, balanced and sustainable development of economic activities, the development of employment and human resources, the protection and improvement of the environment, the elimination of inequalities and the promotion of equality between men and women. The Commission and the Member States shall ensure that the operations financed by the funds are in conformity with the provisions of the Treaty, the instruments adopted under it, and are consistent with other Community policies and operations.

Overall level of allocations for structural operations

In view of the continued priority accorded to economic and social cohesion and as a result of more targeted concentration of structural expenditure in line with this Treaty objective, the European Council considers that the overall amounts for the structural and cohesion funds should be a total of euro 213 billion over the seven-year period, which represents about euro 30 billion a year. This overall level of expenditure will enable the Union to maintain the present average aid intensity levels, thereby consolidating the present overall effort in this field.

---

[24] See the Presidency conclusion—Berlin European Council March 24 and 25, 1999: DN: DOC/99/1, March 26, 1999.

(2) Structural Funds

Overall level of allocations for the structural funds

The European Council considers that the appropriate level of commitment appropriations to be entered in the financial perspective for the structural funds, including transitional support, Community initiatives and innovative actions, should be euro 195 billion, which represents about euro 28 billion a year. 69.7 per cent of the structural funds will be allocated to Objective 1, including 4.3 per cent for transitional support (*i.e.* a total of euro 135.9 billion). 11.5 per cent of the structural funds will be allocated to Objective 2 including 1.4 per cent for transitional support (*i.e.* a total of euro 22.5 billion). 12.3 per cent of the structural funds will be allocated to Objective 3 (*i.e.* a total of euro 24.05 billion).

(3) Eligibility

Objective 1

Objective 1 shall promote the development and structural adjustment of regions whose development is lagging behind. Objective 1 status for the period 2000–2006 will be conferred on:

- current NUTS level II regions whose *per capita* GDP is less than 75 per cent of the Community average;
- the most remote regions (the French overseas Departments, the Azores, Medeira and the Canary Islands), which are all below the 75 per cent threshold;
- areas eligible under Objective 6 for the period 1995–1999 pursuant to Protocol No. 6 to the Act of Accession of Finland and Sweden.

Objective 2

Objective 2 shall support the economic and social conversation of areas facing structural difficulties. These shall include areas undergoing economic and social change in the industrial and service sectors, declining rural areas, urban areas in difficulty and depressed areas dependent on fisheries, defined on the basis of objective criteria laid down in the legislative texts.

The Member States will propose to the Commission a list of areas which meet the objective criteria, subject to a population ceiling to be applicable to each Member State. This population ceiling for each Member State will be fixed by the Commission on the basis of the total population of the areas in each Member State which meet the Community criteria, and the seriousness of structural problems assessed on the basis of total unemployment and long-term unemployment outside Objective 1 regions.

A maximum of 18 per cent of the Union's population will be covered by the new Objective 2. The indicative breakdown of the population at Community level for the different types of Objective 2 region should be 10 per cent for industrial areas, five per cent for rural areas, two per cent for urban areas and one per cent for fishery dependent areas. The industrial and rural areas meeting the Community criteria laid down in the regulation must contain at least 50 per cent of the population covered by Objective 2 in each Member State, except where this is objectively impossible. The total allocation to each Member State under Objective 2 will depend directly on the relative share of each Member State in the total population of the Union eligible for Objective 2.

Objective 3

Objective 3 will lend support to the adaptation and modernisation of policies and systems of education, training and employment. It shall apply outside Objective 1. Each Member State will receive a percentage of the total resources available for Objective 3 on the basis of its share of the total target populations of the Union yielded by indicators selected on the basis of the objective criteria. The European Council considers that the aveage per capital level of assistance under Objective 3 should take account of the priority given to employment, education and training.

Community initiatives and innovative actions

In the light of the added value that Community Initiatives offer over and above the mainstream Objectives, the number of Community initiatives will be reduced to the following three: INTERREG (cross-border, transnational and interregional co-operation), EQUAL (transnational co-operation to combat all forms of discrimination and inequalities in the labour market) and LEADER (rural development). Five per cent of the structural fund commitment appropriations should be set aside for the Community initiatives. At least 50 per cent of appropriations will be allocated to INTERREG, under which due attention should be given to cross-border activities, in particular in the perspective of enlargement, and for Member States which have extensive frontiers with the applicant countries, as well as to improved co-ordination with the PHARE, TACIS and MEDA programmes. Due account will be taken of the social and vocational integration of asylum seekers in the framework of EQUAL. It is agreed that the three new mainstream Objectives should cover the scope of all existing Community Initiatives which have proved their effectiveness but which are no longer retained as such. Due attention will also be given to co-operation with the outermost regions. One per cent of the structural fund allocations will be set aside for innovative actions and technical assistance.

(4) Financial support

Adequate transitional support for regions which are no longer eligible for assistance are an essential counterpart to greater concentration of structural funds, so as to underpin the results secured by structural assistance in ex-Objective 1 regions, and to support the end of the conversion process in areas ceasing to be eligible. The profile of transitional support may be tailored to the specific needs of individual regions, in agreement with the Commission, provided the financial allocation for each region is respected.

Indicative allocations among Member States

In accordance with the Commission's proposals, the allocation of resources to Member States for Objectives 1 and 2 will be based, using transparent procedures, on the following objective criteria: eligible population, regional prosperity, national prosperity and the severity of structural problems, especially the level of unemployment. An appropriate balance will be struck between regional and national prosperity. For Objective 3, the breakdown by Member State shall be based principally on the eligible population, the employment situation and the severity of the problems, such as social exclusion, education and training levels and participation of women in the labour market, with a relative weighting as outlined by the Commission.

Total annual receipts in any Member States from structural operations (*i.e.* including the Cohesion Fund) should not exceed four per cent of national GDP.

Rates of assistance

The European Council, bearing in mind that the actual rates of structural fund assistance applied in practice are often less than the maximum ceilings, agrees that the contribution of the structural funds shall be subject to the following ceilings:

a maximum of 75% of the total eligible cost and, as a general rule, at least 50% of eligible public expenditure in the case of measures carried out in the regions covered by Objective 1. Where the regions are located in a Member State covered by the Cohesion Fund, the Community contribution may rise, in exceptional and duly justified cases, to a maximum of 80% of the total eligible cost and to a maximum of 85% of the total eligible cost for the outermost regions and for the outlying Greek islands which are under a handicap due to their distant location;

a maximum of 50% of the total eligible cost and, as a general rule, at least 25% of eligible public expenditure in the case of measures carried out in areas covered by Objective 2 or Objective 3.

In the case of investment in firms, the contribution of the funds shall comply with the ceilings on the rate of aid and on combinations of aid set in the field of state aids. The European Council also endorses the lower rates proposed by the Commission for contributions of the funds to revenue generating infrastructure investment and investment in firms.

Administration and financial management of the Structural Funds

The administration of the structural funds should be substantially simplified by giving practical effect to decentralising decision-making and striking the right balance between simplification and flexibility so as to ensure that funds are disbursed quickly and effectively. To achieve this, responsibilities of Member States, their partners and the Commission will be clarified, bureaucracy reduced and monitoring, evaluation and control strengthened, thereby ensuring improved and sound financial management.

(5) Cohesion Fund

The European Council considers that the basic objectives of the Cohesion Fund, which was set up to further economic and social cohesion in the Union and solidarity among the Member States by providing a financial contribution to projects in the field of the environment and trans-European networks, are still relevant today. The European Council considers that the four current beneficiaries should continue to be eligible to the fund in 2000, *i.e.* Member States with a *per capita* GNP of less than 90 per cent of the Union average and a programme leading to the fulfilment of the conditions of economic convergence.

In view of the continuing progress achieved towards real convergence and taking account of the new macro-economic context in which the Cohesion Fund now operates, the overall allocation of assistance for Member States participating in the euro will be adjusted so as to take account of the improvement in national prosperity attained over the previous period.

The European Council accordingly considers that for the seven year period 2000–2006, the overall level of resources available to be committed under the Cohesion Fund should be euro 18 billion, which represents about euro 2.615 billion a year. A review of eligibility based on the 90 per cent average GNP criterion will be undertaken at mid-term in 2003. In the event of a Member State becoming ineligible, resources for the Cohesion Fund will be reduced accordingly.

With regard to the economic convergence criterion, the current macro-economic conditionality provisions will continue to apply. Accordingly, no new projects or new project stages shall be financed by the Fund in a Member State in the event of the Council, acting by qualified majority on a recommendation from the Commission, finding that the Member State has not respected the stability and growth pact.

The rate of Community assistance granted by the Cohesion Fund shall remain unchanged at between 80 per cent and 85 per cent of public or equivalent expenditure. This rate may be reduced to take account of a project's capacity to generate revenue and of any application of the polluter-pays principle. The European Council notes that the Commission will ensure that Member States maximise the leverage of fund resources by encouraging greater use of private sources of financing, that it will draw up implementing procedures on the application of the polluter-pays principle, and that in implementing them, it will take account of specific situations in each beneficiary Member State.

The European Council considers that the financial management and control provisions should be consistent with the relevant provisions of the structural funds regulation, subject to taking due account of the specific features of the Cohesion Fund.

(6) Completion of legislative work

The European Council considers that the agreement on the above political questions implies agreement on the content of the following legislative texts related to the structural and Cohesion funds:

6896/99 (General Regulation on the Structural Funds) + COR 1, 2, 3

6881/99 (ERDF Regulation)

6882/99 (FSF Regulation)

6876/99 (FIFG Regulation) + COR 1

6878/99 (Cohesion Fund Regulations) + COR 1

The European Council, recalling the readiness expressed by the Parliament and the Council at the Cardiff European Council to achieve final adoption of the legislative texts before the next European Parliamentary elections, urges both institutions to take the necessary steps to ensure that they are enacted by that deadline, particularly in view of the need to prepare a smooth transition into the new structural funds programming period beginning on January 1, 2000.

(7) Programming

Financial assistance is given in the form of non-reimbursable grants, subject to co-financing from the Member States, and is channelled through three financial instruments: national programmes, Community initiatives and Innovative measures.[25]

National programmes

They account for about 90 per cent of the ERDF budget. At the start of each programming period, Member States submit proposals, in the form of regional development plans or single programming documents, to the European Commission for the use of Structural Funds in their respective countries.

On the basis of those proposals, two to six year regional development programmes are negotiated between the European

[25] This section is based on http://europa.eu.int/comm/dg16/activity/erdf/erdf2en.htm and some parts are borrowed from it.

Commission and each Member State and are implemented in partnership with regional and local authorities concerned.

The designated authorities in the Member States are responsible for organising calls for tenders and project selection. Implementation of the measures and projects is supervised by the Monitoring Committees, which are made up of representatives of the regions, the Member States, the responsible bodies and the Commission. Those Committees oversee the implementation of the programmes on a regular basis and set guidelines where necessary.

The regulations provide for timetables for the various phases. As mentioned, the financing is done through an integrated approach of the Structural Funds. However, each fund has its own characteristic which must be respected; their individual scope can be described as follows.

The ERDF can finance productive investments, infrastructure, local development and SMEs, pilot projects, investment in education and health, Trans-European Networks and R&D.

The ESF may give financial assistance for vocational training, start-up aid, innovation measures, training and education schemes and R&D.

The EAGGF Guidance Section finances the adjustment of agricultural development measures, agri-environmental, afforestation and early retirement measures and other development measures such as promotion of local produce, prevention of natural disasters in remote regions, village renovation, protection of the rural heritage and financial engineering.

The FIFG makes funds available for fishing fleets, aquaculture and coastal waters, fishing port facilities, processing and marketing of fishery and aquaculture products and the search for new markets.

(8) Partnership

This was the key principle underlying the 1989 reform. It is defined as close consultation between the Commission, the Member State concerned and the competent authorities and bodies, including the social partners, designated by the Member State. This principle recognises that regional development cannot be carried out solely through central decision-making; it requires the consent and co-operation of the regions themselves.

The consultation takes place at the national, regional and local or other level, with each party acting as a partner in pursuit of a common goal. This partnership covers the preparation, financing, monitoring and assessment of the various operations.

Since Community action must "complement" action in the field, continual dialogue with all the economic operators is required. The nature of partnership depends on the institutional structure and traditions of each Member State. It, therefore, necessarily can take many forms.

Community initiatives

These programmes differ from mainstream national programmes in that they are initiated at the Community rather than at the national level and are proposed by the Commission to the Member States, with a view to promoting innovative approaches to address specific problems which are of European-wide concern.

The initiatives give the Commission the opportunity to activate special funds for measures of special interest in the Community. Those measures complement those included in the Community Support Frameworks. They are financed by 9 per cent of Structural Fund commitments. Parliament, the Council and the Commission have undertaken to create a special budget line to finance measures to be carried out in the border regions of the countries bordering eastern and central Europe. A Committee for the Community initiatives was set up by the Commission.[26] There are 13 Community Initiatives under the Structural Funds for the period 1994–99. They have three features which give them added value as compared with other measures financed by the structural funds, namely;

- their support for the development of transnational, cross-border and inter-regional co-operation;
- their "bottom-up" method of implementation, and
- the high profile they give, on the spot, to Community measures and priorities.

Operational programmes under the Community initiatives are proposed by the Member States, are then subject to negotiation with the Commission and then implemented in partnership with regional and local authorities concerned.

Innovative measures

These measures are financed under the ERDF Regulation and account for around 1 per cent of the total ERDF budget. They are

[26] For a complete list see Community Structural Funds 1994–1999, ISBN 92-826-6272-1, 28.

the only exception to the principle of programming and permit the Commission, on its own initiative, to finance studies, pilot projects or networks with a view to testing new policy approaches at the Union level. These measures are aimed at exploring new approaches to encourage co-operation and the exchange of experience between actors in local and regional development.

For the period 1994–99, four priority themes govern the allocation of funding in this area:

- innovation for local and regional development (euro 90 million);
- regional and spatial planning (euro 45 million);
- urban development (euro 80 million), and
- interregional co-operation (euro 189 million).

Calls for tender and project selection under the innovative measures are organised by the Commission.

(9) Additionality

To prevent the Community structural funds from being used merely to replace national aids, the 1988 Funds reform introduced the principle of additionality: "the Commission and the Member States shall ensure that the increase in the appropriations for the Funds results in at least an equivalent increase in total volume of official or similar structural aid in the Member State concerned". Since this provision was not sufficient to force certain Member States to implement the principle of additionality, the regulations now specify that each Member State has to maintain, in the whole of the territory concerned, its public structural or comparable expenditure at least at the same level as in the previous programming period. Member States must provide the financial information needed to verify additionality when submitting plans and regularly during the implementation of the CSFs.

Implementing procedures

This important topic covers four elements, details of which are to be found in the above-mentioned regulations;

(1) Adherence to Community policies: need for compatibility of the measures financed by the Structural Funds with other Community policies.

(2) Appraisal, monitoring and evaluation. With regard to appraisal, the regulation provides that "assistance will be allocated where appraisal shows medium-term economic and social benefits commensurate with the resources deployed".
(3) Part-financing rates. The new rates of assistance are set out above under (4) Financial Support.
(4) Payments are generally made up of advances with a final balance of 20 per cent.

The Treaty envisages the grouping of the various funds[27] and the creation of a Cohesion Fund to provide a financial contribution to projects in the fields of environment and Trans-European networks in the area of transport infrastructure.

Further Reading

European Commission, "Economic and social cohesion in the EU: the impact of Member States' own policies", Luxembourg, EUR-OP 1998.

F. Bollen, "Cohesion policy in an even larger Union", EIPASCOPE 1997, No. 3, p. 19.

[27] Art. 130d, 1, E.C.

Chapter Twenty-nine

Research and Technological Development

One of the lengthier chapters of the Treaty,[1] it was added to the Treaty by the SEA and left practically untouched by the Treaties on E.U. and of Amsterdam. The latter only modified the unanimity, required *inter alia*, for setting up joint undertakings, in qualified majority and the co-operation procedure in co-decision, for the other measures. In this field, the Community was assigned its own task, mainly through the implementation of the multiannual framework programme, while, on the other hand, complementing the activities of the Member States. To avoid wasteful duplication, co-ordination is therefore essential and the Treaty provides that "the Community and the Member States shall coordinate their research and technological development activities".[2]

It is interesting to note that the objective of R&TD is not research for its own sake or for scientific purpose, but "strengthening the scientific and technological bases of Community industry and encouraging it to become more competitive at international level".[3] The whole activity of the Community in this field is industrially orientated, whether it is carried out in the undertakings themselves, including small and medium-sized ones, or in research centres and universities. The task of the Community is to encourage such research and to support their efforts to co-operate with one another. This is made easier by the establishment of the internal market,[4] the opening of national public contracts,[5] the definition of common

[1] Arts 163 (ex 130f) to 173 (ex 130p) E.C.
[2] Art. 163(1) (ex 130h(1)) E.C.
[3] Art. 163(1) (ex 130f(1)) E.C.
[4] See above under "Free movement of goods".
[5] See above under "Industrial policy".

standards[6] and the removal of legal[7] and fiscal obstacles to the co-operation. The importance of co-operation between undertakings, research centres and universities is further underlined by the following tasks entrusted to the Community.[8]

The means to achieve the objectives are, firstly, the implementation of the multiannual programmes, secondly cooperation with third countries and international organisation and, thirdly, the dissemination of information.

The fifth *Framework Programme for Research and Technological Development* (R&TD), for the period 1998 to 2002, was adopted at the end of 1998. To give an idea what the implementation of such a programme represents, it might be interesting to examine what it meant in 1997. Nearly 24,000 proposals were received and evaluated across all the specific programmes, 6,000 contracts were signed and euro 3,000 million of Community funds were attributed to research projects, involving 24,000 participants. Cumulatively, more than 15,000 research projects had been established under the Fourth Framework Programme at the end of 1997, amounting to euro 8,200 million in signed contracts, with 1,000 projects ongoing. Strong growth was registered in the level of participation of SMEs (24 per cent of total participants as compared with 18 per cent in 1996) and the budgetary contributions they received: 16 per cent of total contributions in 1997 as against 13 per cent in 1996. This result was achieved largely through the success of stimulation measures (co-operative research and exploratory awards) and take-up actions (for information technologies).

It should be noted that those programmes cover a wide range of subjects cutting across many activities of the Community: Information Technologies, Industry, Energy, Transport and Agriculture, and the Joint Research Centre. In this respect, a new strategy, involving a redirection of Community research activity was developed taking account of the orientations given by the Maastricht Treaty, and a start was made on implementing it.[9] It was developed by the Commission in a document entitled "Research after Maastricht: an assessment, a strategy".[10] In this communication the Commission states that European industry has become less competitive in the world in recent years, due in part to an insufficient level of

---

[6] See *supra* under "Free movement of goods", section 4 "Theory and reality". See Directive 83/189 laying down a Procedure for the Provision of Information in the Field of Technical Standards and Regulations [1983] O.J. L109/8.

[7] See above under "Competition policy".

[8] Art. 164 (ex 130g) E.C.

[9] General Report (1992), p. 98.

[10] [1992] E.C. Bull. 4–29.

expenditure on R&TD. The Commission proposed three guiding principles: redirecting research activities: implementation of priority projects more directly linked to key generic technologies on which the competitiveness of European industry depends. These projects might concern micro-electronics, advances technology in the transport sector, high performance computing, flat screens, environment-friendly industrial technologies or advanced molecular biology; increasing resources: they would increase from euro 2.4 billion in 1992 to 4.2 billion in 1997. They now represent less than 4 per cent of the total financial resources allocated to R&TD in the Member States; strengthening the programme: this should be the case with the fourth framework programme.

It is clear from the previous remarks that the multiannual framework programmes play an important role in the implementation of the research and technological development activities of the Community. Those programmes are adopted by Parliament and the Council acting together, after consulting the ESC.[11] They establish the scientific and technological objectives, fix the relevant priorities, indicate the broad lines of each activity and fix the maximum overall amount for Community financial participation. Those programmes are to be implemented through specific programmes developed for each activity. The rules for the participation of undertakings, research centres and universities in those programmes, and the dissemination of the results, are determined by the Council. The Treaty also provides that supplementary programmes may be financed by certain Member States only; this will, of course, influence the dissemination of the results of such programmes.[12] Also, the Community may participate in programmes carried out by several Member States,[13] while in its own programmes it may make provisions for co-operation with third countries or international organisations.[14]

It is also provided that the Community may set up joint undertakings or any other structure necessary for the execution of its research, technological development and demonstration programmes.[15]

R&TD programmes may be co-financed by the European Regional Development Fund and the European Social Fund in specific regions.[16]

---

[11] Art. 167 (ex 130j) E.C.
[12] Art. 168 (ex 130k) E.C.
[13] Art. 169 (ex 130l) E.C.
[14] Art. 170 (ex 130m) E.C.
[15] Art. 171 (ex 130n) E.C.
[16] See under Chapter Twenty-Eight "Economic and Social Cohesion".

In the second place, the implementation of the R&TD tasks is carried out through the *promotion of co-operation with third countries and international organisations*. In its communication on research after Maastricht, the Commission considered that the Community should internationalise its research effort to a greater extent and contemplate increased involvement in "big science" projects.[17] In any case, the Community did not wait for the new strategy to develop close co-operation with third countries in the field of R&TD. The ESPRIT programme is just one example among many.[18]

In this context mention must be made of the Agreement establishing an International Science and Technology Centre,[19] the participation of the Communities in the European Science Foundation,[20] several Framework Agreements were concluded with third countries like Norway[21] and Switzerland,[22] often on specific subjects.

Thirdly, the results of the Community activities in this field must be *disseminated* and optimised. This is one of the more important aspects of an efficient R&TD programme: what to do with the results. If those are not immediately and properly communicated to the undertakings which need them, such programmes will not fulfil the objectives set out in the Treaty. In 1995 the Commission adopted a Regulation on the dissemination and exploitation of knowledge resulting from the specific R&TD programmes.[23] It lays down general rules on dissemination and protection of knowledge and provides for the implementation of centralised dissemination and exploitation measures.

Finally, one of the tasks of the Community is to stimulate the training and mobility of researchers. This should be made easier by the Community activities with regard to education and training examined elsewhere in this book and, of course, the free movement of persons.

Some of the above-mentioned research is carried out by the Community itself in the Joint Research Centre which was set up in

---

[17] *ibid.* For more information see, *e.g.* General Report (1993) 82–95.
[18] General Report (1984), p. 104; see also Resolution concerning the mid-term review [1986] O.J. C102/1.
[19] [1992] O.J. L409/3 and 10. *id.* between the USA, Japan, the Russian Federation and the Communities: *ibid.* at 1.
[20] [1974] O.J. C7/5.
[21] [1986] O.J. L78/27.
[22] [1988] O.J. L195/75.
[23] Reg. 2897/95 [1995] O.J. L304/11.

pursuance of the Euratom Treaty.[24] The latter is composed of eight institutes which carry out their work in the Centre's four areas of activity: specific research programmes under the framework programme,[25] support for Commission departments,[26] work under contract for outside bodies[27] and exploratory research.[28]

Finally, the Commission must each year send a report to Parliament and the Council on its R&TD activities, the dissemination of results and the work programme for the current year.[29]

Further Reading

Parliament and Council Decision 1999/182 concerning the fifth framework programme for research, technological development and demonstration activities (1998–2002) [1999] O.J. L26/1 of February 1, 1999.

Council Decision 1999/64 concerning the fifth framework programme of Euratom, *ibid* at 34.

Council Decision 1999/65 concerning the rules for the participation of undertakings, research centres and universities and for the dissemination of research results for the implementation of the fifth framework programme, *ibid.* at 46.

---

[24] Art. 8(1) Euratom.

[25] Decs 92/274 and 92/275 [1992] O.J. L141/20 and 27.

[26] Dec. 92/273 [1992] O.J. L141/11.

[27] General Report 1992, p. 101.

[28] It would go far beyond the scope of this book to enumerate the many research programmes financed by the Community. A first source of information thereon are the usual General Reports published by the Commission, *e.g.* General Report (1998) 173(ex 130p).

[29] Art. 104 E.C.

Chapter Thirty
Environment

The first Community environmental legislation emerged in the 1970's. The Community and the Member States started to realise that—especially over the long term—the promotion of economic growth within the Community and the establishment of a single market economy required an underlying cross-border environmental protection regime. However, before the Single European Act of 1987, the Treaty did not explicitly provide for the adoption of environmental measures. Consequently, the early legislation[1] was founded either on the internal market harmonisation provisions[2] or on the possibility for the Council to take the appropriate measures when action proves to be necessary to attain one of the objectives of the Treaty, while the necessary powers have not been provided.[3] In both cases, an unanimous decision by the Council is required, on a proposal from the Commission and after consultation of the Parliament. The Court, on the other hand, relied on the preamble to the Treaty and on the tasks assigned to the Community to justify such measures. As mentioned, the SEA introduced environmental provisions into the Treaty: Title VII "Environment" and into the

[1] *e.g.* Dir. 67/548 [1967] O.J. L196/1, on classification, packaging and labeling of dangerous substances; Dir. 70/157 [1970] O.J. L42/16, on noise levels; Dir. 70/220 [1970] O.J. L76/1, on automobile emissions.

[2] Case 91/79 *Commission v. Italy* [1980] E.C.R. I–1099; [1981] 1 C.M.L.R. 331 and Case 92/79 *Commission v. Italy* [1980] E.C.R. 1115; [1981] 1 C.M.L.R. 331.

[3] Art. 308 (ex 235) E.C. Since the Treaty did not refer to environmental protection as one of its objectives, the Court relied on an interpretation of Art. 2 E.C, which defines as a task of the Community "a harmonious development of economic activities, a continuous and balanced expansion, . . . (and) an accelerated raising of the standard of living" and of the preamble stating that Community goals include "the constant improvement of living and working conditions". In 1985, the Court finally held that environmental protection is one of the Community's "essential objectives": *Procureur de la République v. Association de défense des brûleurs d'huiles usagées* Case 240/83, [1985] E.C.R. I–531(549).

harmonisation provisions.[4] Furthermore, one of the Community tasks was described as the promotion of a "sustainable and non-inflationary growth respecting the environment".

The Amsterdam Treaty of 1997[5] slightly modified the description of those tasks focusing on "a harmonious, balanced and sustainable development of economic activities, . . . sustainable and non-inflationary growth, . . . a high level of protection and improvement of the quality of the environment, the raising of the standard in living and quality of life". This objective was given even more weight by the inclusion, under the "activities" of the Community, of a "policy in the sphere of the environment".[6]

The Maastricht Treaty significantly enhanced the scope of environmental responsibility within the Community by "democratising" the decision-making process; this was achieved by conferring more power upon the Parliament in this sector also. The Community's objectives for environmental protection were listed as follows[7]:

- preservation, protection and improvement of the quality of the environment;
- protection of human health;
- prudent and rational utilisation of natural resources;
- promotion of measures at international level to deal with regional or world-wide environmental problems.

In addition, a unique set of principles serving as guidelines for further environmental regulations was incorporated,[8] such as the precautionary principle,[9] the principle of preventive action, the proximity principle (*i.e.* environmental damage shall be rectified at source), the principle of high level of protection and the "polluter pays" principle.[10] By requiring that "environmental protection requirements shall be a component of the Community's other policies", this

---

[4] Art. 100a E.C. granted the right to adopt measures progressively establishing the internal market and concerning health, safety, environmental protection and consumer protection.

[5] [1997] O.J. C340/181.

[6] Art. 3(l) (ex 3) E.C.

[7] Art. 174 (ex 130r) E.C.

[8] *ibid.*

[9] Although not expressly defined in the Treaty, this principle entails that, despite scientific uncertainty concerning the likelihood of harm, certain measures should be taken before the environmental risk can be clearly evidenced.

[10] This "polluter pays" principle is regarded as the cornerstone of Community environmental policy. References to it are made, *inter alia*, in Dir. 75/439 on the disposal of waste oils [1975] O.J. L194/23 and Dir. 91/689 on dangerous waste [1991] O.J. L377/20, amended by Dir. 94/31 [1994] O.J. L168/28.

so-called integration principle led to a general obligation for Community institutions to seek to conciliate other Treaty objectives (*e.g.* single market economy) with environmental protection, determining the wide scope of environmental responsibility.[11] Finally, the principle of subsidiarity, first mentioned in the SEA in relation with the Environment, was generalised by the Maastricht Treaty: the Community is only to legislate if and in so far as the objectives stated above "cannot be sufficiently achieved by the Member States and can, therefore, by reason of the scale or effects of the proposed action, be better achieved by the Community".[12]

But even where Community action is necessary, the Amsterdam Treaty[13] allows the Member States to maintain or introduce stricter national provisions concerning, *inter alia*, environmental legislation derogating from Community "internal market" harmonisation measures. However, these provisions have to be notified to the Commission. The latter will only approve them if it is satisfied that they are based on "grounds of major needs" or on new scientific evidence relating to the protection of the environment or the working environment. The Commission must also be convinced that those measures are neither means of arbitrary discrimination nor disguised restrictions on E.U. interstate commerce or other obstacles to the functioning of the internal market. Where protective measures adopted by the Council to achieve the environment objectives are concerned,[14] Member States are not prevented from maintaining or introducing more stringent provisions as long as they are "compatible with this Treaty".[15]

As mentioned before, the Maastricht Treaty substantially enhanced the decision-making power of the Parliament in the area of environmental legislation. Where unanimous decisions of the Council, after prior consultation of the Parliament, were required, the

---

[11] The Amsterdam Treaty provides for the integration principle in Art. 6 (ex 3c) E.C.: "environmental protection requirements must be integrated into the definition and implementation of the Community policies and activities referred to in Art. 3, in particular with a view to promoting sustainable development."

[12] Art. 5 (ex 3b) E.C. modified significantly the wording of the old Art. 130r E.C. (4) seemingly to emphasise Community action; it referred to the concept of proportionality as follows: "(a)ny action shall not go beyond what is necessary to achieve the objectives of this Treaty". In this context, mention must be made of the "Protocol on the application of the principles of subsidiarity and proportionality" annexed to the Amsterdam Treaty [1997] O.J. C340/105.

[13] Art. 95(4) and (5) (ex 100a(4) and (5)) E.C.

[14] Art. 174 (ex 130s) E.C.

[15] Art. 176 (ex 130t) E.C.

Treaty now provides for a joint decision of the Council and the Parliament, and a "qualified majority" in the Council.[16]

Since 1973, the Community environmental policy has been developed through the enactment of a series of non-binding "Environmental Action Programmes"[17] by the Parliament and the Council after consultation of the Economic and Social Committee and the Committee of the Regions.[18] Serving as an orientation for future Community action, the recent and most ambitious fifth Programme is entitled "Towards Sustainability". It addresses the need for a greater use of market forces through market instruments and incentives (*e.g.* taxes, eco-labeling, liability schemes, eco-audits, voluntary agreements, deposit/refund systems, etc.). It also introduces the notion of shared responsibility between public authorities, public and private enterprises and the general public, emphasising the need for their wider involvement in environmental affairs. Most significant, though, is the shift among Member States to accept the concept of "sustainable development",[19] as being fundamental to future economic E.U. policy leading to the prudent use of resources and to profound changes of current patterns of development, production, consumption and behaviour.[20]

Noticeably, almost all of the around 300 Community legislative acts aiming at environmental protection are in the form of directives leaving room for each Member State to implement them taking into account its own economic, social and cultural background. Thus, due to the diversity of situations within the various regions of the Community, E.U. environmental policy focuses rather on the

---

[16] Art. 175 (ex 130s) E.C., which refers to Art. 251 (ex 189b) E.C.

[17] Usually passed as "Resolutions": First Action Programme (1973–77) [1973] O.J. C112/1; Second Action Programme (1977–83) [1977] O.J. C139/1; Third Action Programme (1983–87) [1983] O.J. C46/1; Fourth Action Programme (1987–93) [1987] O.J. C328/1; Fifth Action Programme (1993–2000) [1993] O.J. C138/1.

[18] Art. 175(3) (ex 130s(3)) E.C.

[19] Following the Report of the World Commission on Environment and Development (Brundtland Commission), the term "sustainable development" can be defined as "development which meets the needs of the present without compromising the ability of future generations to meet their own needs".

[20] [1992] E.C. Bull. 12–93 in accordance with this realisation process, the Amsterdam Treaty includes the concept of sustainable development into various provisions, namely the preamble of the Treaty on the European Union (in connection with the promotion of environmental protection) and Art. 2 (ex B) E.C. stating that one of the objectives of the Union shall be "to achieve balanced and sustainable development". Nevertheless, in the latter case, specific reference to environmental protection was not made. Furthermore, Art. 2 (ex 2) E.C. stresses "sustainable development" as a Community task, whereas Art. 6 (ex 3c) E.C. combines the integration principle with the accompanying promotion of sustainable economic development.

harmonisation than on the unification of environmental standards.[21] In this context, the major sectors of environmental E.U. concern have been the protection of fresh and sea water,[22] the monitoring of atmospheric pollution,[23] the prevention of noise, the conservation of wild flora and fauna,[24] waste management,[25] the control of chemi-

---

[21] In terms of national environmental legislation within the Member States, substantial differences exist due to diverse social, cultural and economic realities. Unification of standards would often neglect the respective socio-economic situation of a Member State. Therefore, the use of directives shall leave room for each Member State to adjust its laws accordingly. At present, for example, Member States such as Denmark, the Netherlands, Sweden, Austria and Germany are far more concerned about environmental protection than, for instance, Greece, Spain or Italy.

[22] Many directives in this area are concerned with quality standards of water for specific uses (*e.g.* Dir. 75/440 [1975] O.J. L194/96 to help ensure clean drinking water by protecting those rivers, lakes and reservoirs used as drinking water sources; Dir. 76/160 [1976] O.J. L31/1 to safeguard the health of bathers and to maintain the quality of bathing water; Dir. 78/659 [1978] O.J. L222/1 to protect freshwater bodies capable of supporting fish life; Dir. 79/923 [1979] O.J. L281/47 to protect coastal and brackish waters to support shellfish populations; Dir. 80/778 [1980] O.J. L229/11 to safeguard human health by imposing strict quality standards for water intended for direct or indirect human consumption). Various amendments and modifications have followed. Other legislation introduced emission standards for discharges to surface waters and groundwater (*e.g.* framework Dir. 76/464 [1976] O.J. L129/23 on the discharge of dangerous substances into the aquatic environment) and established a system of information exchange on river water quality between the Member States.

[23] In the 1980s, especially under the impression of acid rain pollution, various directives on air quality standards were enacted (*e.g.* Dir. 80/779 [1980] O.J. L229/30 setting up quality standards for sulphur dioxide and suspended particulates; other directives for lead and nitrogen dioxides followed). For new industrial plants prior authorisation schemes were developed verifying, *inter alia*, the use of "green" technologies and the compliance with certain air quality standards to prevent excessive air pollution (framework Dir. 84/360 [1984] O.J. L188/20). Various daughter directives flowed from this, as well as legislation setting up emission standards for industrial plants and motor vehicles. An information exchange system was established by a Council Decision concerning atmospheric pollution in each Member State.

[24] *e.g.* Dir. 92/43 [1992] O.J. L206/7 on the conservation of European wildlife and natural habitats; Dir. 79/409 [1979] O.J. L103/1 on the conservation of wild birds; other legislation banned the import of sea pup skins or the use of leghold traps within the Community and established common rules for the imports of whales and other cetacean products.

[25] *e.g.* framework Dir. 75/442 [1975] O.J. L194/39 on waste management; Dir. 91/689 [1991] O.J. L377/20 on waste management in hazardous waste; Reg. 259/93 [1993] O.J. L30/1 on the supervision and control of shipments of waste within, into and out of the E.U. (legislation implementing the obligations under the Basel Convention (1989) and the Lomé IV Convention (1991)); other directives focused on landfill waste, packaging and packaging waste, waste disposal installations or the encouragement of the production of recyclable/refillable products (*e.g.* containers of liquid).

cals[26] and energy policies. Despite this sector-specific legislation, the Community is in the process of establishing a comprehensive framework of procedural and organisational rules in the field of environmental policy. In 1985, the Council adopted an "environmental impact assessment" procedure. It not only required every private and public project likely to have a significant impact on the environment to undergo an "assessment", but, and this was even more significant, it introduced a preventive policy approach within the Community.[27] In recent years, particular attention has been paid to a shift from "command-and-control" measures (*e.g.* fines, imprisonment, etc.) to market-based incentives[28] as well as to the improvement of public participation and information. A voluntary eco-labeling system was enacted to award consumer products, which reduce environmental impact, with an eco-label and to inform the public about environmentally "friendly" options.[29] In addition, an eco-audit regime allows for voluntary registration of private industrial companies in eco-management and audit schemes aiming at the improvement of the companies environmental performance. They provide, *e.g.* for the introduction of environmental reviews, programmes and management systems, audits and the publication of

[26] *e.g.* framework Dir. 67/548 [1967] O.J. L196/1 on the classification, packaging and labeling of dangerous chemical substances especially in the area of agriculture (use of pesticides and artificial fertiliser, etc.); many amendments have followed; the so-called "Seveso-Directive" 82/501 [1982] O.J. L230/1 on the prevention of major accident hazards of chemical industrial activities trying to set up a better control mechanism concerning actions entailing potential risk; Reg. 2455/92 [1992] O.J. L251/13 establishing a prior informed consent procedure for exports and imports of substances that are already severely restricted within the Community.

[27] Dir. 85/337 [1985] O.J. L175/40; further amendments and modifications followed.

[28] In 1992, the proposal of a combined CO_2/energy tax failed by not reaching the necessary unanimous consent ([1992] O.J. C196/1). Although, recently, the Commission published a communication on eco-taxes and charges in the internal market: COM (97) 009 final, the negotiations appear to steer toward a voluntary system of national energy tax regimes.

[29] Reg. 880/92 [1992] O.J. L99/1. The Commission has to establish the ecological criteria for the award of a Community eco-label for specific product groups. This has already been done for washing machines and dishwashers, soil improver, toilet paper, kitchen rolls, laundry detergents, light bulbs, hair sprays, refrigerators and paint; the main objective is to promote the design, production, marketing and use of products which have a reduced environmental impact during their entire "life-cycle" (Art. 1). So far, more than 180 products have been awarded the eco-label (a flower made up of 12 stars and an "E" for "Europe").

"environmental statements", while exposing them to public scrutiny.[30] Still highly controversial is the establishment of a civil environmental liability regime.

In 1989, the proposal of a civil liability scheme for damage caused by waste calling for a system of unlimited strict liability on the waste producer[31] was heavily criticised and eventually not further approached.[32] In 1993, the Council of Europe initiated the Lugano Convention establishing a civil liability scheme for activities dangerous to the environment[33] and the same year, the Commission published a "Green Paper"[34] addressing the usefulness of a general liability system. This paper proposed a dual system of strict and joint compensation mechanisms, the latter to cover costs of environmental restoration that cannot be individually attributed. In this case, a compensation fund (similar to the U.S. Superfund) should provide financial means for cleaning-up measures.[35] Although, in 1994, the Parliament called upon the Commission to prepare a draft environmental liability directive and, in 1996, the Community's waste management strategy[36] clearly demanded action in this field, a binding environmental liability scheme is yet to be passed. Maybe this is not surprising at a time when economic recession and massive unemployment put pressure on the European governments to privilege economic policies triggering short-term economic results. The Commission, nevertheless, in its Communication on the implementation of the Fifth Action Programme, criticised the lack of "attitude changes and (of) the will . . . to make the necessary progress to move towards sustainability".[37] Nonetheless, in 1992, a directive on the freedom of public access to environmental information came into force; the aim is to trigger public participation in

[30] Reg. 1836/93 [1993] O.J. L168/1; by 1997, some 700 sites had been registered which are, in return, allowed to use a logo on their correspondence papers indicating their participation in the system.

[31] See amended proposal [1991] O.J. C192/6; this approach was based on the preventive action and polluter pays principles and entailed provisions for a compulsory insurance by producers and disposers of waste.

[32] Mainly the industrial and insurance lobby as well as France, Germany and the United Kingdom argued that the establishment of a civil liability regime should be left to each Member State and that the subsidiarity principle did not call for Community action in this area.

[33] This Convention set up an unlimited strict, joint, several and retroactive liability scheme in which access to justice was granted to individuals and non-governmental organisations. But at the end, only eight of the 27 participants signed the document.

[34] Green Paper on remedying environmental damage, COM (93) 47 final.

[35] This fund was to be financed by the industrial sectors most closely linked to the probable source of damage.

[36] COM (96) 399.

[37] COM (95) 624.

the decision-making and in the monitoring process by disseminating environmental information held by public authorities.[38]

Externally, the Community has become party to numerous international Conventions and related Protocols for the protection of the environment.[39] These international Treaties, nevertheless, have without any exception, the form of joint agreements between the Community and its Member States due to the fact that their respective subject-matters usually fall partly within the competence of the Community and partly within that of the Member States (shared competence).[40] Organisationally, the establishment of the European Environmental Agency and the European Environment Information and Observation Network[41] in 1990, was supposed to create an organisational basis for an independent, objective, reliable and comparative collection, screening and evaluation network of environmental data and information.

In addition, in 1993, the Commission set up a European Environmental Forum with general consultative functions.[42] However, the fact that about 90 per cent of Community environmental legislation is in the form of directives, means that the major problem with the environmental law of the Community resides in the too prudent and

---

[38] Dir. 90/313 [1990] O.J. L158/56; this right of information may be restricted in order to prevent the disclosure of business secrets.

[39] *e.g.* Rio de Janeiro Convention on Biological Diversity [1993] O.J. L309/1, Vienna Convention on the Protection of the Ozone Layer and the Montreal Protocol on Substances that Deplete the Ozone Layer; both in [1988] O.J. L297/8, Basel Convention on the Control of Transport of Hazardous Waste [1993] O.J. L39/1, New York Convention on Climate Change [1994] O.J. L33/11, Bonn Convention on the Conservation of Migratory Species of Wild Animals [1982] O.J. L210/10, Paris Convention for the Prevention of Marine Pollution from Land-Based Sources [1975] O.J. L194/5.

[40] Art. 174(4) (ex 130r(4)) E.C.; this provision reserves, again, strong rights for the Member States to conclude international agreements individually and limits the power of the Community accordingly. However, the Treaty only refers in this respect to "their respective fields of competence" without further specification. Therefore, future disputes over the respective limits of each side's competence cannot be excluded until clear-cut criteria for such a distinction—similar to the "Protocol on the application of the principles of subsidiarity and proportionality" added by the Amsterdam Treaty, will be established.

[41] Reg. 1210/90 [1990] O.J. L120/1. The Agency is located in Copenhagen. It is interesting to notice that this institution is the only one set up by the Community, membership in which extends beyond the E.U. to Norway and Iceland, with Switzerland and a number of Central and East European countries expected to join soon. Its 1996's budget was euro 14.5 million.

[42] The Forum consists of 32 members elected from the sectors of economics and of environmental protection.

often insufficient implementation by the Member States.[43] Therefore, in 1992, a financial instrument for the environment ("LIFE") was created, the main objective of which is the development and implementation of E.U. environmental policy by granting financial assistance.[44] In 1993, the establishment of the Cohesion Fund which was designed to finance environmental and transport infrastructure projects in Member States whose gross domestic product is less than 90 per cent of the Community average, made even more financial support available.[45] Finally, the European Investment Bank funds environmental projects that pass a prior environmental assessment procedure.

Further Reading

C. London, "*Droit Communautaire de l'environnement*", Revue Trimestrielle de Droit Européen, 1997, No. 3, p. 629.

R. Wägenbaur and R. Wainwright, "EC energy and environment policy", Yearbook of European Law, 1996, No. 16, p. 59.

---

[43] From the start of the environmental legislation there has been a steadily increase in the number of Court actions initiated by the Commission about lack of proper implementation by the Member States, particularly in the fields of drinking water quality, environmental impact assessments and the protection of wild birds (1978: 25 complaints and cases; 1986: 192; 1992: 587). Finally, a new legal procedure was introduced to enable the Community to exert stronger influence on each Member State's implementation activities. Now, where a Member State does not comply with a judgment of the Court, although it has been previously found in breach of Community law by not implementing appropriately E.U. directives, the Commission can propose and specify to the Court the amount of a lump sum or penalty payment to be paid by the Member State concerned: Art. 228 (ex 171) E.C. The Court may then impose such penalty. In 1997, the first two environmental cases were submitted to the Court both against Germany asking for penalty payments of euro 26,400 and 158,000, per day respectively (both Case C–121/97 *Commission v. Germany*, [1997] O.J. C166/7).

[44] Reg. 1973/92 [1992] O.J. L215/1; its annual budget is about euro 100 million.

[45] Reg. 1164/94 [1994] O.J. L130/1; its budget for the period of 1993 to 1999 contains euro 15.15 billion. Currently, only Greece, Ireland, Portugal and Spain are eligible for financial assistance.

Chapter Thirty-one

Energy Policy

There is no specific Title on Energy in the E.C. Treaty, neither after nor before the modifications introduced by the Treaties on E.U. or of Amsterdam. Of course, coal, previously the main source of energy, has been the object of Community measures since 1952 and the development of nuclear energy is the objective of the Euratom Treaty since 1958. But obviously a concerted effort in the energy field is required from the Member States and the Community, as much as in the areas of agriculture, transport and commercial policy. Consequently, notwithstanding the absence of specific Treaty provisions, the Community has developed and is still expanding and implementing, in close co-operation with the Member States of course, an energy policy. This raises the question of the competence of the Community to do so, since as was explained several times in the foregoing pages, the Community may only exercise those powers which have been explicitly conferred upon it. As shall be seen, the institutions adopted directives, regulations and decisions in the energy field and it is interesting to examine at the onset what empowered the Community to do so.

A typical example is the Directive of the Parliament and the Council concerning common rules for the internal market in electricity.[1] The institutions indicate as legal bases for their act, in the first place, the E.C. Treaty provisions concerning the right of establishment, *i.e.* the right to "issue directives for the coordination of provisions laid down by law, regulation or administrative action in the Member States concerning the taking-up and pursuit of activities as self employed persons".[2] Secondly, the provisions concerning the freedom to provide services,[3] and, thirdly, the Treaty provisions concerning the harmonisation measures necessary for the

[1] [1997] O.J. L27/20.
[2] Art. 47(2) (ex 57(2)) E.C.
[3] Art. 66 E.C. which refers back to several provisions concerning the right of establishment, including the above-mentioned Art. 42(2).

establishment and functioning of the internal market.[4] And, although an energy policy is not provided for in the E.C. Treaty, the reference to the above mentioned provisions are ample justification for the Community to act in this domain.[5] In December 1998, the Council adopted a multiannual framework programme for actions in the energy sector (1998–2002) and connected measures. This programme will primarily contribute to the balanced pursuit of security of supply, competitiveness and protection of the environment. The Council also adopted a multiannual programme of studies, analyses, forecasts and other related work in the energy sector (1998–2002).[6]

According to the Commission[7] the overall objective of the Community's Energy policy is to help ensure security of energy supplies for European citizens and businesses at competitive prices and in environmental compatible ways. More precisely:

- *Manage external dependency to secure future energy supplies.* At the present time the Union gets almost half of its energy supplies from third countries; as energy consumption grows, this is expected to increase to 70 per cent in the year 2020 for gas, and even 90 per cent for oil.
- *Integrate European energy markets to increase competitiveness and foster employment.* European industry pays far more for energy compared to the USA (in the case of the chemical industry 45 per cent more). More competitive energy prices are essential for European industry in the context of the globalisation of the economies.
- *Assure the compatibility of energy and environmental objectives.* Energy is indeed a key factor for addressing environmental changes such as climate change.[8]

The most important actions to achieve the above objectives were set

---

[4] Art. 95(1) (ex 100a(1)) E.C.

[5] The absence of an explicit reference to Energy in the Treaty has nothing to do with the Commission's Communication to the Parliament and the Council concerning the repeal of several Community legislative texts in the field of energy policy [1996] O.J. C221/3.

[6] [1999] O.J. L7/16 and 20; the first Decision is based upon Art. 235 (now 308) E.C. and Euratom, Art. 203; the second one on Art. 235 (now 308) E.C.

[7] See http://europa.eu.int/encomm/dg17/mission.htm (December 1998) on which much of this chapter is based and from which some parts are reproduced here.

[8] See Communication from the Commission to the Parliament, the Council, the ESC and the Committee of the Regions—the energy dimension of climate change: COM (97) 196.

out in a Communication: "An overall view of Energy Policy and Actions".[9]

(1) Security of energy supply and international co-operation

This includes the development of relation with the supplier countries through bilateral and multilateral agreements such as the *Energy Charter*. The Energy Charter Treaty[10] was adopted in 1997 and designed to develop new relations between the main European countries and most of the independent States of the former Soviet Union and Central and Eastern Europe, Canada, the USA and Japan covering trade, investment and energy co-operation. The main aim is to meet the challenge of developing the energy potential of the independent States of the former Soviet Union and Eastern Europe while helping to improve security of supply for the European Community.[11] Another aspect of those relations is the external interconnection of Trans-European Networks.[12]

The actions also aim at the more efficient use of existing resources; a multiannual programme was set up to promote energy efficiency in the Community,[13] the diversification of energy resources through the promotion of new energy sources[14] and the use of renewable sources[15] (hydro-electric, solar, wind, geothermal and bio-fuels) and the implementation of provisions concerning the supply of nuclear materials and safeguard measures.[16] Other actions focus on *energy*

---

[9] COM (97) 167.

[10] See also the Decision with regard to the ECT, the Energy Charter Protocol on energy efficiency and related environmental aspects, and the amendments to the ECT [1998] O.J. L252/21.

[11] [1997] E.C. Bull. 9–26.

[12] See above, Industry Policy and Communication from the Commission to the Parliament and the Council—The external dimension of Trans-European networks: COM (97) 125 and the Communication on Community Guidelines on Trans-European energy Networks: COM (93) 685 final.

[13] Dec. 96/737 concerning a multiannual programme for the promotion of efficiency in the Community [1996] O.J. L335/50.

[14] See, for instance, Communication from the Commission on a Community strategy to promote combined heat and power (CHP) and to dismantle barriers to its development: COM (97) 514 final.

[15] See White Paper on energy for the future—renewable sources of energy: COM (97) 599 final. See also Dec. 94/806 adopting a specific programme for research and technological development, including demonstration, in the field of non-nuclear energy: [1994] O.J. L334/87.

[16] See Communication from the Commission on the nuclear industries in the EU: COM (97) 401 final.

demand, which include the promotion of energy saving and the development of a culture of energy-saving behaviour and rational energy consumption.

In December 1998, the Council adopted a multiannual programme to promote international co-operation in the energy sector (1998–2000).[17]

Finally, some actions concern *international aid and co-operation programmes*. These include actions in the context of general technical assistance programmes: PHARE, TACIS[18] and MEDA and specific actions aiming at taking European priorities into account: the SYNERGY programme.[19] This programme finances international co-operation projects with third countries for developing, formulating and implementing their energy policy in fields of mutual interest. Those projects have to contribute to accomplishing the objectives defined in the Commission's White Paper on "An energy policy for the European Union". Also included are actions for the preparation of the accession of new States, co-operation with international organisations: IEA, IAEA, OECD, ERBD and the World Bank, and the definition of crisis-management measures to be implemented for each type of energy source if needed.

(2) Integrating energy markets

The main objective is the completion of the Internal Energy Market, especially in the fields of electricity and gas. A directive was adopted by the Parliament and the Council concerning common rules for the internal market in electricity.[20] It concerns electrical energy, electricity supply, energy production, energy transport and the internal market. Other actions include the implementation of competition rules, including State aid,[21] the establishment of networks for the transport of energy throughout Europe, taxation of

---

[17] [1999] O.J. L7/23.

[18] See Council Decision adopting a multiannual programme (1998–2002) of actions in the nuclear sector, relating to the safe transport of radioactive materials and safeguards and industrial co-operation to promote certain aspects of the safety of nuclear installations in the countries currently participating in the TACIS programme [1999] O.J. L7/31.

[19] Reg. 701/97 amending a programme to promote international co-operation in the energy sector—Synergy programme [1997] O.J. L104/1.

[20] [1997] O.J. L27/20.

[21] See, for instance, Dec. 93/3632 establishing Community rules for State aid to the coal industry: [1993] O.J. L329/12.

energy products and the promotion of standards for energy products. Those actions are closely linked with Community action in the field of Economic and Social Cohesion. The Commission sent a Communication on energy and social and economic cohesion in the Community to the other institutions[22] and contributions for energy are provided for in the Structural Funds. Energy investments are also financed by the TENs, the EIB and ECSC and Euratom aids and loans.

(3) Promoting sustainable development in the energy field

One of the Commission's main tasks is to ensure the compatibility of energy and environment objectives by reducing harmful emissions from energy production and use in transport and ensuring structural and operational safety of nuclear installations.

(4) Promoting energy technology development

This is carried out in the context of the Research, Development and Demonstration JOULE-THERMIE and Euratom programmes.

(5) Sectoral aspects

Coal comes within the ambit of the European Coal and Steel Community Treaty which will shortly cease to exist. Indeed, it was concluded for a period of fifty years from its entry into force,[23] *i.e.* July 25, 1952. From 2001 on coal will be considered a "good" in the sense of the E.C. Treaty, and subject to its rules. The main problem with this solid fuel is the uneconomic extraction conditions prevailing in all the Member States.[24] Some coal mines are still maintained in operation thanks to massive subsidies from governments. Those aids must, however, first be approved by the Commission. Mention was already made of the Community rules for State aid to the coal industry.[25] In 1997, the Commission still received five notifications

[22] COM (93) 645 final.
[23] ECSC, Art 97.
[24] Coal imported from Australia is cheaper on arrival in Rotterdam than European coal.
[25] [1993] O.J. L329/12.

of new aid schemes or amendments to existing ones; no negative decisions were taken.[26] In December 1998, the Council adopted a multiannual programme of technological actions promoting the clean and efficient use of solid fuels (1998 to 2002).[27]

Oil and petroleum products are, as was indicated, mainly imported from third countries; consequently, the Community attaches great importance to prospection, exploration and production within the Community itself.[28]

As for *natural gas*, which is also produced in limited quantities within the Union, the Community will shortly establish common rules for the internal market in gas[29] which are similar to those for electricity. The common rules for electricity entered into force in February 1997.[30] They are based on a balanced approach to public service obligations and competition rules and on the broad application of the subsidiarity principle, in order to take account of the different gas and electricity systems existing in the Member States. They provide for the opening-up of the market over a period of ten years.[31]

Nuclear energy is submitted to the rules of the Euratom Treaty, which shows great similarities with the E.C. Treaty. One of the main particularities consists in the fact that nuclear fissile materials are the property of the Community. This property right is exercised, *inter alia*, by the right of option on fissile material.[32] Furthermore, all operations concerning nuclear material must be handled by the Supply Agency. The latter will be examined hereafter. Another important aspect is the necessity to safeguard the use of the fissile material for non-military purposes when they have been declared to be destined for peaceful purposes.[33]

---

26 Report on Competition 1996, 94.

27 [1999] O.J. L7/28.

28 See Dir. 94/22 on the conditions for granting and using authorisations for the prospection, exploration and production of hydrocarbons [1994] O.J. L164/3.

29 General Report, 1997, 166.

30 [1997] O.J. L27/20.

31 General Report 1997, 163.

32 See Joined Cases T–458 and 523/93 *ENU v. Commission* [1995] E.C.R. II–2459.

33 See the Agreement for co-operation in the peaceful use of nuclear energy between Euratom and the U.S.: [1996] O.J. L120/1.

(6) Euratom's Supply Agency and safeguards

The property of all special fissionable material within the territory of the Member States is vested in the Community,[34] in so far as this material is subject to Euratom's safeguard control. The latter does not extend to materials "intended to meet defence requirements".[35]

The Treaty provides for the creation of a Supply Agency having a right of option on all ores, source materials and special fissile materials produced in the territories of the Member States. It also has the exclusive right to conclude contracts relating to the supply of ores, source material and special fissile materials coming from inside or outside the Community.[36] The Statute of the Agency was laid down by the Council[37] and various regulations have specified the conditions under which nuclear materials can be acquired, sold or transferred.[38]

Currently, the supply of natural uranium, special fissile material and enrichment services to Community users and the provisions of services for the whole fuel cycle do not present any problems.[39]

The Community depends on imports for some 94 per cent of its supplies of natural uranium.[40]

In this context must also be mentioned the *Euratom safeguards*. In pursuance of the Euratom Treaty, "the Commission must satisfy itself that, in the territories of the Member States, ores, source materials and special fissile materials are not diverted from their intended uses as declared by the users and that the provisions relating to supply and any particular safeguarding obligation assumed by the Community under an agreement concluded with a third State or an international organisation are complied with".[41]

To fulfil those obligations, the Commission must carry out inspections and its inspectors have access to all places and data and all persons who, by reason of their occupation, deal with materials,

---

[34] Art. 86 Euratom Treaty.

[35] *ibid.*, Art. 85.

[36] *ibid.*, Art. 52(2)(b). In 1989, *e.g.* the Agency concluded 184 contracts, 87 for uranium procurement and 97 for the supply of enrichment services and special fissile materials. See Case 7/71 *Commission v. France* [1971] E.C.R. 1003; [1972] C.M.L.R. 453.

[37] J.O. 534/58, [1952–1958] O.J. Spec. Ed. 78.

[38] See J.O. 777/60, [1959–1962] O.J. Sped. Ed. 46 (manner in which demand is to be balanced against supply); J.O. 116/62 and J.O. 4057/66, [1965–1966] O.J. Spec. Ed. 297 (implementation of supply provisions) and J.O. 1460/60 and 240/64 (communications of the Agency).

[39] Twenty-Seventh General Report (1993), p. 109.

[40] *ibid.*

[41] Art. 77 Euratom Treaty.

equipment or installations which are subject to the Euratom safeguards. In certain cases serious irregularities are discovered and the Commission imposes sanctions.[42]

As far as the International Atomic Energy Agency (IAEA) is concerned, joint IAEA-Euratom safeguards are applied in certain Community installations in compliance with the Verification Agreement in force since 1973.

Safeguards provisions are, of course an essential element in all the agreements which the Community has concluded with Third World countries.[43]

Further Reading

European Commission, "European Energy to 2020: a scenario approach", DG XVII, Luxembourg, EUR-OP 1996.

[42] See Twenty-Sixth General Report (1992), p. 236.
[43] See *ibid.*

PART SIX: THE UNION IN THE WORLD

Chapter Thirty-two

The Community's Jurisdiction

In Part Six, the Community's commercial policy, development policy, its relations with international organisations, the bilateral and regional relations and enlargement will be examined. However, before going into details, some general remarks seem necessary. Indeed, the ECSC Treaty explicitly provides that, in international relations, the Coal and Steel Community enjoys the "legal capacity it requires to perform its functions and attain its objectives".[1] The Euratom Treaty confers upon the Atomic Energy Community the authority to enter, within the limits of its powers and jurisdiction, "into obligations by concluding agreements or contracts with third States, an international organisation or a national of a third State".[2] But the E.C. Treaty only refers to the "establishment of a commercial policy towards third countries"[3] and the "association of the overseas countries and territories"[4] and contains a few other specific provisions.[5] The overall situation changed substantially, where the Union is concerned, when the Treaty on E.U. added the Title on "Provisions on a Common Foreign and Security policy", which will be examined hereafter.

However, the absence in the E.C. Treaty of a provision conferring upon the Community a general competence with regard to foreign policy has not prevented it from developing a particularly active one. This was made possible, as will be seen, with the help of the Court. According to the latter the Community is a body created by an international treaty concluded between sovereign States with the task, *inter alia*, of exercising activities in the international field. This body enjoys international legal personality and participates in activities which come within the ambit of international law. However, it is only to the extent that other subjects of international

[1] Art. 6, ECSC. This international capacity is thus strictly limited.
[2] Art. 101, Euratom.
[3] Art. 133 (ex 113), E.C.
[4] Arts 182 to 188 (ex 131–136a) E.C.
[5] See Arts 170 (ex 130m) and 300 (ex 228) E.C.

law recognise the Community as a member of the international community, that it can take initiatives and play an active role in the international sphere. This recognition is no longer a problem. It was rather among the Member States that some disagreement existed as to the extent of the Community's jurisdiction in international affairs.

The question was raised mainly with regard to the Community's treaty-making power; in other words: how much of the Member States' treaty-making power was transferred to the Community? That some powers were transferred is not questioned, but it was not clear whether those powers are to be exercised exclusively by the Community or in conjunction with the Member States.

As far as the first question is concerned, the views of the Court were clearly formulated in 1971[6] and repeated in later judgments. They were based on the Treaty which provides that "the Community shall have legal personality".[7] According to the Court, this provision placed at the head of Part Six of the Treaty devoted to "General and Final Provisions", means that in its external relations the Community enjoys the capacity to enter into international commitments over the whole field of objectives defined in Part One of the Treaty, which Part Six supplements. The following statement is also important:

> "to establish in a particular case whether the Community has authority to enter into international commitments, regard must be had to the whole scheme of Community law no less than to its substantive provisions. Such authority arises not only from express conferment by the Treaty but may equally flow implicitly from other provisions of the Treaty, from the Act of accession and

---

[6] Case 22/70 *Commission v. Council* (better known as the *AETR* case: *Accord Européen de Transport (European Transport Agreement)*) [1971] E.C.R. 263 at 274(14); [1971] C.M.L.R. 335. See also the Opinions of the Court given under Art. 300 (ex 228) E.C.: Opinion 1/75 [1975] E.C.R. 1355: compatibility with the EEC Treaty of a draft "Understanding on a Local Cost Standard" drawn up under the auspices of the OECD; Opinion 1/76 [1977] E.C.R. 741: compatibility of a draft agreement establishing a European lying-up fund for inland waterway vessels; Opinion 1/78 [1979] E.C.R. 2817: compatibility of the draft International Agreement on Natural Rubber negotiated in the UNCTAD; Case C–25/94, *Commission v. Council* [1996] E.C.R. I–1469; Joined Cases 3, 4 and 6/76, *Cornelis Kramer and Others* [1976] E.C.R. 1279; [1976] 2 C.M.L.R. 440; Opinion 2/91 [1993] E.C.R. I–1061; [1993] 3 C.M.L.R. 800 concerning the compatibility of the I.L.O. Convention 170 on safety in the use of chemicals at work and Opinion 1/94 [1994] E.C.R. I–5264.

[7] Art. 281 (ex 210) E.C.

from measures adopted within the framework of those provisions, by the Community institutions."[8]

In other words, whenever Community law has created for the institutions powers within the internal system for the purpose of attaining a specific objective, the Community has authority to enter into the international commitments necessary for the attainment of that objective, even in the absence of an express provision in that connection.[9] This is particularly so in all cases where internal power has already been used in order to adopt measures which come within the attainment of common policies.[10]

With regard to the second question (exclusive or shared jurisdiction) the Court admits a "mixed procedure", *i.e.* both the Community and the Member States are the contracting parties when an agreement covers matters for which the Community is competent and others coming within the ambit of the Member States.[11] But, "each time the Community with a view to implementing a common policy envisaged by the Treaty, adopts provisions laying down common rule, whatever form these may take, the Member States no longer have the right, acting individually or even collectively, to undertake obligations with third countries which affect those rules".[12]

As long as the Community has not exercised its right to conclude agreements, the Member States retain the power to do so.[13] But this authority is only of a transitional nature and Member States are bound by Community obligations in their negotiations with third countries: they may not enter into or renew any commitment which

[8] *ibid.* at 1308(17–18). In its Opinion of 2/91 the Court expressed it as follows: "Whenever Community law created for the Institutions of the Community powers within its internal system for the purpose of attaining a specific objective, the Community has authority to enter into the international commitments necessary for the attainment of that objective even in the absence of an express provision in that connection." See n.6 above.

[9] Opinion 1/76 Lying-up fund (n.6 above) at 755.

[10] *ibid.*

[11] *ibid.* at 756(7). In the Opinion 2/91 (see n.6 above) the Court came to the conclusion that the ILO Convention 170 is a matter which falls within the joint competence of the Member States and the Community. As the Court mentioned in its Opinion 3/94 ([1995] E.C.R. I–4579) with regard to the Uruguay Round multilateral negotiations, the Council adopted Dec. 94/800 concerning the conclusion on behalf of the European Community, "as regards matters within its competence". The other matters were adopted by the Member States.

[12] Case 22/70 *AETR* (n.6 above) at 274(17).

[13] See answer to Parliamentary question no. 173/77 ([1978] O.J. C72/1).

could hinder the Community in the carrying out of the tasks entrusted to it by the Treaty.[14]

The emergence of a Community competence should not, however, be seen as a sudden break; Community law being evolutive, the transfer of power from the Member States to the Community is necessarily gradual.[15]

Then there is also the question of the consequences for the Community and Community law of existing collective international commitments undertaken by the Member States. Here also the Court has, through various judgments, formulated the basic principles. For instance with regard to tariffs and trade policy the Member States have progressively transferred to the Community their jurisdiction. By doing so they have also conferred upon the Community the international rights and obligations connected with the exercise of this jurisdiction, particularly with regard to the General Agreement on Tariffs and Trade (GATT). It follows that the Community itself is bound by that agreement.[16] This constitutes a clear case of substitution of the Community for the Member States in the implementation of multilateral treaties bearing on the subject-matter of the Treaty. As for the rights which derive for the Community from those agreements, their exercise depends on recognition of the Community by the other contracting parties.

The internal problems of the Community in this field may not, of course, obliterate the interests of third countries. In the various Court statements referred to above, this principle was underlined several times.[17] However, third States may not intervene in internal

---

[14] Joined Cases 3, 4 and 6/76 *Kramer* (n.6 above), at 1310(40). See also Art. 307 (ex 234) E.C. existing agreements concluded between one or more Member States and one or more third countries are not affected by the entry into force of the Treaty. Art. 234 takes effect only if the agreement imposes on a Member State an obligation that is incompatible with the Treaty: Case C–324/93 *Evans Medical and MacFarlan Smith* [1995] E.C.R. I–563.

[15] Case 22/70 *AETR* (n.6) above at 281(81–92).

[16] Joined Cases 21–24/72 *International Fruit Company v. Produktschap voor Groenten en Fruit* [1972] E.C.R. 1219 at 1227(18); [1975] 2 C.M.L.R. 1. The Community has assumed those powers in pursuance of EEC, Arts 131 and 133 (ex 111 and 113) E.C. See also Case 38/75 *Nederlandse Spoorwegen v. Inspecteur der invoerrechten en accijnzen* [1975] E.C.R. 1439 at 1450(21); [1976] 1 C.M.L.R. 1; Joined Cases 267–269/81 *Amministrazione delle Finanze dello Stato v. SPI and SAMI* [1983] E.C.R. 801; [1984] 1 C.M.L.R. 334; and Joined Cases 290–291/81 *Singer and Geigy v. Amministrazione delle Finanze dello Stato* [1983] E.C.R. 847.

[17] See, *e.g.* Opinion 1/75 Local Cost Standards (n.6 above) and Opinion 1/76 Laying-up fund (*ibid.*)

matters of the Community and, more particularly, in the determination of the very complex and delicate relationship between the Community and its own Member States.[18]

A last question to be examined here concerns the effects of international commitments undertaken by the Community. In the first place, it should be noted that such commitments constitute "acts of the institutions of the Community" and as such can be challenged in the Court as to their compatibility with the Treaty.[19] In the second place, provisions of international agreements concluded by the Community in conformity with the procedures provided for in the Treaty, "shall be binding on the institutions of the Community and on Member States".[20] Such provisions are directly applicable in the Community. They can also have direct effect. Indeed, an agreement concluded by the Community with third countries must be considered as having direct effect when, taking into account its provisions and the object and nature of the agreement, it contains a clear and precise obligation, which is not submitted, in its implementation or effects, to a subsequent act; international agreements also override conflicting provisions of Member States' domestic law.[21]

The Community's Right of Passive and Active Legation

With regard to diplomatic representation, the only relevant Treaty provisions are to be found in the Protocol on the Privileges and

---

[18] Ruling 1/78 [1978] E.C.R. 2151 compatibility with the Euratom Treaty of a draft Convention of the IAEA on the Physical Protection of Nuclear Materials, Facilities and Transport.

[19] Arts 230 and 234 (ex 173 and 177) E.C.

[20] Art. 300(2) (ex 228(2)) E.C. See also Opinion 1/76 laying-up fund (n.6 above), at 6 and 7. See especially Case 104/81 *Kupferberg* [1982] E.C.R. 3641: according to Art. 228(2) [now 300(2)], Member States are bound in the same manner as the institutions of the Community, by the international agreement which the latter are empowered to conclude. When they ensure respect for commitments arising from an agreement concluded by the Community institutions, they fulfil an obligation, not only in relation to the non-member country concerned, but also and above all in relation to the Community, which has assumed responsibility for the due performance of the agreement. That is why the provisions of such an agreement form an integral part of the Community legal system. It follows from the Community nature of such provisions that their effect in the Community may not be allowed to vary according to whether this application is in practice the responsibility of the Community institutions or of the Member States.

[21] Case 87/75 *Bresciani v. Amministrazione Italiana delle Finanze* [1976] E.C.R. 129 at 141(23), [1976] 2 C.M.L.R. 62. See also Case 65/77, *Razanatsimba* [1977] E.C.R. 2229, [1978] 1 C.M.L.R. 246; Case 12/86 *Demuel* [1987] E.C.R. 3719(14).

Immunities.[22] The Member States in whose territory the Communities have their seat, shall accord the customary diplomatic immunities and privileges to missions of third countries accredited to the Communities.[23] Reference can also be made to the Statement issued after the extraordinary meeting of the Council in January 1966, held in Luxembourg. It provides that the credentials of the Heads of Missions of non-Member States accredited to the Community will be submitted jointly to the President of the Council and the President of the Commission, meeting together for this purpose.

The representatives of the Community in third countries enjoy the same diplomatic immunities and privileges. This is the case also for the Community delegations to various third countries and International Organisations such as the WTO, the OECD, the United Nations and its Specialised Agencies.

Without it being more explicitly provided for in the Treaty, the Community thus exercises the right of active and passive legation.

Further Reading

Nicholas Emiliou, "The Death of Exclusive Competence?", (1996) 21 E.L.Rev. 294.

---

[22] Annexed to the Merger Treaty.

[23] Protocol, Art. 17. For a list of the accredited missions, see "*Corps diplomatique accredité auprès des Communautés Européennes*", Directorate General External Relations.

Chapter Thirty-three
Commercial Policy

Generalities

The European Union is now the largest trading group in the world, accounting for just over 20 per cent of total global trade in goods. This gives the Union the capacity to play a leadership role in global negotiations to liberalise world trade; indeed it is one of the tasks imposed upon the Community by the Treaty: "by establishing a customs union between themselves Member States aim to contribute, in the common interest, to the harmonious development of world trade, the progressive abolition of restrictions on international trade and the lowering of customs barriers".[1] Furthermore, free trade has traditionally been one of the main aims of the Union, because it is heavily dependent on international commerce—more than the US for example. This broad objective has been pursued multilaterally—first in the GATT, now in the World Trade Organisation (WTO)—through regional agreements, and in bilateral relations with other countries. As indicated in the previous chapter, the Community has sole responsibility for trade policy.

One of the first Treaty Articles provides that, in order to carry out the tasks assigned to it, the Community's activities shall include "a common commercial policy".[2] A little further on it states that the Community is based upon a customs union which involves the prohibition within the Community of all customs duties on imports and all charges having equivalent effect, and "the adoption of a common customs tariff in their relations with third countries".[3]

As was pointed out under the heading "free movement of goods", the elimination of internal customs tariffs requires the adoption of a common customs tariff with regard to third countries; without it trade from third countries would be deflected towards the Member State with the lowest tariffs. Customs tariffs furthermore, are one of

[1] Art. 131 (ex 110) E.C.
[2] Art. 3(1)(b) (ex 3(1)(b)) E.C.
[3] Art. 23(1) (ex 9(1)) E.C.

the main instruments of commercial policy, *i.e.* the trade relations with third countries. Since the external customs tariffs had to be "common", the commercial policy itself must be a policy common to the 15 Member States. And, the Treaty provides that "the common commercial policy shall be based on uniform principles, particularly in regard to changes in tariff rates, the conclusion of tariff and trade agreements, the achievement of uniformity in measures of liberalisation, export policy and measures to protect trade such as those to be taken in the event of dumping or subsidies".[4] It was therefore transferred by the Treaty from the national ambit to the Community's jurisdiction.[5]

Unfortunately, this evidence is not fully accepted yet by all the governments, since commercial policy itself is part of external relations in general, which until recently were strictly reserved to the different Member States.

Theoretically, national measures of commercial policy are no longer possible, but can still be taken with the Community's authorisation.[6]

This situation is necessarily detrimental to the conduct of a coherent policy towards third countries, even if it is limited to trade. It is to be hoped therefore, that the Maastricht Treaty's provisions establishing a common foreign and security policy[7] will "communitarise" the whole spectrum of relations with third countries.

However, where customs tariffs are concerned, it was accepted from the beginning that they can only be modified by the Community. Changes in tariff rates and the conclusion of tariff agreements must, however, as was just pointed out, be based on uniform principles. The Treaty provides for two procedures: first, the so-called "autonomous" modification, where the Community acts on its own,[8] but which has become practically impossible since most duties have been "consolidated" in the WTO. And, secondly, those which take place pursuant to agreements with third countries. Those agreements are negotiated by the Commission on the basis of a

---

[4] Art. 133(1) (ex 113(1)) E.C.

[5] Courts' Opinion 1/75 [1975] E.C.R. 1355.

[6] Case 41/76 *Donckerwolcke v. Procureur de la République* [1976] E.C.R. 1921 at 1937(32); [1977] 2 C.M.L.R. 535. See Council Dec. of 27/03/1991 authorising prorogation or tacit renewal of commercial agreements concluded by the Member States [1991] O.J. L83/13. Art. 133 (ex 113) E.C. and Council Dec. 69/494 concerning progressive uniformisation of existing trade agreements. See [1991] O.J. L82/52.

[7] Art. 11 (ex J(1)) TEU.

[8] Art. 26 (ex 28) E.C.

mandate which it proposes to and receives from the Council and are concluded by the latter.[9]

In case the "execution of measures of common commercial policy taken in accordance with the Treaty by any Member State is obstructed by deflection of trade, or where differences between such measures lead to economic difficulties in one or more Member States the Commission must recommend methods for the requisite co-operation between Member States". If that were to fail the Member States shall require authorisation from the Commission to take the necessary protective measures,[10] which may deviate from the provisions regarding free movement of goods.[11] Or, in case of urgency, the Member States can seek authorisation to take those measures themselves. Priority shall, however, be given to those measures which cause the least disturbance to the functioning of the common market.[12]

1. Commercial Policy Instruments and Import and Export Arrangements

(1) Exports

It will be noted that the specific Treaty provisions concerning commercial policy[13] start with aids for exports to third countries. Member States must harmonise the systems whereby they grant aid for export to third countries, to the extent necessary to ensure that competition between enterprises is not distorted. In this connection reference must be made to the OECD Arrangement on Guidelines for Officially Supported Export Credits "Consensus". The application of the agreement was made compulsory for the Member States.[14]

Generally speaking, exports from the Community are free,

---

[9] Art. 133(3) (ex 113(3)) E.C.; these negotiations are conducted in close consultation with a special Committee (the "133 Commitee") composed of national officials appointed by the Council.

[10] Art. 134 (ex 115) E.C.

[11] Case 62/70 *Bock v. Commission* [1971] E.C.R. 897, at 909(14); [1972] C.M.L.R. 160.

[12] *ibid.* See particularly Case 29/75 *Kaufhof v. Commission* [1976] E.C.R. 434 at 443(6) where the Court annulled a Commission decision granting an authorisation under Art. 115 [now 134] because the Commission failed to examine the justification put forward by the Member State and whether the measures were necessary.

[13] Art. 132 (ex 112) E.C.

[14] [1997] O.J. L216/77.

although the Council is empowered[15] to impose restrictions in certain cases. For instance in 1992, the Council adopted a regulation requiring prior authorisation for the export of eight chemical products. This authorisation may not be given if there is reason to believe that the products in question will be used for the development of or production of chemical weapons or that there is a risk of their being delivered directly or indirectly to belligerent countries or to areas of serious international tension.[16]

The Commission supplements Member State's export promotion efforts with a programme based on fairs, trade forums and co-ordinated E.U. initiatives; it is currently giving priority to promoting exports to the Gulf and Asian countries. See Council Decision on the implementation by the Commission of activities relating to the Community market access strategy.[17]

(2) Imports and trade protection

The instruments concerning imports consist mainly in anti-dumping and anti-subsidy measures. The purpose of the anti-dumping measures is to eliminate the prejudice suffered by Community producers of a given product because of imports of a similar product being "dumped". Dumping exists when an exporter applies to export a price which is lower than the so-called "normal value". The latter is normally the price asked for the similar product on the home market.[18] In case the products were sold domestically for a loss, then the normal value would be construed by adding a profit margin to the production costs, the so-called "constructed value".

---

[15] Art. 133 (ex 113) E.C.

[16] General Report (1992), p. 311. See, for instance, the suspension of trade concession to former Yugoslavia: Case C–162/96 *Racke* [1998] E.C.R. I–3655 concerning the EEC/Yugoslavia Co-operation Agreement and the Vienna Convention on the Law of treaties: application of the rule *rebus sic stantibus*.

[17] [1998] O.J. L265/31.

[18] Reg. 384/96 on protection against dumped imports from countries not members of the E.C. [1996] O.J. L56/1, amended by [1996] O.J. L317/1 and [1998] O.J. L128/18. See Guide to the European Communities' anti-dumping and countervailing legislation and questionnaire on lodging complaints, one intended for producers and exporters and one intended for importers. See also Guidelines for the calculation of the amount of subsidy in countervailing duty investigations [1998] O.J. C394/6. Also of interest is Reg. 519/94 on common rules for imports from certain Third World countries [1994] O.J. L67/89, last amended [1997] O.J. L122/1.

Community action, generally speaking, takes the form of provisional anti-dumping duties imposed on the import of the product causing injury. This is followed either by an undertaking from the exporter concerning his export price to the Community or by definitive duties. Such action is taken at the end of a procedure which starts with a complaint containing sufficient proof submitted to the Commission by a majority of the European producers of a given branch or by a Member State. The Commission can then initiate proceedings and an investigation, after consultation of a consultative Committee. The initiation of proceedings is announced in the *Official Journal*. The Commission could also open proceedings on its own initiative, but never does so, deeming the industry better placed to gather the necessary proofs. The complaint should be deposited by producers of a similar product, which, furthermore, must be "communautaire". Next, the existence of dumping and of a prejudice must be ascertained by the Commission. The Commission's investigation covers a period of six months preceding the submission of the complaint. To conduct the investigation the Commission needs the full co-operation of all the interested parties. The Commission cannot however impose coercive measures, but in case of a refusal to furnish the requested information, the Commission may, in pursuance of the WTO Anti-Dumping Code decide on the basis of the existing evidence. Indeed, mention should be made of the fact that the Community rules in this field are based upon the General Agreement for Tariffs and Trade (GATT).

The proceedings are closed either by a decision that there is no need for protective measures, by the expiration or abrogation of the anti-dumping measures or by the nullity of the price undertaking. This means that as long as one of these three events has not occurred, the Council can take a new measure without opening proceedings anew.

Measures can only be imposed by the Community after it has ascertained that there is dumping and that it causes injury to Community producers. This may be a lengthy procedure and reactions to a complaint cannot therefore be immediate. There is however, a further requirement namely that the interest of the Community does require such measures. In practice, injury to a Community industry is considered as constituting a Community interest.

As for the undertaking made by the exporter, it consists in applying a price which will eliminate the dumping effect and the injury to the Community producers. The implementation of the undertaking is verified by periodical reports from the exporter to the Commission.

The anti-dumping duties are established for five years and are levied when the product is put in free circulation. The proceedings and measures described above are similar for anti-subsidy measures; in order to offset any subsidy bestowed, directly or indirectly, in the country of origin or export, upon their manufacture, production, export or transport of any product whose release in the free circulation in the Community causes injury, a countervailing duty may be imposed.

Finally, it should be pointed out that it was established that the regulation could be circumvented by importing spare-parts and assembling them within the Community. Indeed, those products would have been subject to anti-dumping duties had they been imported in a finished state. To prevent this deflexion the Community adopted a regulation concerning the so-called screwdriver plants.[19]

Anti-dumping or countervailing duties imposed by the Community are, of course, subject to the judicial control of the Court; this control had given rise to an abundant case law.

"*Many trading partners, many commercial agreements.*" Those are the words of the Commission[20] to indicate that in addition to full participation in the multilateral negotiation and management activities of the WTO, the E.U. also has a broad range of commercial agreements of differing types with its many partners:

- it has agreements creating customs unions with Turkey, Malta and Cyprus;
- free trade agreements with the three members of the European Economic Area;
- "Europe" agreements (also known as association agreements) with nine Central and Eastern European countries. Those aim to integrate their economies with the Union as quickly as possible;
- preferential agreements with Mediterranean countries and, through the Lomé convention, with 71 African, Caribbean and Pacific countries. These arrangements give their exports privileged access to the E.U. as well as financial and technical assistance;
- non-preferential commercial and economic cooperation agreements with many countries of Latin America and Asia,
- sectoral agreements such as in textiles and clothing guaranteeing Third World producers access to the E.U. market, and

---

[19] Reg. 1761/87 [1987] O.J. L167/9.

[20] Parts of this chapter are based on, or borrowed from, http://europa.eu.int/pol/comm/info_en.htm (December 1998).

- international commodity agreements, such as the Cocoa Agreement, 1993.[21]

2. Relations with Industrialised Countries

(1) The United States

The relations between the United States and the Community are rather ambiguous. On the one hand, both sides claim to attach great importance to closer co-operation and to a strengthening of their relations, and on the other hand, they are involved in what seem petty disputes,[22] threats, retaliation measures, counter-retaliations, WTO panels, etc.

These two economic powers are, however, bound to co-operate very closely in the economic and political fields. This they successfully do, for example, within the Western Economic Summits held every year.

Indeed the E.U. and the U.S. form a global partnership, covering not only trade and economics but also co-operation on a whole range of foreign issues and global challenges. In December 1995, the E.U.–U.S. Summit adopted the New Transatlantic Agenda together with a Joint E.U.–U.S. Action Plan. Building on the consultation mechanism established by the Transatlantic Declaration of 1990, the Agenda and Action Plan move the relationship from one of mere consultation to one of joint action in four broad areas. The promotion of peace and stability, democracy and development around the world; responding to global challenges; contribution to the expansion of world trade and closer economic relations, and building bridges across the Atlantic.

The economic relationship between the two is characterised by close economic interdependence. The E.U. and the U.S. are each others most important partners in trade and in investment. More

---

[21] Dec. 98/489 concerning the conclusion of the International Cocoa Agreement, 1993, on behalf of the Community [1998] O.J. L220/1.

[22] For details about those disputes, consult the General Reports published by the Commission each February; see, e.g. General Report (1993), p. 270. General Report 1997, 333, where mention is made, *inter alia*, of the U.S. legislation with an extraterritorial effect like the Cuban liberty and democratic solidarity (Helms-Burton) act and the Iran and Libya sanctions act (d'Amato), act about which the E.U. and the U.S. reached an understanding in April 1997; see also General Report 1996, point 878; lately the banana dispute.

than three million jobs on either side of the Atlantic depend on this investment. To foster yet more trade across the Atlantic, the Agenda creates the "New Transatlantic Market Place" within which both sides work together to reduce progressively or eliminate barriers that hinder the flow of goods, services and capital between them. This process is aided significantly by the Transatlantic Business Dialogue, a forum in which business leaders from both the E.U. and the U.S. identify the main obstacles to trade across the Atlantic and chart recommended course of action.

Agreements were signed between the parties concerning mutual recognition of technical norms and certificates, establishing a cooperation programme in higher education and vocational education and training,[23] on sanitary measures to protect public and animal health in trade in live animals and animal products[24] and for scientific and technological co-operation.[25]

Notwithstanding the above mentioned disputes, the bilateral dialogue and consultations are increasing both in the economic and in the political fields.[26]

(2) Canada

Links between Europe and Canada have traditionally been close. The first co-operation agreement ever signed by the European Economic Community (as it was at that time) with an industrialised country was with Canada in 1976. This provided for closer business and commercial links, economic co-operation and joint undertakings between industries and companies.

The Community and its Member States and Canada adopted a Joint Declaration in 1996 and an Action Plan on relations between the E.U. and Canada. Less tense than with the United States, the economic relations between Canada and the Community are clouded by numerous disagreements. The worst concerned fish and lasted many years. The Community's constructive policy for the conservation, management and control of fish stocks led in 1992 to a comprehensive agreement being concluded at international level on fishing in international waters outside the Canadian 200-mile exclusive economic zone. The new propensity to co-operate in this

---

23 [1995] O.J. L279/13.
24 [1998] O.J. L118/3.
25 [1998] O.J. L284/37.
26 [1996] E.C. Bull. 12, 171.

field, and on animal health regulations, should enable Canada to settle its bilateral differences with the Community on fisheries and timber exports.

The Community is Canada's biggest partner, after the USA, both in trade and in direct investments.[27]

In order to facilitate trade between the two partners, they signed an Agreement on mutual recognition between the European Community and Canada.[28] They also concluded an Agreement establishing a Co-operation programme in higher education and vocational education and training.[29]

(3) Japan

Relations improved after the E.C.-Japan Joint Declaration adopted in July 1991.[30] The co-operation covers various fields such as trade, the environment, industry, scientific research, social affairs, competition policy and energy. However, the commercial relations with Japan are a constant worry for the Community, as shown in the Commission Communication entitled "A consistent and global approach: a review of the Community's relations with Japan".[31] The Council therefore asked the Commission to analyse on a regular basis statistically the development of trade with Japan in goods and services.[32] The Community's trade balance with Japan started to improve in April 1993 and this trend continued. The apparent improvement, however, is due largely to the recession in Europe reflected in a shrinking market for Japanese exports. The continuing fall in E.C. exports to Japan remains a major source of concern.

Co-operation between the Union and Japan now takes place across a wide range of areas, including science and technology, competition policy, development assistance, macroeconomic and financial affairs and transport. The Commission runs an export promotion programme "Gateway to Japan", which complements the export promotion activities of Member States. It also operates the executive training programme that takes young European business people to Japan for 12 months of in-house training in a Japanese company.

---

[27] General Report (1992), p. 276.
[28] [1998] O.J. L280/3.
[29] [1995] O.J. L300/19.
[30] General Report (1991), p. 272.
[31] COM (92) 219; [1992] E.C. Bull. 5–1992.
[32] [1992] E.C. Bull. 6, 95. General Report (1993), p. 257.

(4) Australia and New Zealand

The relations of the Community with Australia and New Zealand are affected principally by the opposition of those two countries to what they consider to be a subsidised common agricultural policy. While those same countries apply very restrictive measures to the imports of manufactured products, they seem unable to understand that the Community cannot allow itself to rely on imports for most of the agricultural products it needs. A certain degree of self-sufficiency is politically and economically imperative and the Community must therefore maintain its two-tier price system which includes tariffs on imports and restitutions for the exports of agricultural and processed products.

The Council authorised the Commission to negotiate with Australia the first scientific and technical co-operation agreement with a non-European industralised country.[33] Australia welcomed the reform of the common agricultural policy[34] and an agreement was concluded on trade in wine and the protection of wine designations.[35]

The Community is still Australia's second-largest supplier and its eleventh export market. It is its leading partner for services while the Community is also the chief source of cumulative investment and the second home for Australian overseas investments.[36]

Total annual trade is around euro 13 billion with the balance in the Union's favour.

Co-operation between the E.U. and New Zealand is based on preferential agreements largely focused on agricultural products. Thus, butter and lamb imports into the E.U. from New Zealand have enjoyed preferential access for many years. Total trade between the two is about euro 3 billion with a small balance in favour of New Zealand. In 1991, the two sides signed a scientific and technical co-operation agreement covering agriculture, biomass, biotechnology, environment, forest, renewable sources of energy and information technology.

---

[33] General Report (1992), p. 278. Council Dec. of June 27, 1994 [1994] O.J. L188/17.
[34] See "Agriculture" in Part Three.
[35] General Report (1993), p. 189.
[36] General Report (1992), p. 278.

(5) The European Economic Area (EEA)

The *European Economic Area* was born on January 1, 1994; it joins together the three remaining members of the EFTA: Iceland, Liechtenstein and Norway with the Union in one single market. Among other things, it grants those countries the basic freedoms of goods, services, capital and persons, and requires them to adopt most E.U. policies on mergers, State aids, consumer protection, labour markets and the environment.

Work on the application of the internal market legislation to the European Economic Area (EEA) continued, as the Commission reports,[37] apace with the adoption of 90 decisions concerning free movement of goods, capital, services and persons and 17 decisions concerning horizontal and flanking policies. From an institutional point of view, it might be interesting to note that the EEA has a Council, a Joint Committee and a Consultative Committee which meet either in Brussels or in the capital of one of the member countries. From the reports it is clear that the members of the EEA are becoming more and more involved in Community affairs and actually participate in several of its activities: Norway and Iceland, for instance, participate in the European Agency for the Evaluation of Medicinal Products and in other schemes.

Relations with Switzerland, which in a referendum rejected membership of the EEA, will continue to be governed by the existing co-operation agreements.

3. Relations with Mediterranean and Eastern European Countries

Implementation of a new Mediterranean policy started in 1992 with three regulations. One concerning financial co-operation in respect of all the non-member countries of the area,[38] the second concerns the detailed implementation of financial co-operation under the existing protocols with all those countries[39] and the third improving the arrangements for the import into the Community of certain agricultural products originating in Algeria, Cyprus, Egypt, Israel, Jordan, Lebanon, Malta, Morocco, Syria and Tunisia.[40]

Association Agreements exist with Turkey, Cyprus and Malta and

[37] General Report 1997, p. 305.
[38] Reg. 1763/92 [1992] O.J. L181/5.
[39] Reg. 1762/92 [1992] O.J. L181/1.
[40] Reg. 1764/92 [1992] O.J. L181/9.

a Co-operation Agreement was concluded and entered into force with San Marino.[41] Agreements exist also with the Maghreb Countries, Algeria, Morocco and Tunisia, the Mashrek countries, Egypt, Jordan, Lebanon and Syria, and with Israel, West Bank and Gaza Strip ("occupied territories"). Those agreements cover agriculture, energy, industry, distribution trades, infrastructure, education and training, health and environment and scientific co-operation. Those activities are financed by the resources provided for in the financial protocols. In 1992 the Council adopted the fourth Financial Protocols with Algeria, Israel, Jordan and Lebanon in the context of the new Mediterranean policy. Similar protocols with the other countries were already concluded or on the point of being concluded. In December 1994, the Essen European Council endorsed a strategy set out by the Commission in the framework of a Euro-Mediterranean partnership with a view of strengthening the Union's policy for peace, security and welfare of the Mediterranean. The long-term goal was the creation of an extensive trade area, backed up by substantial financial aid.[42]

A Euro-Mediterranean ministerial conference took place in Barcelona in November 1995.[43] The E.U. and its 12 Mediterranean partners[44] adopted a Declaration[45] in which they decided to put their relations on a multilateral and durable footing based on a spirit of partnership and on a work programme. Reinforced and regular political dialogue, enhanced economic and financial co-operation in support of the creation of a free trade area and a further strengthening of the social, cultural and human dimension are the partnerships three key components. Those three facets are being implemented and the process was spurred on by a second Euro-Mediterranean ministerial[46] conference in 1997, in Malta.[47] The concrete implementation is carried out through Euro-Mediterranean association agreements. The existing association or co-operation agreements are being relaunched on the basis of the Barcelona Declaration. The latter also sets the ambitious target of a free zone by 2010 between the Union and the 12 countries from the Southern and Eastern Mediterranean.

---

41 [1991] O.J. C302.

42 General Report (1995) 327.

43 [1995] E.C. Bull. 11, point 1.4.56 and Suppl. 2/95.

44 Algeria, Cyprus, Egypt, Israel, Jordan, Lebanon, Malta, Morocco, Syria, Tunisia, Turkey, Palestinian Authority.

45 The full text of the Declaration and the work programme can be found in [1995] E.C. Bull. 11.

46 27 foreign ministers met in April 1997.

47 General Report (1997) 315.

Current agreements give duty-free access into the E.U. to all, or most, of their industrial products, some concessions for some agricultural produce and financial aid in the form of grants and loans. Turkey has formed a customs union with the E.U., which means complete free trade and adoption of the Union's Common Customs Tariff[48] and E.U. rules on state aid, competition and trade.

The Community has contractual links with *Turkey* since 1963; the association agreement went into force for an unlimited period on December 1, 1964. Turkey applied for membership on April 14, 1987 and on December 14, 1989, the Commission delivered its opinion, which did not lead to the opening of accession negotiations, but to a wider integration into the overall economy of the Union.

(1) Northern Mediterranean

Negotiations for the Accession of *Cyprus* were started in the spring of 1998.[49] After having applied for membership, *Malta* withdrew its request[50]; it was, however, reintroduced or "reactivated", following a change of government, in 1998.

Bosnia and Herzegovina, the *Federal Republic of Yugoslavia* and *Albania*, were high on the list of priorities and preoccupations of the Union. However, Union action was hindered by conflicting approaches from various Member States. Unfortunately for the image of the external policy of the Union, it cannot be said that it played a brilliant role in trying to solve the many problems of that region situated at its very door-step. For more information on those various subjects the reader is referred to the Commission's General Reports published yearly.

A co-operation agreement exists with *Andorra*, in respect of the environment, communications, education, transport, and regional and transfrontier co-operation and veterinary matters. A co-operation and customs union agreement exist with *San Marino*.

Mention must also be made of the Co-operation Agreement between the EEC, on the one part, and the countries parties to the Charter of the Co-operation Council for the Arab States of the Gulf (the State of the United Arab Emirates, the State of Bahrain, the Kingdom of Saudi Arabia, the Sultanate of Oman, the State of Qatar and the State of Kuwait), on the other part, signed in 1988.[51]

---

[48] See under "Free Movement of Goods".
[49] See under "Enlargement".
[50] See General Report 1996, point 815.
[51] [1989] O.J. L54/1.

(2) Central and Eastern European Countries (CEECs)

The collapse of communism led to a surge in the relations between the Union and most of the CEECs, including the signing of association agreements, the so-called "Europe Agreements". These relations have been further deepened since the European Council meeting in Copenhagen in June 1993 which established that those countries that had signed "Europe Agreements" with the E.U. could be eligible for membership. Currently, there are nine such agreements. Six are in force involving Bulgaria, the Czech Republic, Hungary, Poland, Romania and Slovakia, while those with Estonia, Latvia and Lithuania are awaiting ratification (a tenth has been initialled with Slovenia).

These agreements give the signatories associate status and cover both political and economic relations. They establish regular and intensive political dialogue, progressive economic integration and financial assistance. They are of unlimited duration and allow the CEECs up to 10 years to remove economic and commercial barriers, while Union restrictions on the import of their industrial goods was removed by January 1, 1995 with some exemptions for textiles and steel. These exemptions had to be removed by the end of 1997.

Total aid from the E.U. and its Member States to the 12 CEECs (the 10 listed above plus Albania and the former Yugoslav Republic of Macedonia) was euro 33.8 billion between 1990 and 1994, 45 per cent of the total assistance they received. Some euro 5.3 billion were committed under PHARE, the Union's main technical assistance programme for the CEECs for the period 1990–95.

The European Union's PHARE programme which of its own inception was a technical assistance programme has now been given the task of supporting the pre-accession strategy as a structural assistance programme.

(3) Russia

The E.U. is Russia's largest trading partner by far, accounting for close to 40 per cent of the latter's foreign trade. When the Russian and E.U. national parliaments have finally ratified it, future political and economic relations will be governed by a partnership and co-operation agreement signed in 1994. This establishes a political dialogue at all level, regulates the trade in nuclear fuels, allows free E.U. investment in Russia with full repatriation of profits, liberalises the activities of foreign banks in Russia, removes all E.U. quotas on Russian exports apart from certain textile and steel products and allows temporary Russian quotas on some E.U. imports.

Pending ratification, the trade provisions of this agreement have been in force since February 1, 1996 based on an interim agreement signed in July 1995.

At their meeting in Madrid in December 1995, the European Council asserted that on-going relations between the E.U. and a democratic Russia "are essential to stability in Europe". The Heads of State or Government said the E.U. would:

- contribute to Russia's democratic reforms;
- support Russia's economic reforms, her integration into the international economy, the development of trade and investment and the necessary condition for the future establishment of a free trade area between Russia and the E.U.;
- take into account Russia's concerns about NATO enlargement;
- support peaceful settlement of disputes in the CIS area.

TACIS. The E.U.'s future relationship with Russia is being vitally shaped by the TACIS programme, designed to help her make the transition from a centrally planned to a market economy. TACIS projects involve, among other things, help in the restructuring of State enterprises and private sector development, reform of public administration, raising agricultural efficiency and supporting improvements in the safety of nuclear power plants.

Between 1991 and 1995, TACIS made available to Russia more than euro 790 million and nearly 500 projects have been completed or are under way.

(4) The New Independent States (NIS)

Relations with these republics of the former Soviet Union are increasingly regulated by partnership and co-operation agreements whose scope is political, economic, commercial and cultural. They aim to pave the way for the integration of these countries into the wider European economy. In the last two years such agreements have been signed with Russia, Ukraine, Moldova, Kyrgyzstan, Belarus, Kazakhstan, Georgia, Armenia, and Azerbaijan.

Substantial allocations—euro 2,268 million in 1991–1995, including Russia—have been made from the TACIS programme to the NIS to aid their transition to a market economy and to entrench democracy.

4. Multilateral Relations—The Uruguay Round GATT Agreement

(1) GATT[52]

The negotiations for the Uruguay Round started on September 20, 1986 at Puente del Este and ended in Geneva on December 15, 1993. The final text was signed on April 15, 1994.

It was a particularly difficult period for the Community: the enlargement to Portugal and Spain, the launching of the 1992 Internal Market completion programme, the reform of the Common Agricultural Policy, the worst recession since the War, German unification, the Maastricht Treaty's painful birth, the opening of Central and Eastern Europe and the negotiations for the European Economic Area with the EFTA countries. Those are just a few landmarks, but they show that that is how the Union went through very demanding years. However, the Community held together and, in the end, managed to muster the necessary cohesion to arrive at an acceptable outcome of the GATT negotiations. It withstood, more or less, the combined attacks of the United States and the Cairn countries against the CAP which became, unfortunately and unnecessarily, the focal point of the Round.

Nevertheless, from a Community point of view, the results can probably be considered satisfactory. Even with regard to agriculture it can be said that the results are in conformity with the reform as described in the Chapter on Agriculture in Part Four of this book. Community agriculture shall continue to play a role on the world markets and develop its production. As for industrial products, the Union and the main GATT partners decided to reduce their tariffs by an average of 37 per cent, while the developing countries have, for the first time, participated in the global liberalisation effort by consolidating their tariffs at levels compatible with their level of development.

Another new aspect of the Uruguay Round is the inclusion of the services sector and the intellectual property rights. Also important for the Community industry is the updating of the rules concerning disputes settlement, anti-dumping, anti-subsidy and safeguard actions.

---

[52] This summary is based on the Commission's weekly reports.

(2) The World Trade Organisation (WTO)

The Uruguay Round agreement provides for the establishment of the World Trade Organisation, which should permit the attainment of the following objectives. Thanks to the institutional framework of the WTO it will be possible to establish the rules of world trade on a stable basis and on a commitment of the participants to all the results of the negotiation, without exception. As mentioned, it will encompass an effective system for the settlement of disputes and, finally, it will allow a better co-ordination with the International Monetary Fund (IMF) and the Bank for Industrial Reconstruction and Development (BIRD).

The institutions of the WTO consist of the *Ministerial Conference* which meets at least once every two years and takes the basic decisions and a *General Council*, which oversees the functioning of the WTO and the implementation of the ministerial decisions. It is, at the same time, the *Organ for the Settlement of Disputes* and the *Organ for the Examination of the Commercial Policies*.

Councils for goods, services and TRIPs (Trade related Intellectual Property Rights) were set up.

The functioning of the WTO, like that of the GATT, is based on consensus, and when a vote is necessary, decisions are, save exceptions, taken by a majority of the votes cast. However, decisions concerning the interpretation of the Agreement and the granting of exemptions must be taken by a two-third majority of the members. Specific rules are provided for amendments to the Agreement.

The Agreement contains one binding provision concerning the conformity of the national legislations with the rules of the WTO.

Special attention is also given to the tandems "trade and environment" and "trade and competition".

The WTO should permit a reduction of the trade obstacles resulting in an improvement of the free "market access". It should also put an end to the bilateral and unilateral trade measures, which particularly the United States have a tendency to prefer above the agreed upon multilateral arrangements.

The final results of the Uruguay Round were put in the form of various agreements.

(i) The Agreement on Trade in Goods

One of the main preoccupations of the Community was the so-called Balance of Payment (BOP) exception, which was not infrequently used as an instrument of protection by developing countries. The Uruguay Round agreement provides for BOP consultations with a real impact and a reinforced rule for the BOP Committee. Clarifications were also sought on the formation of customs unions and free trade areas. The new text represents a tightening of the GATT disciplines. The same applies to new negotiating rights introduced for the benefit of suppliers with a high rate of dependence on the product for which a concession is withdrawn.

With regard to *market access*, which covers both tariffs and non-tariff measures, tariff reductions of around 37 per cent, as already mentioned were achieved. They will be implemented over a period of 5–10 years, beginning on July 1, 1995. In fact, in major industrial countries access shall be duty free for certain products (construction, agricultural and medical equipment, beer, spirits, pharmaceuticals, paper, toys and furniture). For chemicals there is a harmonisation at very low rates. Another important result is the "binding" of existing rates, which means that they may not be unilaterally increased. Especially important for Community exports are the tariff reductions accepted by countries such as South Korea (10 per cent for Community products), Hong-Kong (zero rate for 35 per cent of its tariffs) and Singapore (bound at 10 per cent). The results for Latin America were rather disappointing, while important reductions were obtained in Asia (down from 100 per cent to 10, 30 or 45 per cent).

Where *agriculture* is concerned the Blair House agreement among others played a major role. The main aspects are: access to the Community market, rebalancing the protection against various imports, internal support from which the so-called compensatory payments are now excluded, Community commitments on exports and a peace clause with regard to WHO panels. The final arrangements concerned mainly the Community and the United States and became possible only after the latter agreed to modify the famous Blair House agreement. Under these arrangements the Community has sufficient flexibility to manage its own internal policies. The commitments on market access will not undermine Community preference and new access opportunities will open up for Community exporters. The export commitments can be met within the framework of the CAP and, finally, the peace clause will ensure that the Community and its producers will not be harassed by panels dispute settlements.

Other agreements were concluded on *textiles and clothing* (delicate compromise taking into account the phasing out of the Multifibre Agreement (MFA) over a transitional period of 13–14 years), *Technical Barriers to Trade* (new Code of Practice concerning technical norms often used to protect a market), *Trade Related Investment Measures* (*TRIMs*) (clarification of GATT rules), *Anti-Dumping* (greater legal certainty and new provisions on standards of review; the new rules are in line with current Union practice on matters such as costs of production, sales at a loss, constructed value, level of trade and fair comparison of prices), *Subsidies* (trade effect oriented approach) and *Safeguards* (disciplines are reinforced).

(ii) Agreement on Trade in Services (GATS)

The objective was to capture all measures affecting the supply of services including the measures at sub-national level. The final package consists of three elements

(a) a general agreement on services: multilateral rules and disciplines and specific consideration is given to developing countries;
(b) national schedules or commitments and lists of exemptions: in terms of initial commitments, the package is far from satisfactory;
(c) Ministerial Decisions establishing future Work Programmes.

However, the most important aspect is that there is for the first time a multilateral agreement aiming at liberalisation of trade in services.

(iii) Trade related Intellectual Property Rights (TRIPs)

The agreement will, *inter alia*, ensure the implementation of existing international treaties (Bern and Paris Conventions), introduce the principle of national treatment, extend the protection for copyrighted works to new areas such as computer programmes, enhance the protection of sound recording, protect the rights of performing artists, establish high levels of protection for trade marks, protect industrial models and designs, geographical indications, etc.

(iv) Memorandum of Agreement on the Settlement of Disputes

The result is a reinforced mechanism very close to an automatic and quasi-jurisdictional system. New also is the possibility of appeal against the decisions of the WTO panels.

(v) Trade Policy Review Mechanism

Concerted and comprehensive surveillance of national trade policies. This mechanism is fully operational.

(vi) Plurilateral Trade Agreements

They concern Civil Aircraft (with regard to indirect subsidies, the negotiations were prolonged for one year), Public Procurement (results are comparable to the procedures laid down in the Union's directives) and Steel (tariff reduction to zero depending on the outcome of a Multinational Steel Agreement which was upheld because of the U.S. actions against flat steel and other steel products).

The Uruguay Round Agreement ends with a *Declaration on the Functioning of the GATT* which, *inter alia*, aims at establishing a link between trade, monetary and financial policies.

Further Reading

European Commission, "Trade in the new World Order", DG VIII, Courier Africa Caribbean-Pacific-European Union", 1997, No. 166, p. 58.

European Commission, "E.U. world trade policies: global partnership, global opportunities", Luxembourg, EUR-OP 1998.

Chapter Thirty-four
Development Co-operation and Common Foreign and Security Policy

1. General

As pointed out at the beginning of Part Six of the book, external relations were developed by the Community out of necessity even in the absence of explicit provisions. The Treaty did, however, provide for several possibilities such as the common commercial policy,[1] relations and co-operation with international organisations[2] and, of course, the general provision allowing the Community to take action to attain one of the objectives of the Treaty even in the absence of explicit provisions.[3]

The Maastricht Treaty introduced in the Treaty the necessary provisions for the Community to carry out a policy in the sphere of development co-operation.[4] The objectives of that policy are to foster sustainable economic and social development, the smooth and gradual integration of the developing countries into the world economy and the campaign against poverty. To those socio-economic objectives is added a political one, *i.e.* the development and consolidation of democracy, the rule of law, human rights and the fundamental freedoms. The whole policy must, on the other hand, comply with the international commitments of the Community.[5]

This development policy must be integrated into all the activities of the Community: it must be taken into account when implementing other policies which are likely to affect developing countries. This is, of course, the real test of a development policy. The best example for an area where there clearly are conflicts with this development policy is the Community's agricultural policy.[6]

[1] Art. 133 (ex 113) E.C.
[2] Arts 302, 303, 304 (ex 229, 230, 231) E.C.
[3] Art. 308 (ex 235) E.C.
[4] Arts 177 to 181 (ex 130u to 130y) E.C.
[5] Art. 177(3) (ex 130u(3)) E.C.
[6] See, *e.g.* below under relations with Latin American countries the measures taken to counteract the effects of the Community's banana policy.

Development cooperation allows the Community to help 71 ACP States, 20 overseas Countries and Territories, and all developing countries for food aid and food security operations, and to co-operate with Development Non-Governmental Organisations (NGOs). Presently, the Commission pursues the following targets: improve the coherence in the Community's approach between all different policies involved with development, improve the collaboration between the policies of the Community and those of the Member States, strengthen the ACP-E.U. relations now extended to South Africa and prepare for the after-Lomé.

Despite growing pressure on public budgets, the Commission was able to report[7] that the European Union and its members remain at the centre of global efforts to promote aid and development in the "South" or "Third World". They are committing up to euro 4 billion a year for this purpose and account for between 45 and 50 per cent of all public aid for development, compared with around 20 per cent from the U.S. and 18 per cent from Japan. The Union itself is responsible for around 15 per cent of the total aid given by Member States whose national interests are served by helping developing countries which both supply them with raw material and offer markets on which to sell their products. The Union is also a vital market for developing countries, absorbing more than 21 per cent of their total exports. It offers free access without offsetting concessions to the products of 71 African, Caribbean and Pacific countries. Virtually all developing countries enjoy special trade provisions of one kind or other.

The E.U.'s aid and development initiatives take two forms;

- regional agreements such as the Lomé Convention examined in the next section, and
- world wide action, *i.e.* Humanitarian aid, Food aid, Generalised System of Preferences (GSP), Project Co-financing and Decentralised Co-operation.

Humanitarian Aid: the Commission's *European Office for Emergency Humanitarian Aid* (ECHO) implements food aid, emergency humanitarian aid (food, medicine, shelter, etc.) and aid to refugees. In recent years, assistance has been granted, among others, to victims of the war in the former Yugoslavia and victims of conflicts in Afghanistan, Armenia, Azerbaijan and Tadjikistan.

Generalised System of Preferences: it gives developing countries duty-free or reduced-duty access for finished and semi-finished

[7] http://europa.eu.int/pol/dev/info_en.htm (December 1998).

products.[8] In 1996, the Council adopted a revised scheme of agricultural preferences based on the same principles as the scheme for the industrial sector and covering a much greater number of products; the scheme came into force on July 1, 1996.[9]

Many more schemes exist through which the Community helps underdeveloped countries; to name but a few; the International Commodity Agreements, the North-South Co-operation on drugs and drug abuse, the North-South Co-operation on health issues, the Co-operation on Eradicating Anti-personnel Mines, Co-operation through Non-governmental Organisations, Rehabilitation Aid, etc.[10]

Contrary to other new policies introduced by the Maastricht Treaty where the powers of the Community are strictly limited, the Treaty here provides for measures to be adopted jointly by the Council and Parliament. Reference is made to multiannual programmes which, obviously, will have to be financed. For this purpose the EIB is also instructed to participate. All this, of course, without prejudice to the co-operation with the ACP countries.[11] The latter is in any case financed by the European Development Fund (EDF) which draws its resources not from the Community budget but from direct contributions from the Member States as was confirmed in a declaration annexed to the Maastricht Treaty.[12] The Community's development co-operation policy is not an exclusive one, the Member States retain the necessary powers to continue to carry out their own development policy.

Consequently, the Treaty provides for co-ordination of those policies and instructs the Community and the Member States to consult each other on their aid programmes, including in international organisations and during international conferences. They may also undertake joint action and Member States shall contribute, if necessary to the implementation of the Community aid programmes. In other words, the Community policy is complementary to those of the Member States and the "division of labour" in this

---

[8] Reg. 3281/94 applying a four year scheme of generalised tariff preferences (1995 to 1998) in respect of certain industrial products originating in developing countries, with more favourable tariff treatment for the least developed countries [1994] O.J. L348/1 extended by Reg. 602/98 [1998] O.J. L80/1.

[9] Reg. 1256/96 applying multiannual schemes of generalised tariff preferences from July 1, 1996 to June 30, 1999 in respect of certain agricultural products originating in developing countries [1996] O.J. L160/1, amended [1998] O.J. L80/1.

[10] The reader will find the necessary information concerning those multiple forms of intervention in the General Reports of the Commission and on the Internet.

[11] Art. 179 (ex 130w) E.C. For ACP co-operation see next section.

[12] Declaration 12 on the EDF.

field shall necessarily be based on the principle of subsidiarity which means that the Community will implement its policy only if the Member States cannot, by themselves, attain the objectives set out in the Treaty.

The Community's co-operation with third countries and international organisations may be the subject of agreements which shall be concluded in accordance with the Treaty provisions on the conclusion of international agreements.[13] After what was just pointed out about the complementary character of the Community action, one might wonder why it was considered necessary to add (once again) that Member States retain their "competence to negotiate in international bodies and to conclude international agreements[14]; that had already been said, but it clearly shows how jealous certain Member States are about their prerogatives in the area of external relations. Obviously this dichotomy does not reinforce the Community's image towards third countries, let alone the efficiency of its international activities.

2. Relations with the African, Caribbean and Pacific Countries

The Fourth Lomé Convention came into force on September 1, 1991.

The main feature of the Community policy towards developing countries is the ACP-EEC Agreement, better known as the Lomé Convention.[15] It establishes commercial, industrial and financial relations between the Community on the one hand, and 71 African, Caribbean and Pacific countries,[16] on the other. It is therefore a bilateral agreement.

This relationship grew out of a quite different set of links which

---

[13] Art. 300 (ex 228) E.C.

[14] Art. 181 (ex 130y) E.C.

[15] The Third Lomé Convention entered into force on May 1, 1986 and expired on February 28, 1990. The negotiations for the renewal were opened in Luxembourg in October 1988.

[16] Angola, Antigua and Barbuda, Bahamas, Barbados, Belize, Benin, Botswana, Burkina Faso, Burundi, Cameroon, Cape Verde, Central African Republic, Chad, Comoros, Congo (Brazzaville), Congo (Kinshasa), Djibouti, Dominica, Equatorial Guinea, Ethiopia, Fiji, Gabon, Gambia, Ghana, Grenada, Guinea, Guinea Bissau, Guyana, Haiti, Ivory Coast, Jamaica, Kenya, Kiribati, Lesotho, Liberia, Madagascar, Malawi, Mali, Mauretania, Mauritius, Mozambique, Niger, Nigeria, Papua New Guinea, Rwanda, St Christopher and Nevis, St Lucia, Dominican Republic, St Vincent and the Grenadines, São Tomé & Principe, Senegal, Seychelles, Sierra

existed when the Community was established. Most of the countries now "associated" with the Community were colonies at the time and the Member States had special responsibilities towards them. The Treaty provides for the association of "overseas countries and territories", in order to increase trade and to promote jointly economic and social development.[17] Consequently, countries which had special relations with Belgium, France, Italy and the Netherlands and after accession Denmark and the United Kingdom were associated with the Community. The Treaty provisions were drafted at a time when most of these overseas countries were still dependent but the principle of a special relationship was maintained after they gained independence.

For a first period of five years, the details and the procedures of the association were determined by an implementing convention[18] annexed to the Treaty.[19] This convention was replaced by an agreement negotiated between the Community and the emerging African and Malgasy States. Known as the Yaoundé I Convention,[20] it still bears the marks of the paternalistic approach most European countries nourished towards their former colonies. A second Yaoundé Convention, similar to the first, came into force on January 1, 1971.[21] It did not apply to the United Kingdom, Ireland and Denmark until January 1, 1975.[22]

An entirely new agreement was signed at Lomé (Togo) on February 28, 1975, between the Community of 10 and 46 countries situated in Africa, the Caribbean and the Pacific.[23] It came into force on April 1, 1976[24] and expired on March 1, 1980. The Lomé II expired in 1985 and the Lomé III in 1990. The Lomé Conventions differ from the Yaounde Conventions in that they aim to establish a kind of partnership between the developing countries and the Community.

Leone, Solomon Islands, Somalia, Sudan, Surinam, Swaziland, Tanzania, Togo, Tonga, Trinidad and Tobago, Tuvalu, Uganda, Vanuatu, Western Samoa, Zambia, Zimbabwe, Namibia. Eritrea was added in October 1993 ([1993] O.J. L280/26) and South Africa in 1997.

17 Art. 131, E.C.

18 This was of course a convention concluded between the Member States, not with the overseas countries.

19 Art. 136, E.C.

20 [1964] O.J. 1431, and 1490.

21 [1970] O.J. L282/1; O.J. Spec. Ser. I(2) 7.

22 Arts 109 and 115(1), Act of Accession.

23 [1976] O.J. L25/1.

24 [1976] O.J. L85/1. Since it expired before the Lomé II Agreement became effective, transitional measures were adopted [1980] O.J. L55/1. The Lomé III, see [1984] E.C. Bull. 11–7 and General Report (1984), p. 275.

In respect of trade co-operation, the ACP countries enjoy, without reciprocity for the Member States, free entry into the Community for most of their agricultural products and for all industrial products originating in ACP countries. The Member States only have the guarantee that they will be treated not less favourably than any other industrialised country and that all of them will be treated equally.

An entirely new feature of the Lomé Conventions is the Stabilisation of Export Earnings (STABEX) and SYSMIN systems. STABEX is a mechanism assuring those ACP countries whose revenues derive mainly from a single product, a certain level of export earnings; to this end they are protected from income fluctuations due to the play of the markets or production hazards.[25] In 1992 this represented transfers to the amount of 330 million ECUs. The second system, in the form of special loans, aims at remedying the harmful effects to the national economy of the situation in the mining sector.

The Lomé Conventions also provide for an undertaking by the Community to purchase from certain ACP countries, at guaranteed prices, cane sugar for an indefinite period and an undertaking from those countries to supply specific quantities annually; this is referred to as the Sugar Protocol.[26]

Another important element is the place assumed by industrial co-operation, with its Industrial Co-operation Committee and Industrial Development Centre. The purpose is to integrate firms and entrepreneurs into the EEC-ACP co-operation.

Mention must also be made of the Regional Co-operation; the Convention devotes considerable resources to it and contains provisions designed to encourage the ACP States towards greater solidarity, with the ultimate goal of genuine regional integration.[27]

The Lomé IV Convention was signed on December 15, 1989 and will remain in force for a period of 10 years commencing on March 1, 1990, with a renewable five-year financial protocol.[28] It offers a number of innovations, the most important of which is support for structural adjustments (balance of payments, budget, public enter-

---

[25] For details see General Report (1997), p. 352.

[26] For the Sugar Protocol see General Report (1989), p. 358.

[27] General Report (1989), p. 361.

[28] A mid-term review took place in 1995 and the Lomé IV Convention was modified by an Agreement signed at Mauritius on November 4, 1995; see "le Courrier" No. 154, January-February 1996 (ISSN 1013-7343). All financial protocols are concluded for five years; the last one was agreed upon at Council level in November 1995. See Council Doc. No. 244/95 (ACP/FIN). Concerning the financing of the Conventions, see Case C–316/91 *Parliament v. Council* [1994] E.C.R. I–625; [1994] 3 C.M.L.R. 149.

prises, debt burden, etc.) and includes a chapter on debt. In addition the ACP-EEC co-operation now covers cultural and social co-operation (population) and the development of services and environmental protection (*e.g.* a ban on the movement of toxic and radioactive waste). The next emphasis will be on the private sector (investment, promotion, protection, support and financing, notably with risk capital) and on-the-spot enhancement of the value of ACP commodities through the development of processing, marketing, distribution and transport activities.

Finally, the Convention strengthens the provisions on human rights and respect for human dignity under which Article 5 specifies the various categories: non-discriminatory treatment, fundamental human rights, civil and political rights, economic, social and cultural rights. The same Article provides that financial resources may be allocated for the promotion of human rights in the ACP States through specific schemes.

The Community also contributes to the development of "non-associated" third countries; India has been the main recipient of the allocated financial aid. The aid programme is intended mainly for the most under-privileged sections of the population in the poorest countries. It has been running since 1976; the emphasis is on the rural sector and improving supplies of foodstuffs.[29]

South Africa. The ACP-E.C. Council of Ministers adopted in April 1997 the protocol governing South Africa's accession to the revised Lomé IV Convention. The protocol provides for the qualified accession: the Republic may participate fully in the institutions and is eligible for instruments such as access to public tenders financed by the eighth EDF, but not for EDF resources.

In accordance with the European Programme for Reconstruction and Development in South Africa[30] the first multiannual indicative programme formalising Community development aid to South Africa for the period 1997 to 1999 was signed in May 1997. It identifies basic social services as focal areas.

Institutional aspects of the Lomé Convention

The Convention provides for three common institutions: the Council of Ministers ("Council"), the Committee of Ambassadors ("Committee") and the Joint Assembly ("Assembly"). The Council is composed of the members of the Council of the Communities and members of the Commission and, on the other side, of a member of

---

[29] See Council Reg. on the implementations of the programme [1981] O.J. L48/8.

[30] Reg. 2259/96 [1996] O.J. L306/5.

the government of each ACP country. It establishes the general guidelines for the implementing activities, takes all the political decisions in view of the objectives of the Convention, and is generally speaking in charge of the implementation of the Convention.[31]

The Committee is composed of the Permanent representatives of the Member States of the E.U., and, on the other hand, of the Heads of Mission of the ACP countries to the E.U. It assists the Council in the implementation of its tasks and follows the application of the Convention.[32]

The Assembly is composed in equal numbers of members of the European Parliament and parliamentarians or other designated persons of the ACP countries. It is a purely consultative body.

3. Asia and Latin-America

(1) Asia

In 1995, *China* became the Union's fourth largest export market and its fourth largest supplier, with the E.U.'s import exceeding its exports. China is the E.U.'s largest supplier of textile and clothing. The legal framework for commercial relations and a programme of co-operation and development are provided by a co-operation agreement signed in 1985. At the end of 1995, the Council issued guidelines for a E.U. strategy towards China, whose objectives emphasised the "smooth and gradual integration of China into the world economy, together with the promotion of democracy, structures based on the rule of law and respect for human rights".

A framework trade and co-operation agreement was negotiated with *South Korea* in 1995 to promote closer economic relations and exchanges of information and mutually beneficial investment. In addition, the E.U. is contributing to the Korean Peninsula Energy Development Organisation in support of the search for peace and stability in the region.

Where *Other Asian Countries* are concerned, the 25 nation summit in Bangkok between European and Asian leaders in March 1996, was a major step towards widening and deepening the dialogue between the two regions. The meeting brought together the 15 E.U. members with the seven members of ASEAN as well as China, Japan and Vietnam.

Co-operation agreements were signed with Cambodia and Laos, while Myanmar (Burma) was withdrawn from the GSP.

---

[31] Convention, Art. 30.
[32] Convention, Art. 31.

Co-operation agreements exist with Bangladesh, India, Pakistan and Sri Lanka in the fields of rural development, food aid, scientific and technical co-operation and industrial and trade promotion.

Under a system of compensation for loss of export earnings for least-developed countries not signatories to the Lomé Convention,[33] Nepal, Bangladesh and Haiti have received Community financial aid.

Diplomatic relations with *Vietnam* were established in 1990.

Financial and technical co-operation with Asia amounted to euro 328.5 million in 1997. The main activities covered a programme to protect E.C.-Asian patents and registered trade-marks, education, environmental technology, energy co-operation, medical co-operation, refugee aid, etc.[34]

(2) Latin-America

The Community has established relations with the Rio Group Countries (Argentina, Bolivia, Brazil, Chile, Columbia, Ecuador, Panama, Paraguay, Peru, Uruguay and Venezuela), the countries of Central America and Mercosur[35] and the Andean group. Then there is also the San José group composed of Costa Rica, El Salvador, Guatemala, Honduras, Nicaragua and Panama; with all those groups the Union holds regular meetings at ministerial level.

Besides those multilateral relations the Community has bilateral relations with a number of Latin-American countries. The last such an agreement was concluded with Mexico in 1997; it aims at "institutionalising" the political dialogue, intensifying co-operation, and strengthening economic and trade relations.

Following the establishment of the common organisation of the banana market a five-year diversification and development programme was established for the Latin-American banana producing countries: Panama, Costa Rica, Nicaragua, Honduras, El Salvador, Guatemala, Columbia, Venezuela, Ecuador, Peru and Bolivia.

Financial and technical co-operation with Latin America, which is the main instrument of aid to the region, amounted to 190.2 million ECUs in 1997. The main economic co-operation activities were geared to trade promotion, training, regional intergration, energy

---

[33] [1987] O.J. L43.

[34] General Report (1992) 299. See Council Decision of December 2, 1993; Agreement on trade in textiles with Hong Kong, Singapore, Macao, Indonesia, the Philippines, China, Bangladesh, Korea, India, Malaysia, Pakistan, Sri Lanka and Thailand [1994] O.J. L110.

[35] General Report (1993) 271.

co-operation, investment promotion, development of democracy in the region, refugee aid, etc.[36]

Common Foreign and Security Policy (CFSP)

The preamble to the Maastricht Treaty refers to the implementation of "a common foreign and security policy including the eventual framing of a common defence policy, which might in time lead to a common defence, thereby reinforcing the European identity and its independence in order to promote peace, security and progress in Europe and in the world". As will appear, the means provided to achieve this lofty objective do not seem to be sufficient; this is due to the opposition from those Member States which resent any encroachment on their so-called national sovereignty, of which, for some, foreign affairs is the symbol.

The external competences of the Community were enlarged in several ways, first, by the simple fact that its internal competences were increased,[37] secondly, by the inclusion in the Treaty of a new external policy, *i.e.* Development Co-operational and finally, by the addition to (not "in") the E.C. Treaty of Provisions on a Common Foreign and Security Policy.[38] With regard to the competences of the Community which existed under the E.C. Treaty, except for the provisions concerning the conclusion of international agreements,[39] not much was changed and the CFSP was not included in the E.C. Treaty but remains outside under different institutional arrangements: it is not the foreign policy of the European Community but of the European Union. The very first Article of the Maastricht Treaty makes this clear when it refers to the Union founded on the European Communities, "supplemented" by the policies and forms of co-operation established by the Treaty.[40]

The implementation of the Common Foreign and Security Policy is the task of both the Union and its Member States and the tasks assigned to them are the following:

---

[36] EEC-Central America Co-operation Agreement: [1986] O.J. L172.

[37] See above, Chapter Twenty-Two "Community's Jurisdiction". As pointed out at the beginning of this book, the Community's competences were enlarged with Education, Culture, Public Health, Consumer protection, Trans-European Networks, etc. Another example is the possibility for the Community to conclude agreements concerning monetary and foreign exchange regime matters; Art. 109(3) E.C.

[38] In short CFSP. Arts 11 (ex J.1) and 21 (ex J.11) TEU.

[39] Art. 300 (ex 228) E.C.

[40] Art. 1 (ex A) TEU.

(a) to safeguard the common values, fundamental interests, independence and integrity of the Union in conformity with the principles of the United Nations Charter;
(b) to strengthen the security of the Union in all ways;
(c) to preserve peace and strengthen international security, in accordance with the principles of the United Nations Charter, as well as the principles of the Helsinki Final Act and the objectives of the Paris Charter, including those on external borders;
(d) to promote international co-operation;
(e) to develop and consolidate democracy and the rule of law, and respect for human rights and fundamental freedoms.[41]

(1) Activities

The Treaty provides for various activities to be carried out by the Member States in the framework of this common policy. Member States shall inform and consult each other within the Council[42] in order to ensure that the Union's influence is extended as effectively as possible by means of concerted and convergent action.[43] The Council must recommend "common strategies" to the European Council and shall implement them, in particular by adopting "joint actions" and "common positions".[44] Joint action address specific situations where operational action by the Union is deemed to be required. The European Council lays down General Guidelines which identified the areas falling within the security sphere which could be the subject of joint action.[45]

The Treaty also lays down the procedure for adopting "joint action".[46] This aspect is extremely important since it constitutes the embryo of a joint foreign policy.

On the basis of general guidelines from the European Council, the Council shall decide on the principle of *joint action*. When it does so

---

[41] *ibid.* Art. 11(1) (ex J(1)).
[42] Identical text in Art. 34(1) (ex K.3(1)) TEU regarding Police and Judicial Co-operation.
[43] Art. 16 (J(6)) TEU.
[44] Art. 13 (ex J(3)) TEU. See, for instance Council decision on the implementation of Joint Action 96/588/CFSP on anti-personnel landmines with a view to co-financing the special appeals from the International Red Cross Committee [1997] O.J. L338/5. See also statement by Denmark (*ibid.* at 4) hiding behind the fact that it doesn't take part in actions of the Union which have defence implications in order to refuse to participate in the financing of the anti-personnel landmines action.
[45] [1997] O.J. L338/5.
[46] Art. 13 (ex J(3)) TEU.

decide, it shall also lay down the specific scope, the general and specific objectives of such joint action, the duration, the means, the procedures and the conditions for implementation. It shall define furthermore, those matters on which decisions are to be taken by a qualified majority; in such a case votes are weighted in the same way as for the Community Council. The subject and principle may, of course be reviewed at all times. Member States shall be committed by the joint action in the position and conduct they adopt. In case national action is to be taken, prior information is to be provided to allow, if necessary, consultation. In case of urgency, Member States may take the necessary measures and in case of difficulty in implementing the joint action the matter shall be referred to the Council for discussion and to seek an appropriated solution.[47]

One of the first joint actions decided by the Council concerned the inaugural conference on the stability pact.[48]

Common positions shall define the approach of the Union to a particular matter of a geographical or thematic nature. Member States shall ensure that their national policies conform to the common position.[49]

Diplomatic and consular missions of the Member States and the Commission Delegations in third countries and international conferences, and their representations to international organisations, shall co-operate in ensuring that the joint actions common positions adopted by the Council are complied with.[50]

(2) Conclusion of International Agreements

The Treaty of Amsterdam introduced important changes. Since the Commission is not directly implicated in the implementation of Title V on foreign and security policy, it could not, as provided for in the E.C. Treaty, make recommendations to the Council. The Treaty therefore provides that when it is necessary to conclude an agreement with one or more States or international organisations in implementation of Title V, the Council, acting unanimously, may authorise the Presidency, assisted by the Commission as appropriate, to open negotiations to that effect. Such agreements shall be concluded by the Council acting unanimously on a recommendation

---

47 *ibid.* Art. 13 (ex J.3(7)).

48 See Joined action adopted by the Council of the European Union [1993] O.J. L339/1 and L316/45.

49 Art. 15 (ex J(5)) TEU.

50 Art. 16 (ex J(6)) TEU.

from the Presidency. The Amsterdam Treaty also changed the provisions concerning the effects of such agreement. While under the E.C. Treaty, Community and Member States are bound by those agreement, the Treaty now provides that a Member State whose representative in the Council states that it has to comply with the requirements of its own constitutional procedure, shall not be bound. At that point the other Member States may decide that the agreement shall apply provisionally to them.[51]

(3) Security, Common Defence Policy and Common Defence

The provisions concerning the security policy have been extensively modified by the Treaty of Amsterdam. The European Council may now decide the progressive framing of a common defence policy and such a decision will have to be adopted by the Member States in accordance with their respective constitutional requirements. It is also stated that the Western European Union (WEU) is an integral part of the development of the Union, providing the latter with access to an operational capability, notably in the context of humanitarian and rescue tasks, peacekeeping tasks and tasks of combat forces in crisis management, including peacekeeping.

The WEU supports the Union in framing the defence aspects of the common foreign and security policy. The inclusion of the WEU in to the Union is envisaged. Such a decision would also have to be ratified by the Member States. The defence policy of the Union may not, however, prejudice the defence policy of certain Member States and respects the obligations of certain Member States, which see their common defence realised in the North Atlantic Treaty Organisation (NATO), under the North Atlantic Treaty.

When the Union avails itself of the WEU, the European Council will establish the necessary guidelines. All Member States may fully participate in the elaboration and implementation of the relevant decisions. The Council shall adopt, in agreement with the institutions of the WEU, the necessary practical arrangements.

The Intergovernmental Conference which negotiated the Amsterdam Treaty adopted two Declarations; one on enhanced co-operation between the E.U. and WUE and another relating to the WUE. The first refers to security clearance of the personnel of the General Secretariat of the Council.[52] The second, very elaborate,

[51] Art. 24 (ex J.14) TEU.
[52] [1997] O.J. C349/125.

contains a Declaration adopted by the Council of ministers of the WEU, on the role of the WEU and its relations with the E.U. and the Atlantic Alliance.[53]

(4) Role of the Institutions

The role of the European institutions within the framework of the foreign and security policy, is rather different from what it is under the E.C. Treaty. Decision making is intergovernmental and therefore the role of the European Council and the Council is, as was just described, fundamental.

In its work the *Council* is seconded by the Political Committee established by the SEA and also by Coreper.[54] The political secretariat and the Council secretariat continue to exist next to each other!

As for the *Commission*, it remains "fully associated with the work carried out" in the CFSP[55] and enjoys a right of initiative, but cannot receive delegation of powers, nor represent the Community in this field.

The European Parliament. It must be consulted by the Presidency on the main aspects and the basic choices and has the assurance that its views are duly taken into consideration. It shall be kept informed by the Presidency and the Commission and has the right to ask questions and make recommendations.[56]

The role of the *Court of Justice* provided for in the provisions on police and judicial co-operation in criminal matters was already examined in the Chapter on the Court. Although this role is limited to giving preliminary rulings on the validity and interpretation of framework decisions and decisions, on the interpretation of Conventions established under the above mentioned provisions, and on the validity and interpretation of the measures implementing them, it is an important step towards guaranteeing the application of the rule of law in that field. This was not provided previously.

With regard to the foreign and security policy, the Treaty of Amsterdam did not confer any jurisdiction on the Court.

As was indicated at the beginning of the book, the Union is "served by a single institutional framework" and the above description gives

[53] *ibid.*
[54] *ibid.* Arts 18(5) and 11(1) (ex J8(5) and J1(1)).
[55] *ibid.* Art. 19 (ex J9) TEU.
[56] Art. 21 (ex J.11) TEU.

some idea about what this means in reality. Although some of the institutions are indeed involved, only the Council, which consists, as is by now well known, of representatives of the Member States, exercises its real function; the others play minor roles compared to the ones that are attributed to them under the E.C. Treaty. It must be said therefore that the single institutional framework barely exists but could constitute the embryo of a more integrated entity in the future.

Further Reading

On-line Publications Catalogue of the Directorate General for Development: http://europa.eu.int/comm/dg08/publication_en.htm

Chapter Thirty-five
Enlargement

Any European State which respects the principles of liberty, democracy, respect for human rights and fundamental freedoms, and the rule of law[1] may apply to become a Member of the Union. It must address its application to the Council, which shall act unanimously after consulting the Commission and after receiving the assent of the European Parliament.[2] In its opinions, the Commission uses objective economic and political criteria to assess each applicant's ability to fulfil in the medium term the obligations arising out of accession. These criteria ensure equal treatment of all applicants and were defined by the European Council in Copenhagen in 1993.[3] An applicant country must have

- stable institutions guaranteeing democracy, the rule of law, human rights and respect for and protection of minorities;
- a functioning market economy and the capacity to cope with competitive pressure and market forces within the Union;
- the ability to take on the obligations of membership, including adherence to the aims of political, economic and monetary union.

The Commission seeks to evaluate the progress each applicant might reasonably be expected to make in the years ahead, bearing in mind that the *acquis communautaire* (established Community law and practice) would continue to evolve. Without prejudice to the actual date of accession, each opinion was therefore based on the foreseeable economic situation in the country and its probable capacity to apply existing Community rules in the medium term.

The Luxembourg European Council took the decisions required to set in motion the overall process. It stressed that the process was a comprehensive, inclusive and ongoing one, which would take place in stages, with each of the applicant countries proceeding at its own

[1] Art 6(1) (ex F) TEU.
[2] Art. 49 (ex O) TEU.
[3] [1993] E.C. Bull. 6, point 1.13.

pace depending upon its degree of preparedness. The process would comprise a single framework and enhanced pre-accession partnership and aid for each applicant country. It was decided to convene bilateral intergovernmental conferences in the spring of 1998 to begin negotiations with Cyprus, Hungary, Poland, Estonia, the Czech Republic and Slovenia.

The present situation of each of the main ten candidates for membership is examined below in alphabetical order.[4]

Bulgaria

The Commission ascertains[5] that the country, following the installation of a new government, is on the way to fulfilling the political criteria, but that progress in establishing a market economy has been limited by the lack of commitment to market-oriented economic policies. It would not be able to cope with competitive pressure and market forces within the Union in the medium term. Bulgaria has neither transposed nor implemented the essential elements of Community law and practice, particularly those on the single market. It is therefore doubtful whether Bulgaria would be able, in the medium term, to assume the obligations of membership. A considerable effort and investment is needed on environment, transport, energy, home affairs, justice and agriculture. It also needs to set up the structures needed to apply and enforce the full body of Community law. The Commission therefore considered that negotiation should start when sufficient progress has been made to fulfil the criteria set out by the Copenhagen European Council.

Czech Republic

The Czech Republic presents, as far as the Commission is concerned,[6] the characteristics of a democracy with stable institutions guaranteeing the rule of law, human rights and respect for and protection of, minorities. It may be regarded as a functioning market economy, able to cope with competitive pressure and market forces within the Union in the medium term. It should also be capable of applying the full body of Community law and practice on

---

[4] All the information provided in this chapter is based on and/or borrowed from the General Reports 1994 to 1997.

[5] [1997] E.C. Bull. Supp. 13.

[6] [1997] E.C. Bull. Supp. 14.

the single market, provided it maintains the effort to transpose the law and speeds up work on actual implementation. A further effort is needed on transposing Community rules on agriculture, environment and energy, and more detailed administrative reforms to provide the country with the structures it needs for effective application and enforcement of the full body of Community law. The Commission advises that accession negotiations should begin.

Estonia

Estonia presents, according to the Commission,[7] the characteristics of a democracy, with stable institutions guaranteeing the rule of law, human rights and respect for and protection of, minorities. However, steps need to be taken to speed up the naturalisation of Russian-speaking non-citizens to enable them to integrate more fully into Estonian society. Estonia may be regarded as a functioning market economy, and should be able to cope with the competitive pressures and market forces within the Union in the medium term. It has made considerable progress in transposing and implementing Community law and practice on the single market, which should enable it to participate fully in the market in the medium term. Some further effort is needed in areas like environment, and the administrative organisation needs to be strengthened if the country is to effectively apply and enforce the full body of Community law. The Commission recommends that accession negotiations with Estonia should begin.

Hungary

Hungary presents, in the opinion of the Commission,[8] the characteristics of a democracy, with stable institutions guaranteeing the rule of law, human rights and respect for and protection of, minorities. It may also be regarded as a functioning market economy, and should be able to cope with the competitive pressure and market forces within the Union in the medium term. It should also be able to take over the body of Community law in the medium term, particularly that on the single market, provided it maintains its efforts of transposition and implementation. Efforts are still needed in the areas of environment, customs and energy; internal structure

[7] [1997] E.C. Bull. Supp. 11.
[8] [1997] E.C. Bull. Supp. 6.

need to be reformed to allow the country to effectively apply and enforce Community rules. The Commission recommended that accession negotiations should begin.

Latvia

In its Opinion[9] the Commission ascertains that Latvia presents the characteristics of a democracy, with stable institutions guaranteeing the rule of law, human rights and respect for and protection of, minorities, but steps have to be taken to speed-up the naturalisation of Russian-speaking non-citizens to enable them to integrate more fully into Latvian society. Latvia has made considerable progress towards establishing a market economy, but would still have serious difficulties in the medium term in coping with competitive pressures and market forces within the Union. It also made considerable progress in transposing and applying Community rules, particularly on the single market. However, further efforts are required for it to be capable of full participation in the market in the medium term. Efforts and investments are needed if Community law is to be applied fully in the environment and agricultural sectors. Similarly the administration will have to be strengthened for Estonia to be able to apply and enforce the full body of Community rules. The Commission recommends that accession negotiations begin when sufficient progress has been made to fulfil the criteria set out by the Copenhagen European Council.

Lithuania

For the Commission[10] Lithuania already presents the characteristics of a democracy, with stable institutions guaranteeing the rule of law, human rights and respect for and protection of, minorities. It has made considerable progress towards establishing a market economy but would still have serious difficulty, in the medium term, in coping with the competitive pressures and market forces within the Union. It has also made considerable progress in transposing and implementing Community law on the single market in particular. Much further effort is needed to make it able to participate fully in the market in the medium term, especially with regard to the Community rules on agriculture, energy and the environment. Also,

---

[9] [1997] E.C. Bull. Supp. 10.
[10] [1997] E.C. Bull. Supp. 2.

the administration will have to be strengthened to provide Lithuania with the structures it needs to apply and enforce the full body of Community rules. The Commission therefore recommends that accession negotiation should begin when sufficient progress has been made to fulfil the accession criteria.

Poland

In its Opinion,[11] the Commission finds that Poland presents the characteristics of a democracy, with institutions guaranteeing the rule of law, human rights and the respect for and the protection of, minorities. It may be regarded as a functioning market economy, and should be able to cope with the competitive pressures and market forces within the Union. Similarly, in the medium term, it should be able to participate fully in the single market provided it maintains the effort to transpose Community law, and steps up, implementation thereof. Further efforts are needed in the areas of agriculture, environment and transport. Also administrative reforms are necessary to permit Poland to implement and enforce the full body of Community rules. The Commission recommends that accession negotiations with Poland should begin.

Romania

Following the installation of a new government, the country is, according to the Commission,[12] on its way to fulfilling the political criteria. It has made considerable progress in establishing a market economy, but would have serious difficulties, in the medium term, in coping with the competitive pressures and market forces within the Union. Romania has neither transposed nor implemented the essential elements of Community law and practice, particularly those on the single market. It is therefore doubtful whether Romania will be in a position to assume the obligations of membership in the medium term. A considerable amount of work is needed on environment, transport, employment, social affairs, home affairs, justice and agriculture. Also, substantial reform of structures is needed to make possible the effective application and enforcement of the full body of Community law. The Commission recommends that accession negotiations begin when sufficient progress has been made to fulfil the accession criteria.

---

[11] [1997] E.C. Bull. Supp. 7.
[12] [1997] E.C. Bull. Supp. 8.

Slovakia

The Commission, in its Opinion,[13] states that Slovakia does not fulfil the political conditions satisfactorily because its institutions are unstable and too detached from political life, and because there are shortcomings in the functioning of its democracy. It adds that this is all the more regrettable as the country would be capable of meeting the economic criteria in the medium term and is firmly committed to adopting Community law and practice, particularly in the single market, even if further progress is still required to ensure effective application. The Commission considers that accession negotiations should only begin when sufficient progress has been made to fulfil the accession criteria set out by the Copenhagen European Council.

Slovenia

Slovenia presented a formal application for membership on June 10, 1996 and the Europe (association) agreement and the interim agreement were signed on June 10 and 11 respectively. The European Parliament gave its assent to the Europe Agreement on October 24, 1996. The Commission gave its Opinion on the membership application in July 1997.[14] Slovenia presents the characteristics of a democracy, with stable institutions guaranteeing the rule of law, human rights and respect for and protection of minorities. It may be regarded as a functioning market economy, able to cope with competition pressure and market forces within the Union in the medium term. However, the Commission is of the opinion that the country will have to make a considerable effort to transpose Community law, particularly with regard to the effective application of the rules on the single market, especially in the areas of environment, employment, social affairs and energy. Slovenia also needs to reinforce its administrative structure so as to be able to effectively apply the full body of Community law. The Commission recommends beginning accession negotiations.

The first step in the negotiations with the applicant countries was the European Conference held in London on March 12, 1998.

The ministerial meeting to launch the accession process with the 11 applicant countries (10 from Central and Eastern Europe and Cyprus) took place in Brussels on March 30, 1998. The next day, ministerial intergovernmental Conferences were held in Brussels

---

[13] [1997] E.C. Bull. Supp. 9.

[14] [1997] E.C. Bull. 7, point 1.4.83; [1997] E.C. Bull. Supp. 15.

with each of the six applicants selected on the basis of the above mentioned Commission's opinions: Cyprus, Czech Republic, Estonia, Hungary, Poland and Slovenia.

Pre-access strategy

Besides the *Regular Reports* of the Commission analysing the progress in the capacity of each candidate to implement the *acquis communautaire*, there are the already mentioned Europe Agreements, the Instrument for Institution building (*Twinning*) and the *Accession Partnership*. Each one will support the candidate country in its preparation for membership by setting out both the priority areas for further work identified from the Commission's Opinions and the financial assistance from the E.U. available to help tackle those problems.

If this pre-access strategy provides for efforts to be made by the candidates to membership, mention must also be made of the preparations to be made by the Community and the actual Member States. Some of those are set out in the Commission's Communication "Agenda 2000" but another very imported one is the reorganisation of the institutional structure of the Community. One of the Protocols annexed by the Amsterdam Treaty to the three existing Treaties (ECSC, E.C. and Euratom) refers to the "institutions with the prospect of enlargement".[15] This protocol, which forms part of the Treaty provides that at the entry into force of the first enlargement of the Union, the Commission shall comprise one national (instead of two from certain of them, as is now the case) of each of the Member States. However, this shall only take place if, "by that date, the weighting of the votes in the Council has been modified, whether by re-weighting of the votes or by dual majority, in a manner acceptable to all Member States, taking into account all relevant elements, notably compensating those Member States which give up the possibility of nominating a second member of the Commission". A second Article of this Protocol provides that at least one year before the membership of the Union exceeds twenty (presently, there are fifteen) a conference of representatives of the governments of the Member States shall carry out a comprehensive review of the composition and functioning of the institutions.

This review and the resulting restructuring of the Institutional system of the Community is an absolute necessity. Indeed, as experience shows, a Community of 15 Member States, let alone 21 and more, cannot function with an institutional structure which was

[15] [1997] O.J. C340/111.

set up for six Member States. The incapacity of the Member States to make this review and its subsequent restructuring at the occasion of the negotiations leading up to the Treaty of Amsterdam constitutes a major failure on their part. This Treaty was supposed to have prepared the Union for enlargement, but neither the objectives set out in the "Agenda 2000", nor the adaptation of the institutions, were achieved. Many efforts are therefore required by both sides before the enlargement can become a reality.

Further Reading

Andrew Evans, "Contextual Problems of E.U. Law: State Aid Control under the European Agreements", (1996) 21 E.L.Rev. 280.

Index